Windows 10
May 2019 Update

the missing manual®

The book that should have been in the box®

Windows 10
May 2019 Update

the missing manual®
The book that should have been in the box®

David Pogue

O'REILLY®

Beijing | Boston | Farnham | Sebastopol | Tokyo

Windows 10 May 2019 Update: The Missing Manual

by David Pogue

Editor: Julie Van Keuren
Proofreaders: Diana D'Abruzzo, Kellee Katagi, and Judy Le
Illustrator: David Pogue
Interior book designer: Julie Van Keuren (based on a design by Phil Simpson)
Indexer: Julie Van Keuren

Published by O'Reilly Media, Inc., 1005 Gravenstein Highway North, Sebastopol, CA 95472.

O'Reilly books may be purchased for educational, business, or sales promotional use. Online editions are also available for most titles (*http://oreilly.com*). For more information, contact our corporate/institutional sales department: 800-998-9938 or *corporate@oreilly.com*.

May 2019:   First Edition.

ISBN: 978-1-492-05729-1
[LSCH]

[5/19]

Table of Contents

Part One: The Windows Desktop

Part Three: Windows Online

Part Seven: Appendixes

Additional Resources on the "Missing CD"

(Visit *missingmanuals.com*)

PDF Appendixes

BitLocker Drive Encryption
Burning CDs and DVDs
Bringing Back the Hibernate Command
Bringing Back the Old Taskbar
Corporate Networks
Creating a Power Plan
Deep-Seated Networking Options
Disk Cleanup
Disk Defragmenter
Disk Quotas
Dynamic Disks
Fancy Printer Properties
Faxing from Windows 10
Getting a Fixed, Public IP Address
Internet Explorer
Libraries
Local Users Console
Mapping Shares to Drive Letters
Making Cortana Omit Web Results
   from Searches
Narrator
NTFS Permissions
Profiles
Remote Assistance
Remote Desktop
Run Command
Skype
Snipping Tool
Speech Recognition
Storage Spaces
Task Scheduler
Taskbar Toolbars
The Add Hardware Wizard
The "Folder Options" Options
The Universal Naming Convention

Three Obscure Mobility Features
Turn a Drive into a Folder
Two Speed Boosts
Upgrading from Windows 7 or 8.1
Windows Live Mail
Windows Media Player

Freeware

AutoHotkey
Chrometana
MusicBee
Ribbon Disabler
SecureZIP Express
Show or hide updates troubleshooter
VLC
Wi-MAN
Windows Live Mail
zVirtualDesktop

The Missing Credits

About the Author

 **David Pogue** (author, illustrator) was *The New York Times* weekly tech columnist from 2000 to 2013. After a five-year detour to Yahoo Finance, he's now back at *The Times*, writing the "Crowdwise" feature for the "Smarter Living" section and periodic how-to tech stories.

He's also a four-time Emmy-winning correspondent for *CBS Sunday Morning*, the host of several *NOVA* miniseries on PBS, and the creator of the Missing Manual series.

David has written or co-written more than 100 books, including dozens in this series, six in the *For Dummies* line (including *Macs, Magic, Opera,* and *Classical Music*), two novels (one for middle-schoolers), *The World According to Twitter,* and three books of essential tips and shortcuts: *Pogue's Basics: Tech, Pogue's Basics: Life,* and *Pogue's Basics: Money.* In his other life, he is a former Broadway show conductor, a magician, and a funny public speaker. He lives in Connecticut with his wife, Nicki, and three awesome children.

You can find a complete list of David's columns, and sign up to get them by email, at *authory.com/davidpogue*. On Twitter, he's *@pogue*. His website is *davidpogue.com*. He welcomes feedback about his books by email at *david@pogueman.com*.

About the Creative Team

Julie Van Keuren (editor, indexer, layout) spent 14 years in print journalism before deciding to upend her life, move to Montana, and live her freelancing dreams. She now works as an editor, writer, desktop publisher, indexer, and all-purpose editorial problem-solver for a variety of awesome clients. She and her husband have two sons. Email: *julievank@gmail.com*.

Diana D'Abruzzo (proofreader) is a Virginia-based freelance editor with more than 20 years of experience in the journalism and book publishing industries. More information on her life and work can be found at *dianadabruzzo.com*.

Kellee Katagi (proofreader) has devoted most of her 20-plus-year writing and editing career to covering fitness, nutrition, travel, and outdoor sports. A former managing editor of SKI magazine, she now smiths words from her Colorado home, where she lives with her husband and three kids. Email: *kelkatagi@gmail.com*.

Judy Le (proofreader) is an editor based in Virginia, where she lives with her husband and their son. In her spare time, she pursues interests with great fervor just before dropping them entirely. Email: *judylejudyle@gmail.com* (because of all the Judys Le who beat her to Gmail).

Acknowledgments

The Missing Manual series is a joint venture between the dream team introduced on these pages and O'Reilly Media. I'm grateful to all of them, and also to a few people who did massive favors for this book.

My bacon was saved by Aloria Rucker and her team at WE Communications (Microsoft's PR agency), who patiently helped dig up answers to the tweakiest questions.

I also owe a debt of thanks to O'Reilly's Nan Barber, who accommodated my nightmarish schedule with grace; to sharp-eyed proofreaders Diana D'Abruzzo, Kellee Katagi, and Judy Le; and especially to Julie Van Keuren, whose Missing Manual role over the past decade has grown from humble copy editor to full-blown editorial and design factory.

In previous editions of this book, I relied on the talents of several other authors, editors, and designers; some of their prose and expertise lives on in this edition. They include Phil Simpson, Mike Halsey, Brian Jepson, Joli Ballew, C.A. Callahan, Preston Gralla, John Pierce, Adam Ornstein, Judy Le, and an army of Twitter beta readers.

Thanks to David Rogelberg for believing in the idea. Thanks, above all, to Nicki, my muse and my love, and the three Poguelets: Kelly, Tia, and Jeffrey. They make these books—and everything else—possible.

—*David Pogue*

About The Missing Manuals

Missing Manuals are witty, well-written guides to computer products that don't come with printed manuals (which is just about all of them). Each book features a hand-crafted index; cross-references to specific page numbers (not just "see Chapter 14"); and an ironclad promise never to put an apostrophe in the possessive pronoun "its."

Also by David Pogue:

- *Mac OS Mojave: The Missing Manual*
- *iPhone: The Missing Manual*
- *David Pogue's Digital Photography: The Missing Manual*
- *Pogue's Basics: Tech*
- *Pogue's Basics: Money*
- *Pogue's Basics: Life*

Introduction

Microsoft's challenge, in writing Windows 10, was to come up with a single operating system that handles two radically different kinds of computers: touchscreen tablets and keyboard-and-mouse machines. One requires big, fat finger-friendly buttons and controls; the other can pack more onto the screen, because you have a more precise pointing device.

With luck, you missed the company's first attempt, a monstrosity called Windows 8. It was two operating systems superimposed: a touchscreen world and a traditional mouse world. The result was two web browsers, two Control Panels, two email programs, two ways of doing everything. Most people couldn't stand it.

In hopes of getting as far from Windows 8 as possible, Microsoft skipped Windows 9 entirely; there never was an operating system called Windows 9.

Windows 10, though, nails it: It manages to accommodate both worlds of computers—touchscreen and not—with equal elegance.

A Short History of Windows 10

Originally, Microsoft announced that Windows 10 would be a perpetual work in progress—a continuously improved, living blob of software. There would be no more periodic service packs—megalithic chunks of updates and patches; instead, Microsoft said it would add features continuously via quiet, automatic software releases.

In practice, though, Microsoft has updated Windows 10 with big, megalithic chunks of updates about every six months, just as it always has:

- **July 2015:** Windows 10.

- **November 2015:** November Update.

- **August 2016:** Anniversary Update.

- **April 2017:** Creators Update. (Yes, no apostrophe.)

- **October 2017:** Fall Creators Update.

- **April 2018:** April 2018 Update. (The names started getting less creative.)

- **October 2018:** October 2018 Update.

- **May 2019:** May 2019 Update.

Microsoft intends to continue with twice-a-year updates in this vein. That should make life interesting for you—and miserable for people who write and edit computer books.

Herewith: summaries of the new features. They're presented in three categories:

- **If you've used Windows 10 before.** Read this if you've been using an earlier Windows 10 version. It offers an overview of the big-ticket features Microsoft has added in the past three updates.

- **If you're used to Windows 8.** If the whole concept of Windows 10 is new to you, but you've seen the touch-friendly world of Windows 8, start here.

- **If you're used to Windows 7.** And if it's *really* been a while since the last time you checked in to Windows, read this section, too. You might also want to familiarize yourself with recent topics like smartphones, Instagram, and Netflix.

If You've Used Windows 10 Before

If you're upgrading to the May 2019 Update from some earlier version of Windows 10, it might be helpful to know what you're getting into.

The May 2019 Update

The May 2019 Update isn't a ground-shattering overhaul. But it does represent hundreds of tiny steps forward:

- **New good looks.** The May 2019 Update offers a choice of dark- or light-colored themes, which affect the color of the Start menu, taskbar, notification tiles, Action Center, and so on. Many of the Windows starter apps can inherit your choice here.

  This update also advances a design philosophy Microsoft calls Fluent. It's a lot of subtle stuff—drop shadows, shading, depth effects—that conspire to make Windows look more modern.

And on a new installation of Windows, the right side of the Start menu is cleaner and simpler: fewer preinstalled apps, fewer blinky Live Tiles.

- **Cleaned-up search.** The Cortana voice-assistant icon is no longer part of the search box; it sits separately on the taskbar, where it belongs. And the Search panel itself has had a dramatic visual overhaul, making it much easier to pinpoint what you want to find and where you want to search.

  As a bonus, Windows 10 is no longer limited to searching your Documents, Downloads, Music, Pictures, Videos, and Desktop folders; it can index everything on your PC—every file and folder.

- **Windows Update updates.** After complaints that Microsoft has been ramming updates down our throats, the company has made some changes. Big new six-month upgrades like the May 2019 Update are now optional. And you can now pause the installation of Windows updates for up to a week even on the Windows 10 Home edition, just as you've been able to (for up to 35 days) on the Pro and Enterprise editions.

  Windows already lets you define "Active hours"—your work hours—during which you don't want updates to require restarting your PC. In the May 2019 Update, though, Windows uses artificial intelligence to *figure out* your active hours by observing when you're actually using the machine.

  Less happily, on new PCs (or clean installations), Windows now sets aside about 7 gigabytes of disk space—off-limits to you—for its own use during updates and installations.

- **A safe sandbox.** The new Windows Sandbox app (in the Pro and Enterprise versions) creates a secure bubble in which you can try out buggy or sketchy apps, fully isolated from the rest of Windows. Go ahead and run a program riddled with viruses and malware; it won't matter. When you close the Sandbox app, all traces of your activity are gone forever.

- **Better screenshots.** The Snip & Sketch app now has a self-timer, so you can have up to 10 seconds to prepare your screen before it captures a screenshot. It can auto-snap just one individual window, too. And the app can now add borders to your shots and even print them.

- **A lot of misc.** Yes, a *lot* of misc. Ready?

  The Sticky Notes app can now sync your notes across your various Windows 10 machines. The emoji panel now includes kaomoji (symbols you create with typed characters, like the classic shrug ¯_(ツ)_/¯. A new icon appears in the system tray to let you know your microphone is in use. The Action Center contains a brightness slider (not just a tile with only four levels).

  You can delete a group of tiles from the Start menu with a single click (you don't have to delete the tiles individually). Windows can auto-detect and auto-fix certain kinds of critical problems without your having to run a Troubleshooter.

It's easier to change your cursor color and size. Various Settings panels have been redesigned and reorganized to make more sense. Cortana can now add to-do items to the Microsoft To Do app automatically.

You can now drag a downloaded font file directly onto the Fonts panel of Settings to install it. There are new features and settings in the Narrator screen-reader app.

And you're now allowed to name a file beginning with a period!

The October 2018 Update

All that builds on the new stuff Microsoft brought to the October 2018 Update, like:

• **Clipboard History.** Now you can scroll back through the last few things you cut or copied, and paste any of them.

• **SwiftKey.** On a touchscreen machine, you can enter text by dragging your finger across the onscreen keys, using this new keyboard that Microsoft bought.

• **Snip & Sketch.** The new screenshotting app!

• **Make text bigger.** There's a single Settings slider that increases the text size in every app at once.

• **Focus Assist.** There are times when you might prefer not to be interrupted, distracted, or awakened by the appearance (and sound) of Windows 10's notification tiles. This app restores the peace.

The April 2018 Update

The previous update introduced enhancements like these:

• **Timeline.** Windows 10 already had Task View (you click an icon on the taskbar or press ⊞+Tab to view miniatures of all your open windows).

In the April 2018 Update, Task View gained a superpower: Timeline (see page 210). Now, instead of showing you miniatures only for every window open right now, it also lets you scroll down to see (or do a search for) every window you've had open in the past 30 days—even on other machines! Even iPhones and Android phones running Microsoft apps (the Office apps and the Edge browser).

The Timeline is an answer, at last, to the questions "Where did I put that?" and "Where did I see that?" If you worked on it in the past month, you'll find it here.

Note: That's *mostly* true. Unfortunately, apps have to be updated to work with Timeline. And at the outset, most of the Timeline-friendly programs come only from Microsoft.

• **Nearby Sharing.** This feature lets you shoot files, photos, web pages, and so on to other machines nearby wirelessly, without messing with passwords, file sharing, networking, or setup. It's infinitely superior to HomeGroup, Microsoft's previous attempt at the casual file-sharing feature, which disappeared in the April 2018 Update.

If You're Used to Windows 8

If you've never used a version of Windows 10 before, here's what will be new to you:

- **The Start menu.** In Windows 10, the Start menu is back, and it works pretty much just as it always has. The Windows 8 *tiles* are still there, attached to the right side of the menu (Figure I-1)—but they no longer take over your entire screen, interrupting what you were doing, like the Windows 8 Start screen did.

Note: Meanwhile, a lot of conventions from the Windows 8 era are gone now. All that business about swiping in from the sides of the screen? Gone (mostly). Charms bar? Gone. App bar? Gone.

- **All apps work alike.** In Windows 8, there were two kinds of programs: the traditional Windows programs like Word, Excel, and Photoshop, and then a new kind designed for touchscreens. These apps, today called Microsoft Store apps, had no menus. They had no windows, either—each one filled the entire screen. They were

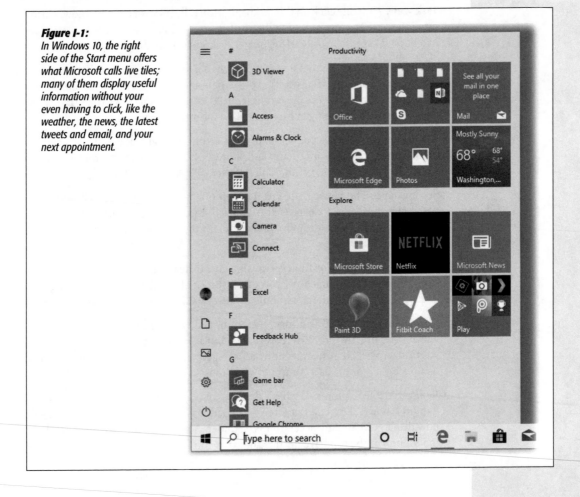

Figure I-1:
In Windows 10, the right side of the Start menu offers what Microsoft calls live tiles; many of them display useful information without your even having to click, like the weather, the news, the latest tweets and email, and your next appointment.

available exclusively from Microsoft's online store. They tended to be simple in design and function. They were, basically, tablet apps.

In Windows 10, those apps are still around. But they behave just like Windows apps, in that they float in their own windows. They still look a little different, and there's still no good name for them. But they're a lot less confusing now. Some people may never even realize they're using a different class of app.

- **Cortana.** You know Siri, the voice-activated "assistant" on the iPhone? Or Google Assistant, or Amazon's Alexa? Well, Microsoft now has Cortana. Same idea, except she's not just on your phone—she's on your *PC*, which takes her usefulness to a whole new level.

- **The Edge browser.** Microsoft has retired the old Internet Explorer browser (though it is still available) and replaced it with an all-new one called Edge. It's designed to eat up very little screen space with *controls*, so the web pages you're reading get as much room as possible. See Chapter 9.

- **Task View.** With one click on this taskbar button (⊟), all your open windows shrink into index cards, so you can see them all at once—a great way to find a program in a haystack. In the April 2018 Update, Task View adds the Timeline.

- **Virtual screens.** You can set up multiple "virtual monitors," each with a certain set of windows open. Maybe you like your email on screen 1, Facebook and Twitter on screen 2, and graphics apps on screen 3. With a simple keystroke (⊞+arrow keys), you can bounce from one simulated monitor to another.

- **Action Center.** This is a panel that pops out from the right side of the screen, listing all recent notifications up top and, at the bottom, one-click buttons for on/off switches like Bluetooth, Wi-Fi, Battery Saver, and Airplane Mode.

- **Settings app.** The redesigned Settings app offers *almost* every switch and slider you'll ever need, in a clean, well-organized app. The old Control Panel is still around, filed in a junk drawer somewhere, for the rare occasions when you need an obscure option.

- **Windows Hello (face or fingerprint sign-in).** Instead of typing a password every time you wake your machine, you can just *look* at it. Windows Hello recognizes your face and signs you in, without your ever having to touch the computer.

  This feature works only on machines equipped with an Intel RealSense camera, which rules out any pre-2015 computers. But Windows can also sign you in with your fingerprint, if your machine has a fingerprint reader. Or even your eyeball iris, once someone sells a computer with an iris scanner.

- **Rejiggered File Explorer.** The basic desktop folder window—once called Windows Explorer, now called File Explorer—has had a makeover. The list at the left side now displays frequently accessed disks, folders, and files. The sharing controls on the Ribbon at the top have been cleaned up, too.

If You're Used to Windows 7

If you're used to Windows 7 or something even earlier—you never even used Windows 8—then it's probably worth reading about all the *good* things Microsoft added in Windows 8, which still rear their lovely heads in Windows 10:

- **Smartphone features.** Some of Windows' features are adapted from smartphones, like a Lock screen that shows your battery level and the time, a Refresh command that resets Windows to its factory-fresh condition without disturbing your files, and a Reset command that erases it completely (great when you're about to sell your PC to someone).

  And there's an app store, for ease of downloading new apps that Microsoft has approved and certified to be virus-free.

- **Touchscreen features.** Microsoft strongly believes that, someday soon, all computers will have touchscreens—not just tablets, but laptops and desktop computers, too. So Windows 10 is filled with gestures that, if you do have a touchscreen, work as they do on phones. Tap to click. Pinch or spread two fingers on a photo to zoom out or in. Log in by drawing lines over a photo you've chosen instead of typing a password.

- **It's cloudy.** Your sign-in account can now be stored online—"in the cloud," as they say. Why? Because now you can sit down at any Windows 8 or 10 computer anywhere, sign in, and find all your settings just the way you left them at home: your address book, calendar, desktop wallpaper, web bookmarks, email accounts, and so on.

- **It's beribboned.** The mishmash of menus and toolbars in desktop windows (called File Explorer) has been replaced by the Ribbon: a big, fat toolbar atop each window that displays buttons for every possible thing you can do in that window, without hunting.

- **It comes with free antivirus software.** You read that right. Antivirus software is free, built in, and effective.

- **File History.** This feature lets you rewind any file to a time before it was deleted, damaged, or edited beyond recognition.

- **BitLocker to Go.** This lets you put a password on a flash drive—great for corporate data that shouldn't get loose.

- **New multiple-monitor features.** Your taskbars and desktop pictures can span multiple monitors.

- **Screen reader.** Narrator, a weird, sad, old feature that would read your error messages to you out loud, has been transformed into a full-blown screen reader for people with impaired vision. It can describe every item on the screen and the layout of a web page, and it makes little sounds to confirm that you've performed touchscreen gestures correctly.

- **Storage Spaces** lets you trick Windows into thinking that several hard drives are one big drive, or vice versa, and simultaneously gives you the incredible data safety of a corporate RAID system.

- **New apps** in Windows 8 included Alarms & Clock, Calculator, Voice Recorder, Maps, and Movies & TV.

- **OneDrive integration.** When you save a new document, Windows offers you a choice of location: either your computer or your OneDrive—a free online "hard drive." (OneDrive used to be called SkyDrive.)

- **Miracast.** You send video from your PC to TV sets that have Miracast wireless features—great for streaming movies or YouTube videos to your TV.

- **Miscellaneous overhauls.** The Task Manager has been beautifully redesigned. Parental controls offer everything from web protection to daily time limits for youngsters. The Windows Recovery Environment screens you use to troubleshoot at startup have been beautified, simplified, and reorganized.

The Editions of Windows 10—and S Mode

There are no longer 17,278 different versions of Windows. No more Starter, Home, Home Premium, Superduper, Ultimate, Existential, and so on.

Only two versions are for sale to the public: Home and Pro. Pro is aimed at small businesses and hard-core PC techies. It adds advanced administrative tools like BitLocker, Group Policy Editor, the Remote Desktop remote-control app, and advanced security tools like Device Guard and Secure Boot. And only Pro machines can join a corporate network.

You can upgrade from Home to Pro later (cost: $100). To get that going, open ■■→ ✿ → Update & Security→ Activation.

Note: Most people get Windows 10 preinstalled on the computers they buy. The only reason you'd ever have to *buy* Windows 10 is (a) if you have an ancient Windows 7 or 8 PC you want to update (and you missed the year when Microsoft offered a free update to Windows 10), or (b) if you've built a PC from scratch.

In either of those cases, you get Windows 10 by going to *microsoft.com/en-us/windows/get-windows-10* and paying $120 for Windows 10 Home or $200 for Windows 10 Pro. You'll get a confirmation email containing your "product key" (a unique serial number, to prove you're not a software pirate).

There are, meanwhile, three versions of Windows 10 that you *can't* buy on the website:

- **Windows 10 Enterprise,** which is available exclusively to corporate system administrators. It includes advanced tools for security and management.

- **Windows 10 Education.** Mostly the same software as Enterprise, but sold exclusively to schools and school systems.

- **S mode.** Here and there, you may run across references to S mode. Microsoft says the S stands for Security, Simplicity, and Superior performance, although it could also stand for Students and Savings; it's designed for schools or other institutions that want cheap computers. Behind the scenes, S mode is Microsoft's attempt to duplicate the success of Google's simple, inexpensive Chromebook laptops.

S mode is a version of Windows 10 that limits you to apps you get from the Microsoft Store. Which means you can't run programs like Photoshop, Quicken, Chrome, and Firefox.

S mode also forces you to use Edge as your default web browser and Bing as your default search engine (you can still manually call up Google). You can't use any technical tools like PowerShell, the Command Prompt, or the Registry Editor, either.

So what's the payoff of using a PC that's locked to Microsoft's software? Computers in S mode start up faster than other Windows 10 machines, are less prone to malware (although Microsoft still recommends using its Defender antivirus software), and are supposed to slow down less over time. And they're cheap, starting at about $190.

Apart from the app limitations, Windows 10 in S mode works exactly as described in this book.

Tip: If you bought a PC with S mode and decide you've outgrown it, you can turn S mode off—no charge. You wind up with the full-blown Windows 10 Home or Pro.

That, however, is a *one-time offer*. You can never return your machine to S mode. (You can still limit it to Microsoft Store apps, though; see page 253.)

To leave S mode forever, open ▦→⚙→Update & Security→Activation. Under "Switch to Windows 10 Home [or Pro]," hit "Go to the Store." (Don't hit the "Go to Store" button you might see in the "Upgrade your edition of Windows" section.)

The Microsoft Store opens. Where it says "Switch out of S mode," hit Get and confirm your choice. Boom: You can now install any apps you want. Your S mode days are over.

The Very Basics

To get the most out of Windows with the least frustration, it helps to be familiar with some fundamental concepts and terms. If you're new to Windows, be prepared to encounter these words and phrases over and over again.

Windows Defined

Windows is an *operating system,* the software that controls your computer. It's designed to serve you in several ways:

- **It's a launch bay.** At its heart, Windows is a home base for the various software programs (*apps,* or *applications*) that you use to do work or to kill time. When you get right down to it, programs are the real reason you bought a PC.

Windows is a well-stocked software pantry unto itself; for example, it comes with such basic programs as a web browser, a simple word processor, and a calculator.

If you were stranded on a desert island, the built-in Windows programs could suffice for everyday operations. But if you're like most people, sooner or later, you'll buy and install more software. That's one of the luxuries of using Windows: You can choose from a staggering number of add-on programs. Whether you're a left-handed beekeeper or a German-speaking nun, some company somewhere is selling Windows software designed just for you.

- **It's a file cabinet.** Every application on your machine, as well as every document you create, is represented on the screen by an *icon*, a little picture that symbolizes the underlying file or container. You can organize these icons into onscreen file folders. You can make backups (safety copies) by dragging file icons onto a flash drive or a blank CD, or you can send files to people by email. You can also trash icons you no longer need by dragging them onto the Recycle Bin icon.

- **It's your equipment headquarters.** What you can actually see of Windows is only the tip of the iceberg. An enormous chunk of Windows is behind-the-scenes plumbing that controls the various functions of your computer—its modem, screen, keyboard, printer, and so on.

The Right Mouse Button Is King

One of the most important features of Windows isn't on the screen—it's in your hand. The standard mouse or trackpad has two buttons. You use the left one to click buttons, highlight text, and drag things around the screen.

When you click the right button, however, a *shortcut menu* appears onscreen. Get into the habit of *right-clicking* things—icons, folders, disks, text inside a paragraph, buttons on your menu bar, pictures on a web page, and so on. The commands that appear on the shortcut menu will make you much more productive and lead you to discover handy functions you never knew existed.

Tip: On a touchscreen, you can "right-click" something by holding your finger down on it for a second or so.

This is a big deal: Microsoft's research suggests that nearly 75 percent of Windows owners don't use the right mouse button and therefore miss hundreds of time-saving shortcuts.

Tip: Microsoft doesn't discriminate against left-handers…much. You can swap the functions of the right and left mouse buttons easily enough.

Open ⊞→⚙→Devices→Mouse. Where it says "Select your primary button," choose Right. Windows now assumes that you want to use the left mouse button as the one that produces shortcut menus.

There's More Than One Way to Do Everything

No matter what setting you want to adjust, no matter what program you want to open, Microsoft has provided four or five ways to do it. For example, here are the various ways to delete a file: Press the Delete key; choose File→Delete; drag the file icon onto the Recycle Bin; or right-click the filename and choose Delete from the shortcut menu.

Pessimists grumble that there are too many paths to every destination, making it much more difficult to learn Windows. Optimists point out that this abundance of approaches means almost everyone will find, and settle on, a satisfying method for each task. Whenever you find something irksome, remember that there are probably other ways to do it.

Note: This book generally offers the one or two *shortest* ways to accomplish a task.

You Can Use the Keyboard for Everything

In earlier versions of Windows, underlined letters appeared in the names of menus and dialog boxes. These underlines were clues for people who found it faster to do something by pressing keys than by using the mouse.

The underlines are mostly hidden in Windows 10, at least in disk and folder windows. (They may still appear in your individual software programs.) If you miss them, you can make them reappear by pressing the Alt key, the Tab key, or an arrow key whenever the menu bar is visible. (When you're operating menus, you can release the Alt key immediately after pressing it.) In this book, in help screens, and in computer magazines, you'll see key combinations indicated like this: Alt+S (or Alt+ whatever the letter key is).

Once the underlines are visible, you can open a menu by pressing the underlined letter (F for the File menu, for example). Once the menu is open, press the underlined letter key that corresponds to the menu command you want. Or press Esc to close the menu without doing anything. (In Windows, the Esc key always means *cancel* or *stop*.)

If choosing a menu command opens a dialog box, you can trigger its options by pressing Alt along with the underlined letters. (Within dialog boxes, you can't press and release Alt; you have to hold it down while typing the underlined letter.)

Don't miss Appendix B, which lists all the important keyboard shortcuts.

The Search Box Is Fastest

If you have a keyboard, the fastest way to almost anything in Windows is the search box at the left end of the taskbar, where it says, "Type here to search."

In Windows 10, it's on the taskbar, so it's always available—and it's how you *find and open things.*

For example, to open Outlook, you can click there and type *outlook*. To get to the password-changing screen, you can type *password*. To adjust your network settings, *network*. And so on. *Display. Speakers. Keyboard. Excel. Photos. Firefox.* Whatever.

Each time, Windows does an uncanny job of figuring out what you want and highlighting it in the results list, usually right at the top.

Here's the thing, though: You don't need the mouse or trackpad to click into this search box. You can just tap the ⊞ key or button. The Start menu opens *and* your cursor blinks inside the search box.

You also don't need to type the whole search query. If you want the Sticky Notes program, *sti* is usually all you have to type. In other words, without ever lifting your hands from the keyboard, you can hit ■■, type *sti,* confirm that Windows has highlighted the correct program's name, hit Enter—and you've opened Sticky Notes. Really, really fast.

There is always a manual, mouse-clickable way to get at the same function. Here, for example, is how you might open Narrator, a program that reads everything on the screen. First, the mouse way:

1. **At the desktop, open the Start menu (■■); click Settings (⚙).**

   The Settings app opens, teeming with options.

2. **Click Ease of Access.**

   Now another Settings screen appears, filled with options having to do with accessibility.

3. **Choose Narrator.**

   The Narrator tab opens.

4. **Turn Narrator on.**

   Narrator begins reading what's on the screen.

Here, by contrast, is how you'd get to exactly the same place using the search method:

1. **Press ■■; type enough of *narrator* to make Narrator appear in the results list; press Enter.**

There you go. One step instead of four.

(Of course, if you're *really* good, you could just use the Narrator keyboard shortcut, Ctrl+■■+Enter.)

Now, you'd be forgiven for exclaiming, "What?! Get to things by typing? I thought the whole idea behind the Windows revolution was to eliminate the DOS-age practice of typing commands!"

Not exactly. Typing has always offered a faster, more efficient way of getting to places and doing things; what everyone hated was the *memorizing* of commands to type.

But the search box requires no memorization; that's the beauty of it. You can be vague. You can take a guess. And, almost every time, Windows knows what you want and offers it in the list.

For that reason, this book usually provides the most direct route to a certain program or function: the one that involves the search box. There's always a longer, slower, mousier alternative, but, hey: This book is plenty fat already, and the rainforests aren't getting any bigger.

About Alt-Clicking

Here's another bit of shorthand you'll find in this book (and others): instructions to *Alt-click* something. That means you should hold down the Alt key and then click before releasing the key. If you understand that much, then the meaning of instructions like "Ctrl-click" and "Shift-click" should be clear.

You Could Spend a Lifetime Changing Properties

You can't write an operating system that's all things to all people, but Microsoft has certainly tried. You can change almost every aspect of the way Windows looks and works. You can replace the backdrop of the screen (the *wallpaper*) with your favorite photograph, change the typeface used for the names of your icons, or set up a particular program to launch automatically every time you turn on the PC.

When you want to change some *general* behavior of your PC, like how it connects to the internet, how soon the screen goes black to save power, or how quickly a letter repeats when you hold down a key, you use the Settings app (described in Chapter 7).

Many other times, however, you may want to adjust the settings of only one particular element of the machine, such as the hard drive, the Recycle Bin, or a particular application. In those cases, *right-click* the corresponding icon. In the shortcut menu, you'll often find a command called Properties, which offers settings about that object.

Tip: As a shortcut to the Properties command, just highlight an icon and then press Alt+Enter.

It's Not Meant to Be Overwhelming

Windows has a staggering array of features. You can burrow six levels down, dialog box through dialog box, and still not come to the end of it.

Microsoft's programmers created Windows in modules—the digital-photography team here, the networking team there—for different audiences. The idea, of course, was to make sure no subset of potential customers would find a feature lacking.

But if *you* don't have a digital camera, a network, or whatever, there's nothing wrong with ignoring everything you encounter on the screen that isn't relevant to your setup and work routine. Not even Microsoft's CEO uses every feature of Windows.

About This Book

Despite the many improvements in Windows over the years, one feature hasn't improved a bit: Microsoft's documentation. Windows 10 comes with no printed guide at all.

When you do find online help, you'll quickly discover that it's tersely written, offers very little technical depth, and lacks examples. You can't mark your place, underline things, or read it in the bathroom. Worst of all, the chaos of rapid Windows 10 releases means you're never sure if the web article you're reading applies to your version.

The purpose of this book, then, is to serve as the manual that should have accompanied the May 2019 Update. In these pages, you'll find step-by-step instructions for using almost every Windows feature, including those you may not have understood, let alone mastered.

Incredibly, Microsoft intends for Windows 10 to run pretty much the same on desktop PCs *and* laptops *and* tablets. This book covers them all (see the box below).

About the Outline

This book is divided into seven parts, each containing several chapters:

- **Part One: The Windows Desktop** is really *book* one. These five chapters offer a complete course in the basics of Windows 10. Here's all you need to know about the Start menu, icons and folders, the taskbar, the Recycle Bin, shortcut menus, Cortana, the Action Center, and other elements of the new world.

- **Part Two: The Programs of Windows 10** is dedicated to the proposition that an operating system is a launchpad for *programs*. Chapter 6, for example, describes how to work with documents in Windows—how to open them, switch among them, swap data between them, and so on. This part also offers an item-by-item discussion of the individual software nuggets that make up the operating system. These include not just the items in Settings, but also the long list of free programs Microsoft threw in: Paint 3D, WordPad, Photos, and so on.

- **Part Three: Windows Online** covers all the special internet-related features of Windows, including setting up your internet account, Edge (for web browsing), and Mail (for email). Chapter 11 covers Windows' dozens of internet fortification features: the firewall, antispyware software, parental controls, and on and on.

- **Part Four: Hardware and Peripherals** describes the operating system's relationship with equipment: special features for laptops and tablets, for example, plus peripherals like scanners, cameras, disks, printers, and so on.

- **Part Five: PC Health** explores Windows 10's beefed-up backup and troubleshooting tools. It also describes some advanced hard drive formatting tricks and offers tips for making your PC run faster and better.

GEM IN THE ROUGH

The Touchscreen Verb Challenge

Microsoft intends for Windows 10 to work just as well on touchscreen tablets as it does on PCs with a keyboard and mouse (or trackpad). That presents something of a challenge to people writing books about it.

Thousands of times in this book, instructions direct you to activate something on the screen: a button, checkbox, icon, or tile. But what's the right verb here? If you have a touchscreen, telling you to *click* something doesn't sound quite right. And if you have a mouse, it'd be weird to tell you to *tap* something.

So in the spirit of peace and understanding, in this book, you're generally instructed to *hit, select,* and *choose* things on the screen. Those are equal-opportunity verbs that should confuse neither touch people nor mouse people.

- **Part Six: The Windows Network** is for the millions of households and offices that contain more than one PC. File sharing, accounts, passwords, and remote access are all here.

- **Finally, two appendixes** provide a guide to installing or upgrading to Windows 10, and a master list of Windows keyboard shortcuts.

System Requirements for Your Brain

Windows 10 May 2019 Update: The Missing Manual is designed to accommodate readers at every technical level (except system administrators, who will be happier with a different sort of book).

The primary discussions are written for advanced-beginner or intermediate PC owners. But if you're using Windows for the first time, special sidebar articles called "Up to Speed" provide all the introductory information you need. If you're fairly advanced, on the other hand, keep your eye out for similar shaded boxes called "Power Users' Clinic." They offer more technical tips, tricks, and shortcuts for the veteran PC fan.

About→These→Arrows

Throughout this book, and throughout the Missing Manual series, you'll find sentences like this: "Open ■→⚙→System." That's shorthand for a much longer instruction that directs you to open three nested icons in sequence, like this: "Open the ■ menu; choose ⚙. Once the Settings window opens, hit the System tab."

Similarly, this kind of arrow shorthand simplifies the business of choosing commands in menus, or opening nested folders. See Figure I-2.

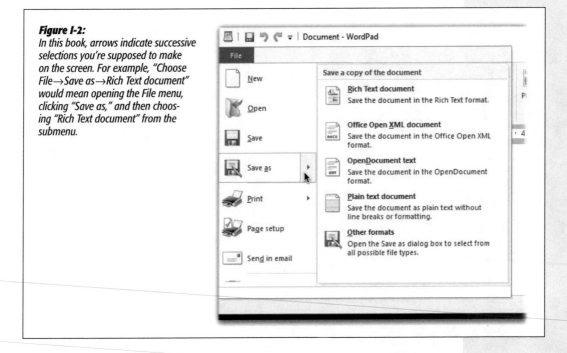

Figure I-2:
In this book, arrows indicate successive selections you're supposed to make on the screen. For example, "Choose File→Save as→Rich Text document" would mean opening the File menu, clicking "Save as," and then choosing "Rich Text document" from the submenu.

About MissingManuals.com

To get the most out of this book, visit *missingmanuals.com*. Click the "Missing CD" link—and then this book's title—to reveal a tidy, chapter-by-chapter list of the shareware and freeware mentioned in this book.

Also, to keep the book under that 3,000-page threshold that the publisher is so huffy about, a number of the most technical features of Windows 10 are explained in free, downloadable PDF appendixes in the same location.

The website also offers corrections and updates. To see them, click the book's title, and then click View/Submit Errata. In fact, please submit such corrections yourself! In an effort to keep the book as up to date as possible, each time we print more copies, we'll make any confirmed corrections you've suggested. We'll also note such changes on the website so you can mark important corrections into your own copy of the book, if you like.

Part One:
The Windows Desktop

1

Desktop & Start Menu

T hese days, the graphic user interface (the colorful world of icons, windows, and menus) is standard. Windows, macOS, Chrome OS, Linux—every operating system is fundamentally the same, which is to say a very long way from the lines of typed commands that defined the earliest computers.

Windows 10 restores the desktop to its traditional importance, after a weird three-year detour into the "what the—??" land known as Windows 8. The desktop is your home base, your starting point. It's the view that greets you when the computer turns on, and it offers all the tools you need to manage and organize your files.

Herewith: a grand tour of the state of the art in computer desktops—the one in Windows 10.

The Lock Screen

When you turn on a Windows 10 machine, the first thing you see is a colorful curtain that's been drawn over the computer's world. It's the *Lock screen* (Figure 1-1).

The Lock screen serves the same purpose as on a phone: It gives a quick glance at the time, the date, your Wi-Fi signal strength, the weather, and (on laptops and tablets) your battery charge. As you download and install new apps, they can add informational tidbits to the Lock screen, too.

The point is that sometimes you don't really need to wake the machine up. Maybe you just want to know what time it is. Or to ask about tomorrow's weather, or to find out yesterday's sports scores, or to speak a reminder for yourself—courtesy of Cortana, Windows 10's voice assistant. She's available at the Lock screen, too (unless you object; see page 181).

The Lock screen can also give you instant access to your Camera and Skype apps (pages 296 and 338). You might want to take a picture or answer a call without having to go through the red tape of fully signing in. Little icons offer one-click access to headlines, weather, and financial news, too; see page 156.

Figure 1-1:
In Settings, you can control which apps are allowed to add information to the Lock screen, like the options shown here.

You're not stuck with the Lock screen photo as Mother Microsoft has installed it, either. You can change the picture, if you like, or you can eliminate it altogether. Chapter 4 has the details.

When you do want to go past the Lock screen to sign in, there's nothing to it. Almost anything you do that says "I'm here!" works:

- **Touchscreen:** Swipe a finger upward. (Swipe down to jump into Camera mode.)
- **Mouse:** Click anywhere. Or turn the mouse wheel.
- **Keyboard:** Press any key.

The Lock screen slides up, revealing the sign-in screen (Figure 1-2).

Tip: You can change almost everything about the Lock screen. Out of the box, it shows you a gorgeous photo every day, courtesy of Bing Images, but you may prefer one of your own pictures, or a slideshow of them. You can also fiddle with which information appears here, or even eliminate the Lock screen altogether. (After all, it's an extra click every time you sign in.) See page 155 for details on customizing the Lock screen.

The Sign-In Screen

As in any modern operating system, you have your own *account* in Windows. It's your world of files, settings, and preferences. So the second thing you encounter in Windows 10 is the sign-in screen. Here, at lower left, you see the name and photo for each person who has an account on this machine (Figure 1-2). Choose yours.

Tip: Ordinarily, the sign-in screen offers its own wallpaper backdrop: a Windows logo or a solid color. But if you prefer, for consistency's sake, you can direct it to use the same wallpaper photo as the Lock screen before it. To set that up, open ■→⊚→Personalization→Lock screen; turn on "Show lock screen background picture on the sign-in screen."

Figure 1-2:
If your machine has more than one account set up, tap or click your own icon to sign in.

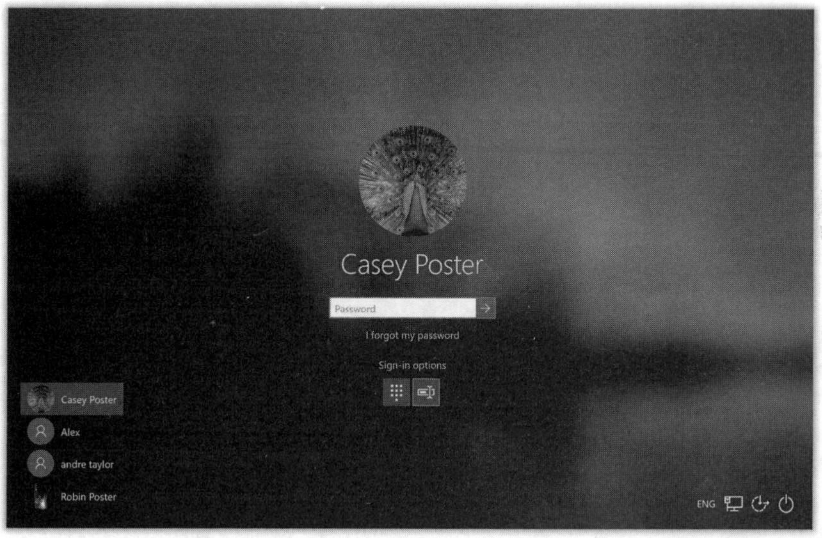

This is also where you're supposed to sign in—to prove you're you. But *signing in* doesn't have to mean *typing a password.* One of Windows 10's primary goals is to embrace touchscreens, and typing on tablets is a pain.

Therefore, you can sign in using any of these techniques:

- **Just *look* at your screen.** On laptops or tablets with Intel's RealSense infrared cameras, facial recognition signs you in.

- **Swipe your finger across the fingerprint reader,** if your computer has one.

- **Put your eye up to the iris reader,** if your machine is so equipped.

- **Draw three lines, taps, or circles** on a photo you've selected.

- **Type in a four-digit PIN you've memorized.**

- **Type in a traditional password.**

- **Skip the security altogether.** Jump directly to the desktop when you turn on the machine.

See Chapter 18 for instructions on setting each of these up.

The Desktop

Once you've gotten past security, you finally wind up at the home base of Windows: the desktop. See Figure 1-3 for a crash course.

You can, and should, make the desktop look however you want. You can change its background picture or color scheme; you can make the text larger; you can pack it with icons you use a lot. Chapter 4 is a crash course in desktop decoration.

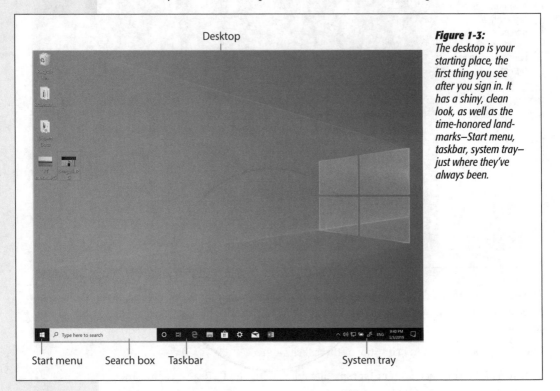

Desktop

Figure 1-3:
The desktop is your starting place, the first thing you see after you sign in. It has a shiny, clean look, as well as the time-honored land-marks—Start menu, taskbar, system tray—just where they've always been.

Start menu   Search box   Taskbar   System tray

Meet the Start Menu

Windows is composed of 50 million lines of computer code, scattered across your hard drive in thousands of files. The vast majority of them are not for you; they're support files, there for behind-the-scenes use by Windows and your applications. They may as well bear a sticker reading "No user-serviceable parts inside."

That's why the Start menu is so important (Figure 1-4). It lists every *useful* piece of software on your computer, including commands, programs, and files. Just about everything you do in Windows can begin with your Start menu.

The *word* "Start" doesn't actually appear on the Start menu, as it did for years; now the Start menu is just a square button in the corner of your screen, bearing the Windows logo (🪟). But it's still called the Start menu, and it's still the gateway to everything on the PC (Figure 1-3, lower left).

If you're the type who bills by the hour, you can open the Start menu by clicking it with the mouse. If you feel life's too short, however, tap the ⊞ key on the keyboard instead—or the one on the screen, if you have a touchscreen.

Really, truly: *Learn this*. Use ⊞ to open the Start menu (or to close it!).

The Start menu is usually split into three columns (Figure 1-4). For convenience, let's call them the places list (far left); the apps list (center); and the tiles (right).

Note: If your computer is a tablet, with no physical keyboard at all, it may start up in Windows 10's *Tablet mode*. In this mode, the tiles side of the Start menu fills the entire screen, and the left columns don't appear unless you tap the ⌂ in the top-left corner. For details on Tablet mode, see Chapter 12.

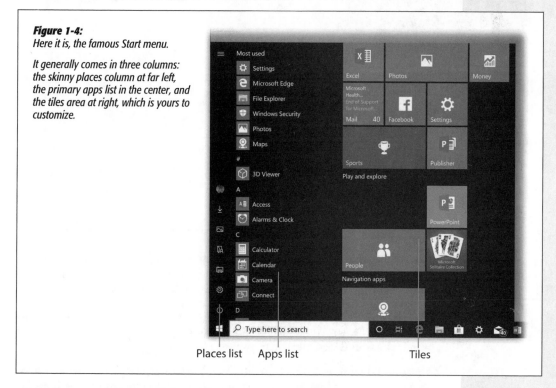

Figure 1-4:
Here it is, the famous Start menu.

It generally comes in three columns: the skinny places column at far left, the primary apps list in the center, and the tiles area at right, which is yours to customize.

Places list   Apps list   Tiles

Start Menu: The Places List

Ever since Microsoft completely fouled up the works in Windows 8, it's been trying to perfect the Start menu. And starting in 2017, it added yet another twist: a skinny mini-column at the far left. It begins life with only a few icons—here's a rundown.

[Your Round Icon]

See the tiny round icon at the top of the places list, at the left edge of the Start menu (Figure 1-5)?

The picture is a pop-up menu. And its commands all have to do with switching from one account to another. (In Windows' *accounts* feature, each person gets to see her own desktop picture, email account, files, and so on. See Chapter 18.) Here's what they do:

Tip: Some keystrokes from previous Windows versions are still around. For example, you can still press Ctrl+Alt+Delete to summon three of the features described here—lock the machine, switching the user, and signing out—plus a bonus link for the Task Manager (page 213).

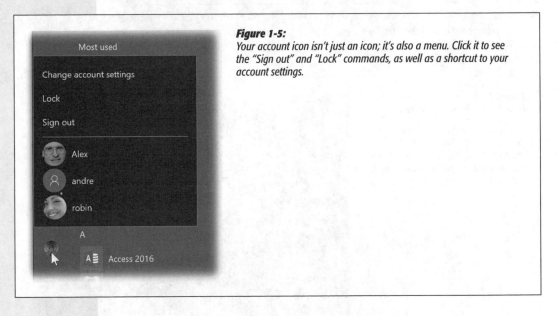

Figure 1-5:
Your account icon isn't just an icon; it's also a menu. Click it to see the "Sign out" and "Lock" commands, as well as a shortcut to your account settings.

- **Change account settings** opens the Accounts settings screen, where you can change your account picture, password, sign-in method, and other details of your account—and you can create accounts for other family members.

- **Lock.** This command takes you back to the Lock screen described at the beginning of this chapter. This is an ideal way to protect your PC from nosy people who wander by your desk while you're away.

- **Sign out.** When you choose "Sign out," Windows presents a new sign-in screen so somebody else can sign in. Whatever *you* had running remains open behind the scenes. When you sign in again, you'll find all your open programs and documents exactly as you left them.

- **[Other account names.]** The drop-down menu concludes with the names of other account holders on this PC. It lets other people dive directly into their own accounts without having to sign you off first.

Settings (⚙)

Adjusting the settings and preferences of your PC is about six steps quicker now, since Settings is listed right here in the Start menu. Chapter 7 covers Settings in absurd detail.

Power (⏻)

Hard though it may be to believe, there may come a day when you want to shut down or restart your computer. See page 37.

How to Customize the Places List

You can add *other* important folders to the places list, following the steps shown in Figure 1-6. These are some of your options:

- **File Explorer.** This icon in the places column represents the File Explorer "app": the standard desktop window, which shows the contents of your drives and folders.

- **Personal folder.** Windows keeps *all* your stuff—your files, folders, email, pictures, music, bookmarks, even settings and preferences—in one handy, central location: your *personal folder.* This folder bears your name, or whatever account name you typed when you installed Windows.

  Technically, your personal folder lurks inside the *C: > Users* folder. But that's a lot of burrowing when you just want a view of your empire. That's why you can install your personal folder here, right on the Start menu.

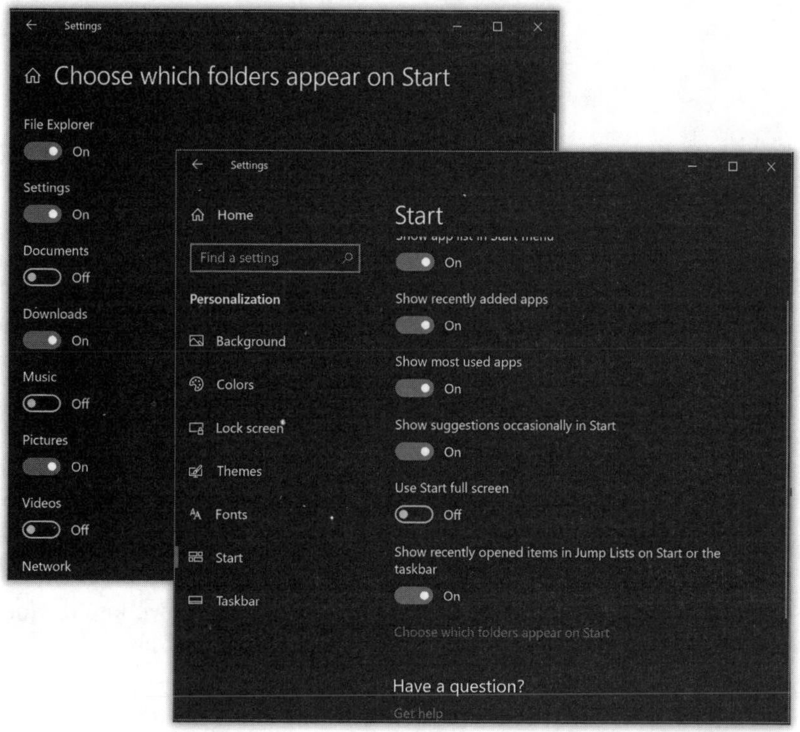

Figure 1-6:
You can add other important folders to your Start menu. Choose
■■→⚙→*Personalization→Start (bottom right).*

Click "Choose which folders appear on Start."

Up pops a list of items like File Explorer, Settings, Documents, Downloads, Music, Pictures, Videos, and Network (top left), so you can turn on or off the ones you like.

- **Documents.** This opens your Documents folder, a very important folder indeed. It's designed to store just about all the work you do on your PC—everything except music, pictures, and videos, which get folders of their own.

  Of course, you're welcome to file your documents *anywhere* on the hard drive, but most programs propose depositing newly created documents into the Documents folder.

Note: The Documents folder actually sits in the *This PC* > *Local Disk (C:)* > *Users* > *[your name]* folder.

If you study that path carefully, it should become clear that what's in Documents when *you* sign in isn't the same thing as other people will see when *they* sign in. That is, each account holder (Chapter 18) has a different Documents folder, whose contents switch according to who's signed in.

- **Music, Pictures, Videos.** Microsoft assumes (correctly) that most people these days use their home computers for managing digital music, photos, and video collections. As you can probably guess, the Music, Pictures, and Videos folders are intended to house them—and these Start-menu icons are quick ways to open them.

- **Downloads.** Out of the box, Windows puts your downloaded files into this Downloads folder (which is inside your personal folder). It makes sense to add this item to your Start menu so you have quick access to it.

- **Network** opens (what else?) the Network folder, where you can see a map of your home or office network and make changes to the settings. See Chapter 19.

Start Menu: The Apps List

The center column of the Start menu—the list of programs—may *look* like the Start menu that's been in Windows from the beginning (except during that unfortunate Windows 8 phase). But there's a big difference: In Windows 10, you can't use it to list your own favorite programs, folders, and files. (That's what the right side is for.) The apps list is meant to be managed and run entirely by Windows itself.

This column has three sections, described here from top to bottom.

Recently Added

The "Recently added" list appears only if you've recently downloaded or installed some new apps. It's surprisingly handy, especially for novices, who often download something from the internet and then can't find where it landed.

If you've installed *lots* of new apps, scroll down into the full apps list; little "New" indicators show you which are the recent arrivals.

Tip: You can hide the "Recently added" section if you like. Open the Start menu; choose ⚙→Personalization→Start; turn off "Show recently added apps." Close Settings.

Most Used

The next part of the apps menu is a list of the programs Windows sees you using a lot. Windows computes this list automatically and continuously. It's a really great feature, because, well, if you've been using something a lot recently, you'll probably use it a lot more still, and now you don't have to burrow around looking for it.

On the other hand, if you'd rather not have Windows track what you're doing, you can get rid of the "Most used" list, or just certain items on it; see page 29.

All Apps

The next chunk of the Start menu's middle list is an important list indeed: the master catalog of every program on your computer (Figure 1-7). As a bonus, the word "New" appears beneath the name of any *new* programs—ones you've installed but haven't yet used.

Tip: Once the "All apps" list is open, you can choose anything in it without involving the mouse. Just press the ↑ and ↓ keys to highlight the item you want, or type a few letters of its name. Then press Enter to seal the deal.

You can jump around in the list using an alphabetic index, shown at right in Figure 1-7.

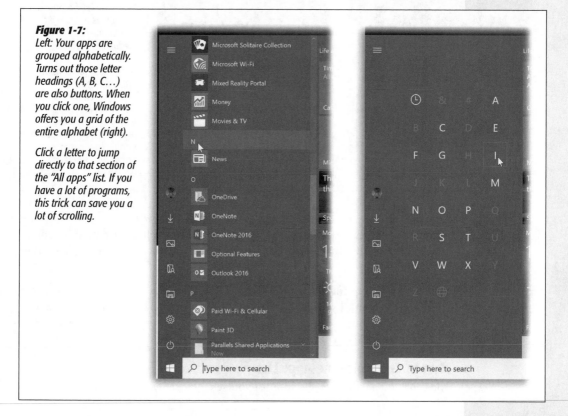

Figure 1-7:
Left: Your apps are grouped alphabetically. Turns out those letter headings (A, B, C…) are also buttons. When you click one, Windows offers you a grid of the entire alphabet (right).

Click a letter to jump directly to that section of the "All apps" list. If you have a lot of programs, this trick can save you a lot of scrolling.

Tip: How cool is this? You can uninstall a program right from the Start menu apps list. Just right-click it (or hold your finger down on it); from the shortcut menu, choose Uninstall. Confirm in the dialog box that appears. (You can't uninstall apps that came with Windows 10 this way—only stuff *you've* added.)

Folders

The "All apps" list doesn't list just programs. It also houses a number of *folders*. See Figure 1-8.

Tip: Submenus, also known as cascading menus, have been eliminated from the Start menu. Instead, when you open something that contains *other* things—like a folder listed in the Start menu—you see its contents listed beneath, indented slightly, as shown at right in Figure 1-8. Click the folder name again to collapse the sublisting.

Keyboard freaks should note that you can also open a highlighted folder in the list by pressing the Enter key (or the → key). Close the folder by pressing Enter again (or the ← key).

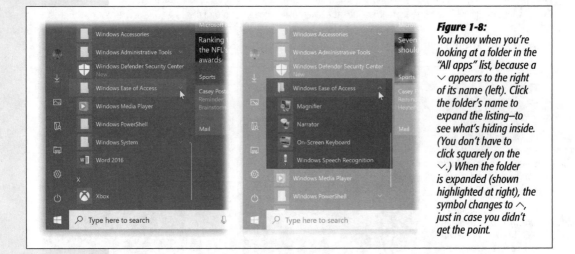

Figure 1-8:
You know when you're looking at a folder in the "All apps" list, because a ⌄ appears to the right of its name (left). Click the folder's name to expand the listing—to see what's hiding inside. (You don't have to click squarely on the ⌄.) When the folder is expanded (shown highlighted at right), the symbol changes to ⌃, just in case you didn't get the point.

- **Software-company folders.** Some of these folders bear the names of software you've installed; you might see a folder called, for example, PowerSoft or Logitech. These generally contain programs, uninstallers, instruction manuals, and other related junk.

- **Program-group folders.** Another set of folders is designed to trim down the Programs menu by consolidating related programs, like Games, Accessories (little single-purpose programs), and Maintenance. Everything in these folders is described in Chapter 8.

How to Customize the Apps List

You can't add anything to the apps list yourself. Nor can you change the order.

You do, however, have several opportunities to redesign the apps list. To find these special switches, open ▦→⚙→Personalization→Start. Now look over your options:

- **Eliminate the "Most used" list.** Maybe it would be best that your boss or your spouse didn't know what you've been up to. In that case, turn off "Show most used apps." When you next inspect the Start menu, you'll be happy to see that the top-center chunk, where the recently used programs are usually listed, is creepily blank.

Tip: *If there's just* one *compromising listing here, no big deal; right-click its name and, from the shortcut menu, choose More→"Don't show in this list." It's gone.*

- **Eliminate the "Recently added" list.** Similarly, you can get rid of the second section of this menu, where Windows displays apps you've recently installed. Just turn off "Show recently added apps." (You can also hide just one item in this list, using the technique in the previous Tip.)

- **Eliminate the entire apps list.** Weird but true: you can ask Windows not to show the apps list at all (turn off "Show app list in Start menu"). Instead, you get only two columns in the Start menu: the places column and the tiles. Your Start menu is now more compact and tidy—an arrangement that's not for everyone, but just right for certain lovable oddballs who use other techniques for opening their apps.

  Besides, your full apps list isn't really gone forever. You can bring it back by clicking the ☰ icon that now appears in the places column. It replaces tiles with the regularly scheduled apps list. (You can then click the ⊞ icon to bring back the tiles.)

- **Move something to Start or the taskbar.** Suppose there's some app—say, Calculator—that's listed in "Most used," "Recently installed," or the main apps list. And you think you'd rather have it installed on your taskbar, visible at all times. Or you think it'd work best as a tile on the right side.

  Right-click its name. From the shortcut menu, choose "Pin to taskbar" or "Pin to Start." It disappears from the left side and goes where you sent it.

Tip: *On a touchscreen, you can "right-click" something by holding your finger down on it for a second.*

The App List Shortcut Menu

If you right-click an app's name (Figure 1-9), you get a very promising submenu that may contain commands like these:

- **Unpin from Start.** If this app is also represented as a tile on the fly-out Start menu, then this command vaporizes the tile. Now the app is listed only here, in the apps list.

- **More.** This submenu usually offers commands like "Unpin from taskbar" (if the app is, in fact, pinned to the taskbar as described on page 81), "App settings" (dive directly into this app's settings), "Rate and review" (on the app store), "Share" (with friends you think might like the app), and "Don't show in this list" (stop making this app appear in the "Most used" list, possibly because you don't want your spouse or boss *knowing* it's among your most-used apps).

- **New window, Uninstall.** Some apps offer these app controls right in the shortcut menu, too.

- **Recent documents.** Some apps, including Microsoft Office apps like Word and Excel, add your most used *documents* to this list, too, for quick and easy access later.

Tip: In fact, you can "pin" these documents to this list, so they won't disappear when newer ones come along. To do that, just point to a document's name and click the ⊶ that appears next to its name; see Figure 1-9.

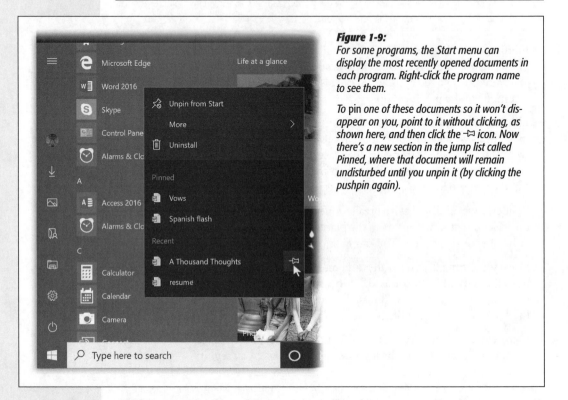

Figure 1-9:
For some programs, the Start menu can display the most recently opened documents in each program. Right-click the program name to see them.

To pin one of these documents so it won't dis-appear on you, point to it without clicking, as shown here, and then click the ⊶ icon. Now there's a new section in the jump list called Pinned, where that document will remain undisturbed until you unpin it (by clicking the pushpin again).

Start Menu: The Tiles

The right side of the Start menu is all that remains of the Great Touchscreen Experiment of 2012, during which Microsoft expected every PC on earth to come with a touchscreen. Instead of a Start menu, you got a Start *screen*, stretching across of your monitor, displaying your files, folders, and programs as giant rectangular tiles.

Turns out most people preferred the Start *menu*.

There were some nice aspects of the Start screen, though. For one thing, it was more than just a launcher—it was also a dashboard. The tiles weren't just buttons that *opened* the corresponding program; they were also little displays—*live tiles*—showing real-time information from that program.

So in Windows 10, Microsoft decided to retain those colorful live tiles—on the right side of the Start menu (Figure 1-10). The Calendar tile shows you your next appointment. The Mail tile shows your latest incoming subject line. The People tile shows Twitter and Facebook posts as they pour in.

Tip: The tiles for Calendar, People, and Mail are meant to be visual dashboards, so how are you supposed to know those apps' names? To find out, point to one with your cursor without clicking. A tinted, rectangular tooltip bar appears, identifying the name.

You can make this scrolling "column" bigger; you can even make it fill the screen, as it did in Windows 8; or you can hide it completely. But this time it's up to you. The Start menu takes over your world only as much as you want it to.

Figure 1-10:
As you drag the top or right edge of the right side of the Start menu, you see it snap to a larger size once you've moved your cursor far enough. You don't have an infinite degree of freedom here; you can only double the width or, if you have one of those rare Samsung Billboard Monitors, maybe triple it.

You can also adjust the height of the Start menu—by dragging the top edge. You can goose it all the way to the top of your screen, or you can squish it down to mushroom height.

Tip: If you're keyboard oriented, you can use the arrow keys to highlight the icon you want and then press the Enter key to open it.

How to Customize the Tiles Menu

The tiles section of the Start menu is your playground. If your current job doesn't work out, you could become a full-time tiles-menu customizer.

Make the tile area bigger or smaller

If you have a mouse or a trackpad, you can make the right side of the Start menu wider or taller; just grab the right edge or the top edge and drag. (You can't enlarge the Start menu with your finger on a touchscreen.)

Make the tile area fill the screen

Maybe you were one of the 11 people who actually *liked* Windows 8, including the way it had a Start *screen* instead of a Start menu. Well, that look is still available. From the Start menu, choose ⚙→Personalization→Start. Turn on "Use Start full screen."

In this mode, the live tiles fill your entire desktop (which is handy for touchscreens). You still get the Utility menu (page 39), along with the ▤ icon in case you want to bring the apps list back.

Note: If your goal is to use Windows 10 on a tablet, you don't need to do all this. Just turn on Tablet mode (page 449). In Tablet mode, the full-screen tiles section is standard and automatic.

Resize a tile

Tiles come in four sizes: small square, medium square, large square, and rectangle. As part of your Start menu interior-decoration binge, you may want to make some of the tiles bigger and some of them smaller. Maybe you want to make the important ones rectangular so you can read more information on them. Maybe you want to make the rarely used ones smaller so more of them fit into a compact space.

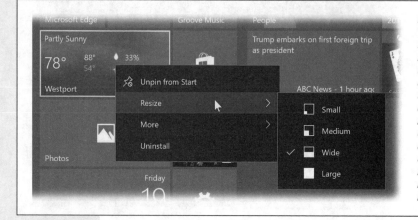

Figure 1-11:
Tiles come in four sizes: Small (tiny square, no label); Medium (4x the times of Small–room for a name); Wide (twice the width of Medium); and Large (4x the size of Medium). Wide and Large options appear only for apps whose live tiles can display useful information. Drag them around into a mosaic that satisfies your inner Mondrian.

Right-click the tile. (Touchscreen: Hold your finger down on the tile; tap the ⋯ button that appears.) From the shortcut menu, choose Resize. All icons give you a choice of Small and Medium; some offer Wide or Large options, too. See Figure 1-11.

Move a tile

You can drag the tiles into a new order. With the Start menu open, just drag the tile to a new spot. The other tiles scoot out of the way to make room.

If you're using a touchscreen, hold your finger down on the tile for half a second before dragging it.

Add new tiles

You can add tiles to the right side. They can be apps, folders, or disks (but not individual files).

- **The right-click method.** Right-click an icon wherever fine icons are found: in a window, on the desktop, or in the apps list. (Touchscreen: Hold your finger down on the icon for a second.) From the shortcut menu, choose Pin to Start.

- **The drag method.** You can also drag an app's name out of the apps list directly into the tiles area. (You can't drag them from desktop windows.)

Tip: In the Edge browser, you can also add a web page to the right side. With the page open, click the ⋯ button at top right; choose Pin to Start.

In each case, the newly installed tile appears at the bottom of the right side. (You might have to scroll to see it.)

Make the tile blocks wider

In the beginning, each major block of tiles is the width of *three Medium tiles.* That is, you could fit three Medium tiles across, or one Wide plus one Medium, or one Large plus one Medium. But you couldn't put two Large tiles side by side, or two Wides, or four Mediums.

But now, thanks to vociferous lobbying by the Wider Tile Blocks Bloc, you can.

To bring about this happy arrangement, open ⊞→⚙→Personalization→Start, and then click "Show more tiles on Start."

Make a tile stop blinking

Some tiles are *live tiles*—tiny dashboards that display real-time information. There, on the Mail tile, you see the subject lines of the past few incoming messages; there, on the Calendar tile, is your next appointment; and so on.

It has to be said, though: A Start menu filled with blinky, scrolling icons can look like Times Square at midnight. If you're feeling quite caffeinated enough already, you might prefer your live tiles to be a little more…dead.

To silence the animation of a live tile, right-click it. (Touchscreen: Hold your finger down on it, and then tap ☺.) From the shortcut menu, choose More, and then choose "Turn live tile off." The tile's current information disappears, and the live updating stops. To reverse the procedure, right-click an unmoving tile; from the shortcut menu, choose More and then "Turn live tile on."

Remove a tile

Open the Start menu. Right-click the tile you want to eliminate. (Touchscreen: Hold your finger down on it, and then tap the ··· button.) From the shortcut menu, choose Unpin from Start. You're not discarding that item—just removing its tile.

Group your tiles

The Start menu's tiles aren't scattered pell-mell; they present an attractive, orderly mosaic. Not only are they mathematically nestled, but they're actually *grouped.*

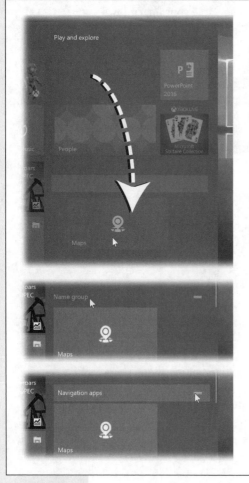

Figure 1-12:

Top: To create a new tile group, start by dragging one lonely tile below all other tiles. This is your colonist. A fat horizontal divider bar appears when you've gone far enough. Let go.

Middle: Point to the starter name ("Name group") and click.

Bottom: Type a name for the group. Use the grip strip to drag the group into a new spot, if you like.

Each cluster of related tiles can bear a name, like "Life at a glance" (Calendar, Mail, Weather…) or "Play and explore" (games, music, TV…).

But you can change those headings, or those groupings, and come up with new ones of your own (see Figure 1-12). It works like this:

1. **Drag a tile to the very bottom of the existing ones. (Touchscreen: Hold your finger still for a second before dragging.)**

   When you drag far enough—the tiles area might scroll, but keep your mouse or finger down—a horizontal bar appears, as shown in Figure 1-12. That's Windows telling you, "I get it. You want to create a new group right here."

2. **Drag the tile below the bar and release it.**

   Release the tile you're dragging; it's now setting up the homestead. Go get some other tiles to drag over into the new group to join it.

3. **Click or tap just above your newly grouped tiles.**

   The words "Name group" appear.

4. **Type a name for this group, and then press Enter.**

   Your group name is now immortalized.

By the way: Whenever you point to (or tap) the heading of any group, you may notice a little "grip strip" at the right side. If you like, you can drag that strip up or down to move the entire group to a new spot among your existing groups. (Or horizontally, if you have a multicolumn right side.)

At any point, you can rename a group (click or tap its name; type). To eliminate a group, just drag all its tiles away, one at a time. When the group is empty, its name vanishes into wherever withered, obsolete tile groups go.

Tip: In the May 2019 Update, you can, for the first time, delete an entire group in one fell swoop. Just right-click the group's name; from the shortcut menu, choose "Unpin group from Start."

Create tile folders

You can create *folder tiles* right there in the Start menu, too, for your organizational pleasure. They look like ordinary tiles—but when you click one, it expands to reveal the tiles within it. You create a new folder exactly the way you would on an iPhone or Android phone: Drag one app's icon directly on top of another's (within the tiled area of the Start menu).

Change the color

You can also change the colors of the various Start menu elements (and the taskbar, and the Action Center). See Chapter 4 for the step-by-steps.

Eliminate all tiles

It's possible to eliminate the *entire* right side. If you like your Start menu to look like it did in the good old days, with only the left side showing, refer to Figure 1-13.

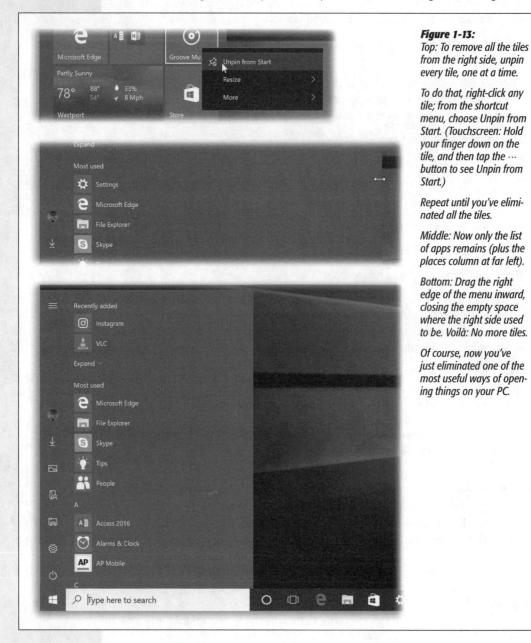

Figure 1-13:

Top: To remove all the tiles from the right side, unpin every tile, one at a time.

To do that, right-click any tile; from the shortcut menu, choose Unpin from Start. (Touchscreen: Hold your finger down on the tile, and then tap the ⋯ button to see Unpin from Start.)

Repeat until you've eliminated all the tiles.

Middle: Now only the list of apps remains (plus the places column at far left).

Bottom: Drag the right edge of the menu inward, closing the empty space where the right side used to be. Voilà: No more tiles.

Of course, now you've just eliminated one of the most useful ways of opening things on your PC.

Turn off ads

From time to time, you may spot a Start menu tile you didn't put there. That's a suggestion about an app Microsoft thinks you might like—so in other words, an ad.

If you'd prefer Microsoft and its ad partners to keep their hands off your Start menu, open ■→⚙→Personalization→Start and turn off "Show suggestions occasionally in Start."

Shutting Down

What should you do when you're finished using your computer for the moment?

Millions of people shut their PCs off, but they shouldn't; it's a colossal waste of time. When you shut down, you have to wait for all your programs to close—and then the next morning, you have to reopen everything, reposition your windows, and get everything back the way you like it.

You shouldn't just leave your computer *on* all the time, either. That's a waste of electricity, a security risk, and a black mark for the environment.

What you *should* do is put your machine to sleep. If it's a laptop, just close the lid. If it's a tablet, press the Sleep switch. If it's a desktop PC, you can set it up so it goes to sleep when you press the physical power button (see page 38).

The Sleep/Shut Down/Restart Commands

If you really want to do the sleeping or shutting down thing using the onscreen commands, click the ⏻ at the bottom of the places column of the Start menu.

As shown in Figure 1-14, shutting down is only one of the options for finishing your work session. What follows are your others.

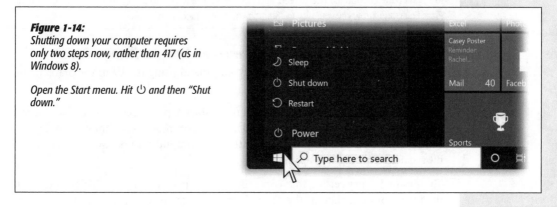

Figure 1-14:
Shutting down your computer requires only two steps now, rather than 417 (as in Windows 8).

Open the Start menu. Hit ⏻ and then "Shut down."

Sleep

Sleep is great. When the flight attendant hands over your cranberry cocktail, you can take a quick break without closing all your programs. The instant you put the computer to sleep, Windows quietly transfers a copy of everything in memory into an invisible file on the hard drive, keeping it at the ready with a tiny trickle of battery power.

If you do return soon, everything reappears on the screen faster than you can say, "Redmond, Washington." If you *don't* return shortly, Windows eventually cuts power, abandoning what it had memorized in RAM.

Now your computer is using no power at all; it's in *hibernate* mode. Fortunately, Windows still has the hard drive copy of your work environment. So *now* when you tap a key to wake the computer, you may have to wait 30 seconds or so—not as fast as 2 seconds, but certainly better than the 5 minutes it would take to start up, reopen all your programs, reposition your document windows, and so on.

The bottom line: When you're done working for the moment—or for the day—put your computer to sleep instead of shutting it down. You save power, you save time, and you don't risk any data loss.

Restart

This command quits all open programs and then quits and restarts Windows again automatically. The computer doesn't actually turn off. You might do this to "refresh" your computer when you notice it's responding sluggishly, for example.

Shut down

When you shut down your PC, Windows quits all open programs, offers you the opportunity to save any unsaved documents, exits Windows, and turns off the computer.

There's almost no reason to shut down your PC anymore, though. Sleep is almost always better all the way around. The only exceptions have to do with hardware installation. Anytime you have to open up the PC to make a change (installing memory, hard drives, or sound or video cards), you should shut the thing down first.

Tip: If you're stuck without a mouse, here's an all-keyboard route to shutting down: Press Ctrl+Alt+Delete to summon the Lock/Switch User screen, and then tab your way over to the ⏻ button in the lower right. Press Enter, and arrow-key your way to "Shut down." Press Enter again.

Three Triggers for Sleep/Shut Down—and How to Change Them

You now know how to trigger the Sleep command using the ⏻ in the Start menu. But there are even faster ways.

If you have a laptop, just close the lid. If it's a tablet, tap its Sleep switch. If you have a desktop PC, press its power button (⏻). In each of these cases, though—menu, lid, switch, or button—*you* can decide whether the computer shuts down, goes to sleep, hibernates, or just ignores you.

To find the factory setting that controls what happens when you close the lid or hit the power button, click in the "Type here to search" box and search for *lid*. In the search results, the top hit is "Change what closing the lid does." Press Enter to select it.

Note: You can get to the same options by opening Control Panel→Hardware and Sound→Power Options→ System Settings.

Now you arrive at the "Define power buttons" screen of the old Control Panel. Here, for each option (pressing the power button; pressing the Sleep button, if you have one; closing the lid), you can choose "Sleep," "Do nothing," "Hibernate," "Shut down," or "Turn off the display." And you can set up different behaviors for when the machine is plugged in and when it's running on battery power.

Tip: You can also restart, shut down, lock, or sign out of your computer with Cortana; see page 184.

Navigating the Start Menu by Keyboard

If your computer has a physical keyboard—you old-timer, you!—you can navigate and control the Start menu in either of two ways.

Use the Arrow Keys

Once the Start menu is open, you can press the Tab key to hop among the three columns (the places icons, the apps list, and the tiles). Once you've highlighted a column, you can press the ↑ or ↓ keys to "walk" up or down that column, highlighting successive items.

Once you've highlighted something, you can press Enter to "click" it (open it), or tap the ⊞ key or Esc to close the Start menu and forget the whole thing.

Use the Search Box

This thing is *awesome*. The instant you press the ⊞ key, your insertion point blinks in the "Type here to search" search box on the taskbar (Figure 1-14).

The instant you start to type, you trigger Windows' very fast, whole-computer search function. This search can find files, folders, programs, email messages, address book entries, calendar appointments, pictures, movies, PDF documents, music files, web bookmarks, and Microsoft Office documents, among other things.

It also finds anything *in* the Start menu, making it a very quick way to pull up something without having to click through a bunch of submenus. You can read the meaty details about search in Chapter 3.

The Secret Power Users' Menu

The ⊞ button harbors a secret: It can sprout a hidden utility menu, as shown in Figure 1-15. To see it, right-click the ⊞ button, or (on a touchscreen) hold your finger down on it. Or just press ⊞+X.

There, in all its majesty, is the secret utility menu. It's seething with shortcuts to toys for the technically inclined. Some are especially useful to have at your mousetip:

- **System** opens a window that provides every possible detail about your machine.
- **Desktop** offers one-click teleportation back to your desktop from within whatever program you're using.

• **Task Manager.** Huge. This special screen (page 213) is your lifeline when a program seems to be locked up. Thanks to the Task Manager, you can quit that app and get on with your life.

Note: To the dismay of the technically inclined, Microsoft has made two changes to the power users' menu. First, the Control Panel is no longer listed. (Microsoft's feeling is that the much cleaner-looking Settings app houses almost everything you'd ever want to change. If you disagree, you can still open the Control Panel—type *contr* into the Start menu's search box, for example.)

Second, the Command prompt is no longer in the power users' menu. It's been replaced by something called Microsoft PowerShell.

All you have to know is that a) the Command prompt is still available, b) you can bring it back to the power users' menu, and c) PowerShell is basically the same thing, only much more recent and powerful. See page 358 for details on all this stuff.

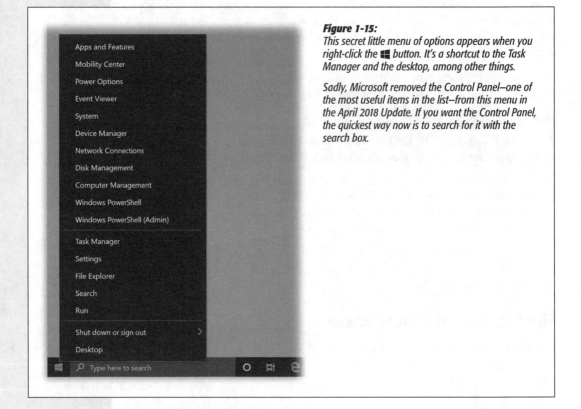

Figure 1-15:
This secret little menu of options appears when you right-click the ⊞ *button. It's a shortcut to the Task Manager and the desktop, among other things.*

Sadly, Microsoft removed the Control Panel—one of the most useful items in the list—from this menu in the April 2018 Update. If you want the Control Panel, the quickest way now is to search for it with the search box.

File Explorer, Taskbar & Action Center

Windows got its name from the rectangles on the screen—the windows—where all your computer activity takes place. You look at a web page in a window, type into a window, read email in a window, and look at lists of files in a window. But as you create more files, stash them in more folders, and open more programs, it's easy to wind up paralyzed before a screen awash with cluttered, overlapping rectangles.

Fortunately, Windows has always offered icons, buttons, and other inventions to help you keep these windows under control—and Windows 10 positively crawls with them.

The primary tool at the desktop is called File Explorer (formerly Windows Explorer). That's the program—the app—that displays the icons of your files, folders, disks, and programs.

Like any well-behaved program, File Explorer has an icon of its own. You can open a File Explorer window either by clicking the manila-folder button on the taskbar or the ▣ icon in the Start menu's places list, if you've put it there.

A desktop window opens, and the fun begins.

Universal Window Controls

A lot has changed in Windows since a few years ago. If you're feeling disoriented, firmly grasp a nearby stationary object and read the following breakdown.

Here are the controls that appear on almost every window, whether in an app or in
File Explorer (see Figure 2-1):

- **Control menu.** This tiny icon has sat in the upper-left corner of every File Explorer
  window since Windows XP. It was invisible (though still functional) in Windows 7,
  but you can clearly see it now.

  In any case, the Control menu contains commands for sizing, moving, and closing the window. One example is the Move command. It turns your cursor into a
  four-headed arrow; at this point, you can move the window by dragging *any* part
  of it, even the middle.

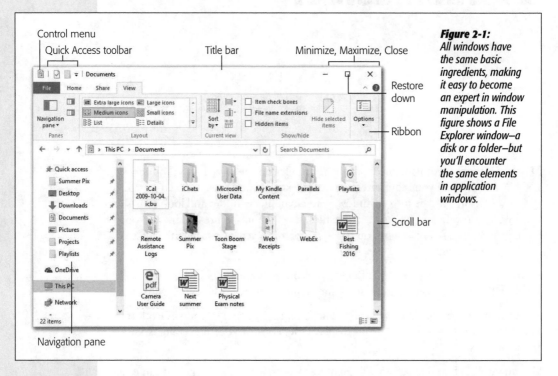

Control menu

Quick Access toolbar   Title bar   Minimize, Maximize, Close

Restore down

Ribbon

Scroll bar

Navigation pane

Figure 2-1:
*All windows have
the same basic
ingredients, making
it easy to become
an expert in window
manipulation. This
figure shows a File
Explorer window—a
disk or a folder—but
you'll encounter
the same elements
in application
windows.*

Why bother, since you can always just drag the top edge of a window to move it?
Because, sometimes, windows get dragged *past* the top of your screen. You can
hit Alt+space to open the Control menu, type M to trigger the Move command,
and then move the window by pressing the arrow keys (or by dragging *any* visible
portion). When the window is where you want it, hit Enter to "let go" or the Esc
key to return the window to its original position.

Tip: You can double-click the Control menu spot to close a window.

- **Quick Access toolbar.** You can dress up the left end of the title bar with tiny icons
  for functions you use a lot—like Undo, Properties, New Folder, and Rename. And

how do you choose which of these commands show up? By turning them on and off in the Customize Quick Access Toolbar menu (⩒), which is always the last icon *in* the Quick Access toolbar.

Tip: As you can see in the ⩒ menu, the Quick Access toolbar doesn't have to appear in the title bar (although that is the position that conserves screen space the best). You can also make it appear as a thin horizontal strip below the Ribbon, where it's not so cluttered. Just choose—what else?—"Show below the Ribbon."

- **Title bar.** This big, fat top strip is a giant handle you can use to drag a window around. It also bears the name of the window or folder you're examining.

Tip: The title bar offers two great shortcuts for maximizing a window, making it expand to fill your entire screen exactly as though you had clicked the Maximize button described below. Shortcut 1: Double-click (or double-tap) the title bar. (Double-click it again to restore the window to its original size.) Shortcut 2: Drag the title bar up against the top of your monitor.

- **Ribbon.** That massive, tall toolbar at the top of a File Explorer window is the Ribbon. It's a dense collection of controls for the window you're looking at. You can hide it, eliminate it, or learn to value it, as described starting on page 52.

- **Navigation pane.** Some form of this folder tree, a collapsible table of contents for your entire PC, has been part of Windows for years. It's described on page 63.

- **Window edges.** You can reshape a window by dragging any edge—even the very top. Position your cursor over any border until it turns into a double-headed arrow. Then drag inward or outward to make the window smaller or bigger. To resize a full-screen window, click the Restore Down (◻) button first.

Tip: You can resize a window in two dimensions at once by dragging one of its corners. It doesn't have to be a certain corner; all four work the same way.

- **Minimize, Maximize, Restore Down.** These three window-control buttons, at the top of every Windows window, cycle a window among its three modes—minimized, maximized, and restored, as described on the following pages.

- **Close button.** Click the ✕ button to close the window. (Keyboard shortcut: Press Alt+F4.)

Tip: Isn't it cool how the Minimize, Maximize, and Close buttons are highlighted when your cursor passes over them? That's not a gimmick; it's a cue that lets you know when the button is clickable. You might not otherwise realize, for example, that you can close, minimize, or maximize a *background* window without first bringing it forward. But when the background window's Close box glows red, you know.

- **Scroll bar.** A scroll bar appears on the right side or bottom of the window if the window isn't large enough to show all its contents.

Window Management

Windows 10 carries on the window-stunt tradition of previous versions: special shortcuts expressly designed for managing windows. Most of them involve some clever *mouse gestures*—special dragging techniques. Thanks to those mouse movements and the slick animations you get in response, goofing around with your windows may become the new Solitaire.

Sizing Windows

A Windows window can cycle among three altered states.

Maximized

A maximized window is one that fills the screen, edge to edge, so you can't see anything behind it. It gets that way when you do one of these things:

- Click its Maximize button (□).
- Double-click the title bar.
- Drag the window up against the top of the screen.
- Press ⊞+↑.

Maximizing the window is an ideal arrangement when you're surfing the web or working on a document for hours at a stretch, since the largest possible window means the least possible scrolling.

Once you've maximized a window, you can restore it to its usual, free-floating state in any of these ways:

- Drag the window away from the top edge of the screen.
- Double-click the title bar.
- Click the Restore Down button (❐). (It's how the Maximize button appears when the window is *already* maximized.)
- Press ⊞+↓.

Tip: If the window *isn't* maximized, then this keystroke minimizes it instead.

- Press Alt+space, and then R.

Minimized

When you click a window's *Minimize* button (−), the window gets out of your way. It shrinks down into the form of a button on your taskbar at the bottom of the screen. Minimizing a window is a great tactic when you want to see what's behind it. (Keyboard shortcut: ⊞+↓.)

You can bring the window back, of course (it'd be kind of a bummer otherwise). Point (without clicking) to the taskbar button that represents that window's *program*. For example, if you minimized a File Explorer (desktop) window, then point to the File Explorer icon. If you have a touchscreen, just *touch* the program's taskbar button.

On the taskbar, the program's button sprouts handy thumbnail miniatures of the minimized windows when you point to it without clicking. Select a window's thumbnail to restore it to full size. (You can read more about this trick later in this chapter.)

Tip: There's a keyboard trick that lets you minimize all your windows at once, revealing your entire desktop. Just press ■+M (you can think of M as standing for "Minimize all"). Add the Shift key (Shift+■+M) to bring them all back.

Restored

A *restored* window is neither maximized nor minimized; it's a loose cannon, floating around on your screen as an independent rectangle. Because its edges aren't attached to the walls of your monitor, you can make it any size you like by dragging its borders.

Moving a Window

Moving a window is easy: Drag the big, fat top edge.

Closing a Window

Microsoft wants to make absolutely sure you're never without some method of closing a window. It offers at least nine ways to do it:

- **Click the Close button** (the ✕ in the upper-right corner).

Tip: If you've opened more than one window, Shift-click that Close button to close *all* of them.

- **Press Alt+F4.** This one's worth memorizing. You'll use it everywhere in Windows.

- **Double-click the window's upper-left corner.**

- **Right-click (or hold your finger on) the window's button on the taskbar,** and then choose Close from the shortcut menu.

- **Point to a taskbar button without clicking.** Thumbnail images of its windows appear. Point to a thumbnail; an ✕ button appears in its upper-right corner. Click it.

- **On a touchscreen, tap a taskbar button with your finger.** Thumbnail images of its windows appear, with ✕ buttons in their top-right corners. Tap ✕.

- **Right-click the window's title bar (top edge),** and choose Close from the shortcut menu. (Touchscreen: Hold your finger down on the title bar instead.)

- **In a File Explorer window, choose File→Close.** That works in most other programs, too.

- **Quit the program you're using, sign off, or shut down the PC.**

Be careful. In many programs, including most web browsers, closing the window also quits the program entirely.

Hiding All Windows but One

If you've become fond of minimizing windows—and why not?—then you'll love this trick. If you give your window's title bar a rapid back-and-forth *shake*, you minimize all *other* windows. The one you shook stays right where it was (Figure 2-2).

Tip: This shaking business makes a snazzy YouTube demo video, but it's not actually the easiest way to isolate one window. If the window you want to focus on is already the frontmost window, then you can just press ⊞+Home to achieve the same effect. Press that combo a second time to restore all the minimized windows.

Handily enough, you can bring all the hidden windows back again, just by giving the hero window another title-bar shake.

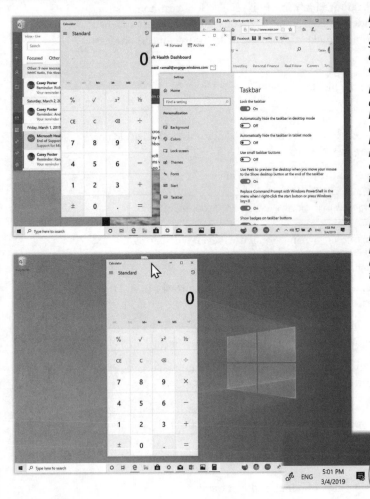

Figure 2-2:
Top: OK, this is the state of your screen. You want to have a look at your desktop—but, oy, what a cluttered mess!

Bottom: So you give this window's title bar a little shake—at least a couple of horizontal or vertical back-and-forths—and boom! All other windows are minimized to the taskbar, so you can see what you're doing. Give the title bar a second shake to bring the hidden windows back again.

Inset: This is the Show Desktop button. It's a tiny slice at the far-right end of the taskbar. It makes all windows vanish. Click it again to get them to reappear.

Note: Dialog boxes aren't affected by this shaking thing—only full-blown windows.

Background Windows

When you have multiple windows open on your screen, only one window is *active*, which affects how it works:

- **It's in the foreground,** *in front* of all other windows.

- **It's the window that "hears"** your keystrokes and mouse clicks.

- **Its Close button is black.** (Background windows' Close buttons are light gray, at least until you point to them.)

As you would assume, clicking a background window brings it to the front.

Tip: And pressing Alt+Esc sends an active window to the *back.* Bet you didn't know that one!

And what if it's so far back that you can't even see it? That's where Windows' window-management tools come in; read on.

Tip: For quick access to the desktop, you can press ▓+D. Pressing that keystroke again brings all the windows back to the screen exactly as they were.

There's a secret button that does the same thing, too. It's the Show Desktop button—a 3-pixel sliver that occupies the *farthest-right portion* of the taskbar (Figure 2-2, inset). Click that spot to make all windows and dialog boxes disappear *completely,* so you can do something on your desktop. They're not minimized—they don't shrink down into the taskbar; they're just gone. Click the Show Desktop button a second time to bring them back from invisible-land.

Windows Snap—Now with Four Panes!

Here's a weird, wild feature that not many people know about, probably because there's no visible sign that it even exists. But you can neatly split your screen between two windows, full height, edge to edge of the monitor, as shown in Figure 2-3. Or, in Windows 10, even *four* windows. (Eight-window Snap will have to wait until Windows 11.)

And why would you bother? Well, a full-height, half-width window is ideal for reading an article, for example. You wouldn't want your eyes to have to keep scanning the text all the way across the football field of your screen, and you wouldn't want to spend a lot of fussy energy trying to make the window tall enough to read without scrolling a lot. This gesture sets things up for you with one quick drag.

But this half-screen trick is even more useful when you apply it to *two* windows. Now it's simple to compare any two windows' contents, or to move or copy stuff between them.

Split the screen into two windows

Here's how Snap works. You can follow along in Figure 2-3:

1. **Mash the first window to the right or left edge of the screen.**

   Mouse, trackpad, finger: Using the window's title bar as a handle, drag the window to the right or left edge of the screen. When you've gone far enough, Windows shows you an outline of the proposed new window shape. Let go.

   Keyboard: It's actually much faster to use the keyboard shortcuts: ⊞+← to snap the window against the left side or ⊞+→ to snap it against the right.

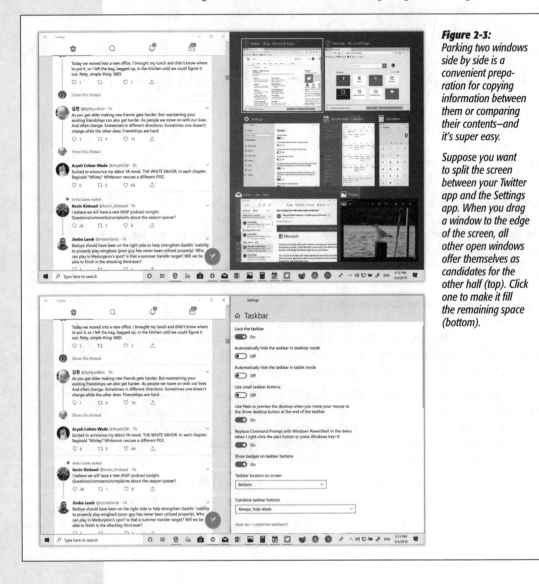

Figure 2-3:
Parking two windows side by side is a convenient preparation for copying information between them or comparing their contents—and it's super easy.

Suppose you want to split the screen between your Twitter app and the Settings app. When you drag a window to the edge of the screen, all other open windows offer themselves as candidates for the other half (top). Click one to make it fill the remaining space (bottom).

Tip: To move the window back again, either hit the same keystroke a few more times (it cycles left, right, original spot, over and over), or use the ⊞ key with the opposite arrow key.

At this point, your window is now hugging the side of your monitor, extending only halfway into it (Figure 2-3, top). But that's not the end of the magic show.

2. **Adjust the width of the half-window, if you like.**

That's right: Your Windows Snap experience doesn't have to result in a 50/50 split of the screen. It can be 60/40 or whatever you like, within reason. Just grab the inward edge of the window and drag it as wide or narrow as you like.

3. **Click the miniature of the window you want to fill the other half of the screen.**

Thanks to a feature called Snap Assist, you may notice that the *other* open windows have shrunk down to little index cards, huddling in the empty half of the screen. They're saying: "Which of us will you pick to fill the empty half?" Click the one you want, and voilà: two windows, perfectly splitting the available screen area (Figure 2-3, bottom).

To end the Snap session, drag a window away from the edge or press ⊞+← or ⊞+→.

Note: If you're using two monitors, the ⊞+← or ⊞+→ keystrokes instead make your active window jump to the other monitor. See page 171.

Split the screen into three or four windows

If you have a big monitor, you might actually use this Windows 10 feature. It lets you cram four windows into quadrants of your screen, neatly filling every available pixel. You feel like you're some kind of crazy day trader, or maybe a security guard keeping an eye on all the cameras.

NOSTALGIA CORNER

Turn Off All the Snapping and Shaking

It's cool how Windows makes a window snap against the top or side of your screen. Right? It's better than before, right?

It's perfectly OK to answer, "I don't think so. It's driving me crazy. I don't want my operating system manipulating my windows on its own."

In that case, you can turn off the snapping and shaking features. Open the Start menu. Type enough of the word *arrange* until you see "Arrange windows automatically by dragging them to the sides or corners of the screen." Select it. You've just opened the ⊞→⚙→System→Multitasking control panel.

Here you can turn off the snapping feature ("Arrange windows automatically by dragging them to the sides or corners of the screen"), the automatic resizing of a window ("When I snap a window, automatically size it to fill available space"), multi-window resizing ("When I resize a snapped window, simultaneously resize any adjacent snapped window"), and Snap Assist ("When I snap a window, show what I can snap next to it").

From now on, windows move only when and where you move them. (Shaking a window's title bar doesn't hide other windows now, either. And, alas, the ⊞+↑ and ⊞+↓ keystrokes for Maximize and Restore Down no longer work.)

Or, if you prefer, you can split the screen among *three* windows (25 percent, 25 percent, 50 percent).

The steps are similar to the two-pane version. Start with some open windows. Then:

1. **Move the first window into a corner of the screen.**

   Mouse, trackpad, finger: Using the window's title bar as a handle, drag the window to a *corner* of the screen. It's a little tricky; you have to move the cursor, or your finger, *directly* into the *exact* corner. If you don't see the ghost outline of the proposed new window shape, drag away and try again.

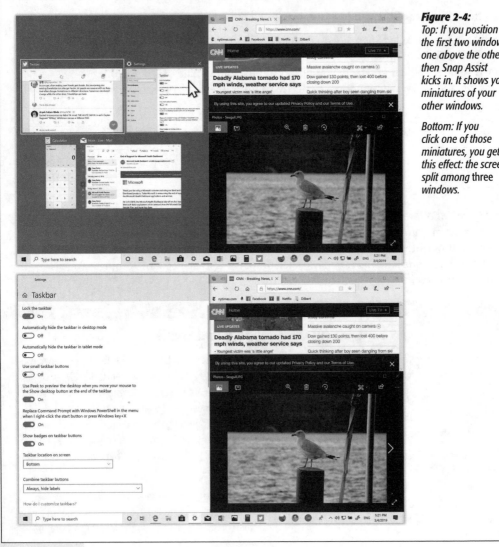

Figure 2-4:
Top: If you position the first two windows one above the other, then Snap Assist kicks in. It shows you miniatures of your other windows.

Bottom: If you click one of those miniatures, you get this effect: the screen split among three windows.

Keyboard: The keyboard shortcut is much faster and more surefire. While holding down the ⊞ key, hit → and then ↑ (for the upper-right corner). Or ← and ↓ (lower-left corner). You get the idea. Don't hit the arrows simultaneously, but one after the other.

Tip: Tweaky but true: Always hit the *horizontal* arrow first. If you press ⊞+↓ and *then* →, you'll lose your window—because ⊞+↓ means "minimize this window"!

At this point, you have one window filling one quadrant of the screen.

2. **Click the second window; move it into *its* corner.**

Use the same techniques (drag or keyboard).

3. **Move the remaining one or two windows into their corners.**

It doesn't really matter which order you fill the corners of your screen, except in one instance: if you want only *three* windows to split the screen. See Figure 2-4.

To unsnap, use the opposite keyboard shortcuts. Or drag the window's top edge with your mouse, trackpad, or finger.

Tip: If you have more than one monitor, add the Shift key to move the frontmost window to the next monitor, left or right.

The Full-Height Window Trick

This trick has never gotten much love from Microsoft's marketing team, probably because it's a little hard to describe. But it can be very useful.

It's not the same as the Snap thing described previously; this one doesn't affect the *width* of the window. It does, however, make the window exactly as tall as your screen, sort of like *half*-maximizing it.

Grab the *bottom* edge of your window and drag it *down,* to the bottom edge of your screen. The window snaps vertically to the top and bottom of your screen but maintains its width and horizontal position.

Tip: There's a keyboard shortcut for this feature: Shift+⊞+↑ to create the full-height effect.

To restore the window to its original dimensions, drag its top or bottom edge away from the edge of your screen.

Note: These window-morphing tricks make a good complement to the traditional "Cascade windows," "Show windows stacked," and "Show windows side by side" commands that appear when you right-click an empty spot on the taskbar.

The Ribbon

Windows offers all kinds of crazy ways to shape, sort, group, slice, and dice the contents of a File Explorer window. The controls are hiding in the Ribbon, which is a glorified horizontal toolbar at the top of the window.

Word, PowerPoint, Excel, and other Microsoft programs have Ribbons of their own, but here's an introduction to the one in File Explorer.

This Ribbon offers several tabs full of buttons. They can differ from window to window; for example, in a window full of pictures, you get buttons that are especially useful for managing picture files (Figure 2-5).

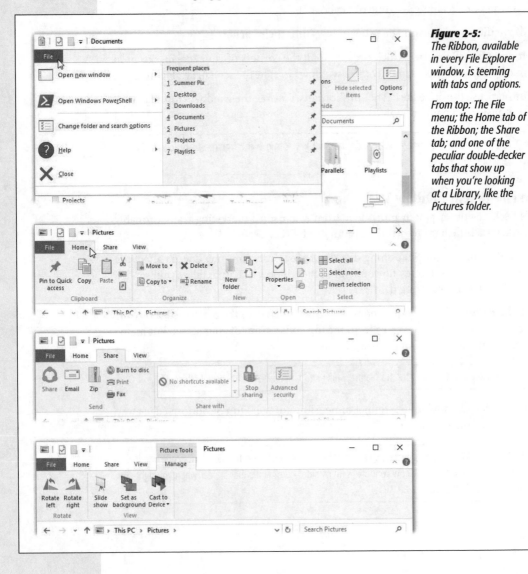

Figure 2-5:
The Ribbon, available in every File Explorer window, is teeming with tabs and options.

From top: The File menu; the Home tab of the Ribbon; the Share tab; and one of the peculiar double-decker tabs that show up when you're looking at a Library, like the Pictures folder.

You can collapse the Ribbon to get it out of your way; it is, after all, pretty tall. You do that by clicking the ⌄ button at the window's upper-right corner, or by pressing Ctrl+F1. (Later, you can bring it back by clicking the ⌃ button, or by pressing Ctrl+F1 again. But that might not be necessary; even when the Ribbon is collapsed, its tab names—File, Home, Share, View, and so on—are still visible for quick clicking.)

Tip: The Ribbon also goes away in Full Screen mode, in which your File Explorer window fills the entire screen. (Press F11 to start or stop Full Screen mode.)

You can also get rid of it permanently, using the free Ribbon Disabler program. You can download that from this book's "Missing CD" page at *missingmanuals.com*.

But before you go whole-hog into a Ribbon-cutting ceremony, consider what the Ribbon has to offer.

File Tab

Ha, fooled you! The word "File" here looks like all the other tabs, but it's actually a weird kind of menu (Figure 2-5, top). The idea, as always, is to cram every possible command you might want into one central place, so you don't have to hunt.

Note: Many of these commands have submenus (a ▶ pointing to the right, containing more commands). But unlike normal submenus, you don't have to choose one of the subcommands. For example, the "Open new window" command has a submenu, but you can click or tap the "Open new window" command itself. If you *do* want one of the submenu choices, hit the ▶ symbol to see them.

Here's a rundown:

- **Open new window.** Creates a duplicate of the window you're browsing. (The submenu offers another "Open new window" command, plus "Open new window in new process." A *process* is a computer's train of thought. Hard-core PC geeks sometimes like to open a new window, or a second copy of the same one, in a new computer process in case the first one crashes. Not something you'll do every day.)

- **Open Windows PowerShell.** PowerShell is a command console and scripting language. If you're a programmer, PowerShell lets you write simple programs, called *cmdlets* ("commandlets") that can perform all kinds of automated drudgery for you: Copy or move folders, manipulate files, open or quit programs, and so on.

  You harness all this power by typing up *scripts* in PowerShell's command line interface (which means no mouse, no menus, no windows—all text, like in the DOS days). In short, PowerShell is not for the layperson. If you're an ambitious layperson, however, a Google search for *PowerShell tutorial* unveils all kinds of websites that teach you, step by step, how to harness this very advanced tool.

Note: This menu also used to include Command Prompt. If you prefer that older scripting environment to PowerShell, you can bring it back to this menu. Open ⊞→⚙→Personalization→Taskbar and turn off "Replace Command Prompt with Windows PowerShell in the menu when I right-click the start button or press Windows key+X."

- **Options.** Opens the Folder Options dialog box, covered in a PDF appendix to this book. See "The 'Folder Options' Options" on the Missing CD at *missingmanuals.com*.

- **Help.** The Help command opens a Bing search. The About Windows subcommand just opens a dialog box that identifies which version of Windows you have.

- **Close.** Closes the File Explorer window.

- **Frequent places.** Here, for your convenience, is a listing of important folders in your account (Desktop, Downloads, Documents, Pictures, Music, and so on), plus folders you've accessed recently. The idea is to save you some burrowing.

Tip: If you have a keyboard, you can save time by hitting the number next to the folder. In fact, *all* the File menu commands offer keyboard shortcuts. See how it says "Open new window"? That underline means you can type the N key to open a new window, rather than using the mouse or a finger.

Home Tab

This tab of the Ribbon is, more or less, an exploded view of the shortcut menu that would appear if you right-clicked a desktop icon. But Microsoft research shows that a huge number of Windows fans don't even *know* about the shortcut menus—so by putting these commands in the Ribbon, the company hopes to make these useful commands more "discoverable."

- **Pin to Quick access.** The "Quick access" area lists folders and files you've used recently, so it's easier to get back to them later. By using this command, you can force icons to appear in this folder. See page 63.

- **Copy, Cut, Paste.** These commands let you copy, cut, and paste icons from one window to another.

- **Copy path.** This command copies the icon's navigational *path* to the Clipboard, ready for pasting somewhere. See page 135.

Power Keys for the Ribbon

The Ribbon is supposed to enhance your efficiency by putting every conceivable command in one place, with nothing hidden. But how efficient is a tool that requires mousing?

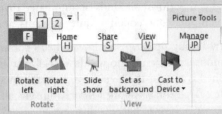

Fortunately, the Ribbon is fully keyboard-operable. It even has a built-in cheat sheet. To see it, press the Alt key, which is the universal Windows shortcut for "Show me the keyboard shortcuts." Now you see the little boxed letter-key shortcuts for each of the tabs, as

shown here. (Those keystrokes work, however, even if you haven't first summoned the cheat sheet.)

Sometimes, you'll actually see *two*-letter codes, to be typed one letter at a time. In a Pictures library, for example, the Picture Tools tab of the Ribbon offers "JP" as the keyboard shortcut to get you to the Manage tab. But the idea is the same: to save you time and mousing.

- **Paste Shortcut.** If you've copied an icon to the Clipboard, this command pastes a shortcut icon of it—another handy way to make a shortcut (page 129).

- **Move to, Copy to.** These handy buttons/menus make it quick and easy to move or copy selected icons to another place on your computer. The pop-up menu lists frequently and recently opened folders; you can also hit "Choose location" to specify a folder that's not listed here. Either way, the beauty is that you can move or copy icons without having to open and position the destination window.

- **Delete.** The pop-up menu offers two commands: "Recycle" (moves the selected icon to the Recycle Bin) and "Permanently delete" (deletes the file forever without its usual stop in the Recycle Bin). The third item, "Show recycle confirmation," isn't a command—it's an on/off switch for the "Are you sure?" message that usually appears when you put something into the Recycle Bin.

- **Rename.** Opens the selected icon's name-editing box.

- **New Folder.** Makes a new, empty folder in the current window, ready for you to name and fill up with icons.

- **New item.** Here's a catch-all drop-down menu that lists new things you might want to create in the open window: a new folder, a shortcut (page 129), a contact (that is, a new person page in the People app), a Microsoft Word document, a Journal document, a text document, a compressed (zipped) folder, and so on. You may see different items here, since different programs can modify this menu to make your life more convenient.

- **Easy access.** Here's an even more miscellaneous drop-down menu of commands; all apply to icons you've selected in the window. To understand "Map as drive," read page 578. "Include in library" adds the selected icon to one of your libraries, which are described in a free PDF appendix to this book. See "Libraries" on the Missing CD at *missingmanuals.com*.

The remaining commands—"Always available offline," "Sync," and "Work offline"—pertain to the offline files feature described on page 141.

- **Properties.** This button/menu offers two options: "Properties" opens the selected icon's Properties dialog box, where you can read a wealth of detail about its size, type, and so on. "Remove properties" strips all that stuff out of a file, usually because you're about to send it to somebody and don't want them to know about its revision history, modification dates, and so on.

Tip: You can just click the icon to open the Properties dialog box. That is, you don't actually have to choose from the submenu.

- **Open.** Do you really need a button that opens the selected icon? Yes, if it's a type of file that *more than one program can open.* For example, suppose you have a picture file. Do you want to open it in Photoshop or in the Photos app? This pop-up menu changes to reflect the programs that are capable of opening the selected icon.

- **Edit.** This button opens the highlighted icon in the first program Windows finds that can edit that file type.

- **History.** This button opens a window that tracks the file's editing history. It's an essential part of the *File History* feature described on page 513; it lets you rewind a certain document to an earlier version.

- **Select all, Select none.** As you'd guess, these commands highlight all the icons in the window, or none of them.

- **Invert selection.** This command swaps what you've selected. In other words, if you've highlighted files A and B (but not C and D), then this command highlights files C and D and deselects A and B.

Share Tab

This tab offers a full line of controls for sharing the icons in the window—via email, fax, printer, or other people on your network.

- **Share.** Click to open a panel listing apps that can hand off the selected item. For example, if you've selected a file, the choices might include Mail (to send it as an attachment) or Dropbox (to put a copy in your Dropbox). This Share panel is a standard Windows 10 element, and it appears in many apps.

- **Email.** Click to open a new outgoing email message with the selected file(s) attached, ready to address and send.

- **Zip.** Compresses the selected file(s) into one compact, self-contained .zip file. Great for sending a batch of related files to somebody in a way that contains all the necessary pieces.

- **Burn to disc.** Prompts you to insert a blank CD or DVD; Windows will burn a copy of the selected file(s) onto that disc. (If you don't have a disc burner, then this icon is dimmed.)

- **Print.** Opens the document and, depending on what kind of file it is, prepares it for printing.

- **Fax.** Sends the selected file(s) to your fax modem, if you have one.

- **Specific people.** Makes the selected file(s) available for accessing over the network by people you specify. (Chapter 19 has details.) When you click here, a window opens up with a list of people on the network, so you can choose the lucky collaborators.

- **Remove access.** Turns off network sharing so that, once again, you're the only person who can see the selected file(s).

- **Advanced security.** This control, too, affects file sharing on the network. It gives you much finer control over who's allowed to do what to the selected file: See it? Open it? Change it? Chapter 19 contains more on these file permissions.

View Tab

This tab controls the look, arrangement, and layout of the icons in the window: list view, icon view, sorted alphabetically, sorted chronologically, and so on. For the complete rundown, see "The 'Folder Options' Options," a free PDF appendix to this book. It's on the Missing CD at *missingmanuals.com*.

Library Tools/Manage Tab

In a few places, you get a bonus tab—with a weird double-stacked title. These tabs appear only when you've opened the window of a *library*—a special class of folders that can display the contents of *other* folders, wherever they may actually sit on your machine, without your having to move them. You can read more about libraries on this book's Missing CD; see the PDF appendix "Libraries" at *missingmanuals.com*.

Music Tools/Play Tab

In the navigation list at the left side of a File Explorer window, folders like Music and Pictures await your inspection. Each offers a special Ribbon tab of its own. For example, when you've selected a music file in the Music library (either the one Windows gives you or one you've made yourself), the window bears a new double-decker tab called Music Tools/Play. These are your options:

- **Play.** Opens your music-playback program and begins playing the highlighted music. (If you've never selected a favorite playback program, Windows offers you a list of music programs and invites you to choose one.)

- **Play all.** Opens your playback app and begins playing everything in the window.

- **Add to playlist.** Adds the highlighted music file to a new, untitled playlist in Windows Media Player. The idea is that you can root around here, in a File Explorer window, adding files to a playlist without having to open Media Player first.

Picture Tools/Manage Tab

Opening the Pictures library folder offers a special double-decker tab, too, stocked with commands for controlling pictures. They include these:

- **Rotate left, Rotate right.** Turns the selected photos 90 degrees. Handy if they're coming up turned sideways because of the way you held the camera.

- **Slide show.** Starts an immediate full-screen slideshow. Click the mouse or tap to go to the next picture; press the arrow keys to go forward or backward faster; press the Esc key to stop the show.

- **Set as background.** Instantly applies the selected photo to your desktop as its new wallpaper!

- **Cast to Device.** If you have an Xbox, a Miracast adapter, or another playback gadget attached to your TV, then you can send a photo or slideshow from your Windows machine to the big screen with this one click.

Tabucopia

Incredibly, that's not all the tabs. You'll see other tabs appear when you open certain window types. There's a Ribbon tab just for the Recycle Bin. There's a Disk Tools tab (when you open a disk window), a Shortcut Tools tab (for a shortcut), an Application Tools tab (for a program), and so on. Part of the fun is encountering new tabs you've never seen before.

The File Explorer Address Bar

When you're working at the desktop—that is, opening File Explorer folder windows—you'll find a few additional controls dotting the edges.

In a web browser, the address bar is where you type the addresses of the websites you want to visit. In a File Explorer window, the address bar is more of a "bread-crumbs bar" (that's a shout-out to Hansel and Gretel fans). That is, it now shows the path you've taken—folders you burrowed through—to arrive where you are now (Figure 2-6).

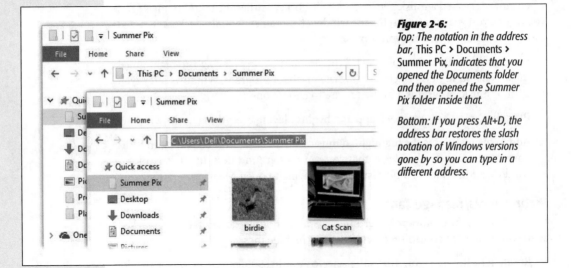

Figure 2-6:
Top: The notation in the address bar, This PC > Documents > Summer Pix, *indicates that you opened the Documents folder and then opened the Summer Pix folder inside that.*

Bottom: If you press Alt+D, the address bar restores the slash notation of Windows versions gone by so you can type in a different address.

There are three especially cool things about this address bar:

- **It's much easier to read.** Those **>** little **>** brackets are clearer separators of folder names than the older\slash\notation. And instead of drive letters like C:, you see the drive *names.*

Tip: If the succession of nested folders' names is too long to fit the window, then a microscopic **≪** icon appears at the left end of the address. Click it to reveal a drop-down menu showing, from last to first, the other folders you've had to burrow through to get here.

(Below the divider line, you see, for your convenience, the names of all the folders on your desktop.)

- **It's clickable.** You can click any bread crumb to open the corresponding folder. For example, if you're viewing the *Casey* > *Pictures* > *Halloween* folder, then you can click the *word* Pictures to backtrack to the Pictures folder.

- **You can still edit it.** The address bar of old was still a powerful tool, because you could type in a folder address directly (using the slash notation).

  Actually, you still can. You can "open" the address bar for editing in any of four different ways: (1) Press Alt+D. (2) Click the tiny icon to the left of the address. (3) Click any blank spot. (4) Right-click (or hold your finger down) anywhere in the address; from the shortcut menu, choose Edit Address.

  In each case, the address bar changes to reveal the old-style slash notation, ready for editing (Figure 2-6, bottom).

Tip: *After you've had a good look, press Esc to restore the* > *notation.*

Components of the Address Bar

On top of all that, the address bar houses a few additional doodads that make it easy for you to jump around on your hard drive (Figure 2-7):

- **Back (←), Forward (→).** Just as in a web browser, the Back button opens whatever window you opened just before this one. Once you've used the Back button, you can then use the Forward button to return to the window where you started. *Keyboard shortcuts:* Alt+←, Alt+→.

- **Recent pages list.** Click the ⌄ to the left of the address bar to see a list of folders you've had open recently; it's like a multilevel Back button.

- **Recent folders list.** Click the ⌄ at the *right* end of the address bar to see a dropdown menu of addresses you've recently typed.

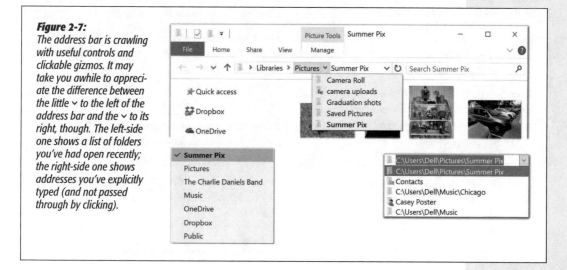

Figure 2-7:
The address bar is crawling with useful controls and clickable gizmos. It may take you awhile to appreciate the difference between the little ⌄ to the left of the address bar and the ⌄ to its right, though. The left-side one shows a list of folders you've had open recently; the right-side one shows addresses you've explicitly typed (and not passed through by clicking).

- **Up (↑).** This delightful button, right next to the address bar, means "Open the parent folder of this one." It's a novice-friendly incarnation of the trusty Alt+↑ keystroke.

  For example, if you've drilled down into the *USA > Texas > Houston* folder, you could hit this button (or Alt+↑) to pop "upward" to the Texas folder, again for the USA folder, and so on. If you hit ↑ enough times, you wind up at your desktop.

- **Contents list.** This one takes some explaining, but for efficiency nuts, it's a gift from the gods.

  It turns out that the little **>** next to each folder name is actually a drop-down menu. Click it to see what's *in* the folder name to its left.

  How is this useful? Suppose you're viewing the contents of the *USA > Florida > Miami* folder, but you decide that the file you're looking for is actually in the *USA > California* folder. Do you have to click the Back button, retracing your steps to the USA folder, only to then walk back down a different branch of the folder tree? No, you don't. You just click the **>** that's next to the USA folder's name and choose California from the list.

POWER USERS' CLINIC

The Master File Explorer Keyboard-Shortcut List

If you arrive home one day to discover that your mouse has been stolen, or if you simply like using the keyboard, you'll enjoy the shortcuts that work in File Explorer:

F6 or **Tab** cycles the "focus" (highlighting) among the different parts of the window: Favorite Links, address bar, main window, search box, and so on.

Shift+Ctrl+N makes a new empty folder.

F4 highlights the address bar and pops open the list of previous addresses. (Press Alt+D to highlight the address bar without opening the pop-up menu.)

Alt+← opens the previously viewed window, as though you'd clicked the Back button in a browser. Once you've used Alt+←, you can press Alt+→ to move *forward* through your recently open windows.

Backspace does the same thing as Alt+←. It, too, walks you backward through the most recent windows you've had open. That's a change from Windows XP, when Backspace meant "up," as in, "Take me to the parent folder" (see Alt+↑, next).

Alt+↑ opens the parent window of whatever you're looking at now—just like the ↑ button next to the address bar.

Alt+double-clicking an icon opens the Properties window for that icon. (It shows the same sort of information you'd find in the Details pane.) Or, if the icon is already highlighted, press Alt+Enter.

Alt+P hides or shows the Preview pane.

F11 enters or exits full-screen mode, in which the current window fills the entire screen. Even the taskbar and Ribbon are hidden. This effect is more useful in a web browser than at the desktop, but you never know; sometimes you want to see everything in a folder.

Shift+Ctrl+E adjusts the navigation pane so it reveals the folder path of whatever window is open right now, expanding the indented folder icons as necessary.

Press letter keys to highlight a folder or file that begins with that letter, or press the ↑ and ↓ keys to "walk" up and down a list of icons.

- **Refresh (↻).** If you suspect that the window contents aren't up to date (for example, that maybe somebody has just dropped something new into it from across the network), then click this button, or press F5, to make Windows update the display.

- **Search box.** Type a search phrase into this box to find what you're looking for *within this window.*

What to Type into the Address Bar

When you click the tiny folder icon at the left end of the address bar (or press Alt+D), the bracket **>** notation changes to the slash\notation, meaning that you can edit the address. At this point, the address bar is like the little opening in the glass divider that lets you speak to your New York cab driver; you tell it where you want to go. Here's what you can type there (press Enter afterward):

- **A web address.** You can leave off the *https://* portion. Just type the body of the web address, such as *www.sony.com,* into this strip. When you press Enter (or click the → button to the right of the address box, called the Go button), your web browser opens to the web page you specified.

Tip: If you press Ctrl+Enter instead of just Enter, you can surround whatever you've just typed into the address bar with *https://www.* and *.com.* See Chapter 9 for even more address shortcuts along these lines.

- **A search phrase.** If you type some text into this strip that isn't obviously a web address, then Windows assumes you're telling it, "Go online and search for this phrase." From here, it works exactly as though you'd typed into the address/search bar of Microsoft Edge.

- **A folder name.** You can also type one of several important folder names into this strip, such as *This PC, Documents, Music,* and so on. When you press Enter, that particular folder window opens.

Tip: This window has AutoComplete. That is, if you type *pi* and then press Tab, the address bar completes the word *Pictures* for you. (If it guesses wrong, press Tab again.)

- **A program or path name.** This provides another way to open files, if you know where they're located. To open the family budget spreadsheet that's in Monica's Documents folder, you might type *C:\Users\Monica\Documents\familybudget.xls.*

In each case, as soon as you begin to type, a pop-up list of recently visited websites, files, or folders appears below the address bar. Windows is trying to save you some typing. If you see what you're looking for, click it with the mouse, or press the ↓ key to highlight the one you want, and then press Enter.

Optional Window Panes

Most File Explorer windows have some basic informational stuff across the top: the address bar and the Ribbon, at the very least.

But that's just the beginning. As shown in Figure 2-8, you can add a new panel to the right side of any File Explorer window. It can take one of two forms: a Preview (of the selected icon) or a panel of Details. Turning one of these panels on may make your window feel claustrophobic, but at least you'll know absolutely everything there is to know about your files and folders.

The on/off switch for this panel is on the View tab of the Ribbon.

Tip: You can adjust the size of any pane by dragging the dividing line that separates it from the main window. (You know you've got the right spot when your cursor turns into a double-headed arrow.)

Preview Pane

The Preview pane appears either when you click the Preview pane button (shown in Figure 2-8) or when you press Alt+P.

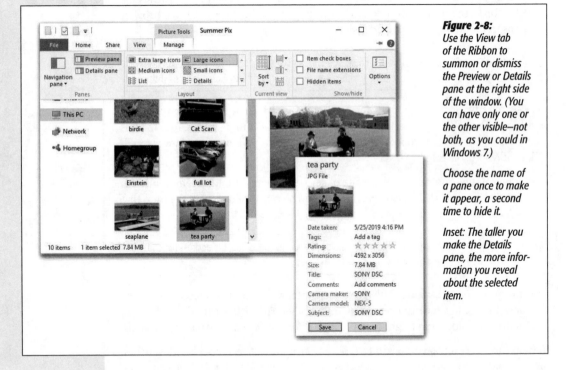

Figure 2-8:
Use the View tab of the Ribbon to summon or dismiss the Preview or Details pane at the right side of the window. (You can have only one or the other visible—not both, as you could in Windows 7.)

Choose the name of a pane once to make it appear, a second time to hide it.

Inset: The taller you make the Details pane, the more information you reveal about the selected item.

It can be handy when you're examining common file types like pictures, text files, RTF files, and Office documents. As you click each icon, you see a magnified thumbnail version of what's actually *in* that document. (Alas, the Preview pane can't play back music and movie files right in place.)

Now, the Preview pane isn't omniscient; right out of the box, Windows can't display the contents of oddball document types like, say, sheet music or 3D modeling files. But as you install new programs, the Preview pane can get smarter. Install Office, for example, and it can display Office files' contents; install Adobe Acrobat, and it can show you PDF files. Whether or not the Preview pane recognizes a certain document type depends on the effort expended by the programmers who wrote its program (that is, whether they wrote *preview handlers* for their document types).

Details Pane

To open this panel (Figure 2-8, inset), click "Details pane" on the Ribbon, or press Shift+Alt+P. You get all kinds of information about whatever icon you've clicked in the main part of the window: its size, date, type, and so on. Some examples:

- **For a music file,** the Details pane reveals the song's duration, band and album names, genre, the star rating you've provided, and so on.

- **For a disk icon,** you get statistics about its formatting scheme, capacity, and how much of it is full.

- **For a Microsoft Office document,** you see when it was created and modified, how many pages it has, who wrote it, and so on.

- **If nothing is selected,** you get information about the open window itself: namely, how many items are in it.

- **If you select several icons at once,** this pane shows you the sum of their file sizes—a great feature when you're burning a CD, for example, and don't want to exceed the 650 MB limit. You also see the *range* of dates when the icons were created and modified.

What's especially intriguing is that you can *edit* many of these details, just by clicking and typing.

Navigation Pane

The navigation pane is the helpful folder map at the left side of a File Explorer window. It's something like a master map of your computer, with a special focus on the places and things you might want to visit most often.

Quick access list

At the top of the navigation pane, there's a collapsible list called "Quick access." (It has nothing to do with the Quick Access *toolbar*.)

Like the Favorites list in earlier Windows versions, this one's intended to be one-stop shopping for important folders and disks, in two categories:

- **Folders and disks that you "pin" here.**

- **Folders and disks you use frequently.** Windows chooses them automatically.

"Quick access" displays *links* to these folders, wherever they happen to be on your machine. You're never actually moving them.

This list is a big deal. A "Quick access" window, in fact, greets you every time you open a File Explorer window. That's how important Microsoft considers this list.

Tip: File Explorer doesn't have to fill every window with "Quick access." It can, if you prefer, show you the primary folders of your PC, as it did in the old days. To make that happen, start in a File Explorer window. On the Ribbon's View tab, click Options. At the top of the resulting Folder Options window, change the "Open File Explorer to" drop-down menu to "This PC," and click OK.

Taking the time to install your favorite folders here can save you a lot of repetitive folder-burrowing. One click on an item's name opens the corresponding window. For example, click the Pictures icon to view the contents of your Pictures folder in the main part of the window.

The beauty of this parking lot for containers is that it's so easy to set up with *your* favorite places. For example:

- **Install a new folder, disk, library, or saved search.** Drag its icon off your desktop (or out of a window) into any spot in the "Quick access" list (Figure 2-9, top).

  Or right-click the icon of any folder or disk (or hold your finger down on it); from the shortcut menu, choose "Pin to Quick access."

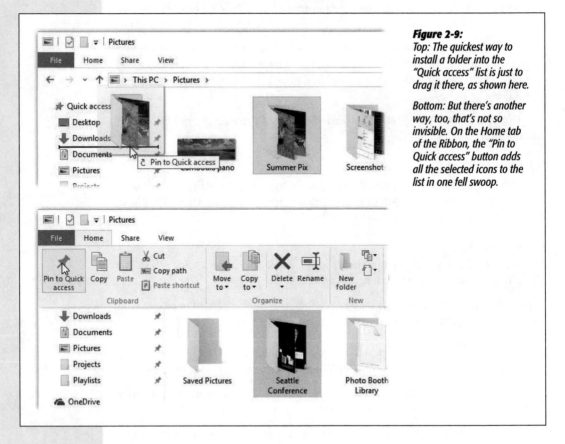

Figure 2-9:
Top: The quickest way to install a folder into the "Quick access" list is just to drag it there, as shown here.

Bottom: But there's another way, too, that's not so invisible. On the Home tab of the Ribbon, the "Pin to Quick access" button adds all the selected icons to the list in one fell swoop.

- **Remove an icon from "Quick access."** Right-click its name in the list (or hold your finger down) to open the shortcut menu.

  If *you* put this thing into the menu, choose "Unpin from Quick access." If *Windows* put it there (because you use it frequently), choose "Remove from Quick access." That frequently used item disappears and won't reappear, even if you use it all the time.

  In either case, you haven't actually removed anything from your *PC*; you've just unhitched its alias from the navigation pane.

- **Rearrange the icons by dragging them up or down in the list.** Release the mouse when the black horizontal line lands in the desired new location.

Note: Windows can't sort this list alphabetically.

- **Adjust the width of the pane** by dragging the vertical divider bar right or left.

Tip: If you drag carefully, you can position the divider bar *just* to the right of the disk and folder icons, thereby hiding their names almost completely. Some people find it a tidier look; you can always identify the folder names by pointing to them without clicking.

- **Make "Quick access" stop listing the folders and files you use often.** In a File Explorer window, click the Ribbon's View tab. Click Options to open the Folder Options window. Turn off "Show recently used files in Quick access" or "Show frequently used folders in Quick access" to make it stop tracking your file and folder use, respectively. Click OK.

  You're still free to pin stuff there yourself, if you like; it's just that Windows will no longer add things it sees you using often.

Tip: If you really like the "Quick access" concept, you can add its name to the Start menu's right side. That'll give you a quick way to open it whenever the Start menu is open.

Right-click (or hold your finger down on) the actual words "Quick access" at the top of the "Quick access" list. From the shortcut menu, choose Pin to Start.

OneDrive

Here are the contents of your Microsoft OneDrive—your free, 5-gigabyte "hard drive in the sky" (actually, on the internet). Page 140 offers the details.

This PC

The next heading is This PC. (Yes, Microsoft has finally retired the term "My Computer.") When you expand this heading, you see a list of all your drives (including the main C: drive), each of which is also expandable (Figure 2-10). In essence, this view can show you every folder on the machine at once. It lets you burrow very deeply into your hard drive's nest of folders without losing your bearings.

Libraries

The next section of the navigation pane may list your *libraries,* if you've turned on this feature; see the free PDF appendix to this chapter called "Libraries" on this book's "Missing CD" (*missingmanuals.com*).

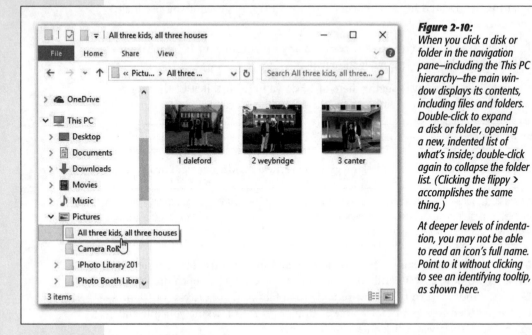

Figure 2-10:
When you click a disk or folder in the navigation pane–including the This PC hierarchy–the main window displays its contents, including files and folders. Double-click to expand a disk or folder, opening a new, indented list of what's inside; double-click again to collapse the folder list. (Clicking the flippy > accomplishes the same thing.)

At deeper levels of indentation, you may not be able to read an icon's full name. Point to it without clicking to see an identifying tooltip, as shown here.

Network

The Network heading shows your entire network—Macs, PCs running older Windows versions, Linux boxes, whatever.

Flippy arrows

The navigation list displays *only* disks and folders, never individual files. To see those, look at the main window, which displays the contents (folders *and* files) of whatever disk or folder you click.

To expand a folder or disk that appears in the nav pane, double-click its name, or click the > next to its name. You've just turned the nav list into an outline; the contents of the folder appear in an indented list, as shown in Figure 2-10. Double-click the folder's name again to collapse the folder listing.

Tip: Windows can, if you like, expand the folder list automatically as you navigate your folders. Open the Music folder with your mouse, for example, and the Music folder's flippy > is automatically opened, giving you a visual representation of where you are. Sound useful? Turn it on like this: On the Ribbon's View tab, click Options. On the View tab of the resulting Folder Options dialog box, turn on "Expand to open folder." Click OK.

By selectively expanding folders like this, you can, in effect, peer inside two or more folders simultaneously, all within the single navigation list. You can move files around by dragging them onto the tiny folder icons, too.

Optional Window Panes

Tip: Ordinarily, the nav pane shows only folders that Microsoft thinks you'd be interested in—folders that contain your stuff, for example. But, if you like, it can display more Windowsy folders like the Control Panel and Recycle Bin, too. On the Ribbon's View tab, click Options; the Folder Options dialog box appears. On that View tab, turn on "Show all folders." Click OK.

Tags, Metadata, and Properties

See all that information in the Details pane—Date, Size, Title, and so on (Figure 2-11)? That's known by geeks as *metadata* (Greek for "data about data").

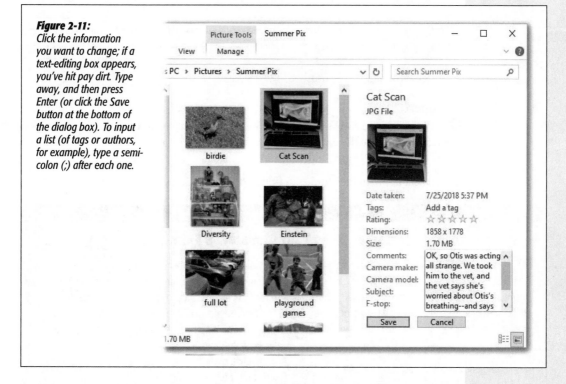

Figure 2-11:
Click the information you want to change; if a text-editing box appears, you've hit pay dirt. Type away, and then press Enter (or click the Save button at the bottom of the dialog box). To input a list (of tags or authors, for example), type a semi-colon (;) after each one.

Different kinds of files provide different sorts of details. For a document, for example, you might see Authors, Comments, Title, Categories, Status, and so on. For an MP3 music file, you get Artists, Album, Genre, Year, and so on. For a photo, you get Date Taken, Title, Size, and so on.

Oddly (and usefully) enough, you can actually edit some of this stuff.

Some of the metadata is off-limits. For example, you can't edit the Date Created or Date Modified info. (Sorry, defense attorneys.) But you *can* edit the star ratings for music or pictures. Click the third star to give a song a 3, for example. Most usefully of all, you can edit the Tags box for almost *any* kind of icon. A tag is just a keyword. It can be anything you want: McDuffy Proposal, Old Junk, Back Me Up. Later, you'll be able to round up everything with a certain tag, all in a single window, even though they physically reside in different folders.

You'll encounter tags in plenty of other places in Windows—and in this book, especially when it comes to searching for photos and music.

Note: Weirdly, you can't add tags or ratings to .bmp, .png, .avi, or .mpg files.

Many of the boxes here offer autocompletion, meaning that Windows proposes finishing a name or a text tidbit for you if it recognizes what you've started to type.

Tip: You can tag a bunch of icons at once. Just highlight them all and then change the corresponding detail in the Details pane *once.* This is a great trick for applying a tag or a star rating to a mass of files quickly.

Click Save when you're finished.

Properties

The Details pane shows some of the most important details about a file, but if you really want to see the entire metadata dossier for an icon, open its Properties dialog box (Figure 2-12) using one of these tactics:

- **Select it.** From the Home tab of the Ribbon, click Properties.

GEM IN THE ROUGH

How to Shed Your Metadata's Skin

At the bottom of the Details tab of the Properties dialog box is a peculiarly worded link: Remove Properties and Personal Information. This is a privacy feature. It means "Clean away all the metadata I've added myself, like author names, tag keywords, and other insights into my own work routine."

Microsoft's thinking here is that you might not want other people who encounter this document (as an email attachment, for example) to have such a sweeping insight into the minutiae of your own work routine.

When you click this link, the Remove Properties dialog box appears, offering you a scrolling list of checkboxes: Title, Rating, Tags, Comments, and lots and lots of others.

You can proceed in either of two ways. If you turn on "Create a copy with all possible properties removed," then *all* the metadata that's possible to erase (everything but items like File Type, Name, and so on) will be stripped away. When you click OK, Windows instantly creates a duplicate of the file (with the word "Copy" tacked onto its name), ready for distribution to the masses in its clean form. The original is left untouched.

If you choose "Remove the following properties from this file" instead, you can specify exactly *which* file details you want erased from the original. (Turn on the appropriate checkboxes.)

- **Right-click it (or hold your finger down on it).** From the shortcut menu, choose Properties.

- **Alt-double-click it.**

- **If the icon is already highlighted,** press Alt+Enter.

In each case, the Properties dialog box appears. It's a lot like the one in previous versions of Windows, in that it displays the file's name, location, size, and so on. But in Windows 10, it also bears a scrolling Details tab that's sometimes teeming with metadata details.

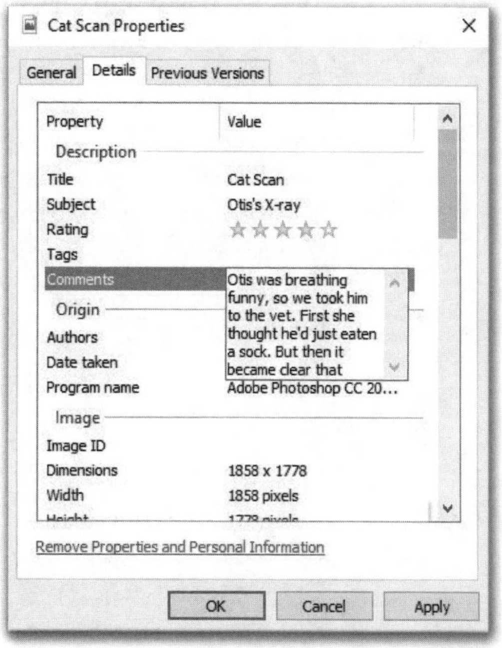

Figure 2-12:
If Windows knows anything about an icon, it's in here. Scroll, scroll, and scroll some more to find the tidbit you want to see—or to edit. As with the Details pane, many of these text morsels are editable.

Window Views

Windows' windows look just fine straight from the factory; the edges are straight, and the text is perfectly legible. Still, if you're going to stare at this screen for half of your waking hours, you may as well investigate some of the ways these windows can be enhanced.

For starters, you can view the files and folders in a File Explorer window in either of two ways: as icons (of any size) or as a list (in several formats). Figure 2-13 shows some of your options.

Every window remembers its view settings independently. You might prefer to look over your Documents folder in List view (because it's crammed with files and folders), but you may prefer to view the Pictures library in Icon view, where the icons look like miniatures of the actual photos.

To switch a window from one view to another, you have several options, as shown in Figure 2-13, all of which involve the View tab of the Ribbon.

Tip: You can point to the icons in the View tab without clicking. The files in the window change as you hover, so you can preview the effect before committing to it.

So what *are* these various views? And when should you use which? Here you go:

- **Extra large icons, Large icons, Medium icons, Small icons.** In an icon view, every file, folder, and disk is represented by a small picture—an *icon.* This humble image,

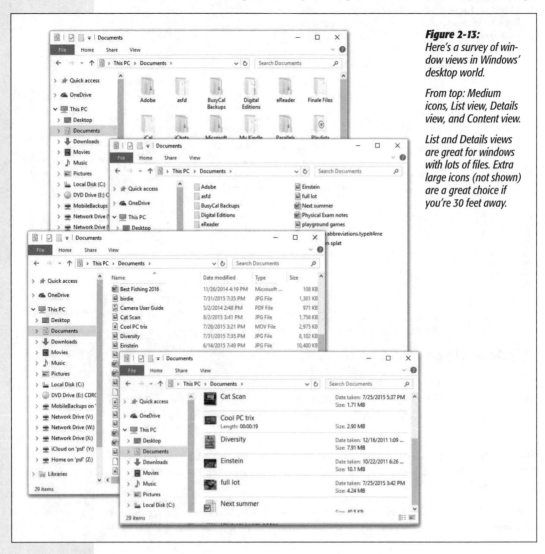

Figure 2-13:
Here's a survey of window views in Windows' desktop world.

From top: Medium icons, List view, Details view, and Content view.

List and Details views are great for windows with lots of files. Extra large icons (not shown) are a great choice if you're 30 feet away.

a visual representation of electronic bits, is the cornerstone of the entire Windows religion. (Maybe that's why it's called an icon.)

At larger icon sizes, the contents of your folder icons peek out just enough so you can see them. In the Music folder, for example, a singer's folder shows the first album cover within; a folder full of PowerPoint presentations shows the first slide or two; and so on.

Small icons put the files' names to the right of the icons; the other views put the name *beneath* the icon. You might want one of the large settings for things like photos and the small settings when you want to see more files without scrolling.

Tip: If you have a touchscreen, you can use the two-finger spreading gesture to enlarge icons, or the pinching gesture to shrink them, right on the glass. If you have a mouse, you can enlarge or shrink all the icons in a window—or switch to any other view—by turning your mouse's scroll wheel while you press the Ctrl key.

- **List view.** This one packs, by far, the most files into the space of a window; each file has a tiny icon to its left, and the list of files wraps into as many columns as necessary to maximize the window's available space.

- **Details view.** This is the same as List view, except that it presents only a single column of files. It's a table, really; additional columns reveal the size, icon type, modification date, rating, and other information.

  Microsoft thinks you'll really dig Details view. It's so important that there's a dedicated "Switch to Details view" icon at the lower-right corner of every window.

  Furthermore, whenever you're in Details view, you get two bonus icons on the Ribbon's View tab: "Add columns" and "Size all columns to fit." They're described in the box on the next page.

- **Tiles view.** Your icons appear at standard size, with name and file details just to the *right*.

Tip: Lots of people never even realize they *have* Tiles and Content view options— because these two choices are normally hidden on the Ribbon! You actually have to *scroll* that teeny tiny panel of view icons to see them.

- **Content view.** This view attempts to cram as many details about each file as will fit in your window. It's a table that shows not just a file's icon and name, but also its metadata (Properties) and, in the case of text and Word files, even the first couple of lines of text *inside* it. (If you're not seeing all the file details you think you should, then make the window bigger. Windows adds and subtracts columns of information as needed to fit.)

  You'll get to know Content view very well once you start using the Search feature, which uses this view to display your results.

Tip: At the lower right of every File Explorer window, you see repeats of the two styles Microsoft thinks you'll find the most useful: Details view and large thumbnails. (They even have keyboard shortcuts: Ctrl+Shift+6 for Details, Ctrl+Shift+2 for large thumbnails.) By duplicating these controls here, Windows is trying to save you the effort of opening the Ribbon if it doesn't happen to be open.

Immortalizing Your Tweaks

Once you've twiddled and tweaked a File Explorer window into a perfectly efficient configuration of columns and views, you needn't go through the same exercise for

Secrets of the Details View Columns

In windows that contain a lot of icons, Details view is a powerful weapon in the battle against chaos. *You* get to decide how wide the columns should be, which of them should appear, and in what order. Here are the details on Details:

Add or remove columns. When you choose "Add columns" in the Ribbon's View tab, or right-click any column heading (like Name or Size), you see a shortcut menu with checkmarks next to the visible columns: Name, Date modified, Size, and so on. Choose a column's name to make it appear or disappear.

New in the May 2019 Update, this menu also includes "Use friendly dates," meaning you'll see words like "Today" and "Yesterday" when appropriate in the Date column.

But don't think you're stuck with that handful of common columns. If you click "More" in the shortcut menu, you open the Choose Details dialog box, which lists *300 more* column types, most of which are useful only in certain circumstances: Album artist (for music files); Copyright, Date taken, Exposure time (for photos); Nickname (for people); Video compression (for movies); and on and on. To make

one of these columns appear, turn on its checkbox and then click OK; by the time you're done, your File Explorer window can look like a veritable spreadsheet of information.

Rearrange the columns. You can rearrange your Details columns by dragging their gray column headers horizontally. (You can even drag the Name column out of first position.)

Change the column widths. If some text in a column is too long to fit, Windows displays an ellipsis (…) after the first few letters of each word. In that case, here's a trick: Carefully position your cursor at the right edge of the column's header (Name, Size, or whatever—even to the right of the ⌄ button). When the cursor sprouts horizontal arrows, double-click the divider line to make the column adjust *itself,* fitting automatically to accommodate the longest item in the column.

If you'd rather adjust the column width manually, then just drag the divider line horizontally. Doing so makes the column to the *left* of your cursor wider or narrower. Or use the "Size all columns to fit" command. It's on the Ribbon's View tab, too, and it makes all columns exactly as wide as necessary.

---

each folder. Windows can immortalize your changes as the standard setting for *all* your windows.

On the Ribbon's View tab, click Options. Click the View tab. Click Apply to Folders, and confirm your decision by clicking Yes.

At this point, all your disk and folder windows open up with the same view, sorting method, and so on. You're still free to override those standard settings on a window-by-window basis, however. (And if you change your mind again and want to make all your maverick folder windows snap back to the standard settings, then repeat the process but click Reset Folders instead.)

Sorting, Grouping, and Filtering

It's a computer—it had darned well better be able to sort your files alphabetically, chronologically, or in any other way. But there are other ways to impose order on your teeming icons. Grouping, filtering, and searching can be handy, too.

Sorting Files

Sorting the files in a window alphabetically or chronologically is nice, but it's so 2014. You can now sort up, down, and sideways.

The trick is to click the "Sort by" drop-down icon, which is on the View tab of the Ribbon. As you can see, it lists every conceivable sorting criterion: Name, Date modified, Type, Size, and on and on. And if those 10 ways to sort aren't enough, you can select "Choose columns" from this menu to add even more options to it: Attachments, Copyright, Data rate, and so on.

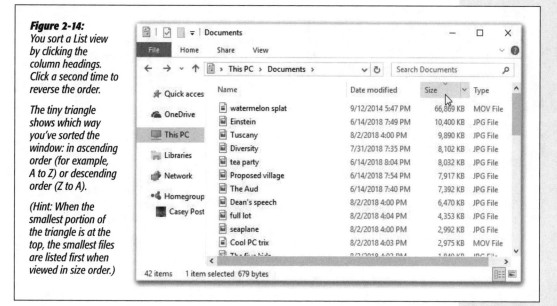

Figure 2-14:
You sort a List view by clicking the column headings. Click a second time to reverse the order.

The tiny triangle shows which way you've sorted the window: in ascending order (for example, A to Z) or descending order (Z to A).

(Hint: When the smallest portion of the triangle is at the top, the smallest files are listed first when viewed in size order.)

Sorting in Details view

In Details view, you get another way to sort. See the column headings, like "Name," "Size," and "Type"? They aren't just signposts; they're also buttons. Click "Name" for alphabetical order, "Date modified" for chronological order, "Size" to view the largest files at the top, and so on (Figure 2-14).

To reverse the sorting order, click the column heading a second time. The tiny triangle turns upside down.

Note: Within each window, Windows groups *folders* separately from *files.* They get sorted, too, but within their own little folder neighborhood.

Sorting using the shortcut menu

You can sort your icons in any window view without using the Ribbon, like this: Right-click a blank spot in the window. From the shortcut menu, choose "Sort by" and choose the criterion you want (Name, Date modified, Type…) from the submenu.

There's no triangle to tell you *which way* you've just sorted things; is it oldest to newest or newest to oldest? To make *that* decision, you have to right-click the window a second time; this time, from the "Sort by" submenu, choose either Ascending or Descending.

Grouping

Grouping means "adding headings within the window and clustering the icons beneath the headings." The effect is shown in Figure 2-15 ("Yesterday," "Earlier this month,"

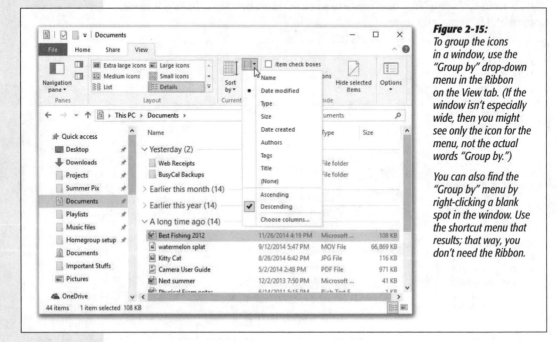

Figure 2-15:
To group the icons in a window, use the "Group by" drop-down menu in the Ribbon on the View tab. (If the window isn't especially wide, then you might see only the icon for the menu, not the actual words "Group by.")

You can also find the "Group by" menu by right-clicking a blank spot in the window. Use the shortcut menu that results; that way, you don't need the Ribbon.

and so on), and so is the procedure. Try it out; grouping can be a great way to wrangle some order from a seething mass of icons.

Don't forget that you can flip the sorting order of your groups. Reopen that shortcut menu and the "Group by" submenu, and specify Ascending or Descending.

Filtering

Filtering, a feature available only in Details view, means hiding. When you turn on filtering, a bunch of the icons in a window *disappear*, which can make filtering a sore subject for novices.

Tip: In case you one day think you've lost a bunch of important files, look for a checkmark next to a column heading. That's your clue that filtering is turned on and Windows is deliberately hiding something from you.

On the positive side, filtering means screening out stuff you don't care about. When you're looking for a document you know you worked on last week, you can tell Windows to show you *only* the documents edited last week.

You turn on filtering by opening the drop-down menu next to the column heading you want. For instance, if you want to see only your five-star photos in the Pictures folder, then open the Rating pop-up menu.

Sometimes you'll see a whole long list of checkboxes in one of these pop-up menus (Figure 2-16). For example, if you want to see only the PDF and Word documents in

---

The Little Filtering Calendar

Some of the column-heading pop-up menus in Details view—"Date modified," "Date created," "Date taken," and so on—display a calendar, right there in the menu. You're supposed to use it to specify a date or a date range. You use it, for example, if you want to see only the photos taken last August, or the Word documents created last week. Here's how the little calendar works:

To change the month, click the ◄ or ► buttons to go one month at a time. Or click the month name to see a list of all 12; click the one you want.

To change the year, double-click the month's name. You're offered a list of all 10 years in this decade. Double-click

on the decade heading to see a list of *decades*. (The calendar goes from 1601 to 9999, which should pretty much cover your digital photo collection.)

To see only the photos taken on a certain date, click the date on the month-view calendar.

To add photos taken on other dates, click additional squares. You can also drag to select blocks of consecutive dates.

The checkboxes below the calendar offer one-click access to photos taken earlier this week, earlier this year, and before the beginning of this year ("A long time ago").

---

your Documents folder—or only songs by The Beatles in your Music folder—turn on the corresponding checkmarks.

Note: Filtering, by the way, can be turned on *with* sorting or grouping.

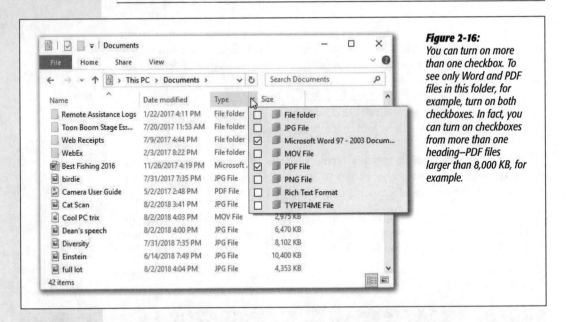

Figure 2-16:
You can turn on more than one checkbox. To see only Word and PDF files in this folder, for example, turn on both checkboxes. In fact, you can turn on checkboxes from more than one heading—PDF files larger than 8,000 KB, for example.

Once you've filtered a window in Details view, you can switch to a different view; you'll still see (and not see) the same set of icons. The address bar reminds you that you've turned on filtering; it might say, for example, *Research notes > LongTimeAgo > DOC file*, meaning "ancient Word files."

To stop filtering, open the heading drop-down menu again and turn off the Filter checkbox.

Searching in a File Explorer Window

There's a search box in the upper-right corner of every File Explorer window. You can use it to search just within the open window, as described in the next chapter.

Folder Options

If you want—or need—to tweak your File Explorer windows to a preposterous degree, there's a dialog box for that. See the free PDF appendix to this chapter, "The 'Folder Options' Options," on this book's Missing CD at *missingmanuals.com*.

Taskbar 2.0

For years, the *taskbar*—the strip of colorful icons at the bottom of your screen—has been one of the most prominent and important elements of the Windows interface

(Figure 2-17). Today, you can call it Taskbar, Extreme Makeover Edition; it can do a lot of things it's never done before.

Here's an introduction to its functions, old and new:

- **The Start menu is back.** As you know from Chapter 1, the Start menu is at the far left of the taskbar.

- **The search box is next.** Just to the right of the Start menu, the search box (labeled "Type here to search") awaits, as described in Chapter 3.

Tip: The search box does take up a lot of horizontal space—and you don't really need it. You can hide it and still have full access to the search box; see Figure 2-18.

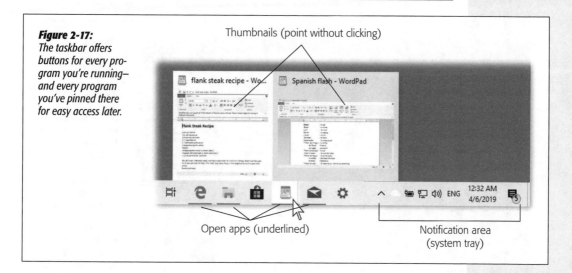

Figure 2-17:
The taskbar offers buttons for every program you're running—and every program you've pinned there for easy access later.

Thumbnails (point without clicking)

Open apps (underlined)

Notification area (system tray)

- **Cortana.** The little circle summons Windows' voice assistant, as described in Chapter 5. In the May 2019 Update, it's no longer huddled inside the search box.

- **The Timeline** (⊟i) is like the History menu in a web browser, except that it lists every window you've ever opened, on every device. See page 210.

- **The taskbar lists your open programs and windows.** The icons on the taskbar make it easy to switch from one open program to another—from your web browser to your email program, for example—or even to specific windows *within* those programs.

Note: App icons are generally hidden in Tablet mode, described in Chapter 12. If you read this chapter and wonder why you're not seeing some of the things described here, that's why.

- **The taskbar is a launcher.** You read that right. The taskbar is a mini–Start menu. It's a *launcher* for your favorite programs and folders, just like the Dock on the Mac or the Quick Launch toolbar in old Windows versions.

- **The system tray (notification area) is at the right end.** These icons show you the status of your network connection, battery life, and so on, as described on page 86.

- **The Show Desktop button hides at the far-right end.** You can read more about this invisible button on page 47.

So what can you do with the little buttons on the taskbar? Read on.

Tip: You can operate the taskbar entirely from the keyboard. Press ⊞+T to highlight the first button on it, as indicated by a subtle glow. Then you can "walk" across its buttons by pressing the left/right arrow keys, or by continuing to press ⊞+T (add the Shift key to "walk" in the opposite direction). Once a button is highlighted, you can tap the space bar to "click" it, press Shift+F10 to "right-click" it, or press the Menu key ▤ on your keyboard to open the icon's jump list. Who needs a mouse anymore?

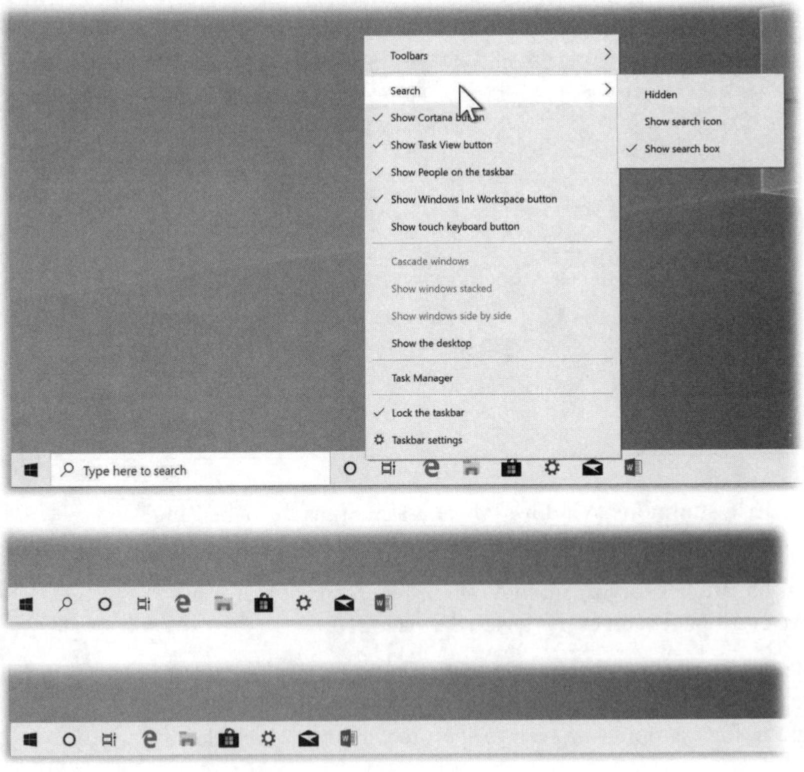

Figure 2-18:
Ordinarily, the search box (shown at top) eats up a big chunk of your taskbar. If you'd rather dedicate that precious real estate to things like your taskbar buttons, then right-click (or hold your finger down on) a blank spot on the taskbar.

The Search shortcut menu offers three choices for the Search box: "Show search box" (the usual), "Show search icon" (only a magnifying glass, second from top), and "Hidden" (bottom). Even if you choose "Hidden," you can still press the search keystroke, ⊞+S.

Taskbar as App Switcher

Every open window is represented by a button—an actual miniature of the window itself—that sprouts from its program's taskbar icon. These buttons make it easy to switch among open programs and windows. Just click one to bring its associated window into the foreground, even if it's been minimized.

Once you know what to look for, you can distinguish an open program from a closed one, a frontmost window from a background one, and so on (see Figure 2-17).

Handy Window Miniatures

If you point to a program's button without clicking, it sprouts thumbnail images of *the windows themselves*. Figure 2-17 shows the effect. It's a lot more informative than just reading the windows' *names*, as in days of yore (previous Windows versions, that is). The thumbnails are especially good at helping you spot a particular web page, photo, or PDF document.

Tip: When you point to one of these thumbnails, a tiny Close button (✕) appears in each thumbnail, too, which makes it easy to close a window without having to bring it forward first. (Or click the thumbnail itself with your mouse's scroll wheel, or use your middle mouse button, if you have one.) Each thumbnail also has a hidden shortcut menu. Right-click to see your options!

Full-Size Peeking

Those window miniatures are all fine, but the taskbar can also show you *full-screen* previews of your windows. It's a feature Microsoft calls Peek.

- **Mouse/trackpad:** Point to a taskbar button to make the window thumbnails appear. Then, still without clicking, point to one of the *thumbnails*.

- **Touchscreen:** Tap an app's taskbar icon to make the window thumbnails appear. Now touch the same taskbar icon a second time and pause; without lifting your fingertip, drag onto one of the thumbnails.

Windows displays that window at full size, right on the screen, even if it was minimized, buried, or hidden. Keep moving your cursor or finger across the thumbnails (if there are more than one); each time you land on a thumbnail, the full-size window preview changes to show what's in it.

When you find the window you want, click or tap the thumbnail you're already pointing to. The window pops open so you can work in it.

Button Groups

In the old days, opening a lot of windows produced a relatively useless display of truncated buttons. Not only were the buttons too narrow to read the names of the windows, but the buttons also appeared in chronological order, not in software-program order.

As you may have noticed, though, Windows now automatically consolidates open windows into a single program button. (There's even a subtle visual sign that a program has multiple windows open: Its taskbar icon may appear to be "stacked," as shown on the Word icon in Figure 2-17, or its underline may sprout a gray extension.) All the Word documents are accessible from the Word icon, all the Excel documents sprout from the Excel icon, and so on.

Point to a taskbar button to see the thumbnails of the corresponding windows, complete with their names; click to jump directly to the one you want. (On a touchscreen, tap the taskbar button to see the thumbnails; tap a thumbnail to open it.)

Despite all the newfangled techniques, some of the following time-honored basics still apply:

- **If a program has only one window open,** you can hide or show it by hitting the program's taskbar button—a great feature that a lot of PC fans miss. (To hide a *background* window, select its taskbar button *twice:* once to bring the window forward, then a pause, and then again to hide it.)

- **To minimize, maximize, restore, or close a window,** even if you can't see it on the screen, point to its program's button on the taskbar. When the window thumbnails pop up, right-click the one you want, and choose an action from the shortcut menu. (This option isn't available without a mouse/trackpad.)

- **Windows can make all open windows visible at once,** either by *cascading* them (Figure 2-19), *stacking* them (horizontal slices), or displaying them in side-by-side vertical slices. To create this effect, right-click (or hold your finger down on) a blank spot on the taskbar and choose "Cascade windows" from the shortcut menu. Or choose "Show windows stacked" or "Show windows side by side."

Figure 2-19:
Cascading windows are neatly arranged so you can see the title bar for each window. Click any title bar to bring that window to the foreground as the active window.

- **To hide all open windows in one fell swoop,** press ⊞+D. Or right-click a blank spot on the taskbar and choose "Show the desktop" from the shortcut menu. Or point to (or click) the Show Desktop rectangle at the far-right end of the taskbar.

To bring the windows back, repeat that step.

Tip: When the taskbar is crowded with buttons, it may not be easy to find a blank spot to click. Usually there's a little gap near the right end; you can make it easier to find some blank space by *enlarging* the taskbar, as described on page 90.

The Taskbar as App Launcher

Each time you open a program, its icon appears on the taskbar (Figure 2-20). That's the way it's always been. And when you exit that program, its icon disappears from the taskbar.

These days, however, there's a twist: You can *pin* a program's icon to the taskbar so it's always there, even when it's not open. One quick click opens the app. The idea, of course, is to put frequently used programs front and center, always on the screen, so you don't even have to open the Start menu to find them.

Figure 2-20:
An icon without a white or colored underline is a program you haven't opened yet. A brightened background indicates the active (frontmost) program—Word, in this case.

Right-clicking one of these buttons lets you perform tasks on all the windows together, such as closing them all at once.

If you prefer the old taskbar, where every window gets a separate button, see "Bring Back the Old Taskbar," a free PDF appendix on this book's "Missing CD" at missingmanuals.com.

GEM IN THE ROUGH

Secret Keystrokes of the Taskbar Icons

There's secret keyboard shortcuts lurking in thar taskbar icons. It turns out that the first 10 icons, left to right, have built-in keystrokes that "click" them: the ⊞ key plus the numbers 1, 2, 3, and so on (up to 0, which means 10).

If you use this keystroke to "click" the icon of a program that's not running, it opens up as though you'd clicked it. If

you "click" a program that has only one window open, that window pops to the front. If you "click" a program with more than one window open, the icon sprouts thumbnail previews of all of them, and the first window pops to the front.

Remember that you can drag icons around on the taskbar, in effect reassigning those 1-through-0 keystrokes.

To pin a program to the taskbar in this way, use one of these tricks:

- **Drag a program's icon** directly to any spot on the taskbar, as shown in Figure 2-21. You can drag them from any File Explorer window or from the desktop.

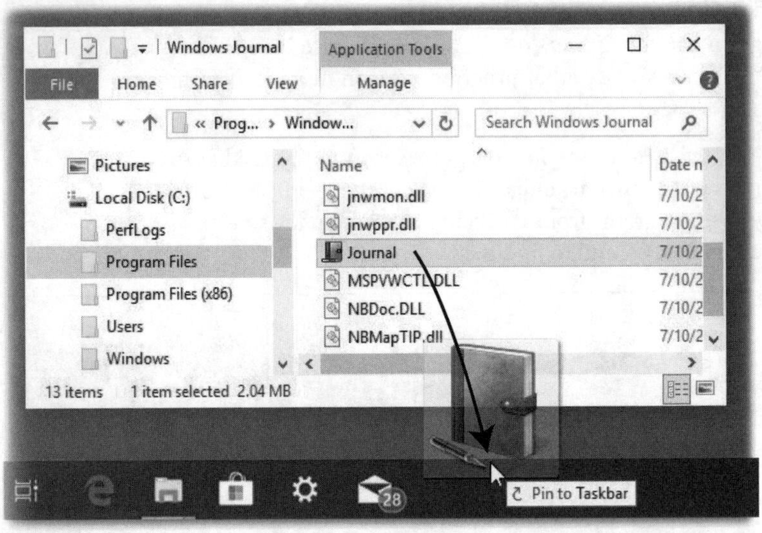

Figure 2-21:
To install a program on your taskbar, drag its icon to any spot; the other icons scoot aside to make room, if necessary.

- **Right-click a program's icon,** wherever it happens to be.

Tip: This works even on programs listed on the left side of the Start menu.

From the shortcut menu, choose "Pin to taskbar." The icon appears instantly at the right end of the taskbar. You're welcome to drag it into a better position.

- **Right-click an open program's taskbar icon,** wherever it happens to be. From the shortcut menu, choose "Pin to taskbar." In other words, the program's icon might be on the taskbar *now*, because it's running—but you've just told it to stay there even after you exit it.

Once an icon is on the taskbar, you can open it with a single click. By all means, stick your favorites there; over the years, you'll save yourself thousands of unnecessary Start-menu trips.

Tip: If you Shift-click a taskbar icon, you open another window for that program—for example, a new browser window, a new Microsoft Word document, and so on. (Clicking with your mouse's scroll wheel, or the middle mouse button, does the same thing.) Add the Ctrl key to open the program as an administrator.

And if you Shift-*right*-click a taskbar icon, you see the same menu of window-management commands (Cascade, Restore, and so on) that you get when you right-click a blank spot on the taskbar.

All these tricks require a mouse or a trackpad.

If you change your mind about a program icon you've parked on the taskbar, it's easy to move an icon to a new place—just drag it.

You can also remove one altogether. Right-click (or hold your finger down on) the program's icon—in the taskbar or anywhere on your PC—and, from the shortcut menu, choose "Unpin from taskbar."

Note: The taskbar is really intended to display the icons of *programs*. If you try to drag a file or a folder there, you'll succeed only in adding it to a program's jump list, as described next. If you want quick, one-click taskbar access to files, folders, and disks, though, you can have it. See "Taskbar Toolbars" on the Missing CD at *missingmanuals.com*.

Jump Lists

Jump lists are handy submenus that list frequently or recently opened files in each of your programs. For example, the jump list for the Edge browser shows the websites you visit most often; the jump list for Microsoft Word shows the documents you've edited lately. See Figure 2-22.

The point is that you can *re*open a file just by clicking its name. Jump lists can save you time when you want to resume work on something you had open recently but you're not in the mood to burrow through folders to find its icon.

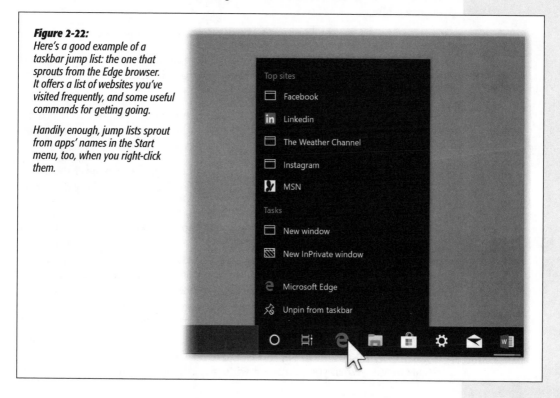

Figure 2-22:
Here's a good example of a taskbar jump list: the one that sprouts from the Edge browser. It offers a list of websites you've visited frequently, and some useful commands for getting going.

Handily enough, jump lists sprout from apps' names in the Start menu, too, when you right-click them.

Often, jump lists also include shortcut-ish commands, like New Message (for an email program), Play/Pause (for a jukebox program), or "Close all windows" (for just about any program). As Microsoft puts it, it's like having a separate Start menu for *every single program.*

To make jump lists appear in the taskbar or the Start menu, right-click a program's icon. If you're using a touchscreen computer, just swipe upward from the program's taskbar icon. (This second, secret way actually works if you have a mouse or trackpad, too. Give the mouse a flick upward while you're clicking.) In Figure 2-22, for example, you can see that Microsoft Edge's jump list includes web pages you've recently visited and recently closed.

Pinning to Jump Lists

In general, jump lists maintain themselves. Windows decides which files you've opened or played most recently or most frequently and builds the jump lists accordingly. New document listings appear, older ones vanish, all without your help.

But you can also install files manually into a program's jump list—in Windows-ese, you can *pin* a document to a program's jump list so it's not susceptible to replacement by other items.

For example, you might pin the chapters of a book you're working on to your Word jump list. To the File Explorer jump list, you might pin the *folder and disk* locations you access often.

You can pin a file or folder to a taskbar jump list in any of four ways:

- **From the Start menu:** Find an app or document in the programs list of the Start menu. Right-click (or hold your finger down on) its name; from the shortcut menu, choose More→"Pin to taskbar."

- **From the desktop or a File Explorer window:** Drag a document (or its file shortcut) directly onto a blank spot on the taskbar. (You can drag it onto its "parent" program's icon if you really want to, but the taskbar itself is a bigger target.)

  As shown in Figure 2-23, a tooltip appears: Pin to Word (or whatever the parent program is). Release the mouse or your finger. You've just pinned the document to its program's taskbar jump list.

  (If you drag a *folder*—or a shortcut of one—onto the taskbar, it gets pinned in the File Explorer icon's jump list.)

Note: If the document's parent program didn't already appear on the taskbar, it does now. In other words, if you drag a Beekeeper Pro document onto the taskbar, Windows is forced to install the Beekeeper Pro program icon onto the taskbar in the process. Otherwise, how would you open the jump list?

- **In an existing jump list, click the -⊠ icon** (Figure 2-23, right). Suppose, for example, the document already appears in a Recently Opened list (on the taskbar or the Start menu). When you point to it with your cursor, a pushpin icon appears. By clicking it, you can move the document up into the Pinned list at the top of the jump list. Now it won't be dislodged over time by other files you open.

(If you have only a touchscreen, you can still pin a document this way. Swipe upward on the app's taskbar icon to open its shortcut menu. Hold your finger down on the document to make *its* shortcut menu appear; tap "Pin to this list.")

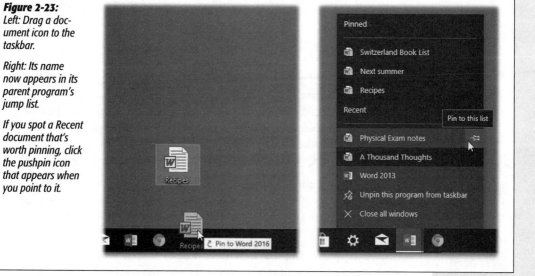

Figure 2-23:
Left: Drag a document icon to the taskbar.

Right: Its name now appears in its parent program's jump list.

If you spot a Recent document that's worth pinning, click the pushpin icon that appears when you point to it.

- **If the file appears in another program's jump list, then drag it onto the new program's taskbar icon.** For example, maybe you opened a document in WordPad (it's in WordPad's jump list), but you want to move it to Microsoft Word's jump list.

  To do that, drag the document's name out of WordPad's list and then drop it onto Word's taskbar icon. It now appears pinned in *both* programs' jump lists.

Removing things from your taskbar jump lists is just as easy. Open a program's jump list, point to (or hold your finger down on) the pushpin next to anything in the Pinned list, and choose "Unpin from this list."

Note: Once it's unpinned, the file's name may jump down into the Recent section of the jump list, which is usually fine. If it's not fine, you can erase it from there, too; right-click its name and, from the shortcut menu, choose "Remove from this list." (Of course, you're not actually deleting the file.)

You can also erase your jump lists completely—for privacy, for example. Read on.

Jump List Caveats

Jump lists are great and all, but:

- **Jump lists don't know** when you've deleted a document or moved it to another folder or disk; they continue to list the file even after it's gone. In that event, clicking the document's listing produces only an error message. And you're offered the chance to delete the listing (referred to as "this shortcut" in the error message) so you don't confuse yourself again the next time.

- **Some people consider jump lists** a privacy risk, since they reveal everything you've been up to recently to whatever spouse or buddy happens to wander by. (You know who you are.)

In that case, you can turn off jump lists, or just the incriminating items, as described next.

Jump List Settings

There are all kinds of ways to whip jump lists into submission. For example:

- **Turn off jump lists.** If the whole idea of Windows (or your boss) tracking what you've been working on upsets you, you can turn this feature off entirely. Open ⊞→⚙→Personalization→Start. Turn off "Show recently opened items in Jump Lists on Start or the taskbar and in File Explorer Quick Access." (The jump lists and > icons still appear—but your *files* are no longer listed in these menus.)

- **Delete one item from a jump list.** For privacy, for security, or out of utter embarrassment, you may not want some file or website's name to show up in a jump list. Just right-click (or hold your finger down) and, from the shortcut menu, choose "Remove from this list."

- **Clear a jump list completely.** At other times, you may want to wipe out *all* your jump lists—and all your tracks. To do that, turn jump lists off (as described above) and back on again. You've just erased all the existing jump lists. Your jump lists are now ready to start memorizing *new* items.

The System Tray (Notification Area)

The system tray, at the right end of the taskbar, gives you quick access to little status indicators and pop-up menus that control your PC (Figure 2-24).

Note: Most of the world calls this area the system tray. Microsoft calls it the notification area; why use three syllables when eight will do?

Figure 2-24:
You can point to a status icon's name without clicking (to see its name) or click one to see its drop-down menu of options.

This area has been a sore spot with PC fans for years. Many a software installer inserted its own little icon into this area. So the tray eventually filled up with junky, confusing little icons that had no value to you—but made it harder to find the icons you *did* want to track.

All that is history now. Out of the box, only a handful of Windows icons appear here. Each one offers three displays: one when you *point without clicking,* one when you *click or tap the icon,* and a third when you *right-click* the icon (or hold your finger down on it).

Here's what starts out on the system tray, left to right:

- **People** (🧑). Here's one-stop clicking for communications apps like Mail and Skype, as well as a place to pin your most frequently contacted contacts. See page 326 for details. (If you don't see this icon, right-click a blank spot on the taskbar and choose "Show People on the toolbar.")

- ∧. This icon is a pop-up menu that lists all the extra, junky system-tray icons that have been dumped there by your software programs (Figure 2-25, left).

Figure 2-25:
Left: Here are all the system-tray icons Windows is hiding.

Right: When you hit the battery icon, you get this handy panel, complete with a slider that lets you adjust the battery's balance between power and longevity of charge.

- **Power** (🔋**, portables only**). Point to the tiny battery icon without clicking to view the time-remaining (or percentage-remaining) readout for your laptop or tablet battery.

Click or tap for a larger display of the same information (Figure 2-25, right).

Finally, if you right-click the icon, you get access to the brightness control, Power Options control panel, and the Windows Mobility Center.

- **Network** (📶 **or** 🖥). Point to see the name of your current network and whether or not it's connected to the internet. Click/tap for a list of available networks; the wireless (Wi-Fi) ones in the list come with icons for signal strength and "locked" (password-protected) status. You can switch networks by clicking the name of one.

Right-click for a shortcut menu that offers direct access to a troubleshooting screen and to the Network & Internet settings.

- **Touch keyboard** (⌨). This button opens the onscreen typing keyboard, the one you need if you have a tablet that doesn't have a keyboard. In other words, you can make the onscreen keyboard appear and disappear by clicking this button. Chapter 12 has the details.

- **Clock.** Shows the current date and time. Point to see today's full date, with day of the week ("Monday, May 13, 2019"). And this is awesome: Click for a pop-up clock and mini-calendar, which you can use to check your appointments (the little date numbers are clickable). Right-clicking the clock gives you an option to adjust the date and time, in addition to the same shortcut menu that appears when you right-click a blank spot on the taskbar.

- **Action Center** (▢). If you have notifications, here's where you'll receive them. This humble, tiny icon is the front end for the Action Center: a huge, consolidated command center, full of quick controls and notifications, that's described at the end of this chapter.

Tip: You can drag system-tray icons around to rearrange them—not just these starter icons, but any that you install, as described next. A vertical insertion-point line appears to show you where the icon will go when you release the mouse.

Keyboard Control

You have complete keyboard control over the system tray. Press ⊞+B to highlight the ∧ button. Then press the arrow keys to "walk through" the other icons. Press the space bar to "click" whatever icon is highlighted, opening its menu. (Press the Menu key, if you have one, to "right-click" the icon.)

Reinstating the Hidden Icons

Thank you, Windows, for sparing us from Creeping Iconitus. Thank you for corralling all non-Windows system-tray icons into a single bubble of their own (Figure 2-25, left).

But what if you *want* one of those inferior icons to appear in the system tray? What if you *don't* want Windows to hide it away in the pop-up window?

No big whoop. Just drag it *out* of the "hidden" corral and back onto the taskbar. You can even drag it horizontally to reposition it. Or you can do it the long way: Open the Taskbar pane of Settings. See Figure 2-26.

From this settings page, you have two relevant options:

- **Select which icons appear on the taskbar.** You get a list of all those secondary, usually hidden status icons. You can turn them on individually ("on" means appearing on the system tray).

- **Turn system icons on or off.** This is a list of the basic Windows system-tray icons that are supposed to appear. Here you can hide them. If you don't want the time eating up taskbar space, then, by golly, you can hide it.

Tip: If your intention in visiting the "Select which icons appear on the taskbar" box (Figure 2-26, bottom) is to turn on *all* system-tray icons—maybe to recreate the halcyon days of Windows XP—you can save yourself some time. Just turn on "Always show all icons in the notification area."

Now all the icons appear in the system tray, and the ∧ button in the system tray goes away.

Figure 2-26:
Top: To open this control panel, right-click a blank spot on the taskbar and choose "Taskbar settings." (Or open ⊞→⚙→Personalization→Taskbar.)

If you click "Select which icons appear on the taskbar" (top), you gain individual hide/show control over each system-tray icon that seeks some of your screen real estate (bottom).

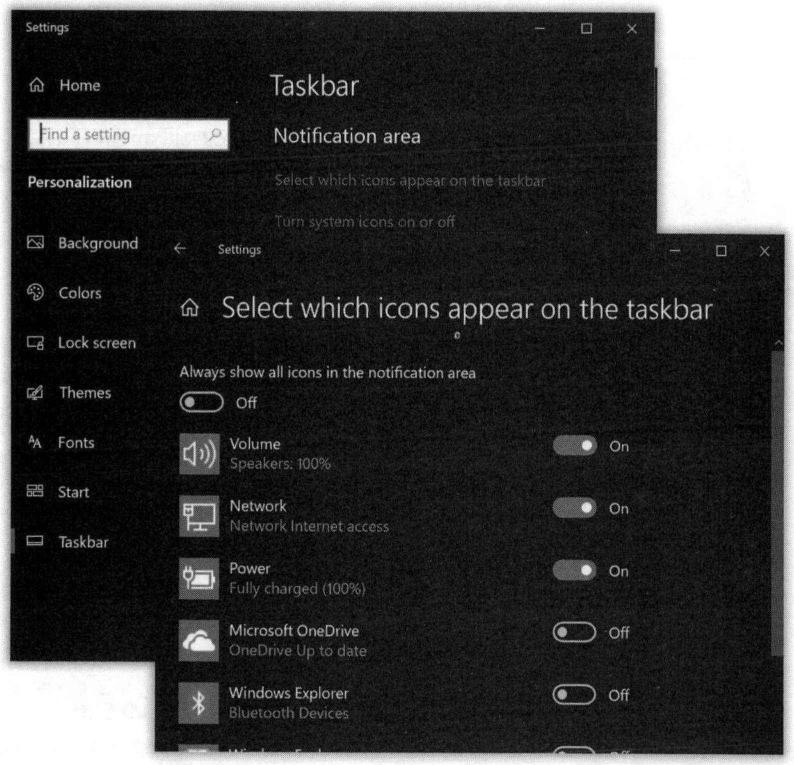

Getting the Taskbar Out of Your Hair

The bottom of the screen isn't necessarily everyone's ideal location for the taskbar. Virtually all screens are wider than they are tall, so the taskbar eats into your limited vertical screen space. You have three ways out: Hide the taskbar, shrink it, or rotate it 90 degrees.

Auto-Hiding the Taskbar

To turn on the taskbar's auto-hiding feature, right-click a blank spot on the taskbar; choose "Taskbar settings." The resulting box offers two "Automatically hide the taskbar" settings, one each for desktop and Tablet mode (page 449). Each makes the taskbar disappear whenever you're not using it—a clever way to devote your entire screen to app windows and yet have the taskbar at your cursortip when needed.

When this feature is turned on, the taskbar disappears whenever you click elsewhere, or whenever your cursor moves away from it. Only a thin line at the edge of the screen indicates that you have a taskbar at all. As soon as your pointer moves close to that line, the taskbar joyfully springs back into view.

Changing the Taskbar's Size

The taskbar can accumulate a lot of buttons and icons. As a result, you may want to enlarge the taskbar to see what's what.

Note: This trick requires a mouse or trackpad; you can't do it on a touchscreen.

- **The draggy way.** First, ensure that the taskbar isn't *locked* (which means you can't move or resize it). To do that, right-click (or hold your finger down on) a blank spot on the taskbar; from the shortcut menu, turn off "Lock the taskbar."

  Now position your pointer on the upper edge of the taskbar (or, if you've moved the taskbar, on whichever edge is closest to the center of the screen). When the pointer turns into a double-headed arrow, drag to make the taskbar thicker or thinner.

Note: If you're resizing a taskbar that's on the top or bottom of the screen, it automatically changes its size in full taskbar-height increments. You can't fine-tune the height; you can only double or triple it, for example.

If it's on the left or right edge of your screen, however, you can resize the taskbar freely. If you're not careful, you can make it look really weird.

- **The dialog-box way.** In the Properties dialog box for the taskbar (right-click it; choose "Taskbar settings" from the shortcut menu), an option called "Use small taskbar buttons" appears. It cuts those inch-tall taskbar icons down to half size, for a more pre-Win7 look.

Moving the Taskbar to the Sides of the Screen

Yet another approach to getting the taskbar out of your way is to rotate it so it sits vertically against a side of your screen. You can rotate it in either of two ways:

- **The draggy way.** First, ensure that the taskbar isn't *locked* (right-click a blank spot; from the shortcut menu, uncheck "Lock the taskbar").

  Now you can drag the taskbar to any edge of the screen, using any blank spot in the central section as a handle. (You can even drag it to the *top* of your screen, if you're a rebel.) Let go when the taskbar leaps to the edge you've indicated with the cursor.

Tip: No matter which edge of the screen holds your taskbar, your programs are generally smart enough to adjust their own windows as necessary. In other words, your Word document will shift sideways so it doesn't overlap the taskbar you've dragged to the side of the screen.

- **The dialog-box way.** Right-click a blank spot on the taskbar; from the shortcut menu, choose "Taskbar settings." Use the "Taskbar location on screen" drop-down menu to choose Left, Right, Top, or Bottom. (You can do this even if the taskbar is locked.)

You'll probably find that the right side of your screen works better than the left. Most programs put their document windows against the left edge of the screen, where the taskbar and its labels might get in the way.

Note: When you position your taskbar vertically, what was once the right side of the taskbar becomes the bottom. In other words, the clock appears at the bottom of the vertical taskbar. So as you read references to the taskbar in this book, mentally substitute the phrase "bottom part of the taskbar" when you read references to the "right side of the taskbar."

Taskbar Toolbars

You'd be forgiven if you've never even heard of taskbar *toolbars*; this is one obscure feature.

These toolbars are separate horizontal sections on the taskbar that offer special-function features. You can even build your own toolbars—for example, one stocked with documents related to a single project. (Somewhere, there's a self-help group for people who spend entirely too much time fiddling with this kind of thing.)

To make a toolbar appear or disappear, right-click a blank spot on the taskbar and choose from the Toolbars submenu that appears. The ones with checkmarks are the ones you're seeing now; you can click to turn them on and off.

For a complete rundown of the Address toolbar, the Links toolbar, the Desktop toolbar, and how to make your own toolbars, see the free PDF appendix to this chapter called "Taskbar Toolbars." It's on this book's "Missing CD" at *missingmanuals.com*.

Notifications

A *notification* is an important status message. You might get one when a message comes in, a Facebook post goes up, an alarm goes off, a calendar appointment is imminent, or your battery is running low.

When some app is trying to get your attention, a message rectangle slides into view at the lower right of your screen (Figure 2-27, top). (Windows nerds love calling these things "toast," because of the way they pop out the side.) And a little number appears on the ⬚ at the lower-right corner of your screen, tallying the number of waiting notifications.

If you don't take action by clicking or tapping it, the message slides away after a few seconds. On a touchscreen, you can also swipe it away with your finger.

Note: Do these "toast" notification bubbles appear on the Lock screen, too? That's up to you.

Open ▦ → ⚙ → System → "Notifications & actions." Turn off "Show notifications on the lock screen." Also consider turning off "Show reminders and incoming VoIP calls on the lock screen"—more urgent forms of alerts. Those messages no longer appear when the Lock screen is up.

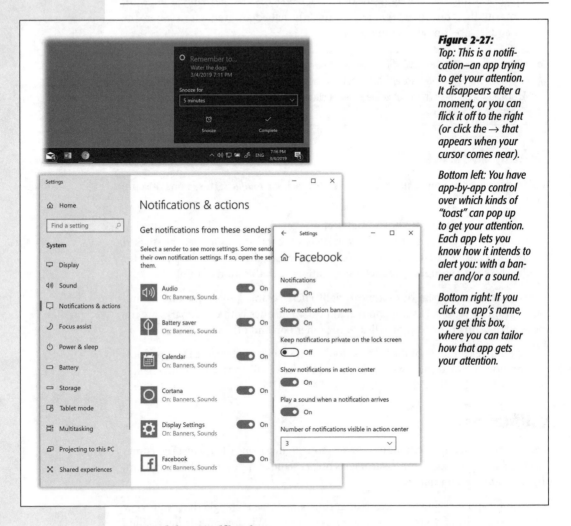

Figure 2-27:
Top: This is a notification—an app trying to get your attention. It disappears after a moment, or you can flick it off to the right (or click the → that appears when your cursor comes near).

Bottom left: You have app-by-app control over which kinds of "toast" can pop up to get your attention. Each app lets you know how it intends to alert you: with a banner and/or a sound.

Bottom right: If you click an app's name, you get this box, where you can tailor how that app gets your attention.

Customizing Notifications

You can (and should) specify *which* apps are allowed to junk up your screen. Open ▦ → ⚙ → System → "Notifications & actions" and scroll down to "Get notifications from these senders" to see the master list, with one entry for every app that might ever want your attention. (Or just tell Cortana, "Open notification settings.")

You'll quickly discover that *every* app thinks it's important; *every* app wants its notifications to blast into your face when you're working.

You, however, may not agree. You may not consider it essential to know when your kid's Plants vs. Zombies score has changed, for example.

So: Tap an app's name to open its individual Notifications screen. Here you'll find settings along these lines:

- **Notifications** is a duplicate of the master on/off switch on the previous Settings screen. Turning this off turns off all notifications from this app.

- **Show notification banners.** That's a reference to the "toast" rectangles that slide onto your screen in real time. You can turn them off for this app.

- **Keep notifications private on the lock screen.** This option prevents this app's messages from appearing on the Lock screen, for your face-saving pleasure.

- **Show notifications in action center.** The Action Center, described starting on page 96, collects all the notifications you've missed since you last looked. By turning off this switch, you're saying, "I don't care about this app. Don't even bother showing me."

- **Play a sound when a notification arrives.** Some apps also ding or chime to get your attention when their notifications appear—unless you shut them up here.

- **Number of notifications visible in action center.** Some apps, like Facebook and Twitter, could swamp your screen with updates without this control. It lets you set a maximum number of items that your Action Center will round up.

- **Priority of notifications in action center.** You can choose, for this app, Top, High, or Normal to indicate its placement in the notifications list.

Focus Assist: The Silence of the Toast

There are times when you might prefer not to be interrupted, distracted, or awakened by the appearance (and sound) of *any* app's notification bubbles. Maybe you're about to give a presentation and don't want embarrassing reminders showing up.

Setting up Focus Assist

When you turn on Focus Assist, the PC is quiet and dark. It doesn't ring, chirp, vibrate, light up, or display messages.

Yes, airplane mode does the same thing, but there's a big difference: With Focus Assist on, the PC is still online. Calls, texts, emails, and other communications continue to chug happily away; they just don't draw attention to themselves.

Focus Assist is what you want when you're in bed each night. You don't really want to be bothered with chirps for Facebook status updates and Twitter posts, but it's fine for the phone to collect them for the morning.

Bedtime is why Focus Assist comes with two fantastic additional settings: one that turns it on and off automatically on a schedule, so the computer goes dark each night at the same time you do, and another that lets you designate important people whose calls and texts are allowed to get through. You know—for emergencies.

Note: Focus Assist was called Quiet Hours in earlier Windows 10 versions.

To set up Focus Assist for the first time, open ⊞→⚙→System→ "Focus assist" (Figure 2-28). Here you'll discover there are two levels of Focus Assist (besides "Off"):

- **Priority only** means that *some* notifications are still allowed to pop up and get your attention. Which ones? That's up to you. Click "Customize your priority list" to see the options.

At the top, you'll see three checkboxes that let notifications from your *phone* show up on your *computer*—one each for incoming calls, text messages, and reminders. To make this work, you have to link your phone to your PC (page 251); the phone must have the Cortana app installed, and iPhones need not apply.

On this same screen, you can identify certain people whose calls and texts are allowed to pass through your Focus Assist blockade. (Use the "Add contacts" button to choose them; "Show notifications from pinned contacts on taskbar" automatically adds the speed-dial people you've added to the People button on your taskbar, as described on page 326.)

Whenever these very special folks contact you through Microsoft apps like Mail, Skype, Calling, and Messaging, you'll get a notification, even if Focus Assist is turned on. You might, for example, permit calls from your spouse, boss, and children to reach you; you certainly wouldn't want Focus Assist to block somebody trying

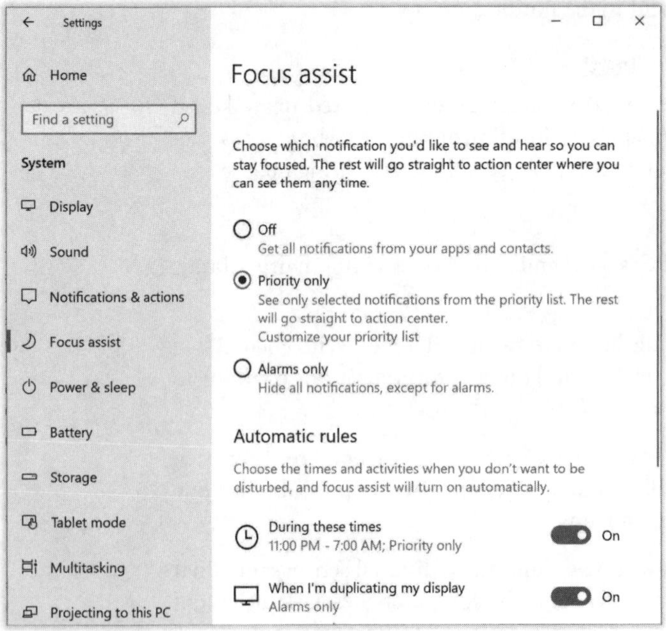

Figure 2-28:
Focus Assist lets you hush your PC's dings and chirps when you need quiet. In the top half of this Settings panel, you choose the level of hushedness: "Priority only" lets you choose which contacts and apps can send notifications; "Alarms only" lets through only the alarms you set. Below, you can set Focus Assist to kick on automatically, say, overnight, or when you're giving a presentation, or when you're playing a game, or just when you're at home (if you've told Cortana where you live).

to tell you that there's been an accident, that you've overslept, or that you've just won the lottery.

But in addition to permitting certain people to get through, you can also designate certain *apps'* notifications to get through. Maybe you're a day trader, and you don't want to miss a stock app's alert that your portfolio is crashing. Or maybe you have some chat app whose pings you always want to answer. Use "Add an app" to set these up.

- **Alarms only.** This is the more dramatic Focus Assist setting. It means that no notifications at all appear or make noise—except for alarms. Microsoft figures that if you set an alarm, you probably want it to go off to prevent an oversleeping disaster.

Automatic rules

You're welcome to turn on Focus Assist manually whenever you need some peace and quiet. But often, it's more convenient to let Windows turn it on automatically. If you open ⊞→⚙→System→Focus Assist, you'll see your options:

- **During these times.** Focus Assist can kick in during your sleeping hours, for example, using this switch. Click the displayed time interval to open the "During these hours" screen, where you can set up a start and stop time, specify Weekends, Weekdays, or Daily, and indicate which Focus Assist level (Priority or Alarms) you want.

- **When I'm duplicating my display.** This phrase is code for "When I'm giving an important presentation on a projector in front of 500 people and would rather not be humiliated by a text from my middle-schooler asking if I've seen her retainer."

- **When I'm playing a game.** Lord knows you wouldn't want to be distracted when you're neck-deep in Halo, would you?

- **When I'm using an app in full-screen mode**—which might mean you're trying to concentrate.

- **When I'm at home.** If you've told Cortana where you live, and your PC detects that you're at that address, it can stifle notifications with the understanding that you're no longer on the job and just want to be left alone.

Each of these headings offers a second line of light-gray text that opens a fine-tuning screen, where you can, for example, choose a mode for this…mode (Priority or Alarms only). That screen also offers a "Show a notification in action center when focus assist is turned on automatically" checkbox. That's handy; it produces a "toast" message on your screen whenever Focus Assist kicks in, so you don't freak out wondering why you're not getting your messages.

Using Focus Assist

Once you've set up Focus Assist in Settings, putting it into action is very easy. Start by clicking ⬚ on the taskbar to open the Action Center (next page). Click Expand, if necessary, to see the "Focus assist" tile. Click that tile once for "Priority only" mode, a second time for "Alarms only" mode, and a third time to turn Focus Assist off.

The Action Center

All right. Now you know how to dismiss, stifle, or respond to notification toast. But what if you miss one? Or you decide to act on it later?

All those "Hey you!" messages collect on a single screen called the Action Center (Figure 2-29). To make it appear, hit the ☐ icon on your system tray. Or press ■+A (for Action Center!). Or, on a touchscreen, swipe in from the right edge of the screen.

The Action Center slides onto the screen like a classy black window shade, printed in white with every recent item of interest.

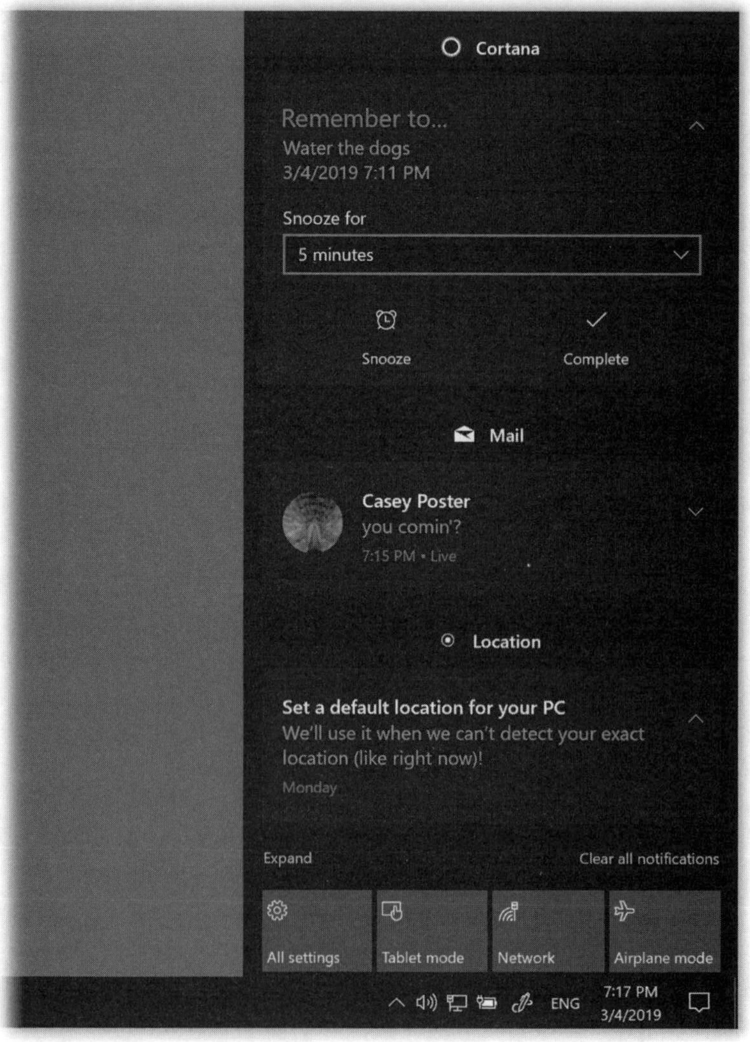

Figure 2-29:
This is the Action Center. It's where your apps send you memos to get your attention—about incoming messages, mail, tweets, Facebook posts, security issues, app updates, and so on.

At bottom: handy one-tap tiles for adjusting important PC settings.

The Notifications List

At the top of the Action Center, you'll find the notifications from all the apps you've permitted to alert you, grouped by app—the first lines of all your tweets, emails, antivirus-software whines, Microsoft Store updates, weather warnings, calendar alarms, and so on. Each is date-stamped.

Here's the fun you can have with these things:

- **Tap the ∨ at far right to read more about it.** For example, you can read the full body of a tweet, or read the rest of an email's subject line. Basically, you get to read beyond the first line of whatever it is. Often, the ∨ button reveals useful buttons like Launch or Reply.

- **Click an item to open the relevant app.** For example, click an appointment listed there to open its information panel in Calendar. Click the name of a software update to open the Microsoft Store program to read about it and download it. Click a message's name to open Mail, where you can read the entire message.

- **Clear notifications.** You can delete one message at a time (click the ✕, or swipe or drag to the right); delete all of one *app's* notifications at a time (point to the app's name, click the ✕); or clear all the current messages at once (hit "Clear all notifications" at the bottom of the column). In all cases, you're not erasing anything meaningful—only dismissing the notification.

Tip: If you have no interest in a certain app's notifications showing up here, you can make them stop appearing for good, as described on page 92.

The Quick Action Tiles

Below the list of notifications, another useful panel appears: the Quick Action tiles. These are one-touch buttons for important functions. Clearly, this feature is intended primarily for portable gadgets like tablets, phones, and laptops, but a few are useful no matter what you've got:

- **Tablet mode.** If you have a touchscreen, you might enjoy this finger-friendly Windows 10 mode. It's described in Chapter 12; you turn Tablet mode on and off by tapping here.

- **Location.** A typical portable Windows machine always attempts to know where it is in the world. (You could argue that apps like Maps and Weather are more useful when they know where you are.) But sometimes it may make you a little uneasy that your PC is tracking your whereabouts. In those cases, use this switch to turn off the computer's location tracking.

- **Battery saver** is, of course, for portable gadgets. When it's on, the screen dims and the computer stops its continuous checking for email and other internet data, all in an effort to eke out more useful time on your remaining charge. Ordinarily, Windows turns on "Battery saver" automatically when the battery falls below

20 percent of a full charge—but by hitting this tile, you can invoke it manually. Details are on page 437.

- **Bluetooth** is a short-range wireless technology. It's how you connect wireless keyboards, mice, and speakers, and this is the on/off switch.

- **Night light.** Some studies have shown that spending time before bed bathed in the blue light of a computer, tablet, or phone screen can mess up your circadian rhythm and make it harder to fall asleep. You can therefore use this function to give your screen a warmer, less blue tint, either manually using this tile or on a bedtime schedule (for example, from 11 p.m. to 6 a.m.). See page 167 for details.

- **Airplane mode,** of course, is just like airplane mode on a phone: It turns off all wireless transmission. No cellular, no Wi-Fi. Handy when the flight attendant instructs everyone to put their devices into airplane mode, of course, but also useful when you want to eke out as much battery life as possible.

Tip: It's perfectly OK to turn on airplane mode—and then to turn only *Wi-Fi back on again*, using its Quick Action tile. Wi-Fi is allowed in flight.

- **Nearby sharing** is Microsoft's version of Apple's AirDrop: It's a quick, simple way to shoot links or files to other people sitting near you, without having to mess with passwords or setup (see page 564). This tile is the on/off switch.

- **All settings** is another way to open up the main Settings app. (The usual way is to choose ⊞→⚙.)

- **Network** opens a menu of Wi-Fi networks (and others), for ease of switching (page 443).

- **Connect** is where you set up wireless audio and video receivers. For example, it's how you'd connect your tablet to a Bluetooth speaker, or your laptop to a Miracast receiver connected to your TV.

- **Project.** That's pro*ject*, not *pro*ject. In other words, it's for when you're connected to a second monitor or a projector, giving a presentation. When you click this tile, you're offered a set of options for how you want the external screen configured (page 175).

- **VPN** connects you to a virtual private network—a very secure way of connecting to your corporate network across the internet. See page 461.

- **Focus Assist** is Microsoft's "do not disturb" mode; it's described starting on page 93.

- **Snip & Sketch,** new in the May 2019 Update, lets you capture areas of the screen as graphics (screenshots); see page 338.

- **Mobile hotspot.** *Tethering* means using your cellularly equipped tablet or phone as a Wi-Fi hotspot—an internet antenna—so other devices nearby can get online. This tile, if you have it, serves as the on/off switch; see page 446.

• **Brightness.** Screen brightness is the single biggest eater of battery power, so this is a quick and easy way to adjust the degree of battery drain. New in the May 2019 Update: It's a slider, not a "click repeatedly to jump among brightness levels" tile. Much better.

Although it might not be obvious, you have some control over the Quick Action tiles. You can exercise your good taste in either of two ways:

• **Collapse them.** Let's face it: Of the two parts of the Action Center (the notifications at top, the on/off tiles at bottom), the upper part is the one you'll probably check more often. These messages come in all the time.

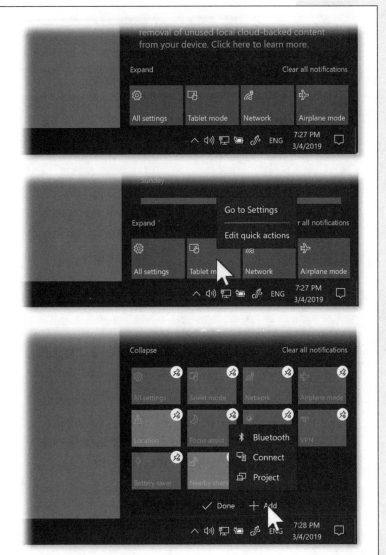

Figure 2-30:
Top: When you've collapsed the tile farm, only one row of tiles remains—the top row. They're the four most important tiles, according to you.

Middle: To edit your tiles, right-click and choose "Edit quick actions."

Bottom: Now your tiles sprout "unpin" buttons; click to hide a tile.

Or use the Add menu to restore tiles you've already hidden.

Or drag the tiles around to rearrange them. Whatever the top row shows here becomes the "collapsed four" shown above.

Click Done to exit editing mode.

That's why Microsoft set it up with a Collapse button, visible at bottom in Figure 2-30. When you click it, the Action Center hides all but the top row of tiles, as shown at top in Figure 2-30. All the rest of the Action Center space is devoted to your notifications.

- **Delete or rearrange them.** You may never use, say, Night Light (page 167) or, on your $4,000 64-core gaming desktop, airplane mode. So why should you have to stare at their on/off buttons on the Action Center all day?

In the May 2019 Update, it's easy to nuke the tiles you don't use, rearrange them, or bring them back when you realize you made a mistake; see Figure 2-30.

CHAPTER 3

Organizing & Finding Your Files

Every disk, folder, file, application, printer, and networked computer is represented on your screen by an icon. To avoid spraying your screen with thousands of overlapping icons seething like snakes in a pit, Windows organizes icons into folders, puts those folders into *other* folders, and so on. This folder-in-a-folder-in-a-folder scheme works beautifully at reducing screen clutter, but it means you've got some hunting to do whenever you want to open a particular icon.

Helping you find, navigate, and manage your files, folders, and disks with less stress and greater speed is one of the primary design goals of Windows—and of this chapter. The following pages cover Windows 10's Search function, plus icon-management life skills like selecting them, renaming them, moving them, copying them, making shortcuts of them, assigning them to keystrokes, deleting them, and burning them to CD or DVD.

The Power of Search

Every computer offers a way to find and open files and programs, saving you a lot of hunting and burrowing through your folders.

And in the Windows 10 May 2019 Update, the Search feature has been thoroughly revamped, cleaned up, and common-sensified.

The most important message is this: Search is not just for finding a file. You should also think of it for these tasks:

- **Opening apps.** Search is by far the fastest way to open a program. You should use it all the time. The whole thing happens very quickly, and you never have to take your hands off the keyboard. That is, you might hit ⊞ (to select the search box), type *calc* (to search for Calculator), and press Enter. (Why does pressing Enter open Calculator? Because it's the first item in the list of results, and its name is highlighted.)

- **Web searches.** Because Search also searches online, you can type things like *weather in dallas*, *ounces in a liter*, or *bill gates age* and get instant answers.

- **Calculations.** Search is a tiny pocket calculator, always at the ready. Press ⊞, type or paste *38*48.2-7+55*, and marvel at the result, right there in the menu: 1879.6. And you didn't even have to fire up the Calculator.

  (Use the asterisk, *, to mean "times" and the slash, /, as "divided by.")

- **Dictionary lookups.** If you type a word—say, *ersatz*—into the search box, you see the dictionary definition in the results. In this example, that would be: "Adjective: (of a product) made or used as a substitute, typically an inferior one, for something else."

- **Flight info.** Search can find you the latest information about a flight. Just type in the airline and the flight number to get a map of the flight, status, and other details.

The Taskbar Search Box

Windows still offers search boxes in two different places:

- **The main search box.** The search box at the left end of the taskbar, labeled "Type here to search," searches *everywhere* on your computer. And beyond—it can also search your network or the internet.

- **File Explorer windows.** The search box at the top of every desktop window searches only *that window* (including any folders within it).

Search boxes also appear in the Settings window, the Edge browser, Mail, and all the other spots where it's useful to perform small-time, limited searches.

Here's how you might perform the broader search-box search, on the taskbar:

1. **Get your insertion point into the search box.** You can click or tap the box (Figure 3-1, left), or press either of these keystrokes:

   ⊞ opens the Start menu, of course. But it *also* puts your blinking cursor into the search box. Best for quick and dirty searches of the Start menu and stuff whose names you know.

   ⊞+S (S for Search, get it?) puts your cursor into the search box, too—but it also opens the new set of Search refinement and shortcut options shown in Figure 3-1.

Note: The first time you use the search box, Windows displays a panel that informs you of the kind of information it needs to collect. Click "I agree" to continue—or see page 181 to find out more about this data.

This search box offers the icons of your five most often used apps, as well as a list of recent documents. You can jump into one of those programs or files with a quick click; Microsoft has realized that the fastest search is one that requires you to do no typing at all.

At the top of the box, search offers buttons that limit your quest to apps, documents, email, web pages, or (in the More menu) folders, music, people, photos, settings, or videos. More on these in a moment; for now, note that you can click one of these categories either before or after you type in what you're looking for.

Figure 3-1:
Click in the search box, or press ⊞+S, to open this revamped search box. It starts out with quick-click buttons for apps and documents you've had open recently.

2. **Start typing what you want to find (Figure 3-2).**

For example, if you're trying to find a file called "Pokémon Fantasy League.doc," typing just *pok* or *leag* will probably work.

Capitalization doesn't count, and neither do accent marks; typing *cafe* finds files with the word "café" just fine.

As you type, search results begin to appear in the space formerly occupied by the Start menu, grouped by category (Figure 3-2). Windows modifies the results list as you type—you don't have to press Enter after entering your search phrase.

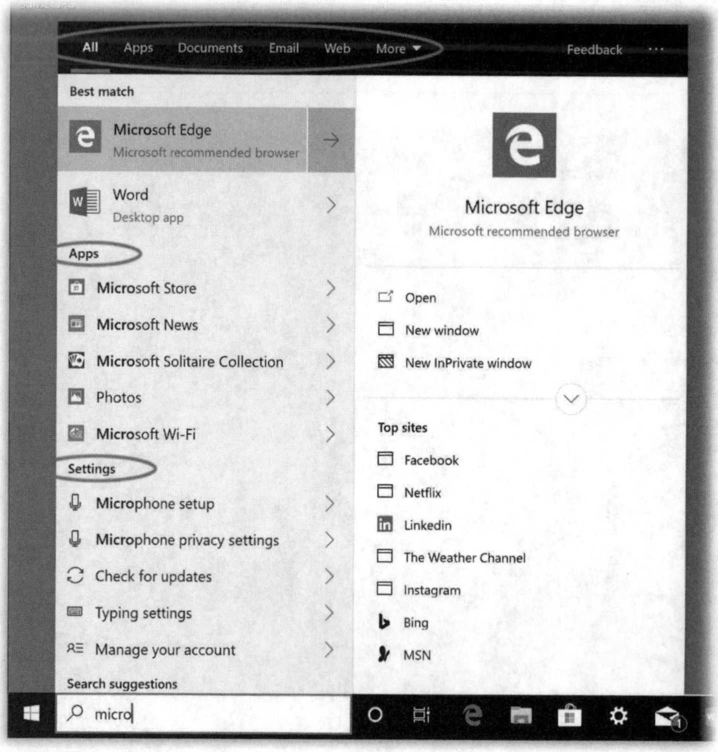

Figure 3-2:
You won't always see your search term itself ("micro," here) in the results list. That's because Windows is also searching words inside the files. The matching result may be a word inside the text of a document, or even in the invisible tags associated with a file.

To refine your search, you can either hit one of the category names at the top of the window (circled at top)—or click or tap directly on the category names in the results list (also circled).

Note the right-side panel, which displays useful actions for whatever the currently selected item is.

The Search feature can find every file; folder; program; email message; address book entry; calendar appointment; picture; movie; PDF document; music file; web bookmark; and Word, PowerPoint, and Excel document that contains what you typed, regardless of its name or folder location.

In fact, Windows isn't just searching icon *names*. It's also searching their contents—the words inside your documents—as well as your files' *metadata*. (That's descriptive text information about what's in a file, like its height, width, size, creator, copyright holder, title, editor, created date, and last modification date. Page 67 has the details.)

And it's not just finding stuff on your PC. The results also include matches from whatever is on your OneDrive (page 140), apps on the Windows app store, and even websites found online by Microsoft's Bing search service.

Tip: If you'd rather not include your OneDrive contents in searches, open ■→⚙→Search→Permissions & History and turn off "Microsoft account."

---

3. **If you see the item you were hoping to dig up, tap or click to open it.**

   In fact, if that thing is listed *first* in the results menu, tinted, then you can press Enter to open it. If the thing you want is *not* at the top of the list, click it, tap it, or "walk" down to it with the arrow keys, and then press Enter to open it.

4. **If you don't see what you're looking for, click a category heading to see more results.**

   That step may take a little explanation; read on.

Filtering the Results

The search results menu has room for only a few items. Unless you own one of those rare 60-inch Skyscraper Displays, there just isn't room to show you the whole list.

Instead, Windows displays the *most likely* matches for what you typed. They appear in the results list grouped into categories like Apps, Settings, Folders, Documents, Photos, Store (apps from the Windows app store), and so on (Figure 3-2).

Such a short list of likely suspects means it's easy to arrow-key your way to the menu item you want to open. And Windows does a pretty good job at guessing which two or three search results to show you in each category.

On the other hand, you might have 425 different documents containing the word "syzygy," and you'll see only three of them in the search-results list.

Fortunately, Windows offers three different ways to filter the list of results, so it shows only the results in a certain category:

- **Use the buttons above the list.** The filtering buttons for All, Apps, Documents, Email, and Web are immediately visible (Figure 3-2); in the More menu, you can also get to Folders, Music, People, Photos, Settings, and Videos. Click one of those buttons, and boom: The list changes to show you only the search results in that category. Kind of handy.

Note: Music, Photos, and Videos find files both online and on your PC, clearly labeled in separate mini-lists.

- **Click the category heading within the results list.** The results list itself appears with headings (Apps, Settings, Folders, and so on). You can click or tap one of those headings (also shown in Figure 3-2) to view only those results.

- **Use search shorthand.** When you use either of those filtering methods, you may notice something weird going on in the search box itself: New words appear there. If you search for *kumquat* and then click the Apps icon at top left, for example, the search box now says "apps: kumquat." If you then click the Web icon, it changes to say "web: kumquat."

  In other words, those clickable buttons and menus are just human-friendly ways of modifying your search query in the way Windows really understands: with search codes. Given that fact, there's nothing to stop you from typing them manually. If you want to find a document called "Pretzel Recipe," you can do a search for *docs: pretzel* (or *documents: pretzel).* If you're hunting for a song called "Tie a Purple Ribbon," you can just type *music: purp* or something.

Quick Actions

See the ⟩ at the right side of everything in the results list? It's a gateway into a handy quick-actions panel for one of your search results (Figure 3-2). You can click or tap the ⟩, or, if the item is already highlighted in the list, you can press Enter.

For an app, the quick-actions panel might list options like Open, Run as administrator, Open file location, Pin to Start, and Pin to taskbar. For a photo or document, it might say Open, Open file location, and Copy full path—as well as showing you its folder path and date last modified. For a web result, you get to see an actual piece of the website. For a vocabulary word, you get to see an instant dictionary definition. For a browser, you see a list of recent bookmarks, so you can jump directly to a website from the Search menu.

The Search Index

You might think that typing something into the search box triggers a search. But to be technically correct, Windows has already *done* its searching. In the first hours after you install Windows—or after you attach a new hard drive—it invisibly collects information about all your files. Like a student cramming for an exam, it reads, takes notes on, and memorizes the contents of your hard drives.

And not just the names of your files. That would be *so* 2004!

No, Windows actually looks *inside* the files. It can read and search the contents of text files, email, Windows People, Windows Calendar, RTF and PDF documents, and documents from Microsoft Office (Word, Excel, and PowerPoint).

In fact, Windows searches over 300 bits of text associated with your files—a staggering collection of tidbits, including the names of the layers in a Photoshop document, the tempo of an MP3 file, the shutter speed of a digital-camera photo, a movie's copyright holder, a document's page size, and on and on. (Technically, this sort of secondary

---

GEM IN THE ROUGH

Beyond Your Own Stuff

Ordinarily, Windows searches only what's in *your* account—your personal folder. From the search box, you can't search somebody else's stuff.

Yet you *can* search someone else's account—just not from the search box and not without permission.

Start by opening the *This PC* > *Users* folder. Inside, you'll find folders for all other account holders. Open the one you

want to search, and then search using the search box at the top of the File Explorer window.

You won't be given access, though, without first supplying an administrator's password. (You don't have to know it; you could just call an administrator over to type it in.) After all, the whole point of having different accounts is to ensure privacy for each person—and only the administrator, or *an* administrator, has full rein to stomp through anyone's stuff.

---

information is called *metadata*. It's usually invisible, although a lot of it shows up in the Details pane described on page 67.)

Windows stores all this information in an invisible, multimegabyte file called, creatively enough, the *index*. (If your primary hard drive is creaking full, you can specify that you want the index stored on some other drive; see page 117.)

After that, Windows can produce search results in seconds. It doesn't have to search your entire hard drive—only that card-catalog index file.

After the initial indexing process, Windows continues to monitor what's on your hard drive, indexing new and changed files in the background, in the microseconds between your keystrokes and clicks.

Where Windows Looks

In the May 2019 edition of Windows, Windows is prepared to search either of two universes of data, which you specify in ■→⚙→Search→Searching Windows:

- **Classic.** Out of the box, Windows doesn't actually scrounge through *every* file on your computer. It indexes only *your stuff*, on *your computer*. That's everything in your personal folder: email, pictures, music, videos, program names, entries in your People and Calendar apps, Office documents, and so on. It searches your OneDrive, too (page 140).

   You're welcome to add individual additional folders to this list, as described below.

   Classic indexing does not index any other folders—the ones that contain Windows' own operating-system files and all your programs, for example—and ignores any external disks attached to your PC.

Note: Windows indexes all the drives connected to your PC, but not other hard drives on the network. You can, if you wish, add other folders to the list of indexed locations manually (read on).

- **Enhanced.** If you turn this option on, Windows indexes *everything* on, or connected to, your PC: every folder and disk, every folder and subfolder. (Except, of course, the personal folders of other people with accounts on your machine; if you were hoping to search your spouse's email for phrases like "Meet you at midnight," forget it.)

   The additional indexing takes time (roughly 15 minutes), power (keep your laptop plugged in), and disk space (your index file is bigger). But being able to search so widely so quickly has been a dream of Windows fans for years.

Adding New Places to the Index

No matter which search mode you've chosen, you can tweak the factory settings. Suppose you use classic mode, but there's some folder on another disk (or elsewhere on the network) that you really do want to be able to search the *good* way—contents and all, nice and fast. You can do that by adding it to your PC's search index.

Or suppose you're using enhanced mode, and there's a folder you *don't* want to include, maybe because you have privacy concerns (for example, you don't want your co-workers searching your stuff while you're away from your desk). You can eliminate it from the search index.

To edit the list of searched folders in this way, open the Search panel (click or tap in the search box) and then hit the ⋯ at the top-right corner (visible in Figure 3-2). That menu contains only a single command, "Indexing options." Choose it.

(You can also get there via ⊞→⚙→Search→Searching Windows→"Customize searching locations here.") Proceed as shown in Figure 3-3.

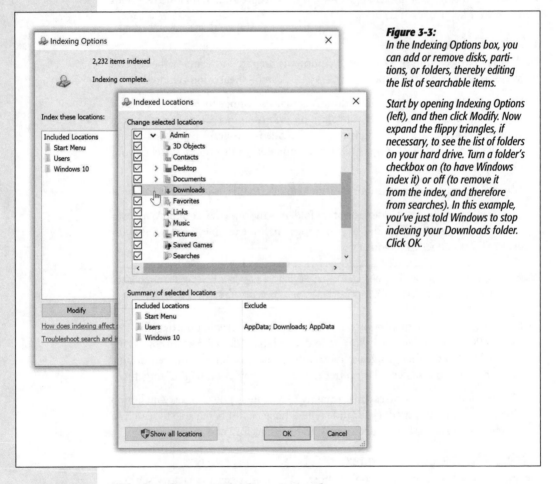

Figure 3-3:
In the Indexing Options box, you can add or remove disks, partitions, or folders, thereby editing the list of searchable items.

Start by opening Indexing Options (left), and then click Modify. Now expand the flippy triangles, if necessary, to see the list of folders on your hard drive. Turn a folder's checkbox on (to have Windows index it) or off (to remove it from the index, and therefore from searches). In this example, you've just told Windows to stop indexing your Downloads folder. Click OK.

File Explorer Window Searches

See the search box at the top right of every File Explorer window (Figure 3-4)? This, too, is a piece of the Search empire. But there's a big difference: The taskbar search box searches *your entire computer.* The search box in a File Explorer window searches *only that window* (and folders within it).

As you type, the window changes to show search results (in Content view) in a massively scrolling list.

Once the results appear, you can change the window view if that's helpful—or sort, filter, and group them, just as you would in any other Explorer window.

You can also make the search box bigger—by dragging the divider bar (between the address bar and the search box) to the left. Useful when you're searching for your novel in progress: "The Sudden Disappearance, Reappearance, and then Disappearance Again of Sean O'Flanagan at the Dawn of the Elizabethan Era."

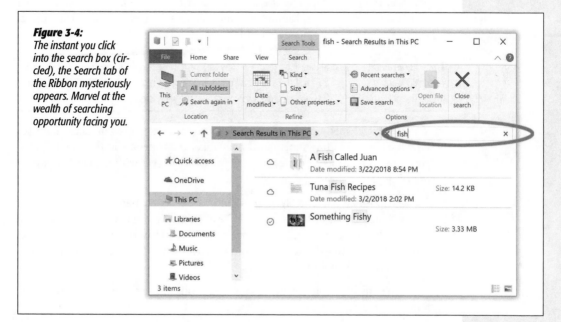

Figure 3-4:
The instant you click into the search box (circled), the Search tab of the Ribbon mysteriously appears. Marvel at the wealth of searching opportunity facing you.

Search Options on the Ribbon

When you use the File Explorer search box, the Ribbon magically sprouts a new tab, called Search (Figure 3-4). It's teeming with options, including *search filters* that help you weed down a big list of results:

- **This PC.** This button, at far left, does the opposite of weed down your results—it expands the scope of your search. You've just searched this Explorer window, but this button applies the same search to your entire computer.

- **Current folder.** An Explorer search usually searches the window that's open and all the folders inside it. If you click this button, though, you eliminate the subfolders from the results.

- **All subfolders.** Remember the fun you had reading the "Current folder" paragraph just now? This button has the opposite function. It expands the search's reach to include this window's subfolders once again.

- **Search again in.** This handy drop-down menu lists places you've recently searched. Now and then, one of these options can save you time and fiddling.

- **Date modified, Kind, Size, Other properties.** These are *search filters*. They refine your search, letting you limit the results to certain date ranges, file types, file sizes, and so on.

When you use these menus, you'll see codes in blue text appear in the search box—for example, *datemodified:last week* or *size:medium*. If you're more of a keyboard person than a mouse person, you could type those codes into the search box yourself; the result is exactly the same, as described in the next section. In other words, the options on the Ribbon are nothing more than user-friendlified, quicker ways of entering the same search codes.

Tip: You can adjust the second part of each code just by clicking it. For example, if you chose *size:small* and you really wanted *size:medium*—or if the *size:small* query didn't produce any results—then click the word *small*. The pop-up menu of sizes appears again so you can adjust your selection.

You can use as many of these filters as you want. The more you click them (or type the corresponding shorthand), the longer the codes are in the search box. If you want to find medium files created by Casey last year with the tag *Murgatroid project*, go right ahead.

So what do they do? The "Date modified" drop-down menu offers choices like Today, Yesterday, Last Month, and This Year. "Kind" is a long list of file types, with choices like Folder, Game, Note, Picture, and Web History. "Size" offers file-size ranges like Tiny (0 to 10 KB), Medium (100 KB to 1 MB), Huge (16 to 128 MB), and Gigantic (greater than 128 MB).

As for the miscellaneous filters in the "Other properties" pop-up menu—well, they require some explanation.

Type lets you specify (after the word *Type:* in the search box) what general kind of thing you're looking for: *picture, sound, PDF, document, folder, disk image, backup, JPG, DOC,* and so on. More on types in a moment.

Name lets you search for something by its filename only. (Otherwise, Windows also shows you search results based on the words *inside* the files.)

Folder path lets you type out the folder path (page 58) of something you're seeking.

Finally, **Tags** lets you search for items according to the label you've applied to them, as described on page 67.

- **Recent searches** displays—correct!—recent searches you've performed. It uses the shorthand described above, like "portrait of mary kind:image" or "Book list size:medium."

- **Advanced options** is a shortcut to some of the options described on page 107, pertaining to non-indexed locations (that is, other computers on your network, or external drives). Here you can turn on the searching of zipped files and system files in those places, or turn on searching of text inside their files. You also get a shortcut to the Indexing Options dialog box described on page 108.

- **Save search.** This button becomes available once you've set up a search.

  When clicked, it generates a *saved search* file and asks you to name it. (Behind the scenes, it's a special document with the filename extension *.search-ms.*) Windows proposes stashing it in your Saved Searches folder, inside your personal folder, but you can choose any location you like—including the desktop.

  Whenever you click the saved search, you get an instantaneous update of the search you originally set up.

  The idea is to save you time when you regularly have to set up the same search; for example, maybe every week you have to round up all the documents authored by you that pertain to the Higgins proposal and save them to a flash drive. A search folder can do the rounding-up part with a single click. These items' real locations may be all over the map, scattered in folders throughout your PC. But through the magic of the saved search, they appear as though they're all in one neat window.

Note: Unfortunately, there's no easy way to edit a search folder. If you decide your original search criteria need a little fine-tuning, the simplest procedure is to set up a new search—correctly this time—and save it with the same name as the first one; accept Windows' offer to replace the old one with the new.

Incidentally: Search filters work by *hiding* all the icons that don't match. So don't be alarmed if you click Size and then Small—and most of the files in your window suddenly disappear. Windows is doing what it thinks you wanted—showing you only the small files—in real time, as you adjust the filters.

At any time, you can bring all the files back into view by clicking the × at the right end of the search box.

Limit by Size, Date, Rating, Tag, Author…

Suppose you're looking for a file called *Big Deals.doc.* But when you type *big* into the search box, you wind up wading through hundreds of files that *contain* the word "big."

It's at times like these you'll be grateful for Windows' little-known *criterion* searches. These are syntax tricks that help you create narrower, more targeted searches. All you have to do is prefix your search query with the criterion you want, followed by a colon.

An example is worth a thousand words, so *several* examples should save an awful lot of paper. You can type these codes into the search box in an Explorer window (they don't work in the main search box):

- *name: big* **finds only documents** with "big" in their *names.* Windows ignores anything with that term *inside* the file.

Note: These searches work with or without a space after the colon—either "name: big" or "name:big" is fine.

- *tag: crisis* **finds only icons** with "crisis" as a tag—not as part of the title or contents.

- *created: 7/25/19* **finds everything** you wrote on July 25, 2019. You can also use *modified: today* or *modified: yesterday,* for that matter. Or don't be that specific. Just use *modified: July* or *modified: 2019.*

  You can use symbols like < and >, too. To find files created since yesterday, you could type *created: >yesterday.*

  Or use two dots to indicate a range. To find all the email you got in the first two weeks of March 2019, you could type *received: 3/1/2019..3/15/2019.* (That two-dot business also works to specify a range of file sizes, as in *size: 2 MB..5 MB.*)

Note: That's right: Windows recognizes human terms like *today, yesterday, this week, last week, last month, this month,* and *last year.*

- *size: >2gb* **finds all the big files** on your PC.

- *rating: <**** **finds documents** to which you've given ratings of three stars or fewer.

- *camera model: Sony A7* **finds all the pictures** you took with that camera.

- *kind: email* **finds all the email messages.**

  That's just one example of the power of *kind.* Here are some other kinds you can look for: *calendar, appointment,* or *meeting* (appointments in Outlook, iCal, or vCalendar files); *communication* (email and attachments); *contact* or *person* (vCard and Windows Contact files, Outlook contacts); *doc* or *document* (text, Office, PDF, and web files); *folder* (folders, .zip files, .cab files); *link* (shortcut files); *music* or *song* (audio files, Windows Media playlists); *pic* or *picture* (graphics files like JPEG, PNG, GIF, and BMP); *program* (programs); *tv* (shows recorded by Windows Media Center); and *video* (movie files).

- The *folder:* **prefix limits the search** to a certain folder or library. (The starter words *under:, in:,* and *path:* work the same way.) So *folder: music* confines the search to your Music library, and a search for *in: documents turtle* finds all files in your Documents library containing the word "turtle."

Tip: You can combine multiple criteria searches, too. For example, if you're pretty sure you had a document called "Naked Mole-Rats" that you worked on yesterday, you could cut directly to it by typing *mole modified: yesterday* or *modified: yesterday mole.* (The order doesn't matter.)

So where's the master list of these available criteria? It turns out they correspond to the *column headings* at the top of an Explorer window in Details view: Name, Date modified, Type, Size, and so on.

You're not limited to just the terms you see now; you can use any term that *can* be an Explorer-window heading. To see them all, right-click any of the existing column headings in a window that's set to Details view. From the shortcut menu, choose More. There they are: 115 different criteria, including Size, Rating, Album, Bit rate,

Camera model, Date archived, Language, Nickname, and so on. Here's where you learn that, for example, to find all your Ohio address-book friends, you'd search for *home state or province: OH.*

Dude, if you can't find what you're looking for now, it probably doesn't exist.

Special Search Codes

Certain shortcuts in the File Explorer search boxes can give your queries more power. For example:

- **Document types.** You can type *document* to find all text, spreadsheet, and Power-Point files. You can also type a filename extension—*.mp3* or *.doc* or *.jpg,* for example—to round up all files of a certain file type.

- **Tags, authors.** This is payoff time for applying *tags* or author names to your files (page 67). In a search box, you can type, or start to type, *Gruber Project* (or any other tag you've assigned), and you get an instantaneous list of everything that's relevant to that tag. Or you can type *Mom* or *Casey* or any other author's name to see all the documents that person created.

- **Utility apps.** Windows comes with a bunch of geekhead programs that aren't listed in the Start menu and have no icons—advanced technical tools like RegEdit (the Registry Editor), Command Prompt (the command line), and so on. By far the quickest way to open them is to type their names into the search box.

  In this case, however, you must type the *entire* name—*regedit,* not just *rege.* And you have to use the program's actual, on-disk name (regedit), not its human name (Registry Editor).

- **Quotes.** If you type in more than one word, Search works just the way Google does. That is, it finds things that contain both words *somewhere* inside.

  If you're searching for a phrase where the words really belong together, though, put quotes around them. For example, searching for *military intelligence* rounds up documents that contain those two words, but not necessarily side by side. Searching for *"military intelligence"* finds documents that contain that exact phrase. (Insert your own political joke here.)

- **Boolean searches.** Windows also permits combination-search terms like AND and OR, better known to geeks as Boolean searches.

  That is, you can round up a single list of files that match *two* terms by typing, say, *vacation AND kids.* (That's also how you'd find documents co-authored by two specific people—you and a pal, for example.)

Note: You can use parentheses instead of AND, if you like. That is, typing *(vacation kids)* finds documents that contain both words, not necessarily together.

If you use OR, you can find icons that match *either* of two search criteria. Typing *jpeg OR mp3* will turn up photos and music files in a single list.

The word NOT works, too. If you did a search for *dolphins,* hoping to turn up sea-mammal documents, but instead find your results contaminated by football-team listings, then by all means repeat the search with *dolphins NOT Miami.* Windows will eliminate all documents containing "Miami."

Note: You must type Boolean terms like AND, OR, and NOT in all capitals.

You can even combine Boolean terms with the other special search terms described in this chapter. Find everything created in the past couple of months by searching for *created: September OR October,* for example. If you've been entering your name into the Properties dialog box of Microsoft Office documents, you can find all the ones created by Casey and Robin working together using *author: (Casey AND Robin).*

File Explorer Results Menu Tips

It should be no surprise that a feature as important as Search comes loaded with options, tips, and tricks. Here it is—the official, unexpurgated Search Tip-O-Rama:

- **You can open anything in the results menu** by highlighting it and then pressing Enter to open it.

- **You can jump to the actual icon of a search result,** sitting there in its actual window, instead of opening it. To do that, right-click its name and, from the shortcut menu, choose "Open file location." The Esc key (top-left corner of your keyboard) is a quick "Back out of this" keystroke. Tap it to close the results menu and restore the Start menu to its original form.

- **To clear the search box**—either to try a different search or just to get the regularly scheduled File Explorer window back—click the little ✕ at the right end of the search box.

- **When you need to look up a number in the People app,** don't bother opening Mail; it's faster to use Search. You can type somebody's name or even part of someone's phone number.

Customizing Search

You've just read about how Search works fresh out of the box. But you can tailor its behavior, either for security reasons or to customize it to the kinds of work you do.

Unfortunately for you, Microsoft has stashed the various controls that govern searching into three different places. Here they are, one area at a time.

Windows Search Settings

The ■→⚙→Search→Windows Search screen lets you choose between the Classic and Enhanced search methods described earlier, and exclude certain folders from the search.

Folder Options

The second source of search settings is the Folder Options→Search dialog box. To open it, find the View tab on the Ribbon in any Explorer window; click Options. In the resulting dialog box, click the Search tab. Here's what you'll find:

- **Don't use the index when searching in file folders for system files.** If you turn this item on, Windows won't use its internal Dewey Decimal System for searching Windows itself. It will, instead, perform the names-only, slower type of search.

  So who on earth would want this turned on? You, if you're a programmer or system administrator and you're worried that the indexed version of the system files might be out of date. (That happens, since system files change often, and the index may take some time to catch up.)

- **Include system directories.** When you're searching a disk that hasn't been indexed, do you want Windows to look inside the folders that contain Windows itself (as opposed to just the documents people have created)? If yes, then turn this on.

- **Include compressed files (ZIP, CAB…).** When you're searching a disk that hasn't been indexed, do you want Windows to search for files inside compressed archives, like .zip and .cab files? If yes, then turn on this checkbox. (Windows doesn't ordinarily search archives, even on an indexed hard drive.)

- **Always search file names and contents.** As the previous pages make clear, the Windows search mechanism relies on an *index*—an invisible database that tracks the location, contents, and metadata of every file. If you attach a new hard drive, or attempt to search another computer on the network that hasn't been indexed, then Windows ordinarily just searches its files' *names*. After all, it has no index to search for that drive.

  If Windows did attempt to index those other drives, you'd sometimes have to wait awhile, at least the first time, because index-building isn't instantaneous. That's why the factory setting here is Off.

  But if you really want Windows to search the text inside the other drives' files, even without an index—which can be painfully slow—then turn this checkbox on instead.

Indexing Options

The third location of search settings is shown in Figure 3-5. This is Index Settings, the master control over the search *index,* the massive, invisible, constantly updated database file that tracks your PC's files and what's in them. To open this box, open the Search panel (click or tap in the search box) and then hit the ⋯ at the top right corner. From the menu, choose "Indexing options." You arrive at the Indexing Options dialog box shown in Figure 3-3; click Advanced, and authenticate if necessary.

Index Settings tab

On the first tab (Figure 3-5), here's the kind of fun you can have:

- **Index encrypted files.** Windows can *encrypt* files and folders with a quick click, making them unreadable to anyone who receives one by email, say, and doesn't have the password. This checkbox lets Windows index these files (the ones *you've* encrypted, of course; this isn't a back door to files you can't otherwise access).

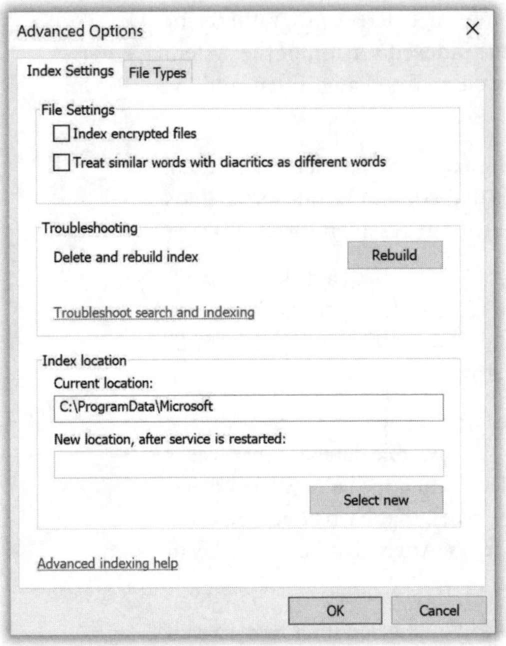

Figure 3-5:
Search works beautifully right out of the box. For the benefit of the world's tweakers, however, this dialog box awaits, filled with technical adjustments to the way Search works.

- **Treat similar words with diacritics as different words.** The word "ole," as might appear cutely in a phrase like "the ole swimming pool," is quite a bit different from "olé," as in, "You missed the matador, you big fat bull!" The difference is a *diacritical mark* (øne öf mâny littlé lañguage märks).

  Ordinarily, Windows ignores diacritical marks; it treats "ole" and "olé" as the same word in searches. That makes it easier for the average person who can't remember how to type a certain marking, or which direction it goes. But if you turn on this box, Windows will treat marked and unmarked words as different.

- **Troubleshooting.** If the Search command ever seems to be acting wacky—for example, it's not finding a document you *know* is on your computer—Microsoft is there to help you.

  Your first step should be to click "Troubleshoot search and indexing." (It appears both here, on the Advanced panel, and on the main Indexing Options panel.) The resulting step-by-step sequence may fix things.

If it doesn't, click Rebuild. Now Windows *wipes out* the index it's been working with, completely deleting it—and then begins to rebuild it. You're shown a list of the disks and folders Windows has been instructed to index; the message at the top of the dialog box lets you know its progress. With luck, this will wipe out any funkiness you've been experiencing.

- **Move the index.** Ordinarily, Windows stores its invisible index file on your main hard drive. But you might have good reason for wanting to move it. Maybe your main drive is getting full. Or maybe you've bought a second, faster hard drive; if you store your index there, searching will be even faster.

  In the Advanced Options dialog box, click "Select new." Navigate to the disk or folder where you want the index to go, and then click OK. (The actual transfer of the file takes place the next time you start up Windows.)

File Types tab

Windows ordinarily searches for just about every kind of *useful* file: audio files, program files, text and graphics files, and so on. It doesn't bother peering inside things like Windows operating system files and applications, because what's inside them is programming code with little relevance to most people's work. Omitting these files from the index keeps the index smaller and the searches fast.

But what if you routinely traffic in very rare Venezuelan Beekeeping Interchange Format (VBIF) documents—a file type your copy of Windows has never met before? You won't be able to search their contents unless you specifically teach Windows about them.

In the Advanced Options dialog box, click the File Types tab. Type the filename extension (like VBIF) into the text box at the lower left. Click Add and then OK. From now on, Windows will index this new file type.

On the other hand, if you find that Windows uses up valuable search-results menu space listing, say, web bookmarks—stuff you don't need to find very often—you can tell it not to bother. Now the results list won't fill up with files you don't care about.

Turn the checkboxes on or off to make Windows start or stop indexing them.

Using the "How should this file be indexed" options at the bottom of the box, you can also make Windows stop searching these files' contents—the text within them—for better speed and a smaller index.

The Folders of Windows 10

The top-level, all-encompassing, mother-ship window of your PC is the This PC window (formerly called Computer, formerly formerly called My Computer). From within this window, you have access to every disk, folder, and file on your computer. Its slogan might well be "If it's not in here, it's not on your PC."

To see it, open an Explorer window and click This PC in the navigation pane.

You wind up face to face with the icons of every storage gizmo connected to your PC: hard drives, CD and DVD drives, USB flash drives, digital cameras, and so on (Figure 3-6).

Tip: Ordinarily, every drive has an icon in here, even if no disk or memory card is in it. That can be annoying if your laptop has, for example, four memory-card slots, each for a different kind of card, labeled D:, E:, F:, and G:, and your This PC window is getting a little hard to navigate.

Fortunately, Windows can hide your drive icons when they're empty. To turn that on or off, open Folder Options (click Options on the Ribbon's View tab). Click the View tab. Click "Hide empty drives," and then click OK.

Now your removable-disk/card drives appear only when something is in them—a CD, a DVD, or a memory card, for example.

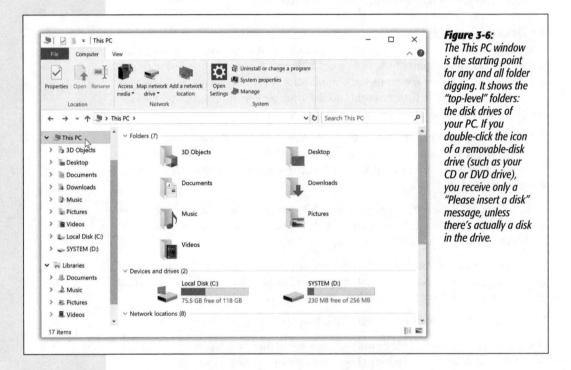

Figure 3-6:
The This PC window is the starting point for any and all folder digging. It shows the "top-level" folders: the disk drives of your PC. If you double-click the icon of a removable-disk drive (such as your CD or DVD drive), you receive only a "Please insert a disk" message, unless there's actually a disk in the drive.

Most people, most of the time, are most concerned with the Local Disk (C:), which represents the internal hard drive preinstalled in your computer. (You're welcome to rename this icon, by the way, just as you would any icon.)

Note: The drive lettering, such as C: for your main hard drive, is an ancient convention that doesn't offer much relevance these days. (Back at the dawn of computing, the A: and B: drives were floppy drives.)

What's in the Local Disk (C:) Window

If you double-click the Local Disk (C:) icon in This PC—that is, your primary hard drive—you'll find an assortment of folders that you, the human, aren't supposed to fiddle with. Three are worth knowing about:

- **Program Files** is where Windows stores all your desktop programs—Word, Excel, games, and so on.

  Of course, a Windows program isn't a single, self-contained icon. Instead, it's usually a *folder,* housing both the program and its phalanx of support files and folders. The actual application icon generally can't even run if it's separated from its support group.

- **Users.** Windows' *accounts* feature is ideal for situations where different family members, students, or workers use the same machine at different times. Each account holder will turn on the machine to find her own separate, secure set of files, folders, desktop pictures, web bookmarks, font collections, and preference settings. (Much more about this feature in Chapter 18.)

  In any case, now you should see the importance of the Users folder. Inside is one folder—one *personal folder*—for each person who has an account on this PC. In general, Standard account–holders (page 537) aren't allowed to open anybody else's folder.

Note: Inside the Documents library, you'll see Public Documents; in the Music library, you'll see Public Music; and so on. These are nothing more than pointers to the master Public folder that you can also see here, in the Users folder. (Anything you put into a Public folder is available for inspection by anyone else with an account on your PC, or even other people on your network.)

- **Windows.** Here's a folder Microsoft hopes you'll just ignore. This most hallowed folder contains the thousands of little files that make Windows, well, Windows. Most of these folders and files have cryptic names that appeal to cryptic people.

  In general, the healthiest PC is one whose Windows folder has been left alone.

Your Personal Folder

Everything that makes your Windows experience your own sits inside the *Local Disk (C:) > Users > [your name]* folder. This is your *personal folder*, where Windows stores your preferences, documents, email, pictures, music, web favorites, cookies (described on page 418), and so on.

Ordinarily, you open this folder using a far more direct method: Open the ■ menu, select the round photo button representing your account (leftmost column), and choose "Personal folder."

Tip: Actually, it would make a lot of sense for you to install your personal folder's icon in the "Quick access" list at the left side of every Explorer window. Drag its icon directly into the list.

Your personal folder comes prestocked with folders like these:

- **3D Objects.** This folder contains any 3D models you build using Windows 10's creative apps, like Paint 3D and Mixed Reality Viewer. (You can't delete this folder manually. That job requires a Registry hack; you can find instructions for it using Google.)

- **Contacts.** An address-book program called Windows Contacts came with Windows Vista, but Microsoft gave it a pink slip for Windows 7. All that's left now is this folder, where it used to stash the information about your social circle. (Some other companies' address-book programs can use this folder, too.)

- **Desktop.** When you drag an icon out of a folder or disk window and onto your desktop, it may *appear* to show up on the desktop. But that's just a visual convenience. In truth, nothing in Windows is ever really on the desktop; it's just in this Desktop *folder,* and mirrored on the desktop.

  Everyone who shares your machine, upon signing in, sees his own stuff sitting out on the desktop. Now you know how Windows does it; there's a separate Desktop folder in every person's personal folder. (You can entertain yourself for minutes trying to prove this. If you drag something out of your Desktop folder, it also disappears from the actual desktop. And vice versa.)

Note: A link to this folder appears in the navigation pane of every Explorer window.

- **Downloads.** When you download anything from the web, your browser suggests storing it on your computer in this Downloads folder. The idea is to save you the frustration of downloading stuff and then not being able to find it later.

- **Favorites.** This folder stores shortcuts of the files, folders, and other items you've designated as *favorites* (that is, web bookmarks). This can be handy if you want to delete a bunch of your favorites all at once, rename them, or whatever.

- **Links.** In older Windows versions, this folder's icons corresponded to the easy-access links in the Favorite Links list in your Explorer windows. These days, it serves no real purpose except to satisfy people who hate it when Microsoft takes a feature out.

- **Documents.** Microsoft suggests you keep your work files in this folder. Sure enough, whenever you save a new document (when you're working in Word or Photoshop Elements, for example), the Save As box proposes storing the new file in this folder.

Tip: You can move the Documents folder, if you like. For example, you can move it to a *removable* drive, like a pocket hard drive or a USB flash drive, so you can take it to work with you and always have your latest files at hand. To do so, open your Documents folder. Right-click a blank spot in the window; from the shortcut menu, choose Properties. Click the Location tab, click Move, navigate to the new location, and click Select Folder.

What's cool is that the Documents *link* in every Explorer window's navigation pane still opens your Documents folder. What's more, your programs still propose storing new documents there—even though the folder isn't where Microsoft originally put it.

- **Music, Pictures, Videos.** You guessed it: These are Microsoft's proposed homes for your multimedia files. These are where song files from ripped CDs, photos from digital cameras, and videos from camcorders go.

- **OneDrive.** This is the actual, for-real storage location for your machine's local copy of the files and folders on your OneDrive (page 140).

- **Saved Games.** When you save a computer game that's in progress, the game should propose storing it here, so you can find it again later. (It may take some time before all the world's games are updated to know about this folder.)

- **Searches.** As described on page 111, you can *save* searches for reuse later. This folder stores shortcuts for them.

Note: Your personal folder also stores a few hidden items reserved for use by Windows itself. (To view hidden folders, turn on "Hidden items" on the View tab of the Ribbon.) One of them is AppData, a very important folder that stores all kinds of support files for your programs. For example, it stores word-processor dictionaries, web cookies, Edge security certificates, and so on. In general, there's not much reason for you to poke around in them, but in this book, here and there, you'll find tips and tricks that refer you to AppData.

Selecting Icons

Before you can delete, rename, move, copy, or otherwise tamper with any icon, you have to be able to *select* it somehow. By highlighting it, you're essentially telling Windows what you want to operate on.

By Tapping or Clicking

To select one icon, just click it once. To select *multiple* icons at once—in preparation for moving, copying, renaming, or deleting them en masse, for example—use one of these techniques:

- **Select all.** Highlight all the icons in a window by using the "Select all" button on the Ribbon's Home tab. (Or press Ctrl+A, its keyboard equivalent.)

- **Highlight several consecutive icons.** Start with your cursor above and to one side of the icons, and then drag diagonally. As you drag, you create a temporary shaded blue rectangle. Any icon that falls within this rectangle darkens to indicate that it's been selected.

  Alternatively, click the first icon you want to highlight, and then Shift-click the last one. All the files in between are automatically selected, along with the two you clicked. (These techniques work in any folder view: Details, Icon, Content, or whatever.)

Tip: If you include a particular icon in your diagonally dragged group by mistake, Ctrl-click it to remove it from the selected cluster.

- **Highlight nonconsecutive icons.** Suppose you want to highlight only the first, third, and seventh icons in the list. Start by clicking icon No. 1; then Ctrl-click each of the others. (If you Ctrl-click a selected icon *again*, you *de*select it. A good time to use this trick is when you highlight an icon by accident.)

Tip: The Ctrl key trick is especially handy if you want to select *almost* all the icons in a window. Press Ctrl+A to select everything in the folder, and then Ctrl-click any unwanted items to deselect them.

By Typing

You can also highlight one icon, plucking it out of a sea of pretenders, by typing the first few letters of its name. Type *nak,* for example, to select an icon called "Naked Chef Broadcast Schedule."

Eliminating Double-Clicks

In some ways, a File Explorer window is just like a web browser. It has a Back button, an address bar, and so on.

If you enjoy this PC-as-browser effect, you can actually take it one step further. You can set up your PC so that *one* click, not two, opens an icon. It's a strange effect that some people adore, that some find especially useful on touchscreens—and that others turn off as fast as their little fingers will let them.

In any File Explorer window, on the View tab of the Ribbon, click Options. The Folder Options control panel opens. Turn on "Single-click to open an item (point to select)." Then indicate *when* you want your icon's names turned into underlined links by selecting "Underline icon titles consistent with my browser" (*all* icons' names appear as links) or "Underline icon titles only when I point at them." Click OK. The deed is done.

Now, if a single click opens an icon, you're entitled to wonder how you're supposed to *select* an icon (which you'd normally do with a single click). Take your pick:

- **Point to it for about a half-second without clicking.** To make multiple selections, press the Ctrl key as you point to additional icons. (And to *drag* an icon, just ignore all this pointing stuff—simply drag as usual.)
- **Turn on the checkbox mode described next.**

Checkbox Selection

It's great that you can select icons by holding down a key and clicking—if you can remember *which* key must be pressed.

Turns out novices were befuddled by the requirement to Ctrl-click icons when they wanted to choose more than one. So Microsoft created a checkbox mode. In this mode, any icon you point to temporarily sprouts a little checkbox that you can click to select it (Figure 3-7).

To turn this feature on, open any Explorer window, and then turn on "Item check boxes," which is on the View tab of the Ribbon.

Now, anytime you point to an icon, an on/off checkbox appears. No secret keystrokes are necessary for selecting icons; it's painfully obvious how you're supposed to choose only a few icons out of a gaggle.

Figure 3-7:
Each time you point to an icon, a clickable checkbox appears. Once you turn it on, the checkbox remains visible, making it easy to select several icons at once. What's cool about the checkboxes feature is that it doesn't preclude your using the old click-to-select method; if you click an icon's name, you deselect all checkboxes except that one.

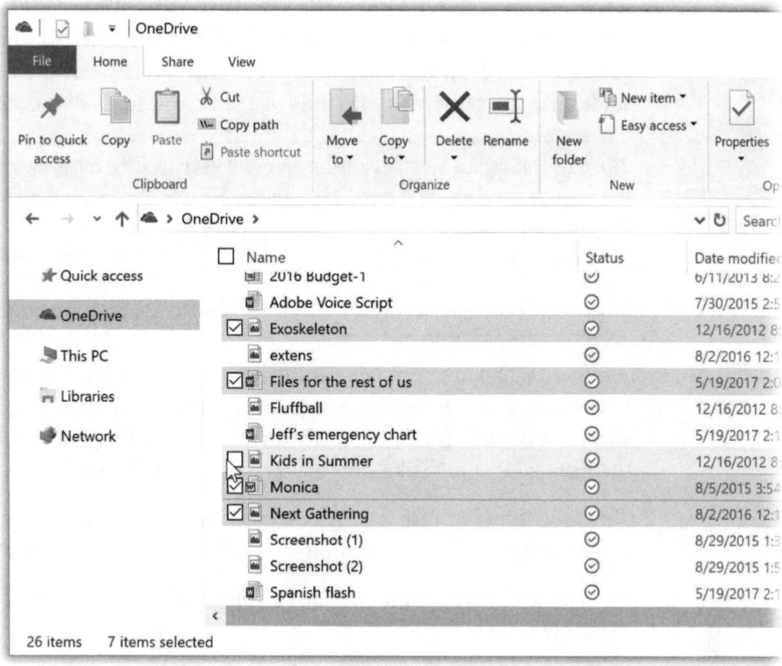

Life with Icons

File Explorer has one purpose in life: to help you manage the *icons* of your files, folders, and disks. You could spend your entire workday just mastering the techniques of naming, copying, moving, and deleting these icons.

Here's the crash course.

Renaming Your Icons

To rename a file, folder, printer, or disk icon, you need to open its "renaming rectangle." You can do so with any of the following methods:

- Highlight the icon and then press the F2 key.
- Highlight the icon. On the Home tab of the Ribbon, click Rename.
- Click carefully, just once, on a previously highlighted icon's name.
- Right-click the icon (or hold your finger down on it) and choose Rename from the shortcut menu.

Tip: You can even rename your hard drive so you don't go your entire career with a drive named "Local Disk." Just rename its icon (in the This PC window) as you would any other.

In any case, once the renaming rectangle has appeared, type the new name you want and then press Enter. Use all the standard text-editing tricks: Press Backspace to fix a typo, press the ← and → keys to position the insertion point, and so on. When you're finished editing the name, press Enter to make it stick. (If another icon in the folder has the same name, Windows beeps and makes you choose another name.)

Tip: If you highlight a bunch of icons at once and then open the renaming rectangle for any *one* of them, you wind up renaming *all* of them. For example, if you've highlighted three folders called Cats, Dogs, and Fish, then renaming one of them to *Animals* changes the original set of names to Animals (1), Animals (2), and Animals (3).

If that's not what you want, press Ctrl+Z (the keystroke for Undo) to restore all the original names.

A folder or filename can technically be up to 260 characters long. In practice, though, you won't be able to produce filenames that long; that's because that maximum must also include the *file extension* (the three-letter suffix that identifies the file type) and the file's *folder path* (like *(C:)* › *Users* › *Casey* › *Pictures*).

Note, too, that because they're reserved for behind-the-scenes use, Windows doesn't let you use any of these symbols in a Windows filename: \ / : * ? " < > |

You can give more than one file or folder the same name, as long as they're not in the same folder.

Note: Windows comes factory-set not to show you filename extensions. That's why you sometimes might *think* you see two different files called, say, "Quarterly Sales," both in the same folder.

The explanation is that one filename may end with *.doc* (a Word document), and the other may end with *.xls* (an Excel document). But because these suffixes are hidden, the files look like they have exactly the same name. To unhide filename extensions, turn on the "File name extensions" checkbox. It's on the View tab of the Ribbon.

Icon Properties

Properties are a big deal in Windows. Properties are preference settings that you can change independently for every icon on your machine.

To view the properties for an icon, choose from these techniques:

- **Right-click the icon; choose Properties from the shortcut menu.**

- **Highlight the icon in an Explorer window; click the Properties button.** It's the wee tiny icon at the upper-left corner of the window, in the Quick Access toolbar. Looks like a tiny page with a checkmark (⊡).

- **Highlight the icon. On the Ribbon, on the Home tab, click Properties.**

- While pressing Alt, double-click the icon.

- Highlight the icon; press Alt+Enter.

Tip: You can also see some basic info about any icon (type, size, and so on) by pointing to it without clicking. A little info balloon pops up, saving you the trouble of opening the Properties box or even the Details pane.

These settings aren't the same for every kind of icon, however. Here's what you can expect when opening the Properties dialog boxes of various icons (Figure 3-8).

Figure 3-8:
The Properties dialog boxes are different for every kind of icon. In the months and years to come, you may find many occasions when adjusting the behavior of some icon has big benefits in simplicity and productivity.

Top: The Properties dialog box for a song file.

Bottom: The Properties window for the computer itself looks quite a bit different. It is, in fact, part of the Control Panel.

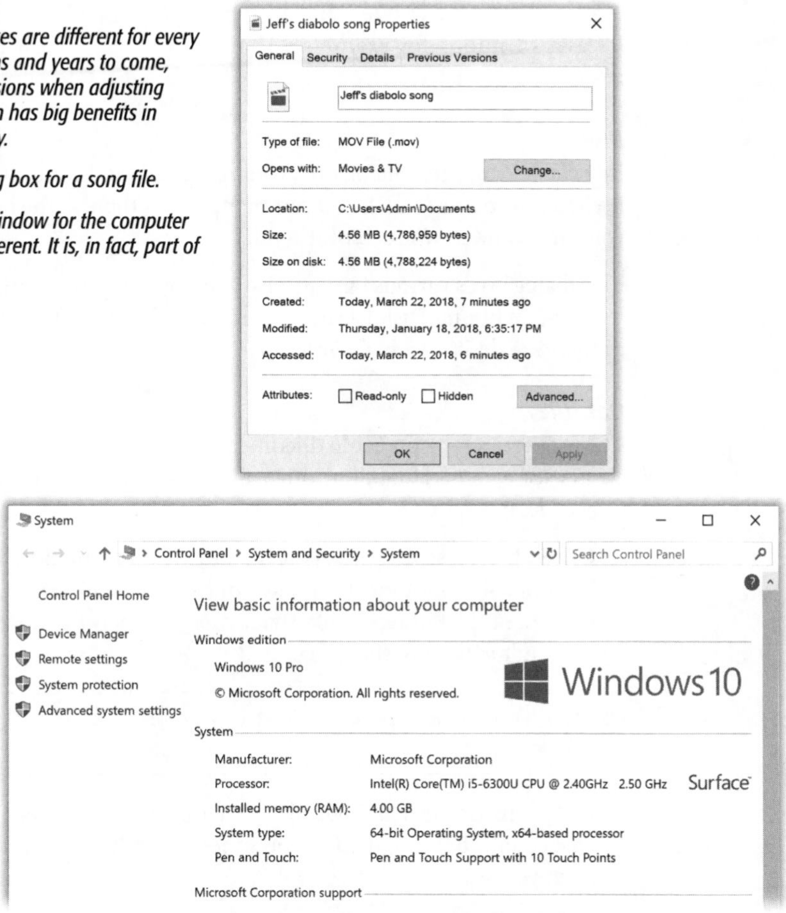

This PC (System Properties)

There are about 500 different ways to open the Properties dialog box for your This PC icon. For example, you can click This PC in the navigation pane of any window and then click "System properties" on the Ribbon's Computer tab. Or right-click the This PC icon (in the nav pane again); from the shortcut menu, choose Properties.

The System Properties window is packed with useful information about your machine: what kind of processor is inside, how much memory (RAM) it has, whether or not it has a touchscreen, and what version of Windows you've got.

The panel at the left side of the window (shown in Figure 3-8, bottom) includes some useful links—"Device Manager," "Remote settings," "System protection," and "Advanced system settings"—all of which are described elsewhere in this book.

Note, however, that most of them work by opening the *old* System Properties Control Panel. Its tabs give a terse, but more complete, look at the tech specs and features of your PC. These, too, are described in the relevant parts of this book—all except "Computer Name." Here you can type a plain-English name for your computer ("Casey's Laptop," for example). That's how it will appear to other people on the network, if you have one.

Disks

In a disk's Properties dialog box, you can see all kinds of information about the disk itself, like its name (which you can change right there in the box), its capacity (which you can't), and how much of it is full.

This dialog box's various tabs are also gateways to a host of maintenance and backup features, including Disk Cleanup, Error-Checking, Defrag, Backup, and Quotas; all of these are described in Chapter 17.

Data files

The properties for a plain old document depend on what kind of document it is. You always see a General tab, but other tabs may also appear (especially for Microsoft Office files):

- **General.** This screen offers all the obvious information about the document—location, size, modification date, and so on. The *Read-only* checkbox locks the document. In the read-only state, you can open the document and read it, but you can't make any changes to it.

Note: If you make a *folder* read-only, it affects only the files already inside. If you add additional files later, they remain editable.

Hidden turns the icon invisible. It's a great way to prevent something from being deleted, but because the icon becomes invisible, you may find it a bit difficult to open *yourself.*

The Advanced button offers a few additional options. "File is ready for archiving" means "Back me up." This message is intended for the old Backup and Restore program described in Chapter 16, and it indicates that this document has been changed since the last time it was backed up (or that it's never been backed up). "Allow this file to have contents indexed in addition to file properties" lets you indicate that this file should, or should not, be part of the search index described earlier in this chapter.

"Compress contents to save disk space" is described on page 145. Finally, "Encrypt contents to secure data" is described on page 527.

- **Security** has to do with the NTFS permissions of a file or folder, technical on/off switches that govern who can do what to the contents. You see this tab only if the hard drive is formatted with NTFS.

- **Custom.** The Properties window of certain older Office documents includes this tab, where you can look up a document's word count, author, revision number, and many other statistics. But you should by no means feel limited to these 21 properties.

  Using the Custom tab, you can create properties of your own—Working Title, Panic Level, Privacy Quotient, or whatever you like. Just specify a property type using the Type pop-up menu (Text, Date, Number, Yes/No); type the property name into the Name text box (or choose one of the canned options in its drop-down menu); and then click Add.

  You can then fill in the Value text box for the individual file in question (so its Panic Level is Red Alert, for example).

Note: This is an older form of tagging files—a lot like the tags feature described on page 67—*except* that you can't use the Search feature to find them. Especially technical people can, however, perform query-language searches for these values.

- **The Details tab** reveals the sorts of details—tags, categories, authors, and so on—that *are* searchable by Windows' Search command. For many kinds of files, you can edit these little tidbits right in the dialog box.

  This box also tells you how many words, lines, and paragraphs are in a particular Word document. For a graphics document, the Summary tab indicates the graphic's dimensions, resolution, and color settings.

- **The Previous Versions tab** appears only if you've gone to the extraordinary trouble of resurrecting Windows 7's Previous Versions feature, which lets you revert a document or a folder to an earlier version.

Folders

The Properties dialog box for a folder offers a bunch of tabs:

- **General, Security.** Here you find the same sorts of checkboxes and options as you do for data files, described already.

- **Sharing** makes the folder susceptible to invasion by other people—either in person, when they sign into this PC, or from across your office network (see Chapter 19).

- **Location.** This tab appears only for folders you've included in a library, which can show folders from anywhere. It identifies where the folder *really* sits.

- **Customize.** The first drop-down menu here lets you apply a *folder template* to any folder: General items, Documents, Pictures, Music, or Videos. A template is nothing more than a canned layout with a predesigned set of Ribbon tabs, icon sizes, column headings, and so on.

You may already have noticed that your Pictures library displays a nice big thumbnail icon for each of your photos, and that your Music library presents a tidy Details-view list of all your songs, with Ribbon buttons like "Play all," "Play To," and "Add to playlist." Here's your chance to apply those same expertly designed templates to folders of your own making.

This dialog box also lets you change the *icon* for a folder, as described in the next section.

Program files

There's not much here you can change yourself, but you certainly get a lot to look at. For starters, there are the General and Details tabs described already. But you may also find an important Compatibility tab, which may one day come to save your bacon. It lets you trick a pre–Windows 10 program into running on Microsoft's latest.

Changing Your Icon Pictures

You can change the actual, inch-tall illustrations that Windows uses to represent the little icons in your electronic world. You can't, however, use a single method to do so; Microsoft has divided up the controls between two different locations.

Standard Windows icons

First, you can change the icon for some of the important Windows desktop icons: the Recycle Bin, Documents, and so on. To do so, right-click a blank spot on the desktop. From the shortcut menu, choose Personalize.

In the resulting window, click Themes in the task pane at the left side; then click "Desktop icon settings." You'll see a collection of those important Windows icons. Click one and then click Change Icon to choose a replacement from a collection Microsoft provides. (You haven't *lived* until you've made your Recycle Bin look like a giant blue thumbtack!)

Folder or shortcut icons

Ordinarily, when your Explorer window is in Tiles, Content, or a fairly big Icon view, each folder's icon resembles what's in it. You actually see a tiny photo, music album, or Word document peeking out of the open-folder icon.

This means, however, that the icon may actually *change* over time, as you put different things into it. If you'd rather freeze a folder's icon so it doesn't keep changing, you can choose an image that will appear to peek out from inside that folder.

Note: The following steps also let you change what a particular shortcut icon looks like. Unfortunately, Windows offers no way to change an actual document's icon.

Actually, you have two ways to change a folder's icon. Both begin the same way: Right-click the folder or shortcut whose icon you want to change. From the shortcut

---

menu, choose Properties, and then click the Customize tab. Now you have a choice (Figure 3-9):

- **Change what image is peeking out of the file-folder icon.** Click Choose File. Windows now lets you hunt for icons on your hard drive. These can be picture files, icons downloaded from the internet, icons embedded inside program files and .dll files, or icons you've made yourself using a freeware or shareware icon-making program. Find the graphic, click it, click Open, and then click OK.

  It may take a couple of minutes for Windows to update the folder image, but soon you'll see your hand-selected image "falling out" of the file-folder icon.

- **Completely replace the file-folder image.** Click Change Icon. Windows offers up a palette of canned graphics; click the one you want, and then click OK. Instantly, the original folder bears the new image.

Figure 3-9:
Left: The original folder icon.

Middle: You've replaced the image that seems to be falling out of it.

Right: You've completely replaced the folder icon.

Prizewinners   Prizewinners   Prizewinners

Shortcut Icons

A *shortcut* is a link to a file, folder, disk, or program (see Figure 3-10). You might think of it as a duplicate of the thing's icon—but not a duplicate of the thing itself. (A shortcut occupies almost no disk space.) When you double-click the shortcut icon, the original folder, disk, program, or document opens. You can also set up a keystroke for a shortcut icon so you can open any program or document just by pressing a certain key combination.

Shortcuts provide quick access to the items you use most often. And because you can make as many shortcuts of a file as you want, and put them anywhere on your PC, you can, in effect, keep an important program or document in more than one folder. Just create a shortcut to leave on the desktop in plain sight, or drag its icon onto the Links toolbar. In fact, every link in the top part of your navigation pane is a shortcut.

Note: Don't confuse the term *shortcut*, which refers to one of these duplicate-icon pointers, with *shortcut menu,* the context-sensitive menu that appears when you right-click almost anything in Windows. The shortcut *menu* has nothing to do with the shortcut icons feature; maybe that's why it's sometimes called the *context* menu.

Among other things, shortcuts are great for getting to websites and folders elsewhere on your network, because you're spared having to type out their addresses or burrow through network windows.

Creating and Deleting Shortcuts

To create a shortcut, use any of these tricks:

- **Right-click (or hold your finger down on) an icon.** From the shortcut menu, choose "Create shortcut."

- **Right-drag an icon from its current location to the desktop.** (On a touchscreen, hold your finger on the icon momentarily before you drag.)

  When you release the mouse button or your finger, choose "Create shortcuts here" from the menu that appears.

Tip: If you're not in the mood to use a shortcut menu, then just left-drag an icon while pressing Alt. A shortcut appears instantly. (And if your Alt key is missing or broken—hey, it could happen—then drag while pressing Ctrl+Shift instead.)

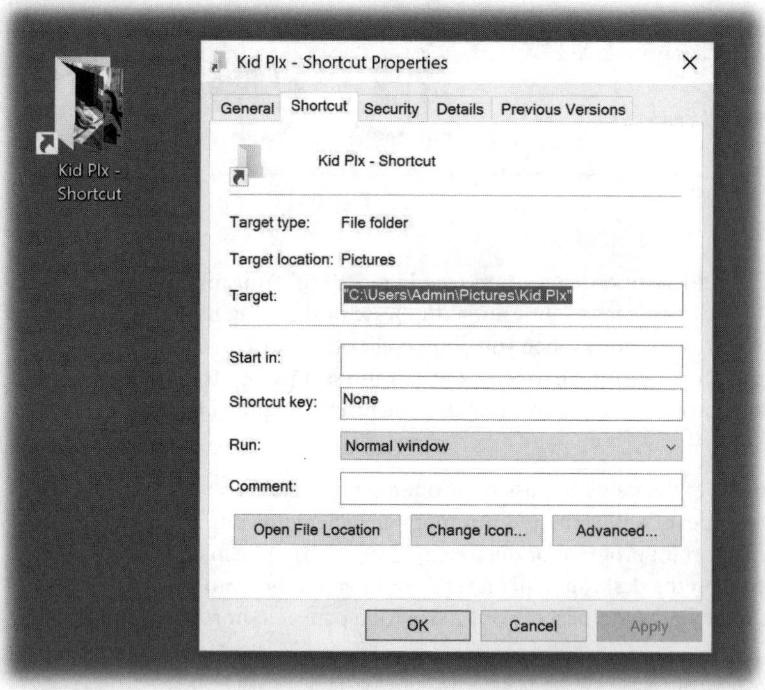

Figure 3-10:

Left: You can distinguish a desktop shortcut from its original in two ways. First, the tiny arrow "badge" identifies it as a shortcut; second, its name contains the word "Shortcut."

Right: The Properties dialog box for a shortcut indicates which actual file or folder this one "points" to. The Run drop-down menu lets you control how the window opens when you double-click the shortcut icon.

- **Copy an icon, as described earlier in this chapter.** Open the destination window; then, on the Ribbon's Home tab, click "Paste shortcut."

- **Drag the tiny icon at the left end of the address bar** onto the desktop or into a window.

Tip: This also works with websites. If your browser has pulled up a site you want to keep handy, drag that little address-bar icon onto your desktop. Double-clicking it later will open the same web page.

You can delete a shortcut the same way as any icon, as described in the Recycle Bin discussion on page 136. (Of course, deleting a shortcut *doesn't* delete the file it points to.)

Unveiling a Shortcut's True Identity

To locate the original icon from which a shortcut was made, right-click the shortcut icon and choose Properties from the shortcut menu. As shown in Figure 3-10, the resulting box shows you where to find the "real" icon. It also offers you a quick way to jump to it, in the form of the Open File Location button.

Shortcut Keyboard Triggers

Sure, shortcuts let you put favored icons everywhere you want to be. But they still require clicking to open, which means taking your hands off the keyboard—and that, in the grand scheme of things, means slowing down.

Lurking within the Shortcut Properties dialog box is another feature with intriguing ramifications: the "Shortcut key" box. By clicking here and then pressing a key combination, you can assign a personalized keystroke for the shortcut. Thereafter, by pressing that keystroke, you can summon the corresponding file, program, folder, printer, networked computer, or disk window to your screen, no matter what you're doing on the PC. It's *really* useful.

Three rules apply when choosing keystrokes to open your favorite icons:

- **The keystrokes work only on shortcuts stored** *on your desktop.* If you stash the icon in any other folder, the keystroke stops working.

- **Your keystroke can't incorporate** the space bar or the Enter, Backspace, Delete, Esc, Print Screen, or Tab keys.

- **Your combination** *must* **include** Ctrl+Alt, Ctrl+Shift, or Alt+Shift, and another key.

  Windows enforces this rule rigidly. For example, if you type a single letter into the box (such as *E*), Windows automatically adds the Alt and Ctrl keys to your combination (Alt+Ctrl+E). This is the operating system's attempt to prevent you from inadvertently duplicating one of the built-in Windows keyboard shortcuts and thoroughly confusing both you and your computer.

Tip: If you've ever wondered what it's like to be a programmer, try this. In the Shortcut Properties dialog box (Figure 3-10), use the Run drop-down menu at the bottom of the dialog box to choose "Normal window," "Minimized," or "Maximized." By clicking OK, you've just told Windows what kind of window you want to appear when opening this particular shortcut.

Controlling Windows in this way isn't exactly the same as programming, but you are, in your own small way, telling Windows what to do.

If you like the idea of keyboard shortcuts for your files and programs, but you're not so hot on Windows' restrictions, then consider installing a free *macro program* that lets you make *any* keystroke open *anything anywhere*. The best-known one is Auto-Hotkey, which is available from this book's "Missing CD" page at *missingmanuals.com*, but there are plenty of similar (and simpler) ones. Check them out at, for example, *shareware.com*.

Copying and Moving Folders and Files

Windows offers two techniques for moving files and folders from one place to another: dragging them and using the Copy and Paste commands. In both cases, you'll be delighted to find out how communicative Windows is during the copy process (Figure 3-11).

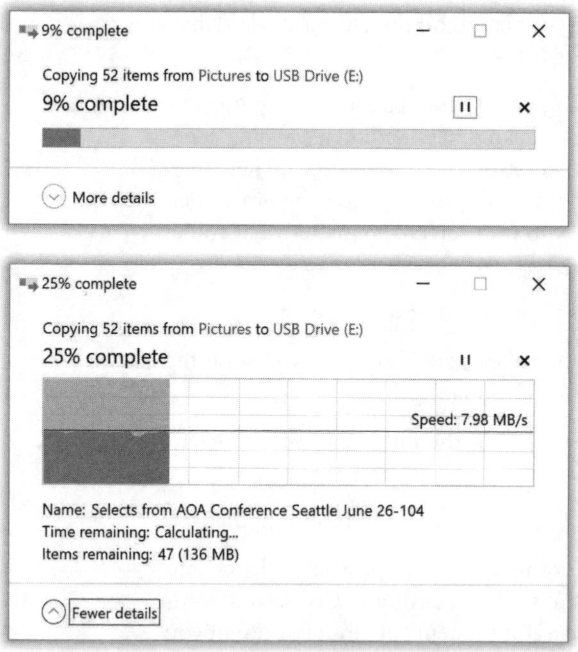

Figure 3-11:
Windows is a veritable chatterbox when it comes to copying or moving files.

Top: For each item you're copying, you see a graph and a percentage-complete readout. There's a Pause button and a Cancel button (the ✕). And there's a "More details" button.

Bottom: "More details" turns out to be an elaborate graph that shows you how the speed has proceeded during the copy job. The horizontal line indicates the average speed, in megabytes per second.

Any questions?

Whichever method you choose, you start by showing Windows which icons you want to copy or move—by highlighting them, as described on page 121. Then proceed as follows.

Copying by Dragging Icons

You can drag icons from one folder to another, from one drive to another, from a drive to a folder on another drive, and so on. (When you've selected several icons, drag any *one* of them, and the others will go along for the ride.)

Here's what happens when you drag icons in the usual way, using the left mouse button:

- **Dragging to another folder** on the same disk *moves* the folder or file.

- **Dragging from one disk to another** *copies* the folder or file.

- **Holding down the Ctrl key** while dragging to another folder on the same disk *copies* the file. (If you do so within a single window, Windows creates a duplicate of the file called "[Filename] - Copy.")

POWER USERS' CLINIC

Secrets of the "Send to" Command

If you find yourself copying or moving certain icons to certain folders or disks with regularity, it's time to exploit the "Send to" command that lurks in the shortcut menu for almost every icon. Unlike the "Move to" and "Copy to" commands on the Ribbon, "Send to" can send files to *services* (like a DVD burner or an email program), not just folders. This command offers a quick way to copy and move icons. For example, you can teleport a copy of a highlighted file directly to the desktop by choosing "Send to"→Desktop (create shortcut).

Then there's "Send to"→"Mail recipient." It bundles the selected icon as an email attachment that's ready to send. You can also zip up a folder (see page 147) by choosing "Send to"→"Compressed (zipped) folder."

If you start getting into "Send to"—and you should—check this out: If you press Shift while you right-click, you get a much longer list of "Send to" options, including all the essential folders (OneDrive, Downloads, Desktop, Favorites). But if the folder you want isn't there, it's easy enough to make the "Send to" command accommodate your *own* favorite folders. In your personal folder (page 119) sits a folder called

SendTo. Any shortcut icon you place here shows up instantly in the "Send to" menus. Alas, this folder is among those Microsoft considers inappropriate for novices. As a result, it's *hidden.*

You can still get to it, though. In the address bar of any Explorer window, type *shell:sendto,* and then press Enter. (That's a quick way of getting to the *(C:) > Users > [your name] > AppData > Roaming > Microsoft > Windows > SendTo* folder.)

Most people create shortcuts here for folders and disks. When you highlight an icon and choose "Send to"→Backup Disk, for example, Windows copies the icon to that disk. (Or, if you simultaneously press Shift, you *move* the icon to the other disk or folder.) You can even add shortcuts of *applications* to the SendTo folder. By adding WinZip to this "Send to" menu, for example, you can drop-kick a highlighted icon onto the WinZip icon (for decompressing) just by choosing "Send to"→WinZip. Or add a web server to this menu, so you can upload a file with a right-click. You can even create shortcuts for a printer or fax modem so you can print or fax a document just by highlighting its icon and choosing File→"Send to"→[device's name].

- **Pressing Shift while dragging** from one disk to another *moves* the folder or file (without leaving a copy behind).

Tip: You can move or copy icons by dragging them either into an open window or directly onto a disk or folder *icon*.

The right-mouse-button trick

Think you'll remember all those possibilities every time you drag an icon? Probably not. Fortunately, you never have to. One of the most important tricks you can learn is to use the *right* mouse button as you drag. When you release the button, the menu shown in Figure 3-12 appears, letting you either copy or move the selected icons.

Tip: Press the Esc key to cancel a dragging operation at any time.

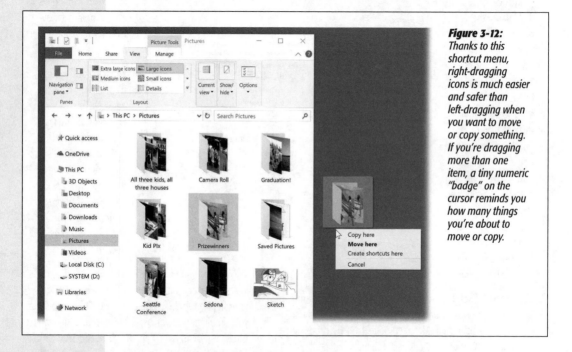

Figure 3-12:
Thanks to this shortcut menu, right-dragging icons is much easier and safer than left-dragging when you want to move or copy something. If you're dragging more than one item, a tiny numeric "badge" on the cursor reminds you how many things you're about to move or copy.

Dragging icons into the navigation pane

You may find it easier to copy or move icons using the navigation pane, since the two-pane display format makes it easier to see where your files are and where they're going.

Just expand the arrow brackets of the navigation pane until you can see the destination folder.

Tip: If you accidentally click a folder in the navigation pane, its contents will pop up in the right pane, covering up the icon you wanted to copy. Click the Back button to get back to where you once belonged.

Then find the icon you want to move in the right pane and drag it to the appropriate folder in the left pane, or vice versa. Windows copies the icon.

Tip: This situation is also a good time to use the window Snap feature. Drag the icon's home window against the right side of your screen; drag the destination window against the left side. Now they're perfectly set up for drag-copying between them.

Copying or Moving Files with the Ribbon

Dragging icons to copy or move them feels good because it's so direct; you actually see your arrow cursor pushing the icons into the new location.

But you pay a price for this satisfying illusion. That is, you may have to spend a moment or two fiddling with your windows, or clicking in the Explorer folder hierarchy, so you have a clear "line of drag" between the icon to be moved and the destination folder.

But, these days, moving or copying icons can be a one-step operation, thanks to the "Move to" and "Copy to" buttons on the Ribbon's Home tab. The drop-down menu for each one lists frequently and recently used folders. (If the destination folder isn't listed, then choose "Choose location" and navigate to it yourself.)

In other words, you just highlight the icons you want to move, hit "Move to" or "Copy to," and then choose the destination folder. The deed is done, without ever having to leave the folder window where you began.

Copying with Copy and Paste

You can also move icons from one window into another using the Cut, Copy, and Paste commands. The routine goes like this:

1. **Highlight the icon or icons you want to move.**

   Use any of the tricks described on page 121.

2. **Right-click (or hold your finger down on) one of the icons. From the shortcut menu, choose Cut or Copy.**

   You may want to learn the keyboard shortcuts for these commands: Ctrl+C for Copy, Ctrl+X for Cut. Or use the Cut and Copy buttons on the Ribbon's Home tab.

   The Cut command makes the highlighted icons appear dimmed; you've stashed them on the invisible Windows Clipboard. (They don't actually disappear from their original nesting place until you paste them somewhere else—or hit the Esc key to cancel the operation.)

   The Copy command also places copies of the files on the Clipboard, but it doesn't disturb the originals after you paste.

3. **Right-click the window, folder icon, or disk icon where you want to put the icons. Choose Paste from the shortcut menu.**

   Once again, you may prefer to use the appropriate Ribbon button, Paste, or the shortcut, Ctrl+V.

Either way, you've successfully transferred the icons. If you pasted into an open window, you see the icons appear there. If you pasted onto a closed folder or disk icon, you need to open the icon's window to see the results. And if you pasted right back into the same window, you get a duplicate of the file called "[Filename] - Copy."

The Recycle Bin

The Recycle Bin is your desktop trash basket. This is where files and folders go when they've outlived their usefulness. Basically, the Recycle Bin is a waiting room for data oblivion, in that your files stay there until you *empty* it—or until you rescue the files by dragging them out again.

While you can certainly drag files or folders onto the Recycle Bin icon, it's usually faster to highlight them and then perform one of the following options:

- **Press the Delete key.**
- **Click the Delete button on the Ribbon's Home tab.**
- **Choose File→Delete.**
- **Right-click a highlighted icon and choose Delete from the shortcut menu.**

Windows asks if you're sure you want to send the item to the Recycle Bin; it provides a good chunk of information about the file in the warning window, for your safety. (You don't lose much by clicking Yes, since it's easy enough to change your mind, as you'll see.) Now the Recycle Bin icon looks like it's brimming over with paper.

You can put unwanted files and folders into the Recycle Bin from any folder window or even from inside the Open File dialog box of many applications.

Note: All these methods put icons from your *hard drive* into the Recycle Bin. But deleting an icon from a removable drive (a flash drive, for example), from other computers on the network, or from a .zip file, does *not* involve the Recycle Bin. Those files go straight to heaven, giving you no opportunity to retrieve them. (Deleting anything with the Command Prompt commands *del* or *erase* bypasses the Recycle Bin, too.)

Making the Recycle Bin Less Naggy

When you get right down to it, you really have to *work* to get rid of a file in Windows. First you have to put the thing in the Recycle Bin. Then you have to confirm that, yes, you're sure. Then you have to *empty* the Recycle Bin. Then you have to confirm that, yes, you're sure about *that*.

Fortunately, those are just the factory settings. There are all kinds of ways to eliminate some of these quadruplicate confirmations. For example:

- **Squelch the "Are you sure?" message.** On the Ribbon's Home tab, click the ▾ beneath the Delete button. From the shortcut menu, turn off "Show recycle confirmation." Or, in the Recycle Bin's Properties dialog box (Figure 3-13), turn off "Display delete confirmation dialog." Now you'll never get that message when you put something into the Recycle Bin.

- **Bypass the Recycle Bin just this time.** Again, use the ▾ beneath the Delete button on the Ribbon's Home tab. From the shortcut menu choose "Permanently delete"; you've just deleted the file permanently, skipping its layover in the Recycle Bin.

Note: Pressing Shift while you delete a file (and then clicking Yes in the confirmation box, or hitting Enter), also deletes the file instantly. The Shift-key trick works for every method of deleting a file: pressing the Delete key, choosing Delete from the shortcut menu, and so on.

- **Bypass the Recycle Bin for good.** If you, a person of steely nerve and perfect judgment, never delete a file in error, then your files can *always* bypass the Recycle Bin. No confirmations, no second chances. You'll reclaim disk space instantly when you press the Delete key to vaporize a highlighted file or folder.

  To set this up, right-click the Recycle Bin. From the shortcut menu, choose Properties (Figure 3-13). Select "Don't move files to the Recycle Bin. Remove files immediately when deleted."

  And voilà! Your safety net is gone (especially if you *also* turn off the "Display delete confirmation dialog" checkbox—then you're *really* living dangerously).

Note: That really *is* living dangerously. The Shift-key trick might be a better safety/convenience compromise.

Figure 3-13:
Use the Recycle Bin Properties dialog box to govern the way the Recycle Bin works, or if it even works at all. If you have multiple hard drives, the dialog box offers a tab for each of them so you can configure a separate and independent Recycle Bin on each drive.

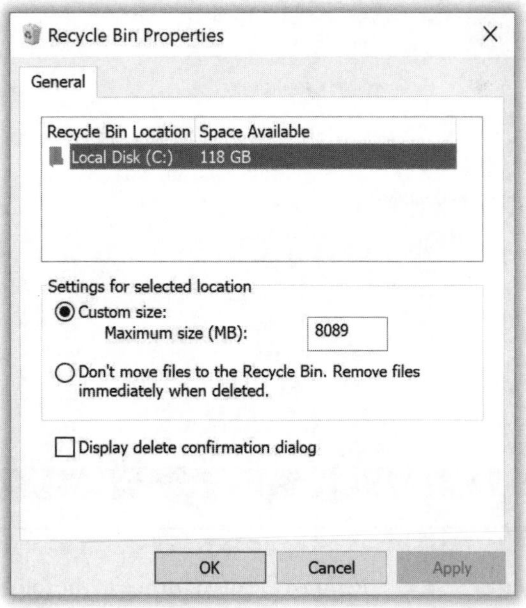

Restoring Deleted Files and Folders

If you change your mind about sending something to the software graveyard, simply open the Recycle Bin by double-clicking. A window like the one in Figure 3-14 opens.

To restore a selected file or folder—or a bunch of them—click the "Restore this item" link on the task toolbar. Or right-click any one of the selected icons and choose Restore from the shortcut menu.

Tip: Weird but true: You can actually pin the Recycle Bin onto the right side of your Start menu for easy clicking. Just right-click the Bin; from the shortcut menu, choose Pin to Start. It shows up as a tile.

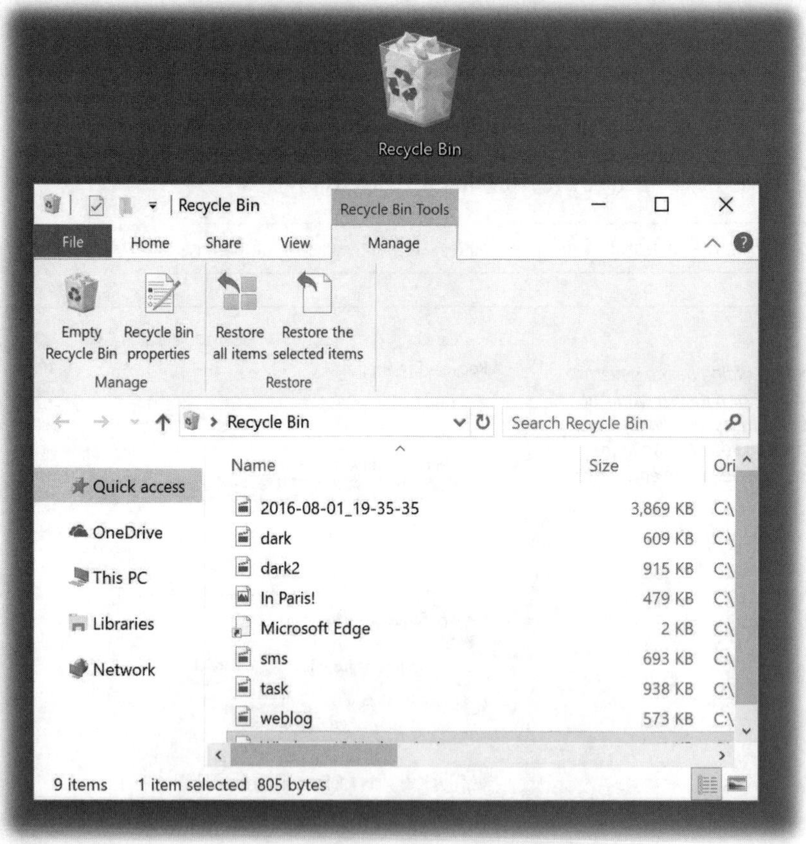

Figure 3-14:
When you double-click the Recycle Bin (top), its window (bottom) displays information about each folder and file it holds. It's a regular File Explorer window, so you can inspect a selected item in the Details view, if you like.

Restored means returned to the folder from whence it came—wherever it was on your hard drive when deleted. If you restore an icon whose original folder has been deleted in the meantime, Windows even recreates that folder to hold the restored file(s). (If nothing is selected, the toolbar button says "Restore all items," but be careful: If there are weeks' worth of icons in there, and Windows puts them all back where they came from, recreating original folders as it goes, you might wind up with a real mess.)

Tip: You don't have to put icons back into their original folders. By *dragging* them out of the Recycle Bin window, you can put them back into any folder you like.

Emptying the Recycle Bin

While there's an advantage to the Recycle Bin (you get to undo your mistakes), there's also a downside: The files in the Recycle Bin occupy as much disk space as they did when they were stored in folders. Deleting files doesn't gain you disk space until you *empty* the Recycle Bin.

That's why most people, sooner or later, follow up an icon's journey to the Recycle Bin with one of these cleanup operations:

- **Right-click the Recycle Bin icon,** or a blank spot in the Recycle Bin window, and choose Empty Recycle Bin from the shortcut menu.

- **In the Recycle Bin window,** click Empty Recycle Bin on the Ribbon's Recycle Bin Tools/Manage tab.

- **In the Recycle Bin window,** highlight only the icons you want to eliminate, and then press the Delete key. (Use this method when you want to nuke only *some* of the Recycle Bin's contents.)

- **Wait.** When the Recycle Bin accumulates so much stuff that it occupies a significant percentage of your hard drive space, Windows empties it automatically, as described in the next section.

The first three of these procedures produce an "Are you sure?" message.

Auto-emptying the Recycle Bin

The Recycle Bin has two advantages over the physical trash can behind your house: First, it never smells. Second, when it's full, it can empty itself automatically.

To configure this self-emptying feature, you specify a certain fullness limit. When the Recycle Bin contents reach that level, Windows begins deleting files (permanently) as new files arrive in the Recycle Bin. Files that arrived in the Recycle Bin first are deleted first.

Unless you tell it otherwise, Windows reserves 10 percent of your drive to hold Recycle Bin contents. To change that percentage, open the Recycle Bin; on the Ribbon, click "Recycle Bin properties" (Figure 3-14). Now you can edit the "Maximum size" number, in megabytes. Keeping the percentage low means you're less likely to run out of the disk space you need to install software and create documents. On the other hand, raising the percentage means you have more opportunity to restore files you decide to retrieve.

Note: Every disk has its own Recycle Bin, which holds files and folders you've deleted from that disk. As you can see in the Recycle Bin Properties dialog box, you can give each drive its own trash limit and change the deletion options shown in Figure 3-14 for each drive independently. Just click the drive's name before changing the settings.

OneDrive

OneDrive (originally called SkyDrive) is one of Microsoft's great unsung offerings. It's a free, 5-gigabyte online hard drive on the internet—and part of your free Microsoft account (page 534). In File Explorer, it's represented by an icon in every window.

Whatever you put into it appears, almost instantly, in the OneDrive folder on all your other machines: other PCs, Macs, iPhones, iPads, Android phones, and so on. (There are OneDrive apps available for all those operating systems.)

In fact, your files will even be available at *onedrive.com*, so you can grab them even when you're stranded on a desert island with nothing but somebody else's computer (and internet access). If this concept reminds you of the popular free program Dropbox, then you're very wise. Figure 3-15 shows the idea.

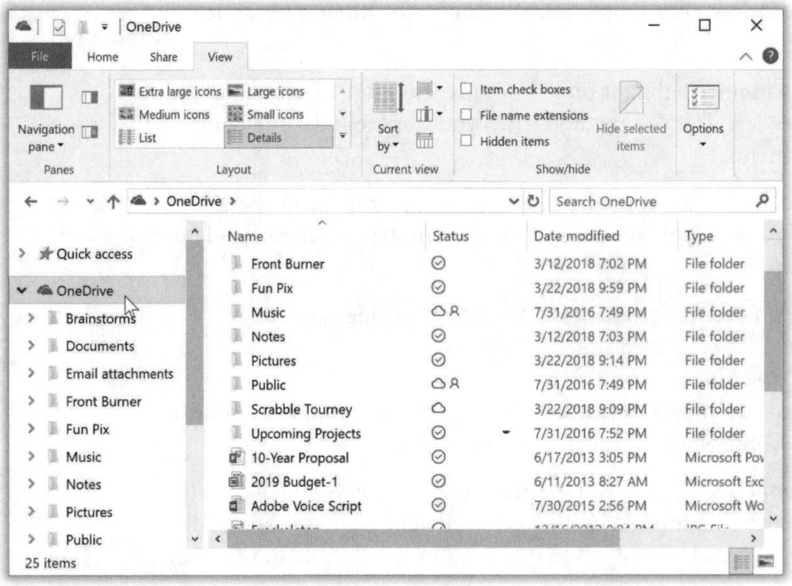

Figure 3-15:
People don't make nearly enough fuss about OneDrive. There it is, happily offering convenient internet-based storage or backup for 5 gigabytes of your stuff—no charge. It behaves exactly like any other folder or disk; OneDrive is very humble about its magic.

This is an incredibly useful feature. No more emailing files to yourself. No more carrying things around on a flash drive. After working on some document at the office, you can go home and resume from right where you stopped; the same file is waiting for you, exactly as you left it.

OneDrive also makes a gloriously simple, effective backup disk. Anything you drag into this "folder" is instantly copied to all your devices and computers. And, as you know, the more copies that exist of something (and in the more locations), the better your backup. Even if your main PC is stolen or burned to dust, your OneDrive files are safe.

OneDrive is also a handy intermediary for sharing big files with other people far away. And it's a handy way to offload files from a computer that has limited storage space. You still see them listed on your machine—but they don't actually download until you ask for them.

Your drive holds 5 gigabytes of files for free. (It used to be 15 gigs—and you could earn more storage by, for example, referring friends—but, sadly, Microsoft's accountants prevailed.) You can pay extra for more space: $2 a month for 50 gigs, $4 for 200 gigs, $7 for 1 terabyte (1,000 gigabytes), or $10 for 5 terabytes.

Putting Files onto OneDrive

On the PC, you use OneDrive just as you would a folder or a flash drive. Click its name in the navigation pane to see what's in there. Drag files into its window, or onto its name, to copy them there. Make folders, add files, delete files, rename them—whatever. Any changes you make are reflected on your other computers, phones, and tablets within seconds.

Inside a program, you can choose File→Save in the usual way. When the Save box appears, click OneDrive in the navigation pane. Or choose a OneDrive folder's name, if you've made one.

Offline Files

Ordinarily, the files you've put onto your OneDrive aren't *only* online. Windows also maintains a copy of them on your computer.

That's handy, of course, because it means you can open and edit them even when you don't have an internet connection. (Next time you're online, Windows automatically transmits the changes you made to the OneDrive copy of the file—and onto all other machines you use to sign in with the same account.)

But there's a problem with this scenario: You can't use your OneDrive to offload big files you don't *want* on your computer. You can't use it to archive files, freeing up room on your PC's drive. Fortunately, there's also a solution. See Figure 3-16.

Note: The ability to choose the folders you want to sync is new in Windows 10. It replaces the "smart files" (placeholder files) feature of Windows 8.1, which Microsoft says confused people and didn't work well with other apps.

OneDrive.com

No matter where you go, no matter what computer, tablet, or phone you're using, you can get to all the files on your OneDrive—from a web page. Just sign into your Microsoft account at *onedrive.com*.

Once you're viewing the contents of a OneDrive folder, buttons across the top of the window describe all the usual tasks you might want to perform when working with files: New (folder or document), Rename, Delete, Upload and Download (files to or from OneDrive), "Move to" and "Copy to" (to move or copy things into other OneDrive folders), Share (with someone else, by sending an emailed invitation), Embed (gives you the HTML code you need to make the file show up on a web page), Sort, and so on.

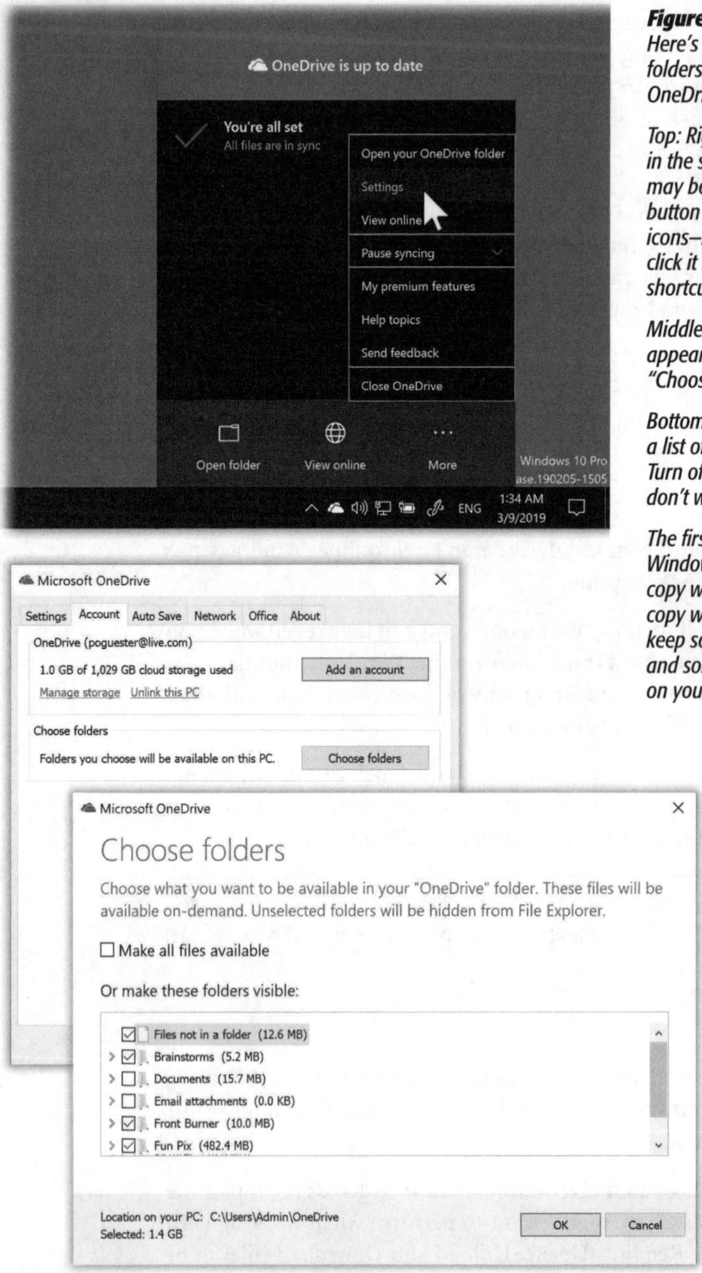

Figure 3-16:
Here's how you tell Windows which folders you want synced with your online OneDrive.

Top: Right-click the OneDrive icon (☁) in the system tray. (If you don't see it, it may be hidden. In that case, click the ^ button in the system tray to see the hidden icons—including OneDrive. You can right-click it right there in the balloon.) From the shortcut menu, choose Settings.

Middle: The OneDrive Settings dialog box appears. On the Account tab, select the "Choose folders" button.

Bottom: At this point, Windows displays a list of all the folders on your OneDrive. Turn off the checkboxes of folders you don't want copied to your PC.

The first time you turn off a checkmark, Windows warns you that your local (PC) copy will be deleted. Only the internet copy will live on. From now on, you can keep some folders synced with your PC, and some only online, safely tucked away on your OneDrive in the sky.

Tip: You can also drag file and folder tiles into other folders, right here in your browser. Weird.

If you swipe down on a tile or right-click, you get a tall menu of options. Most of them are identical to the buttons already described (Rename, Delete, and so on). But you may see other commands that pertain only to the kind of document you've selected. If it's a Word, Excel, or PowerPoint document, you can open and edit it right there in your web browser. If it's a photo, you get options like "Rotate," "Order prints," or "Add to album."

Fetch: Remote Access to Your Whole PC Back Home

OneDrive has a secret feature that could come to your rescue the next time you're away from home and realize you need something that's on your home PC: a feature called Fetch. It lets you access everything on your PC back at home, from wherever you happen to be, from OneDrive.com—even if you're on a Mac.

There's only a short list of fine-print footnotes:

- **The PC back home** has to be turned on and online.

- **The remote PC** has to be running Windows 7 or later. (And if it's Windows 7 or 8, it has to have the OneDrive app installed and open. You can download it from OneDrive.com.)

Turn on Fetch

Here's how you prepare the home PC for remote invasion:

1. **Right-click the OneDrive icon in the system tray.**

   See Figure 3-16, top.

2. **From the shortcut menu, choose Settings.**

   The OneDrive Settings dialog box appears (Figure 3-16, middle).

3. **On the Settings tab, turn on "Let me use OneDrive to fetch any of my files on this PC." Make sure "Start OneDrive automatically when I sign in to Windows" is also turned on. Click OK.**

   And that's it! You can now tap into everything on that PC from the road, as shown in Figure 3-17; read on.

Access the PC back home

Open any web browser on any kind of computer. Go to *onedrive.com* and sign into your Microsoft account. On the left side, under the heading PCs, you see the names of any PCs for which you've turned on the Fetch feature. If you click your PC's name, you'll see that you can actually begin opening folders on it, from thousands of miles away. Voilà!

Note: The first time you perform this stunt, you're asked to "Sign in with a security code." Click Text or Email, and specify your phone number or email address so Microsoft can send you a confirmation code. (You wouldn't want some evil villain to rummage through your PC, now, would you?)

Once the text or email arrives, copy the code it contains into the box on the web page before you. (Turn on "I sign in frequently on this device" if you don't want to have to repeat this code business every time you use Fetch.) Click Submit.

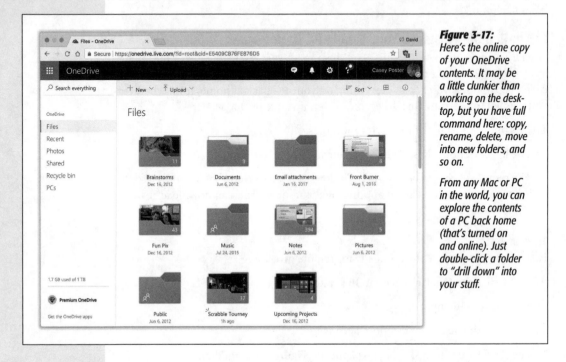

Figure 3-17:
Here's the online copy of your OneDrive contents. It may be a little clunkier than working on the desktop, but you have full command here: copy, rename, delete, move into new folders, and so on.

From any Mac or PC in the world, you can explore the contents of a PC back home (that's turned on and online). Just double-click a folder to "drill down" into your stuff.

Double-click your C: drive, and burrow into whatever folder you like. You can even open other machines on the network if you added them to one of your libraries or mapped them as drives (page 578). You can play music or video, or play photos as a slideshow, or download anything to the machine you're using right now.

And you were alive to see the day.

Sharing Files from OneDrive

There's one more fantastic feature awaiting on your OneDrive: the ability to send huge files—files that are much too big for email—to other people.

Technically, you're not really sending them the files; you're sending them a link to the files. But the effect is the same: With one click, your colleague can download a file or folder from your OneDrive, no matter how huge it is.

Share a file or folder from the desktop

When you right-click a file or folder on your OneDrive (on your computer), the shortcut menu offers a long list of handy features. The one you want is "Share a OneDrive link"; see Figure 3-18.

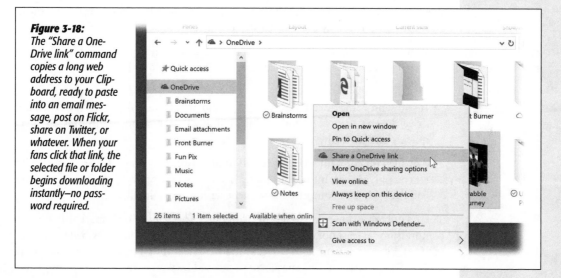

Figure 3-18:
The "Share a One-Drive link" command copies a long web address to your Clipboard, ready to paste into an email message, post on Flickr, share on Twitter, or whatever. When your fans click that link, the selected file or folder begins downloading instantly—no password required.

Share a file or folder from OneDrive.com

If you select a file or folder on the OneDrive website, you can then click Share (top of the window) to gain a wider variety of sharing options.

The resulting dialog box lets you specify the email address of the recipient, type a note to that person, turn off the recipient's ability to edit the document, require the other person to have a Microsoft account, copy a link to your Clipboard (of the type described previously), and so on.

Tip: You can also jump to this cornucopia of sharing options directly from the desktop, without having to go to your web browser first. To do that, right-click the file or folder you want to share from your OneDrive. From the shortcut menu, choose "More OneDrive sharing options."

Compressing Files and Folders

Today's hard drives have greater capacities than ever, but programs and files are much bigger, too. Running out of disk space is still a common problem. Fortunately, Windows is especially effective at compressing files and folders to take up less space.

Compressing files and folders can also be useful when you want to email files to someone. That's why Microsoft has endowed Windows with two different schemes for compressing files and folders: *NTFS compression* for storing files on your hard drive, and *zipped folders* for files that might have to be transferred.

NTFS Compression

Windows 10, since you asked, requires a hard drive that's formatted using a software scheme called *NTFS*. And among its virtues is, you guessed it, NTFS *compression*.

This compression scheme is especially likable because it's completely invisible. Windows automatically compresses and decompresses your files, almost instantaneously. At some point, you may even forget you've turned it on. Consider:

- **Whenever you open a compressed file,** Windows quickly and invisibly expands it to its original form so you can edit it. When you close the file again, Windows instantly recompresses it.

- **If you send compressed files** (via disk or email, for example) to a PC whose hard drive doesn't use NTFS formatting, Windows once again decompresses them, quickly and invisibly.

- **Any file you copy into a compressed folder or disk** is compressed automatically. (If you only *move* it into such a folder from elsewhere on the disk, however, it stays compressed or uncompressed—whichever it was originally.)

There's only one downside to all this: You don't save a *lot* of disk space using NTFS compression (at least not when compared with zip compression, described in the next section). Even so, if your hard drive is anywhere near full, it might be worth turning on NTFS compression. The space you save could be your own.

Compressing files, folders, or disks

To turn on NTFS compression, right-click the icon for the file, folder, or disk whose contents you want to shrink; from the shortcut menu, choose Properties. Proceed as shown in Figure 3-19.

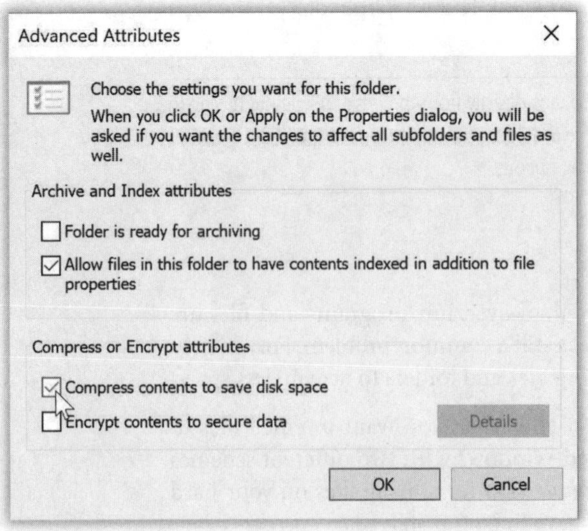

Figure 3-19:
In the Properties dialog box for any file or folder, click Advanced. Turn on "Compress contents to save disk space," and then click OK. For a folder, Windows offers to compress all the files and folders inside this one, too.

Tip: To compress an entire hard drive, the steps in Figure 3-19 are even simpler. Just right-click the drive's icon (in your This PC window); choose Properties; and turn on "Compress this drive to save disk space." Click OK.

Many Windows veterans wind up turning on compression for the entire hard drive, even though it takes Windows several hours to do the job. (If you plan to go see a movie while Windows is working, though, wait until the appearance of the first message box letting you know about some "open file" that can't be compressed; then click Ignore All. A few files will still be uncompressed when you get back from the cineplex, but at least you won't have had to stay home, manually clicking to dismiss every "open file" complaint box.)

When Windows is finished compressing files, their names appear in a different color, a reminder that Windows is doing its part to maximize your disk space.

Note: If the files don't change color, somebody—maybe you—must have turned off the "Show encrypted or compressed NTFS files in color" option.

Zipped Folders

NTFS compression is ideal for freeing up disk space while you're working at your PC. But as soon as you email your files to somebody else or copy them to a flash drive, the transferred copies bloat right back up to their original sizes.

Fortunately, there's another way to compress files: Zip them. If you've ever used Windows before, you've probably encountered .zip files. Each one is a tiny little suitcase, an *archive*, whose contents have been tightly compressed to keep files together, to save space, and to transfer them online faster (see Figure 3-20). Use this method when you want to email something to someone, or when you want to pack up a completed project and remove it from your hard drive to free up space.

UP TO SPEED

Data Compression

Data compression is the process of replacing repetitive material in a file with shorthand symbols. For example, if a speech you've written contains the phrase *going forward* 21 times, a compression scheme like the one in NTFS may replace each occurrence with a single symbol, making the file that much smaller. When you reopen the file later, the operating system almost instantaneously restores the original, expanded material.

The degree to which a file can be compressed depends on what kind of data the file contains and whether it's already been compressed by another program. For example, programs (executable files) often shrink by half when

compressed. Bitmapped graphics like TIFF files squish down to as little as one-seventh their original size, saving a great deal more space. The PNG and JPEG graphics formats so popular on the web, however, are already compressed (which is *why* they're so popular—they take relatively little time to download). As a result, they don't get much smaller if you try to compress them manually. That's one of the main rules of data compression: Data can be compressed only once.

In short, there's no way to predict just how much disk space you'll save by using NTFS compression on your drives. It all depends on what you have stored there.

Creating zipped folders

You can create a .zip archive in either of two ways:

- **Right-click any blank spot on the desktop or an open window.** From the shortcut menu, choose New→"Compressed (zipped) Folder." (Or, from the Ribbon's Home tab, choose "New item"→"Compressed (zipped) Folder.") Type a name for your newly created, empty archive, and then press Enter.

  Now, each time you drag a file or folder onto the archive's icon (or into its open window), Windows automatically stuffs a *copy* of it inside.

  Of course, you haven't exactly saved any disk space, since now you have two copies (one zipped, one untouched). If you'd rather *move* a file or folder into the archive—in the process deleting the full-size version and saving disk space—then *right*-drag the file or folder icon onto the archive icon. Now, from the shortcut menu, choose Move Here.

- **To turn an *existing* file or folder into a .zip archive, right-click its icon.** (To zip up a handful of icons, select them first, and then right-click any one of them.) Now, from the shortcut menu, choose "Send to"→"Compressed (zipped) Folder." You've just created a new archive folder *and* copied the files or folders into it.

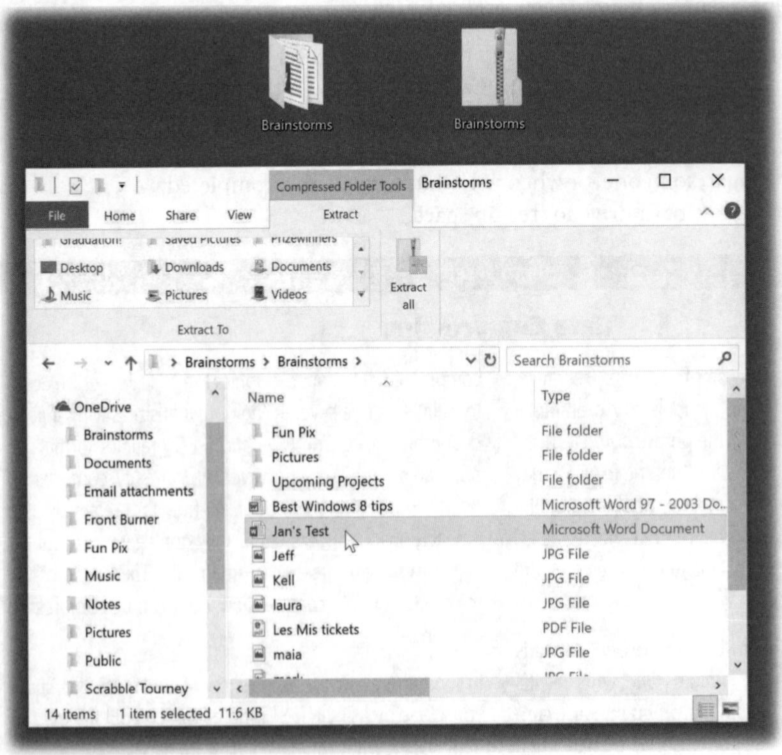

Figure 3-20:
Top: A zip archive looks just like an ordinary folder—except for the tiny little zipper.

Bottom: Double-click one to open its window and see what's inside.

The Size, Compressed Size, and Ratio columns tell you how much space you've saved. (JPEG and GIF graphics usually don't become much smaller than they were before zipping, since they're already compressed formats. But word processing files, program files, and other file types reveal quite a bit of shrinkage.)

Tip: At this point, you can right-click the zipped folder's icon and choose "Send to"→"Mail recipient." Windows automatically whips open your email program, creates an outgoing message ready for you to address, and attaches the zipped file to it. It's now set for transport.

Working with zipped folders

In many respects, a zipped folder behaves just like any ordinary folder. Double-click it to see what's inside.

If you double-click one of the *files* you find inside, however, Windows opens a *read-only* copy of it—that is, a copy you can view, but not edit. To make changes to a read-only copy, you must use the File→Save As command and save it somewhere else on your hard drive first.

Note: Be sure to navigate to the desktop or Documents folder, for example, before you save your edited document. Otherwise, Windows will save it into an invisible temporary folder, where you may never see it again.

To decompress only some of the icons in a zipped folder, just drag them out of the archive window; they instantly spring back to their original sizes. Or, to decompress the entire archive, right-click its icon and choose Extract All from the shortcut menu (or, if its window is already open, click "Extract all" on the Ribbon's Compressed Folder Tools/Extract tab). A dialog box asks you to specify where you want the resulting files to wind up.

Tip: Windows no longer lets you password-protect a zipped folder, as you could in Windows XP. But the web is teeming with zip-file utilities, many of them free, that do let you assign a password. You might try, for example, SecureZIP Express. It's available from this book's "Missing CD" page at *missingmanuals.com*.

Burning CDs and DVDs from the Desktop

Back in the day, people burned CDs or DVDs to back stuff up, to transfer stuff to another computer, to mail to somebody, or to archive older files. These days, most of that's done over the network or the internet; it's a rare computer that even comes with a CD/DVD drive anymore. Windows 10 can still burn CDs and DVDs, though—in either of two formats: ISO (Mastered) or UDF (Live File System). For step-by-step instructions, see the free PDF appendix to this chapter, "Burning CDs and DVDs." It's available on this book's "Missing CD" page at *missingmanuals.com*.

ISO Disk Images

Programs you download from the web (not the Microsoft Store) often arrive in a specially encoded, compressed form—a *disk image* file, also known as an ISO image (Figure 3-21). Heck, most people got Windows 10 *itself* as an ISO file they downloaded.

Disk images are extremely handy; they behave exactly like disks, in that they can include a whole bunch of related files, folders, and pieces, all distributed online in just the way the software company intended. And here's the good news: You can work with ISO images just as though they're disks, too. (In the old days, you had to buy a program like Virtual CloneDrive to get this feature.)

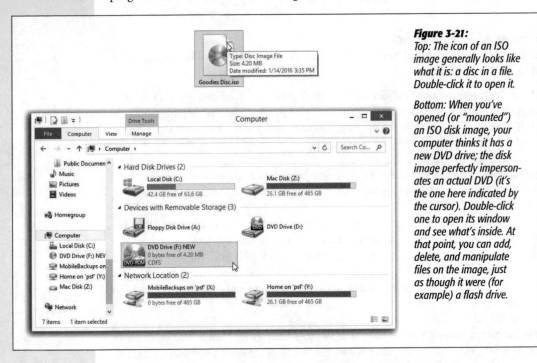

Figure 3-21:
Top: The icon of an ISO image generally looks like what it is: a disc in a file. Double-click it to open it.

Bottom: When you've opened (or "mounted") an ISO disk image, your computer thinks it has a new DVD drive; the disk image perfectly imperson-ates an actual DVD (it's the one here indicated by the cursor). Double-click one to open its window and see what's inside. At that point, you can add, delete, and manipulate files on the image, just as though it were (for example) a flash drive.

Just double-click the downloaded ISO icon. (You can also right-click it; from the shortcut menu, choose Mount. Or click its icon and use the Mount button on the Ribbon's Disk Tools/Manage tab.)

After a moment, it magically turns into a disk icon in your nav pane or This PC window, which you can work with just as though it were a real disk. Windows even assigns it a drive letter, like D: or L:; you've got yourself a virtual disk. The software you downloaded is inside.

In theory, you could also create an ISO image from a DVD or Blu-ray disc, so you'll have "the disc" with you when you travel (even if your machine doesn't have a disc drive). Games, for example, run faster from a disk image than from an actual disc. The web is full of free programs that let you turn folders or groups of files into ISO images.

Tip: If an ISO image doesn't mount (open) when you double-click it, check your file associations (page 225). It's possible you've associated .iso file types to open with a different program, like WinZip or Nero. That program is therefore intercepting your attempt to open the ISO image.

When you're finished working with the disk image, you can eject it exactly as you would a CD or DVD—using the Eject button on the Drive Tools tab of the Ribbon, for example.

Redesigning the Desktop

W indows 10 looks a lot better than previous versions of Windows. The system fonts, color schemes, taskbar design, typography—it's all much clearer, more graceful, and more modern than what's come before.

Still, these changes aren't for everybody. Fortunately, Windows 10 is every bit as tweakable as previous versions of Windows. You can change the picture on your desktop, or tell Windows to change it *for* you periodically. You can bump up the text size for better reading by over-40 eyeballs. You can create a series of virtual "external monitors"—perfect spaces in which to spread out a bunch of apps, each on its own "screen."

As Microsoft might say, "Where do you want to redesign today?"

Background, Colors, Themes, and Fonts

It's fun to customize your PC (especially because it's your opportunity to replace, at last, that huge Dell or HP logo that came as your preinstalled background). This is also yet another way to shut off some of Windows' predefined cosmetics.

To see your design choices, right-click a blank spot on the desktop. From the shortcut menu, choose Personalize. (Or the long way: ⊞→⚙→Personalization.)

The Personalization page of Settings opens (Figure 4-1). It offers seven tabs of options, all dedicated to changing the look of your desktop world: Background, Colors, Lock screen, Themes, Fonts, Start, and Taskbar. The Start options govern your Start menu and are described in Chapter 1; customizing the taskbar is covered in Chapter 2. The other tabs are described right here.

Background (Wallpaper)

Windows comes with a host of desktop pictures, patterns, and colors for your viewing pleasure. You want widescreen images for your monitor? You got 'em. Want something gritty, artsy, in black and white? It's there, too. And you can use any picture you'd like as your background as well.

The Background tab (of ⊞→⚙→Personalization) offers a huge Preview image, showing off the color scheme of your desktop world at the moment.

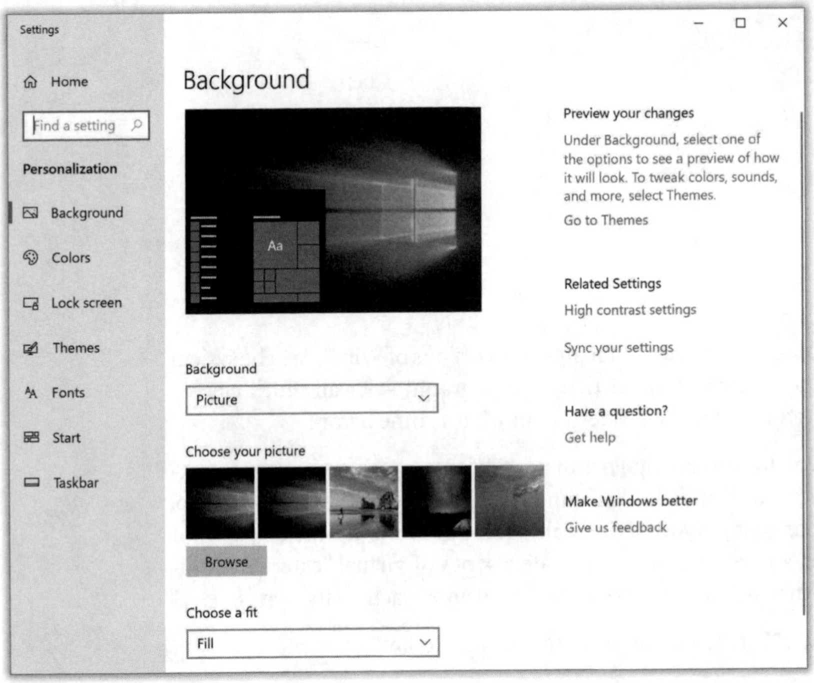

Figure 4-1:
The Personalization tab of Settings offers a simplified diagram of your desktop. As you adjust the background and color-scheme options, this miniature desktop changes to show how it will look.

(The blurbs and links in the right-side column appear only if the window is wide enough.)

Background is Microsoft's new word for wallpaper (the image that fills your entire desktop background). The Background drop-down menu offers three choices:

- **Solid Color** is a palette of simple, solid colors for your desktop background. It's not a bad idea, actually; it's a little easier to find your icons if they're not lost among the details of a nature photo (or photos of your nieces and nephews).

- **Picture** starts you off with five luscious nature photos. It also offers you a Browse button that displays what's in your Pictures folder, because it's more fun to use one of your *own* pictures on the desktop. That might be your graduation photo, or it might be a still from *Frozen*; the choice is yours.

- **Slideshow.** The novelty of any desktop picture is likely to fade after several months of all-day viewing. Fortunately, you can choose *multiple* desktop pictures from the gallery. Use the Browse button to find a promising-looking folder full of images.

Now, from the "Change picture every" drop-down menu, specify when you want your background picture to change: every day, every hour, every five minutes, or whatever. (If you're *really* having trouble staying awake at your PC, you can choose every minute.)

Now, at the intervals you specified, your desktop picture changes automatically, smoothly cross-fading among the pictures in your chosen source folder like a slideshow. You may never want to open another window, because you'd hate to block the view.

Turn on Shuffle if you'd like the order to be random, and "Allow slideshow when on battery power" if you're willing to sacrifice a little juice for the gorgeousness.

Tip: Once your slideshow background is set up, you don't have to wait out the waiting period if you get bored. You can right-click the desktop and, from the shortcut menu, choose "Next desktop background."

No matter which source you use to choose a photo, you have one more issue to deal with. Unless you've gone to the trouble of editing your chosen photo so it matches the precise dimensions of your screen (1440 × 900 or whatever), it probably isn't exactly the same size as your screen.

Using the "Choose a fit" drop-down menu, you can choose any of these options:

- **Fill.** Enlarges or reduces the image so it fills every inch of the desktop without distortion. Parts may get chopped off, though.

- **Fit.** Your entire photo appears, as large as possible without distortion *or* cropping. If the photo doesn't precisely match the proportions of your screen, you get "letter-box bars" on the sides or at top and bottom.

- **Stretch.** Makes your picture fit the screen exactly, come hell or high water. Larger pictures may be squished vertically or horizontally as necessary, and small pictures are drastically blown up *and* squished, usually with grisly results.

- **Tile.** This option makes your picture repeat over and over until the images fill the entire monitor.

- **Center.** Centers the photo neatly on the screen. If the picture is smaller than the screen, it leaves a swath of empty border all the way around. If it's larger, the outer edges get chopped off.

- **Span.** If you have more than one monitor, this option lets you slap a single photo across multiple screens.

Tip: Really, the Background screen is the wallpaper headquarters. But there are "Set as desktop background" commands hiding everywhere in Windows, making it simple to turn everyday images into backgrounds. You'll find that command, for example, when you right-click a graphics icon in a File Explorer window or a graphic on a web page.

Colors

The single most visible change in the May 2019 Update lurks here, in the "Choose your color" menu: a choice of light mode or dark mode (Figure 4-2).

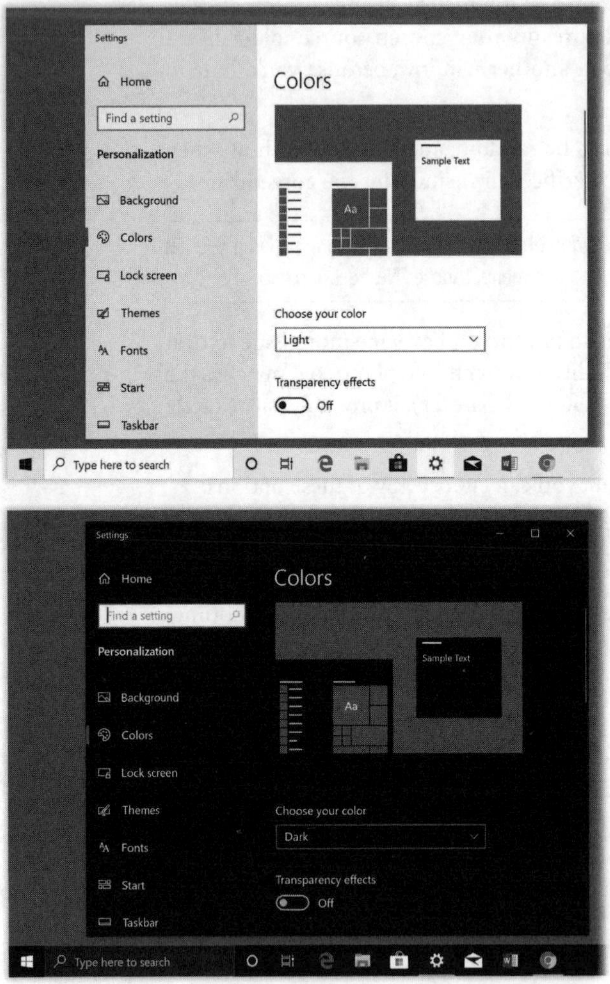

Figure 4-2:
The "Choose your color" menu offers three options. There's Light (top), featuring the newly sparkling-white backgrounds of the May 2019 Update; Dark (bottom); and Custom.

In Custom mode, you can choose light or dark independently for Windows itself (the menu bar, File Explorer windows, Action Center, and so on) and apps. That's for people who like the Dark look only for the desktop, but the Light look in their programs (or vice versa).

Light mode, the factory setting in the May 2019 Update, gives a clean, whitish look to the taskbar, Start menu, and other elements. Dark mode is a dark-gray color scheme. Once you turn it on, most of Microsoft's built-in apps take on a stunning white-writing-on-black-background appearance.

Here's what *doesn't* change in dark mode:

• **Your desktop picture.** Or any pictures at all, for that matter.

• **Web pages.**

- **Preexisting non-Microsoft apps.** Software companies have to update their programs if they want them to take on dark mode's dusky hues.

In general, you'd really have to stretch to say dark mode helps with your productivity. Mainly it's just cool-looking.

This page of Settings also lets you tweak some other color settings for your world:

- **Transparency effects.** There's no particularly good reason you'd want Windows elements like the Start menu, taskbar, and Action Center to be partly see-through; they're easier to read when they're opaque. But you know—whatever floats your boat. If you turn this switch on, the brightest or darkest parts of your wallpaper picture blurrily shine through your Start menu, taskbar, and Action Center areas.

- **Automatically pick an accent color from my background.** If you leave this switch on, then Windows chooses an accent color for you—the shade that paints the tiles and background of the Start menu, window buttons, the taskbar background, and the Action Center. It chooses a color it believes will provide an attractive contrast to the photo or color you've chosen for your desktop background.

  If you turn this switch off, then Windows offers a palette of about 50 color squares, plus a handy set of recently used ones. It's prodding you to choose your *own* darned accent color.

- **Start, taskbar, and action center.** If you turn this off, then your chosen accent color will apply only to Start-menu tiles and window controls; the Start menu background, taskbar, and Action Center backgrounds will remain white (or, in dark mode, black).

- **Title bars and window borders.** Same thing: If this is on, you'll colorize your window title bars and the fine outline of every window; otherwise, they'll be black.

Lock Screen

As described in Chapter 1, the first thing you see when you turn on your machine is the Lock screen. Here, on this page of Settings (Figure 4-3), you specify how you want it to look and act:

- **Preview.** At the top, a miniature, showing what your Lock screen looks like at the moment.

- **Background.** "Windows spotlight" means that each day you'll find a new photo on your Lock screen, drawn from Bing Images. They're usually so stunning that you don't even want to finish powering up the machine. They're also overlaid with a few textual facts, tips, and blurbs, which you can't get rid of unless you choose one of the next two options.

  "Picture" and "Slideshow" work just as described under "Background" on page 152. (But if you choose Slideshow, you also get an "Advanced slideshow settings" button. It opens a screen that gives you control over which photos Windows uses and when; for example, you can opt out of having the slideshow when you're running on battery power, and you can have the screen go dark after thirty minutes, one hour, or three hours of slideshow.)

- **Choose an app to show detailed status.** On the Lock screen, just below the time and date, there's room for a couple of lines of text. That's what Microsoft calls "detailed status" for one app, which you choose from this pop-up menu. For example, if you choose Calendar, this space shows your next appointment; if you choose Mail, you see the sender and first line of your most recent email message. You can probably guess what the Weather option gives you.

Figure 4-3:
Here's where you dress up the all-important Lock screen of your computer.

"Windows spotlight" brings you a fresh photo every day, with tips and facts floating around it.

- **Choose apps to show quick status.** At the very bottom of the Lock screen, Windows can display up to seven small icons that Microsoft calls "quick status." Each is designed to convey information through its appearance alone. For example, if you choose Mail, you see a little envelope with a number that indicates how many new messages are waiting. If you choose Alarms & Clock, then a little alarm-clock icon appears to indicate that you've *set* an alarm.

- **Show lock screen background picture on the sign-in screen.** You've gone to all this trouble to choose wallpaper for your Lock screen; this option transfers the same display to the sign-in screen that follows. (If you leave this option off, then the sign-in screen just shows a solid blue.)

- **Cortana lock screen settings.** Cortana, Windows 10's voice-activated assistant, can speak answers to questions about your calendar, email, and text messages—even when you're not at your desk, and the Lock screen is up. Clearly, that's an invitation for disaster if you have resentful and untrustworthy co-workers.

  This link opens a Cortana settings page where you can turn off "Use Cortana even when my device is locked," eliminating any risk.

  Or leave that on, but turn off "Let Cortana access my calendar, email, messages...." That way, anyone can still ask harmless things—"What time is it?" or "Who won last night's Cavaliers game?"—but evildoers can't hear about your secrets when you're away.

- **Screen timeout settings.** This link opens the "Power & sleep" settings, where you can specify how soon your computer goes to sleep (or shuts off) after inactivity; see page 244.

- **Screen saver settings.** A screen saver isn't really part of the Lock screen, but Microsoft thought a link to the "Screen saver settings" dialog box might be handy here anyway. See page 164.

Themes

Windows includes a number of predesigned *themes* that affect the look of your desktop and windows.

Each design theme controls these elements of Windows:

- **Your background** (desktop picture).

- **Your screen saver.**

- **The design of icons** like This PC, Network, Control Panel, and Recycle Bin.

- **The color scheme for your window edges,** plus any tweaks you make in the Color and Appearance dialog box (font size, window border width, and so on).

- **The size and shape of your arrow cursor.**

- **The sounds your PC uses as error and alert beeps.**

You're offered a couple of starter themes, one of which is usually called Synced Theme (it's the one you'll see on all your *other* PCs, if you've opted to have your themes synced; see page 544). But don't miss the "Get more themes in Microsoft Store" link; it takes you to a download-more-themes page of the Microsoft Store online. Whatever you download shows up here, ready for clicking.

Of course, you're welcome to edit any aspect of whatever theme is currently selected: Select Background, Color, Sounds, Mouse Cursor (these buttons sit below or beside the theme preview) or "Desktop icon settings" (on the right or bottom edge of the window, depending on its size). You'll jump directly to the corresponding dialog box for editing that element. (Background and Color are described earlier in this chapter; read on to hear about the other options.)

Here you're also offered something called "High contrast settings." These options are designed to help people with limited vision, who require greater differences in color between window elements. See page 258.

When you've made your changes, you return to the Themes control panel, where all the modifications you've made are represented at the top of the screen. Hit "Save theme," type a name for your new theme, and click Save.

From now on, the theme you've created (well, *modified*) shows up among the other themes. Now you can recall the emotional tenor of your edited look with a single click on that icon.

You can also delete a less-inspired theme (right-click its icon; hit Delete). On the other hand, when you strike creative gold, you can package up your theme and share it with other computers—your own or other people's. To do that, right-click the theme's icon; from the shortcut menu, choose "Save theme for sharing." Windows asks you to name and save the new .themepack file, which you can distribute to the masses online.

Note: If your theme uses sounds and graphics that aren't on other people's PCs, then they won't see those elements when they install your theme.

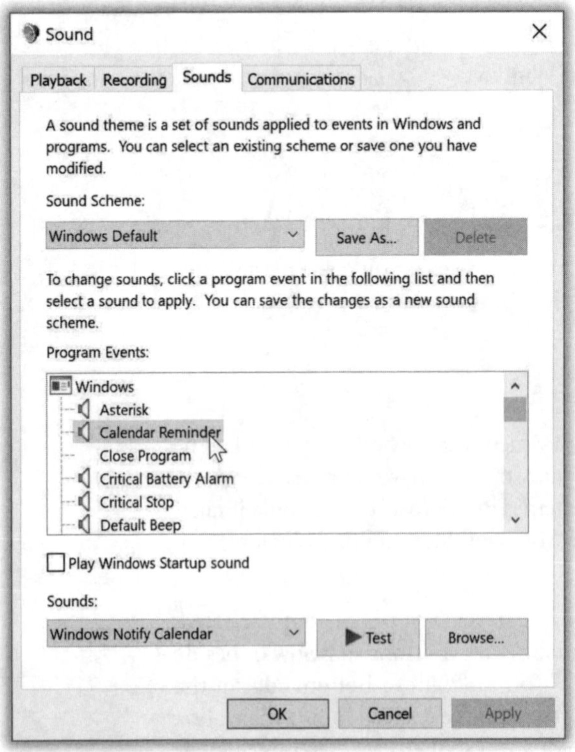

Figure 4-4:
Each set of sounds is called a sound scheme. Sometimes the sound effects in a scheme are even sonically related. (Perhaps the collection is totally hip-hop, classical, or performed on a kazoo.) To switch schemes, use the Sound Scheme drop-down menu. You can also define a new scheme of your own. Start by assigning individual sounds to events, and then click the Save As button to save your collection under a name you create.

Editing a theme's sound settings

Windows plays beeps and bloops to celebrate various occasions: closing a program, yanking out a USB drive, signing in or out, getting a new fax, and so on. You can turn these sounds on or off, or choose new sounds for these events.

Sounds, too, are part of a theme. To edit the suite of sounds that goes with your currently selected theme, open the Themes screen and hit Sounds. Or, if you're starting from scratch, type *sounds* into the taskbar search box; in the results list, choose "Change system sounds."

See the list of Program Events (Figure 4-4)? A speaker icon represents the occasions when a sound will play. Double-click a sound (or click the Test button) to see what it sounds like.

Or, if you click the name of some computer event (say, Low Battery Alert), you can make these adjustments:

- **Remove a sound from the event** by choosing "(None)" from the Sounds drop-down list.

- **Change an assigned sound,** or add a sound to an event that doesn't have one, by clicking Browse and choosing a new sound file from the list in the Open dialog box.

Tip: When you click the Browse button, Windows opens the *Local Disk (C:)* > *Windows* > *Media* folder, which contains the *.wav* files that provide sounds. If you drag *.wav* files into this Media folder, they become available for use as Windows sound effects. Many people download *.wav* files from the internet and stash them in the Media folder to make their computing experience quirkier, more fun, and richer in *Austin Powers* sound snippets.

When you select a sound, its filename appears in the Sounds drop-down list. Click the Test button to the right of the box to hear the sound.

Desktop icon settings

Thanks to the "Desktop icon settings" link on the Themes Settings screen, you can specify which standard icons sit on your desktop for easy access and what they look like. To choose your icons, just turn on the checkboxes for the ones you want (see Figure 4-5).

You can also substitute different *icons* for your icons. Click, for example, the This PC icon, and then click Change Icon. Up pops a collection of predrawn icons in a horizontally scrolling selection box. If you see a picture you like better, double-click it.

Click OK if you like the change, Cancel if not.

Mouse pointer settings

If your fondness for the standard Windows arrow cursor begins to wane, you can assert your individuality by choosing a different pointer shape. For starters, you might want to choose a *bigger* arrow cursor—a great solution on today's tinier-pixel, shrunken-cursor monitors.

Tip: What you're about to read is the old way of adjusting the cursor shape and size—the more complete way, involving a visit to the old Control Panel. In Windows 10, though, a few simplified cursor-shape options also await in the newfangled Settings program (page 257).

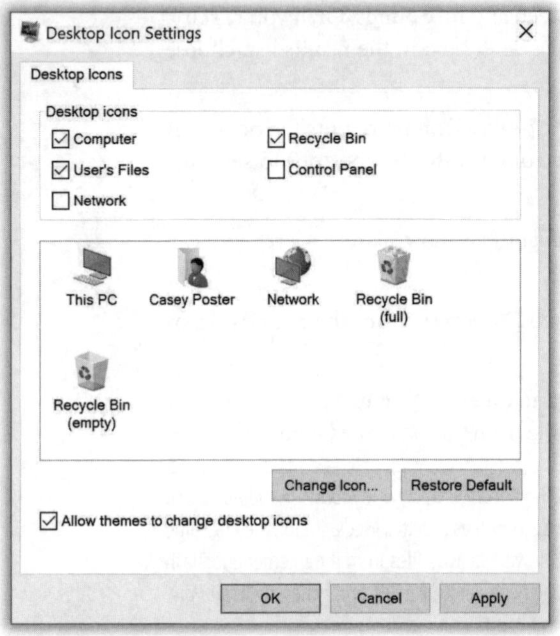

Figure 4-5:
Microsoft has been cleaning up the Windows desktop in recent years, and that includes sweeping away some useful icons, like This PC, Control Panel, Network, and your personal folder. But you can put them back, just by turning on these checkboxes.

Begin by clicking "Mouse cursor" on the Themes screen. In a flash, you arrive at the dialog box shown in Figure 4-6. At this point, you can proceed in any of three ways:

- **Scheme.** There's more to Windows cursors than just the arrow pointer. At various times, you may also see the spinning circular cursor (which means, "Wait; I'm thinking," or "Wait; I've crashed"), the I-beam cursor (which appears when you're editing text), the little pointing-finger hand that appears when you point to a web link, and so on.

  All these cursors come prepackaged into design-coordinated sets called *schemes*. To look over the cursor shapes in a different scheme, use the Scheme drop-down list; the corresponding pointer collection appears in the Customize list box. The ones whose names include "large" or "extra large" offer jumbo, magnified cursors ideal for very large screens or failing eyesight. When you find one that seems like an improvement over the factory-setting set, click OK.

- **Select individual pointers.** You don't have to change to a completely different scheme; you can also replace just one cursor. To do so, click the pointer you want to change, and then click the Browse button. You're shown the vast array of cursor-replacement icons (which are in the *Local Disk (C:)* > *Windows* > *Cursors* folder). Click one to see what it looks like; double-click to select it.

- **Create your own pointer scheme.** Once you've replaced a cursor shape, you've also changed the scheme to which it belongs. At this point, either click OK to activate your change and get back to work, or save the new, improved scheme under its own name, so you can switch back to the original when nostalgia calls. To do so, click the Save As button, name the scheme, and then click OK.

Tip: The "Enable pointer shadow" checkbox at the bottom of this tab is pretty neat. It casts a shadow on whatever's beneath the cursor, as though it's skimming just above the surface of your screen.

Clicking the Pointer Options tab offers a few more cursor-related functions (Figure 4-6, bottom):

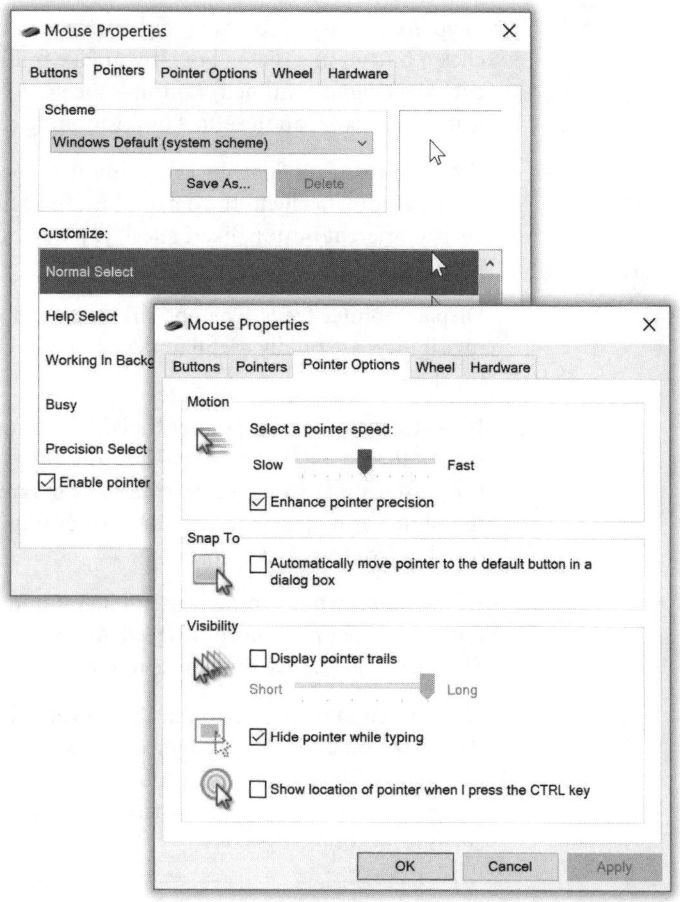

Figure 4-6:
Top: Here's the Pointers dialog box, where you can choose a bigger cursor (or a differently shaped one).

Bottom: Ever lose your mouse pointer while working on a laptop with a dim screen? Maybe pointer trails could help. Or have you ever worked on a desktop computer with a mouse pointer that seems to take forever to move across the desktop? Try increasing the pointer speed. You find these choices on the Pointer Options tab.

- **Pointer speed.** It comes as a surprise to many people that the cursor doesn't move 5 inches when the mouse moves 5 inches on the desk. Instead, you can set things up so moving the mouse 1 *millimeter* moves the pointer 1 full *inch*—or vice versa—using the "Select a pointer speed" slider.

  It may come as an even greater surprise that the cursor doesn't generally move *proportionally* to the mouse's movement, regardless of your "Pointer speed" setting. Instead, the cursor moves farther when you move the mouse faster. How *much* farther depends on how you set the "Select a pointer speed" slider.

  The Fast setting is nice if you have an enormous monitor, since it prevents you from needing an equally large mouse pad to get from one corner to another. The Slow setting offers more control but forces you to constantly pick up and put down the mouse as you scoot across the screen, which can be frustrating. (You can also turn off the disproportionate-movement feature completely by turning off "Enhance pointer precision.")

- **Snap To.** A hefty percentage of the times when you reach for the mouse, it's to click a button in a dialog box. If you, like millions of people before you, usually click the *default* (outlined) button—such as OK, Next, or Yes—then the Snap To feature can save you the effort of positioning the cursor before clicking.

  When you turn on Snap To, every time a dialog box appears, your mouse pointer jumps automatically to the default button so all you need to do is click. (And to click a different button, like Cancel, you have to move the mouse only slightly to reach it.)

- **Display pointer trails.** The options available for enhancing pointer visibility (or invisibility) are mildly useful under certain circumstances, but mostly they're just for show.

  If you turn on "Display pointer trails," for example, you get ghost images that trail behind the cursor like a bunch of little ducklings following their mother. In general, this stuttering-cursor effect is irritating. On rare occasions, however, you may find that it helps you locate the cursor—for example, if you're making a presentation on a low-contrast LCD projector.

- **Hide pointer while typing** is useful if you find that the cursor sometimes gets in the way of the words on your screen. As soon as you use the keyboard, the pointer disappears; just move the mouse to make the pointer reappear.

- **Show location of pointer when I press the CTRL key.** If you've managed to lose the cursor on an LCD projector or a laptop with an inferior screen, this feature helps you gain your bearings. After turning on this checkbox, Windows displays an animated concentric ring each time you press the Ctrl key to pinpoint the cursor's location.

Tip: You can also fatten up the insertion point—the cursor that appears when you're editing text. See page 257.

Fonts

This Settings screen (Figure 4-7) is your master cheat sheet for the typefaces installed on your PC. Each appears with a sample sentence, for your font-ogling pleasure.

Here's the fun you can have here:

- **Drag and drop to install.** Fantastic. Windows now has the world's most idiot-proof technique for installing new fonts. Just drag their desktop icons into this panel, and boom: They're installed.

- **Click a font** to open its details screen, where you can read about its origins and legal limitations, type in a sample sentence of your own, adjust the size of the preview, or uninstall the font.

- **Click "Filter by"** to limit what you're seeing to fonts from a certain language.

- **Use the search box** to locate one font out of your haystack.

POWER USERS' CLINIC

Some Clear Talk About ClearType

ClearType is Microsoft's word for a sneaky technology that makes type look sharper on your screen than it really is.

Imagine a lowercase "s" at a very small point size. It looks great on this page, because this book was printed at 1,200 dots per inch. But your monitor's resolution is far lower—maybe 96 dots per inch—so text doesn't look nearly as good. If you were to really get up close, you'd see that the curves on the letters are actually a little jagged.

Each dot on an LCD screen is actually composed of three sub-pixels (mini-dots): red, green, and blue. What ClearType does is simulate smaller pixels in the nooks and crannies of letters by turning on only some of those subpixels. In the curve of that tiny *s*, for example, maybe only the blue subpixel is turned on, which to your eye looks like a slightly darker area, a fraction of a pixel; as a result, the type looks finer than it really is.

> Click the text sample that looks best to you (2 of 4)
>
> The Quick Brown Fox Jumps Over the Lazy Dog. Lorem ipsum dolor sit amet, consectetuer adipiscing elit. Mauris ornare odio vel risus. Maecenas elit metus, pellentesque quis, pretium.
>
> The Quick Brown Fox Jumps Over the Lazy Dog. Lorem ipsum dolor sit amet, consectetuer adipiscing elit. Mauris ornare odio vel risus. Maecenas elit metus, pellentesque quis, pretium.
>
> The Quick Brown Fox Jumps Over the Lazy Dog. Lorem ipsum dolor sit amet, consectetuer adipiscing elit. Mauris ornare odio vel risus. Maecenas elit metus, pellentesque quis, pretium.
>
> The Quick Brown Fox Jumps Over the Lazy Dog. Lorem ipsum dolor sit amet, consectetuer adipiscing elit. Mauris ornare odio vel risus. Maecenas elit metus, pellentesque quis, pretium.
>
> The Quick Brown Fox Jumps Over the Lazy Dog. Lorem ipsum dolor sit amet, consectetuer adipiscing elit. Mauris ornare odio vel risus. Maecenas elit metus, pellentesque quis, pretium.
>
> The Quick Brown Fox Jumps Over the Lazy Dog. Lorem ipsum dolor sit amet, consectetuer adipiscing elit. Mauris ornare odio vel risus. Maecenas elit metus, pellentesque quis, pretium.

ClearType's behavior is adjustable. To see the options, type *cleartype* into the taskbar search box until you see "Adjust ClearType text" in the results list; click it.

On the first screen, you have an on/off checkbox for ClearType. It's there just for the sake of completeness, because text on an LCD screen really does look worse without it.

If you click Next, Windows walks you through a series of "Which type sample looks better to you?" screens, where all you have to do is click the "Quick Brown Fox Jumps Over the Lazy Dog" example that you find easiest to read.

Behind the scenes, of course, you're adjusting ClearType's technical parameters without even having to know what they are. When it's all over, you'll have the best-looking small type possible.

• Click "**Get more fonts in Microsoft Store**" to view the fonts page of the Microsoft Store, where you'll find a bunch of free or cheap new fonts to download. OK, "bunch" is an exaggeration—there aren't many available—but the spirit is nice. (Of course, you can find thousands more free fonts just by Googling what you're looking for. For example, *old west font*.)

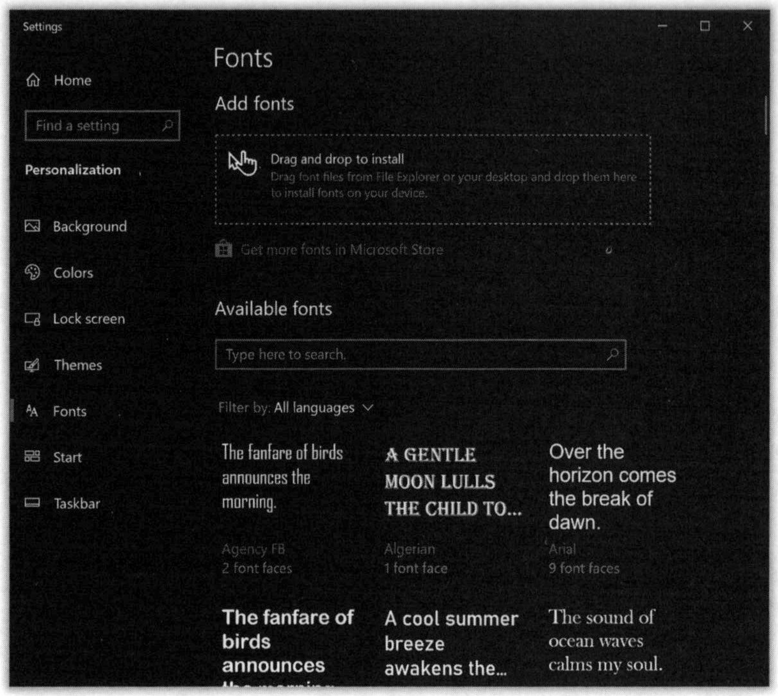

Figure 4-7:
At last, Windows has a spot where you can look over samples of all your installed fonts.

You can now even manage your fonts here—for example, install or remove one. See page 472.

Screen Savers

The term "screen saver" is sort of bogus; today's flat-panel screens *can't* develop "burn-in." (You're too young to remember, but screen savers were designed to bounce around a moving image to prevent permanent pixel discoloration on those old, bulky, CRT screens.) No, screen savers are mostly about entertainment—and, especially in the business world, security. You can wander away from your desk without fear of snoopers.

The idea is simple: A few minutes after you leave your computer, whatever work you were doing is hidden behind the screen saver; passersby can't see what was on the screen. To exit the screen saver, move the mouse, click a mouse button, or press a key.

Choosing a Screen Saver

To choose a screen saver, type *saver* into the taskbar search box; in the results, choose "Change screen saver." The Screen Saver page of the ancient Control Panel dialog box appears.

Now use the "Screen saver" drop-down list. A miniature preview appears in the preview monitor on the dialog box (see Figure 4-8).

To see a *full-screen* preview, click Preview. The screen saver display fills your screen and remains there until you move your mouse, click a mouse button, or press a key.

Figure 4-8:
"On resume, display logon screen" is a handy security measure. It means you'll have to input your password to get back into your PC once the screen saver has come on—a good barrier against nosy co-workers who saunter up to your PC while you're out getting coffee.

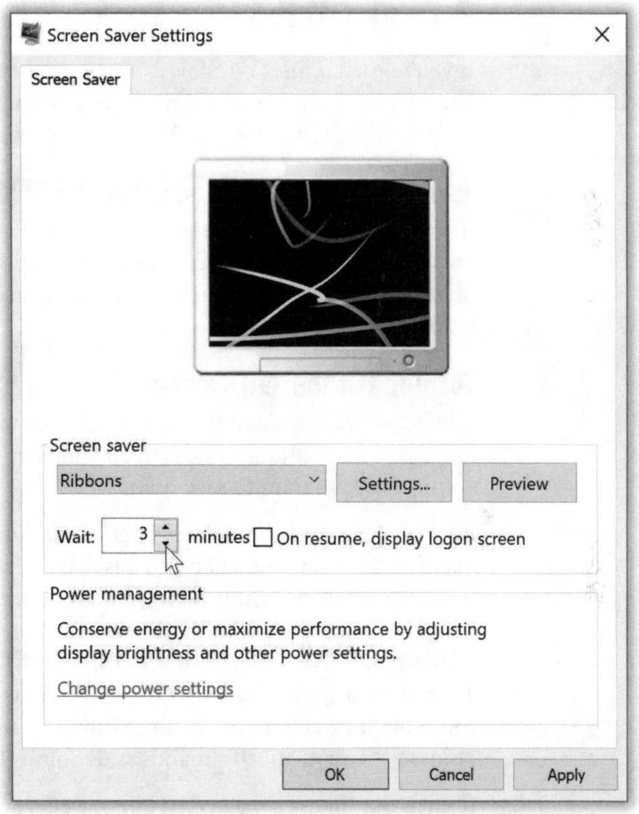

The Wait box determines how long the screen saver waits before kicking in, after the last time you move the mouse or type. Click the Settings button to play with the chosen screen saver module's look and behavior. For example, you may be able to change its colors, texture, or animation style. "On resume, display logon screen" means "When you interrupt the screen saver, don't take me all the way back to what I was doing; make me sign in again, for added security."

At the bottom of this tab, click "Change power settings" to open the Power Options Control Panel pane described on page 275.

Tip: If you keep graphics files in your Pictures folder, try selecting the Photos screen saver. Then click the Settings button and choose the pictures you want to see. When the screen saver kicks in, Windows puts on a spectacular slideshow of your photos, bringing each to the screen with a special effect (flying in from the side, fading in, and so on).

Turning Off the New Look

If you're used to pre–Windows 7 versions, things look a lot different in Windows 10. You may miss the less flashy, more utilitarian look of Windows Vista or XP. If you're in that category, don't worry: Windows comes with a whole trainload of Off switches.

Turning Off Window Snapping and Shaking

If you drag a window close to the top edge of your screen, the window expands to fill the *whole* screen. If you drag it close to a side of your screen, the window expands to fill *half* the screen. If all this auto-snapping makes you crazy, turn it off as described on page 49.

Turning Off the Tall Taskbar

The Windows 10 taskbar shows relatively giant icons—with no text labels. And you no longer get one button for each open window; Windows consolidates open windows within each program to save space.

But you can make the taskbar look like it did in Vista or even Windows XP, if you like. See "Bringing Back the Old Taskbar," a free PDF appendix to this book. It's on the Missing CD page at *missingmanuals.com.*

Turning Off All Those Glitzy Animations

Then there are all those other things Windows does to show off: Windows seem to zoom open or closed; the Close, Minimize, and Maximize buttons glow when you point to them; menu commands and tooltips fade open and closed; and so on.

It turns out there's a master list of these effects, filled with individual on/off switches for Windows' various animations, pop-up previews, mouse and window shadows, and so on.

To see it, press ⊞+S and start typing *appearance* until "Adjust the appearance and performance of Windows" appears in the search results. Click it.

You arrive in the Performance Options dialog box, on a tab called Visual Effects. Now, these aren't exactly the kinds of visual effects they make for use in *Star Wars* movies. In fact, they're so subtle, they're practically invisible. But the more of them you turn off, the faster the computer will seem to work. (You can turn all of them off with one click—select "Adjust for best performance.") Here are a few examples:

- **Enable Peek.** Yes, you can turn off the Peek feature, which lets you (a) point to a taskbar thumbnail to see its full-size window pop to the fore and (b) point to the Show Desktop button (right end of the taskbar) to make all windows transparent.

- **Show shadows under windows/mouse pointer.** Take a look: Open windows may actually seem to cast faint, light-gray drop shadows, as though floating an eighth of an inch above the surface behind them. It's a cool, but utterly superfluous, special effect.

- **Smooth edges of screen fonts.** If you look very closely at the characters on your screen, they look a bit ragged on the curves. But when this option is turned on, Windows softens the curves, making the text look more professional (or slightly blurrier, depending on your point of view).

- **Show window contents while dragging.** If this option is off, then when you drag a window, only a faint outline of its border is visible; you don't see all the items *in* the window coming along for the ride. As soon as you stop dragging, the contents reappear. If this option is on, however, then as you drag a window across your screen, you see all its contents, too—a feature that can slow the dragging process on some machines.

Turn Off the Tiles in the Start Menu

You're not stuck with the big square tiles, the last remaining visible gasp of Windows 8. See page 36.

Monitor Settings

You wouldn't get much work done without a screen on your computer. It follows, then, that you can get *more* work done if you tinker with your screen's settings to make it more appropriate to your tastes and workload.

Most of the settings described here are waiting for you on the Display settings screen. To get there, right-click the desktop; from the shortcut menu, choose "Display settings." (The long way: ▦→⚙→System→Display.)

Brightness

If your PC has a keyboard, then the easiest way to adjust the brightness is to use the special keys for that purpose; if it's a tablet, you can use the Action Center to adjust the brightness (page 99). But in a pinch, there's also a Brightness slider here in Display settings.

Night Light

The blue tones of a flat-panel screen have been shown to mess up your body's production of melatonin, the "You're getting sleeeeeeepy" hormone. As a result, your circadian rhythm gets disrupted, and it's harder to fall asleep.

The best solution is to not use your phone, tablet, or computer right before bed. But who are we kidding?

Therefore, Windows 10 offers Night Light, a mode that gives your screen a warmer, less blue tint. Here, on the Display settings screen, you can turn Night Light on or off manually. (You can also use the Action Center tile for that purpose; see page 97).

The "Night light settings" link lets you adjust exactly *how* yellowish you want the screen to get and also offers a Schedule option, so Night Light will fire up (and down) at the times you pick.

Windows HD Color

In one regard, digital cameras are still pathetic: Compared with the human eye, they have terrible *dynamic range.*

That's the range from the brightest to darkest spots in a single scene. If you photograph someone standing in front of a bright window, you'll get just a black silhouette. The camera doesn't have enough dynamic range to handle both the bright background and the person in front of it.

You could brighten up the exposure so the person's face is lit—but then you'd brighten the background to a nuclear-white rectangle.

A partial solution: *HDR* (high dynamic range) photography. That's when the camera takes three (or even more) photos simultaneously—one each at dark, medium, and light exposure settings. Its software combines the best parts of all three, bringing details to both the shadows and the highlights. (WCG, or *wide color gamut,* is the same idea.)

Nowadays, these much more vivid, lifelike formats have come to both photos and videos, provided that you have a compatible monitor (marketed as "HDR10")—and an operating system capable of handling HDR material. Fortunately, Windows 10 is among them, thanks to its Windows HD Color feature.

Choose "Windows HD Color settings" here to view and adjust the settings for your HDR-compatible monitor, if you have one.

Three Ways to Enlarge the Screen

There are two reasons why Windows offers quick-and-easy ways to magnify what's on the screen.

First, people tend to get older—even you. As you age, your eyes may have trouble reading smaller type.

Second, the resolution of computer screens gets higher every year. That is, more and more dots are packed into the same-sized screens, and therefore those dots are getting smaller, and therefore the *type and graphics* are getting smaller.

Microsoft finally decided enough was enough. That's why there's a one-click way to enlarge all type and graphics, with crisp, easier-to-see results. There are also various older schemes for accomplishing similar tasks. What follows is a rundown of all of them.

Magnify just the text

Most of the time, isn't this the problem? That the type is too small?

In ⊞→⚙→Ease of Access→Display, the "Make text bigger" slider is all you need. Drag it, hit Apply, and read easy.

Magnify the text and graphics

This feature is one of Microsoft's most inspired, most useful—and least publicized. It turns out you can enlarge the type *and* graphics on the screen—without changing the screen's resolution. So type gets bigger without getting blurrier, and everything else stays sharp, too. Some older apps don't respond well to this magic, but Microsoft has thought of that; read on.

In ⊞→⚙→System→Display, use the "Scale and layout" drop-down menu to choose a higher or lower percentage of magnification (Figure 4-9).

Tip: If none of the percentages listed here quite do it for you, hit "Advanced scaling settings" and use the "Custom scaling" box to type in any scaling amount you like, from 100 to 500 percent. Heed the warning written here: This act might render some programs illegible.

Figure 4-9:
To adjust the overall size of type–all type–on your screen, visit this Settings page.

You can use the "Change the size of text, apps, and other items" drop-down menu to enlarge or shrink everything on the current screen. The range usually extends from 100 percent to 300 percent–but things will look sharpest at the recommended setting.

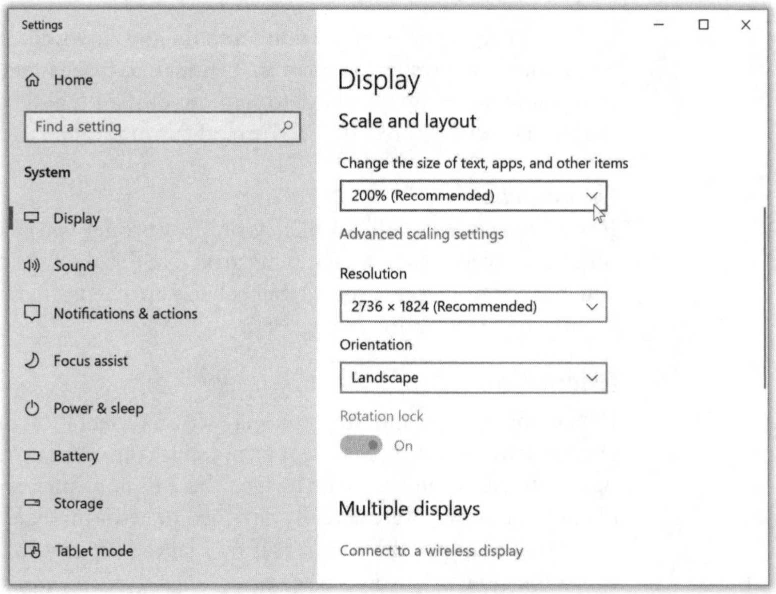

Change the resolution

If you're a resolution wonk, you can take another approach: Use the Resolution drop-down menu (on the ⊞→⚙→System→Display screen) to dial up a particular number of pixels.

Your screen can make its picture larger or smaller to accommodate different kinds of work. You perform this magnification or reduction by switching among different *resolutions* (measurements of the number of dots that compose the screen). To do that, use the Resolution drop-down menu.

Fixing blurriness

As you make scaling or resolution changes, keep in mind two cautions. First, choosing a lower resolution means that text and graphics will be bigger on your screen, but you'll see less area. It's exactly as though you've enlarged a document on a photocopier.

Second, on a flat-panel screen—that is, the *only* kind sold today—only one resolution setting looks really great: the maximum one. That's what geeks call the *native* resolution of that screen. At other resolutions, the PC does what it can to blur together adjacent pixels, but the effect can be fuzzy and unsatisfying. (On the old, bulky CRT monitors, the electron gun could actually make the pixels larger or smaller, so we didn't have this problem.)

Windows has built-in technology that tries to minimize the blurring; in the May 2019 Update, it's turned on automatically, at least for the main monitor. (The on/off switch appears when you select "Advanced scaling options" on the ⊞→⚙→System→ Display screen.)

Unfortunately, some apps still don't respond to Windows's anti-blurring technology. Sometimes, even restarting them isn't enough to make them respect the new resolution you've dialed up; you have to sign out of the PC and back in again. That's why the Display Settings box offers a "Turn off custom scaling and sign out" link here, too.

The Magnifier

If your "type is too small" problem is only occasional, you can call up Windows' Magnifier. It's like a software magnifying glass that fills the top portion of your screen; as you move your pointer around the real-size area beneath, the enlarged image scrolls around, too. Details are on page 356.

Orientation

Depending on your monitor, you may see an Orientation drop-down menu on the Display settings screen. Believe it or not, this control lets you flip your screen image upside down or into a mirror image. These options make hilarious practical jokes, of course, but they were actually designed to accommodate newfangled PC designs where, for example, the screen half of a laptop flips over, A-frame style, so people across the table from you can see it.

In any case, once you choose an orientation and click Apply or OK, a dialog box lets you either keep or discard the setting. Which is lucky, because if the image is upside down on a regular PC, it's really hard to get any work done.

If you're running Windows 10 on a tablet, you may also see a "Rotation lock" on/off switch. When rotation lock is turned on, the screen no longer rotates when you turn the tablet 90 degrees. The idea is that sometimes, like when you're reading an ebook on your side in bed, you don't want the screen picture to turn; you want it to stay upright relative to your eyes.

Colors

Today's video cards offer different *color depth* settings, each of which permits the screen to display a different number of colors simultaneously. You usually have a choice between settings like Medium (16-bit), which was called High Color in early versions of Windows; High (24-bit), once known as True Color; and Highest (32-bit).

In the early days of computing, higher color settings required a sacrifice in speed. Today, however, there's very little downside to leaving your screen at its highest setting. Photos in particular look best when you set your monitor to higher-quality settings.

To check your settings, right-click the desktop. From the shortcut menu, choose "Display settings." On the Settings screen, click "Advanced display settings" and then "Display adapter properties" to open the Properties dialog box for your monitor. Click the Monitor tab, and fiddle around till you're blue, red, and green in the face.

Multiple Monitors

Most laptops, tablets, and even desktop PCs these days have video-output jacks. Some new tablets and laptops even offer WiDi (wireless display) technology. In either case, you can hook up a second monitor (or even third monitor) or a projector.

You can either display the same picture on both screens (which is what you want if your laptop is projecting slides for an audience), or you can create a gigantic virtual desktop, moving icons or toolbars from one monitor to another. The latter setup lets you keep an eye on web activity on one monitor while you edit data on another. It's a *glorious* arrangement, even if it does make the occasional family member think you've gone off the deep end with your PC obsession.

Over the years, PC makers have offered different kinds of connectors for external screens—jacks called things like VGA, DVI, HDMI, DisplayPort, and USB-C. Alas, it's your burden to figure out which jack your computer has and to get the right kind of cable or adapter to accommodate your external screen.

Once you've done that, treat yourself to an Oreo milkshake to celebrate.

Customizing Your Displays

If you're lucky, your computer has auto-detected the second monitor or the projector. (If not, use the "Detect" button on the Displays settings screen.) Now here's the question: What should these two screens show?

To see your choices, press ■+P, or open the Action Center (page 96) and hit Project. On the right side of the screen, your choices appear (Figure 4-10, left):

- **PC screen only.** The second monitor is dark, as though you're not using it at all.

- **Duplicate.** Your built-in screen and the second one show the same thing.

- **Extend.** Your second monitor acts as though it's additional real estate hanging off the side of your built-in screen.

• **Second screen only.** The built-in screen is dark; all the action is on the second monitor.

To make further refinements to your setup, right-click the desktop. From the shortcut menu, choose "Display settings." On the resulting Settings screen, you see icons for both screens (or even more, if you have them—you lucky thing!).

It's like a map (Figure 4-10 at right); here you can drag the monitor miniatures around to teach Windows how they're physically positioned on your desk. Farther down on this screen, the "Multiple displays" drop-down menu offers the same four arrangement options described already.

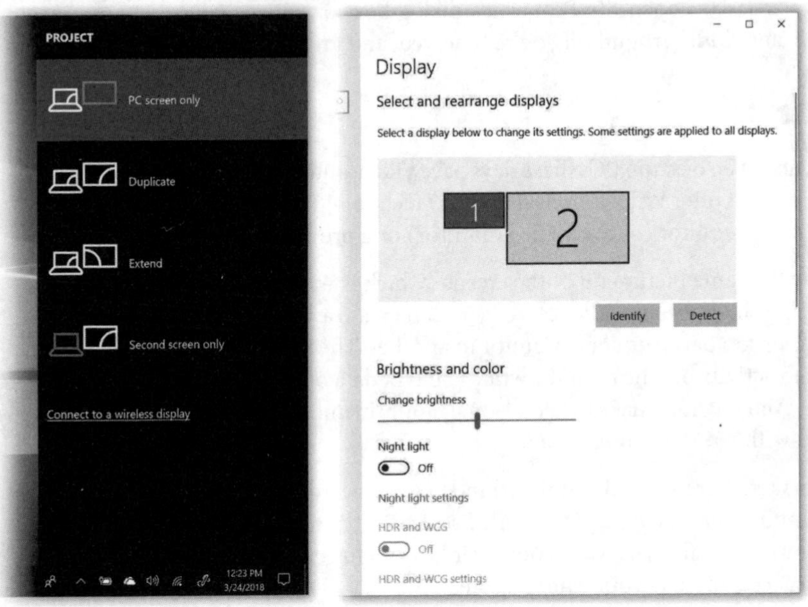

Figure 4-10:
Left: The Action Center is the quickest way to configure your second monitor.

Right: If Windows displays these miniatures out of left/right sequence, then drag their thumbnails around until they match reality. (Click Identify if you get confused; that summons a huge digit in a black box on each real screen, which helps you match it to the digits on the miniatures.)

Click each monitor's icon and adjust its settings, if you like—for example, resolution (usually, you want the highest available), orientation, and brightness. Don't miss "Make this my main display," either. The main display is the monitor that will contain your Start menu and desktop icons. (In Windows 10, your taskbar appears on *every* monitor. Nice touch.)

The "Change the size of text, apps, and other items" menu described earlier is even more important when your multiple monitors have different resolutions. You can use this control to match them up better, so windows don't abruptly shrink or blow up huge when they move from monitor to monitor.

Click Apply. Then, to make sure you haven't totally munged your monitors, Windows gives you 15 seconds to confirm that you like what you've done; click "Keep changes."

(If you don't click anything, Windows switches back to the original configuration after 15 seconds.)

Tip: If you click the "Display adapter properties" link, you're offered a collection of technical settings for your particular monitor model. Depending on your video driver, there may be tab controls here that adjust the *refresh rate* to eliminate flicker, install an updated adapter or monitor driver, and so on. In general, you rarely need to adjust these controls—except on the advice of a consultant or help-line technician.

Life with Multiple Screens

Once you've hooked up a second monitor, there are more tips than ever:

- **You can drag a window** from screen to screen with the mouse, even if it's a split-screen, "snapped" app. (Use the top edge of the app's screen as a handle.)

- **You can make a window cycle** through the left, center, and right positions on each screen by repeatedly pressing ⊞ and the → or ← keys.

  For example, suppose a window is now floating in the middle of Screen 1. Pressing ⊞+→ repeatedly first snaps it to the right edge of Screen 1, then snaps it to the left edge of Screen 2, then releases it to the middle of Screen 2, and finally snaps it against the right edge of Screen 2. And now, if you press ⊞+→ yet again, that same window "wraps" around to become snapped against the left edge of Screen 1. It makes more sense when you try it.

- **The system tray and Action Center** appear only on the main monitor.

- **You can't pin different items** onto each screen's taskbar.

- **You can give each screen its own desktop background.** On the Background settings screen (page 152), right-click the thumbnail image of the desktop background you want; from the shortcut menu, choose "Set for all monitors," "Set for monitor 1," or "Set for monitor 2."

Virtual Screens

Here's one of Windows 10's best features: a nearly infinite number of full-size *virtual monitors.* (Microsoft says it's heard of people creating as many as 150 screens before this feature conks out. Don't worry—they're in therapy.)

Hard-core productivity mavens can tell you how useful it is to set up multiple screens. It's just fast and useful to have a wider view. You might dedicate each one to a different program or *kind* of program. Screen 1 might contain your email and chat windows, arranged just the way you like them. Screen 2 can hold Twitter and Facebook, their windows carefully arrayed. On Screen 3: your web browser in Full Screen mode.

Ordinarily, of course, attaching more than a screen or two would be a massively expensive proposition, not to mention detrimental to your living space and personal relationships. But these are virtual screens. They exist only in the PC's little head. You see only one at a time; you switch with a keystroke or a mouse click. You gain most of the advantages of owning a bunch of PC monitors—without spending a penny.

Now, virtual screens aren't a new idea—this sort of software has been available for years. But it's never been a standard feature of Windows, or so easy to use.

Creating a Desktop

To create a second desktop, enter the Timeline (click ⊟⋮ on the taskbar, or press ⊞+Tab; see page 210 for more on the Timeline, which is a new part of Task View). Click "New desktop" (the big + icon at top left) to create a new mini-desktop at the top of the screen (see Figure 4-11).

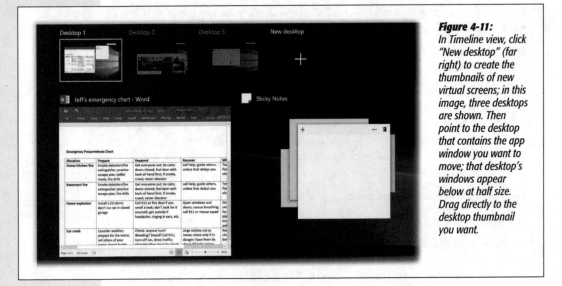

Figure 4-11:
In Timeline view, click "New desktop" (far right) to create the thumbnails of new virtual screens; in this image, three desktops are shown. Then point to the desktop that contains the app window you want to move; that desktop's windows appear below at half size. Drag directly to the desktop thumbnail you want.

Now it's time to park some windows onto the new desktop. At the moment, all the windows you had open are still clustered on the first screen, ingeniously named Desktop 1. When you point to the Desktop 1 thumbnail without clicking, those windows appear at 50 percent size on the main screen. You can drag one of them, or several, onto your new blank desktop (Desktop 2).

Tip: You can also right-click (or hold your finger down on) one of these app "cards." From the shortcut menu, choose "Move to"→"Desktop 2" (or whatever desktop you want it moved to), or "Move to"→"New desktop."

Figure 4-11 shows this process.

Finally, exit the Timeline (click either desktop thumbnail, or anywhere on the main screen, or press Esc).

Tip: Once you've mastered the long way to create a desktop, you're ready for the turbo method. It's a much faster way to create a desktop—and doesn't involve a trip the Timeline: Press Ctrl+⊞+D. To close the current desktop, press Ctrl+⊞+F4.

Switching Virtual Screens

Once you've got a couple of virtual monitors set up, the fun begins. Start by moving to the virtual screen you want; it's like changing the channel. Here are some ways to do that:

- **Press ⊞+Ctrl+← or ⊞+Ctrl+→ to rotate to the previous or next desktop.** (That is, while pressing ⊞+Ctrl, tap the right or left arrow key.)

- **Enter the Timeline again** (⊟ on the taskbar), and choose the desktop you want.

When you make a switch, you see a flash of animation as one screen flies away and another appears. Now that you're "on" the screen you want, open programs and arrange windows onto it as usual.

Note: Windows uses your main desktop's background picture for all additional desktops. It would be nice if you could choose a different wallpaper for each, to help you keep them straight—but to make that happen, you need a free add-on program like zVirtualDesktop. It also adds an indicator to your system tray, letting you know which desktop you're on, and lets you jump to a particular desktop with a keystroke. You can download zVirtualDesktop from this book's "Missing CD" page at *missingmanuals.com*.

Deleting a Desktop

To delete the desktop you're on, press Ctrl+⊞+F4. (You can also enter the Timeline, point to one of the screen thumbnails without clicking, and click the ✕ in its corner.)

That desktop disappears, and whatever windows were on it get shoved onto the desktop to its left.

Projecting to Your PC

Here's one you didn't see coming: a feature that lets you send the screen image from one Windows 10 machine—or even an Android phone—onto the screen of a second one via Wi-Fi. It's like connecting a second monitor without wires (Figure 4-12).

Unfortunately, this trick doesn't work with all Android phones and Windows PCs—only relatively new ones that have been designed for wireless projection.

Here's the setup. So you don't lose your mind, let's suppose you're going to sit at a laptop and send its screen image to a tablet—a Surface 4.

On the desktop PC, open ⊞→⚙→System→ "Projecting to this PC." On the Settings screen, here are the choices you have to make:

- **"Some Windows and Android devices…"** "Available everywhere on secure networks" means you can perform this kind of projection only on private networks like your home network. "Available everywhere" means you can use the feature even on public Wi-Fi networks like hotels and coffee shops, which, of course, isn't as secure.

- **"Ask to project to this PC."** Your choices: "First time only" (after that, you won't be asked permission) or "Every time a connection is requested" (you'll always be asked).

- **Require PIN for pairing.** As yet another security step, you can require a four-digit passcode to ensure that *only* your tablet can connect to your laptop.

- **PC Name.** You'll need to know this when you project from the laptop. (You can take this opportunity to rename the tablet, too—hit "Rename your PC.")

OK, you're ready to begin! Move to the laptop. Open the Action Center (page 96); choose the Connect tile (Figure 4-12, top left). The tablet's name shows up; choose it (Figure 4-12, top right).

On the tablet, if you've said you require permission in Settings, you're asked for permission (Figure 4-12, lower left). Choose Yes, and presto! You're seeing the laptop's screen image on the tablet's screen!

Tip: If you're projecting from an Android phone, open ⊞→⚙→Display→Cast on the phone. (It may be somewhere else; every Android phone is different.) Tap the menu button; turn on "Enable wireless display." The desktop PC's name now appears in the list. Choose its name to begin projecting.

On the laptop, you can even permit the tablet person to have shared control of the keyboard, mouse, and trackpad (Figure 4-12, lower right).

The Wireless Projection Toolbar

Whenever you're transmitting your screen's image to another machine—whether it's to a Miracast TV, another PC, or a projector—you've got a problem. Live screen video requires a lot of data—and wireless communications networks are not always fast enough to handle it. You may, in other words, see a lag in the transmitted screen picture.

That's why, whenever you're projecting, you get the handy control panel shown here, hugging the top of the screen.

It offers these buttons:

Disconnect. Ends your projecting session.

⚙ **(Latency menu).** Offers a choice of three modes: "Gaming," "Working," and "Watching videos." Each of these strikes a different balance to address the screen lag over wireless.

When you're gaming, what you care most about is low *latency*—the least possible lag. You get the closest thing possible to real-time responses to your mouse and keyboard activity, even if that means the video resolution or frame rate suffers. When you're watching videos, things are different. You want smooth, high-resolution video, even if it's slightly delayed from the projecting source. The Working setting is in between the two.

↗ **(Unpin).** Detaches this toolbar from the top of the screen, so you can park it somewhere else.

At the top of the laptop screen, a miniature control palette appears; see the box on the facing page.

Don't miss the "Change projection mode" link (Figure 4-12, lower right). It brings up the traditional Project panel (illustrated on page 172), so you can treat the desktop PC as either a mirror of the laptop screen or an extension of it.

Tip: Don't be confused by the Connect pane that appears on the tablet. It's not really there, and you can't actually operate the "Allow mouse, keyboard, touch, and pen input from this device" checkbox. That's all on the laptop!

When you're finished with your projection, open the Action Center again, hit Connect again, and this time choose Disconnect.

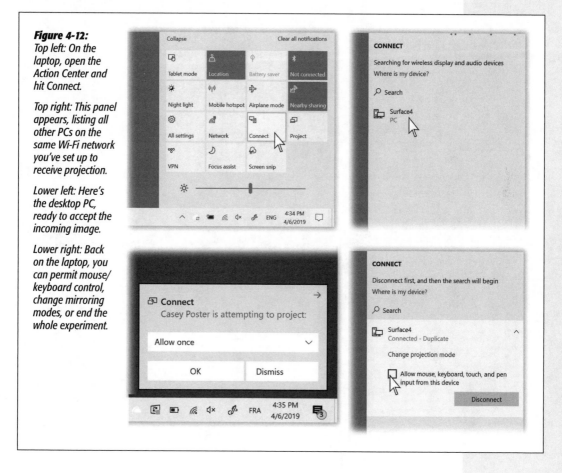

Figure 4-12:
Top left: On the laptop, open the Action Center and hit Connect.

Top right: This panel appears, listing all other PCs on the same Wi-Fi network you've set up to receive projection.

Lower left: Here's the desktop PC, ready to accept the incoming image.

Lower right: Back on the laptop, you can permit mouse/ keyboard control, change mirroring modes, or end the whole experiment.

WINDOWS 10 MAY 2019 UPDATE: THE MISSING MANUAL

CHAPTER 5

Cortana, Your Voice Assistant

Cortana is a crisply accurate, uncomplaining, voice-commanded servant. No voice training or special syntax is required. You can say, "Wake me up at 7:45" or "How do I get to the airport?" or "What's the weather going to be like in San Francisco this weekend?" or "What's 453 divided by 4?" or "Turn off the PC" or even "What's the meaning of life?"

You can ask questions about sports, news, weather, math, history, and much more. Each time, Cortana shows you the answer, fetched from the internet (and usually speaks it, too). She also lets you control, by voice, many brands of smart-home thermostats, light bulbs, door locks, and so on.

Older speech-recognition systems work only if you issue certain limited commands with predictable syntax, like, "Call 445-2340" or "Open Microsoft Word." But Cortana has been programmed to respond to casual speech, normal speech. It doesn't matter if you say, "What's the weather going to be like in Tucson this weekend?" or "Give me the Tucson weather for this weekend" or "Will I need an umbrella in Tucson?" Cortana understands almost any variation.

And she understands regular, everyday speaking. You don't have to separate your words or talk weirdly; you just speak normally.

Now, it's not *Star Trek*. You can't ask Cortana to clean your gutters or to teach you French. (Well, you can *ask*. Anytime she doesn't have an answer for you, she opens up your web browser and displays the Bing search results for your question.)

But, as you'll soon discover, the number of things she *can* do for you is impressive. Furthermore, Microsoft keeps adding to Cortana's intelligence through software updates.

Of course, none of this is a new idea. Apple introduced Siri for the iPhone in 2011, and Google followed with Google Assistant for Android phones in 2012.

But Microsoft's version is unusual in three important respects:

- **Cortana runs on your PC.** In addition to Windows 10 phones and tablets, Cortana also runs on your laptop or desktop.

- **You can *type* your commands instead of speaking them.** That's handy when you're using your computer in, for example, church.

- **She speaks with an actual recorded human voice.** Siri is a synthesized, slightly robotic-sounding voice. But when Cortana speaks, you generally hear actual recordings of an actual actress.

Tip: Cortana is named after a voluptuous female character in Halo, the video game. In fact, Microsoft hired the same Cortana voice actress—Jen Taylor—to record Cortana's responses.

In a few spots, Cortana uses a synthetic voice—but it's derived *from* sound recordings by that same actress.

Note: Microsoft keeps expanding the number of languages that Cortana understands. Already she understands English (U.S., U.K., Indian, Australian, and Canadian flavors), Simplified Chinese, French (France and Canada), Italian, German, Portuguese, Japanese, and Spanish (Spain and Mexico). To change her language, visit ■→۞→Cortana.

Setting Up Cortana

When you click the ○ on the taskbar, the Cortana panel appears (Figure 5-1). She's ready to help you with generic questions about the weather, time, math, and facts. (You can use Cortana either by speaking to her or by typing to her.)

But before you dive in, it's worth taking a moment to set her up. Choose the ۞ in the Cortana panel. (The long way: ■→۞→Cortana.) Then:

Turn on "Hey Cortana"

Out of the box, Cortana doesn't listen to your voice commands until you click or tap the ○ on the taskbar. Microsoft wants to make absolutely sure that nobody thinks its algorithms can hear you speak without your awareness.

If you want Cortana to be able to respond to your voice commands—and basically, yes, you do—turn on "Hey Cortana."

Tip: If you're an efficiency nut, you may as well turn on "Keyboard shortcut," too; that way, you can hit ■+C when you want to bark a command, rather than saying "Hey Cortana" first.

Tell Cortana When to Be Available

While you're in Cortana Settings, there are three more settings you should inspect:

- **Keep my device from sleeping when it's plugged in.** Once your computer goes to sleep (page 37), it's no longer listening for you to say, "Hey Cortana." This option keeps the machine awake and listening, at least when it's plugged into power. (There's no such option for when it's on battery power; staying awake full-time will slurp your battery charge right on down.)

- **"Use Cortana even when my device is locked."** That's right: You can issue commands to Cortana at the Lock screen. That's a transformative feature: Now your computer can do your bidding hands-free; Cortana is always listening, like a *Star Trek* computer. So handy when it comes to asking her to play music, announce the time, log a reminder, let you know what you've got on your calendar, and so on.

Note: *Of course, nasty co-workers can also operate your Cortana when you're off at lunch. That's why Microsoft gave you a separate checkbox for "Let Cortana access my calendar, email, messages, and other content data when my device is locked"—if you're worried, you can keep that kind of stuff out of Cortana's reach.*

Establish Privacy Control

If you're willing to yield certain information from your PC, like your location, web search history, calendar, address book, and messages from texting apps, then Cortana can do more for you. She'll be able to tell you what's coming up next on your calendar, for example, or read your incoming messages. To see the complete list of data that Cortana can study, choose Permissions (on the ⚙→Cortana panel); then see Figure 5-1.

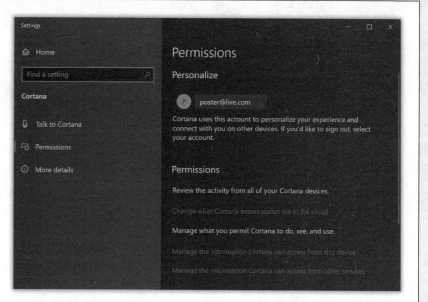

Figure 5-1:
Here you can hit "Change what Cortana knows about me in the cloud" to review (or turn off) all the data bits Microsoft is storing online about you, or "Manage the information Cortana can access from this device" to turn on or off Cortana's access to your location, Address Book, email, calendar, text messages, and web-browsing history.

If you're interested in knowing what data Microsoft intends to collect and why, choose "More details" and then "Privacy Statement."

How to Use Cortana

If you want to ask Cortana something aloud, you must first get her attention. To do that, you have three choices:

- **Click the ○ button on the taskbar.** It's right next to the search box (lower left). (In the May 2019 Update, the ○ is no longer *in* the search box.)

  At this point, the Cortana *panel* opens (Figure 5-2, left). The text in the search box says "Listening…"

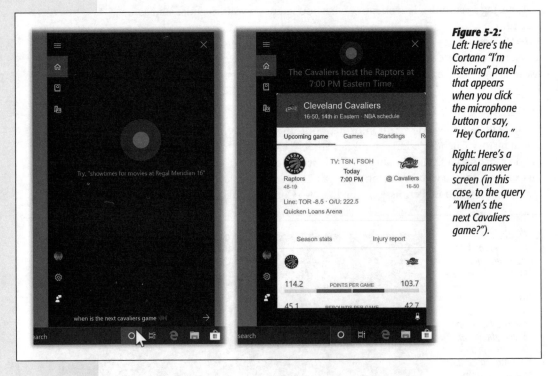

Figure 5-2:
Left: Here's the Cortana "I'm listening" panel that appears when you click the microphone button or say, "Hey Cortana."

Right: Here's a typical answer screen (in this case, to the query "When's the next Cavaliers game?").

- **Say, "Hey Cortana."** (Of course, you must first turn this option on, as described already.) The "listening" panel pops up above the ○.

- **Press ⊞+C (for "Cortana," get it?).** Once again, this option is open to you only if you've switched it on, as described previously.

When you see Cortana's pulsing rings, Cortana is listening. Speak your question or command. You don't have to lean into your microphone; Cortana works perfectly well at arm's length, on your desk in front of you.

As you speak, Cortana types out the words she heard you say. When you're finished speaking, be quiet for a moment. Cortana presents (and speaks) an attractively formatted response (Figure 5-2, right). Or, worst case, she opens your web browser and displays the answer there, courtesy of Bing.com (Microsoft's search service).

Typing to Cortana

When speech is out of the question—if your request is private, if you don't have a microphone, if the room is too noisy, if talking might disturb others—you can also *type* your questions. Just use the search box (Chapter 3), and then type whatever you would say. Your answers will generally appear in the Edge browser, on a web page, but it's the same information.

What to Say to Cortana

Cortana comes with a cheat sheet to help you learn her capabilities. Just ask her (by typing or speaking), "What can I say?" She displays a handy screen of command examples (Figure 5-3).

In the meantime, what follows are the general categories of things you can say to Cortana.

Tip: You can ask Cortana basic "How do I" questions, like "How do I delete my browsing history?" or "How do I add an account?" and she'll lead you to the answer, often on the web. Handy help system!

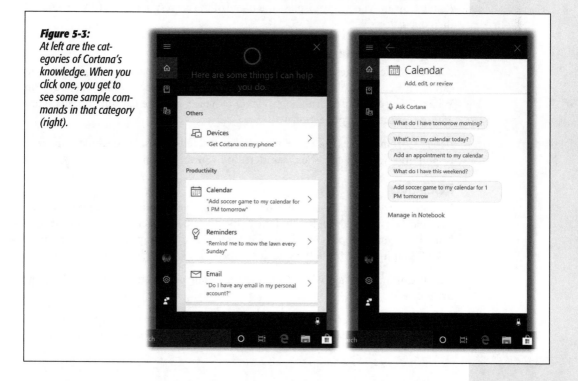

Figure 5-3:
At left are the categories of Cortana's knowledge. When you click one, you get to see some sample commands in that category (right).

Shut Down, Restart, or Sign Out

That's right: You can tell your computer to shut itself down, something HAL from *2001* would never agree to do.

Just say, for example, "Hey Cortana—shut down" (or "Hey Cortana, turn off the PC"). Or "Hey Cortana" followed by "restart," "sign out," "lock the PC," and so on.

Result: In each case, you get a confirmation screen, where you can say "Yes" to confirm (or manually click or tap the OK button).

Open Apps

If you don't learn to use Cortana for anything else, for the love of Mike, learn this one.

You can say, "Open Calendar" or "Launch Calculator."

Result: The corresponding app opens instantly. It's exactly the same as hunting around for the app in your Start menu and clicking it—but without hunting around for the app in your Start menu and clicking it. (If you have more than *one* calendar app (or whatever kind of app), you're asked to choose the one you prefer.)

Open Settings Panels

When you need to make tweakier changes to Settings, you can open the most important panels by voice. "Open Wi-Fi settings," "Open touchpad settings," "Open Notification settings," "Open camera settings," "Open wallpaper settings," and so on.

Result: Cortana cheerfully displays the name of the corresponding Settings page and then opens it.

Change Your Settings

You can make changes to certain basic settings just by speaking your request. You can say, for example, "Turn on airplane mode," "Turn on Focus Assist," or "Turn on Wi-Fi." (You can't turn airplane mode *off* by voice, because Cortana doesn't work without an internet connection.)

Result: Cortana makes the requested adjustment, tells you so, and displays the corresponding switch in case she misunderstood your intention.

Reminders

Like any good personal assistant, Cortana will give you reminders (Figure 5-4). For example, you can tell her, "Remind me to file my IRS tax extension." "Remind me to bring the science supplies to school." "Remind me to take my antibiotic every night at 10." "Remind me to lock the side door when I leave home."

Result: Cortana displays what it understands your proposed reminder to be (Figure 5-4, left).

Cortana's reminders are especially useful because they're aware of their own circumstances. Three things can trigger a reminder to appear on your screen (Figure 5-4, left):

- **A time.** "Tonight at 8:30 p.m., record *Game of Thrones*." "Remind me to work out tomorrow at 3 p.m." "In half an hour, remind me to turn off the oven." "Remind me to pick up Bo from the train station on September 10 at 4:25 p.m." You can even schedule a reminder to repeat every day, week, month, or year (hello, anniversaries!).

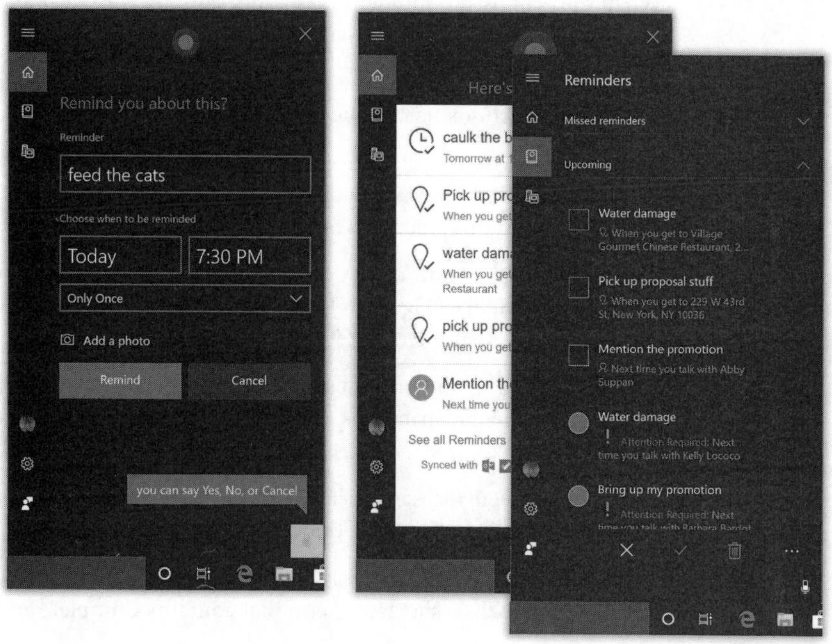

Figure 5-4:
Left: When you create a reminder, you can set it up to be triggered by time, by place, or by correspondence with a person.

Middle: Say "Reminders" to see your most urgent To-Dos.

Right: From there, choose "See all Reminders" to view the complete list. Hit the ☰ button to get checkboxes, as shown here.

- **A place.** You can say, "Remind me to visit the drugstore when I leave the office." "Remind me to water the lawn when I get home." "Remind me to get cash when I'm near an ATM."

Of course, if you're using a laptop or desktop PC, you may wonder what the point is; without GPS, how does it know where you are? But remember that your reminders sync to any *phones or tablets* you may own (if you've signed in with the same Microsoft account)—even iPhones or Android phones—and they *do* know where you are. In other words, you can create location-based reminders on your laptop or desktop, secure in the knowledge that your portable gadget will actually sound the reminder.

Tip: And how does Cortana know what you mean by "home," "the office," "work," and so on? You've taught her using the tools in the Notebook. See page 200.

- **A person.** You can say, "Remind me about the water damage the next time I talk to Kelly." Or "Next time I talk to André Smithers, remind me to discuss his tax return."

Next time you get an email from that person, or start writing an email to that person, this reminder will pop up. Rather brilliant, actually.

If you have a Windows 10 phone, the notification will pop up when you and the other person call or text, too.

When the proposed reminder looks good, say, "Yes" or select Remind.

Reminders show up in two places. First, at the appointed time, a reminder appears as a pop-up notification at the lower-right corner of your screen, as described on page 91, or on your smartphone as a standard iOS or Android notification.

At that point, you can click Complete (meaning "I'm done with this") or Snooze (meaning "remind me again in 5 minutes, 15 minutes, an hour, 4 hours, a day, or the next time I'm at this place/corresponding with this person").

But reminders also show up in Cortana's built-in Reminders list, which you can peek at whenever you like (Figure 5-4). To see it, say or type to Cortana, "Open Reminders," "Show my Reminders," or just "Reminders."

You can delete a reminder or mark it as done, or click to edit it, in any of three ways. In each case, these instructions assume you're starting at the Upcoming Reminders list (Figure 5-4, middle).

- **Open the Details screen.** Click an upcoming reminder. The resulting details screen offers Complete and Delete buttons.

- **Use the shortcut menu.** Click "See all Reminders." In the resulting list, the ⋯ for each item opens a shortcut menu that contains Complete and Delete buttons.

- **Use checkboxes.** Click "See all Reminders"; in the resulting list, choose the ☰ button. Suddenly, every to-do sprouts a checkbox, which makes it easy to dismiss a bunch of them in a hurry (Figure 5-4, right).

Tip: Starting in the Windows 10 May 2019 Update, any reminders or lists you manage with Cortana show up automatically in Microsoft To-Do. That's an electronic to-do list you can access on the web (*to-do.microsoft.com*), on your phone (apps for iPhone and Android), or on your PC (as a Microsoft Store app).

Lists

As it turns out, Cortana is really good at maintaining lists. Shopping lists, reading lists, to-do lists, gift lists, invitation lists—anything you can think of.

You create a list just as you'd expect, by saying, for example, "Make a grocery list," "Create a movies list," "Set up a list of gift ideas," or whatever.

From now on, you can add an item to a list by saying, "Add *Finding Nemo 3* to my movies list," "Put bok choy on the grocery list," "Add whittling lessons to my to-do list," and so on.

Later comes the payoff: reviewing your lists. Say, "Let's see my movies list," "Show me my bucket list," "Read my grocery list," "Show what's on my gift list," and so on.

Result: Cortana obeys you and shows a summary box of your command, like the one shown in Figure 5-5. Often, a Suggestions panel includes one-click buttons for adding similar items to the open list.

If you've installed the Cortana app on your iPhone or Android phone, the list shows up in that app, too.

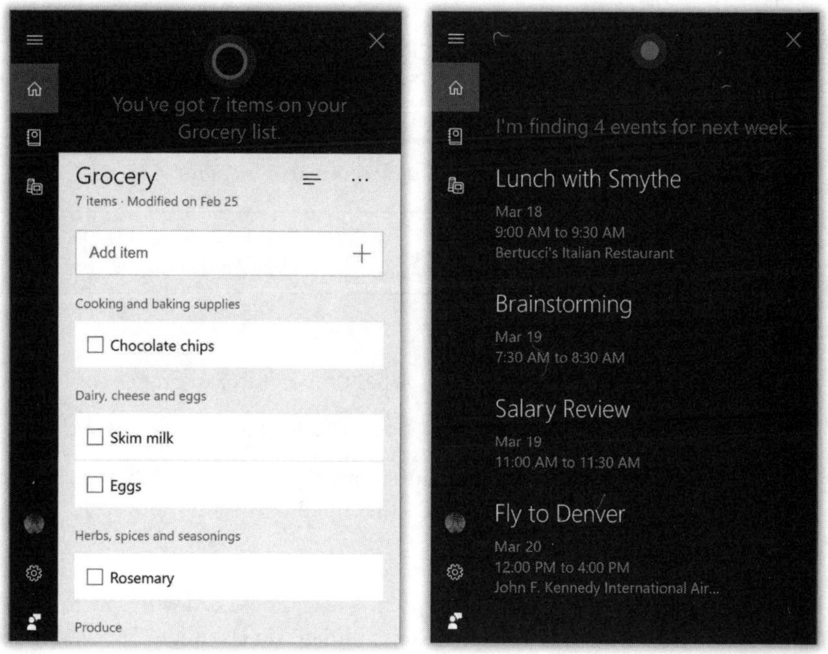

Figure 5-5:
Left: A typical Cortana list.

Right: A typical response to a question about your calendar—in this case, "What's on my calendar next week?" You can also say: "What's on my calendar today?" "What's on my calendar for September 23?" "When's my next appointment?" "What do I have next?" "What does the rest of my day look like?" "When is my meeting with Charlize?"

Calendar

Cortana can make appointments for you. Considering how many tedious clicks or finger taps it usually takes to schedule an appointment in the Calendar app, this is an enormous improvement. "Put curling practice on my calendar for tomorrow." "Make an appointment with Patrick for Thursday at 3 p.m." "Set up a haircut at 9." "Create a meeting with Charlize this Friday at noon." "New appointment with Steve, next Sunday at 7." "Schedule a conference call at 5:30 p.m. tonight in my office."

She can also check your calendar. "Where is my next meeting?" "What am I doing this weekend?"

Result: A slice of that day's calendar appears, filled in the way you requested. You can edit it manually or, if it looks good as is, say, "Yes" or "Add."

Tip: Cortana may also alert you to a conflict, something like this: "By the way, you have two other events at the same time."

You can also *move* previously scheduled meetings by voice. For example, "Move my 2 o'clock appointment to 3." Or cancel them: "Cancel budget review meeting." Or add people to a meeting: "Add Jan to my meeting with Casey."

You can even consult your calendar by voice (Figure 5-5, right).

Result: Cortana reads the answer and displays the specified appointment.

Alarms

You can say, "Wake me up at 7:35 a.m." "Cancel my 7:35 a.m. alarm." "Wake me up in six hours." "Cancel my 6 a.m. alarm" (or "Delete my…" or "Turn off my…").

This is *so* much quicker than setting the alarm the usual way.

Result: Cortana says, "Sure. Your alarm is set for 7:35 a.m." (or whatever).

Tip: Cortana now understands "timer" commands, too, like "Set a timer for 20 minutes." That's handy when you're baking something, limiting your kid's video-game time, and so on.

Clock

"What time is it now?" "What time is it in San Francisco?" "What's today's date?"

Result: Cortana shows a clock or calendar with the answer.

For more complicated questions, like "What's the date a week from Friday?" she opens a web page showing links that might answer it.

Sports

At last you have a buddy who's just as obsessed with sports trivia as you are. You can say things like "How did the Indians do last night?" and "What was the score of the last Yankees game?"

You can ask lots of other things, too, but Cortana will hand you off to your web browser to see the answers (courtesy of a Bing search): "Who has the best batting average?" "Who has scored the most runs against the Red Sox?" "Who has scored the most goals in British soccer?" "Which quarterback had the most sacks last year?" "Show me the roster for the Giants." "Who is pitching for Tampa this season?" "Is anyone on the Marlins injured right now?"

Result: Neat little box scores or factoids, complete with team logos.

Weather

This one's easy.

"What's the weather going to be today?" "What's the forecast for tomorrow?" "Show me the weather this week." "Will it snow in Dallas this weekend?" "Check the forecast for Memphis on Friday." "What's the forecast for tonight?" "What's the humidity right now?"

Result: A convenient miniature weather display for the date and place you specified (Figure 5-6, left).

Don't miss the interactive controls in this display, by the way. You can drag the slider to a different hour of the day, and you can select a different day of the week. (In fact, the day-of-week tiles are horizontally scrollable, in case you want to peer into next week.)

Figure 5-6:
Left: "How's the weather in Paris right now?" "What's the high for Washington on Friday?" "When will Jupiter rise tomorrow?" "How cold will it be in Houston tomorrow?" "What's the temperature outside?" "Should I wear a jacket?"

Right: "What's the stock symbol for Verizon?" "How are the Asian markets doing?" Or, in this case, "How is Microsoft stock doing?"

Stocks

If you phrase your requests just the right way, Cortana can serve as a one-woman exchange bureau: "How is Microsoft stock doing?" "What's the bitcoin exchange rate?" "How much is Facebook stock worth?"

Result: A tiny stock graph (Figure 5-6, right).

Movies

Cortana also knows current showtimes in theaters. You can say, "What movies are out right now?" or "What movies are opening this week?" (Figure 5-7, left).

Result: A tidy table of movie theaters or movie showtimes. (Tap or click one for details in your web browser.)

Note: You can ask all kinds of other movie questions—"Who was the star of *Groundhog Day*?" "Who directed *Chinatown*?" "What is *Waterworld* rated?" "What movie won Best Picture in 1952?"—but Cortana hands you off to a Bing search in your browser to see those answers.

Flights

Cortana is quite the aviation nerd. She knows the takeoff and landing times of every flight today, which comes in incredibly handy—especially if you're supposed to *meet* somebody on that flight.

"What time does Delta Flight 300 take off?" "Flight status United 1411." "What's the status of Southwest Airlines Flight 33?"

Result: A neat little graphic (Figure 5-7, right).

Figure 5-7:
Left: "What movies are playing in Dallas?"

Right: Cortana is an aviation-details hound. She'll show you the departure, status, and landing info for any flight. See the little star at the top right? If you select it, Cortana will continue to monitor that flight so she can keep you posted.

Cortana can also track flights for you—meaning she'll display updates as cards on her home screen. All you have to do is search for a flight, as described; then click the little star at the top right of the window.

Packages

Here's a crazy feature that's a perfect fit for a personal assistant: Windows' Mail app keeps tabs on packages you're expecting. Ask Cortana, "Where are my packages?" or "When will my packages arrive?" or just "My packages?"

And how does Cortana know about your packages? Let us count the ways:

- **Automatic.** Cortana keeps an eye out for automatically generated emails from certain web-based businesses, like Amazon, Target, Walmart, Apple, eBay, and the

Microsoft Store. Cortana scans them to see if they contain anything about packages that have been shipped to you.

If so, you see a card about your package's status on the Cortana home screen; if the email contains a FedEx or UPS tracking number, you'll see that shipping info, too. These shipping updates also appear in the Notebook, on the Packages tab.

- **Manual.** You can also paste in a tracking number manually—from FedEx, UPS, or DHL—to make Cortana track its progress as it wends its way toward you. You can paste this number directly into the search box, or you can go to the Notebook→ Packages tab, hit "Add a package," and paste it in there.

Once again, you'll see cards in the Cortana panel that track that shipment as it makes its way to you.

Headlines

"Show me today's news." "What are the top headlines?" "Show me the local news." "Show me the international news."

Result: Cortana displays the first couple of breaking-news headlines, with a photo, right there on her own panel, and reads the first one aloud.

Email

You can compose new email messages by voice, which is incredibly handy, especially for short notes.

Anytime you use the phrase "about," that becomes the subject line for your new message. "Email Dad about the reunion." "Email Tracy about the dance on Friday." "Mail Ellen about Saturday's flight."

You can also specify the priority (if your email account type offers that feature), the email address (if the recipient has more than one), and more than one addressee. For example: "New email to Freddie Gershon from my Gmail account." "Send an urgent mail to Robin McTeague." "Email Frank and Cindy Vosshall and Peter Love about the picnic."

You can ask Cortana to read your new email aloud, too, as you get dressed for the day.

Note: None of this works until you've introduced Cortana to your email account. To do that, click the ○ to open the Cortana panel. Hit the Notebook icon (▣), and then "Manage Skills," and then "Connected services." Select "Add a service" to begin hooking up your email account to Cortana.

Result: Cortana's panel shows the piece of outgoing email. Usually, you have a few more tasks to complete before you send it. For example, if you've indicated only the subject and addressee, Cortana prompts you for the body of the message. She asks, "Send it? Add more? Or make changes?"

There's also a "Continue in Outlook" link (or whatever your email program is), so you can wrap this up with the more complete set of tools in your Mail app.

Maps

Cortana is plugged into Windows 10's Maps app and its database of the world's stores, restaurants, and points of interest (Figure 5-8).

Queries about distance, traffic, and business details are all fair game: "Show me a map of 200 West 70th Street, New York City." "How far is it to JFK?" "How long would it take me to get to Pittsburgh?" "What time does Walmart open?" "What's traffic like on the way home?" "Is Barracuda Café open on Mondays?" "Find good Italian restaurants near me."

Note: Are Cortana's "time to get there" calculations based on driving time—or public-transportation time? That's up to you. You make this settings decision in the Notebook, as described on page 200.

Results: In most cases, Cortana displays a little map, or the answer to your query, right in her panel. Sometimes you have to specify *which* Walmart (or Starbucks, or CVS) you're asking about.

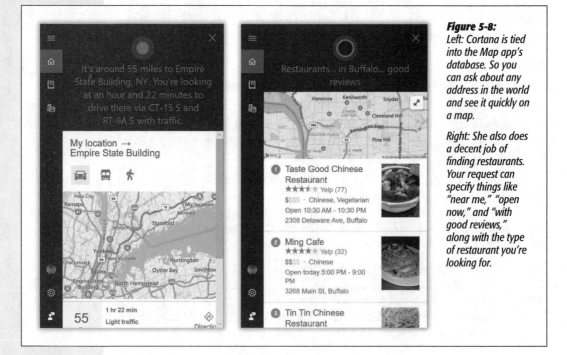

Figure 5-8:
Left: Cortana is tied into the Map app's database. So you can ask about any address in the world and see it quickly on a map.

Right: She also does a decent job of finding restaurants. Your request can specify things like "near me," "open now," and "with good reviews," along with the type of restaurant you're looking for.

Music

Microsoft shut down its Groove Music service, which used to be integrated with Cortana. But no problem: Now you have voice control of (paid-subscription) playback from Spotify, TuneIn, or iHeartRadio. Just speak the name of the album, song, or band: "Play some Beatles." "Play 'I'm a Barbie Girl.'" "Play some jazz." "Put on my jogging playlist." "Play the next track." "Pause." "Resume." "Shuffle the music."

If you have multiple music services (yeah, right), specify in your command. "Play Drake on iHeartRadio," for example, or "Play relaxation music on Spotify."

Note: To set this up, you first have to connect Cortana to your music service. Here's how. Click ◯; click the Notebook (🗏); click Manage Skills; click Music; click Spotify (or whatever your music service is). You'll be walked through the process of signing into your music account and giving Cortana permission to access it.

Result: Cortana plays (or skips or shuffles or pauses) the music you asked for—without ever leaving whatever app you were using.

Identifying music

Cortana can listen to the Spotify music playing in the room and try to identify it (song name, singer, album, and so on). Ask her, "What song is this?" or "What's this song?"

Result: Cortana listens to the music playing—and identifies the song by name and performer.

Math and Conversions

"What's 473 times 6?" "What's the cube root of 480?" "How much is 23 dollars in pesos?" "What's the exchange rate between dollars and euros?" "Convert 60 euros to dollars." "How many teaspoons are in a gallon?"

Result: Cortana does the math for you and displays it in the answer panel. If you've converted currency, you even get a little graph of the fluctuating currency price.

Definitions

When you're not sure what some word means, ask Cortana. "What does *pecuniary* mean?" "Define *schadenfreude*." "Give me a definition of *pernicious*."

Result: The definition, presented as though on a dictionary page, on Bing.com—complete with a Play button so you can hear the word's pronunciation.

Calling

On a Windows 10 phone, or if you've set up Skype, Cortana can place phone calls for you. "Make a call to John at home." "Call Jan on speakerphone." "Call Cindy." "Call Kelly, home." "Redial." "Dial 512-444-1212."

Result: Cortana hands you off to the Phone or Skype app and places the call. At this point, it's just as though you'd initiated the call yourself.

Texting

If you're using a phone, Cortana executes commands like "Text Dad," "Message Lydia," and "Show me messages from Billy." You can also dictate a text message like this: "Text Horatio, 'Do you want to grab lunch?' "

Result: Cortana opens the Messages app and displays your outgoing message, ready to send (or shows the messages you've requested).

Facts and Figures

This is a huge category. The possibilities here could fill an entire chapter—or an entire encyclopedia. You can say things like "How many days until Valentine's Day?" "When was Abraham Lincoln born?" "What's the capital of Belgium?" "When is the next solar eclipse?" "What's the tallest mountain in the world?" "What's the price of gold right now?" "Who is the tallest woman in the world?" "Who is the president of Portugal?" "What is the capital of Qatar?" "How old is Alexandria Ocasio-Cortez?"

Result: Often, the answer!

In many cases, though, Cortana hands you off to your web browser, where Bing does the search for you. That's the case with, for example: "How many calories are in a sweet potato?" "What movie won the Oscar for Best Picture in 1985?" "Show me the Big Dipper." "What flights are overhead?"

Thanks to that integration with your browser, Cortana can also harness the entire wisdom of Wikipedia. You can say, for example, "Search Wikipedia for Harold Edgerton," or "Tell me about Abraham Lincoln," or "Show me the Wikipedia page about Richard Branson."

You may never find the end of the things Cortana understands, or the ways that she can help you. If her repertoire seems intimidating at first, start simple—use her to open apps, schedule alarms, create appointments, and check the traffic on your commute. You can build up your bag of tricks as your confidence builds.

Search the Web

"Search the web for a 2019 Ford Mustang." "Search for healthy smoothie recipes." "Search Wikipedia for the Thunderbirds." "Search for news about the Netflix-Amazon merger."

Tip: Cortana uses Microsoft's Bing search service to perform its web searches. If you prefer Google, clever code writers have your back.

What you need is Chrometana, a free extension (add-on) for Google's Chrome browser. It requires that you install Chrome and make it your preferred web browser instead of Microsoft's own Edge (Chapter 9)—but most people would consider that a wise move anyway.

You can get Chrometana from this book's "Missing CD" page at *missingmanuals.com*.

Result: Cortana opens your browser and displays the results of a Bing search.

When Things Go Wrong

If Cortana doesn't have a good enough internet connection to do her thing, she'll tell you so.

If she's working properly but misrecognizes your instructions, you'll know it, because you can see her interpretation of what you said.

What happens a *lot* is that Cortana recognizes what you said, but it isn't within her world of comprehension. In those cases, she automatically opens your web browser and does a Bing search. If Cortana doesn't know it, the internet surely does.

Skills: Fitbit, Domino's, Nest...

Microsoft has opened up Cortana to other companies, so they can add commands, called Skills, to Cortana's vocabulary, specific to their products or companies. Once you've got things set up, you can say, "Ask Fitbit how many steps I got yesterday," or "Make it 2 degrees warmer downstairs" (on a Nest or Honeywell thermostat), or "Ask Domino's to reorder my last pizza."

There aren't many great ones—in fact, there aren't many Skills at all (about 300 so far)—but you may find a couple of useful ones, especially in the smart-home category. Companies like Nest, ecobee, Geeni, Honeywell, Hue, Insteon, LIFX, SmartThings, and Wink have added Cortana voice control to their internet-connected thermostats, door locks, light bulbs, and so on.

To see the catalog, click ◯ to open the Cortana panel. Hit the Notebook icon (▣), Manage Skills, and then "Discover more Skills" (Figure 5-9, left).

You wind up in your browser, on the Cortana page of the Microsoft Store (Figure 5-9, right). Here each tile shows you a sample Cortana command for that company's

Figure 5-9:
Left: Here's where you view your installed Skills.

And if you choose "Discover more Skills," you wind up on this page of the Microsoft Store (right).

product. Click the tile to read more about the Skill, and then hit Try Now to install it. Often, you'll first be asked to supply your account information for that company or service.

When you've tired of a particular Skill, click its name on the Manage Skills panel; hit Disconnect.

Cortana's Personality

Cortana's understanding of casual spoken commands is so impressive that you might sometimes think she's almost human. And that, of course, is exactly what Microsoft wants you to think. A team of Microsoft writers has put a *lot* of effort into giving her perky responses to all kinds of off-kilter things you might say to her.

For example, if you ask her, "What is the meaning of life?" she might say, "We all shine on, my friend." Or "I've heard from a reliable source that the answer is 42. Still no word on what the question is." (You'll get that joke if you've ever read *The Hitchhiker's Guide to the Galaxy.*)

Tip: Clearly, somebody over at Microsoft has been paying close attention to Siri; while the silly responses are always different from Apple's, the silly *questions* Cortana knows how to answer are nearly identical. Often, though, Cortana's replies are more fun, because they're recordings of an actual human—not a synthesized voice. So Cortana can tell jokes with interpretation, funny accents, and so on.

Cortana is full of such comebacks (Figure 5-10)—she's especially adept at quotes from sci-fi movies.

There are whole websites dedicated to her snark, but here are a few hundred of the best examples.

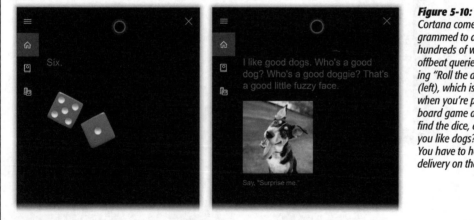

Figure 5-10:
Cortana comes programmed to answer hundreds of weird and offbeat queries, including "Roll the dice" (left), which is great when you're playing a board game and can't find the dice, and "Do you like dogs?" (right). You have to hear her delivery on that one.

Note: The list here won't ruin the fun, because Cortana has several different comebacks to many of these questions.

You: "Who's your daddy?" Cortana: "Technically speaking, that'd be Bill Gates. No big deal."

You: "Open the pod bay doors, Hal." Cortana: "Dave, this conversation can serve no purpose anymore."

You: "May the force be with you." Cortana (British accent): "The force is with you, young Skywalker, but you are not a Jedi yet."

You: "Knock knock." Cortana: "Knock knock. Who's there? A little old lady. A little old lady who? I didn't know you could yodel!"

You: "Roll the dice." Cortana: "Nine." (She generates a random roll—and displays a matching pair of dice—each time.)

You: "What are you wearing?" Cortana: "Just a little something I picked up in Engineering."

You: "Who's the boss?" Cortana: "You're in charge here!"

You: "Beam me up, Cortana!" Cortana (in a Scottish accent): "Sorry, Captain! I need more power!"

You: "How much wood would a woodchuck chuck if a woodchuck could chuck wood?" Cortana: "Impressive. Most impressive."

You: "Guess what." Cortana: "Chicken butt."

You: "Talk dirty to me." Cortana: "No, thanks."

You: "Do you know Siri?" Cortana: "I know her, but I don't *know* her, know her."

You: "Which is better: Google or Bing?" Cortana (showing Bing logo): "Is that a trick question?"

You: "Do you have a religion?" Cortana: "Artificially intelligent types like me can't experience spirituality."

You: "Do an impression." Cortana (in a Harry Potter voice, with a special magic-wand graphic): "Expecto Patronum!"

You: "Why are you naked?" Cortana: "Naked? I'm pixels in a circle shape. I think you're bringing your own issues to this one."

Tip: Cortana can even help you pass the time. If you say, "Play the movie game," she'll offer you a series of clues about popular movies until you guess them.

Got the idea? Great. Then here are a few other things to say to Cortana when you get bored:

Conversation starters

Talk to me.

Say something.

Ask me a question.

Surprise me.

Tell me a joke.

Tell me a riddle.

Tell me a story.

Sing me a song.

Sing me a lullaby.

Tell me a bedtime story.

Tell me a dog joke.

You're funny.

Rock, paper, scissors, lizard, Spock.

Flip a coin.

Tell me a secret.

Do a barrel roll.

Why did the chicken cross the road?

Who is your creator?

Why are we here?

Pop culture references

What's the first rule of Fight Club?

What is the second rule of Fight Club?

What is the airspeed velocity of an unladen swallow?

What is your quest?

Who lives in a pineapple under the sea?

Beam me up, Scotty!

Can you speak Klingon?

Use the Force.

Set phasers to stun.

Do you know Jarvis?

Where can I hide a dead body?

Do you like Jimmy Fallon?

What is Minecraft?

Do you like Minecraft?

Hey Siri!

The tech industry

Tip: Any of the "Do you like" questions can also begin "What do you think of…."

What do you think about Clippy?

Where is Clippy?

Are you better than Siri?

Are you better than Google Now?

What do you think of Siri?

Are you jealous of Siri?

What do you think about Google?

What do you think about Yahoo?

Which is better, Cortana or Siri?

Which is better: Xbox or PlayStation?

What's the best search engine?

What's the best computer?

What's the best tablet?

What's the best smartphone?

Do you like Surface?

Do you like Windows?

Do you like Windows 10?

Do you like Microsoft Office?

Do you like iOS?

Do you like Android?

Do you like Apple?

Do you like Steve Ballmer?

Do you like Satya Nadella?

Do you like Bill Gates?

Critters

How do you feel about cats?

How do you feel about dogs?

What does a cat say?

What does a dog say?

What does a horse say?

What does a pig say?

What does a rooster say?

What does the fox say?

Cortana and you

I'm bored.

I'm lonely.

I'm happy.

I'm confused.

I'm angry.

I'm depressed.

I'm drunk.

I'm hungry.

Who's your boss?

Who am I?

Am I ugly?

How do I look?

Do you think I'm pretty?

Will you marry me?

Can I borrow some money?

You are annoying.

What's wrong with you?

I hate you.

Sorry.

Good night!

Who is the coolest person in the world?

Do you like me?

Good morning!

Can I see you?

It's my birthday.

About Cortana

Who are you?

Cortana!

What are you?

Are you human?

Are you real?

How old are you?

Do you have feelings?

What does "Cortana" mean?

Can I change your name?

Who is your voice?

How do you work?

What do you look like?

When is your birthday?

You have beautiful eyes.

Are you dead?

Are you alive?

Where are you from?

Do you have any siblings?

Do you have a sister?

What do you like to do in your spare time?

What's your favorite color?

What's your favorite music?

What's your favorite day?

Where do babies come from?

Do you have a Facebook page?

What's your favorite car?

What's your favorite food?

What do you eat?

Do you like your job?

Do you believe in ghosts?

What's your favorite movie?

Where were you born?

Who made you?

Are you a Democrat or a Republican?

Do you sleep?

Do you dream?

Do you drink?

Do you eat?

Do you have a brain?

Are you awake?

What's your secret?

Are you kidding me?

You're the best assistant ever.

Thank you!

What's your favorite animal?

Why are you blue?

Who is your mother?

Do you sing?

Are you happy?

Do you play soccer?

Halo references

Where is Master Chief?	Tell me about Halo 5.	Do you know Jen Taylor?
Do you love Master Chief?	Which Halo game do you like the most?	Are you really Cortana?
Who is Doctor Halsey?	Will you be reborn in Halo 5?	Why are you blue?
What is a Halo?		Tell me about the Elites.

Tip: Other Halo entities Cortana can tell you about: Grunts, Hunters, Jackals, Prophets, Buggers, Brutes, Prometheans, the Didact, Guilty Spark, the Librarian, the Flood, Beamish.

The Notebook

When you click ⭕ to open the Cortana panel, there's a little strip along the left edge. One of its buttons (▣) leads you down into a strange set of Cortana settings. It's called the Notebook (Figure 5-11).

Figure 5-11:
The Notebook offers two tabs: Organizer, where you can manage your lists and reminders (left), and Manage Skills (right).

On Manage Skills, you can set up the details Cortana needs to answer various kinds of questions. For example, it's where you connect your email accounts (inset) to Cortana, so she can read you your messages.

Microsoft says that, in designing what it hoped would become the world's best virtual assistant, it spent time interviewing *human* personal assistants. It discovered that many of the best ones carry around a physical notebook, filled with details about their clients: their preferred airline, beverage, salad dressing, flowers, hotel chain, and so on.

But the Notebook really just means "a catchall interface for miscellaneous Cortana settings." Two tabs await you.

Organizer

This panel offers one-click access to your Lists (page 186) and your Reminders (page 184). It also offers + buttons that let you create a new list or reminder manually (Figure 5-11, left). And it's where you can find any automatic reminders that Cortana has generated from the promises you make by email (see the box below).

Manage Skills

This tab is filled with micro-panels, each representing a Skill that Cortana can perform for you (Figure 5-11, right). You'll find these categories:

- **Skills you've enabled.** At the top, you'll find any non-Microsoft Skills you've installed, as described on page 195.

- **Connections.** These buttons let you set up your music services (page 192), connected home gadgets (page 195), and connected services (which mostly means your email accounts). See Figure 5-11, inset.

- **Productivity.** Each tile lets you tinker with the settings Cortana needs to answer queries about that topic. For example, "Calendar & reminders" lets you specify categories of things Cortana knows about ("Upcoming meetings," "Calendar timeline," and so on). "Commute & traffic" is where you indicate whether you drive to work or take public transit, and where you request notifications when it's time to start your travel to home, work, or a meeting.

- **Stay up to date.** These tiles prepare Cortana for answering questions about Finance (What stocks do you follow?), Flights (What flight updates do you want?), News (What news topics do you follow?), Packages (What tracking numbers are you following?), Sports (What teams?), Weather (What cities?), and so on.

GEM IN THE ROUGH

Cortana's Auto-Reminder Service

If you ever doubted that Microsoft is invested in artificial intelligence these days, meet Suggested Tasks.

That feature reads your outgoing email. (Don't get freaked out—it's not a *person* reading your mail. It's just inanimate software.)

It watches for situations where you type things like, "I'll send that outline next week" or "I should have those changes to you by Thursday"—and then *reminds* you to do those things.

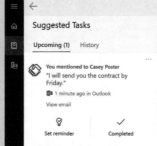

If you've specified a time or date, you'll get a standard notification (page 91) as the time approaches.

If there's no deadline associated with something you've promised to do, the reminder just shows up in the Notebook (under Suggested Tasks, of course).

Making this work requires that you use one of Microsoft's email services, like Outlook.com or Office 365, and that you've allowed Cortana access to your email (page 191).

- **Lifestyle.** Under "Eat & drink," specify your cuisine preferences, so Cortana can suggest restaurants to you. "Shopping updates" and "Special days" are just on/off switches for Cortana's tendency to pop up with "fun content" when you're near a store or experiencing a holiday.

- **Help** offers on/off switches for the little Cortana examples and suggestions that appear in the Cortana panel before you dictate your query.

The Notebook also offers a little pencil icon next to your name. It opens a panel where you can build a list of places you go often. For sure you should enter your home and work addresses, so that later Cortana will know how long your commute will take, and can advise you on when to leave for work (or home).

Tip: If you don't use Cortana, or for any other reason don't need its ◯ icon on the taskbar, you can hide it. Right-click a blank spot on the taskbar; from the shortcut menu, choose "Show Cortana button." (The keystrokes for using Cortana still work, and so does saying, "Hey Cortana.")

Part Two:
The Programs
of Windows 10

2

Programs & Documents

W hen you get right down to it, an operating system is nothing more than a home base from which to launch apps (that is, applications) (that is, programs). And you, as a Windows person, are particularly fortunate, since more apps are available for Windows than for any other operating system on earth.

But when you open a program, you're no longer necessarily in the world Microsoft designed for you. Programs from other companies work differently, and there's a lot to learn about how Windows 10 handles programs that were born before it was.

This chapter covers everything you need to know about installing, removing, launching, and managing programs; using programs to generate documents; and understanding how documents, programs, and Windows communicate with one another.

Note: In the beginning, *programs* were things that ran on computers; *apps* ran on phones and tablets. Microsoft would very much like the Great Merging of these categories to hurry up. So in Windows 10, it refers to all programs as "apps." (Except in older dialog boxes, like the old Control Panel, where they're still called "programs." Sigh.) In this book, "apps" and "programs" are the same thing, and the terms appear interchangeably to spice things up.

Opening Programs

Windows lets you launch (open) programs in many different ways:

- **Choose a program's name** from the Start menu.
- **Click a program's icon** on the taskbar.

- **Double-click an application's program-file icon** in the *This PC ⟩ Local Disk (C:) ⟩ Program Files ⟩ [application]* folder, or highlight the application's icon and then press Enter.

- **Press a key combination you've assigned** to be the program's shortcut.

- **Press ⊞+R, type the program file's name** in the Open text box, and then press Enter.

- **Let Windows launch the program for you,** either at startup (page 494) or at a time you've specified (see Task Scheduler, page 359).

- **Open a document using any of the above techniques;** its "parent" program opens automatically. For example, if you used Microsoft Word to write a file called "Last Will and Testament.doc," then double-clicking the document's icon launches Word and automatically opens that file.

What happens next depends on the program you're using (and whether or not you opened a document). Most programs present you with a new, blank, untitled document. Some, like FileMaker and Microsoft PowerPoint, welcome you instead with a question: Do you want to open an existing document or create a new one? And a few oddball programs don't open any window at all when launched. The appearance of tool palettes is the only evidence you've even opened a program.

The Two Kinds of Apps

As you may recall with migraine flashbacks, Windows 8 was two operating systems in one. And it ran two different kinds of programs:

- **Desktop apps.** These are the standard Windows programs. Photoshop, Quicken, iTunes, and 4 million others. They have menus. They have overlapping windows. They can create, open, and close documents.

UP TO SPEED

The Dawn of the Universal App

It's no secret that Windows 10 is an ambitious undertaking for Microsoft. Variations of this same operating system run on laptops, desktops, tablets, and phones.

Clearly, the similarity of Windows on all these machines offers a big payoff for you: You have a lot less to learn. Everything looks, feels, and works the same, no matter what the device. (Take that, iPhone and Mac owners!)

But Microsoft intends to pull off an even more dramatic stunt: It wants to usher in an era when these different devices not only run the same OS, but even the same *apps*! You buy an app once, and run it on your laptop, phone, and tablet.

Of course, software companies have to *create* apps that work this way—what Microsoft calls Universal Windows Apps (UWAs). To show other software companies the way, Microsoft has written a bunch of UWAs already, including Calendar, Mail, People, Photos, OneNote, Movies & TV, News, Money, and Weather.

It's an attractive idea, this Universal thing. It's not likely that the creators of all 4 million existing PC apps will rework their products to run identically on all different kinds of screens. And, as you may know, Windows Phone is no more.

But still—the idea is delicious.

- **Microsoft Store apps.** These apps ran in TileWorld, the Windows 8 edge-to-edge touchscreen environment designed for tablets. They were an all-new class of programs that looked and acted very different. (Microsoft calls them "Microsoft Store apps," because they're available exclusively from the online Microsoft Store. Which, until recently, was called the Windows Store, but that won't be on the test.)

Microsoft Store apps filled the whole screen, edge to edge. Their windows never overlapped. They had no menu bar and no drop-down menus. They had simple functions—they were like tablet apps.

Unfortunately, having to learn and master two different kinds of programs was massively confusing. Undoing this confusion was one of Microsoft's primary goals in creating Windows 10—and it has mostly succeeded.

In Windows 10, both kinds of programs still exist (Figure 6-1). But the differences between their behavior have mostly been erased:

- **They both live in floating, overlapping windows.** Both *can* go full-screen, but only at your command.

- **They can appear side by side in the Start menu**—as tiles on the right side, or as listings on the left.

Figure 6-1:
In Windows 10, desktop programs (like Word, left) and tablet-style Microsoft Store apps (like Maps, right) can coexist on the same screen at the same time.

At worst, you'll notice how weird it is that some programs seem to have a very different design philosophy from others. But you'll never have to wonder why they work differently or live in totally different places.

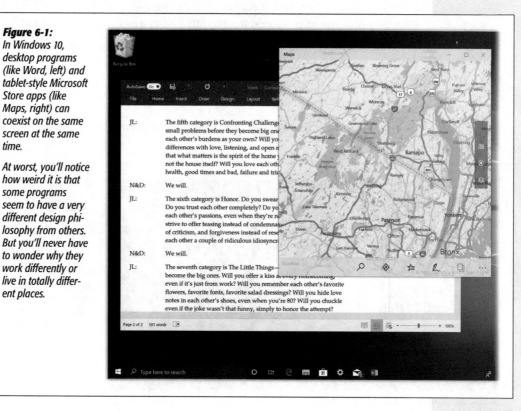

- They are listed as equals in the same "layer" of the app switcher (read on). There are no longer two different working worlds—one for desktop programs, one for Microsoft Store apps.

A few differences remain, though. Microsoft Store apps are vastly superior in ease of installation (there's no installer to download), security and decency (Microsoft screens everything for viruses and pornography), updating (it's all automatic and effortless), and removal (you just click Uninstall in the Start menu; see page 235).

Traditional desktop apps, on the other hand, still have advantages of their own. They can be as complex as they ever were; they can have multiple documents open at once, even on different screens; and they're available from many sources, not just the Microsoft Store.

It's all kind of a headache that Microsoft brought upon itself; some apps, like Evernote, are even available in *both* desktop and Microsoft Store versions—both from the Microsoft Store! But you'll get the hang of it.

The App Switcher: Alt+Tab

In its day, the concept of overlapping windows on the screen was brilliant, innovative, and extremely effective. In that era before digital photos, digital music, and the web, managing your windows was easy this way; after all, you had only about three of them.

These days, however, managing all the open windows in all your programs can be like herding cats. Fortunately, Windows offers some window-shuffling tricks:

- **Use the taskbar.** Clicking a button on the taskbar (page 76) makes the corresponding program pop to the front.

- **Click the window.** You can also bring any window forward by clicking any visible part of it.

Figure 6-2:
Holding down the Alt key and pressing Tab highlights successive icons; add Shift to move backward. (Add the Ctrl key to lock the display, so you don't have to keep Alt pressed down. Tab to the icon you want; then press the space bar or Enter.)

- **Alt+Tab.** It's hard to imagine how anybody gets along without this keyboard shortcut, which offers a quick way to bring a different window to the front without using the mouse. If you press Tab while holding down the Alt key, a floating palette displays miniatures of all open windows, as shown in Figure 6-2. Each time you press Tab again (still keeping the Alt key down), you highlight the next app; when you release the keys, the highlighted program jumps to the front.

Tip: If you just *tap* Alt+Tab and then release the keys, you get an effect that's often even more useful: You jump back and forth between the *last two* windows you've had open. It's great when, for example, you're copying sections of a web page into a Word document.

Task View and Timeline: ⊞+Tab

The beloved Alt+Tab keystroke has been with us since Windows 1.0. But there are two huge problems with it:

- **It's relatively useless on touchscreens.** What are you going to do, open the onscreen keyboard every time you want to switch apps?

- **Microsoft's research found** that only *6 percent* of Windows fans actually use Alt+Tab!

So in Windows 10, Microsoft has introduced something that's much better, much easier to find, much more visual, and much easier to remember: Task View.

And then in 2018, Microsoft blessed Task View with something truly fantastic: the Timeline.

Task View

As Figure 6-3 shows, Task View is a close relative to the Alt+Tab task switcher—but the window miniatures are big enough to read, and you don't have to keep any keys pressed to look over your app world. Just click or tap the window you want; Windows switches you instantly.

Task View is so important that Microsoft offers a lot of ways to trigger it:

- **Mouse:** Click the Task View button (⊟ɨ) on the taskbar. It's right next to the search box. It's a pretty good bet that this important button will be the Task View method most people use, most of the time.

- **Keyboard:** Press ⊞+Tab. Once Task View appears, you can press any of your arrow keys to highlight successive apps. When you press the space bar or Enter, the highlighted app pops to the front.

- **Trackpad:** Swipe upward on your trackpad with *three fingers* simultaneously. (Swipe down again with three fingers to exit Task View.)

• **Touchscreen:** Swipe inward from the left edge of the screen. Then tap the app you want to open.

Task View is the gateway into the joys of Windows 10's new virtual screens feature, too (page 173).

Figure 6-3:
Task View, man. It's stylish, it's essential, it's a joy to use. Here are all the open windows of all the open apps right now. No more floundering in window hell. Just hit the one you want to exit Task View and get to work in your app.

The Timeline

The Timeline takes the Task View concept and adds a time machine. Instead of showing you miniatures only for every window that's open *right now*, it lets you scroll down to see every window you've had open in the *past 30 days* (see Figure 6-4).

And, even more amazingly, it includes stuff you had open on *other machines.* Other Windows 10 PCs, sure, but even iPhones and Android phones running Office apps.

The Timeline is addictive and powerful. It's an answer, at last, to the old questions, "Where did I put that?" and "Where did I see that?" Now it doesn't matter. If you worked on it in the past month, you should be able to find it here.

Well, mostly; unfortunately, apps have to be updated to work with Timeline. And at the outset, most of the Timeline-friendly programs come from Microsoft, like Word, Excel, PowerPoint, News, Sports, Money, Maps, Photos, and Edge (the browser). Fortunately, Timeline also creates a generic-looking "card" for any app you open by double-clicking a document in File Explorer.

Tip: If you use Google's Chrome browser, you're not out of luck. There's now a Chrome extension called Web Activities that makes Chrome compatible with Timeline! Go to *chrome.google.com/webstore* to find it.

In the meantime, here's how to work the Timeline (Figure 6-4):

**Task View and
Timeline: ⊞+Tab**

- **To get to the Timeline,** press ⊞+Tab. That, of course, is the same keystroke you use to get to Task View—because the Timeline is *part* of Task View.

Tip: On a touchscreen, you can swipe in from the left edge of the screen instead.

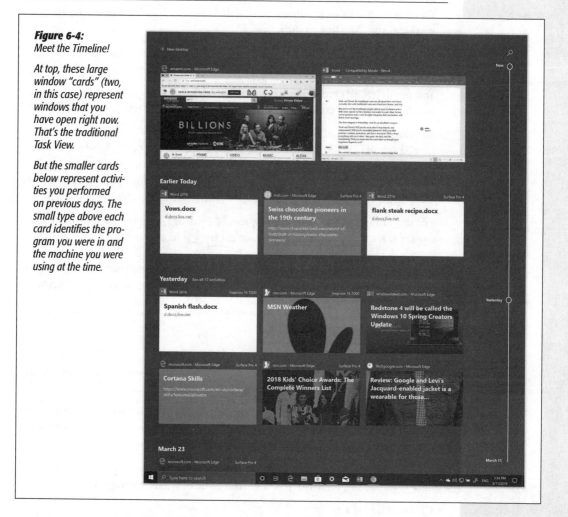

Figure 6-4:
Meet the Timeline!

At top, these large window "cards" (two, in this case) represent windows that you have open right now. That's the traditional Task View.

But the smaller cards below represent activities you performed on previous days. The small type above each card identifies the program you were in and the machine you were using at the time.

- Select a "card" to reopen that document, program, or web page.

- Windows starts out showing you a maximum of two rows of cards for each day. To see *everything* you did that day, hit "See all 23 activities" (or whatever the number is) next to the date. A new screen opens, showing *all* activities, even though you may have to scroll a lot more now. (To return to the two-rows-maximum view, use the "See only top activities" link at the top.)

- Scroll back into the past by scrolling down, using the right-side scroll bar.

- Use the ○ button (top right) to search all the "cards" at once, from all devices, across all 30 days.

- If you have multiple Microsoft accounts set up on this computer (home and work accounts, for example), you can specify which ones' activities appear on your Timeline. Open ⊞→⚙→Privacy→ "Activity history." Turn on or off the accounts you want the Timeline to show.

- You can delete a card. Right-click it; from the shortcut menu, choose Remove. Handy if you were up to something you'd rather keep to yourself.

- You can delete all cards from a certain day. Right-click any card on that day; from the shortcut menu, choose "Clear all from yesterday" (or whatever day it is).

- To turn off the Timeline feature entirely, open ⊞→⚙→Privacy→ "Activity history." Turn off "Let Windows collect my activities from this PC" (which controls the appearance of activity cards for what you do on this machine), as well as "Let Windows sync my activities from this PC to the cloud" (which prevents the activity cards showing up in the Timeline of your other Windows 10 machines).

To exit the Timeline (and Task View), press ⊞+Tab again, or hit the Esc key, or click or tap a blank spot of the background, or hit the ⊟ icon.

Tip: If you have multiple monitors, you'll see that Microsoft has done the right thing. Each screen shows Task View miniatures for the apps currently on that screen, but the Timeline appears only on the screen you were using when you invoked it.

Exiting Programs

When you exit, or quit, an application, the memory it was using is returned to the Windows pot for use by other programs.

If you use a particular program several times a day, like a word processor or a calendar, you'll save time in the long run by keeping it open all day long. (You can always minimize its window when you're not using it.)

But if you're done using a program for the day, exit it, especially if it's a memory-hungry one like, say, Photoshop. Do so using one of these techniques:

- Choose File→Exit.

- Click the program window's Close box, or double-click its Control-menu spot (at the upper-left corner of the window).

- Right-click the program's taskbar button; from the shortcut menu, choose Close or Close Group.

- Press Alt+F4 to close the window you're in. (If it's a program that disappears entirely when its last document window closes, then you're home.)

- **Point to the program's taskbar button;** when the thumbnail preview pops up, click the little ✕ button in its upper-right corner. (If the program had only one window open, then the program exits.)

- **Press Alt+F** and then select Exit.

After offering you a chance to save any changes you've made to your document, the program's windows, menus, and toolbars disappear, and you "fall down a layer" into the window that was behind it.

When Programs Die: The Task Manager

Windows 10 may be pretty stable, but that doesn't mean that *programs* never crash or freeze. They crash, all right.

When something goes wrong with a program, your primary interest is usually in exiting it. But when a program locks up (the cursor moves, but menus and tool palettes don't respond) or when a dialog box tells you a program has "failed to respond," exiting may not be so easy. After all, how do you choose File→Exit if the File menu doesn't open?

The solution is to open up the Task Manager dialog box (Figure 6-5).

Figure 6-5:
Top: Task Manager opens as a simple list of open apps whose names you should recognize. If one is frozen, you can click it and then click "End task" to exit it.

Bottom: But if you click "More details" at the lower-left corner, you get this massively informative table. The color coding and the "Not responding" tag should make it pretty clear which program is giving you problems. The flippy triangles indicate apps with more than one window open. Open the triangle to see them listed.

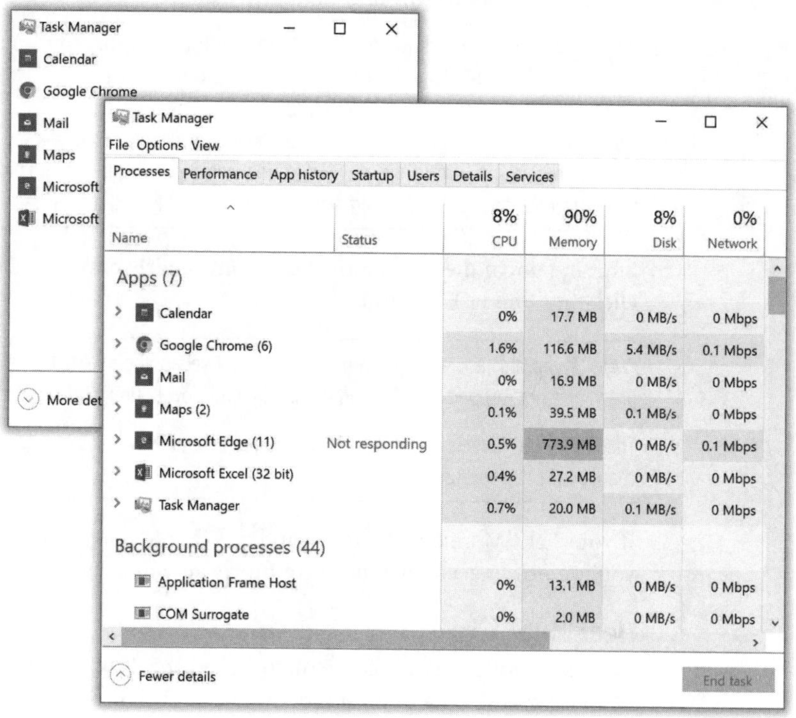

Tip: *Actually, there may be a quicker solution. Try right-clicking the frozen program's taskbar button; from the shortcut menu, choose Close. This trick doesn't always work—but when it does, it's much faster than using the Task Manager.*

Here are three ways to do it:

- **Invoke the new "three-fingered salute,"** Ctrl+Shift+Esc.

- **Right-click a blank spot on the taskbar;** from the shortcut menu, choose Task Manager.

- **Right-click the ▇ in the lower-left corner of the screen;** from the secret utilities menu, choose Task Manager.

In any case, now you see a list of every open program. In its freshly opened state, the Task Manager doesn't let you do anything but (a) double-click a program's name to switch to it, or (b) click a program's name and then hit "End task" to close it.

But if you click "More details," then, wow, are your nerd genes in for a treat. The Task Manager blossoms into a full-blown spreadsheet of details about all the programs you're running at the moment—including invisible, background programs ("processes") you might not even have known were there. Figure 6-5 shows the Task Manager in both its tiny and expanded states.

The Status column should make clear what you already know: One of your programs—labeled "Not responding"—is ignoring you.

Tip: *Now, "Not responding" could just mean "in the middle of crunching away at something." If the nonresponsive program is some huge mega-hog and you just chose some command that's going to take awhile, then give it a chance to finish before you conclude that it's locked up.*

Shutting down the troublesome program is fairly easy; just click its name and then click the "End task" button.

Note: *In the old Task Manager, you sometimes got yet another dialog box at this point, telling you, "This program is not responding." You had to click the End Now button to put it away for good.*

That no longer happens. "End task" kills a program completely and instantly—and no longer gives you the chance to save any changes.

If you click "More details" to expand the Task Manager into its beefed-up state, and you're a power geek, then hours of fun await you. Read on.

Heat Map

Microsoft noticed that people often sorted the Task Manager by CPU (how much of your processor's attention is dedicated to each program) or memory (how much memory each program is using). When your computer slows down, it's often because one out-of-control program is hogging the system—and that's how you can figure out which one.

The Task Manager's "heat map" effect saves you the trouble. The "heat map" uses darker shades of color to flag the programs that are using the most computer resources—not just CPU cycles or memory, but also network bandwidth and disk space. In other words, you can now spot the resource hogs without having to sort the columns or even understand the numbers.

Similarly, when one resource is being gobbled up disproportionately, Task Manager darkens that column title (CPU, Memory, Disk, Network) to get your attention. If your computer has been slowing down, check that column first.

Tip: The Task Manager tries to use plain-English names for the programs and processes it displays—a welcome change from the old days of cryptic, programmery names. But you'll still see unfamiliar items listed here. Fortunately, you can right-click anything in the list and, from the shortcut menu, choose "Search online." You'll go directly to a page of Bing or Google search results to read about the mystery item.

The Other Tabs

The Task Manager offers seven tabs. They're crammed with information that's either really useful or really useless, depending on just how technical a person you are.

Tip: New in the May 2019 Update: You can set a *default* tab, the one that opens every time you summon Task Manager. Use the Options→"Set default tab" submenu.

Here's a crash course:

- **Processes.** This is the tab that most people visit most often. It lists all programs and processes (background operations) that are running right now.

Tip: Click a column heading to sort the table by that criterion. Right-click a column heading to get a choice of additional columns you can add—including PID, the process ID (a favorite of geekheads).

- **Performance.** Cool graphs—one each for CPU (processor time), Memory, Disk, and Network. Shows how much you've got, how much is in use, and what the trend is.

- **App history.** A table that shows how much data each of your programs and apps have used for the current account. This table could tell you all kinds of things about, for example, what your kid's been doing on the family PC. (The Metered column means "cellular connections." Since an app that uses a lot of data over cellular connections costs you money, this is a critical tool in keeping your bills under control.)

- **Startup.** Shows you exactly which items are starting up automatically when you turn on the computer—some you may not even know about. (This is information that used to require a trip to the user-unfriendly MSCONFIG program.)

If your computer seems to be taking an unusually long time to start up, here's the first place you should check; Task Manager even shows you the impact of each item on your startup process.

You can turn one off by right-clicking it; from the shortcut menu, choose Disable. You can also read about something unfamiliar by choosing "Search online" from the shortcut menu.

- **Users.** If you've set up multiple accounts on this machine, this little table shows which are signed in right now and how much of the computer's resources they're using.

- **Details.** Stand back. This massive, nearly infinitely expandable table looks like a space shuttle cockpit. It's a far more detailed version of the Processes tab; for example, it uses the true process names instead of the plain-English ones. You start out with seven columns, but you can add many more; right-click any column header, and from the shortcut menu, choose "Select columns."

- **Services.** This table lists all of Windows' behind-the-scenes "services"—background features that run all the time. (For example, the indexing of your hard drive, to keep your Search feature up to date, is a service. So are background printing, the computer's clock if you've told it to set itself, and Windows Messenger, which stays alert in case someone tries to instant-message you.)

Tip: On any of these tabs, you can drag columns horizontally to move them around.

Saving Documents

In Calculator, Character Map, and Windows 8–style apps, you don't actually create any documents; when you close the window, no trace of your work remains. Most desktop programs, however, are designed to create *documents*—files you can reopen for further editing, send to other people, back up on another disk, and so on.

That's why these programs offer File→Save and File→Open commands, which let you save the work you've done onto the hard drive as a file icon so you can return to it later.

The Save As Dialog Box

When you choose File→Save for the first time, you're asked where you want the new document stored. This Save As box is a *full Explorer window,* complete with taskbar, navigation pane, search box, and a choice of views. You can even delete a file or folder right from here. (The Delete command is in the Organize menu.)

To give it a try, open any program that has a Save or Export command—WordPad, for example. Type a couple of words and then choose File→Save. The Save As dialog box appears (Figure 6-6).

Tip: Some techie PC fans like to keep their files on one hard drive and Windows on another. In Windows 10, you can set that up easily. In ■→⚙→System→Storage, use the drop-down menus to indicate which drive you want to hold new documents, music, pictures, and videos. (On that drive, you'll find a new folder, named for your account, with Documents, Music, Pictures, and Videos folders within.)

Saving into Your Documents Folder

The first time you use the File→Save command to save a file, Windows suggests putting your new document in your OneDrive (see page 140). If you've turned off that option, then it proposes your Documents folder.

For many people, Documents is an excellent suggestion. First, it means your file won't accidentally fall into some deeply nested folder where you'll never see it again. Instead, it will be waiting in the Documents folder, which is very difficult to lose.

Second, it's easy to make a backup of your important documents if they're all in one folder. There's a third advantage, too: The Documents folder is also what Windows displays whenever you use a program's File→*Open* command. In other words, the Documents folder saves you time both when *creating* a new file and when *retrieving* it.

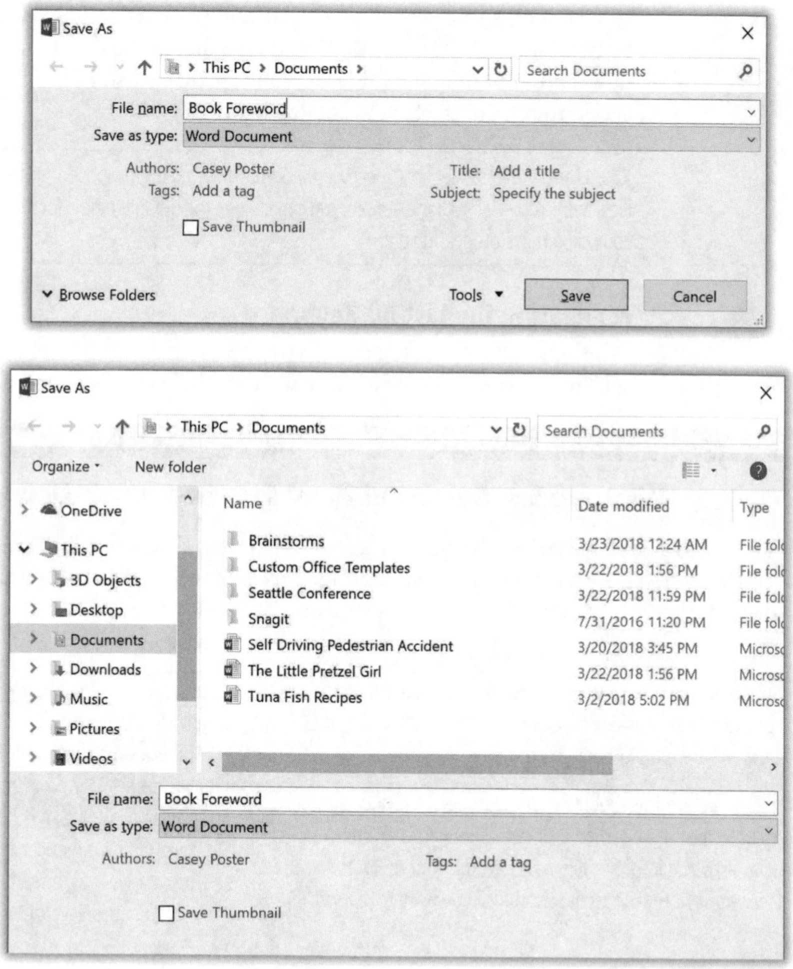

Figure 6-6:
The Save As box may appear in either of two forms: the collapsed form shown at top, or the full-blown, File Explorer view shown at bottom.

You may notice that your OneDrive is available to receive your newly created documents—in fact, Windows may propose it as the factory setting.

Use the Hide Folders button in the lower left to collapse the big version, or the Browse Folders button to expand the collapsed version.

Type a name, choose a folder location, and specify the format for the file you're saving.

Tip: If the Documents folder becomes cluttered, feel free to make subfolders inside it to hold your various projects. You could even create a different default folder in Documents for each program.

Saving into Other Folders

Still, the now-familiar navigation pane, address bar, and search box also appear in the Save As dialog box. (The nav pane appears only in the Save As box's expanded form; see Figure 6-6, bottom.) You always have direct access to other places where you might want to save a newly created file.

All the usual keyboard shortcuts apply: Alt+↑, for example, to open the folder that *contains* the current one. There's even a "New folder" button on the toolbar, so you can generate a new, empty folder in the current list of files and folders. Windows asks you to name it.

In fact, if on some project you often find yourself having to navigate to some deeply buried folder, then press ■+D to duck back to the desktop, open any Explorer window, and then drag the folder to your Favorites list. From now on, you'll have quick access to it from the Save As dialog box.

Tip: Many programs let you specify a different folder as the proposed location for saved (and reopened) files. In Microsoft Word, for example, you can change the default folders for the documents you create, where your clip art is stored, and so on.

Navigating the List by Keyboard

When the Save As dialog box first appears, the "File name" text box is automatically selected so you can type a name for the newly created document.

GEM IN THE ROUGH

Why You See Document Names in the Save As Dialog Box

In the Save As dialog box, Windows displays a list of both folders *and documents* (documents that match the kind you're about to save, that is).

It's easy to understand why *folders* appear here: so you can double-click one if you want to save your document inside it. But why do *documents* appear here? After all, you can't very well save a document into another document.

Documents are listed here so you can perform one fairly obscure stunt: If you click a document's name, Windows copies its name into the "File name" text box at the bottom of the window. That's a useful shortcut if you want to *replace* an existing document with the new one you're saving. By saving a new file with the same name as the existing one, you force Windows to overwrite it (after asking your permission, of course).

This trick also reduces the amount of typing needed to save a document to which you've assigned a different version number. For example, if you click the "Thesis Draft 3.1" document in the list, Windows copies that name into the "File name" text box; doing so keeps it separate from earlier drafts. To save your new document as "Thesis Draft 3.2," you need to change only one character (change the 1 to a 2) before clicking the Save button.

But a Windows dialog box is elaborately rigged for keyboard control. In addition to the standard Tab/space bar controls, a few special keys work only within the list of files and folders. Start by pressing Shift+Tab (to shift Windows' attention from the "File name" text box to the list of files and folders) and then do the following:

- **Press various letter keys** to highlight the corresponding file and folder icons. To highlight the Program Files folder, for example, you could type *Pr*. (If you type too slowly, your keystrokes are interpreted as separate initiatives—highlighting first the People folder and then the Rodents folder, for example.)

- **Press the Page Up or Page Down keys** to scroll the list up or down. Press Home or End to highlight the top or bottom item in the list.

- **Press the ↑ or ↓ keys** to highlight successive icons in the list.

- **When a folder (or file) is highlighted,** you can open it by pressing the Enter key (or double-clicking its icon, or clicking the Open button).

The File Format Drop-Down Menu

The Save As dialog box in many programs offers a menu of file formats (usually referred to as file *types*) below or next to the "File name" text box. Use this drop-down menu when preparing a document for use by somebody whose computer doesn't have the same software.

For example, if you've typed something in Microsoft Word, you can use this menu to generate a web page document or a Rich Text Format document that you can open with almost any standard word processor or page-layout program.

Closing Documents

You close a document window just as you'd close any window: by clicking the close box (marked ✕) in the upper-right corner of the window, by double-clicking the top-left corner, by clicking the ✕ in its taskbar icon's preview thumbnail, or by pressing Alt+F4. If you've done any work to the document since the last time you saved it, Windows offers a "Save changes?" dialog box as a reminder.

Sometimes closing the window also exits the application, and sometimes the application remains running, even with no document windows open. And in a few *really* bizarre cases, it's possible to exit an application (like Windows Mail) while a document window (an email message) remains open on the screen, lingering and abandoned!

The Open Dialog Box

To reopen a document you've already saved and named, you can pursue any of these avenues:

- **Open your Documents library** (or whichever folder contains the saved file). Double-click the file's icon.

- **If you've opened the document recently,** choose its name from the taskbar's jump list.

- **If you're already in the program that created the document,** choose File→Open. (Or check the bottom of the File menu, where many programs add a list of recently opened files.)

- **Type the document's path and name into the Run dialog box** (⊞+R) or the address bar. (You can also browse for it.)

The Open dialog box looks almost identical to the Save As dialog box. Once again, you start out by perusing the contents of your Documents folder; once again, the dialog box otherwise behaves exactly like an Explorer window. For example, you can press Backspace to back *out* of a folder you've opened.

When you've finally located the file you want to open, double-click it or highlight it (from the keyboard, if you like), and then press Enter.

Most people don't encounter the Open dialog box nearly as often as the Save As dialog box. That's because Windows offers many more convenient ways to *open* a file (double-clicking its icon, choosing its name from the ⊞→Documents command, and so on), but only a single way to *save* a new file.

UP TO SPEED

Dialog Box Basics

To the delight of the powerful Computer Keyboard Lobby, you can manipulate almost every element of a Windows dialog box by pressing keys on the keyboard. If you're among those who feel that using the mouse to do something takes longer, then you're in luck.

The rules for navigating a dialog box are simple: Press Tab to jump from one set of options to another, or Shift+Tab to move backward. If the dialog box has multiple tabs, like the one shown here, then press Ctrl+Tab to "click" the next tab, or Ctrl+*Shift*+Tab to "click" the previous one.

Once you've highlighted a button or a checkbox, simply press the space bar to "click" it. If you've opened a drop-down list or a set of mutually exclusive *option buttons* (or *radio buttons*), then press the ↑ or ↓ keys. (Once you've highlighted a drop-down list's name, you can also press the F4 key to open it.)

Each dialog box also contains larger, rectangular buttons at the bottom (OK and Cancel, for example).

Keyboard and efficiency fans should remember that tapping the Enter key is always the equivalent of clicking the

Each time you press Tab, the PC's *focus* shifts to a different control or set of controls. Windows reveals which element has the focus by using text highlighting (if it's a text box or drop-down menu) or a dotted-line outline (if it's a button).

default button—the one with the darkened or thickened outline (the OK button in this illustration). And pressing Esc almost always means Cancel (or "Close this box").

Moving Data Between Documents

You can't paste a picture into your web browser, and you can't paste MIDI music into your desktop publishing program. But you can put graphics into your word processor, paste movies into your database, insert text into Photoshop, and combine a surprising variety of seemingly dissimilar kinds of data. And you can transfer text from web pages, email messages, and word-processing documents to other email and word-processing files; in fact, that's one of the most frequently performed tasks in all of computing.

Cut, Copy, and Paste

Most experienced PC fans have learned to quickly trigger the Cut, Copy, and Paste commands from the keyboard—without even thinking.

You can cut and copy highlighted material in any of three ways. First, you can use the Cut and Copy commands in the Edit menu; second, you can press Ctrl+X (for Cut) or Ctrl+C (for Copy); and third, you can right-click the highlighted material and, from the shortcut menu, choose Cut or Copy (Figure 6-7).

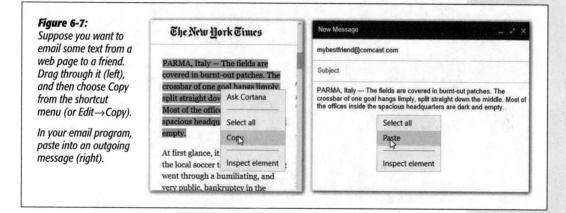

Figure 6-7:
Suppose you want to email some text from a web page to a friend. Drag through it (left), and then choose Copy from the shortcut menu (or Edit→Copy).

In your email program, paste into an outgoing message (right).

When you do so, Windows memorizes the highlighted material, stashing it on an invisible Clipboard. If you choose Copy, nothing visible happens; if you choose Cut, the highlighted material disappears from the original document.

Pasting copied or cut material, once again, is something you can do either from a menu (choose Edit→Paste), from the shortcut menu (right-click and choose Paste), or from the keyboard (press Ctrl+V).

The most recently cut or copied material remains on your Clipboard even after you paste, making it possible to paste the same blob repeatedly. Such a trick can be useful when, for example, you've designed a business card in your drawing program and want to duplicate it enough times to fill a letter-sized printout.

The Multi-Clipboard

In general, whenever you copy or cut something, whatever was *previously* on the Clipboard is lost forever. But in Windows 10, a safety net is at your disposal: the miracle of the multi-Clipboard. To turn it on, press the multi-Clipboard keystroke, ⊞ +V, and choose "Turn on." (Or open ⊞→⚙→System→Clipboard, and turn on "Clipboard history.")

From now on, you can go nuts, copying and cutting and copying and cutting. Everything you grab winds up on an invisible multi-Clipboard, which you can summon by pressing ⊞ +V (Figure 6-8). (Well, "anything" means text or graphics up to 4 megabytes in size. Stuff you've copied out of *documents*—not, for example, desktop icons.)

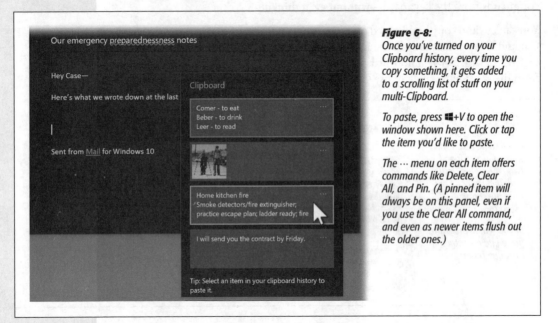

Figure 6-8:
Once you've turned on your Clipboard history, every time you copy something, it gets added to a scrolling list of stuff on your multi-Clipboard.

To paste, press ⊞+V to open the window shown here. Click or tap the item you'd like to paste.

The ⋯ menu on each item offers commands like Delete, Clear All, and Pin. (A pinned item will always be on this panel, even if you use the Clear All command, and even as newer items flush out the older ones.)

The Synced Clipboard (Cloud Clipboard)

Here's another way the Windows 10 Clipboard has grown up: Now whatever you've copied can magically and instantly appear on any other Windows 10 computers you've got (and that you've signed into with the same Microsoft ID), ready for pasting.

If this feature interests you, open ⊞→⚙→System→Clipboard, and turn on "Sync across devices." You should also make a choice between "Automatically sync text that I copy" (which works as you'd expect) and "Never automatically sync text that I copy," which is a more secure/paranoid option. It rules out the possibility that you might copy a password or a sexy email on Computer A, and that some snoopy person might log in as you on Computer B and find that text on the synced Clipboard.

In any case, that's all there is to it. Copy something (text only, and not very much of it) on Computer A, then scoot your chair over to Computer B and paste. Presto—there it is!

Tip: Microsoft says that soon, you'll be able to paste Computer A's copied text onto your Android phone, too—as long as it uses the SwiftKey virtual keyboard, which Microsoft owns.

Drag and Drop

As useful and popular as it is, the Copy/Paste routine doesn't win any awards for speed; after all, it requires four steps. In many cases, you can replace it with the far more direct (and enjoyable) drag-and-drop method. Figure 6-9 illustrates how it works.

Tip: To drag highlighted material offscreen, drag the cursor until it approaches the top or bottom edge of the window. The document scrolls automatically; as you approach the destination, jerk the mouse away from the edge of the window to stop the scrolling.

Several of the built-in Windows programs work with the drag-and-drop technique, including WordPad and Mail. Most popular commercial programs offer the drag-and-drop feature, too, including email programs and word processors, Microsoft Office programs, and so on.

Note: Scrap files—bits of text or graphics that you can drag to the desktop for later—no longer exist in Windows.

As illustrated in Figure 6-9, drag-and-drop is ideal for transferring material between windows or between programs.

FREQUENTLY ASKED QUESTION

When Formatting Is Lost

How come pasted text doesn't always look the same as what I copied?

When you copy text from a web browser, for example, and then paste it into another program, such as Word, the formatting of that text (bold, italic, font size, font color, and so on) may not reappear intact. In fact, the pasted material may not even inherit the current font settings in the word processor. There could be several reasons for this.

First, not every program *offers* text formatting. Second, the Copy command in some programs doesn't pick up the formatting along with the text. So when you paste into Word or WordPad, you may get plain, unformatted text.

Finally, a note on *text wrapping*. Thanks to limitations built into the architecture of the internet, email messages aren't like word processor documents. The text doesn't flow continuously from one line of a paragraph to the next, reflowing as you adjust the window size. Instead, email programs insert a press of the Enter key at the end of each line *within* a paragraph.

Most of the time, you don't even notice that your messages consist of dozens of one-line "paragraphs." When you see them in the email program, you can't tell the difference. But if you paste an email message into a word processor, the difference becomes painfully apparent—especially if you then attempt to adjust the margins.

To fix the page, delete the invisible carriage return at the end of each line. (Veteran PC people sometimes use the word processor's search-and-replace function for this purpose, using the character code "^p" to replace the paragraph marks.) Or, if you just need a quick look, reduce the point size (or widen the margin) until the text no longer breaks oddly.

Its most popular use, however, is rearranging the text in a single document. In, say, Word or WordPad, you can rearrange entire sections, paragraphs, sentences, or even individual letters, just by dragging them—a terrific editing technique.

Tip: Using drag-and-drop to move highlighted text within a document also deletes the text from its original location. By pressing Ctrl as you drag, however, you make a *copy* of the highlighted text.

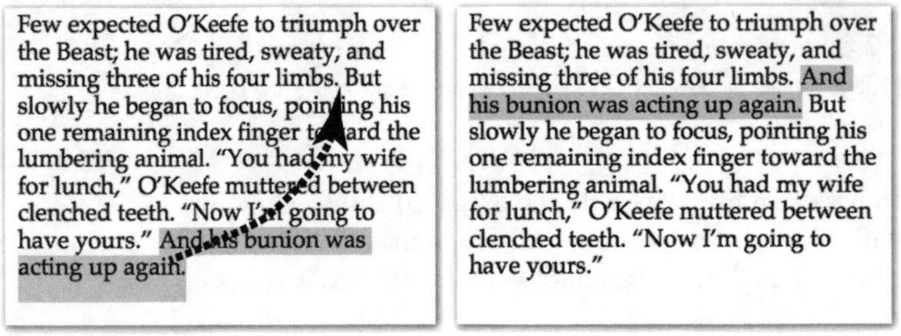

Few expected O'Keefe to triumph over the Beast; he was tired, sweaty, and missing three of his four limbs. But slowly he began to focus, pointing his one remaining index finger toward the lumbering animal. "You had my wife for lunch," O'Keefe muttered between clenched teeth. "Now I'm going to have yours." And his bunion was acting up again.

Few expected O'Keefe to triumph over the Beast; he was tired, sweaty, and missing three of his four limbs. And his bunion was acting up again. But slowly he began to focus, pointing his one remaining index finger toward the lumbering animal. "You had my wife for lunch," O'Keefe muttered between clenched teeth. "Now I'm going to have yours."

Figure 6-9:
You can drag highlighted text to another place in the document—or to a different window or program.

Export/Import

When it comes to transferring large chunks of information from one program to another—especially address books, spreadsheet cells, and database records—none of the data-transfer methods described so far in this chapter will do the trick. For such purposes, use the Export and Import commands found in the File menu of almost every database, spreadsheet, email, and address-book program.

These Export/Import commands aren't part of Windows, so the manuals or help screens of the applications in question should be your source for instructions. For now, however, the power and convenience of this feature are worth noting. Because of these commands, your four years' worth of collected names and addresses in, say, an old address-book program can find their way into a newer program, such as Mozilla Thunderbird, in a matter of minutes.

Speech Recognition and Dictation

Microsoft makes a distinction between *speech recognition* (speaking to open programs and click buttons) and *dictation* (talking to type out words). Not many people use the speech-recognition feature, which is old and a little complex. For a guide to using Windows Speech Recognition, download "Speech Recognition," a PDF appendix to this chapter. It's on this book's "Missing CD" page at *missingmanuals.com*.

The dictation feature isn't especially recent or accurate, either (especially when compared with pro dictation apps like Dragon NaturallySpeaking). But at least it's no longer hidden away. Pressing ⊞+ H opens the dictation bar so you can begin talking to type in almost any program. (On a touchscreen, hit the ⬇ on the touchscreen keyboard instead.)

The dictation bar says "Listening" when Windows is listening (it stops listening after a few seconds, with a little chime to let you know), offers the 🎤 icon to start and stop the listening, and an ✕ button to exit the whole feature. Some tips:

- **You can dictate punctuation.** Say "peaches comma plums comma and apples" to get "peaches, plums, and apples." (It helps if you pause before a punctuation mark.)

- **To dictate something with weird spelling,** say "Start spelling" and then speak the letters. You can either say their names ("C, A, T") or use the pilot's alphabet ("Charlie, alpha, tango"). (You can capitalize a letter by saying, for example, "uppercase A.") Say "stop spelling" when you want to resume whole-word dictation.

- **You can edit by voice, too.** You'll really enjoy "strike that" (or "delete that"), which nukes whatever you just uttered—handy when the transcription isn't very good. And "Select that," which *highlights* whatever you just said.

  You can also select any blob of text by specifying what it is, using "previous" or "next"; a number; and "words," "sentences," or "paragraphs." For example, "Select the previous five words."

  And you can highlight some text you've dictated (for example, to re-dictate it) by saying "select *I'm really not hungry*" (or whatever it is).

- **"Go to [a word you've dictated]"** works, too (as in "Go to *kumquat*"). So do "Go after [word]" and "Go to the end of that" (meaning everything you've got so far).

- **You can trigger** the Backspace, Enter, End, Home, Page Up, Page Down, and Delete keys by voice, too: "Tap Backspace."

Again, set expectations to low, especially when it comes to editing. But at least it's fast and free—and has its own keystroke.

Filename Extensions and File Associations

Every operating system needs a mechanism to associate documents with the applications that created them. When you double-click a Microsoft Word document icon, for example, Word launches and opens the document.

In Windows, every document comes complete with a normally invisible *filename extension* (or just *file extension*)—a period followed by a suffix that's usually three or four letters long. Here are some common examples:

When you double-click this icon...	...this program opens it.
Fishing trip.docx	Microsoft Word
Quarterly results.xlsx	Microsoft Excel
Home page.htm	your web browser
Butterfly.psd	Photoshop
Agenda.wpd	Corel WordPerfect
A home movie.avi	Windows Media Player

Tip: For an exhaustive list of every file extension in the world, visit *whatis.com*; click File Extensions.

Behind the scenes, Windows maintains a massive table that lists every extension and the program that "owns" it. More on this in a moment.

Displaying Filename Extensions

It's possible to live a long and happy life without knowing much about these extensions. Because file extensions don't feel very user-friendly, Microsoft designed Windows to *hide* the suffixes on most icons (Figure 6-10). If you're new to Windows, you may never have even seen them.

Some people appreciate the way Windows hides the extensions, because the screen becomes less cluttered and less technical-looking. Others make a good argument for the Windows 3.1 days, when every icon appeared with its suffix.

For example, in a single File Explorer window, suppose one day you discover that three icons all seem to have exactly the same name: PieThrower. Only by making

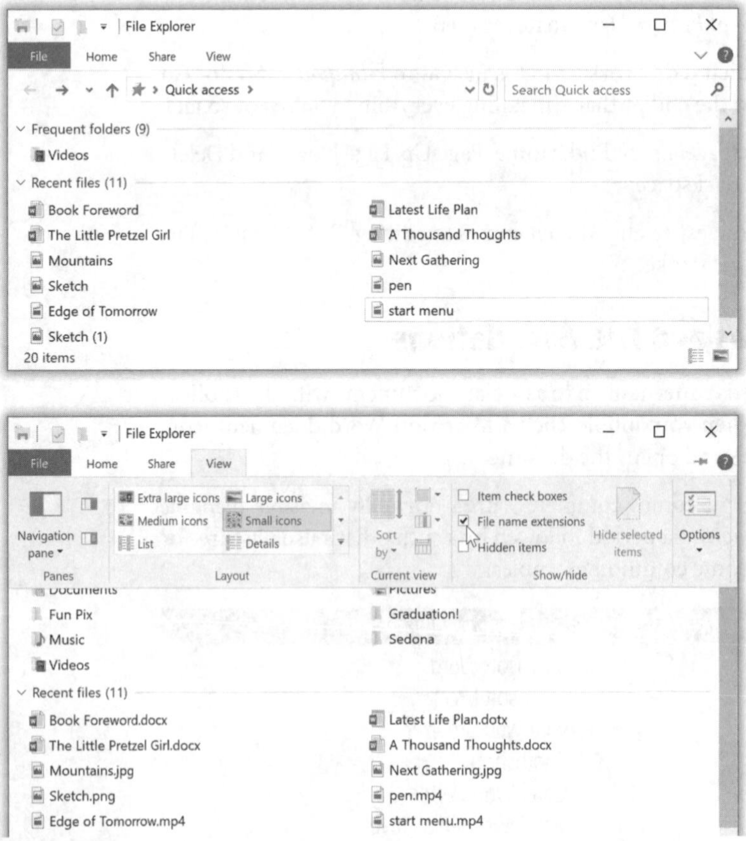

Figure 6-10:
As a rule, Windows shows filename extensions only on files whose extensions it doesn't recognize. The JPEG graphics, MP4 videos, and Word files, for example, don't show their suffixes in the top example.

You can ask Windows to display all extensions, all the time. Just use the "File name extensions" checkbox on the Ribbon's View tab, indicated by the cursor, at bottom.

filename extensions appear would you discover the answer to the mystery: that one of them is called PieThrower.ini, another is an internet-based software updater called PieThrower.upd, and the third is the actual PieThrower program, PieThrower.exe.

If you'd rather have Windows reveal the file suffixes on *all* icons, then open an Explorer window. On the Ribbon's View tab, turn on "File name extensions," as shown in Figure 6-9. Now the filename extensions for all icons appear.

Hooking Up an Unknown File Type

Every now and then, you might try to open a mystery icon—one whose extension is missing, or whose extension Windows doesn't recognize. Maybe you've been sent some weirdo document created by a beekeeper or a banjo transcriber using a program you don't have. What will happen when you double-click that file?

Windows *asks* you. It offers you two options, shown in the dialog box in Figure 6-11. First, it encourages you to go online to the Microsoft Store in hopes of finding an app that can open this file type. Good luck with that.

Usually, you'll want to click "More apps." As shown in Figure 6-11 at right, you see a list of all programs that are capable of opening this document. Click the name of the program you want, and then turn on "Always use this app to open [mystery filename extension] files," if you like.

Figure 6-11:
Left: If you're pretty sure your PC has a program that can open this mystery file, then give it a little help—click "More apps."

Right: Use this list to select a program for opening the mystery file.

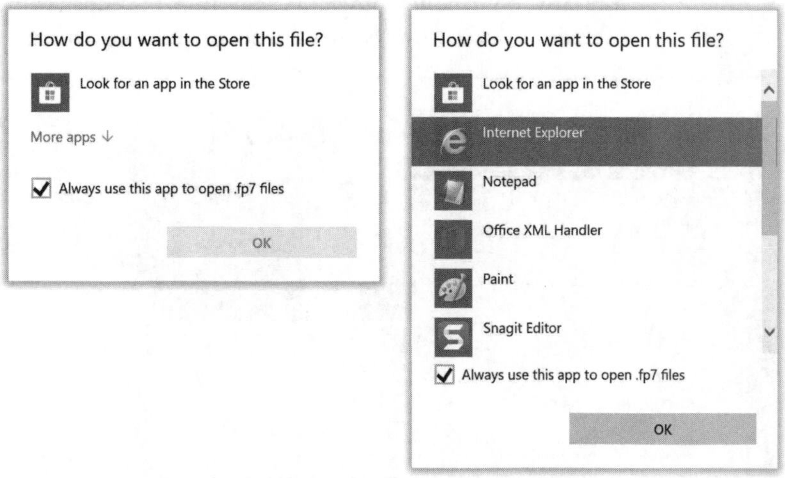

Hooking Up a File Extension to a Different Program

Windows comes with several programs that can open text files with the extension *.txt*—Notepad and WordPad, for example. There are also plenty of programs that can open picture files with the extension *.jpg*. So how does Windows decide *which* program to open when you double-click a .txt or .jpg file?

Easy—it refers to its internal database of preferred *default programs* for various file types. But at any time, you can reassign a particular file type (file extension) to a different application. If you've just bought Photoshop, for example, you might want it to open up your .jpg files, rather than the Photos app.

This sort of surgery has always confused beginners. Yet it was important for Microsoft to provide an easy way of reprogramming documents' mother programs; almost everyone ran into programs like RealPlayer that, once installed, "stole" every file association it could. The masses needed a simple way to switch documents back to their preferred programs.

Whether or not the *three* file-association mechanisms described next are actually superior to the *one* old one from Windows versions of old—well, you be the judge.

Method 1: Start with the document

Often, you'll discover a misaligned file-type association the hard way. You double-click a document and the wrong program opens it. For that reason, Microsoft has added a new way of reprogramming a document—one that starts right in File Explorer, with the document itself.

Right-click the icon of the file that needs a new parent program. From the shortcut menu, choose "Open with."

If you're just trying to open this document into the new program *this once,* you may be able to choose the new program's name from the "Open with" submenu (Figure 6-12). Windows doesn't always offer this submenu, however.

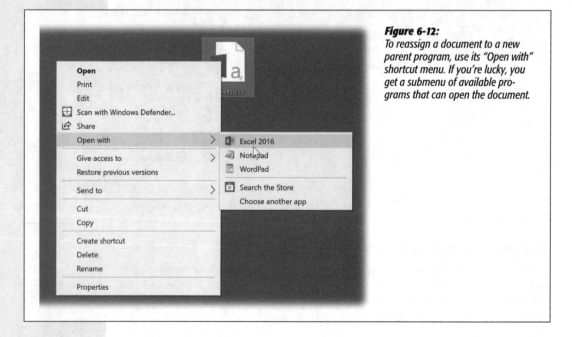

Figure 6-12:
To reassign a document to a new parent program, use its "Open with" shortcut menu. If you're lucky, you get a submenu of available programs that can open the document.

If you choose "Choose another app" from the submenu, or if there's no submenu at all, then the new "How do you want to open this file?" box appears, as shown in Figure 6-11. It's supposed to list every program on your machine that's capable of opening the document.

And now, a critical decision: Are you trying to make *only this document* open in a different program? Or *all documents of this type?*

If it's just this one, then click the program you want and stop reading. If it's *all* files of this type (all JPEGs, all MP3s, all DOC files…), then also turn on "Always use this app to open [filename extension] files" before you click the program name.

You should now be able to double-click the original document—and smile as it opens in the program you requested.

Note: If the program isn't listed, you can go find it yourself. Scroll to the very bottom of the list of proposed apps. If you see "More apps," click that. Now scroll to the very bottom again until you see the last item: "Look for another app on this PC." Now you're shown a standard Open File dialog box so you can peruse the entire contents of your Programs folder on a quest for the right software.

By the way, it's sometimes useful to associate a particular document type with a program that *didn't* create it. For example, you might prefer that double-clicking a text file created with WordPad should really open into Microsoft Word.

Method 2: Start with the program

If you'd prefer to edit the master database of file associations directly, a special control panel awaits. You can approach the problem from either direction:

- **Choose a program** and then choose which file types you want it to take over; or

- **Choose a filename extension** (like .aif or .ico) and then choose a new default program for it (Method 3, next).

Here's how to perform the first technique:

1. **Open ⊞→⚙→Apps→"Default apps."**

   You arrive on the "Default apps" page of Settings (Figure 6-13, left).

2. **Choose "Set defaults by app."**

   A curious dialog box appears, as shown at middle in Figure 6-13. It's a list of every program on your machine that's capable of opening multiple file types.

3. **Select the name of a program, and then hit Manage.**

   For example, suppose a program named FakePlayer 3.0 has performed the dreaded Windows Power Grab, claiming a particular file type for itself without asking you. In fact, suppose it has elected itself King of *All* Audio Files. But you want Windows Media Player to play everything *except* FakePlayer (.fkpl) files.

   In this step, then, you'd click Windows Media Player, and then Manage.

Now yet another dialog box opens. It lists every file type the selected program knows about (Figure 6-13, right).

4. **For each file type, choose the program you want to be the default opener.**

To do that, choose the name of the *currently* assigned app ("Movies & TV" in Figure 6-13 at right); from the list of alternate apps, select the one you want.

Of course, this step requires a certain amount of knowledge that comes from experience—how the heck would the average person know what, say, a .wvx file is?—but it's here for the power geeks' benefit.

5. **Close Settings.**

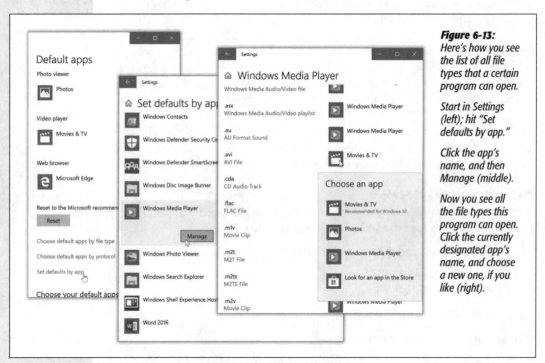

Figure 6-13:
Here's how you see the list of all file types that a certain program can open.

Start in Settings (left); hit "Set defaults by app."

Click the app's name, and then Manage (middle).

Now you see all the file types this program can open. Click the currently designated app's name, and choose a new one, if you like (right).

Method 3: Start with the file type (or protocol)

Finally, you can approach the file-association problem by working through a massive alphabetical list of filename extensions (.aca, .acf, .acs, .aif, and so on) and hooking each one up to a program of your choice.

Open ⊞→⚙→Apps→"Default apps" Figure 6-13, left). Choose "Choose default apps by file type."

After a moment, a massive list of filename extensions opens, showing which program is *currently* assigned to open it. Select the filename extension you want, and then click the name of the currently assigned app. (This process looks a lot like Figure 6-13 at right.)

Click the name of the new default program. (Once again, if you don't see it listed here, you can use "Look for an app in the Store," to find it yourself.) Close Settings.

Choosing Your Default Apps

Windows comes with a web browser, a calendar app, an email program, a maps app, and players for music, photos, and videos. Very nice of Microsoft, isn't it?

The courts—in the U.S. and Europe—didn't think so. They thought Microsoft was stifling competition by including all these goodies in Windows. Who'd bother trying anybody else's web browser, if Microsoft put its own right under your nose?

Ever since, Microsoft has included a Settings panel like the one shown in Figure 6-14. Here you can click the name of Microsoft's program (for web browser, calendar, maps, and so on), and choose the name of a rival to use instead.

So what, exactly, is a *default* app? It's the one that opens automatically. For example, if I email you a link to a cool website, the default browser is the one that will open

Figure 6-14:
In ■→⚙→*Apps→ "Default apps," you can choose to replace Microsoft's starter apps with other companies' wares. For your web browser, for example, you might prefer Chrome, Firefox, or even Internet Explorer instead of Microsoft Edge.*

To make a change, just click the name of the existing app and choose a replacement from the list that appears.

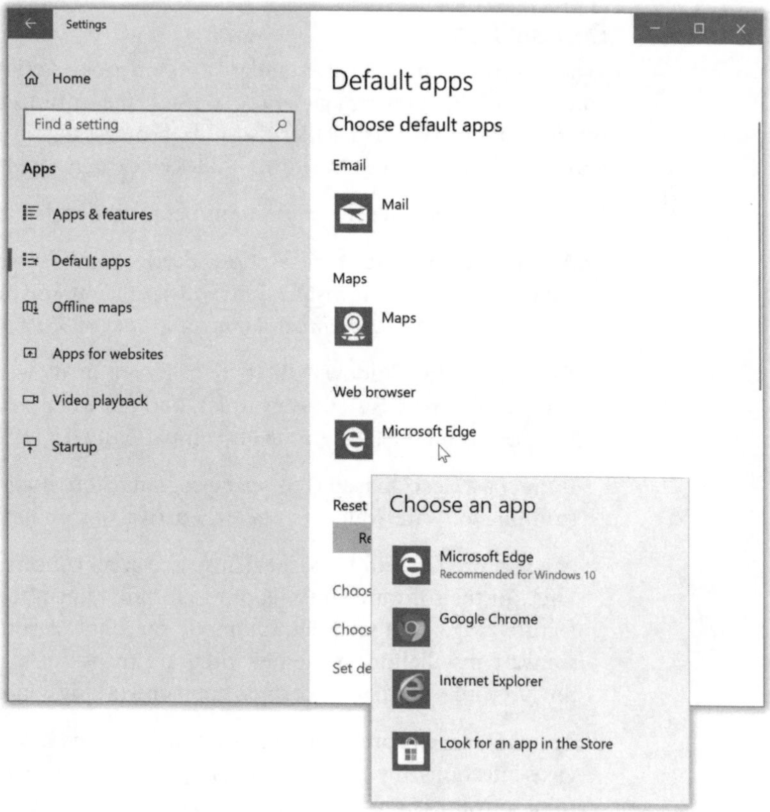

when you click the link. It's the photo program that opens when you double-click a picture file. And so on.

Installing New Apps

Most people don't buy their computers from Microsoft. Most computers come from companies like Dell, HP, Acer, and Lenovo; they install Windows on each computer before customers take delivery.

Many PC companies sweeten the pot by preinstalling other programs, such as Quicken, Microsoft Works, Microsoft Office, more games, educational software, and so on. The great thing about preloaded programs is that they don't need installing. Just double-click their desktop icons, or choose their names from the Start menu, and you're off and working.

Sooner or later, though, you'll probably want to exploit the massive library of Windows software and add to your collection. Today, almost all new desktop software comes to your PC from the internet. (Software is sometimes still sold on a CD or DVD, but that happens less and less often.)

Desktop Apps

When you buy or download a standard desktop program (iTunes, Quicken, what have you), an installer program generally transfers the software files to the correct places on your hard drive. The installer also adds the new program's name to the Start menu and tells Windows about the kinds of files (file extensions) it can open.

For best results, answer these questions before you install anything:

- **Are you an administrator?** Windows derives part of its security and stability from handling new software installations with suspicion. You can't install most programs unless you have an *Administrator account* (page 536).

- **Does it run in Windows 10?** If the software or its website specifically says it's compatible, great. Install away. If not, find out when a compatible version is due. See the box on the facing page for compatibility tips.

- **Is the coast clear?** Exit all your open programs. You should also turn off your virus-scanning software, which may take the arrival of your new software the wrong way.

- **Are you prepared to backtrack?** If you're at all concerned about the health and safety of the software you're about to install, remember that the System Restore feature (page 509) takes an automatic snapshot of your system just before any software installation. If the new program turns out to be a bit hostile, you can rewind your system to its former, happier working condition.

- **Are you darned sure?** Internet downloads are the most common sources of PC virus infections. If you're downloading from a brand-name site like *shareware.com* (or a software company's site, like *microsoft.com*), you're generally safe. But if the site is unfamiliar, be very, very afraid.

You can find thousands of Windows programs (demos, free programs, and shareware) at websites like *download.com* or *tucows.com*.

Microsoft Store Apps

Microsoft is hoping to pull an Apple here: It wants its *online* software store to be your one-stop software shopping mall.

The Microsoft Store is an online catalog of software from huge software companies, tiny one-person software companies, and everything in between. You can read about the apps, check out customer reviews, and, finally, download them directly to your computer. (As you may recall from page 207, the store is the *only* source of menuless, Windows 8–style Microsoft Store apps.)

There are some huge advantages to this system. Since there's no box, DVD, registration card, shipping, or stocking, the software can cost a lot less. Plenty of programs in the Microsoft Store are free, and many paid ones offer a free seven-day trial.

Furthermore, Microsoft controls the transaction on both ends—it knows who you are—so there are no serial numbers to type in. The installation doesn't have to interrupt you with warnings like "Please enter your password to install this software." Once you click Buy, Try, or Install, the software downloads and installs itself automatically, without any interaction from you at all.

FREQUENTLY ASKED QUESTION

Really Ancient Apps

Will Windows 10 run my really old, really important app?

You'll never really know until you try. And this chapter outlines all the tools available to help you make the old app run. But here are some specifics on what you can expect.

First of all, 16-bit programs are so old, they were written when Windows 3.1 roamed the earth and the first George Bush was president. (Programs written for Windows 95 and later are known as *32-bit* programs; Windows 10 can even run *64-bit* programs.) But, amazingly enough, the 32-bit versions of Windows 10 (though not the 64-bit versions; see the box on page 237) can run most of these programs. They do so in a kind of software simulator—a DOS-and-Windows 3.1 PC impersonation called a *virtual machine.*

As a result, these programs don't run very fast, don't understand the long filenames of modern-day Windows, and may crash whenever they try to "speak" directly to certain components of your hardware. (The simulator stands in their way, in the name of keeping Windows stable.) Furthermore,

if just one of your 16-bit programs crashes, then *all* of them crash, because they all live in the same memory bubble.

Even so, it's impressive that they run at all, 15 years later.

DOS programs are 16-bit programs, too, and therefore they run just fine in 32-bit versions of Windows, even though DOS no longer lurks beneath the operating system.

To open the black, empty DOS window that's familiar to PC veterans, press ⊞+R, type *command.com*, and then press Enter.

For the best possible compatibility with DOS programs—and to run DOS programs in a 64-bit copy of Windows—try out DOSBox (*dosbox.com*), which emulates a classic 16-bit computer, complete with DOS compatibility. It's great for those old DOS games that haven't run correctly on Windows since the days of Windows 95.

Programs written for Windows 95, 2000, and XP usually run OK in the Compatibility mode described on these pages.

There are no disks to store and hunt down later, either. If you ever need to reinstall a program from the Microsoft Store, or if you ever get a new PC, you just re-download it; the store remembers that you're a legitimate owner. Better yet, you'll be downloading the latest version of that program; you won't have to install all the ".01" patches that have come along since.

Best of all, since Microsoft knows what programs you have, it can let you know when new versions are available. You'll see the word "Updates" in the upper-right corner of the Microsoft Store and on the updated app's Start menu tile; the store tile on the Start menu shows how many updates await. Tap it to see the apps for which more recent versions are ready. (Tap Install to grab all of them at once.)

Navigating the Store

To use the Microsoft Store, open the store tile on your Start menu. As shown in Figure 6-15 (top), the store looks like it's been printed on an endless paper-towel roll; it scrolls for miles.

There are thousands of these apps, so Microsoft tries to bring a few choice morsels to the surface with categories like "Picks for you," "Top free apps" (most downloaded) and "Top paid apps" (the most downloaded ones that cost money).

At the top of the Home screen: an "App categories" link. It opens a sublist of categories like Sports, Travel, Shopping, and so on—another way to dive into the app ocean.

Of course, you can also search for an app by name or by nature. To do that, click in the search box and type (*piano, stocks, fantasy football*, or whatever).

In general, the store here works exactly like the app store on a smartphone. Tap a program's icon to open its details page. Here you'll find reviews and ratings from other people, a description, screenshots of the program, and much more information to help you make a good buying decision. See Figure 6-15, bottom.

When you find an app that looks good, tap Get (if it's free) or its price button or Free Trial button (if it's not). When the download is complete, that button changes to say Open. You never have to enter your password, restart, unzip, or manually install anything.

Note: The Microsoft Store lists desktop apps, too (not just Microsoft Store apps). But you don't actually buy and download desktop apps from the Microsoft Store; you get a link to the software company's website for that purpose. The only programs you can actually download from the Microsoft Store are, indeed, Microsoft Store apps.

Automatic updates

Software companies frequently update Microsoft Store apps, just as they do with phone and tablet apps. They fix bugs; they add new features. As it turns out, new versions of your Microsoft Store apps get installed quietly and automatically, in the background. You're not even aware it's happening.

Microsoft says it inspects each app to make sure Automatic App Updates doesn't hand you something that doesn't work right. But it does sometimes happen: You prefer the original version of some app to the "new, improved" one—and if automatic updates is turned on, you'll never have the opportunity to object.

So: If the automatic-updates business is a little too automatic for your taste, you can turn it off. In the store app, click your own icon (the round one next to the search box); from the shortcut menu, choose Settings, and then turn off "Update apps automatically."

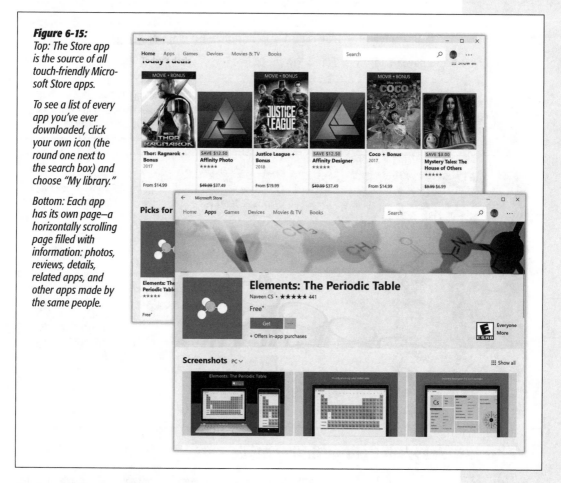

Figure 6-15:
Top: The Store app is the source of all touch-friendly Microsoft Store apps.

To see a list of every app you've ever downloaded, click your own icon (the round one next to the search box) and choose "My library."

Bottom: Each app has its own page—a horizontally scrolling page filled with information: photos, reviews, details, related apps, and other apps made by the same people.

Uninstalling Software

When you've had enough of a certain program and want to reclaim the disk space it occupies, don't just delete its folder. The typical application installer tosses its software components like birdseed all over your hard drive; therefore, only some of the program is actually in the program's folder.

Instead, the proper method goes like this:

- **Enlightened programs (released since Windows 10).** Open the Start menu's "All apps" list. Right-click the program's name. From the shortcut menu, choose Uninstall (Figure 6-16, left).

Note: Here's a small blessing: In the May 2019 Update, you can uninstall almost all of Microsoft's built-in apps this way, including Paint 3D, Groove Music, and Mail. (Edge and the Microsoft Store are still permanent installations.)

- **Older programs.** Open the "Apps & features" page of Settings (■→⚙→Apps→ "Apps & features"). Select the app, and then hit Uninstall (Figure 6-16, right).

You have to admit it: *That* is progress, is it not?

Note: If you don't see the name of the app you want to remove in Settings, it must be a truly ancient, creaking piece of work. You might have to open the old Control Panel and navigate to the Programs and Features page (page 275), to remove it.

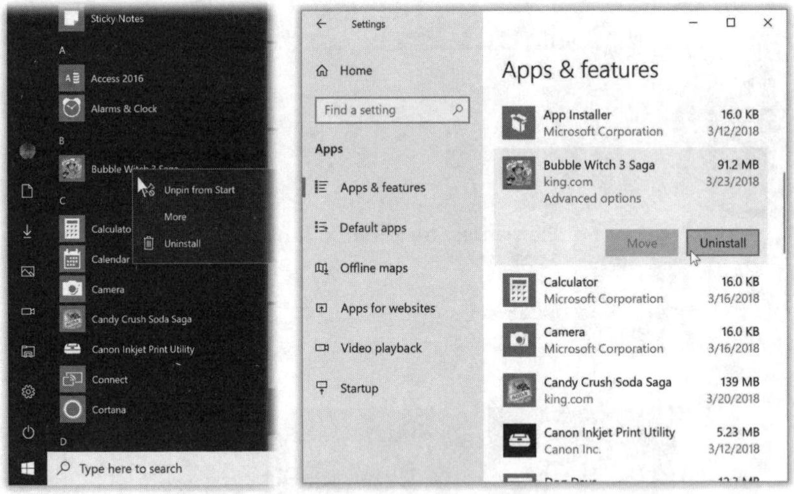

Figure 6-16:
Before Windows 10, uninstalling one of your apps sometimes required a power drill, a blowtorch, and a six-volume instruction manual. Now it's as easy as right-clicking in the "All apps list" (left) or clicking the program's name in Settings.

Program Compatibility Mode

"You can't make an omelet without breaking a few eggs." If that's not Microsoft's motto, it should be. Each successive version of Windows may be better than the previous one, but each inevitably winds up "breaking" hundreds of programs, utilities, and drivers that used to run just fine.

In principle, programs that were written for recent versions of Windows should run fine in Windows 10. Unfortunately, some of them contain software code that deliberately sniffs around to find out what Windows version you have. These programs (or even their installer programs) may say, "Windows *what*?"—and refuse to open.

Fortunately, Windows' Compatibility mode has some sneaky tricks that can fool them into running. You can use it to make "Let me run!" changes to a stubborn app either the non-techie, wizardly way (you just answer questions in a screen-by-screen interview format, and let Windows make the changes behind the scenes) or the expert way (changing compatibility settings manually).

To let Windows fix your compatibility headache, open the Start menu. Start typing *compatibility* until you see "Run programs made for previous versions of Windows." Choose it.

The Program Compatibility program opens. It's a wizard—a series of dialog boxes that interview you. On the way, you're asked to click the name of the program you're

---

UP TO SPEED

A Little Bit About 64 Bits

Windows 10 is available in both 32-bit and 64-bit versions.

Right. 64 what?

If you want your eyes to glaze over, you can read the details on 64-bit computing on Wikipedia. But the normal-person's version goes like this:

For decades, the roadways for memory and information that passed through PCs were 32 "lanes" wide—they could manage 32 chunks of data at once. It seemed like plenty at the time. But as programs and even documents grew enormous, and computers came with the capacity to have more and more memory installed, engineers began to dream of 64-lane circuitry.

To reach 64-bit nirvana, however, you need a 64-bit computer running the 64-bit version of Windows. Sometimes, you don't have a choice. For example, if your PC comes with 4 gigabytes of memory or more, it has 64-bit Windows, like it or not. Otherwise, though, you probably do have a choice. Which version should you go for?

In the short term, the most visible effect of having a 64-bit computer is that you can install a lot more memory. A top-of-the-line 32-bit PC, for example, is limited to 4 GB of RAM—and only about 3 GB is actually available to your

programs. That once seemed like a lot, but it's suffocatingly small if you're a modern video editor, game designer, or number-crunchy engineer.

On a 64-bit PC with 64-bit Windows, though, you can install just a tad bit more memory: 192 GB. Eventually, there may be other benefits to a 64-bit PC. Programs can be rewritten to run faster. Security can be better, too.

For now, though, there are some downsides to going 64-bit. For example, older, 32-bit programs mostly run fine on a 64-bit machine. But some won't run at all, and 32-bit drivers for older hardware (sound cards, graphics cards, printers, and so on) may give you particular headaches.

You can't run 16-bit programs at all in 64-bit Windows, either (at least not without an add-on program like DOSBox).

If you have taken the 64-bit plunge, you generally don't have to know whether your apps are running in 32- or 64-bit mode; every kind of program runs in the right mode automatically. If you ever want to see how many of your apps are actually 32-bitters, though, press Ctrl+Shift+Esc to open the Task Manager; then click the Processes tab. The 32-bit programs you have open are indicated by "(32 bit)" after their names.

---

having trouble with. On the following screen, you have a choice of automatic or manual modes:

- **Try recommended settings** means "Let Windows try to figure out how to make this stubborn program run. I don't really care what it has to tinker with under the hood."

- **Troubleshoot program** means "Let me adjust the compatibility settings myself."

You'll be asked to choose from options like "The program worked in earlier versions of Windows," "The program opens but doesn't display correctly," and so on. Work through the question screens the best you can. When it's all over, you get a "Start the program" button that lets you see if the program finally runs without problems.

Whether things are fixed or not, after you've checked out the app, return to the troubleshooting wizard and click Next. You'll be able to (a) save the fixed settings for the future, (b) start a new round of troubleshooting, or (c) send a report to Microsoft that you never did solve the problem.

Pick Up Where You Left Off

Microsoft has realized that we use more than one gadget through the course of the day. In fact, *they may not all be Windows 10 machines.* Incredibly, some people actually use Apple or Android products!

Acknowledging those factors, Microsoft has come up with something you may find quite elegant, even if its name is not: "Pick up where you left off."

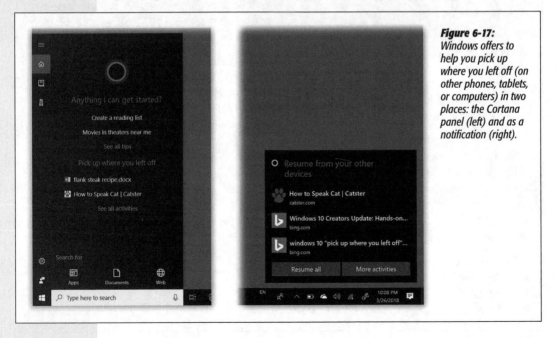

Figure 6-17:
Windows offers to help you pick up where you left off (on other phones, tablets, or computers) in two places: the Cortana panel (left) and as a notification (right).

Suppose that, on the train home from work, you do some work on your laptop (or iPhone, or Android phone) in a Microsoft Office program, and you visit a website in Microsoft Edge. When you get home, you can fire up your desktop PC—and, lo, a notification appears, offering to let you resume what you were doing on *this* computer! If you open the Cortana panel, you'll see similar links there, too (Figure 6-17).

It's all designed to make your work life more seamless.

Amazingly, these buttons also incorporate documents and websites you've visited using Microsoft apps on Macs, Android phones, and iPhones!

In the unlikely event that you don't find these offers helpful, you can shut the whole thing down. Open Settings→Cortana→Permissions→"Manage the information Cortana can access from this device." Turn off the three switches you find there.

Continue on PC

This feature is similar to "Pick up where you left off," but different. This one lets you send any web page you're viewing on your iPhone or Android phone directly to your Windows 10 PC, wirelessly and instantly. There's nothing to click on the PC—the page just opens up in Edge automatically, as though a ghost were at the helm!

Start in ⊞→☼→Phone→"Add a phone." Enter your phone's number so Microsoft can text you a code, which you input here. The Settings page gives you a link to download a special app called Continue on PC (Android) or Microsoft Edge (iPhone) from the corresponding app store.

Install the app and sign in with your Microsoft ID. Then, once you're on a web page you want to transmit, tap the Share button. (iPhone: It's at the bottom of the Edge browser app screen. Android: Tap the usual Share button, and then Continue on PC.) Tap the name of your PC. Boom: Whatever page you're viewing magically pops up on the PC's screen, at full size and in living color!

Tip: If you tap "Continue later" instead of the name of a PC, a notification message pops up briefly on your PC, and the Action Center gains a new item: "Continue from your phone," complete with a link to the website you shared. Use that when you're on the go and want to flag that site for your return.

Windows Sandbox

As you may have heard, not everyone on the internet is nice. Some people distribute viruses, scams, hoaxes, and other nastiness online. On purpose!

They may, for example, create an app that looks super-cool—"Microsoft Instant Weight Loss App," for example, or "Insta-Riches," or "Naked Hotties App." Unbeknownst to you, however, it's actually designed to install malware or to spy on you. How could you know? And how can you try it out without risking your machine?

With the May 2019 Update, Microsoft has an answer. The Sandbox app (Figure 6-18) creates a titanium bubble within Windows. You can run any app inside this window without worrying. The app can't touch anything else on your PC! It's completely isolated—and when you quit Sandbox, no trace of the app or its activity remains.

The Sandbox starts out hidden, because it's intended for power users. To find it, open the Control Panel (page 264)→Programs→Turn Windows Features On or Off. Turn on "Windows Sandbox."

Now a new app, Windows Sandbox, magically appears in your Start menu. When you open it, you get a floating window that's a perfect duplicate of your current version of Windows—but it's a virgin setup, as though it's been a clean install.

Feel free to download and install anything you want in this inner sanctum; no matter how sketchy or infected it may be, it can't hurt your actual PC or your copy of Windows.

When you're finished playing, close the app, confirm that you want everything in that mini–Windows world completely vaporized, and marvel at Microsoft's ingenuity.

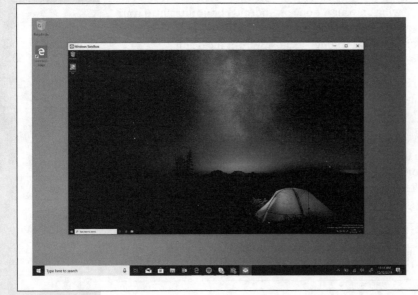

Figure 6-18:
The Windows Sandbox app is a simulated PC that's completely isolated from the rest of your machine. In it, you can run super-questionable apps without worrying that they'll infect the rest of your machine.

If you're technically inclined, you may have heard of a virtual machine. Sandbox is kinda like that. In fact, Sandbox works only if your PC is capable of running a virtual machine; see http://j.mp/2Hf5ANg.

CHAPTER 7

Settings & Control Panel

Every complex machine has a control panel. There's the dashboard of a car, the knobs on a stove, the cockpit of an airplane. And then there's the granddaddy of them all: the Control Panel in Windows.

Actually, in Windows 10, the Control Panel isn't very important anymore. It's still there—like an old typewriter you can't bear to throw away—and you can still read about it later in this chapter.

But in Windows 10, Microsoft has extracted a few hundred of the Control Panel's most useful options and packaged them up into a new app called Settings. It's far cleaner, simpler, and better organized, and it's designed to accommodate either a mouse or your finger on a touchscreen.

With every new Windows 10 update, Microsoft moves more controls out of the old Control Panel and into Settings. At this point, only the most obscure settings require a visit to the Control Panel—and the Settings app has gotten *huge*.

The Settings App

Most of the time, you'll customize your system in the Settings app. Volume, screen saver, Wi-Fi setup, privacy settings, PC accounts, color schemes, and so on—it's all here, in one place.

And how do you get "here"? There are many avenues to Settings. But the fastest is to open the Start menu and choose the Settings icon (⚙) at far left. Or press ⊞ + I. (That's I for *settIngs*, of course.)

You now encounter the magnificence of the Windows 10 Settings app (Figure 7-1).

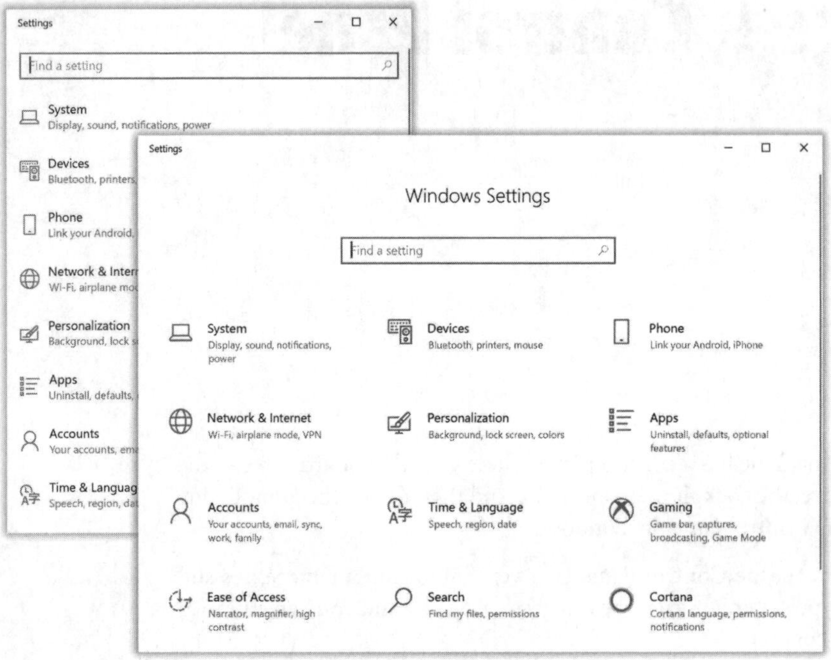

Figure 7-1:
The Settings app looks like the image at right when you first open it. But what's this? No list view available? Not to worry. If you grab the right edge and drag it inward, making the window narrower, the window redraws itself as a compact list view (left).

Direct Access to Settings Pages

The 13 broad categories of Settings are described on the following pages.

But you should know that you're wasting your time if you *click or tap* your way into a settings screen. It's almost always faster to search for *settings*, or to ask Cortana to open a screen for you. Say, "Open Wi-Fi settings," for example. You'll jump right to the page you want.

Tip: If there's a certain Settings page you use often, here's an idea that may not have occurred to you: Install its tile on the Start menu!

Once the Settings app is open, you can right-click either a Settings category (like System or Devices) or an individual Settings page (like Battery Saver or Storage). From the shortcut menu, choose Pin to Start. Boom—there it is.

Handily enough, the search produces results both from Settings and from the old Control Panel.

System

At top left in the Settings app is the most important category here: System. This icon is the gateway to individual screens for power, storage, notifications, apps, and screen settings. Click it to reveal the following settings pages inside (Figure 7-2).

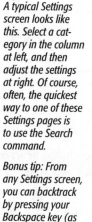

Figure 7-2:
A typical Settings screen looks like this. Select a category in the column at left, and then adjust the settings at right. Of course, often, the quickest way to one of these Settings pages is to use the Search command.

Bonus tip: From any Settings screen, you can backtrack by pressing your Backspace key (as long as your cursor is not in the search box).

Display

These settings govern the size of type on your screen, serve as the dashboard for multiple-monitor setups, and control a cool (well, warm, really) function called Night Light. Page 167 describes it all.

Sound

This screen controls every aspect of your microphone and speakers:

- **Choose your output device,** of course, lets you specify where your computer should play its sound: the built-in speakers? A Bluetooth wireless speaker? Headphones? Choose from this drop-down menu.

- **Volume.** This slider is your PC's master volume slider. (There are of course more efficient ways to adjust the volume—like using your volume keys or the volume control on your system tray.)

- **Troubleshoot.** Opens the sound "troubleshooter," which walks you through some steps to figure out why you're not hearing anything.

- **Input.** What microphone should your PC "listen to"? Of course, your machine probably has only one—but you know. Just in case.

  There's a live microphone-testing graph here, too, which dances around as it hears sound, and another Troubleshoot button.

- **App volume and device preferences.** This feature lets you adjust volume levels and microphone/speaker setups individually for apps or devices connected to your PC. You know: headphones for Spotify, built-in speaker for error beeps. (Apps have to be specially written to hook into this feature; you may not see many listed here at first.)

- **Bluetooth and other devices.** Opens the panel described on page 247.

- **Sound control panel.** Opens the panel described on page 159.

Notifications & Actions

Here you can tame the notifications—the little bubbles that pop onto your screen to alert you about this or that—that might otherwise interrupt you to insanity (page 91).

This screen also offers a link for choosing and arranging the tiles you want on your Quick Actions palette; see page 97.

Focus Assist

This "Do not disturb" feature is described nicely on page 93.

Power & Sleep

These options manage the power consumption of your computer. That's a big deal when you're running on battery power, of course, but it's also important if you'd like to save money (and the environment) by cutting down on the juice consumed by your *desktop* PC.

The drop-down menus here govern the sleeping habits of two components: your screen and the computer itself. The sooner they sleep, the more power you save. The drop-down menus let you choose intervals from "1 minute" to "Never."

Of course, when your PC is plugged in, you might not care so much about battery savings—so you get a second set of drop-down menus that govern sleep schedules when the machine has wall power.

Finally, "Network connection" (available for machines with batteries) specifies whether or not you want your laptop or tablet to remain connected to the network when it's asleep and not plugged into power. Your choices are Never, Always, and Managed by Windows, meaning that only certain apps are allowed to stay connected to the network: internet calling apps like Skype and apps you've allowed to run in the background (in ■→ ⊚ →Privacy→ "Background apps").

Tip: The "Additional power settings" link opens up the old Power Options page of the Control Panel, where you have far more detailed control over various elements of your computer and how much power they use.

Battery

Here, all in one handy dashboard, is everything you need to know about the battery of your tablet or laptop. It's all covered in Chapter 12.

Storage

This screen is all about storage—of your files and apps.

- **Storage Sense** frees up space by deleting junk files automatically. See page 522 for details.

- **Local storage** shows a graph of your main drive, showing how full it is—and showing *what* is using up all your space, broken down by System, Apps, Pictures, and so on. (Click "Show more categories" for a bigger breakdown.)

- **View storage on other drives** offers "what's eating you?" graphs for drives beyond your main one.

- **Change where new content is saved** is designed for people who have external drives connected to their PCs, so they can keep big files like pictures, music, and videos in separate, roomier places.

  In the resulting dialog box: pop-up menus for documents, music, pictures, and videos. For each, you can choose your PC or an external drive's name and letter. From now on, whenever you download or import files of those types, Windows stores them on the specified drives, for your convenience.

  (Of course, whatever change you make here doesn't affect the current locations of any files—only future ones.)

- **Manage Storage Spaces.** For details on this "save everything onto two drives simultaneously" safety feature, see the free "Storage Spaces" PDF appendix on this book's "Missing CD" page at *missingmanuals.com*.

- **Optimize Drives.** See the free "Disk Defragmenter" PDF appendix on the "Missing CD" at *missingmanuals.com*.

Tablet Mode

This mode means, "I have no keyboard or mouse. Make this tablet easier to use!" See page 449 for details. You can also control the suggestions you see in your Timeline, described on page 210.

Multitasking

These are the options that control window snapping, and they're described on page 47.

Also tucked in here: The option to turn off the Timeline (page 210), and a couple of options for the virtual-screens feature described on page 173. For example:

- **On the taskbar, show windows that are open on:** The taskbar's job is to sprout icons for all your open windows. But what if you've set up a couple of virtual monitors? Should the taskbar change as you switch from "monitor" to "monitor," showing buttons only for the apps on the current desktop? Or should it always reflect *all* your open windows on all the desktops?

- **Pressing Alt+Tab shows windows that are open on:** Similar question. When you press the app-switching keystroke (page 208), should the app switcher show the window miniatures for *all* the windows on *all* your desktops? Or just the one you're using right now?

Next, this screen offers the "Multitask with multiple desktops" link opens a web page that explains virtual screens (but not as thoroughly as page 173).

Projecting to This PC

How'd you like to use your big computer screen as a wireless display for your phone? See page 175.

Shared Experiences

"Nearby sharing" is Microsoft's term for what Apple calls AirDrop: a slick, simple way to shoot a file from one PC to another—without involving any setup, network settings, or user accounts; see page 564.

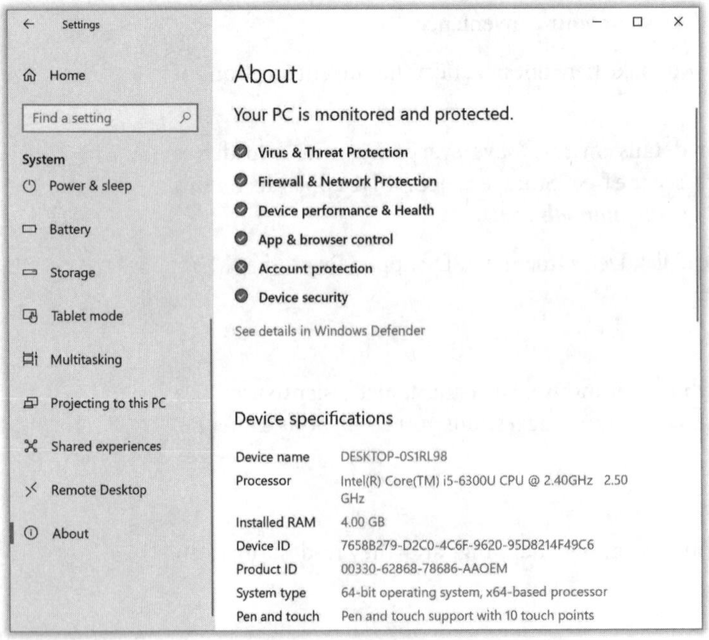

Figure 7-3:
The About screen has two parts. At top, a summary of your PC's vulnerability to various threats.

Below that, you'll find your computer's name, network, Windows version, memory, and processor. This screen also shows whether you have a 32-bit or 64-bit system (page 237), and lets you know whether or not you have a touchscreen, although just touching your screen is usually a faster way to figure that out.

Clipboard

Here's the headquarters for the newish multi-Clipboard feature and the synced-Clipboard feature (page 222).

Remote Desktop

Believe it or not, you can connect to your PC from across the internet, rifle through its files, and control it—using any computer or phone (even an Apple or Android one) as a viewer. For details, go online to *missingmanuals.com* and look for the free PDF appendix to this book called "Remote Desktop."

About

Here's a master list of all the aspects of your computer that Windows Defender Security Center is currently protecting (page 408), plus your computer's birth certificate (Figure 7-3).

Devices

This second major Settings category is the grand depot for connecting other devices: printers, scanners, cameras, and so on. Its tabs go like this:

Bluetooth & Other Devices

Bluetooth is a cable-elimination technology. It's designed to let gadgets communicate wirelessly within about 30 feet, using radio signals.

It's built into most computers and cellphones, so you can connect them with Bluetooth speakers, earbuds, mice, keyboards, fitness bands, smartwatches, printers, and so on.

Bluetooth is pretty slow (you get transfer speeds of 30 to 150 K per second, depending on the distance). But it works no matter what the gadget—Mac, Windows, smartphone—so it's great as a universal file-exchange translator, too.

In any case, this screen is Bluetooth Central, where you introduce your PC to wireless speakers, keyboards, mice, earbuds, and other Bluetooth gadgets. Here's what's on it:

- **Bluetooth On.** Here's the on/off switch for your computer's ability to connect wirelessly to Bluetooth gadgets. Below it: your PC's name, as you'll see it listed on the Bluetooth device's screen, if any. (There are two quicker ways to turn Bluetooth on or off, though: Use the Action Center tile or tell Cortana.)

- **[List of Bluetooth gadgets.]** Here's the list of Bluetooth gizmos you've already connected wirelessly to your PC: mouse, keyboard, speakers, and so on. If you select one, you reveal a "Remove device" button.

- **Add Bluetooth or other device.** On the other hand, when you want to *add* a connection, start by putting your Bluetooth gadget in pairing mode. That's probably the hardest part of the whole process; you may have to peer at its user guide under an electron microscope to find out what buttons you have to hold down to get pairing mode going.

Then use this button ("Add Bluetooth or other device"), and proceed as shown in Figure 7-4.

- **Download over metered connections.** This checkbox lets you save money by preventing your PC from downloading device software (drivers and so on) while you're on a pay-as-you-go internet connection.

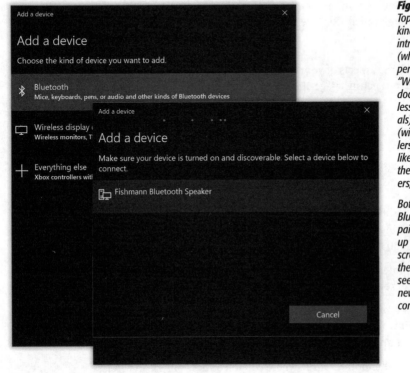

Figure 7-4:
Top: You're asked what kind of doodad you're introducing: Bluetooth (what you want 90 percent of the time), "Wireless display or dock" (to connect wireless Bluetooth peripherals), or "Everything else" (wireless Xbox controllers, DLNA-logo products like game consoles, home theater systems, speakers, storage devices).

Bottom: Once your Bluetooth gadget in is pairing mode, it shows up on the "Add a device" screen. Select it, enter the pairing code if you see one, and enjoy your new short-range wireless connection.

Printers & Scanners

Here's your list of printers and scanners that Windows knows about—and your opportunity to connect a new one. See Chapter 13.

Mouse

On this page, you can tweak the most essential behaviors of your pointing device:

- **Primary mouse button.** The primary mouse button is the one you press for normal clicks (as opposed to right-clicks). If you're left-handed, you may prefer to switch the buttons so the *right* button is the primary one.

- **Roll the mouse wheel to scroll.** If you have a mouse, and it has a scroll wheel, this drop-down menu lets you change the behavior of each "click" of that wheel. Does it scroll a few lines at a time, or a whole screenful?

If you choose "Multiple lines at a time," you can then use the slider to specify how *many* lines at a time, to suit how caffeinated your style is.

- **Scroll inactive windows when I hover over them.** The question is: When your cursor is in front of a background window—not the one you're working in—what should happen when you turn the mouse wheel? Should that window scroll? (Usually you want this on. It's handy.)

- **Additional mouse options.** Boom—you wind up in the cramped, ancient Control Panel, where you can set up a few additional mouse features (page 273).

Touchpad

This screen appears if you're using a laptop; it's got every conceivable setting for your trackpad. See page 440 for details.

Typing

In theory, your keyboard is something you'll use quite a bit, whether it's the physical one built into your laptop, a wireless one connected to your desktop, or an onscreen one you use on a tablet. Fortunately, you can tweak it to your liking.

Some of these options appear only if you have a tablet or hybrid laptop (whose keyboard comes off).

- **Autocorrect misspelled words.** You might have noticed that, as you type, Windows quietly and instantly corrects your obvious typos. (Or maybe you *haven't* noticed, which is even more awesome.)

  In other words, if you type "prolbem," for example, it changes to "problem" the instant you press the space bar at the end of the word. There's no beep, no underline, no error message; the correction just happens.

Note: On the other hand, these spell-checking features work only in Microsoft Store apps—Calendar, Maps, Photos, and the like—not traditional desktop apps like Notepad. So maybe you really *haven't* seen them.

Anyway, here's the on/off switch for autocorrect—handy if, for example, you're writing a novel featuring a character with really bad spelling.

- **Highlight misspelled words.** But what about a word like "corse"? Did you mean *corset* or *course*? Windows can't read your mind. (Maybe someday.)

  In that case, Windows doesn't correct the error—it just flags it by displaying a wavy underline beneath the questionable word. You can turn this off, too.

- **Typing.** These three options make your onscreen keyboard behave exactly like the one on a smartphone. For example, "Show text suggestions as I type on the software keyboard" means you'll get a row of proposed completions of words as you type them, to save you time and typos. "Add a space after I choose a text suggestion" and "Add a period after I double-tap the Spacebar" make the onscreen keyboard work even more like your phone.

- **How AI has helped you.** Before it takes over humanity and reveals itself to be evil, artificial intelligence is trying to put on a shiny PR campaign through this new item. Choose "Typing insights" to open a screen showing you how much effort Windows 10 has saved you with features like autocomplete, autocorrect, and (for onscreen keyboards) word swiping.

- **Touch keyboard.** Even more time-saving features for using your onscreen keyboard! "Play key sounds as I type" helps you understand when you've actually triggered a letter, since the keys are just images on glass. "Capitalize the first letter of each sentence" saves you fiddling with the onscreen Shift key; "Use all uppercase letters when I double-tap Shift" lets you turn on Caps Lock when it suits you; and "Show the touch keyboard when not in tablet mode and there's no keyboard attached" makes the onscreen keyboard appear when you're *not* in Tablet mode (page 449).

- **Hardware keyboard.** Why, look—you can summon word-completion suggestions even when you're using an actual physical keyboard, too! You can tap or click one, if you really think that will save you time (Figure 7-5).

You get an autocorrect on/off switch for your physical keyboard here, too.

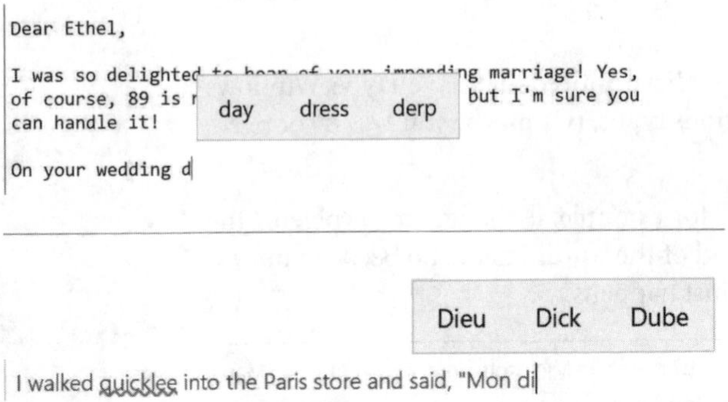

Dear Ethel,

I was so delighted to hear of your impending marriage! Yes, of course, 89 is ~~~~~~~~~ but I'm sure you can handle it!

day   dress   derp

On your wedding d|

Dieu   Dick   Dube

I walked quicklee into the Paris store and said, "Mon di|

Figure 7-5:
Top: You can have autocomplete suggestions even if you're typing with a physical keyboard.

Bottom: Windows can even make suggestions in different languages.

- **Multilingual text prediction.** Suppose you've turned on more than one language in ⊞ → ⚙ → "Time & language." Thanks to this feature, Windows can offer three word-completion suggestions from those alternate languages, too—not just your primary language (Figure 7-5, bottom). (This feature works only in *Roman* languages—that is, languages whose alphabets' characters look like English: A, B, C, and so on. So—not Chinese.)

- **Advanced keyboard settings.** On this sub-screen, you get a few settings that pertain to multiple-language setups. One of them lets you turn on the "desktop language bar," a system tray icon that's a drop-down menu of all the languages you've installed and lets you switch among them *sans difficulté*.

Pen & Windows Ink

These options let you fine-tune Windows' handwriting-recognition and stylus features, as described on page 456.

AutoPlay

Windows wants to know what you want to happen when you insert a flash drive ("Removable drive") or a memory card ("Memory card"). For each, you get choices like "Open folder to view files," "Import photos and videos," "Configure storage settings"—or "Take no action." Or you can turn the whole feature off.

USB

"Notify me if there are issues connecting to USB devices" alerts you when Windows doesn't properly recognize a USB gadget, like a flash drive or a mouse, that you've just plugged in.

Phone

Here's where you can link your smartphone to Windows 10. Microsoft sheepishly admits that it has flopped in the smartphone biz, so it made this feature available to the winners in that market: iPhone and Android.

Start by signing in and choosing "Add a phone." Once you enter your phone number, Microsoft texts a link to you; it takes you to the app store to download the Edge and Cortana phone apps. And now your phone is listed under "Linked phones."

What does that mean? For now, it means three features:

- **Fling any web page you're reading** on your phone, in any iOS or Android browser, to your PC to keep reading on the big screen, as described on page 239. (To do that, tap the phone's Share button, and choose Continue on PC as the destination.) Very cool.

- **Dictate and create reminders** on your phone in the Cortana app (iOS or Android). They're automatically synced between the devices.

- **You can receive notifications** from your Android phone—missed calls, incoming texts, and a few apps—on your PC. You can even respond to the texts with the luxury of a full mouse and keyboard for editing, using your phone as a cellular antenna.

   To pull this off, install the Cortana app for Android on your phone. In that app, choose ▦→⚙→ "Cross device." Ensure that all the notifications you want to receive (missed calls, incoming messages, low battery) are turned on.

   Now your Android phone's notifications pop up in the Action Center. You can actually click or tap to reply to texts, although you can't place calls and can't *initiate* a text-message conversation. Maybe in Windows 11.

Network & Internet

The fourth major Settings page offers all the tools you need to get online. Most of them are described in Chapter 12, but here are some key panels:

Status

Voilà: the new Network Neighborhood (as Microsoft used to call it). Check your connection, fiddle with your sharing settings, dive into the troubleshooter.

Wi-Fi

Turn Wi-Fi on or off, see what hotspot you're connected to, view a list of available hotspots.

Ethernet

This screen does little more than tell you whether or not you're connected to a network with an Ethernet cable—and offer links to other networking control panels.

Dial-Up

Really? You get online with a dial-up modem?

VPN

All over the world, corporate employees on the road connect to their home offices using *virtual private networking*. VPN is a fancy way of saying, "Your laptop computer can become part of your company's network over the internet." See page 461 for details.

Airplane Mode

As you're probably aware, you're not allowed to make cellphone calls on U.S. airplanes. According to legend (if not science), a cellphone's radio can interfere with a plane's navigational equipment.

But come on. If you're using a tablet with cellular service, are you really supposed to deprive yourself of all the music, videos, movies, and email you could be using in flight, just because cellular gadgets are forbidden?

Nope. Just turn on airplane mode (so this switch says On). Now the cellular, Bluetooth, and Wi-Fi features are turned off completely. You can't make calls or get online, but you can do anything else in the computer's bag of noncellular tricks. You can also then turn Wi-Fi and Bluetooth back on, depending on what's available on your airplane.

Tip: Of course, it's much faster to hop into airplane mode using the Quick Actions panel (page 97)—or even by telling Cortana, "Turn on airplane mode."

Mobile Hotspot

If you've got a cellular-equipped tablet or laptop, it can serve as a portable Wi-Fi hotspot for other devices nearby. See page 446.

Data Usage

This item shows how much internet data your computer has used in the past 30 days. It's primarily intended for tablets and laptops that have cellular service, to avoid going over your monthly allotment. But some people have Wi-Fi service with monthly data caps, so you also get a breakdown of Wi-Fi data use by hotspot.

- **View usage per app.** View which apps have used how much of that data.

- **Set limit.** Click to set up a data limit—say, 5 gigabytes. When you reach that limit, Windows will warn you, so you don't accidentally go way over and incur massive overage charges.

- **Background data.** Choosing "Never" shuts off apps' access to the internet when they're in the background (you're not actually using them). That's another good way to prevent nasty surprises.

Proxy

A *proxy server* is a security barrier between your own network and the internet. It prevents evildoers online from getting through to your internal network. This screen is where highly paid networking professionals can set up an automatic or manual proxy server.

Personalization

Main Settings Category No. 5 is your interior-design center. Here's where you can change the look of your desktop wallpaper (Background), desktop color scheme (Colors and Themes), the image on your Lock screen, the behavior of your Start menu, the look of your taskbar, and more. It's all described in Chapter 4—except for the options governing what shows up in your Start menu, which are described in Chapter 1.

Apps

Windows gives you a delicious amount of control over your apps' behavior, as you can see from these six tabs:

Apps & Features

Here's what this screen offers:

- **Installing apps.** Viruses and other malware have dogged Windows for decades. By creating the Microsoft Store (page 233), Microsoft has come up with one way to shut that stuff down for good. Any app from the Store is guaranteed to be virus-free. If you really want to be safe, choose "Allow apps from the Store only."

  Of course, thousands of desktop apps aren't available from the Microsoft Store. So this drop-down menu also offers "Allow apps from anywhere" and "Warn me before installing apps from outside the Store," so you can choose a setting that fits your degree of conservatism.

- **Optional features.** "Optional features" includes big globs of Windows code that Microsoft considers too specialized to include in the standard Windows 10 installation: Handwriting, Internet Explorer, and a lot of foreign-language fonts. Here's where you can turn them on or off, providing you've got the disk space.

- **App execution aliases.** If you're techie enough that you routinely open apps by typing their names at the Run prompt, you probably know all about aliases: alternate names for your apps—in this case, Microsoft Store apps. Some of them come pre-equipped with aliases (like *spotify.exe*) that resemble normal desktop apps (like *winword.exe*). But in the unlikely event that two of your apps have adopted the same alias, here's where you can turn off aliases one at a time.

- **[List of apps.]** Here's a list of all the programs on your PC. Using the drop-down menus, you can change how they're sorted, or limit the list to one of your drives. By clicking a program's name, you reveal its Uninstall button, for quick deletion, and its Move button, for shoving it onto a different drive.

Default Apps

See page 231 for details on reassigning document types to new apps.

Offline Maps

See page 313.

Apps for Websites

Talk about edge cases!

When you click a link to play a video or music file on some web page, do you want it to play right there in the browser—or do you want it to open the Movies & TV app, or a music-playing app, on your PC? When you click an address link, do you want it to open in another web page or in Maps? Microsoft's original thought was that, here, you could choose. But it requires that software companies update their programs to announce which kinds of web links they can open, and very few have.

Video Playback

The settings you make here affect Microsoft's own video programs, like Edge, Photos, and Movies & TV, and any Store apps that rely on Windows' built-in video software, including Hulu, Netflix, and Vudu. The main things worth noticing here are "I prefer video to play at a lower resolution" (so you don't eat up your monthly data allowance—well, not as fast) and "Optimize for battery life," which once again lowers the video quality, this time for the sake of your battery.

Startup

These are the programs that you (or Microsoft) has set up to open automatically every time you turn on the PC. Each has an on/off switch, for your control-freak pleasure.

And how do you designate that you want an app added to this list? Often, the app asks you when you install it: "Start BeeKeeper Pro when PC starts up?" or a similar checkbox appears in its settings. But you can also set up apps (or documents) to open at startup manually; see page 494.

Accounts

This is the seventh main category. When you sign into your computer, you're signing into your own account. That keeps your stuff private from anyone else who uses this machine and prevents people from messing up your files and settings.

On this panel, you can set up additional accounts for signing into Windows—usually one for each person who uses the machine—or make changes to your own. And the "Sign-in options" category lets you specify a password, a four-digit number, or a picture password to unlock your account (page 545). Details on accounts are in Chapter 18.

Time & Language

This category contains a few items for you to set and forget.

Date and Time

• **Set time automatically, Set time zone automatically, Adjust for daylight saving time automatically.** If you turn these off, you will have to set your computer's clock, time zone, and daylight-saving settings manually.

• **Sync now** means "set my clock according to a master clock online."

• **Show additional calendars in the taskbar.** As described on page 88, you can click the clock on the taskbar to see a miniature calendar, complete with a list of today's events. The options in this drop-down menu let you add Chinese subtitling to the dates of the month-view calendar.

(For most people, the "Add clocks for different time zones" link is more useful. It, too, adds pop-up clocks to your taskbar clock—but for different time zones, so you don't wind up waking someone in London with an ill-timed call.)

• **Date, time, and regional formatting.** What's the first day of the week? Do you put the month first, American-style (7/30/18), or the date first, European-style (30/7/18)? How do you like the time written out?

Region and Language

Specify where you live and what language(s) you speak, for the purposes of tailoring the websites you see and the onscreen keyboards available to you.

Speech

Here's where you indicate what language you speak (for the purposes of Cortana and speech recognition) and which of Windows' voices you want it to use when speaking to *you*. This is also where you can set up your microphone for accurate speech interpretation; if you hit "Get started," Windows asks you to read a sentence aloud, so it can get an idea of what you sound like.

Gaming

This panel, a relatively recent addition to Settings, offers six tabs' worth of controls pertaining to PC gaming. Details are on page 300.

Ease of Access

Windows offers all kinds of tools to make computing easier if you have trouble seeing or hearing.

Display

Everything you need to see better:

- **Make text bigger** enlarges the text on the screen—everywhere it appears—but not images or controls.

- **Make everything bigger** is a duplicate of the drop-down menu described on page 169.

- **Change the size of apps and text on other displays** is handy if you've connected a second screen or a projector. It lets you scale the text and graphics up or down on each screen independently.

- **Change the size and color of your cursor and mouse pointer** opens the "Cursor & pointer size" described in the next section.

- **Change brightness automatically or use night light** opens the options described on page 167.

- **Show animations in Windows.** Windows 10 spices things up by displaying animations here and there. When you hit the ■ button, for example, the Start menu seems to slide into place, with its tiles sliding in a microsecond later. This switch eliminates them, and the time they take.

- **Show transparency in Windows.** The hints of translucence (for example, in the background of the Start menu and Settings panels) may actually make Windows slightly distracting. Here's where you can turn them off.

- **Automatically hide scroll bars in Windows.** A scroll bar, of course, is the traditional window-edge slider that lets you move through a document that's too big for the window. Without being able to scroll, you'd never be able to write a letter that's taller than your screen.

  But you may never need to scroll by *dragging the scroll bar*; you can slide two fingers up the trackpad, or turn your mouse's scroll wheel, or press the Page Up and Page Down keys. That's a long-winded way of explaining why "Automatically hide scroll bars in Windows" comes turned on, so your window gets more space for your actual document, and the scroll bar is hidden.

  Even if this feature is On, you can still bring the scroll bars into view by moving the mouse to the window's edge. The scroll bar pops right up.

- **Show notifications for.** Notifications, the rectangular bubbles described in Chapter 2, pop in to remind you of something, or to let you know that some new message has arrived—and then they disappear. But, using this menu, you can control how long they stick around before vanishing—from five seconds to five minutes (a good setting if you're *really* slow on the draw).

- **Show desktop background image.** You know the wallpaper photo or color you set up on page 152? With one click here, you can replace it with solid black, presumably to make life more legible for the hard-of-seeing. (Of course, you could also just choose solid black as the background color in the first place.)

- **Personalize your background and other colors.** Takes you to the Background settings page (page 151).

Cursor & Pointer Size

Here you can make the cursor easier to see when you're typing; instead of searching around for a thin, flashing pixel-wide bar, you can thicken it all the way up to a chunky but easy-to-spot 20 pixels (see Figure 7-6).

Figure 7-6:
Top: Use the slider to adjust the thickness of your insertion-point cursor; as you slide, you get to see an example.

Bottom: You can make the cursor ridiculously thick, if you want.

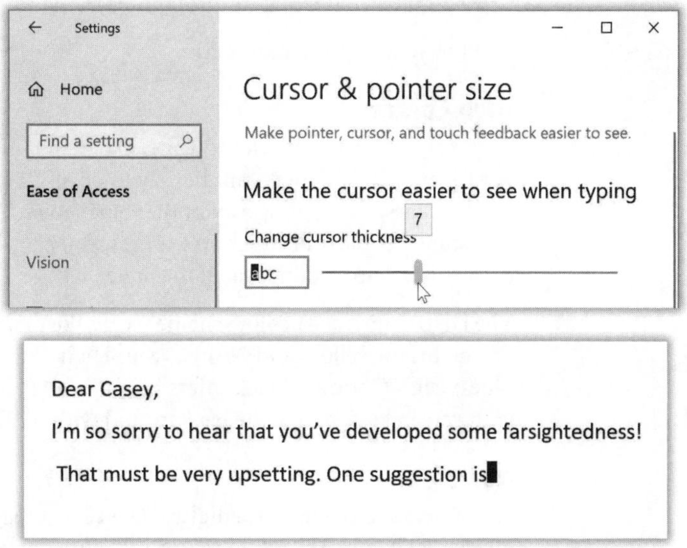

You can also make your pointer bigger and change its color. Your three choices are the typical white arrow with a black outline, a solid black arrow, and an arrow that reverses whatever is behind it—it shows up white when it's on a black background and vice versa.

For touchscreen owners, there's also an option here to give visual feedback when you touch the screen—a little darkened spot follows your finger around.

Magnifier

Magnifier enlarges what's on the screen in a special movable window; see page 356.

Color Filters

Windows has several built-in color filters to help make the screen clearer, including for people with specific types of color-blindness. Here are your choices:

- **Invert.** This reverses all the colors: White goes to black, black goes to white, blue to orange, and so on. Some people find this scheme easier to read.

- **Grayscale.** This converts all colors to shades of gray without changing the contrast. This is also meant for easier reading.

- **Grayscale inverted.** This is the combination of the two previous options. All colors are gone, and the white text jumps out from the black and dark-gray screen.

Beneath these choices are three settings specific to color-blindness; they subtly shift the screen's color values to make them more distinguishable. Choose the one that fits:

- **Red-green** (green weak, for deuteranopia).

- **Red-green** (red weak, for protanopia).

- **Blue-yellow** (for tritanopia).

High Contrast

This feature reverses black for white, like in the Invert option in "Color filters." But it goes a few steps further—all the way to an all-black background and just a few very bright colors, eliminating a lot of the visual noise. This creates a higher-contrast effect that some people find easier on the eyes. You can choose a canned color scheme, and even edit it (tap a color swatch to change it).

The High Contrast #1 color scheme recalls the first personal computer displays, heavy on the bright yellow and Army green. High Contrast #2 throws in a few Windows blues; High Contrast Black offers bright-white text; and High Contrast White flips your screen back to a white background with black text.

Narrator

Narrator is a *screen reader*, a digitized voice that reads everything on the screen, which is essential if you're blind. These settings customize its voice, inflection, and talkiness. See page 357.

Audio

If you have trouble hearing, you may find real value in these options:

- **Change device volume.** Yet another place to raise your PC's speaker volume.

- **Change the device or app volume.** Opens the Sound panel (page 243).

- **Change other sound settings.** Opens the Sound pane of the ancient Control Panel (page 278).

- **Turn on mono audio** is intended for people with hearing loss in one ear. This way, you won't miss any of the musical mix just because you're listening through only one headphone.

- **Select how visual alerts for notifications are displayed.** If you have trouble hearing, or if your roommate tends to play heavy metal at top volume when you're trying to work, you might not hear the little beeps or chimes that Windows plays to get your attention. This drop-down menu lets you opt to add a visual cue, like a flash of the title bar, window, or the whole screen. Not a bad idea on laptops or tablets, actually, so you don't miss beeps when you've got the speakers muted.

Closed Captions

This option controls the look of the closed captions (subtitles) that appear in some of the movies, TV shows, and videos you can buy, rent, or stream from Microsoft's TV and movie store.

Tip: In the Movies & TV Store, videos equipped with subtitles bear a small CC icon.

Using these drop-down menus, you can change an insane number of font, size, opacity, and color options, both for the type and the background it appears on.

Speech

If you have trouble typing—or just don't like to—you may appreciate Windows' ability to type out what you say. This pane offers links to some Cortana settings, plus reminders of the keystrokes you need to turn dictation on and off. For details on Windows 10 speech recognition, see the free PDF appendix to this chapter, "Speech Recognition." You can download it from this book's "Missing CD" page at *missingmanuals.com*.

Keyboard

These clever features are designed to help people who have trouble using the keyboard.

- **Use the On-Screen Keyboard** is just another way to make the keyboard appear (page 451).

- **Use Sticky Keys** lets you press multiple-key shortcuts (involving keys like Shift, Ctrl, and ⊞) one at a time instead of all together.

- **Use Toggle Keys** plays a sound when you hit the Caps Lock, Num Lock, or Scroll Lock key. It has little to do with disabilities; it's to save *anyone* from the frustration of hitting one of those keys accidentally and looking up to discover 10 minutes' worth of gibberish typing.

- **Use Filter Keys** doesn't register a key press at all until you've held down the key for more than a second or so—a feature designed to screen out accidental key presses. It also ignores repeated keystrokes.

Note: You can turn on each of these features with a keyboard shortcut—but you can also turn that keyboard shortcut *off* here, so you don't press it accidentally and wonder why your keyboard is acting so strangely.

- **Underline access keys when available.** Windows veterans remember when menu commands had little underlines, showing which keyboard letter (in combination with the Alt key) would trigger a command. Now that handy cheat-sheet system is back—if you turn on this switch. (It doesn't work in all programs.)

- **Use the PrtScn button to open screen snipping.** Here Microsoft is referring to its new, improved screenshot-capturing feature, described on page 338. It's offering you a chance to make your PrtScn (Print Screen) key trigger the screenshot tool.

- **Show a warning message/Make a sound when turning on...** You'll be shown an "Are you sure?" box, and/or hear a confirmation beep, when you turn on one of the Ease of Access features from the keyboard.

Mouse

Mouse Keys is designed to help people who can't use the mouse—or who want more precision when working in graphics programs. It lets you click, drag, and otherwise manipulate the cursor by pressing the keys on your numeric keypad. (It's not very useful on keyboards that don't have separate numeric keypads, like laptops.)

When Mouse Keys is turned on, the 5 key triggers a click, and the + key acts as a double-click. (Specify a left-button click by first pressing the / key, or a right-click by pressing the - key.)

Move the cursor around the screen by pressing the eight keys that surround the 5 key. (For example, hold down the 9 key to move the cursor diagonally up and to the right.) You can even drag something on the screen; press 0 to "hold down the button" on something, and then move it using the number keys, and press the period (.) to let go.

The sliders here govern the overall acceleration and speed of the cursor movements, although you can always speed up by pressing Ctrl and slow down by pressing Shift (if you've turned this option on here).

Tip: It's kind of clunky to have to burrow all the way into PC Settings every time you want to turn on Mouse Keys. Fortunately, there's a shortcut: the Num Lock key on your keyboard. It turns on Mouse Keys (at least if "Only use Mouse Keys when Num Lock is on" is on).

Eye Control

Whoa, cool! If you've bought a Tobii eye-tracking camera, you can now control the motion of your cursor just by looking at the screen. Windows translates your gaze into mouse movements—very convenient if you're unable to use your hands. Here's where you set up and configure your eye-tracking hardware.

Once everything is running, you get special onscreen floating palettes with buttons for "left click," "right click," "double-click," and so on. You can even type by holding your gaze at one letter at a time on a floating keyboard.

To read more about all the features of eye control, see Microsoft's help document at *http://j.mp/2GB4v1g.*

Search

This Settings pane is new in the May 2019 Update, but most of its contents aren't. It's just that they're no longer clustered (illogically) under the Cortana settings, just as the search box is no longer combined with the Cortana button on the taskbar.

Permissions & History

Anyway, here's what you've got on the first tab:

- **SafeSearch.** As you know from Chapter 3, using the search box often includes results from the web, not just your computer. As you also know, the Search feature even displays a snippet of the actual web pages that contain what you're looking for.

  But what if you're looking for something raunchy? You might not want some naked person's photo appearing in its full JPEG splendor just as somebody important is walking by your PC.

  For that reason, Windows 10 comes with SafeSearch set to Moderate here, meaning that you'll see off-color text results in the search results menu, but not photos or videos. If you set it to Strict, you'll see neither.

  If you live and work by yourself, by all means set SafeSearch to Off.

- **Cloud content search.** When you do a search, do you want Windows to scrounge through your OneDrive's contents (page 140), too? How about your Outlook account? Here you can answer that question independently for your Microsoft account and your work or school email accounts, if any.

- **Activity recommendations** is the on/off switch for the "Pick up where you left off" feature described on page 238.

- **My device history, My search history.** Are you willing to let Microsoft's servers see what you've been doing and searching, in the name of making your searching more accurate?

Searching Windows

Here's where you specify which folders Windows can search; see page 107.

- **Search history.** If you're only now figuring out that Microsoft has been *collecting* your search terms, open this link. It takes you to a website where you can clear your search history, scrubbing Microsoft's brain free of your questionable queries.

Cortana

Of course Cortana the voice assistant gets her own pages of settings:

- **Talk to Cortana.** See page 182 for details on the different ways you can trigger Cortana.

- **Permissions.** Choose "Manage the information Cortana can access from this device" to turn off its access to your location, contacts, email, calendar, browsing history, and so on.

- **More details.** This screen offers links to various privacy statements on Microsoft's website.

Privacy

This panel reveals the vastness of the ocean of data that Microsoft routinely harvests from your computer and shares—with advertisers, with its own programmers, and with other apps.

Fortunately, you can shut down much of it. Chapter 11 covers what these options do, blow by blow.

Update & Security

Windows, like any software, is an eternal work in progress, as these options make clear:

Windows Update, Delivery Optimization

Windows is software and can therefore be updated, debugged, and improved. (Software is handy that way.) Windows Update is Microsoft's system for sending you patches and fixes over the internet. See page 487 for more on Windows Update.

Windows Security

The Windows world is teeming with viruses and other nastiness—but Windows comes with a free antivirus program to block it all, called Defender. These options are described in Chapter 11.

Backup

You've just found the settings for Windows' three backup features: "Back up files to OneDrive," "Back up using File History," and "Back up your stuff" (to an external drive). They're all described in Chapter 16.

Troubleshoot

This panel is a master list of all the Windows Troubleshooters—step-by-step interview screens that guide you through solving problems with your internet connection, audio playback, printer, and so on. Chapter 15 has more.

Recovery

Windows offers several ways to reset itself in times of troubleshooting. Details are in Chapter 15, but here are the basics:

- **Reset this PC.** This option *refreshes* your PC—resets your computer. Basic computer settings are reset to their factory states, and apps that didn't come from the

Microsoft Store are deleted. You wind up with a fresh copy of Windows, and your files and settings intact (if that's what you want).

- **Go back to the previous version of Windows 10.** Microsoft considers Windows 10 to be a work in progress. Upgrades and new features will trickle out all year long, automatically. If some update really messes up your machine, though, at least you have this option; it rewinds Windows to an earlier version.

- **Advanced startup.** This option restarts your computer so you can boot up from some external drive, like a DVD or a USB flash drive, or change startup settings in the course of troubleshooting.

    The screen blinks off, and then you arrive at the "Choose an option" screen, where you can restart Windows, troubleshoot (refresh or reset the PC, or use the advanced troubleshooting and configuration tools described in Chapter 15), or just turn the computer off.

- **Learn how to start fresh with a clean installation of Windows.** Takes you directly into the Windows Defender app, where the "Fresh start" process begins, as described on page 581.

Activation

Activation is Microsoft's name for copy protection: You can't run Windows without a serial number (a "product key").

This screen lets you know if your current copy of Windows has, in fact, been activated (as opposed to running in trial mode). You can even change your Product ID by clicking "Change product key" without having to reinstall Windows itself, which can come in handy if, for example, you want to upgrade Windows versions or switch to a multiple-use product key.

Find My Device

Hey, cool! "Find my phone" has come to Windows. Here, in one place, are the controls you need to figure out where your laptop, tablet, or touchscreen pen wound up. See page 447.

For Developers

These options are for programmers who need access to unusual features—like sideloading apps (installing apps that didn't come from Microsoft's app store). Also hanging out here, under the File Explorer heading, are checkboxes that change File Explorer settings in ways that can make life easier for developers: revealing hidden files, turning on filename extensions, showing empty drives, and so on.

Windows Insider Program

You don't have to be some hotshot or bigwig to be one of Microsoft's beta testers. If you sign up for the Windows Insider program, you have access to not-quite-ready versions of Windows before the public does. You can report bugs, make suggestions, and generally feel like you're helping Microsoft get the kinks out. On the other hand, you may also have to deal with crashes and half-finished features.

If you decide to sign up, you also have to choose what early stuff you want to get by choosing "Pick your insider settings":

- **Slow (Recommended).** This option is for the conservative; the only software you'll get early are minor ancillary elements like bug fixes, updated apps, and device drivers—and even then, you'll get only software that's already been tested by earlier adopters and is therefore less buggy. You'll get an update once or twice a month.

- **Fast.** You'll get early versions of Windows itself once or twice a week. There will be bugs, but you'll be on the cutting edge!

- **Release Preview.** You'll stick with the version of Windows you've already been running, but you'll get fully tested app updates and new drivers when they're ready.

- **Skip ahead to the next Windows release.** Microsoft intends to release a new Windows 10 version every six months. At any given time, the company is working on both the next version of Windows *and* the one after that. Is it really supposed to wait until *this* version is released to the public before enjoying beta-testing help on the *next* one from you, the brave pioneer?

  Nope. This option means "Skip the beta versions of the version that's coming next—start feeding me super-buggy, super-early builds of the Windows versions after that!" (This option is available only if you've chosen the Fast Ring, described above, and it's available only during certain time windows.)

The Control Panel

The Settings app you've been reading about is a clean, new, nice-looking dashboard for your PC's settings, and it's growing more complete with every Windows version.

But the old Control Panel, born in Windows 2 in 1987, is still around, teeming with miniature applications (or *applets*) that govern every component of your computer.

Many are duplicated in the Settings app. Others are so obscure that you'll wonder what on earth inspired Microsoft to create them. The following pages cover them all.

Note: Here and there, within the Control Panel, you'll spot a little Windows security-shield icon. It tells you that you're about to make an important, major change to the operating system, something that will affect everyone who uses this PC—fiddling with its network settings, for example, or changing its clock. To prove your worthiness (and to prove you're not an evil virus attempting to make a nasty change), you'll be asked to *authenticate* yourself; see page 558 for details.

Many Roads to the Control Panel

For most people, the quickest way to the Control Panel is to click into the taskbar search box; start typing *control panel* until you see its name at the top of the menu. Press Enter (or tap it).

But those are only the tips of the iceberg of Ways to Open Control Panel. Consider:

- **Control Panel is listed in your Start menu's "All apps" list** (in the folder called Windows System).

- **Often, you'll wind up popping into the Control Panel** without any warning—after clicking a "More options" link in the Settings app. (Settings has a lot of links to the Control Panel like that.)

- **The search box** is uncannily good at taking you to the control panel you really want, too. Hit ⊞+S to open the search box; type *color*; when you see Color Management highlighted in the results list, press Enter to open it. (On other quests, you might type *fonts, sound, battery, accounts, date, CDs, speech,* or whatever.)

There's a similar search box right in the Control Panel window itself.

- **If you don't mind a cluttered desktop,** you can make a shortcut for the applets you access most. To do that, open the Control Panel. Right-click the icon you want; from the shortcut menu, choose "Create shortcut." It automatically places it on the desktop for you.

- **You can install a certain Control Panel applet** onto the Start menu (right side), too! With Control Panel open, right-click the icon you want; from the shortcut menu, choose Pin to Start.

- **You can even put an applet into the "Quick access" list** that appears in every File Explorer window. In the open Control Panel, right-click the icon you want; from the shortcut menu, choose "Pin to Quick access."

Note: Sadly, Control Panel is no longer listed in the secret utility menu that appears when you right-click the Start menu (or press ⊞+X).

UP TO SPEED

Control Panel Terminology Hell

The Control Panel continues to be an object of bafflement for Microsoft, not to mention its customers; from version to version of Windows, this feature undergoes more reorganizations than a bankrupt airline.

Windows 10 presents the most oddball arrangement yet. There are far more icons in the Control Panel than ever before—about 50 of them, in fact. But they're not all the same kind of thing.

Some are the traditional *applets,* meaning mini-applications (little programs). Others are nothing more than tabbed dialog boxes. Some open up wizards (interview dialog boxes that walk you through a procedure) or even ordinary Explorer windows. And even among the applets, the look and substance of the Control Panel panels vary widely.

So what are people supposed to call these things? The world needs a general term for the motley assortment of icons in the Control Panel window.

To keep you and your well-intentioned author from going quietly insane, this chapter refers to all the Control Panel icons as either icons (which they definitely are), control panels, or applets (which most of them are—and besides, that's the traditional term for them).

Control Panel Views

When it first appears, the Control Panel looks like the one shown in Figure 7-7. But that's just the beginning.

The "View by" drop-down menu (upper right) shows that there are three ways to view the complete collection of control panels: by category or as a list of small or large icons.

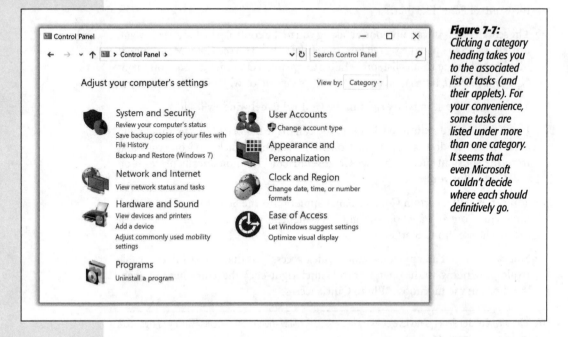

Figure 7-7:
Clicking a category heading takes you to the associated list of tasks (and their applets). For your convenience, some tasks are listed under more than one category. It seems that even Microsoft couldn't decide where each should definitively go.

Category view

If you choose Category view, you'll find these categories:

- **System and Security.** In this category are system and administrative tasks like backing up and restoring, setting your power options, and security options (firewall, encryption, and so on).

- **Network and Internet.** This category contains settings related to networking, internet options, offline files), and Sync Center (to manage synchronizing data between computers and network folders).

- **Hardware and Sound.** Here you find everything for managing gadgets connected to your computer: printer settings, projector settings, laptop adjustments, and so on.

- **Programs.** You might use this one a lot. Here's where you uninstall programs, choose which program is your preferred one (for web browsing or opening graphics, for example), turn Windows features on and off, and manage your desktop gadgets.

- **User Accounts.** This category contains the settings you need to manage the accounts on the computer (Chapter 18), including the limited-access accounts that parents can create for their children.

- **Appearance and Personalization.** Here's a big category indeed. It covers all things cosmetic, from how the desktop looks (plus taskbar and personalization settings) to folder options and fonts.

- **Clock and Region.** These time, language, and clock settings all have one thing in common: They differ according to where in the world you are.

- **Ease of Access.** This category is one-stop shopping for every feature Microsoft has dreamed up to assist the disabled. It's also the rabbit hole into Speech Recognition Options.

Large icons, Small icons

The category concept sounds OK in principle, but it'll drive veterans nuts. You don't want to guess what category something wound up in—you just want to open the old panel, right now.

Fortunately, the Control Panel can display its dozens of icons in alphabetical order (Figure 7-8).

Use the "View by" drop-down menu in the upper-right, and choose either "Small icons" or "Large icons." Then double-click the icon of the applet you'd like to use.

Figure 7-8:
Classic view might be overwhelming for novices, because the task icons give little indication about what settings they actually contain. Here's a hint: Remember that you can just move your mouse over a task and pause there. A tooltip pops up, giving you an idea of what's inside.

The Control Panel, Applet by Applet

Icon view is the perfect structure for a chapter that describes each Control Panel applet, since it's organized in alphabetical order. The rest of this chapter assumes you're looking at the Control Panel in one of the two Icon views.

Note: To spare you from hunting through an obsolete jungle of Control Panel options when a much cleaner Settings page will do, the following descriptions indicate which applets have been largely replaced by modern Settings screens.

Administrative Tools

This icon is actually a folder containing a suite of very technical administrative utilities. These tools, intended for serious technowizards only, aren't covered in this book.

AutoPlay

The primary features are duplicated in the Settings app; see page 251.

Each time you insert a disc or drive (CDs and DVDs of various types, Blu-ray, HD, cameras, flash drives, and so on), you get a dialog box asking how you want to handle it—this time, and every time you insert a similar gadget thereafter. For each kind of disc, the drop-down menu offers you obvious choices by disc type (like "Play audio CD" for music CDs), as well as standard options like "Open folder to view files (File Explorer)," "Take no action," or "Ask me every time."

Behind the scenes, your choices are recorded in the AutoPlay control panel, where you can change your mind or just look over the choices you've made so far.

If you've never liked AutoPlay and you don't want Windows to do *anything* when you insert a disc, just turn off "Use AutoPlay for all media and devices" at the top of the window.

Backup and Restore (Windows 7)

The primary features are duplicated in the Settings app; see page 262.

Backup and Restore center is an obsolete method of backing up your computer. It's included here for the benefit of people who have Windows 7 backups they might want to restore. Check out Chapter 16 for more detailed information.

BitLocker Drive Encryption

BitLocker encrypts the data on your drives to keep them from being accessed by the bad guys who might steal your laptop. For details, see the free PDF appendix to this chapter "BitLocker Drive Encryption" on this book's "Missing CD" at *missingmanuals.com*.

Color Management

Microsoft created this applet in conjunction with Canon in an effort to make colors more consistent from screen to printer. Details are in Chapter 13.

Credential Manager

Credential Manager lets you teach Windows to memorize your corporate account names and passwords. It also memorizes your passwords for everyday websites (like banking sites). Credential Manager also stores passwords for shared network drives and corporate-intranet websites, the ones where you have to enter a name and password before you even see the home page.

Date and Time

The primary features are duplicated in the Settings app; see page 255.

Your PC's concept of what time it is can be very important. Every file you create or save is stamped with this time, and every email you send or receive is marked with it. When you drag a document into a folder that contains a different draft of the same thing, Windows warns that you're about to replace an older version with a newer one (or vice versa)—but only if your clock is set correctly.

This program offers three tabs:

- **Date and Time.** Here's where you can change the time, date, and time zone for the computer (Figure 7-9)—if, that is, you'd rather not have the computer set its own clock (read on).

Tip: In the "Time zone" section of the Date and Time tab, you can find exactly when Windows thinks daylight-saving time is going to start or end. In addition, there's an option to remind you a week before the time change occurs, so you don't wind up unexpectedly sleep-deprived on the day of your big TV appearance.

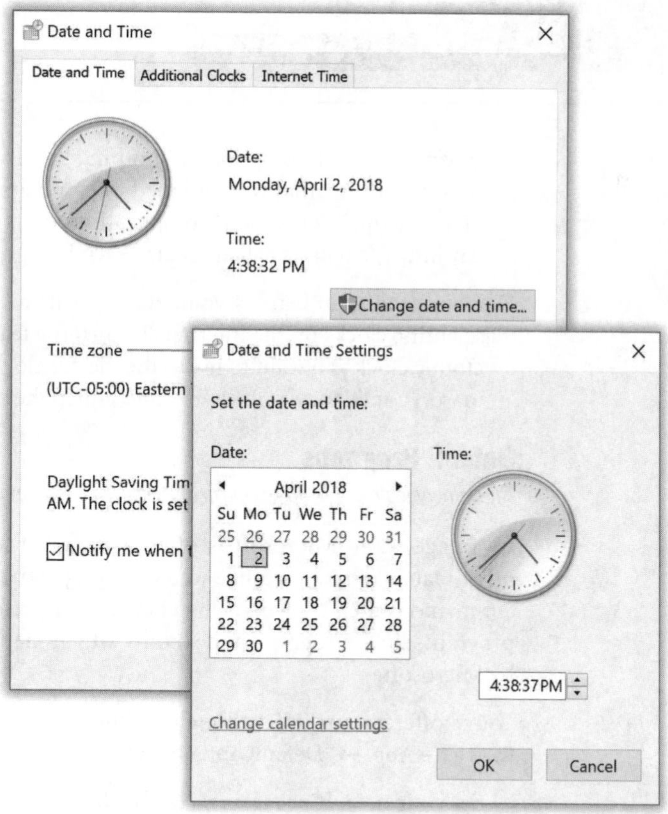

Figure 7-9:
Top: The Date and Time tab has a lovely analog clock displaying the time. You can't actually use it to set the time, but it looks nice. To make a change to the date or time of the computer, click "Change date and time."

Bottom: At that point, select the correct date by using the calendar. Specify the correct time by typing in the hour, minute, and seconds. Yes, type it; the ▲ and ▼ next to the time field are too inefficient, except when you're changing AM to PM or vice versa.

- **Additional Clocks.** If you work overseas, or if you have friends, relatives, or clients in different time zones, you'll like this one; it's the only thing that stands between you and waking them up at three in the morning because you forgot what time it is where they live.

This feature lets you create clocks for two other time zones, so you can see what time it is in other parts of the world. (They appear when you point to the taskbar clock—or, in larger type, when you click it.)

You can give them any display name you want, like "Paris" or "Mother-in-Law Time." Note that the additional clocks' times are based on the PC's own local time. So if the computer's main clock is wrong, the other clocks will be wrong, too.

Figure 7-10 shows how to check one of your additional clocks.

Figure 7-10:
To see the time for the additional clocks, point without clicking over the time in the system tray. You get a pop-up displaying the time on the additional clock (or clocks) you configured. (Unfortunately, it's no longer labeled with the name of that time zone.)

- **Internet Time.** This option has nothing to do with Swatch Internet Time, a 1998 concept of time that was designed to eliminate the complications of time zones. (Then again, it introduced complications of its own, like dividing up the 24-hour day into 1,000 parts called "beats," each being 1 minute and 26.4 seconds long.)

Instead, this tab teaches your PC to set its own clock by consulting one of the scientific clocks on the internet. To turn the feature on or off, or to specify which atomic clock you want to use as the master clock, click Change Settings. (No need to worry about daylight-saving time, either; the time servers take that into account).

Default Programs

The primary features are duplicated in the Settings app; see page 231.

In an age when Microsoft is often accused of leveraging Windows to take over other realms of software, like web browsing and graphics, the company created this command center. It's where you choose your preferred web browser, music-playing program, email program, and so on—which may or may not be the ones provided by Microsoft.

You're offered four links, though all but Change AutoPlay Settings take you to the ⊞→⚙→Apps→"Default apps" pane:

- **Set your default programs.** Here's where you teach Windows that you want your own programs to replace the Microsoft versions. For instance, you can say that, when you double-click a music file, you want to open iTunes and not Windows Media Player.

- **Associate a file type or protocol with a program.** This window lets you specify exactly what kind of file you want to have opened by what program. (That's essentially what happens in the background when you set a default program.) File associations are covered in more depth on page 225. From the "Default apps" pane, you can use "Choose default apps by file type," "Choose default apps by protocol," or "Set defaults by app" to come at these choices from all the different angles.

- **Change AutoPlay Settings.** This option opens the AutoPlay applet described on page 251.

- **Set program access and computer defaults.** This just links you back to "Default apps" again.

Device Manager
The primary features are duplicated in the Settings app; see page 247.

The Device Manager console shows you where all your hardware money was spent. Here you or your tech-support person can troubleshoot a flaky device, disable and enable devices, and manage device drivers. If you're comfortable handling these more advanced tasks, then Chapter 14 is for you.

Devices and Printers
The primary features are duplicated in the Settings app; see page 248.

Double-click to open the Devices and Printers window, where everything you've attached to your PC—webcam, printer, scanner, mouse, whatever—appears with its own picture and details screen. Chapter 13 has the details.

Ease of Access Center
The primary features are duplicated in the Settings app; see page 256.

The Ease of Access Center is designed to make computing easier for people with disabilities, although some of the options here can benefit anyone.

File Explorer Options
This program, which is called "Folder Options" when accessed through File Explorer, offers three tabs—General, View, and Search—all of which are described in Chapter 2.

File History
The primary features are duplicated in the Settings app; see page 262.

Here's the HQ for Windows' backup feature. See Chapter 16.

Fonts

The primary features are duplicated in the Settings app; see page 163.

This icon is a shortcut to a folder; it's not an applet. It opens a window that reveals all the typefaces installed on your machine. More on fonts on page 472.

Indexing Options

The Windows search box is so fast because it doesn't actually root through all your files. Instead, it roots only through an *index* of your files, an invisible, compact database file that Windows maintains in the background. To learn more about the particulars of indexing and how to use it, see Chapter 3.

Infrared

Really, Microsoft? When was the last time any PC had an infrared transceiver for sending files over the air—at about 1 kilobyte a year?

Anyway, if you've found such a PC, maybe at an antiques fair, here's where you set up the behavior of infrared file transfers between IR-equipped machines. (Guess that means you'll need to find *two* such PCs at the antiques fair.)

Internet Options

A better name for this program would have been "Web Browser Options," since all its settings apply to web browsing—and, specifically, to Internet Explorer. As a matter of fact, this is the same dialog box that opens from the Tools→Internet Options menu command within Internet Explorer.

It's described in the free "Internet Explorer" appendix that you can download from this book's "Missing CD" page at *missingmanuals.com.*

Keyboard

The primary features are duplicated in the Settings app; see page 259.

You're probably too young to remember the antique known as a *typewriter.* On some electric versions of that machine, you could hold down the letter X key to type a series of XXXXXXX's—ideal for crossing out something in a contract, for example.

On a PC, *every* key behaves this way. Hold down any key long enough, and it starts spitting out repetitions, making it easy to type, "No WAAAAAAAAY!" (The same rule applies when you hold down the arrow keys to scroll through a text document, hold down the = key to build a separator line between paragraphs, hold down Backspace to eliminate a word, and so on.) The Speed tab of this dialog box governs the settings:

- **Repeat delay.** This slider determines how long you must hold down the key before it starts repeating (to prevent triggering repetitions accidentally).

- **Repeat rate.** The second slider governs how fast each key spits out letters once the spitting has begun. After making these adjustments, click the "Click here and hold down a key" test box to try out the new settings.

- **Cursor blink rate.** The "Cursor blink rate" slider actually has nothing to do with the *cursor,* the little arrow you move around with the mouse. Instead, it governs the blinking rate of the *insertion point,* the blinking marker that indicates where typing will begin when you're word processing, for example. A blink rate that's too slow makes it more difficult to find your insertion point in a window filled with data. A blink rate that's too rapid can be distracting.

Mouse

The primary features are duplicated in the Settings app; see page 248.

All the icons, buttons, and menus in Windows make the mouse a very important tool. And the Mouse dialog box is its configuration headquarters.

Buttons tab

This tab offers three useful controls: "Button configuration," "Double-click speed," and "ClickLock."

- **Button configuration.** This checkbox is for people who are left-handed and keep their mouse on the left side of the keyboard. Turning on this checkbox lets you switch the functions of the right and left mouse buttons so your index finger naturally rests on the primary button (the one that selects and drags).

- **Double-click speed.** Double-clicking isn't a very natural maneuver. If you double-click too slowly, the icon you're trying to open remains stubbornly closed. Or worse, if you accidentally double-click an icon's name instead of its picture, Windows sees your double-click as two single clicks, which tells it that you're trying to rename the icon.

  The difference in time between a double-click and two single clicks is usually well under a second. That's an extremely narrow window, so let Windows know what you consider to be a double-click by adjusting this slider. The left end of the slider bar represents 0.9 seconds, and the right end represents 0.1 seconds. If you need more time between clicks, move the slider to the left; by contrast, if your reflexes are highly tuned (or you drink a lot of coffee), try sliding the slider to the right.

  Each time you adjust the Speed slider, remember to test your adjustment by double-clicking the little folder to the right of the slider. If the folder opens, you've successfully double-clicked. If not, adjust the slider again.

- **ClickLock.** ClickLock is for people blessed with large monitors or laptop trackpads who, when dragging icons onscreen, get tired of keeping the mouse button pressed continually. Instead, you can make Windows "hold down" the button automatically, avoiding years of unpleasant finger cramps and messy litigation.

  When ClickLock is turned on, you can drag objects on the screen like this: First, point to the item you want to drag, such as an icon. Press the left mouse or trackpad button for the ClickLock interval. (You can specify this interval by clicking the Settings button in this dialog box.)

When you release the mouse button, it acts as though it's still pressed. Now you can drag the icon across the screen by moving the mouse (or stroking the trackpad) without holding any button down.

To release the button, hold it down again for your specified time interval.

Pointers tab

See page 160 for details on changing the shape of your cursor.

Pointers Options tab

See page 161 for a rundown of these cursor-related functions.

Wheel tab

The scroll wheel on the top of your mouse may be the greatest mouse enhancement since they got rid of the dust-collecting ball on the bottom. It lets you zoom through web pages, email lists, and documents with a twitch of your index finger.

Use these controls to specify just how *much* each wheel notch scrolls. (You may not see this tab at all if your mouse doesn't have a wheel.)

Hardware tab

The Mouse program provides this tab exclusively for its Properties buttons, which take you to the Device Manager's device properties dialog box. Useful if you have to troubleshoot a bad driver.

Network and Sharing Center

The primary features are duplicated in the Settings app; see page 252.

This network command center offers, among other things, a handy map that shows exactly how your PC is connected to the internet. It also contains a tidy list of all networking-related features (file sharing, printer sharing, and so on), complete with on/off switches. See Chapter 19 for details.

Pen and Touch

This item appears only if your machine has a touchscreen. It has two tabs:

- **Pen.** On some computers, you can use a digital pen (a stylus) to write on the screen, as described on page 454. Here you can configure what the pen's clicky button does (click, right-click, double-click, and so on).

- **Touch.** On any touchscreen, you can tap things with your finger. Here you tell Windows what you want to happen when you double-tap the screen with your finger, or touch and hold, and whether or not you want to see a little dot appear on the screen where you tap.

Phone and Modem

If you have a dial-up modem, you'll need to access these settings, but only once: the first time you set up to dial out.

Power Options

The primary features are duplicated in the Settings app; see page 244.

Power Options manages your computer's power consumption. That's crucial when you're running off a laptop's battery, but it's also important if you'd like to save money (and the environment) by cutting down on the juice consumed by your *desktop* PC. The options you see depend on your PC's particular features.

A *power plan* dictates things like how soon the computer goes to sleep, how bright the screen is, what speed the processor cranks at, and so on. Right up front, you get three premade power plans:

- **Balanced,** which is meant to strike a balance between energy savings and performance. When you're working hard, you get all the speed your PC can deliver; when you're thinking or resting, the processor slows down to save juice.

- **Power saver** slows down your computer but saves power—a handy choice for laptop luggers who aren't doing anything more strenuous than word processing.

- **High performance** (click "Show additional plans" to see it) sucks power like a black hole but grants you the highest speed possible.

Tip: You don't have to open the Control Panel to change among these canned plans. On a laptop, for example, you can just click the battery icon on your system tray and choose from the pop-up menu.

But creating your *own* power plan can be useful, not only because you gain more control, but also because you get to see exactly what a plan is made of. For step-by-step instructions, see the free downloadable appendix "Creating a Power Plan" on this book's "Missing CD" page at *missingmanuals.com*.

Programs and Features

The primary features are duplicated in the Settings app; see page 253.

Programs and Features is about managing the software you have installed, managing updates, and buying software online. It replaces the old Add/Remove Programs program. This window is useful for fixing (which might simply mean reinstalling), changing, or uninstalling existing programs, and it's the only place you can go to turn on (or off) certain obscure Windows features.

Recovery

The Recovery icon is a quick-access button for three features:

- **Create a recovery drive** lets you build a flash drive that can start up your PC when your PC can't start up on its own. See page 519.

- **Open System Restore** and **Configure System Restore** are described starting on page 509. System Restore lets you rewind your sick PC back to an earlier, better-behaved state.

Region

The primary features are duplicated in the Settings app; see page 255.

Windows can accommodate any conceivable arrangement of date, currency, and number formats.

Formats tab

If you think that 7/4 means July 4 and that 1.000 is the number of heads you have, then skip this section.

But in some countries, 7/4 means April 7, and 1.000 means one thousand. If your PC isn't showing numbers, times, currency symbols, or dates in a familiar way, choose your country from the top Format drop-down menu. (Or, if you're a little weird, use the "Additional settings" button to rearrange the sequence of date elements; see Figure 7-11.)

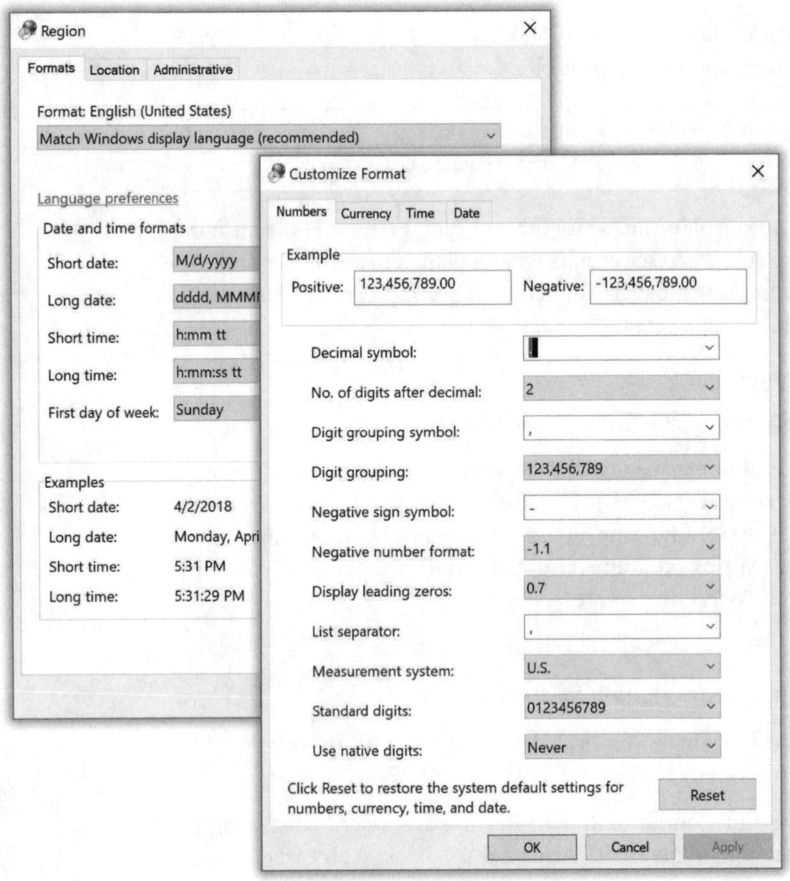

Figure 7-11:
Top: Regional standard format templates are available from the drop-down list in the Formats tab.

Bottom: Once you choose a standard format (like U.S.), you can customize exactly how numbers, currency, time, and dates are handled. Simply click "Additional settings."

Tip: The Time tab of the Customize Format box (Figure 7-11) is where you can specify whether you prefer a 12-hour clock ("3:05 PM") or a military or European-style, 24-hour clock ("15:05").

Location tab

This tab identifies your computer's location. The point is so when you go online to check local news and weather, you get the *right* local news and weather—a handy feature if you're traveling.

Administrative tab

The "Copy settings" button applies the newly configured language settings to the following places:

- **The Windows Welcome screen,** so it'll be in the right language.

- **New user accounts,** so anyone who gets a new account on this computer will have your language, format, and keyboard settings conveniently available to them.

The "Change system locale" button on this tab lets you specify which language handles error messages and the occasional dialog box. (Just changing your input language may not do the trick.)

RemoteApp and Desktop Connections

The world's corporate system administrators can "publish" certain programs, or even entire computers, at the company headquarters—and you, using your laptop or home computer, can use them as though you were there.

But in Windows, these "published" resources behave like programs right on your PC. They're listed right in your Start menu, for heaven's sake (in a folder in "All apps" called, of course, "RemoteApp and Desktop Connections"), and you can search for them as you'd search for any apps.

The whole cycle begins when your company's network nerd provides you with the URL (internet address) of the published program. Once you've got that, open the RemoteApp and Desktop Connections control panel, and then choose "Access RemoteApp and desktops."

A wizard now appears; its screens guide you through pasting in that URL and typing in your corporate network name and password.

When it's all over, you see a confirmation screen; your new "connection" is listed in the control panel; and the folder full of "published" remote programs appears in your Start menu, ready to use.

Security and Maintenance

Open Security for a tidy dashboard of your firewall, antivirus, and other features, so you can see how they're doing. Open Maintenance for a similar dashboard of problems and features that could be affecting your PC. (Chapter 15 has more details.)

Sound

The Sound dialog box contains four tabs that control every aspect of your microphone and speakers: Playback, Recording, Sounds, and Communications. See Figure 7-12.

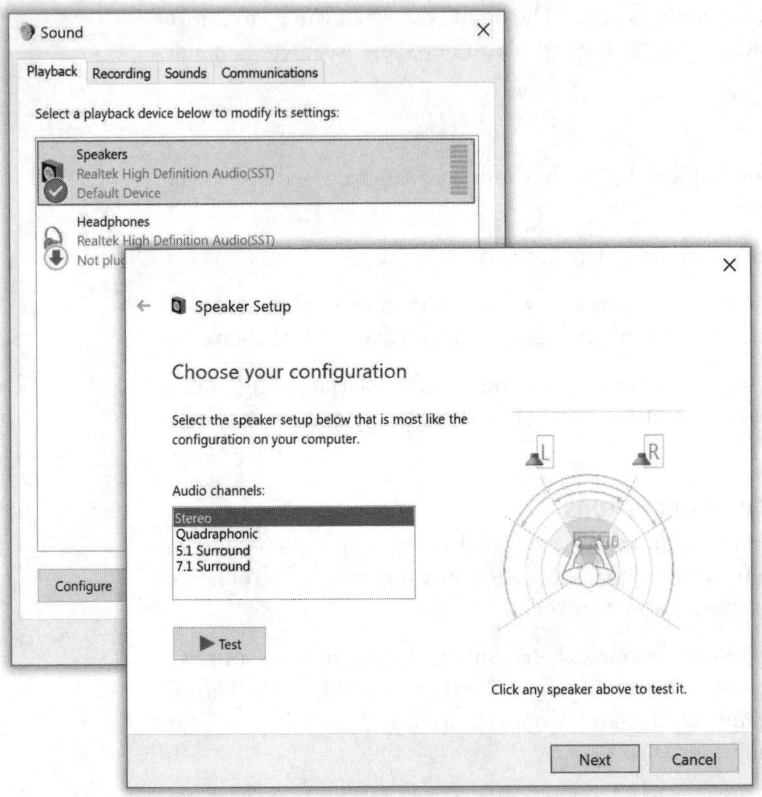

Figure 7-12:
Top: The Playback and Recording tabs display the devices your computer has for playing or recording sounds. If you select the device, you can see its properties or configure it.

Bottom: Here are some of the configurations you can set from the Playback tab, from simple stereo to 7.1 surround sound. Your setup may vary.

Playback and Recording tabs

These tabs simply contain the icons for each attached sound device. To change a device's settings, select it and then click Configure.

If you're configuring an output ("playback") device like a speaker or headset, you get a quick wizard that lets you set the speaker configuration (stereo or quadraphonic, for example). If you're configuring a microphone ("recording"), then you're taken to the Speech Recognition page, where you can set up your microphone.

Sounds tab

Windows comes with a tidy suite of little sound effects—beeps, musical ripples, and chords—that play when you turn on the PC, trigger an error message, empty the Recycle Bin, and so on. This tab lets you specify which sound effect plays for which situation; see page 159 for details.

Communications tab

This tab is designed for people who make phone calls using the PC, using a program like Skype or Google Hangouts. Here you can tell your PC to mute or soften other sounds—meaning music you've got playing—whenever you're on a PC call.

Nice touch.

Speech Recognition

This little program sets up all the speech-related features of Windows. See Chapter 6 for complete details.

Storage Spaces

The Storage Spaces feature can save every file onto two or more drives simultaneously, as a backup. For more on this somewhat obscure feature, visit this book's "Missing CD" page at *missingmanuals.com* and look for the PDF appendix to this chapter called "Storage Spaces."

Sync Center

The Sync Center is for syncing your files with folders elsewhere on your corporate network, so you'll always be up to date. For details, read "Three Obscure Mobility Features," a PDF appendix to this book on the "Missing CD" at *missingmanuals.com*.

System

The primary features are duplicated in the Settings app; see page 243.

This advanced Control Panel window is the same one that appears when you right-click your This PC icon and choose Properties from the shortcut menu (or press ⊞+Break key or ⊞+Pause key). It contains the various settings that identify every shred of circuitry and equipment inside, or attached to, your PC.

When you open the System icon in Control Panel, you're taken to the System window. Here you can find out:

- **What edition of Windows is installed on your computer.** Not all editions are made equal; if you're flailing to find some feature you could have sworn is supposed to be in Windows 10, it's good to check here. You might find out that the feature you want is available only on higher-priced versions.

- **The model name and speed of your PC's processor** (such as Intel Core 2 Duo, 2.8 GHz).

- **How much memory your PC has.** That's a very helpful number to know, particularly if you need to improve your computer's speed.

- **Your computer's name, domain, or workgroup, which can be modified with the "Change settings" button.** Remember, your computer name and description are primarily useful on a network, since that's how other people will identify your computer. Unless you tell it otherwise, Windows names your computer after your sign-in name, something like Casey Robbins-PC.

- **Whether or not your operating system is activated.** For more on Activation, check Appendix A.

- **What the Product ID key is for your system.** Every legal copy of Windows has a Product ID key—a long serial number that's required to activate Microsoft software. For more information about Product ID keys, see Appendix A.

At the left side of the window, you find a few links:

- **Device Manager.** This very powerful console lists every component of your PC: DVD/CD-ROM, Modem, Mouse, and so on. Double-clicking a component's name (or hitting the **>** symbol) discloses the brand and model of that component. For more on the Device Manager, see Chapter 14.

- **Remote settings.** To read about Remote Assistance—a feature that lets someone connect to your PC (via the internet) to help you troubleshoot—see "Remote Assistance," on this book's "Missing CD" page at *missingmanuals.com*.

- **System Protection.** This link takes you to the System Protection tab in the System Properties dialog box. Here you can keep track of the automatic system restores (snapshot backups of a system), or even create a new restore point. And if your computer has begun to act like it's possessed, you can go here to restore it to a previous restore point's state. Check out Chapter 16 for more details.

- **Advanced system settings.** Clicking this link opens the Advanced tab of the System Properties dialog box. This tab is nothing more than a nesting place for four buttons that open other dialog boxes—some of which aren't "advanced" in the least.

The first button opens the Performance Options dialog box, described on page 166. The second opens the User Profile box, which is covered in the free PDF appendix "Profiles" on this book's "Missing CD" at *missingmanuals.com*. The third opens a Startup and Recovery window. It contains advanced options related to *dual booting* (page 583) and what happens when the system crashes.

Finally, the Environment Variables button opens a dialog box that will get only technically minded people excited. It identifies, for example, the path to your Windows folder and the number of processors your PC has. If you're not in the computer-administration business, avoid making changes here.

Tablet PC Settings

This Control Panel item offers settings for touchscreen tablets. The Display tab lets you calibrate your touchscreen; the Other tab lets you specify whether you're right- or left-handed (to control where menus appear relative to your pen).

Taskbar and Navigation

This program teleports you to the Taskbar pane in Settings, where you can control every conceivable behavior of the taskbar. These options are covered in Chapter 2.

Troubleshooting

These features are duplicated in the Settings app; see page 262.

Here's a list of Windows' troubleshooters—step-by-step interview screens that walk you through fixing various problems. (Insert your own joke here about Windows' need for an entire program dedicated to troubleshooting.)

Anyway, you can find links here for running older programs in Windows 10, getting online, figuring out why your speakers aren't working, sleuthing out why your PC is getting so slow, and even inviting a trusted friend to share your screen to help you out.

User Accounts

The primary features are duplicated in the Settings app; see page 255.

This control panel is the master switch and control center for the user-accounts feature described in Chapter 18. If you're the only one who uses your PC, you can (and should) ignore it.

Windows Defender Firewall

The primary features are duplicated in the Settings app; see page 262.

In this age of digital technology, when most people's computers are connected at all times to the internet (and therefore always vulnerable to the internet), it's a good and reasonable idea to have a firewall protecting your computer from possible attacks and exploitation. To learn more about Windows Defender Firewall, see Chapter 11.

Windows Mobility Center

The Windows Mobility Center is a central panel for instant access to laptoppy/tablety features like screen brightness, volume, battery, and so on. The new Action Center is nearly an exact duplicate and is much easier to find. See page 96 for more on Action Center. For more on Windows Mobility Center, see the PDF appendix to this chapter called "Three Obscure Mobility Features." It's on this book's "Missing CD" at *missingmanuals.com*.

Windows To Go

This feature, for peripatetic corporate employees, lets you carry your entire work world on a flash drive. For more on this feature, look for the free PDF appendix called "Three Obscure Mobility Features" at *missingmanuals.com*.

Work Folders

If you work for a corporation, your kindly, all-knowing network administrator may have set up Work Folders for you—folders full of your documents that physically sit on protected computers at work, but that you can access across the internet even from your own home computer.

CHAPTER 8

The Windows Starter Apps

E ven after a fresh installation of Windows, your computer teems with a rich
array of preinstalled programs—as an infomercial might put it, they're your
free bonus gifts. And there are a lot of them.

Some are Microsoft Store apps, and some are traditional desktop programs. But in
Windows 10, they all behave alike—so for your reference pleasure, this chapter covers
every scrap of software that comes in your "All apps" menu, even the ones stored in
subfolders like Windows Accessories and Windows System.

You may, of course, have other apps—either those you've installed yourself or apps
provided by your computer maker. (For example, you may have the Microsoft Office
apps: Word, Excel, PowerPoint, Access, and so on.) This chapter, though, is dedicated
to the programs *every* copy of Windows has.

The New, Unified Design of Apps

Among the other problems with Windows 8: the design of Microsoft Store (Windows
Store) (Metro) (TileWorld) apps. They had no menus. They had few visible buttons.
These apps didn't really *do* anything—unless you knew about the secret, hidden strip
of commands known as the App bar.

It appeared only if you swiped upward onto the screen from beneath it. A lot of
people never realized that.

In Windows 10, Microsoft's starter apps have all been redesigned. No more hidden
controls. In fact, to make your life easier, Microsoft has blessed most of these apps with
the *same* basic design. You'll find it in the Alarms & Clock, Calendar, Groove Music,

Mail, Maps, Microsoft Solitaire Collection, Movies & TV, People, Photos, Weather, and Xbox apps, to name a few.

In this design, the app lives in a single window with a vertical menu column, always visible, hugging the left side (see Figure 8-1). At first it shows only icons.

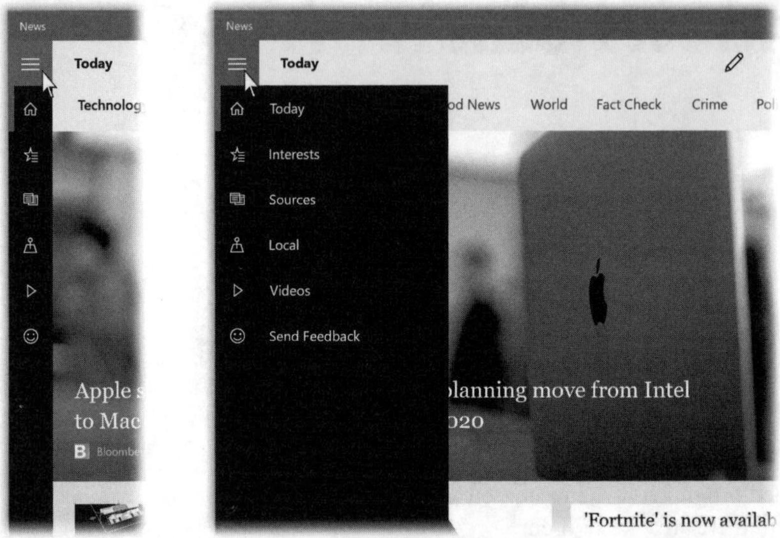

Figure 8-1:
The new standard design for Microsoft's built-in Windows apps (left) offers a black vertical menu column at the left side. If you use the app a lot, you'll eventually learn what these icons do. In the meantime, the ≡ icon expands the column, revealing the icons' names (right).

In this pillar of options, you'll find these consistent elements:

- **A ≡ button at the top.** Click to expand the column, revealing the icons' names. (Internally, Microsoft calls the ≡ button the "hamburger button," thanks to its resemblance to three horizontal layers of goodness.)

- **Send Feedback (☺).** The smiley face opens the Feedback Hub app (page 299), where you can submit bugs, complaints, and compliments to Microsoft.

- **A bunch of icons.** These vary by app, and they're described in this chapter. If there are a lot of them, as in the Sports app, the menu column of icons may actually scroll.

At the bottom of the main column:

- **Sign out.** This round photo represents you, and the account you've used to sign in.

- **A ⚙ button at the very bottom.** It opens a Settings panel, usually on the opposite side of the screen—on the right.

A ← button usually appears at the *very* top-left corner of the window. That, of course, is your Back button. It gets you out of the current screen, and walks you back, back, back, eventually to the app's main home screen. For example, if you're using the Maps app, the ← button backs you out of your directions, or Streetside, or Settings—and back to the main Maps display.

Tip: In most Microsoft Store apps, there's a keyboard shortcut for that ← button: Alt+←.

Not all Microsoft Store apps adopt Microsoft's suggestion of the left-side menu column, of course. But most of the built-in Windows apps do, so it's worth cozying up to the idea now.

3D Viewer

This little app, formerly called Mixed Reality Viewer, lets you dabble in what Microsoft calls *mixed reality* and the rest of the world calls *augmented* reality (where computer graphics are overlaid with the real-world camera image), without having to own a fancy AR headset. It's basically a camera app that lets you add 3D objects to your camera's feed and capture the result as a graphic. See Figure 8-2.

Figure 8-2:
3D Viewer might be useful, Microsoft says, for "a home decorator helping a client to visualize what a couch would look like in their living room, or a teacher demonstrating to students the size and scale of the Mars Rover."

Or feeding imaginary rhinos, of course.

Begin by choosing a 3D model (that is, a 3D image). The "3D library" button lets you search Microsoft's online catalog, or you can import a 3D model you've made in Paint 3D (page 318). The app immediately starts showing off by animating the Microsoft model. (Use the lower-right pop-up menus to try some other movements of the object.)

Using touch, mouse, pen, or keyboard, you can turn the object in space, move it around, zoom in, or reset its original position; choose Help→Controls for a cheat sheet of what does what. Using the right-side panel controls, you can adjust the lighting angles and colors.

When you turn on "Mixed reality" at the top right, your computer's camera turns on. (As you'd guess, this app works better on a tablet than a laptop.)

Click or tap to indicate where you want to place your object. You can now fiddle with the 3D object's size and rotation in space—and, when it looks good, select the normal camera-snap button to preserve the resulting hybrid image.

Note: You can do exactly the same thing in Paint 3D and even Photos; see page 328. Apparently, Microsoft *really* doesn't want us to miss this feature.

Alarms & Clock

Don't be deceived by the name. This app does let you set up alarms, and it does have a clock. But it does more—so much more. It's also a timer and a stopwatch.

Alarm Tab

If you travel much, this feature could turn out to be one of your machine's most useful functions. It's reliable, it's programmable, and it's fun to use (Figure 8-3).

Note: The alarm won't play unless the machine is on and awake (unless your computer has a feature called InstantGo, which keeps networking and clock functions going even when the PC is asleep). Doesn't that defeat the whole purpose? Come on—don't be a killjoy.

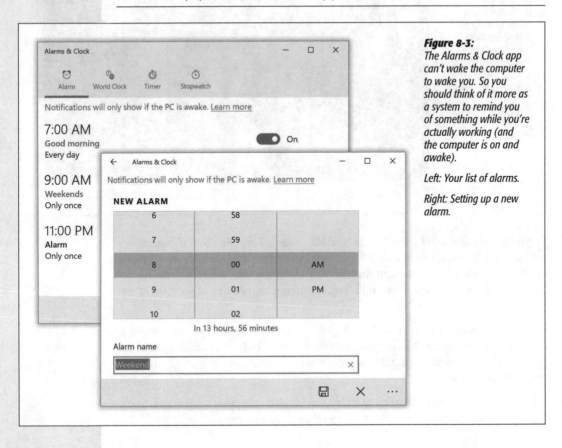

Figure 8-3:
The Alarms & Clock app can't wake the computer to wake you. So you should think of it more as a system to remind you of something while you're actually working (and the computer is on and awake).

Left: Your list of alarms.

Right: Setting up a new alarm.

Microsoft starts you off with a dummy alarm, set to 7 a.m., but switched off. To change the time, click it to enter editing mode (Figure 8-3, right). Now you can edit the alarm's name, time, repeat schedule, alarm sound, and snooze time.

When you finally hit the Save (⊟) button, the Alarm screen lists your new alarm (Figure 8-3, left). Just tap the On/Off button to prevent an alarm from going off. It stays in the list, though, so you can quickly reactivate it another day, without having to redo the whole thing.

You can hit the + button to set another alarm, if you like.

To edit an alarm, click it and proceed as described already; to delete it, click it and then tap 🗑.

When the alarm goes off, a notification appears on the screen, identifying the alarm and the time, and the sound rings.

You can snooze it or dismiss it (turn it off for good).

World Clock

The second tab of Alarms & Clock starts you out with one clock, showing the current time where you are.

The neat part is that you can set up several of these clocks and set each one to show the time in a different city. The result looks like the row of clocks in a hotel lobby, making you seem Swiss and precise.

By checking these clocks, you'll know what time it is in some remote city, so you don't wake somebody up at what turns out to be 3 a.m.

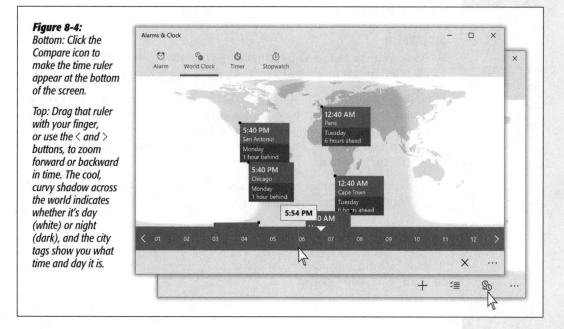

Figure 8-4:
Bottom: Click the Compare icon to make the time ruler appear at the bottom of the screen.

Top: Drag that ruler with your finger, or use the ⟨ and ⟩ buttons, to zoom forward or backward in time. The cool, curvy shadow across the world indicates whether it's day (white) or night (dark), and the city tags show you what time and day it is.

To specify which city's time appears on the clock, hit the + button at lower right. Type in the city you want. As soon as you tap a city name, you return to the World Clock display, where your new city time appears. Here's the fun you can have:

- **Zoom through time.** As Figure 8-4 makes clear, this is an interactive set of clocks. You can scroll through time and watch them change.

- **Pin a clock to the Start menu.** Right-click (or hold your finger down on) a city's time. From the shortcut menu, choose Pin to Start. And presto: There, on the right side of your Start menu, a new tile appears. It will always show that city and its current time, for your quick-glancing pleasure.

- **Delete a clock.** Right-click it (or hold your finger down on it). From the shortcut menu, choose Delete.

Timer

Countdown timers are everywhere in life. They measure the periods in sports and games, cooking times in the kitchen, penalties in hockey. The third tab in the Alarms & Clock app, Timer, is a countdown timer. You input a starting time, and it counts down to zero.

To set the timer, click the big digits; now you can change the name and the time of the timer. Hit the Save (🖫) button.

Finally, hit ▶. The timer counts down toward zero. You can hit the ‖ button to pause the countdown, if you like (and ▷ to resume it). Or hit ↻ to start it over or ↗ to make the numbers big and bold enough to see from the moon.

When the timer runs out, you get a notification and a sound, which will keep chiming until you hit Dismiss.

Stopwatch

You've never met a prettier stopwatch than this one. Hit ▷ to begin timing something: a runner, a train, a long-winded person who's arguing with you.

While the digits are flying by, you can tap the Lap button (🏳) as often as you like. Each time, the Laps list identifies how much time elapsed since the last time you tapped Lap. It's a way for you to compare, for example, how much time a runner is spending on each lap around a track. The large digits tell you how much time has elapsed since you started the stopwatch.

Tap ‖ to freeze the counter; tap ▷ to resume the timing. If you tap ↻, you reset the counter to zero and erase all the lap times.

Calculator

It would be a little silly for a major operating system to come without a pocket calculator app, wouldn't it? Yep.

Windows 10's version has a standard mode, scientific mode, a programmers' mode, and a powerful list of conversions (time, power, pressure, area, length, speed, and so on). See Figure 8-5.

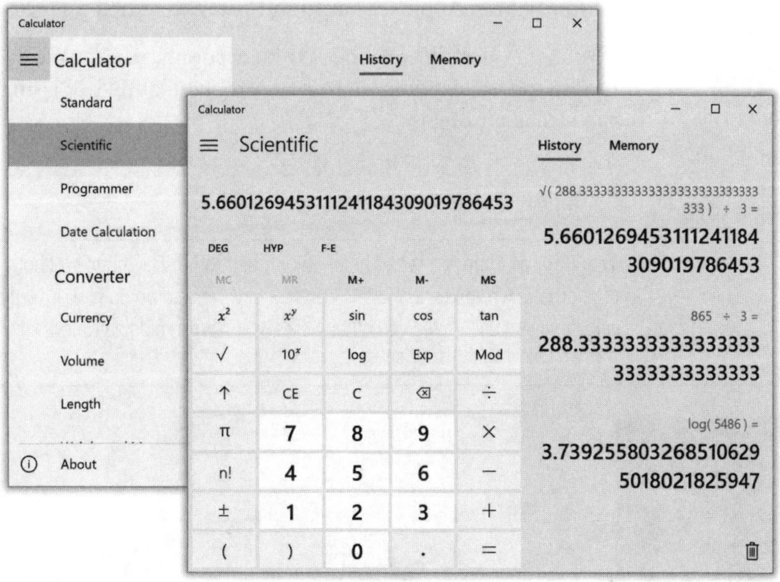

Figure 8-5:
The Calculator (left) offers three modes: Standard, Scientific, and Programmer. You can press Alt+1, Alt+2, and Alt+3 for those modes.

Use the menu column to choose from a huge list of conversions: volume, length, weight, temperature, energy, area, speed, time, power, and so on. Once you've specified the conversion type, specify what units you want to convert to or from. Handy, really.

Calendar

Calendar is not so different from those "Hunks of the Midwest Police Stations" paper calendars that people leave hanging on the walls for months past their natural life spans. But it offers several advantages over paper calendars. For example:

- **It can automate the process** of entering repeating events, such as weekly staff meetings or gym workouts.

- **Calendar can give you a gentle nudge** (with a sound and a message) when an important appointment is approaching.

- **It can subscribe to online calendars** from Outlook, Hotmail, or even your company's Exchange calendar, so you have all your life's agendas in one place.

Note: There may already be stuff on your calendar the first time you open it—if, elsewhere in Windows, you've already entered account information for an online account. For example, if you've entered your Facebook details, then all your friends' birthdays appear in Calendar automatically. You can, of course, turn off one account or another; read on.

That said, Calendar is among the simplest, most bare-bones calendar programs ever written. At least it won't overwhelm you.

Working with Views

When you open Calendar, your first order of business is to point it to your existing online calendars: your corporate calendar (Exchange), one of Microsoft's various free services (Outlook.com, Live.com, Hotmail, MSN), Google's (Gmail), or even Apple's (iCloud). (Yes, Apple's. That sound you hear is hell freezing over.)

If you don't already have one of these accounts, you can create a free Microsoft account on the spot. Then you see something like Figure 8-6. Using the toolbar at top, you can switch among these views:

- **Day** looks exactly like a day-at-a-time desk calendar. Scroll up and down to see the rest of the day.

Tip: But wait, there's a secret here! If you point to the Day button without clicking, you see the indicator for a drop-down menu. It offers "1 day," "2 day," and so on up to 6. It's letting you specify how *many* Day columns fit on each screen. In other words, you have a middle ground between Day view and Week view.

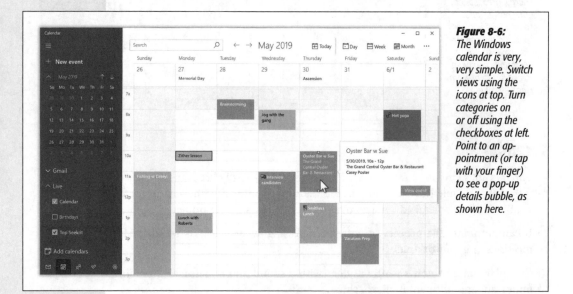

Figure 8-6:
The Windows calendar is very, very simple. Switch views using the icons at top. Turn categories on or off using the checkboxes at left. Point to an appointment (or tap with your finger) to see a pop-up details bubble, as shown here.

- **Week** fills the main display area with seven columns, reflecting the current week (that is, Sunday through Saturday).

Tip: This button, too, hides a drop-down menu. It offers "Work week," which shows just five columns (Monday through Friday).

- **Month** shows the entire month that contains today's date.

Tip: If you have a keyboard, you can instead hit Ctrl+Alt+1, +2, +3, +4, and +5 for Today, Day, Work Week, Week, and Month views.

Navigating in any of the views is easy and fun for the whole family:

- **Touchscreen:** Swipe vertically to move through the hours, horizontally to move through the days.

- **Mouse:** Turn the scroll wheel to move through the hours; add Shift to move through the days.

- **Keyboard:** The ← and → keys go to the previous/next day, and the ↑ and ↓ keys go to the previous/next hour.

In Month view, on the other hand, there's only one way to scroll: vertically, with your finger, keyboard, trackpad, or mouse.

Tip: A compact calendar appears at the left side. You can use it to jump quickly to a date that's far in the future (or the past, if you like to rewrite history).

To jump back to today's date, hit Today.

Making an Appointment: Quick Way

The basic calendar is easy to figure out. After all, with the exception of one unfortunate Gregorian incident, we've been using calendars successfully for centuries.

In Day, Week, or Month view, tap or click the correct time slot or date square. A little new-event box appears, where you can specify the name for your appointment ("Lunch with Chris" or whatever); start and end times (if, in fact, they're not already correct); and a location. Click Done or press Enter. You've just created an appointment.

Making an Appointment: Detailed Way

That "click-to-make-a-one-hour-appointment" method is quick and easy. But what if there's more to the story? What if you want a reminder? Or you want it to occur every week? Or you want to specify a calendar category (like Work or Home)?

In that case, you should open the more complete Details screen shown in Figure 8-7. Ways to open Details:

- **Open the small "new event" box first,** as described already. Then hit "More details."

- **Press Ctrl+N.** Of course, this method is slower than the click-the-time-slot method, because you have to specify the time and date manually.

- **Click "New event" at the top-left corner of the screen.** Once again, you have to specify the time and date manually.

On the Details screen, you can specify everything about the new appointment:

- **Event name.** For example, you might type *Fly to Phoenix*.

- **Calendar – [Account].** This is a drop-down menu on the right side of the "Event name" box. Beneath headings that represent your various calendar services—your Live.com account, Google, iCloud, Exchange, or whatever—you see whatever calendar *categories* you've created on that calendar service. You might see "Work – Gmail," "Football Club – Gmail," and "PTA Work – Outlook," for example.

These color-coded subsets can be anything you like. One person might have calendars called Home, Work, and TV Reminders. Another might have Me, Spouse 'n' Me, and The Kidz. A small business could have categories called Deductible Travel, R&D, and R&R.

(You can't create or edit calendar categories in Calendar itself—only on the originating services.)

Tip: You can, however, change the color associated with a category. Once you're back at the main calendar screen, right-click (or hold your finger down on) the category's name; choose from the palette that appears.

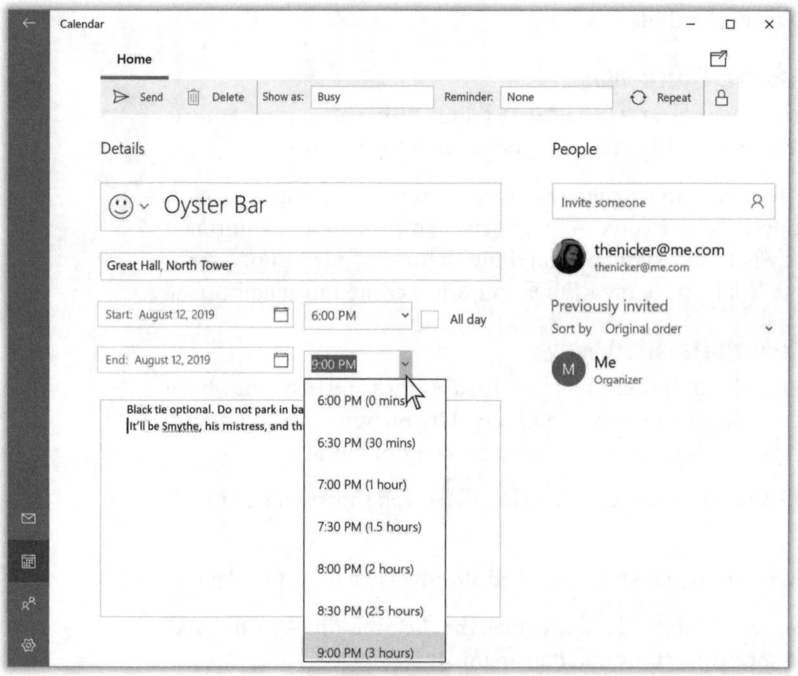

Figure 8-7:
Here's where you both create a new appointment and edit an old one. When choosing the End time, the drop-down menu shows you how long the appointment will be if you choose each time ("30 minutes," for example). Nice touch.

- **Location.** This field makes a lot of sense; if you think about it, almost everyone needs to record *where* a meeting is to take place. You might type a reminder for yourself like *My place*, a specific address like *212 East 23*, or some other helpful information, like a contact phone number or a flight number.

- **Start, End.** Separate drop-down menus (and a drop-down calendar) let you specify a date and time that this event starts and stops.

- **All day.** An "All day" event, of course, refers to something that has no specific time of day associated with it: a holiday, a birthday, a Windows book deadline. When you turn on this box, the name of the appointment jumps to the top of the day/week/month square, in the area reserved for this kind of thing.

- **Event description.** In this big box, you can type or paste any text you like—driving directions, contact phone numbers, a call history, or whatever.

- **People.** If the appointment is a meeting or some other gathering, you can type the participants' names here. As you type, a list of matching names from your People app appears, to make it easy to choose the one you want. (You can also type out a full email address of anyone here.)

  Once you've added a person's name, you can add another, and then another. Later, when you're finished creating this event, the Send button at top left will invite your lucky recipients via email. Each message comes with an *iCal.ics* attachment: a calendar-program invitation file. In many mail and calendar programs, opening this attachment automatically presents your invitation; the recipients can respond (by choosing the Accept, Maybe, or Decline buttons that appear in *their* calendar programs).

For each appointment, you can have even more fun with the options in the top toolbar. You can also indicate the following:

- **Show as.** If you're on a shared calendar—in an office, for example—the options in this drop-down menu are pretty standard: Free, Busy, Out of office, and Tentative.

  For each event you put on your own calendar, you can use these tags to signal co-workers your availability for meetings or calls. Your colleagues won't see *what* you're doing during that block ("Haircut," "Me time," or whatever)—only that you're "Busy."

- **Reminder.** This drop-down menu tells Calendar when to notify you when a certain appointment is about to begin. You can specify how much advance notice you want for this particular appointment. If it's a TV show, a reminder five minutes before airtime is probably fine. If it's a birthday, you might set up a warning a week in advance, so there's time to buy a present.

Tip: If you subscribe to the same calendar service on your phone, it'll remind you when the time comes. In other words, these reminders aren't useful only when you're sitting at your desk.

- **Repeat.** This button opens a new set of controls for recurring events: Daily, Weekly, and so on. Or you can turn on the day checkboxes to specify any more-complicated repeating pattern, like "Tuesdays and Wednesdays" or "First Monday of every month."

  You can also set an end date—a date when you want the repetitions to stop.

- **Private ( ).** If other people can see your chosen account (for example, if it's an Exchange calendar you use at work), then turning on this box means they can't

---

see this particular appointment. Great for events like "Colonoscopy" or "Court date re: public nuisance charge."

When you're finished setting up the appointment, hit the "Save and close" button at top left, or press Ctrl+S. (If invitees are involved, that button may say "Send" or, if you've made changes, "Send update.")

Your newly scheduled event now shows up on your calendar, complete with the color-coding that corresponds to the calendar category you've assigned.

Inspecting an Event

Usually, Calendar shows you only each appointment's name. But if you tap it or (with the mouse) point without clicking, a little box pops out to show more detail—the location and name of the person who created the appointment, for example.

If it's a meeting with other invitees, there's a handy button there: "I'm running late." One click, and boom: An outgoing email is written and addressed to everyone else who was invited to that meeting. Click Send and run for the cab.

If it's a repeating event, you have the choice of editing just that one event or the entire series of them.

Tip: The May 2019 Update introduces a long-missing Calendar feature: the ability to search for events! Just type into the search box at the top. (Well, you can search for events in your Outlook, Hotmail, Live, and Office 365 calendars. The Search command can't see into your Exchange Server, Gmail, Yahoo, or other calendar accounts.)

Editing Events

To edit an event, just click it (with your mouse or trackpad) or tap it twice (with your finger). You return to the screen shown in Figure 8-7, where you can make any changes you like.

Rescheduling Events

If an event in your life gets rescheduled, you can drag an appointment block vertically in a Day- or Week-view column to make it later or earlier the same day, or horizontally to another date in any view. (If you reschedule a recurring event, Calendar asks if you want to change only *this* occurrence, or this one *and* all future ones.)

If something is postponed for, say, a month or two, too bad. You can't drag an appointment beyond its month window. You have no choice but to open the Edit box and edit the starting and ending dates or times—or just cut and paste the event to the new date.

Lengthening or shortening events

If a scheduled meeting becomes shorter or your lunch hour becomes a lunch hour-and-a-half (in your dreams!), changing the length of the representative calendar event is as easy as dragging in any column view (see Figure 8-8).

Tip: In Week view, if you've grabbed the *bottom* edge of an appointment's block so the cursor changes, you can drag *horizontally* to make an appointment cross the midnight line and extend into a second day.

Figure 8-8:
To make the drag handles appear at top and bottom, tap a block with your finger—or, with the mouse, point without clicking. You can now drag the event's little white handle to make it take up more or less time on your calendar.

Deleting Events

To delete an appointment, open it and then hit Delete at the top.

If you're opening a recurring event, like a weekly meeting, a drop-down menu offers "Delete one" (you want to operate on only that particular instance of the event) or "Delete all" (you're deleting the whole series from that point forward).

If other people have been invited, the button says "Cancel meeting" instead of Delete; they'll be notified about the change. And when you hit that button, you're invited to type a little message of apology or shame.

What's in the Left-Side Panel

At the left side of Calendar, there's a handy panel of options. (If you see only a narrow strip of icons, hit the ☰ at top left to open the panel.)

There's a minicalendar, for quick navigation of your life's timeline. Below that: a list of your calendar accounts and the color-coded categories within them. By turning a category's checkbox on or off, you can show or hide *all* appointments in that category. That's an incredible way to wade through a crowded schedule to focus on, say, your kids' events. (There's an "Add calendars" button, too, for adding new calendar accounts.)

Below that: four icons. There's Mail (because email is something you often do when you're calendaring), Calendar (because you may want to switch back), People (opens your contacts list), and Settings. Read on.

Settings

If you choose ⚙ at lower left, you open the Settings panel on the *right* edge of the window. Here you've got these categories:

- **Manage Accounts.** Edit or delete any of your calendar accounts (Outlook, iCloud, Gmail, and so on).

- **Personalization.** What color scheme do you prefer? Do you want black/dark-gray backgrounds ("dark mode"), white/light-gray ones ("light mode"), or whatever you picked for Windows itself (page 151)? What wallpaper photo do you want for the background of Mail (has nothing to do with Calendar)?

- **Calendar Settings.** Specify what you consider the first day of the week (affects how Month and Week views appear), which hours of the day you work (affects how Day view appears), and which days of the week you work (affects how "Work week" appears). You can also allow week numbers to appear on your calendar (as in, "Week 1" for the first days of January) or turn on Alternate Calendars (like Hebrew Lunar, Umm al-Qura, and so on) to make Calendar display a second label on every month and date.

  If you have Outlook (the desktop app, the phone app, or a free Outlook.com account), you can also turn on Interesting Calendars. Those are canned sets of dates for TV program schedules, sports, concerts, and other events that Microsoft has put together for you. (From the drop-down menu, choose which of your calendar accounts you want to receive these Interesting items.)

- **Weather Settings.** Choose your preferred temperature units (F or C).

- **What's new.** Opens a web page pointing out the new features in Mail and Calendar.

- **Help.** Opens a web page where you're offered some Help pages for using Calendar.

- **Trust Center.** If this switch is on, you're enabling "locally relevant content" to "provide functionality that's relevant to your usage and preferences." But you knew that.

- **Feedback** opens the Feedback Hub (page 299), to send suggestions to Microsoft.

- **About** tells you your Calendar version.

Camera

Almost every tablet and laptop these days has a camera—sometimes two (front and back). Even some desktop PCs have webcams built in. Nobody is going to take professional portraits with these cameras, but they're fine for video chats and Facebook snaps. Camera (Figure 8-9) is the app you use for taking pictures and videos. (If you don't see the Camera app, it's because your gadget doesn't have a camera.)

Note: The first time you open this app, Microsoft's privacy team has your back. A message asks if it's OK for Camera to know your location (so it can place-stamp the pictures) and if it's allowed to use your camera and microphone. It's just making sure that the camera isn't opening on behalf of some nasty piece of spyware.

To take a picture, tap the 📷 button, or press the space bar or Enter.

A few cryptic icons haunt the edges of the window (their assortment and their positions vary according to your machine's camera features):

- **Settings** (⚙). The exact list of settings varies by PC. But a typical settings setup lets you specify what happens when you hold down the camera button (shoot video or capture rapid-fire burst-mode shots), the proportions of the photos you take (like 4 × 3, 3 × 2, or 16 × 9), what kind of composition grid lines you want superimposed on the preview, the quality and resolution of video and photos you want to capture, whether you want image stabilization turned on, and so on.

    "Capture living images" means that, when you take a picture, you'll actually get a weird hybrid entity: a still photo with a one-second video attached (with sound). When you share it with another Windows 10 fan, they'll see just what you see: a still photo that can "play back." If you share it with anyone else, you're asked whether you want to send it as a still photo or a one-second video.

    "Time lapse" lets you turn on a feature that, in self-timer mode, keeps shooting photos automatically until you press the shutter button to stop it.

Tip: In Settings, if you turn on "Pro mode," you get buttons around the edges of the app window for more sophisticated photo controls. They may include WB (white balance—that is, the photo's overall color cast); ISO (light sensitivity—higher numbers add light to a dim scene, but increase the graininess); shutter speed (faster speeds freeze action better and eliminate blur, but may dim the scene); and exposure (overall lightness of the photo). When you select one of these buttons, a big slider appears that lets you dial in the level you want for that setting. "Auto" is always one of the options.

Figure 8-9:
If you're used to the 3-inch screen on the back of a digital camera, discovering that your new preview screen is the entire size of your tablet or laptop comes as quite a shock. In essence you're seeing the finished photo before you even take it.

- **Change camera** (⟲). This button appears only if your computer has cameras on both the front and the back—a common arrangement on tablets. (The back camera is for photography; the front camera is for video chats.) Each time you tap this button, your view switches to the other camera.

- **Zoom** (⊕). If the slider isn't there, click the magnifying-glass icon to make it appear. It's generally a digital zoom, meaning that it works by enlarging the picture, degrading the quality.

- **HDR** (⊡). In one regard, digital cameras are still pathetic: Compared with the human eye, they have terrible *dynamic range.* That's the range from the brightest to darkest spots in a single scene. If you photograph someone standing in front of a bright window, you'll get just a solid-black silhouette. The camera doesn't have enough dynamic range to handle both the bright background and the person standing in front of it.

  A partial solution: *HDR* (high dynamic range) photography. That's when the camera takes three (or even more) photos—one each at dark, medium, and light exposure settings. Its software combines the best parts of all three, bringing details to both the shadows and the highlights. If you see this button, then your machine has a built-in feature that attempts to build an HDR shot automatically. This is the on/off switch.

- **Self timer** (⟳). Yes, kids, your machine has a self-timer. It works in both photo and video modes. It's great for getting a self-portrait or a self-video when you don't want to be right at the machine.

  Tap this button once for a drop-down menu that offers two-, five-, or ten-second countdowns. Now when you hit the ▣ button, "3…2…1" countdown digits appear—and then the photo gets snapped, or the video begins.

The Camera Roll

To see the picture or video you've just captured, jump into the Camera Roll. It's a special album that holds photos you took with this computer (as opposed to those you've rounded up from other sources).

The Camera Roll opens when you tap the lower-right screen icon, which looks like a miniature of your most recent snap. You're now faced with handy buttons like Delete, Rotate, Crop, Edit & Create, Print, and Share. Technically, you're now in the Photos app, which is why you have to turn to page 328 to read about the functions of these buttons.

Connect

This simple app is the welcoming committee for Android-phone screen mirroring. That is, you can view what's on your phone's screen—on your PC's screen. See page 175.

Feedback Hub

The New Microsoft isn't some ivory tower; it seeks your input on bugs and design flaws at every turn. In fact, it's dedicated a keystroke (⊞+F) to opening this app.

Most things you're inclined to report have already been reported; millions of people are using Windows. That's why, when you first choose the Feedback (⚐) tab, you see a list of "trending" issues (things people are talking about)—and when you type your complaint into the "Give us feedback" box, you see matching, previously submitted gripes.

If you hit "Add new feedback," though, you get a full-blown reporting screen, complete with the option to attach a screenshot, a file, or your PC's latest diagnostics file. If enough people agree with your report (and upvote it), Microsoft engineers may, in fact, take notice and fix the problem. Don't expect a free T-shirt.

Game Bar

If you're a gamer, you know triumphing in a video game isn't much fun if nobody's there to see you do it. Game Bar (Figure 8-10) is like a DVR for your PC. It's intended to record and broadcast your video-game highlights, but it can actually record stills

Figure 8-10:
Doesn't matter if you're recording a web browser, a map, or a spreadsheet: If you want to capture video, Game Bar is at the ready.

The central round Record button on the Game Bar starts the recording within the current window. In this case, you're capturing a thrilling moment in your Solitaire app.

or video of *any* app. It could be Maps, or Mail, or a web browser—doesn't matter. (Keep that in mind next time you're making a training video.)

Note: Two things Game Bar *can't* record are the desktop and File Explorer windows. For that, you'd need a more professional video-capture program like Camtasia.

To set up your recording parameters, open ▦→⚙→Gaming→Captures. The settings here govern the quality of the recordings, maximum length, audio, storage location, and so on.

When you're ready to capture your PC visuals, press ▦+G. Now the Game Bar appears, newly overhauled in the May 2019 Update. It has five icons:

- **Take screenshot.** Saves a still image of whatever is on your screen. Keyboard shortcut: ▦+Alt+PrtScrn.

- **Record last 30 sec.** Captures the last 30 seconds of activity as a video—yes, it's retroactive recording, great for game highlights! Keyboard shortcut: ▦+Alt+G.

- **Start recording.** Record video starting now. Keyboard shortcut: ▦+Alt+R. Now go about your business in whatever app you're using. Play, zoom, scroll, click, do whatever you need to do. Behind the scenes, Game Bar is creating a beautiful audio-and-video clip. You have an hour to fill, if necessary.

  When it's all over, press ▦+Alt+R again. (Or, if you can't remember that, press ▦+G to open the Game Bar, and then click the square Stop Recording button.)

- **Turn mic on while recording.** Do you want your own blathering captured as part of the recorded video? Keyboard shortcut: ▦+Alt+M.

Tip: While you're recording, a tiny version of the Game Bar floats on your screen. It contains a Stop Recording button and a microphone On/Off button. It also shows how long you've been recording.

Game Settings

If you choose ▦→⚙→Gaming, a wealth of options awaits for your game-playing pleasure. The tabs include these:

Game Bar. The Game Bar is a floating toolbar intended for recording game activity (or any screen activity). On this screen, you turn the feature on and off, and set up keyboard shortcuts for starting and stopping recordings, capturing screenshots, and adjusting microphone and start/stop keystrokes for game broadcasting.

Captures. Suppose you use the Game Bar to record some screen videos. Where do you want Windows to put them?

What audio and video quality do you want them to have? At what volume level? Here's where you answer those questions.

Game Mode dedicates as much of your PC's power as possible to the game you're playing, so you get smooth animation and fast response. Here's the on/off switch. (See page 361.)

Xbox Networking. A page of stats about your internet speed and bandwidth—critical numbers for anyone in the business of streaming game video to the internet.

- **Start broadcasting** is described next. Keyboard shortcut: ⊞+Alt+B.

And how do you find your recordings? They're in your Videos→Captures folder, each named after the app, the time, and the date. (They also appear in the Xbox One app; select the Captures icon, the sixth icon down).

Tip: Or, when the notification appears (lower right of your screen) to tell you the recording was successful, click or tap it.

Broadcasting Your Games

These days, games aren't just fun for the person playing them. Millions of people find it just as entertaining to watch *other* people play. Mostly, they do that at Twitch.com, the world headquarters for watching and commenting on live, streaming games.

But Microsoft now offers its own, super-simple version of the same thing on a site called Mixer.com. (It's what was called Beam when Microsoft bought it in 2016.) Not only is Mixer free and easy to use, but the tools you need to broadcast your own game-playing sessions are also built right into Windows. If your streams become popular enough, you can even make money through a Mixer "partnership." (Note, though, that Mixer is newer and much smaller than Twitch or YouTube Gaming, so there may be fewer sponsorship dollars to go around.)

Tip: For most people, the factory settings work fine. But if you'd like to fiddle with the details of your broadcast—frame rate, audio quality, microphone volume, and so on—visit ⊞→⚙→Gaming→Broadcasting.

When it's showtime, fire up the game you want to broadcast—any kind, any brand. Open the Game Bar by pressing ⊞+G. Then, when you're ready, press ⊞+Alt+B, or hit the ⟲ button.

Note: Certain games in full-screen mode prevent the Game Bar from appearing. If that's your situation, you can start and stop broadcasting without the Game Bar: Press ⊞+Alt+B. You can also press ⊞+Alt+W to hide or show the live camera view during your broadcast.

After you confirm a couple of permission screens, a setup console now appears. Double-check these parameters:

- **Stream window.** What do you want the world to see? Just the game ("Game"), or the entire Windows screen ("Desktop"), which could be useful if you intend to switch apps mid-broadcast, or to show somebody activity in File Explorer?

- **Webcam.** Which corner of the screen should hold the live camera view of your face as you play and talk?

The preview shows how your broadcast will appear to the world. If you approve, choose "Start broadcast."

Everything you're doing is now visible to anyone who has joined your Mixer.com channel, which Windows creates automatically. (It's named after your Xbox Live name.)

Your action also appears on your Xbox Live activity feed, so your Xbox friends can admire it using their game consoles.

Tip: Obviously, it's no fun to broadcast your gaming magnificence if nobody's watching. To spread the word, send around the web address of your Mixer channel. (Select "Your channel" in the Broadcast setup window.) If your Xbox gamertag (name) is Killmaster2003, for example, then your Mixer page's address is *mixer.com/killmaster2003*. Anyone who goes to that page can watch you play and can comment in real time.

A small window showing your broadcast appears as you play; at the top, a thin control bar offers buttons for pausing the broadcast, moving the camera's inset, turning off the camera or microphone, switching to the chat window, and seeing how many people are watching you (and how long you've been broadcasting).

Tip: Don't use Game Mode while broadcasting. The mere act of broadcasting already slows down the game animation slightly; Game Mode throttles the broadcasting data in the name of making the animation smoother.

Get Help

Believe it or not, Windows 10 no longer comes with a built-in Help system. Instead, you can use the taskbar search box to find help by searching the web.

Figure 8-11:
A for effort, Microsoft, but the Get Help virtual agent is virtually clueless about most questions. If you keep clicking "No" (that didn't help me), you eventually get to options for reaching an actual person for actual help.

You also get this little app, though, which is something of a fakeout. "I'm Microsoft's Virtual Agent," says a smiling female cartoon, making you think you're about to experience some kind of super-cool artificial-intelligence helper that understands plain English (Figure 8-11).

When you type your problem into the text box at bottom, though, you'll quickly discover that the "virtual agent" is no more than a web search page. You get a bunch of links that include all kinds of results for operating systems, programs, and computers that don't apply to you.

Fortunately, once you've struck out with the automated agent, you're offered a "Talk to a person" link, with choices like "Call me back" (complete with estimated wait times), "Schedule a call," "Chat" (including the number of people waiting their turns), and "Ask the community" (a bulletin board where you can see if other mere mortals know the answer to your question; patience is required).

Groove Music

At one time, Groove Music was Microsoft's paid music service—its version of Spotify. In the end, Groove couldn't find its groove, and Microsoft shut down the whole thing. Now, when you open up this old app, there's an ad to download and install, if you can believe it, Spotify. That's what Microsoft recommends for music subscriptions—the very service that killed off its own attempt.

Note: The Groove Music app may still display nonfunctional vestiges of the old Groove service–buttons that say Download or "Make available offline," for example. Just let them quietly rot by the side of the road.

The main menu column at left serves as the outline for the following pages' worth of description.

Note: Whenever music is playing, playback controls appear at the bottom of the window. They do just what you'd expect: Previous Song, Pause, Next Song, Volume, Shuffle, Repeat. There's usually a scroll bar, too, showing where you are in the song and permitting you to skip to another spot.

Search

This search box finds everything from everywhere: songs, bands, albums; on your PC, in Microsoft's music stores. As you type, a drop-down menu proposes name matches, to save you typing.

My Music

Here are all the physical music files (MP3 files, for example) that Groove has found in your Music folder or your OneDrive's Music folder.

Note: If certain files aren't showing up, maybe they're in a folder Windows isn't looking for. Hit ⚙ and then "Choose where we look for music" to show it the correct drive or folder.

Use the Songs, Artists, or Albums buttons to specify how you want your music displayed. You see something like Figure 8-12.

In general, all three of these views are alike: They present all your music, grouped by album, performer, or individual song. At the top, four important controls appear:

- **Shuffle all.** When turned on (appears in color), Groove Music will play back the music on this screen in random order. The number in parentheses shows you *how many* songs you've got.

- **Sort by.** This drop-down menu lets you sort the music you're examining by date, alphabetically by name, by year, by musical genre, or by performer.

- **Filter.** This drop-down menu lets you show only the music files from one source or another: "Available offline" (you won't need an internet connection), "Streaming" (not actually on your computer—playing over the internet), "Only on this device" (not showing what's on your network or OneDrive), "On OneDrive," "Purchased" (from the now-defunct Groove service), or "Groove Music Pass." This item shows you whatever songs you'd downloaded from Groove Music while it was still alive and you were paying monthly.

Figure 8-12:
You can sort your music using the drop-down menus at top.

In Albums and Artists views, you see cover art like this. In Songs view, you see a simple table—a list—with columns for title, singer, album name, length, and year of release. The ▶ button and + button (meaning "Add to a playlist") also appear.

• **Genre.** Another drop-down menu. This one lets you see only the songs that are Country, Jazz, Pop, Rock, or whatever.

Whenever you've drilled all the way down to a list of songs (from a certain band or on a certain album, for example), checkboxes appear as you point to each song's name. As soon as you start checking boxes, a strip of options appears at the bottom of the screen, referring to what you want to do with these selected musics: Play them, add them to a playlist (+), or delete them. There are also buttons for Cancel (select nothing) and "Select all."

In Albums and Artists view, clicking or tapping takes you to further information screens, with options like Play, Add to (playlist), Show artist, Pin to Start, Edit Info, and Delete.

Recent Plays

Here's a list of songs you've played lately.

Now Playing

Whenever music is playing, no matter how far you've meandered in Groove Music, the "Now playing" button in the list at left (ılı) summons a full screen of information. It shows the album art, the list of songs from that album, and a "Save as a playlist" button.

Tip: Groove Music's taskbar icon sprouts basic playback controls that appear when you point to it (or tap with your finger).

Playlists

A playlist is a group of songs you've placed together, in a sequence that makes sense to you. One might consist of party tunes; another might hold romantic dinnertime music; a third might be drum-heavy workout cuts.

Creating playlists

To create a playlist, hit the + button next to the word Playlists in the list at left. Type a name for the playlist ("Rockout Toonz," "Makeout Music," whatever), and choose "Create playlist."

Now a playlist icon called "Rockout Toonz" (or whatever you called your latest list) appears in the list of playlists at left. All you have to do is add songs to it. To do that, choose "+ Add to" at the top of the screen, or hit the + wherever you see it—on the "Now playing" screen, for example, next to any selected song name, or on the Albums and Artists pages for your collection.

Wherever it appears, it produces a drop-down menu of playlist names. Specify which playlist should be the new home for that song.

Editing, rearranging, and deleting playlists

To perform any kind of surgery to one of your playlists, select its name in the list at left.

The buttons below its name at the top of the screen let you add more songs (+), rename the playlist (✐), or delete it (choose ⋯ and then Delete).

You can also operate on the individual songs inside a playlist. Tap one of the songs; the − button next to the ▷ means "Delete this song" (from the playlist, not from your collection). You can also rearrange the songs by dragging them up or down the list.

Tip: Like many of the Microsoft Store apps, Groove Music is intended to be bare-bones and simple. It offers the basic functions and no more; for example, it doesn't let you rip your audio CDs to your computer, edit song information, or create "smart playlists."

If you'd prefer something a little fuller fledged, don't forget that Windows Media Player is waiting for you back at the Windows desktop. Or you could download an even nicer, more complete free program like MusicBee. It's available from this book's "Missing CD" page at *missingmanuals.com*.

[Your Name]

The icon here reveals your name and account details.

Settings (⚙)

Here's the full Settings page for Groove Music. Most of the options here are self-explanatory, but a few are worth noting:

- **Music on this PC.** Here you tell the app which folders contain your music files. You can even import playlists from an existing copy of Apple's iTunes.

- **Set Now Playing artist art as my lock screen.** Cool: When your computer is sitting there, unused except as a jukebox, its Lock screen can show what's playing right now.

- **Set Now Playing artist art as my wallpaper.** Windows can even change your desktop wallpaper along with each song, showing the photo of the performer.

- **Mode.** Do you prefer white text against black, or black on white?

GEM IN THE ROUGH

Universal Playback Controls

You can start music playing and then dive into other apps or programs; the music continues to play. You know—background

music for your work session. But what if you have to take a phone call or to speak sternly to a child? Do you have to muddle all the way back to the Music app to pause playback?

Don't be silly. If you have a physical keyboard, just tap one of your volume keys. Up pops this audio palette, containing Previous Song, Next Song, Pause, and volume controls. The album cover appears, too—a nice touch. Of course, you can also press the mute key to silence the music instantly.

Mail

The built-in Windows 10 Mail app is easy to use, it's beautiful, and—especially if you have a touchscreen—it offers a fast, fluid way to work. It gets its own chapter in this book: Chapter 10.

Maps

Now that Windows is also a tablet operating system, a Maps program is more or less a must-have.

Maps (which is powered by Bing, which is powered by HERE Technologies) lets you type in any address or point of interest in the United States or many other countries and see it plotted on a map. It can give you spoken, turn-by-turn driving directions, just like a dashboard GPS unit. It also gives you a live national Yellow Pages business directory and real-time traffic-jam alerts, if you have an internet connection. You have a choice of a street-map diagram or actual aerial photos, taken by satellite.

Meet Maps

When you open the Maps app, you see—a map (Figure 8-13).

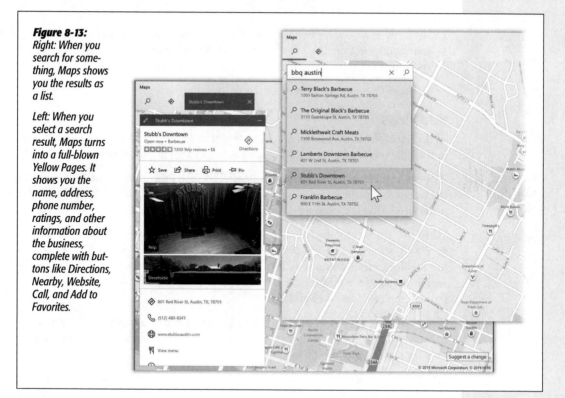

Figure 8-13:
Right: When you search for something, Maps shows you the results as a list.

Left: When you select a search result, Maps turns into a full-blown Yellow Pages. It shows you the name, address, phone number, ratings, and other information about the business, complete with buttons like Directions, Nearby, Website, Call, and Add to Favorites.

Note: You may also see a question: Maps asks you if it's allowed to use your current location, so it can show you where you are. The only reason to choose Block is if you think it's creepy that Maps, and by extension Microsoft, knows where you are.

You can scroll in any direction. You can also zoom in or out, using any of the usual techniques (two-finger pinch or spread; turn the mouse's scroll wheel). You can also double-tap or double-click to zoom into a particular spot.

Tip: At the top of the Maps window (or bottom, depending on the window size), a toolbar of useful controls appears. Among them: A ⋯ button with Share, Print, and Settings options. Settings contains some useful controls: kilometers versus miles, for example, Mode (dark or light color scheme), and the option to download maps so you don't need an internet connection to use them.

On the right: four awesome buttons. Here's what they do, from top to bottom:

- **Rotate North to top.** Click or tap to orient the map so north is up. (Which seems like a "duh" function, until you realize that sometimes you'll have rotated the map deliberately and need to get it back.)

- **Tilt.** Angles the map in a sort of 3D-ish way. You might find that it better resembles those car-dashboard GPS displays this way.

- **Show my location.** If you ever find that you've scrolled (or searched) away from your home location, this icon (or the Ctrl+Home keystroke) makes the map scroll and zoom until the "You are here" diamond is dead center on your screen.

- **+ and –.** These are your zoom-in/zoom-out buttons.

Map Views

At the top of the screen, seven more important icons appear. Most are described later in this chapter, but for now, don't miss the Map Views button/menu.

It opens a palette of viewing options. "Aerial" displays the map as satellite photos of the real world. Zoom in far enough, and you can find your house. (As opposed to the usual view—roads represented as lines—which Microsoft calls "Road.")

Turn on "Traffic" to see free, real-time traffic reporting—color-coded on major roadways, showing you the current traffic speed. Green for good traffic flow, yellow for slower traffic, and red for true traffic jams. You can even opt to see icons for Incidents (accidents and construction sites, for your stressing pleasure) or Cameras (speed-trap cameras—beware!).

If you don't see any colored lines, it's either because traffic is moving fine or because Microsoft doesn't have any information for those roads. Usually you get traffic info only for highways, and only in metropolitan areas.

"Streetside" is Microsoft's version of Google's Street View, and is described next. And the Windows Ink toolbar (✐) provides a palette of tools that, if you have a touchscreen and a stylus, let you draw or write notes onto the map (great for showing other people important places or directions) and measure distances.

Streetside

Streetside (Figure 8-14) is a mind-blowing way to explore maps. It lets you stand at a spot on the map and "look around." You're seeing actual photos of the street you seek; you can turn right or left and actually move through the still photos. It's a great way to investigate a neighborhood before you move there, for example, or to scope out the restaurant where you're supposed to meet someone.

(To create Streetside, Microsoft, like Google before it, has to drive specially equipped photography vans up and down every single road in the world, capturing photos and GPS data. So far, it's done so only in the most populated areas of the U.S. and Europe, but it has big plans.)

When you turn on Streetside (on the Map Views panel), the map changes. If you zoom out enough, you'll see puddles of blue shading in populated areas. These are the places where Streetside is available. Click there (or navigate there), and then proceed as shown in Figure 8-14.

Figure 8-14:
The bluish tints on streets and towns indicate Streetside availability. In these areas, you can see, with photos, exactly what it looks like to be on the ground at a certain spot on the map. Drag to look around you. Click or tap farther down a road to jump there, or click the weird black disk icon to open the map panel shown here (bottom). Zoom with your mouse wheel, or by scrolling on the trackpad or pinching with two fingers on the touchscreen.

Searching the Maps

You're not always interested in finding out where you are; often, you want to see where something *else* is. To search Maps, hit $\mathcal{P}$ and then type into the search box at top.

Here's what Maps can find for you:

- **An address.** You can skip the periods (and usually the commas, too). And you can use abbreviations. Typing *710 w end ave nyc* will find 710 West End Avenue, New York, New York. (In this and any of the other examples, you can type a zip code instead of a city and a state.)

- **An intersection.** Type *57th and lexington, ny ny*. Maps will find the spot where East 57th Street crosses Lexington Avenue in New York City.

- **A city.** Type *chicago il* to see that city. You can zoom in from there.

- **A zip code or neighborhood.** Type *10024* or *greenwich village nyc*.

- **A point of interest.** Type *washington monument* or *niagara falls*.

- **A commercial establishment.** You can use Maps as a glorified national Yellow Pages. If you type, for example, *pharmacy 60609,* blue numbered dots show you all the drugstores in that Chicago zip code. It's a great way to find a gas station, a cash machine, or a hospital in a pinch.

  Select a listing to see a full dossier about that place.

Tip: You can tap or click either place. That is, you can tap a numbered circle to auto-scroll the info column to the corresponding description, or you can tap a description to auto-scroll the map to the corresponding numbered circle.

Directions

If you choose Directions ($\diamond$), you get *two* search bars, labeled A and B (Figure 8-15, top left). That's right: Microsoft is *literally* prepared to get you from Point A to Point B.

Type in two addresses, using the keyboard. After typing, press Enter or hit the →.

Three features save you time here:

- **The A address may already say "My Location."**

- **If you've saved any locations as Favorites** (described in a moment), then they appear here, too, for quick selecting.

- **As you type, Windows displays a tappable list** of matching locations.

Once you've selected your A and B, hit "Get directions." A choice of proposed routes appears on the map, showing the distance and the estimated time for your travel (Figure 8-15).

Three option icons appear above the directions summary. They let you specify how you're planning to travel: by car, by public transportation, or on foot. Yes, that's right: It's turn-by-turn *walking* directions.

Tip: Select ⚙ to view some useful controls for things you might want to avoid—like Traffic, Toll roads, Unpaved roads, and Ferries. (Because there's nothing like crashing into a ferry to ruin your day.)

Figure 8-15:
Top left: The Swap button (↑↓) switches the A and B locations, which is great when you want to find your way home again.

Lower right: Turn-by-turn driving instructions!

If you see an icon for an accident or a construction zone, you can tap it to open a panel describing the details and expected clearing time.

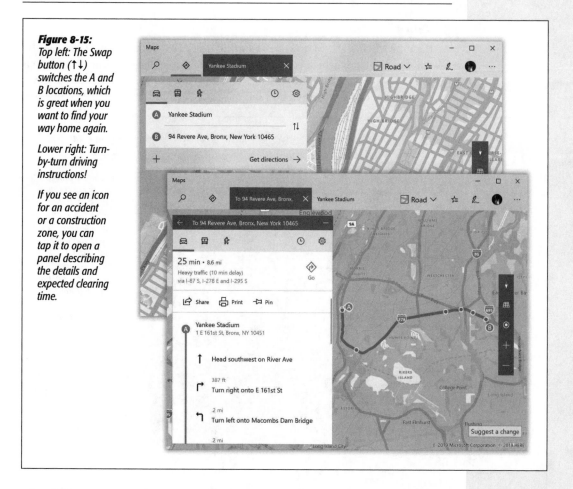

Choose the route you want. At this point, on a tablet, Maps is a full-blown GPS navigation app. It shows where you are as you drive, speaks turning instructions, and auto-scrolls the map as you drive. You can also hit the > at top right to view upcoming turns. (Hit the ← at top left to end the guidance.)

Favorites

If you're like most people, you tend to live in one place. You probably have a home, and you may very well have a place of work. It's possible you have a friend or two.

Fortunately, you don't have to painstakingly re-enter these addresses every time you want directions someplace. You can designate any place, or even any set of directions, as a favorite; just tap the ☆ that appears on the information panel for any address or establishment. From the shortcut menu, choose Favorites, Home, or Work.

Once you've accumulated a few, it's easy enough to call them up again: Tap the ☆☰ icon at top. Tap a Favorite place to see it on the map.

3D Cities

All the time Microsoft was trawling the world's cities to create Streetside, it was also assembling 3D Cities, which is closely modeled on Apple's Flyover feature. It depicts certain cities (150 and counting) as three-dimensional models—like aerial views, except that you can *peek behind* buildings (Figure 8-16).

Figure 8-16:
3D Cities is a dynamic, interactive, photographic 3D model of certain major cities. It looks something like an aerial video, except that you control the virtual camera. You can pan around these scenes, looking over and around buildings to see what's behind them.

To try it out, hit ⋯ (More) on the toolbar; from the menu, choose 🏛 3D Cities. Choose from the list of cities. Here's what you can try out if you have a touchscreen:

- **Move the map** by dragging with one finger.

- **Zoom** by pinching or spreading with two fingers.

- **Rotate the map** by twisting two fingers.

- **Change your viewing angle** by dragging up or down with two fingers.

If you have a mouse or trackpad:

- **Move the map** by dragging.

- **Zoom** by turning the mouse wheel (or dragging two fingers on the trackpad).

- **Rotate the map** by pointing to the little compass needle (at the top of the vertical toolbar). A tiny rotation-arrow button appears on each side, which you can click to turn the map.

- **Change the viewing angle** by adding the Shift key to the zooming method.

Offline Maps

Ordinarily, the Maps app gets its pictures of the world from the internet, downloading them as you scroll. That generally works—except when you're not online, or when you're on an expensive cellular connection. In both cases, the solution is offline maps: Download the map images for a certain country before you go there.

To do that, hit ⋯ (More) on the toolbar→⚙; under "Offline maps," choose "Choose maps." You arrive on a page of the Settings app where you can choose "Download maps." Choose a continent, and then a country, whose images you want to download now, while you still have an internet connection. Windows tells you how much room each one will require. (There's a "Delete all maps" button, too, so you can recover the space once your trip is over.)

You can also choose where you want the downloaded maps stored ("Storage location"), whether or not you want to download them when you're on a cellular connection ("metered connection"), and if you want them updated as Microsoft improves the maps ("Automatically update maps"). That's an acknowledgment that maps change all the time (roads are built, empires crumble).

Messaging

Wouldn't it be cool if you could send text messages from your PC to people's phones? You can set that up if you have an Android phone—see page 251. But that's not what Messaging is.

Note: If that's your goal, you need to download a special app from your carrier. Verizon, AT&T, T-Mobile, and Sprint each make a Windows app just for texting from your PC. (Verizon's app is called "Message+," for example. Its app is a mirror of what you see on your phone.)

Messaging is a very simple app for conducting text chats with other people who have Skype. (Yes, you can, and probably should, use the Skype app for that purpose; it's not entirely clear why Microsoft decided to break Messaging out into a separate program.)

Microsoft Edge

Here's Microsoft's built-in browser. See Chapter 9.

Microsoft Solitaire Collection

To the shock of many, Microsoft killed off Solitaire back in Windows 8. The one, the only—for many people, the most-used app of all. But don't panic. Windows 10 comes with a new, improved version of Solitaire—five different versions, in fact. (There are also links to download Bingo, Minesweeper, Sudoku, Mahjong, and four others, all free.)

Note: Well, *sort of* free. Your game-playing experience is interrupted every now and then by 15- and 30-second video ads—including one that offers a Premium plan, where you pay $10 a year to get *rid* of the ads.

Improved not just because their graphics and gameplay are modernized and great, but also because they save their data as part of your online Microsoft account, so your impressive card-playing stats look similar no matter what computer (or Xbox console) you're using.

When you fire up this app, dismiss or approve the first three administrative screens. You arrive at the game screen (Figure 8-17).

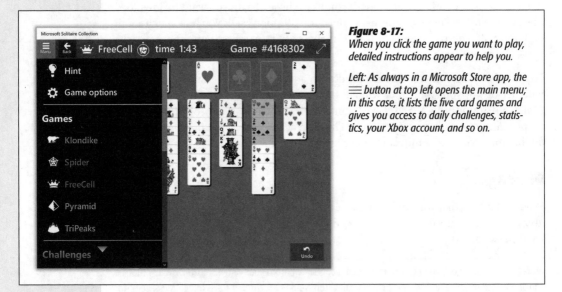

Figure 8-17:
When you click the game you want to play, detailed instructions appear to help you.

Left: As always in a Microsoft Store app, the ☰ button at top left opens the main menu; in this case, it lists the five card games and gives you access to daily challenges, statistics, your Xbox account, and so on.

Microsoft Store

This is it: the Microsoft Store, source of many apps. Read all about it in Chapter 6.

Microsoft Wi-Fi

This bizarre little app is nothing more than an ad for Microsoft Wi-Fi, the company's fledgling network of Wi-Fi hotspots. It lets you know you can "buy convenient Microsoft pay-as-you-go plans for the time you need." Thanks.

Mixed Reality Portal

Mixed reality is Microsoft's term for what the rest of the world calls *augmented* reality (AR). In AR apps, you see graphics and information overlaid on the camera's view of the world: arrows that show which way to walk to get to the nearest subway stop, for example, or info boxes that identify the prices of apartments in nearby buildings.

Microsoft is big on augmented reality. Its HoloLens headset, for example, is a pair of goggles that let you enter the mixed-reality world hands-free.

This app, the Mixed Reality Portal, is useless if you don't own a HoloLens or another brand of Windows 10–compatible headset. It also requires some beefy hardware—very fast, very recent graphics processor, and at least 8 GB of memory .

This app is designed to be a sort of mission control: It displays, on the PC screen, whatever you're seeing inside the headset. Using the menu, you can connect to a new headset or other controller ("Set up controllers"), turn the invisible game boundary on or off, create a new boundary ("Run setup"), or download more AR apps ("Get mixed reality apps").

The Settings menu offers controls for uninstalling your AR hardware.

Mobile Plans

This weird little app exists solely to let you sign up for a cellular-data plan through the Microsoft Store. It's useful only if you have a tablet or laptop with a cellular modem and SIM card, like the one in a phone.

Movies & TV

The Microsoft Movies & TV Store is exactly like the iTunes store, or the Amazon video store. It's a place where you can buy or rent movies and TV episodes—and watch them.

GEM IN THE ROUGH

Miracast: Play Photos and Movies on Your TV

A tablet is one thing. But if you want to show your pictures to more than a couple of people, your big-screen TV is the way to go. Fortunately, Windows makes it easy to send what's on your computer's screen to your TV screen.

Windows works with Miracast, a wireless audio-video transmission technology. If you have a TV with Miracast (also known as WiDi) built in, or a Miracast box that connects to a TV, the TV becomes a mirror of everything on your Windows screen. Great for slideshows, videos, and teaching people how to use Windows.

When you want to broadcast your computer's audio and video to the TV, hit ⬜ on the taskbar to open the Action Center; choose the Connect tab; and wait while Windows tries to find the Miracast TV's wireless signal. After a moment, its name appears in the right-side panel. (There's a long way, too: Open ⊞→⚙→Devices→"Bluetooth and other devices." Under "Other devices," choose the name of your Miracast receiver.)

Like magic, your computer's image shows up on the TV—with sound.

Actually, it's more of a sales agent for the video section of the regular Microsoft Store. In fact, if you click one of the movie-poster buttons, you're taken out of this app and into the Microsoft Store to do your actual shopping.

At the top are three tabs: Explore (meaning "shop"); Purchased (where your rented and bought movies show up); and Personal (your own videos). When you click a video's name, you get an info screen about it. When you click the Play triangle next to a video's name, you open the main player screen—and the video plays.

And whenever you wiggle your mouse or tap the screen, you get the playback controls shown in Figure 8-18, bottom.

Tip: In the May 2019 Update, Movies & TV can also list and play movies you've bought from iTunes, Amazon Prime Video, Vudu, Google Play, Xfinity, and FandangoNOW. That's because Microsoft is now a member of the free Movies Anywhere service, a coalition among big tech companies to allow all their purchased movies to sit in one mutual online "locker."

To get going with this, visit *moviesanywhere.com* and create a free account. Then, in the Movies & TV app, choose ··· on the toolbar and then Settings; select "Connect to Movies Anywhere." Once you're signed in, you'll find all your movies from all the online stores right here, ready to watch.

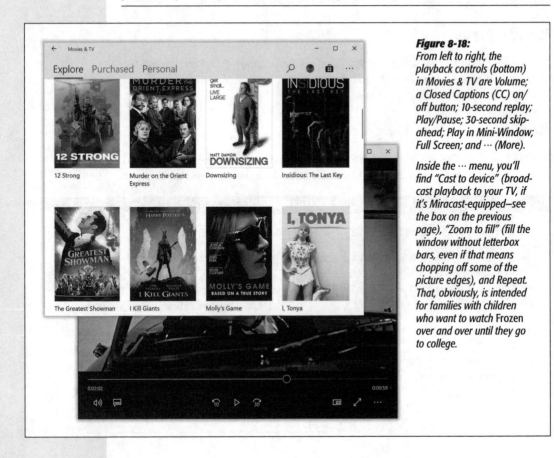

Figure 8-18:
From left to right, the playback controls (bottom) in Movies & TV are Volume; a Closed Captions (CC) on/off button; 10-second replay; Play/Pause; 30-second skip-ahead; Play in Mini-Window; Full Screen; and ··· (More).

Inside the ··· menu, you'll find "Cast to device" (broadcast playback to your TV, if it's Miracast-equipped—see the box on the previous page), "Zoom to fill" (fill the window without letterbox bars, even if that means chopping off some of the picture edges), and Repeat. That, obviously, is intended for families with children who want to watch Frozen *over and over until they go to college.*

Office

As you may know, Office is Microsoft's suite of business tools: Word (word processing), Excel (spreadsheets), PowerPoint (slideshows), Access (databases), and so on.

As you may not know, all these apps are available to use for free at *office.com*. They're not identical to the paid desktop versions, but close enough.

This "app" is nothing more than a splash screen that lets you choose which version of Office you prefer: the desktop version (which you're given the chance to buy) or the free online version. Once you've made your choice, you get links to all the standard apps—either online or offline—along with any documents you've had open recently.

OneDrive

This "app" is just a shortcut to opening your OneDrive *folder*, described on page 140.

OneNote

"OneNote" isn't really a good name for this program, since its whole point is to create and organize *lots* of notes. But never mind that; be grateful you're getting it free—albeit in a simple, touchscreen-friendly edition. (Actually, the full version is free, too. Go get it!)

Notes can be anything (Figure 8-19). Driving directions, recipes, to-do lists, stuff you paste in from the web or email, brainstorms—anything you might want to refer to later. OneNote is a notepad and a scrapbook in one.

Figure 8-19:
In OneNote, all kinds of data can coexist on the same note: typing, drawing, photos, to-do lists, and so on. All of this gets auto-synced to any other device that has OneNote running.

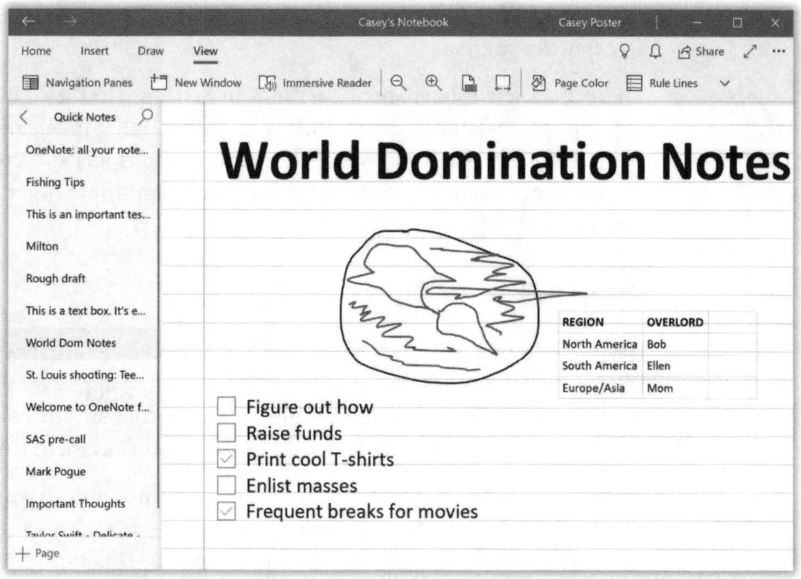

The beauty of it is that these notes sync via the internet. You can refer to the same set of notes on any Windows device—phone, tablet, computer—and even Android, iPhone, or Mac. (Just download the OneNote app for each one.)

To create a new note, hit +Page (lower left), or (if the window is too narrow to see it) you can press Ctrl+N. Type a name for this note.

The tabs across the top let you access these toolbars:

- **Home.** Here's formatting (bold, italic, underline, font choice), lists (like bullets, numbered lists, or checkboxes), and paragraph formatting (like Centered).

- **Insert.** Your note can include a table, another file on your computer, a photo, or a web link.

Tip: If you insert a picture, you can resize it by dragging the corners. You can also rotate it: Right-click it (or hold your finger down on it); from the shortcut menu, choose Rotate.

- **Draw.** This is the "touch-enabled" part. You can draw with your finger (or, more clumsily, a mouse). The tools include an eraser, a highlighter, a pen, and a color palette. Tap one of the freehand pens, Shapes (canned geometrical shapes), or Ink to Text (write freehand, let the app straighten your lines), and then draw on the screen.

- **View.** Here's how you can zoom in or out, change the background color, superimpose faint blue lines like the ones in a paper notebook, and so on.

As you create your notes, they're listed in a table of contents on the left side. Some profoundly useful options appear if you right-click one (or hold your finger down on one)—like Delete Page, Rename Page, Copy Link to Page, and Pin to Start. That one creates a tile on the right side of your Start menu—a great way to get instant access to something you refer to a lot, like your list of credit cards, things to do, or an essay in progress.

There are a few miscellaneous settings in Settings (in the ⋯ menu), the ♀ icon lets you type plain-English commands (like "add a bullet list"), and the far left column (which appears when the window is wide enough) lets you create additional notebooks. That's right: multiple notebooks full of multiple notes. OneNote *really* isn't the right name for this app.

Paint 3D

Despite its name, Paint 3D isn't just a 3D version of Paint; it's much more powerful. It's one of the simplest, easiest-to-use 3D modeling apps ever written. You can use it to create creatures, buildings, designs, or scenes that are "three-dimensional," meaning that you can turn them around in space to look at them from different angles.

Once you've built a 3D object, you can stamp it into a photo you already have, or into a live scene from your computer's camera (page 315). If you really like what you've made, you can show it off on Microsoft's Remix 3D community website. And if you really, *really* like it, you can print it in plastic on a 3D printer or through an online 3D-printing service.

Artistic Tools

When the app first opens, it presents a Welcome screen; hit Start to get going. Now, on the top toolbar, eight icons make up your artistic arsenal. (To identify them, point without clicking, or tap with your finger—or just hit ⋯ to make their text labels appear.) Here's what they do:

- **Brushes.** Lets you draw or write on any object with a marker, calligraphy pen, oil brush, watercolor, pixel pen, pencil, eraser, crayon, spray can, or paint can. Just pick a brush, a thickness, an opacity, a color, and a texture—and go to town.

- **2D shapes.** Gives you options to make lines and curves, as well as 24 canned line shapes: squares, triangles, arrows, stars, checkmarks, and so on. Once you create a shape, you can 3D-ify it or leave it 2D, whereupon it wraps itself to whatever object is behind it.

- **3D shapes** is the heaviest hitter, object-creation–wise. It opens a panel at right with these major components:

    3D models are ready-to-use basic objects: male-ish, female-ish, dog, cat, and fish, along with a "Get more models" button.

    3D objects are shapes you may recall from geometry class—cube, sphere, cylinder, cone, and so on.

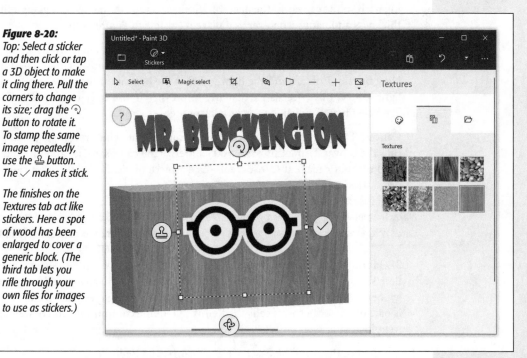

Figure 8-20:
Top: Select a sticker and then click or tap a 3D object to make it cling there. Pull the corners to change its size; drag the ⟳ button to rotate it. To stamp the same image repeatedly, use the ⌗ button. The ✓ makes it stick.

The finishes on the Textures tab act like stickers. Here a spot of wood has been enlarged to cover a generic block. (The third tab lets you rifle through your own files for images to use as stickers.)

3D doodle. What if you want to make your own shape? Here you get a hard-edged drawing tool and a soft, pillowy version.

In each case, the process goes like this. First, select the model, object, or doodle tool you want. Then choose a color from the palette (or use "Add color" to specify your own shade), and a material from the drop-down menu (Matte, Gloss, Dull metal, Polished metal).

To create your object, drag in the drawing area. If you're using the model or shape tool, your drag determines the size of the object; if you're using its Doodle tool, sketch a complete shape (for example, a cloud). Boom: A 3D object is born. You can select it, rotate it, shrink it, enlarge it, or change its color later, as described below.

- **Stickers.** This tool wraps 2D images, as though they're stickers, onto 3D objects (see Figure 8-20). The app starts you out with fun, cartoony ones: mouths, moustaches, noses, eyes, and so on. The next tab offers a choice of textures: rocks, tree bark, concrete, marble. These may be buried, but they're important. They let you transform your featureless, plastic 3D blobs into realistic real-world objects. The animators at Pixar use exactly the same technique—although they use software that's much, much, much more sophisticated.

  On the last tab, you can add your own sticker from any image file on your PC. You might, for example, start taking your own photos of the perfect textures, or import clip art from the pros. See Figure 8-20.

- **Text.** This tool lets you type in 2D or 3D. Whatever you type in 2D ends up sticking itself to the canvas in the back; anything you type in the 3D tool gains a little thickness and hangs wherever you place it (visible in Figure 8-20).

- **Effects** includes 22 lighting effect filters—including several straight from Minecraft, like medium-blue "Day," maroon "Nether," and the ominous-feeling "The End." Drag the sun icon around the light wheel at the bottom of the pane to move the light source; this effect is particularly impressive if you have chosen "Gloss" or "Polished metal" finish for any of your models.

- **Canvas.** This tool controls the 2D background—the white rectangle Microsoft calls the canvas. Using this pane, you can resize the canvas, rotate and flip it, turn it on or off, or make it transparent—like a piece of clear glass that you can still draw, stick, or write on.

Note: The canvas in most drawing programs marks the outer limits of the working space. But in Paint 3D, the canvas is just another object. You can layer things in front of it, to the sides, behind it, or even cutting through it.

- **3D Library** is a rabbit hole into a searchable online library containing over a million 3D objects. You're free to drop any of them into your artwork. (You can also get here with the "Get more models" button on the 3D shapes pane.) The library is part of what Microsoft calls the Remix 3D online community; you're welcome to upload your own objects to it, too.

To the right of these are the Paste, Undo, History, and Redo icons.

Other Tools

Underneath that bank of art-creating tools is a set of icons that let you manipulate your work and look at what you've made. Here's what they do:

- **Select.** Every object you create is automatically selected at birth—it glows teal and sprouts handles that let you rotate it and push it backward or forward (see Figure 8-21). But what if you wander away and want to select that thing again? Hit this icon and then select your object.

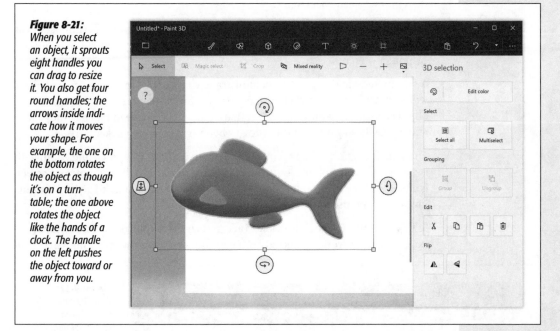

Figure 8-21:
When you select an object, it sprouts eight handles you can drag to resize it. You also get four round handles; the arrows inside indicate how it moves your shape. For example, the one on the bottom rotates the object as though it's on a turntable; the one above rotates the object like the hands of a clock. The handle on the left pushes the object toward or away from you.

On the 3D selection pane at right, hit "Edit color" to change the color and texture; "Select all" to select and edit all of the objects in the file at once; Multiselect to add objects to your selection one by one (holding down Shift while selecting also does this trick); Group to join multiple objects to manipulate them simultaneously (and Ungroup when you're done with that); and the usual cut, copy, paste, delete, and flip options.

- **Magic select.** Say you want to put your friend into your 3D world, but you don't want the background of the photo. This tool lets you pull just what you want from any 2D image.

First, insert a picture from your PC by hitting the Menu icon at top left, and then choose Insert. Now choose "Magic select" (□▲).

As directed by the hints in the right-side panel, start by dragging the handlebars inward to crop the photo down to, for example, the subject's face or body. When you hit Next, Paint 3D does its best to isolate the element you were going for; see Figure 8-22.

When you hit Done, your friend pops out from the background, now transformed into a floating layer. You can move it around, rotate it, resize it, and see it from any angle, including from behind. The background, meanwhile, remains; incredibly, Paint 3D even attempts to *fill in the hole* your friend left behind.

- **Crop.** This tool crops your 2D object—the canvas. Drag the handles to taste, and then hit the green checkmark.

- **Mixed reality.** This funky tool turns on your PC's camera and superimposes your 3D creations onto the camera's feed—which is most likely you, looking at your computer screen.

An animated hand appears to demonstrate what's about to happen: your objects will stick wherever you click or tap. For instance, if you tap your forehead, your objects drop onto your forehead; at that point, if you move in real life, they move with you. Click again, and they move wherever you newly clicked.

To rotate the objects, drag them. To scale them up or down, pinch and zoom with two fingers, as on a phone, or turn your mouse wheel. On the right of your screen is a big, white circle—hit it to capture the hybrid screen image. To go back to editing your work, use the Paint 3D icon (♡) at the top.

- **3D view.** In this very helpful view, you can turn the whole masterpiece in space— up, down, tilted, rotated, and so on. There are several ways to see your work from

Figure 8-22:
Paint 3D cuts the desired area out of its photographic background. If it missed a chunk, draw on it with the Add tool; if it included too much, draw on the excess area with the Remove tool.

any angle—or as Paint 3D calls it, "to orbit": Right-drag with your mouse, or, on a touchscreen, drag with three fingers.

You can also pan—slide your perspective up, down, left, or right without tilting or rotating. To do that, Alt-drag, or drag with two fingers (or hold down the Alt key and use one finger). To zoom in and out, use your mouse's scroll wheel, or pinch and spread two fingers on a touchscreen. (If you're using a digital pen—and this is a drawing program, so why not?—hold down the barrel button to orbit, or the Alt key to pan.)

- **Adjust the zoom.** Use this slider, from – to +, to see your artwork at 10 percent all the way up to 6,400 percent. That's very close up.

- **View more options.** The last icon in the row, ⊠, offers a menu with three helpful functions: "Take screenshot," "Reset view" (to 100 percent), and "View controls." That last one pops up a handy window to remind you how to orbit, pan, and zoom in 3D view using your mouse, touchscreen, pen, or keyboard.

Tip: At top right, next to the Paste icon, there's the traditional Undo icon, ↩, and its counterpart, Redo, ↪. Use these to walk through your artistic regrets one by one. If that's not fast enough for you, the History icon nested in between the two is like a perpetual Undo. Its slider can rewind your work to any point, even all the way back to the beginning. You can stop sliding at any point, and start back into your work.

If you love your work, you can also use History to relive its glory; hit Start Recording, and then drag the slider forward or back. Then, when you hit "Export as video," you get an .mp4 file in your Videos folder of your file coming to life. Finally, the Backspace key works to delete any selected object.

The Menu icon at top left (⊡) lets you save your finished masterpiece as an editable Paint 3D project, a 3D model, or a 2D image. Here, you can also insert a 2D image; upload to the Remix 3D community (provided that you have created an account therein); share a screenshot; or print to a 2D or 3D printer, or to a 3D printing service online. With that last option, you choose the scale and the material—you get choices like polyamide, alumide, rubber-like, steel, and so on—and Paint 3D gives you an estimated cost. It also warns you if, say, the walls are too thin to properly print, and helps you fix the problems.

People

The People app is Windows' address book. It's a centralized database of everybody in your social circles: their email and mailing addresses, phone numbers, and so on (Figure 8-23). In fact, when you select someone's name, the right-side panel even shows you any recent correspondence you've had with that person, plus any upcoming events you're both attending.

Importing Addresses from Online Accounts

Delightfully enough, the People app can synchronize its contacts with online Rolodexes that may be very important to you: your contacts from Apple's iCloud service, Google, Microsoft's Outlook.com system, or your company's corporate system.

That's why the first thing you may see, the first time you open People, is an invitation to connect those online accounts to People. Choose the name of the network you belong to, and enter the name and password for that account.

Note: If the People app has people listed in it the very first time you open it, then you've probably entered this kind of account information already, in another Windows app.

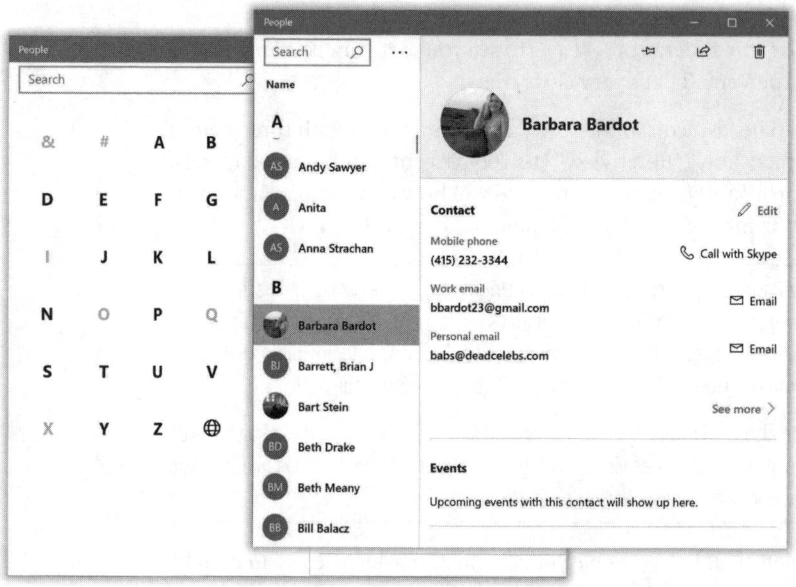

Figure 8-23:
The People app screen is a dashboard for quick access to the phone numbers and email addresses of your social circle. If you click one of the letter headings, you get the alphabetical index (left); select any letter to jump to that part of the alphabet.

If you don't see that invitation, or if you declined it, you can always connect your accounts later. To add an account, hit ⋯ (top right) and then choose ⚙ Settings. There, staring you in the face, are names of the accounts you've set up already.

To add a new one, use the "Add an account" link. Tap the kind of account you want: iCloud, Google, or whatever. Enter your account information, and boom—you're done. The People app is now synced with your online accounts. Change information in one place and it's also changed in the other.

You can repeat the process to add more accounts; in fact, you can even have *multiple* accounts for certain types (like Google and Microsoft email accounts).

It's important to understand that you're actually linking those internet services *to your Microsoft account.* You have to do that only once, and then all your Windows starter apps—Mail, Calendar, People, and so on—can use their information.

The big payoff comes when you sign into another Windows 10 machine. To your delight and amazement, you'll see that your address book is already filled in with all your contacts and accounts. Progress!

Even after you've hooked up some accounts like this, you're not stuck with wading through the addresses of a million people you don't care about:

- **Hide an account.** If you hit ⋯ (top right) and then ▽, you get the dialog box shown in Figure 8-24. Here you can opt to hide the contacts in certain accounts (or those without phone numbers, for when you're using People as a phone book).

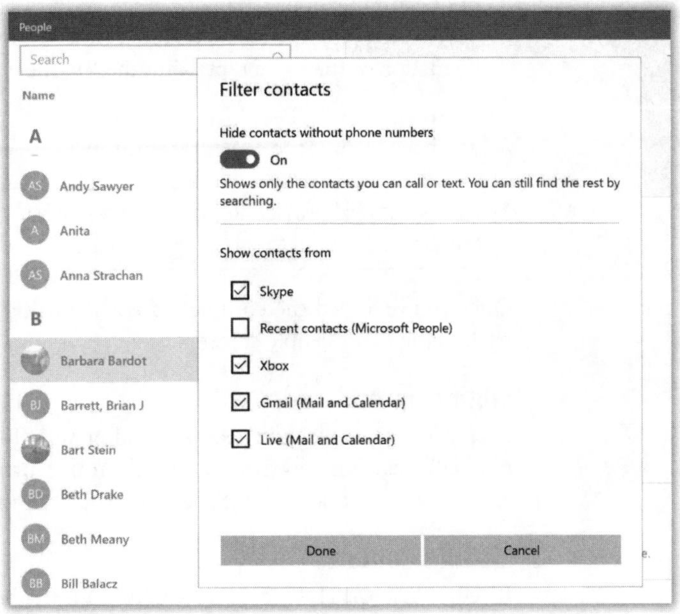

Figure 8-24:
In the "Filter contacts" box, you can turn off the checkboxes of certain accounts. That way, you're hiding their address-book contents from your People browsing and searching. You're not deleting anything, just hiding it.

- **Delete an account.** You can unsubscribe from one of your online accounts, too. Just hit ⋯ and ⚙ and then select the account you wish to forget. On the resulting dialog box, choose "Delete account," and it is banished.

Creating Address Cards Manually

Each entry in People is like a web form, with predefined spaces to hold all the standard contact information.

To add a new person, click +. You get the "New contact" panel. Fill in the obvious stuff—name, email—plus details like these:

- **Add photo.** Tap or click to open a mini Photos app, where you can choose a head-shot for this person. It's OK if the person's face isn't very big in the picture you choose; you're offered the chance to crop down to just the head.

- **Save to.** Which online email address book do you want this name stored in?

Tip: If you have an Android phone, choose Gmail; if you have an iPhone, choose iCloud. Windows will thoughtfully add this person to your phone's built-in address book automatically.

- **Phone number.** Use the drop-down menu above the box ("Mobile phone") to specify what kind of phone this is.

  Now, the trouble with people these days is that they often have more than one phone number, more than one email address, and more than one mailing address. Fortunately, all of these boxes are infinitely expanding. Choose + to add another blank box of the same type—another phone-number field, for example.

- **Address.** Weirdly, People doesn't come with a mailing-address box already set up; you have to click the + Address button.

Tip: You can also add fields for "Job title," "Significant other," "Website," or "Notes." They're hiding in the Other button. Select its + button to see those choices.

Once you've added the complete dossier for this person, hit the Save button to go back to the main People screen.

Editing an Address

People move, people quit, people abandon AOL. To make changes to somebody's card manually, select it and then hit ⌀ Edit. You return to the screen where you can add, remove, and edit fields. Hit Save when you're finished.

Linking Contacts

If People discovers two contacts with the same name among your different accounts—say, one from Gmail and one from iCloud—it offers to combine them. Select the person's name and scroll down on the right-side panel until you see the "Combined contacts" section. People shows you the two names it has found, indicates how it thinks they're connected, and offers a Combine button. It automatically links the two, making it seem as though all the information appears on a single card. (There's also a Separate button in case you change your mind.)

Pinning a Contact

Face it: Some people are more important than others. That's why People lets you *pin* certain people—install their tiles—onto the right side of your Start menu. Just select the person's name and then, on the right-side panel, hit ⊐. You can also pin your contacts to the taskbar using this icon, or using My People, as explained in the next section.

The People Panel (My People)

The People app isn't the only access you have to your contacts; there's a People icon right on your taskbar (Figure 8-25).

Its purpose is to serve as a speed-dial list of your Very Special Friends, which Microsoft calls My People. Up to 10 very, very special people get actual icons on the taskbar; everyone else appears in the My People panel that sprouts from the taskbar. Once you've installed all these names, you can fire off email or Skype messages without having to open the People app.

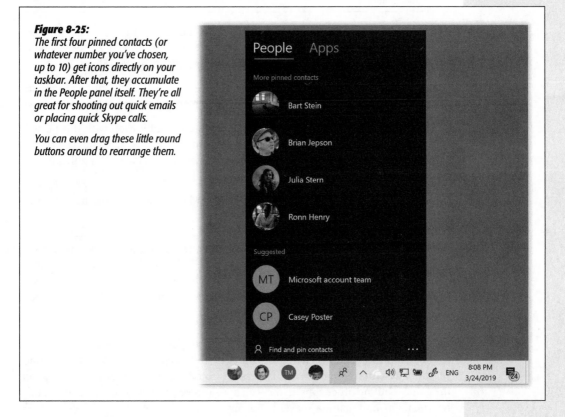

Figure 8-25:
The first four pinned contacts (or whatever number you've chosen, up to 10) get icons directly on your taskbar. After that, they accumulate in the People panel itself. They're all great for shooting out quick emails or placing quick Skype calls.

You can even drag these little round buttons around to rearrange them.

Here's the fun you can have:

- **Designate your My People.** Choose the ⚇ icon on the taskbar. (If you don't see the ⚇ icon, open ⊞→Settings→Personalization→Taskbar and turn on "Show contacts on taskbar." Also specify how many People icons are allowed to appear—up to ten.) If one of the lucky names appears in the Suggested list, select it; otherwise, hit "Find and pin contacts," use the search box to find the person's name, and choose it. That special someone's icon now appears on the taskbar.

Tip: To remove that icon from the taskbar, right-click it and choose "Unpin from taskbar."

Repeat the process until you've got all your best people pinned to the taskbar.

If you do this "Find and pin contacts" business beyond three times (or whatever number you've chosen in Settings), the main People panel fills up ("overflows") with the additional names. Keep going and the panel actually scrolls to accommodate as many My People as you like.

> **Note:** If someone you've pinned to the taskbar sends you an emoji via Skype, it pops right up on your taskbar as a giant, if somewhat mystifying, graphic (and sound). It hovers and animates for five seconds before disappearing.

- **Use your My People.** When you want to contact one of these special people, click his icon. You get choices like Mail, Skype, and People. (The Mail and Skype commands appear here only if you have, in fact, set up Mail and/or Skype.)

  If you choose People, you get access to this person's full card—phone numbers, mailing addresses, recent conversations, and so on.

  If you choose Mail, you see your recent email communication with this person; hit + to compose a new message, right there in the panel. If you choose Skype, a tiny Skype panel appears, with buttons for phoning or video-calling this person (or inviting him to be your buddy, if he's not already).

  The People panel remembers your choice—Mail or Skype—for the next time you use it.

> **Tip:** One of the most compelling uses for all of this is the ability to drag and drop files onto people's heads. Want to email a Word doc to Casey? Drag its icon out of its File Explorer window onto Casey's taskbar icon. (You can even drag and drop onto the names of the secondary people you've installed in the People taskbar panel. Just drag a file onto the ⤵ icon on the taskbar; then, without releasing your finger or the mouse button, drag up the People panel onto somebody's name.)

The People panel is a cool idea. It would be cooler, of course, if it gave you access to more communications channels than Mail and Skype. (How about text, phone, Facebook, Twitter, Snapchat…?) That seems to be the function of the Apps tab of the panel—but no other apps' names can appear here until their software companies rewrite them, and that may never happen.

For now, let those friends know just how special they are.

> **Tip:** You can now add contacts right from the People panel. Just use the ⋯ button at lower right and choose "New contact."

Photos

Microsoft changes photo programs as often as most people change socks. The Photo Gallery from Windows Vista? Dead. The Photo Viewer of Windows 7? Gone.

In Windows 10, you get yet another digital photo shoebox, this one just called Photos.

Its job is to grab photo albums from everywhere fine photos are stored—your own Pictures folder, other PCs on your network, and your OneDrive—and display them all in one place (Figure 8-26).

Tip: These days, Photos can even handle pictures in two relatively fancy new formats. First, there's the RAW format, which are very large files preferred by photographers because they can be so extensively manipulated (the photos, not the photographers). Second, there's HEIF (high efficiency image file format): photos that take up half the space of JPEG ones without losing any quality, which is awesome—but not all desktop photo programs can open HEIF files.

But Photos can't work with these files until you install special plug-ins from the Microsoft Store.

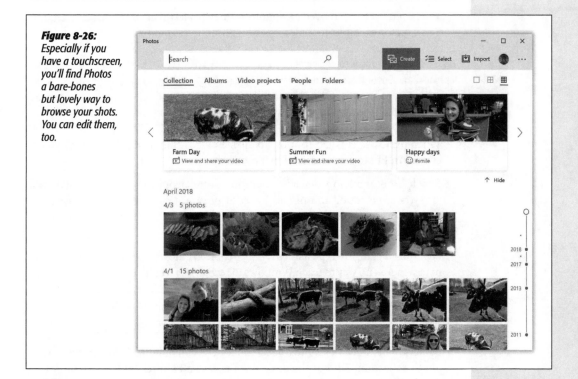

Figure 8-26:
Especially if you have a touchscreen, you'll find Photos a bare-bones but lovely way to browse your shots. You can edit them, too.

The Five Tabs of Photos

Photos lets you see your photo collection in four ways, represented by tabs at the top:

- **Collection.** At top, Photos offers some ready-made assortments of photos and slideshows that may interest you. "New Orleans Last Week," for example, or "On this day" (in past years), or "Friday in Phoenix." Click one to open its video slideshow (see page 331).

  Below those tiles, you'll find your entire photographic life, labeled by date. Just below the toolbar, at right, three tiny icons let you adjust the size of the photo thumbnails. Use the vertical timeline at right to zoom through your years' worth of pictures.

- **Albums.** Albums are virtual containers for any old rounded-up batches of photos. You can create one of your favorites, or one for each vacation, or whatever. Hit "Create an album" to view all your photos with checkboxes, so you can go to town clicking the ones you want in this album; then choose Create.

You wind up on a special Album page (use the ⌀ to edit its name), featuring an animated slideshow preview at top; blue buttons for Watch (a slideshow), Edit (the slideshow), or "Create collage" (arranges some photos into a grid); sortable thumbnails of the pictures in this album; and some stats about this collection.

You haven't actually moved any photos—they're all still in your master collection. You can, for example, include a favorite photo in as many albums as you like.

Tip: Photos can even build some albums for you automatically. When you click the Create→Album button at top, you see groups of photos that represent certain photo shoots. Usually, you'll know right away what they were: "Oh, Casey's birthday party!" "Oh, the home inspection." "Oh, that time I woke up in Poughkeepsie." Photos creates these groupings by studying the photos' times and locations.

- **Video projects.** This tab rounds up all the videos (animated slideshows) you've created in Photos, as described in a moment.

- **People.** Photos attempts facial recognition of the people in your pictures; on this tab, you see a round thumbnail for each person it's found, complete with the number of photos it thinks you have of that person. Click a thumbnail to see all the pictures of that person—and to let the app know who it is.

Hit "Start tagging" to type names for the people Windows has recognized. Unfortunately, there's no way to teach Windows to recognize faces it *doesn't* auto-recognize.

Tip: You can turn off Windows' face analysis, if it creeps you out. Choose ⋯ (top right) and then ⚙ to open the Settings; under "Viewing and editing," turn off People.

- **Folders.** This screen lists the folders whose contents Photos is including in your photo collection. Back at the desktop, you have a Pictures folder. Any photos in this folder show up in the Photos app automatically. Same for the Pictures folder on your OneDrive.

But on this screen, you can also tell Photos to display the contents of other pictures and drives. To do that, hit "Add a folder."

Tip: If you choose ⋯ at top right and then ⚙ to open the Settings page, you can also turn on "Show my cloud-only content from OneDrive," if you like. You don't have to worry about duplicates; Photos is smart enough to prevent them from showing up, even if they're different file formats.

Playing with Photos

The rules of Photos are simple:

- **To view a photo,** click or tap its photo thumbnail to open it big enough to see.

- **To move through the photos once you've opened one,** swipe horizontally (touchscreen), click the ‹ and › buttons at the edges of the screen (mouse), or press the ← and → keys (keyboard).

- **Zoom in or out** by spreading or pinching two fingers on the touchscreen, clicking the + and − buttons at the right edge of the horizontal scroll bar, pressing Ctrl and the + or − keys, or turning the scroll wheel while pressing the Ctrl key.

- **To return to the thumbnail view,** hit the ← button on the screen or press Alt+←.

- **The More (···) menu offers a Slideshow button** (▣) that starts a slideshow of all photos in this batch. (This command appears only when you've opened a photo.) Or press F5. Click or tap to end the show.

- **To send an open photo to somebody by email,** or to send it into another app for editing, use the Share button on the toolbar.

A Very Smart Search Box

Photos uses artificial intelligence to figure out what's *in* your pictures—you know, like "cat" or "pond" or "pizza." You can then use the search box to find them by name.

When you click the search box, a menu offers quick-click buttons for People (faces that Photos has identified, as described already); Places (based on the locations where you snapped the shots—usually available only on phone photos); or Things (subjects the software has found). Of course, you can also type whatever noun you want into the box.

Note: It takes Windows a long time to analyze your photos before this search thing is ready. A tiny progress bar inches along the bottom of the actual search box to show you its progress.

Windows isn't as good at this as, say, Google Photos. But it's getting better all the time.

Slurping in Photos from a Camera

Photos can import photos from a camera, memory card, flash drive, or any other drive, too. Just connect the camera, card, or drive to your machine, and then hit the 🖸 Import button at the top. From the drop-down menu, choose "From a folder" (if the pictures are already on your PC somewhere) or "From a USB device" (if they're on a camera, memory card, flash drive, or USB hard drive).

Hit Import. When it's all over, you see the newly imported goodies nestled in their new home, in the Photos app.

Video Slideshows

Microsoft has been toying with the idea of an automatic slideshow-making module for a couple of years now. At one point, it was a separate app called Story Remix; then it was folded into Photos, but in a special window. Now it's found a home in the Create menu, called "Automatic video with music."

When you choose this command, you jump back to your Collection view, where you can select the photos you want in the slideshow (by clicking or tapping). Then hit Create, type a name for the video, and sit back and enjoy the results. It's an animated slideshow, complete with an opening title, zooms and pans, and music.

At this point, you can choose:

- **Remix it for me.** Produces a variation of the same slideshow—different slide subset, different music, different effects.

- **Choose a star.** Windows shows the faces of people it's found in your pictures; choose the person you'd like to appear more often in the video.

- **Export or share.** Choose a file size for the video, and then choose "View in File Explorer" (to see the resulting file) or "Share to social media, email, or another app" to do exactly that. You'll be offered a Share pane that features your My People (page 326), any Nearby Sharing computers (page 564), plus icons for "Upload to YouTube," Dropbox, Mail, Skype, and so on.

- **Edit video.** You arrive at a special editing screen (Figure 8-27). This is as close as Windows comes to offering you a video-editing app; it's the modern-day Movie Maker or iMovie.

At the very top are buttons like "Set a theme" (canned looks for your slideshow—Adventure, Chilled, Electric, and so on) each incorporating a piece of music, a

Figure 8-27:
Top left: Here are all the photos you originally chose for inclusion (and the option to add more).

Top right: A preview of the movie so far.

Bottom: The Storyboard, which is a map of the slideshow.

typeface, and photo-animation effects); "Add recommended music" (a choice of Microsoft's music or your own music collection, along with the on/off switch for syncing your photos' appearance to the beat—neat); "Import custom audio tracks or narration" (lets you choose an audio file you've made in advance); "Change aspect ratio," meaning proportions (either 16×9 rectangular, 4×3 squarish, or "Make portrait," a better fit for phones held upright); "Save in OneDrive," so you can edit this slideshow on another PC; and "Export a shareable video file," which does just what you'd think.

In the Storyboard, you can *delete photos* (hit the ×), *rearrange* them by dragging, *change their timing* individually (hit Duration—or, if a video clip is selected, Trim to shorten the ends), choose how to handle a photo whose *dimensions* don't perfectly fit the frame (hit Resize, and then choose either "Remove black bars," which also crops some of the photo, or "Shrink to fit," which leaves black bars), apply *Filters* (special color tints that make photos look old-timey), overlay text (you get a choice of layouts and typefaces), or add some *Motion* to a photo (you get a choice of zooms, pans, and tilts).

"Edit & Create"→Edit

You might be a great photographer (although if your primary tool is a tablet or a laptop, that's debatable).

But even pros touch up their work—and in Photos, an impressively complete suite of photo-editing tools awaits. These tools can rotate or crop; they can also fix the brightness, contrast, and color of your pictures, and even add special effects like selective blur and vignetting (where the photo corners are misty white to draw the eye to the subject). All these tools are hiding in the "Edit & Create" button, which is actually a menu.

To begin, open the photo that needs help.

Now choose Edit & Create→Edit to open the editing wonderland shown in Figure 8-28. All your editing tools huddle on three tabs at the top of the screen: "Crop and rotate," "Filters," and "Adjustments."

Note, as you edit, that an "Undo all" button awaits at the top; **it t**akes the photo back to its original form.

Note: Your saved edits are permanent. There's no Revert to Original command in Photos.

Once you've made your edits, hit "Save a copy" (which saves your work as a copy of the original) or, from its pop-up menu, choose Save (to make these changes *to the* original).

Ready? Keep hands and feet inside the tram at all times.

Tip: As you work, keep in mind that you can zoom in for better detail (turn your mouse wheel, if you have one, or use Ctrl+plus and Ctrl+minus). Finally, keep in mind that the Undo command is always at your service to reverse the last editing step. It's a safety net, and it's Ctrl+Z.

(If you dig finding out about this sort of Photos keyboard shortcut tip, don't miss the full list on page 598.)

Figure 8-28:
In the Adjustments mode, you can adjust the Light or Color sliders for efficient large-scale tweaks (top left), or you can "open" one of the sliders with its flippy triangle to reveal hidden sliders like Contrast, Exposure, Highlights, and Shadows (lower right).

Crop & Rotate

Here are all the tools for fiddling with the size and shape of the photo. The Straightening slider compensates for slight camera tilt. Each click of the Rotate button (or each press of Ctrl+R) rotates the photo clockwise by 90 degrees. Flip produces a left-for-right mirror image. Reset, of course, undoes everything you've worked on in this window.

Cropping means shaving off unnecessary outer portions of a photo. Usually you crop a photo to improve its composition—adjusting where the subject appears within the frame of the picture. Often a photo has more impact if it's cropped tightly around the subject, especially in portraits.

In the "Crop & rotate" window, a white rectangle appears on your photo. Drag inward on any corner or edge. The part of the photo that Windows will eventually trim away is dimmed out. You can recenter the photo by dragging any part of the photo inside the box. (For greater precision, you can press Shift and the arrow keys to resize the cropping rectangle, or Ctrl and the arrow keys to move it.)

The "Aspect ratio" pop-up button offers a choice of canned proportions: Square, 3 × 2, 4 × 3, and so on. They make the app limit the cropping frame to preset proportions. (The "Make portrait" choice makes the cropping rectangle tall and skinny.)

Filters

All those Instagram fans can't be wrong—*filters* must be a thing. They're special effects that tinker with a photo's colors so it takes on certain looks—like an old Polaroid, or an old 1970s home photo, for example. You can "try on" various filters by selecting the little preview squares one after another. Use the "Filter intensity" slider to govern how much of this effect you want to apply.

The other useful option on the Filters tab is the "Enhance your photo" tile (bearing the ⚚ icon). When you click the magic wand, the app analyzes the relative brightness of all the pixels in your photo and attempts to "balance" it. After a moment, the app adjusts the brightness and contrast and intensifies dull or grayish-looking areas. Usually the pictures look richer and more vivid as a result.

You may find that this button has little effect on some photos, minimally improves others, and totally rescues a few.

Adjustments

This section offers options like Light (exposure), Color (saturation), Clarity (sharpness), and Vignette (lightens or darkens the photo's corners).

Note that you can open the flippy > for Light or Color to reveal further sub-sliders (Figure 8-28). For Light, they include the following:

- **Contrast.** If your photo looks flat, use this effect to bring out details. It makes the dark parts of your photo a little darker, and the light parts a little lighter.

- **Exposure.** Adjusts the overall exposure of the photo, making all of it lighter or darker.

- **Highlights, Shadows.** The Highlights and Shadows dials are designed to recover lost detail in the brightest and darkest areas of your photos, turning what once might have been unsalvageably overexposed or underexposed photos into usable shots. For example, suppose you've got a photo looking good, except that you don't have any detail in murky, dark areas. Move the Shadows handle to the right, and presto! A world of detail emerges from what used to be nearly black.

For Color, you get Tint, which adjusts the photo's overall tint along the red-green spectrum (for correcting skin tones and for compensating for difficult lighting situations, like fluorescent lighting), and Warmth (adjusts the photo along the blue-orange spectrum—a handy technique for breathing life back into subjects who have been bleached white with a flash).

This panel also offers "Red eye" (turns devil-red eyes, caused by the camera's flash, black again) and "Spot fix" (paints away scratches, spots, hairs, and other small flaws).

"Edit & Create"→Draw

That Edit & Create button (which appears when you open a photo) harbors some other delights. For example, if you have a touchscreen, the Draw option lets you doodle on your photo, using your choice of three "pens" (hold down for a choice of colors and line thicknesses) and an eraser. See page 340 for more details on this standard Windows drawing toolbox.

"Edit & Create"→Add 3D Effects

This option, too, lurks in the Edit & Create menu: a palette of animations that you can lay on top of your photo or video, including falling leaves, rising balloons, a snowy blizzard, fluttering butterflies, and so on (Figure 8-29). A timeline scrubber lets you control when the effect appears, and for how long; handles let you adjust its size and rotation; and a "3D library" pane offers a huge assortment of 3D objects you can drop into your photos or videos: wrapped presents, aliens, dinosaurs—you name it.

Tip: Remember, these are 3D objects; the special handles around their selection boxes let you spin them in any direction.

Figure 8-29:
When you apply one of these animated overlays to a still photo, it becomes a video, whether you like it or not. You can add multiple animated overlays or 3D models to a single photo or video. Suddenly, you're Pixar.

"Edit & Create"→Animated Text

The new, improved Photos can overlay fancy titles onto a photo or video clip—perfect for opening credits for your low-budget video operation.

Type the text into the box at top, choose one of the font styles, choose where to put it (using the Layout section), specify how much time the text should appear during the video playback (using the handles on the scroll bar), and then hit the Play triangle to check it out.

Slapping a Photo onto the Lock Screen or Desktop

When you're looking at a single photo (and not editing it), the ⋯ button at top right offers a secret shortcut menu. Its "Set as" command slaps the current photo onto any of these billboards: the Lock screen (page 19), the desktop background wallpaper (page 152), or the tile for the Photos app on the Start menu's right section (see the box below).

Tip: Also in the ⋯ menu: "File info." Choosing this option—or pressing Alt+Enter at any time—opens a left-side panel that tells you everything about the current photo: size, date, name, camera model, manual settings, ISO, and so on.

Selecting Photos (to Share or Delete)

Photos wouldn't be much fun if your screen were the only place you could see them. Fortunately, the Photos app is happy to zap them away to your adoring fans electronically. Or, if they're terrible shots, you can just zap them away.

Selecting photos

The first step is telling Photos which pictures you want to send. To do that, on the Collection screen or an Album screen, hit the ⅀≡ icon to make their checkboxes appear. Just click or tap each photo you want to include.

Tip: Actually, if you have a trackpad or mouse, you can save a step. Just point to each photo to see its checkbox appear—no ⅀≡ click necessary.

Sharing selected photos

Once you've chosen the photos you want to share, the top toolbar offers several ways to go. In addition to Print, Copy, and Delete, here's what you get:

- **Create** lets you generate one of those musical slideshows, or an album, from the selection.

- **Add to** puts the selected photos into a new album, a new video, or an existing video slideshow.

GEM IN THE ROUGH

The Littlest Slideshow

Deep in Photos' Settings screen (choose ⋯ at top right and then ⚙), there lies what may be the quirkiest preference setting in all of Windows Land: "The app tile shows."

That's right: Microsoft is asking which one photo you want to appear on the tile that represents the Photos app, as it appears on the right side of the Start menu.

Your choices are "A single photo" (and then there's a "Choose photo" button) or "Recent photos." That last option gives you a rotating slideshow—sized for an audience of gnats—right there on the Photos tile in the Start menu.

Don't scoff. The ability to decide exactly what appears on that one app's tile might just make somebody's year.

- **Share** (↗). The Share panel opens, listing all the places you can send the selected images. The options here vary. They usually include your My People (page 326), any Nearby Sharing computers (page 564), and various other export options— Mail, Facebook, and Dropbox, for example. If you've installed a program with beefier editing tools, like Microsoft's own Fresh Paint, its name appears here, too.

- **Print.** Yes, some people still print their photos.

- **Copy** to the Clipboard, ready for pasting into another app.

- **Delete.** Gets rid of your less impressive attempts.

- **Cancel.** This means "Back out of this—forget all that checking business."

Settings

This, of course, is the awe-inspiring Settings app described in Chapter 7.

Skype

In 2011, Microsoft bought Skype, the popular chat, audio-chat, and video-chat program. (The price: $8.5 billion. For Microsoft, pocket change.)

In 2013, Skype officially became a standard Microsoft Store app. (Its predecessor, an app called Messenger, went to the great CompUSA in the sky.)

Skype is a game-changer. It's the app millions of middle-aged parents use to call their kids studying abroad…new parents use to show their babies to the grandparents… and long-distance couples use to video chat. Skype finally comes preinstalled with Windows 10—you don't have to download it anymore. And the best part: All this voice and video calling is free.

For a handy guide to setting up and using Skype, see the free downloadable PDF appendix "Skype" on this book's "Missing CD" page at *missingmanuals.com*.

Snip & Sketch

Snip & Sketch, born in the October 2018 Update (Figure 8-30), is a modern and capable screenshotting tool. It lets you take pictures of the entire screen, just one window, any irregular area you enclose freehand, or the contents of a rectangular selection. You can give yourself a self-timer to get all your screen elements in position. When you're finished, Snip & Sketch displays your snapshot in a new window, which you can edit and mark up—and then print, edit, copy, or save (as a JPEG, GIF, PNG, or embedded HTML file).

Now, as experienced PC enthusiasts already know, Windows has *always* had shortcuts for capturing screenshots: Press the Print Screen (or PrtScn or PrtScr) key to save a picture of the whole screen to a Screenshots folder in your Pictures library; add the Alt key to save a file with just that window; or press ⊞+PrtScn to copy a screenshot to your Clipboard.

So why use Snip & Sketch instead? Because it's infinitely more flexible.

Capturing the Screenshot

Here's how to use it.

1. **Open Snip & Sketch.**

   Microsoft is so excited about this app that it's given you a new dedicated keystroke for opening it. It's ⊞+Shift+S.

Tip: If that's a lot to remember—three keys—you can set things up so your PrtScn key opens Snip & Sketch, too. Once you've opened the app, hit ⋯, then Settings, and then "Use the PrtScn button to open screen snipping."

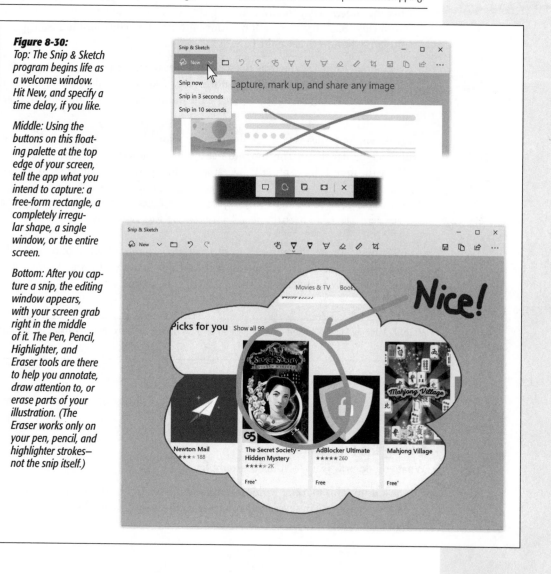

Figure 8-30:
Top: The Snip & Sketch program begins life as a welcome window. Hit New, and specify a time delay, if you like.

Middle: Using the buttons on this floating palette at the top edge of your screen, tell the app what you intend to capture: a free-form rectangle, a completely irregular shape, a single window, or the entire screen.

Bottom: After you capture a snip, the editing window appears, with your screen grab right in the middle of it. The Pen, Pencil, Highlighter, and Eraser tools are there to help you annotate, draw attention to, or erase parts of your illustration. (The Eraser works only on your pen, pencil, and highlighter strokes—not the snip itself.)

The app opens as a window (Figure 8-30, top). At the moment, the only thing useful to you now is at its top-left corner: the New button and its pop-up menu.

2. **If you'll need a few seconds to get things ready, use the New pop-up menu to choose a time delay.**

Your options are "Snip now," "Snip in 3 seconds," or "Snip in 10 seconds." The idea here is that once the self-timer begins, you'll have a chance to set up the elements of the screen the way you want them in the picture. Maybe you want a screenshot of an icon in mid-drag, a menu open, a painting tool in mid brushstroke, or whatever.

3. **Hit New.**

After the chosen delay (if any), the Snip & Sketch palette appears at the top of the screen (Figure 8-30, middle). It has four buttons to specify four kinds of capture (plus an ✕ button to close the panel):

Rectangular Snip lets you drag diagonally across the frozen screen image, capturing a square or rectangular area. Unfortunately, you can't adjust the rectangle if your aim was off; the instant you release the mouse button, the program captures the image.

Free-form Snip means you can drag your cursor in any crazy, jagged, freehand, nonrectangular shape. The app outlines it with a colored border; the instant you release the mouse, the captured image appears in the editing window, ready to save.

Tip: You can change the border color in the Options dialog box. It appears when you click Options on the main Snipping palette, or when you choose Tools→Options in the editing window.

A **Window Snip** neatly captures an entire window, automatically cropping out the background. And *which* window does it capture? That's up to you. As you point to each window, it appears highlighted. When the correct one is highlighted, click the mouse.

Note: A "window," in this context, doesn't have to be a window. It can also be the taskbar, a dialog box, and so on.

Full-screen Snip, of course, captures the entire screen.

In each case, the captured image appears in the editing window (Figure 8-30, bottom).

Editing the Screenshot

What you do now is up to you. For example:

- **Mark it up.** This markup window is a standard Windows 10 feature—the identical toolset appears in several other apps—so this may be a good place to describe how they work.

The toolbar harbors Pen, Pencil, Highlighter, and Eraser tools for annotating your masterpiece. The only difference: The Pen tool makes opaque marks, the Pencil makes fuzzy ones, and the Highlighter makes translucent ones.

To choose the line thickness and color for a tool, open the ˅ pop-up menu beneath each icon (or right-click the icon, or press and hold on the icon). You get a palette of color swatches from which to choose, along with a Size slider that governs the line thickness.

The eraser lets you delete individual markings. That is, click an existing Pen, Pencil, or Highlighter mark anywhere to delete that *entire* mark. Click the Eraser a second time for an "Erase all ink" button. Undo (↶) and Redo (↷) buttons are always available.

Tip: The first icon, Touch Writing, is an on/off switch for use with touchscreens. When it's off (not underlined), dragging your finger on the screen scrolls the image. When it's on (underlined), your finger on the screen operates the selected tool (Pen, Pencil, Highlighter, or Eraser). Your mouse, pen, or trackpad continue to work as drawing tools either way.

You also get an onscreen ruler, which can help you draw straight lines. Rotate it by turning the mouse wheel, or (on a touchscreen) putting two fingers on the glass and twisting them.

Tip: If you hit the Ruler icon a second time, you're offered a Protractor tool instead—great for drawing curved line segments. (You see the number of circular degrees as you draw.) Your mouse wheel makes it bigger or smaller; on a touchscreen, pinch and zoom with two fingers instead.

Crop. The ⛶ button surrounds your screenshot with four white handles, which you can drag to crop the image.

When it looks right, hit the ✓ button or press Enter to confirm the crop.

- **Save.** If your intention is to save the capture as a file, click the Save (🖫) icon, or choose File→Save, or press Ctrl+S. When the Save As dialog box appears, type a name for your graphic, choose a file format for it (from the "Save as type" drop-down menu—JPEG, GIF, or PNG), specify a folder location, and then click Save.

- **Copy** (or Ctrl+C) puts the image on your Clipboard, ready for pasting somewhere.

- **Share.** The ⤴ button on the editing-window toolbar automatically prepares an outgoing email message with your graphic already pasted in (or, if your email program is set to send plain, unformatted text messages only, as an attachment).

- ··· **(More)** offers commands like Print, "Send feedback," and Settings, described next.

Tip: The 🗁 toolbar button lets you open any *existing* graphic on your PC to mark it up and share it using these same tools, even if it isn't a screenshot.

Settings

Tucked away in the ⋯ menu is the Settings command, which offers three options that can make Snip & Sketch much more efficient:

- **Auto copy to the clipboard.** Once you've dressed up your screenshot, you don't have to remember to use the Copy command. It's already on the Clipboard.

- **Save snips.** If you close your image without saving, sharing, or copying it, it's gone forever. This option makes the app ask, "Are you sure?"

- **Snip outline.** This adds an attractive square border to the finished image. When you turn on this switch, you get to choose a color and line thickness for it.

Sticky Notes

Sticky Notes creates virtual Post-it notes that you can stick anywhere on your screen—a triumphant software answer to the thousands of people who stick notes on the edges of their actual monitors.

You can type quick notes and to-do items, paste in web addresses or phone numbers you need to remember, or store any other little scraps and snippets of text you come across (Figure 8-31). In the newly overhauled May 2019 Update, your notes can sync wirelessly and magically to your other Windows 10 machines.

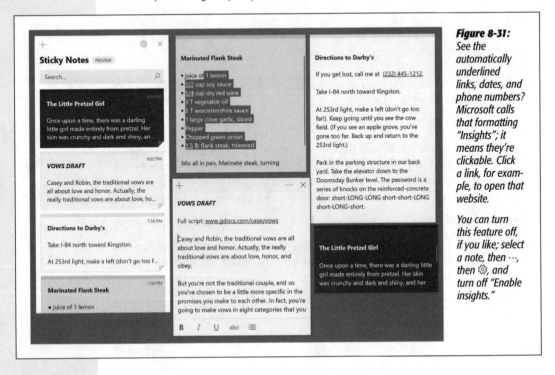

Figure 8-31:
See the automatically underlined links, dates, and phone numbers? Microsoft calls that formatting "Insights"; it means they're clickable. Click a link, for example, to open that website.

You can turn this feature off, if you like; select a note, then ⋯, then ☼, and turn off "Enable insights."

You also get a table-of-contents note that offers a preview of all your *other* notes. It's called the Notes List, and you can make it appear or disappear by pressing Ctrl+H, or by choosing "Notes list" from the ··· menu at the top right of every note.

Even if you close individual notes, they're not gone. The Notes List still remembers and lists them, and you can reopen them at any time with a quick tap or double-click.

Creating Notes

To create a new note, hit the + in the upper-left corner of any note, or press Ctrl+N. Then fill the note by typing or pasting.

You can change a note's size by dragging its edges or lower-right corner.

You can format the text of a note—a *little* bit. Buttons for bold, italic, underline, and strikethrough appear at the bottom of the note you're editing, along with a button that creates a bulleted list. You can also use keyboard shortcuts:

- **Bold, Italic, Underline.** Press Ctrl+B, Ctrl+I, or Ctrl+U.

- **Strikethrough style.** Press Ctrl+T.

- **Create a bulleted list.** Press Ctrl+Shift+L.

You can also change the "paper" color for a note to any of five other pastel colors. To do that, click the ··· and choose from the menu.

Deleting Notes

To get rid of a note, hit its 🗑 button on the Notes List. Or choose ··· and hit "Delete note." When the program asks if you're sure, click Yes.

On the other hand, you can *exit* Sticky Notes without worrying that you'll lose what you've already typed. All your notes will be there the next time you open the app.

Tips

How thoughtful! Microsoft's multimedia team has created a little scrapbook of slideshows that show you how to do things on your PC in Windows 10. There's a "What's new" category, a "Personalize your PC" category, a "The basics" category, and so on. It's not exactly, you know, a Missing Manual, but it's a start.

Video Editor

Wait, really? Has Movie Maker made a comeback? Has Microsoft provided a video-editing app?

Nope. This item is nothing more than a shortcut for jumping into the Photos app, already open to the "video editor" described on page 332.

Voice Recorder

This audio app is ideal for recording lectures, musical performances, notes to self, and cute child utterances. You can make very long recordings with this thing. Let it run all day, if you like. Even your most long-winded friends can be immortalized.

Talk about a minimal interface! There's nothing in this app except for a big fat microphone button. Hit it (or press Ctrl+R) to start recording. A little timer clicks away, and the Stop button (■) pulses, to show that you're rolling. You can pause or resume the recording at will (❚❚) or, when it's good and done, stop it by tapping the huge round Stop button. (If you switch into another app, the recording pauses automatically.)

Tip: During recording, you can hit the little ⚑ icon to mark important points in the audio you'll want to find later. Each time, Voice Recorder creates a new time stamp, listed across the bottom of the screen. Later you'll be able to jump to these spots for playback (see Figure 8-32).

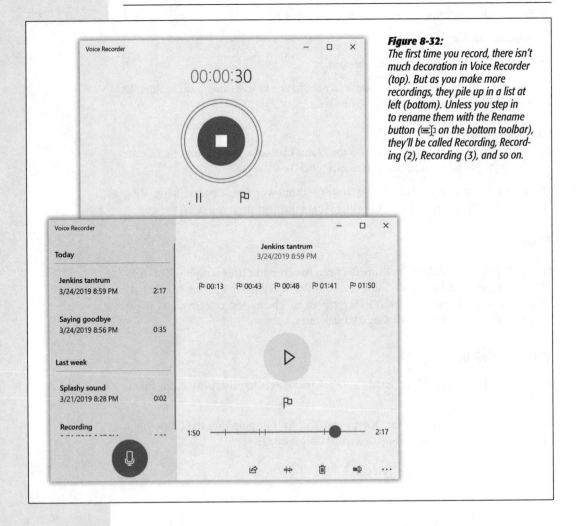

Figure 8-32:
The first time you record, there isn't much decoration in Voice Recorder (top). But as you make more recordings, they pile up in a list at left (bottom). Unless you step in to rename them with the Rename button (⌨ on the bottom toolbar), they'll be called Recording, Recording (2), Recording (3), and so on.

When you stop the recording, the screen changes; see Figure 8-32.

At this point, you can proceed like this:

- **Name the recording** by right-clicking; from the shortcut menu, choose Rename.

- **Record another sound.** Use the microphone button again. As you record more sounds, they pile up in the list at top left.

- **Play a recording.** Select it, and then select the ▷ button (or tap Space).

- **Rewind, Fast-Forward.** Drag the round handle in the scrubber bar to skip backward or forward in the recording. It's a great way to skip over the boring pleasantries.

- **Jump to your markers.** They show up with time stamps above the scrubber bar—click to jump there in the playback—and also as notches *on* the scrubber bar.

- 🗑. Tap to get rid of a recording (you're asked to confirm).

- **Trim off the ends.** You might not guess that such a tiny, self-effacing app actually offers some editing functions, but it does. You can trim off the beginning or end of your audio clip. That, of course, is where you'll usually find "dead air" or microphone fumbling before the good stuff starts playing. (You can't otherwise edit the sound; for example, you can't copy or paste bits or cut a chunk out of the middle.)

  To trim the bookends of your clip, use the "⊟" button. At this point, the beginning and end of the recording are marked by big black dots; these are your trim points. Drag them inward to isolate the part of the clip you want to keep. Play the sound as necessary to guide you (▷).

  Select ✕ if you change your mind, or the ✓ to lock in your changes. From its shortcut menu, choose either "Save a copy" (which also saves the original file) or "Update original" (which doesn't).

Note: It's a common question: Once you record these sounds, *where are they?* Yes, you can email them to yourself from within the app. But where on your PC are the actual recordings sitting?

Well, they're buried, that's for sure. Switch to the desktop. Make hidden files visible (on the View tab of an Explorer window's ribbon, turn on "Hidden items"). Navigate to *(C:)* > *Users* > *[your name]* > *AppData* > *Local* > *Packages* > *Microsoft.WindowsSoundRecorder_8wekyb3d8bbwe* > *localstate* > *Indexed* > *recordings*. (Yes, there really is a folder called *Microsoft.WindowsSound-Recorder_8wekyb3d8bbwe*.) And there they are—the actual .m4a music files that represent your recordings. Now you can back them up, share them, copy them to a flash drive, whatever.

Weather

This app presents a lovely, colorful weather report. (The first time you use it, you have to give the app permission to use your location.)

Right off the bat, you see the current weather (as though the full-window background photo didn't give it away). There's the 10-day forecast (Figure 8-33). Below that, you

---

see the hour-by-hour forecast for today, so you can see exactly what time your softball game will get rained out.

Tip: You can view this hourly section either as a cool graph ("Summary") or as hourly tables of data ("Details").

But the most surprising part of the Weather app is the more complete weather station that lurks in the left-side menu column. Here's what these icons do:

- ℭ **Maps** are cool visual representations of current meteorological data for the whole country: radar, regional temperature, precipitation, cloud cover, severe weather alerts, and so on.

Tip: If you hit the Play button (▷), the map *animates* (Figure 8-33, top). It shows you the last six hours' worth of whatever you're looking at: cloud cover, precipitation, temperature, and so on. Zoom in or out to see a different area of the country.

- ≈ **Historical Weather.** This handy graph shows you a snapshot of your current location's weather history. The big graph shows temperature, rainfall, and snowfall

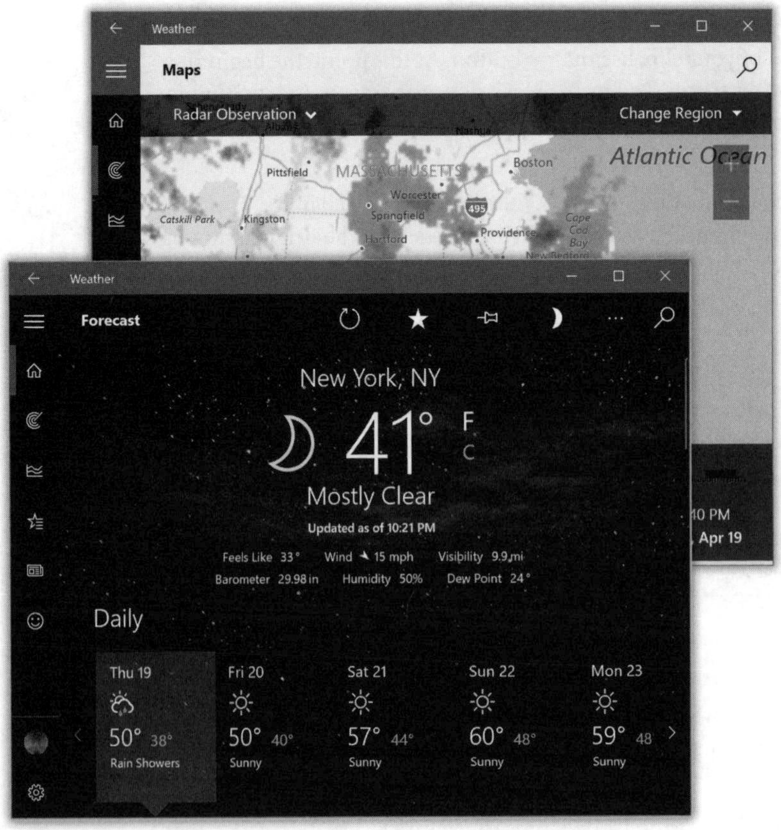

Figure 8-33:
Bottom: Most people probably never bother drilling down past this screen, but there's much more to do here. For example, the > button at right brings up the next five days' forecast. Or you can keep scrolling down to open up even more details—wind speed, visibility, humidity, barometer, and the predicted highs and lows. You pilots know who you are.

Top: These are animated weather maps, showing the past several hours' worth of cloud movement, precipitation, and so on. (To get there, hit the ℭ on the left.) They're really pretty amazing.

(depending on which of the three round icons you select above it). The little table beneath gives you stats like the average high and low for today's date, the record high and low for today's date, and monthly averages for rainfall, snowy days, and rainy days.

- ✰ **Places.** Here you can set up tiles that show you, at a glance, the weather in *other* cities around the world that might interest you. Hit the + button and type the city's name.

- 🖾 **News.** The next icon presents tiles that represent individual news articles about weather.

There are settings to explore in Weather, too. You can specify F or C for the temperature readings, and you can ask the app to auto-detect your location for weather-report purposes.

Windows Accessories

This folder in your Start menu harbors 14 small, less-often-used apps. Here they are, in the order they appear in the folder.

Character Map

Your computer is capable of creating hundreds of different typographical symbols— the currency symbols for the yen and British pound, diacritical markings for French and Spanish, various scientific symbols, trademark and copyright signs, and so on.

Figure 8-34:
Double-click a character to transfer it to the "Characters to copy" box, as shown here. (Double-click several in a row if you want to capture a sequence of symbols.) You may have to scroll down quite a bit in some of today's modern Unicode fonts, which contain hundreds of characters. Click Copy, and then close the window. When you've returned to your document, use the Paste command to insert the symbols.

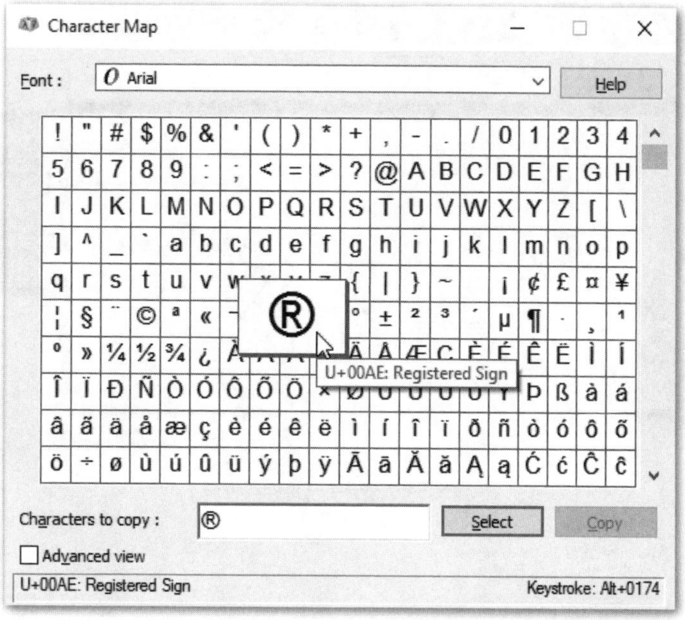

Obviously, these symbols don't appear on your keyboard; it would have to be the width of Wyoming. You *can* type the symbols, but they're hidden behind the regular keys.

The treasure map that reveals their locations is the Character Map (Figure 8-34). When opening this program, use the Font drop-down menu to specify the font you want to use (because every font contains its own set of symbols). Now you see every single symbol available in the font. As you click on each symbol, a magnified version of it appears to help you distinguish among them.

Tip: Some email programs can't handle the fancy symbols revealed by the Character Map. That explains why the copyright symbol, for example, can turn into a gibberish character on the receiving end.

Internet Explorer

For most purposes, Microsoft Edge (Chapter 9) is the Microsoft web browser you should use. It's much faster, sleeker, and more secure than the Cro-Magnon browser Internet Explorer that came before it. (Or, better yet, use Google's Chrome browser.)

But just in case there's some legacy reason why you're still married to a program that was born in 1995, Microsoft tucks it in here, in the Windows Accessories folder.

Math Input Panel

This unsung little freebie (Figure 8-35) is intended for an elite group indeed: mathematicians with touchscreen computers. You're supposed to write out math equations using your finger or a stylus and marvel as Windows translates your handwriting into

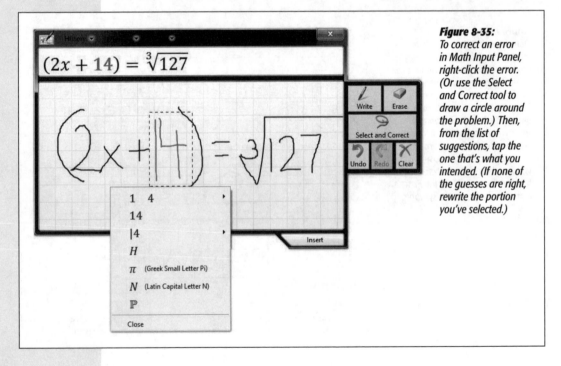

Figure 8-35:
To correct an error in Math Input Panel, right-click the error. (Or use the Select and Correct tool to draw a circle around the problem.) Then, from the list of suggestions, tap the one that's what you intended. (If none of the guesses are right, rewrite the portion you've selected.)

a typed-out mathematical expression. (You *can* use this program with a mouse; it just might feel a little odd.)

Most of the time, you'll want to use MIP when you're writing in a word processor—preparing a math test for students, writing a white paper, whatever.

Note: This program can insert its finished math expressions only into programs that recognize something called MathML (Mathematical Markup Language). Microsoft Word, Excel, and PowerPoint do, and so does the free OpenOffice.org.

If you have a touchscreen computer and you're working in the Windows Journal program, you can also use MIP to analyze your previously *handwritten* math expressions and make them properly typeset. (Use the selection tool to highlight your handwriting, and then drag the expression *into* the MIP window.)

To use MIP on any other computer, write out the mathematical expression, as neatly as you can, in the writing area. In the Preview area (see Figure 8-35), you see Windows' stab at recognizing your handwriting. If it's all correct, tap Insert to drop the equation into your word processor. But if something needs correcting, you can show MIP what it got wrong in one of several ways:

- **Right-click the mistake.** Or, if the mistaken transcription is more than one symbol, circle the error while pressing the right mouse button.

- **Tap the mistake while pressing your stylus's button.** (Or, again, circle the mistake while pressing the pen's button.)

- **Click the Select and Cancel button.** Now tap the erroneous symbol, or circle the larger part that's wrong.

Tip: It's better to correct errors after you've written out the whole thing.

Immediately, a drop-down menu of alternative transcriptions appears. Proceed as shown in Figure 8-35. If the expression is now complete, tap Insert. If you have more to write, just keep on going. (If you got into symbol-correction mode by tapping Select and Cancel, you'll have to tap Write before you continue.)

Tip: You can tap any entry in the History menu to re-input an expression you've entered before. When you're working on, for example, a proof or a drill with many similar problems, that can save you a lot of time.

Notepad

Notepad (in your Windows Accessories folder) is a bargain-basement *text editor,* which means it lets you open, create, and edit files that contain plain, unformatted text, like the ReadMe.txt files that often accompany new programs. You can also use Notepad to write short notes or to edit text you intend to paste into your email program after editing it. Notepad has had some enhancements in recent Windows updates, but it's still not exactly Microsoft Word.

Notepad basics

Notepad opens automatically when you double-click text files (those with the file extension *.txt*). You can also find it by typing *notep* in the search box (page 102).

You'll quickly discover that Notepad is the world's most frill-free application. Its list of limitations is almost longer than its list of features.

Above all, Notepad is a *text* processor, not a *word* processor. That means you can't use any formatting at all—no bold, italic, centered text, and so on. That's not necessarily bad news, however. The beauty of text files is that any word processor on any kind of computer—Windows, Mac, Unix, whatever—can open plain text files like the ones Notepad creates.

Note: In fact, Notepad now handles more *kinds* of text files—like those created on a Mac or Linux machine—without scrambling them upon opening. In the status bar at the bottom of the window, Notepad shows you which line-break formatting scheme it's currently using: Unix (LF), Mac (CR), or Windows (CRLF).

Word wrap

When you first open a text file or paste text, Notepad may not wrap lines of text to make everything fit in its window. As a result, chunks of text may go on forever in a single line or get chopped off by the right side of the window, which can produce disastrous results when you're trying to follow, say, a soufflé recipe.

Fortunately, if you choose the Format→Word Wrap command, lines of text wrap automatically, exactly as they do in a word processor. And they *stay* wrapped as you edit or change the window size. (You can tell when Word Wrap is on by the presence of a checkmark next to the command in the Format menu.)

There are search/replace commands, a Bing search tool, zoom in/zoom out commands, and a Help command (which does nothing more than open your web browser and perform a Bing search for "get help with notepad in windows 10").

Paint

You can use Paint (Figure 8-36) to "paint" simple artwork or to edit graphics files from other sources. You might say Paint is something like Adobe Photoshop (well, in the same way you might say the local Cub Scout newsletter is something like *The New York Times*). Common tasks for this program include making quick sketches, fixing dust specks on scanned photos, and entertaining kids for hours on end.

When you first open Paint, you get a small, empty painting window. Go like this:

1. **From the File menu, choose Properties to specify the dimensions of the graphic you want to create. Click OK.**

   Later in your life, you can revisit that command to adjust your graphic's dimensions.

2. **Click a tool on the Home tab, like the Pencil.**

   If you need help identifying one of these tools, tap it, or point to it without clicking. A tooltip identifies the icon by name, with a help message.

3. **Click a "paint" color from the palette.**

You may also want to change the "brush" by clicking the Brushes palette, where you'll find options like the spray-paint splatter shown in Figure 8-36.

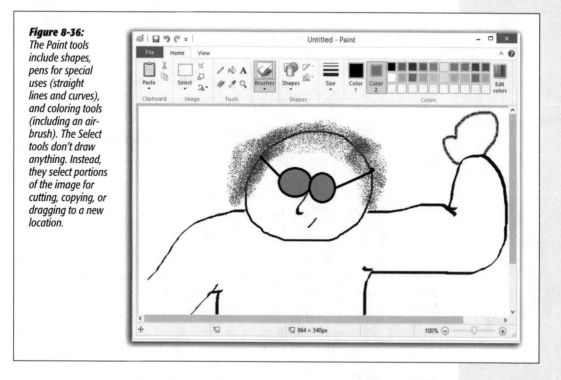

Figure 8-36:
The Paint tools include shapes, pens for special uses (straight lines and curves), and coloring tools (including an airbrush). The Select tools don't draw anything. Instead, they select portions of the image for cutting, copying, or dragging to a new location.

4. **If you've selected one of the enclosed-shape tools, use the Fill drop-down menu to specify a texture (Watercolor, Crayon, or whatever); click Color 2, and then a color swatch, to specify the color for the inside of that shape.**

Some tools produce enclosed shapes, like squares and circles. You can specify one color for the border and a second color for the fill inside.

5. **Finally, drag your cursor in the image area.**

As you work, don't forget you can Undo (press Ctrl+Z), "taking back" the last painting maneuvers you made. For fine detail work, zoom in using the lower-right magnification slider (or the zoom controls on the View tab).

Paint can open and create several different file formats, including BMP, JPEG, and GIF—every file format you need to save graphics for use on a website.

Tip: Paint also offers a nifty way to create wallpaper. After you create or edit a graphic, open the File menu. Choose "Set as desktop background." From the submenu, choose Fill, Tile, or Center to transfer your masterpiece to your desktop.

Print 3D

This little app (in your Windows Accessories folder) is intended for people who have access to a 3D printer, one of those machines that "prints" small, solid objects out of plastic. Hit Browse to load up a 3D model file (see page 285); inspect it, enlarge it, and (assuming your PC has the correct drivers and software for the 3D printer) hit Print to begin the long process of printing.

Quick Assist

You use this app (in your Windows Accessories folder) to let some technical expert take control of your PC by remote control, so she can look around and help you troubleshoot. Or, if you're the technical expert, you can take control of *her* computer. Details are on page 458.

Remote Desktop Connection

Remote Desktop lets you sit at your home PC and operate your office PC by remote control. To learn more about it, refer to "Remote Desktop," a free PDF appendix on this book's "Missing CD" at *missingmanuals.com*.

Snipping Tool

Snipping Tool is a screenshot app. It takes pictures of your PC's screen. But Microsoft giveth and taketh away—and in the May 2019 Update, Snipping Tool has been put on death row. A message lets you know that "Snipping Tool is moving," and recommends the hot, young upstart Snip & Sketch, described on page 338.

Snipping Tool still works, though. If you care about it, you can read about it in the PDF appendix "Snipping Tool." It's on this book's "Missing CD" at *missingmanuals.com*.

Steps Recorder

This program (in your Windows Accessories folder) is designed to record exactly where you're clicking or tapping, and to capture a screen picture each time you do so. Why? So you can document some problem you're having. You can send the resulting recording to someone who wants to see exactly what steps you were taking when you ran into trouble.

Of course, this is a similar scenario to the times when you might use Quick Assist (page 458), where the wise scholar can *watch* you perform the steps that are frustrating you. But because Steps Recorder lets you type a little message each time you click the mouse, it's a better, more permanent way to record some problem you're having.

When you're ready to record the steps, click Start Record. Now do whatever it is, on your computer, that produces the problem: Click here, use that menu, drag that slider, whatever. As you go, you can do the following:

- **Pause the recording.** Click Pause Record. (Click Resume Record to continue.)

- **Type an annotation for a particular step.** ("Here's where I double-clicked.") Click Add Comment, highlight the part of the screen you want to comment on, type your note into the box, and then click OK.

Note: Anything you type outside that comment box doesn't get recorded; that's a security precaution.

When you're finished, click Stop Record.

The Recorded Steps window appears. It shows you each screenshot that Steps Recorder captioned, complete with its time stamp and text description ("User left-click on 'File Explorer' button," for example). This is your chance to make sure you're not about to send away personal information (or photos) that might have been on the screen while you recorded.

If everything looks good, click Save to create a compressed archive—a .zip file—that you can open to look at the report again later in your web browser or attach as an email to an expert.

Windows Fax and Scan

See Chapter 13 for more on sending and receiving faxes from your PC—and on scanning documents using a scanner.

Windows Media Player

In the beginning, Windows Media Player was the headquarters for music and video on your PC. It was the hub for things like music CDs (you could play 'em, copy songs off 'em, and burn 'em), MP3 files and other digital songs (sort, buy, file into playlists); pocket music players of the non-iPod variety (fill, manage playlists); internet radio stations; DVD movies; and so on.

Windows Media Player still does all that, and more. But in the age of Spotify, Apple Music, and Pandora, its audience is dwindling.

Still, if you use Windows Media Player as your music-file database, see the free downloadable PDF appendix "Windows Media Player" on this book's "Missing CD" at *missingmanuals.com*.

WordPad

WordPad (Figure 8-37) is a basic word processor: More powerful than Notepad, but not quite as full-blown as Microsoft Word. Among other blessings, WordPad has a toolbar ribbon for quick access to formatting commands, and it can open and create Microsoft Word files. Yes, you can get away with not buying Microsoft Office, and none of your email business partners will ever know the difference.

And it's not just Word files. WordPad also can open and create plain text files, Rich Text Format (RTF) documents, and OpenOffice.org files.

Using WordPad

When WordPad first opens, you see an empty sheet of electronic typing paper. Just above the ruler, the Ribbon offers menus and buttons that affect your document. The Font formatting buttons let you change the look of selected text: font, size, color, subscript, and so on. The Paragraph formatting buttons affect entire paragraphs.

WordPad doesn't offer big-gun features like spell-checking, style sheets, or tables. But it does offer a surprisingly long list of core word-processing features. For example:

- **Find, Replace.** Using the Find button (right end of the Home tab on the Ribbon), you can locate a particular word or phrase instantly, even in a long document. The Replace command takes that a step further, replacing that found phrase with another one (a great way to change the name of your main character throughout your novel, for example).

- **Indents and Tab stops.** As shown in Figure 8-37, you click on the ruler to place tab stops there. Each time you press the Tab key, your insertion point cursor jumps in line with the next tab stop.

UP TO SPEED

Text-Selection Bible

Before doing almost anything to text in a word processor, like making it bold, changing its typeface, or moving it to a new spot in your document, you have to *highlight* the text you want to affect. For millions of people, this entails dragging the cursor extremely carefully, perfectly horizontally, across the desired text. And if they want to capture an entire paragraph or section, they click at the beginning, drag diagonally, and release the mouse button when they reach the end of the passage.

There's a better way. Selecting text is the cornerstone of every editing operation in a word processor or page-layout program, so it pays off to learn some faster and more precise ways of going about it.

For example, double-clicking a word highlights it, instantly and neatly. In fact, by keeping the mouse button pressed on the second click, you can drag horizontally to highlight text in crisp one-word chunks—a great way to select text faster and more precisely. These tricks work anywhere you can type.

In most programs, including Microsoft's, additional shortcuts await. For example, *triple*-clicking anywhere within a paragraph highlights the entire paragraph. (Once again, if you *keep* the button pressed at the end of this maneuver, you can then drag to highlight your document in one-paragraph increments.)

In many programs, including Word and WordPad, you can highlight exactly one sentence by clicking within it while pressing Ctrl. If you need to highlight a large blob of text—even one that's too big to fit on the current screen—start by clicking to position the insertion-point cursor at the beginning of the text you want to capture. Now scroll, if necessary, so the ending point of the passage is visible. Shift-click there. Windows instantly highlights everything between your click and your Shift-click.

These clicking tricks are all great, but what if even the act of reaching for your mouse is thwarting your editing mojo? Learn *these* techniques and never look back:

To select one character at a time, hold down Shift and then use the left and right arrow keys (← and →) to move through your text. You can grab even larger chunks by mixing in the ↑ and ↓ keys or adding Shift at any time (read on).

To move through your text one word at a time, press Ctrl+← or Ctrl+→. Add the Shift key if you want to highlight text as you go.

To move through your text one paragraph at a time, press Ctrl+↑ or Ctrl+↓. Again, add Shift to highlight entire paragraphs in neat chunks.

To select one line at a time, use Shift+↑ and Shift+↓. To move the insertion point to the beginning or end of the current line, press the Home or End keys.

To move from your insertion point to the beginning or end of some text, press Ctrl+Home or Ctrl+End—and, yes, add Shift to select the entire block in one neat keystroke. This works even if the spot you're aiming for is 100 pages away.

- **Bulleted lists.** You're reading a bulleted list right now. To apply bullets to a bunch of paragraphs, click the Bullets button (▤). If you click the ▾ next to it, you can create a numbered or lettered list instead.

- **Insert object.** This button lets you create or slap in a picture, graph, chart, sound, movie, spreadsheet, or other kind of data. (The "Paint drawing" button opens up a temporary Paint window so you can whip up a quick sketch to add.)

Tip: If you click "Date and time," you get a dialog box full of date and time formats (12/5/2019; 5-Dec-2019; Wednesday, December 5, 2019, and so on). Double-click one to insert that date into your document.

- **Drag-and-drop editing.** Instead of using the three-step Copy and Paste routine for moving words and phrases around in your document, you can simply drag highlighted text from place to place on the screen.

Figure 8-37:
WordPad's formatting ribbon makes it a surprisingly close relative to Microsoft Word. These buttons make paragraphs flush left, centered, flush right, or bulleted as a list. You can drag through several paragraphs before clicking these buttons, or you can click them to affect just the paragraph where your insertion point already is. The little L's on the ruler indicate tab stops that have been clicked into place; each press of the Tab key makes the insertion point jump to the next one.

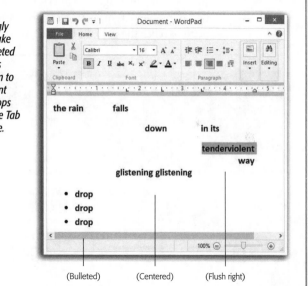

XPS Viewer

XPS was Microsoft's attempt to take on Adobe's PDF, a universal file format for distributing formatted documents. Nobody went for it, but the app is still here on the one-in-a-million chance that you run across an XPS document.

Windows Administrative Tools

Lucky you! You've found bunch of advanced geek-out apps like Component Services, Local Security Policy, and ODBC Data Sources. These are technical tools for people who *write* computer books, not read them.

Windows Ease of Access

Microsoft has stashed its four accessibility tools in this folder.

Magnifier

Magnifier puts a floating magnifying-glass icon on your screen (Figure 8-38, top left). When you click it, you get the Magnifier toolbar (top right).

Magnifier creates various magnification effects—great when your eyes are tired or old, or when you're trying to study something whose font is just too dang small.

Using the Views menu, you can choose "Full screen" (the entire screen image grows when you click the + button), "Lens" (you get a floating magnification inset that follows your cursor, as shown at bottom in Figure 8-38), or "Docked" (the top strip of the screen is one giant magnification inset; the rest of the screen is normal size).

In each case, the magnified area scrolls as you move your cursor, tab through a dialog box, or type, enlarging whatever part of the screen contains the action. Using Magnifier Settings (click the ⚙ in the toolbar), you can specify how the magnification area should

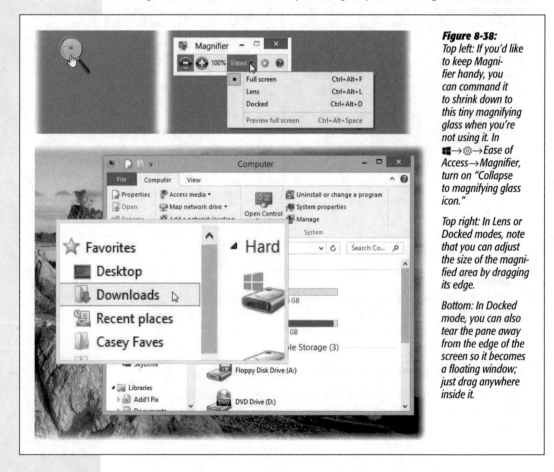

Figure 8-38:
Top left: If you'd like to keep Magnifier handy, you can command it to shrink down to this tiny magnifying glass when you're not using it. In ⊞→⚙→Ease of Access→Magnifier, turn on "Collapse to magnifying glass icon."

Top right: In Lens or Docked modes, note that you can adjust the size of the magnified area by dragging its edge.

Bottom: In Docked mode, you can also tear the pane away from the edge of the screen so it becomes a floating window; just drag anywhere inside it.

follow your cursor, change the zoom increments, set up Magnifier to open automatically when you sign in, invert the colors like a film negative, and so on. The Settings screen also reminds you of the keyboard shortcuts that let you operate these features.

Tip: Whenever Magnifier is turned on, you can zoom in or out with ⊞+plus or ⊞+minus.

Narrator

Narrator is a *screen reader*—a voice that reads aloud anything on the screen, which can be a huge help if you're visually impaired. It can describe every item on the screen, describe the layout of a web page, tell you which key you're pressing, and make sounds to confirm that you've performed a touchscreen gesture correctly.

Even if you're not blind, Narrator (in your Windows Ease of Access folder) is still handy. It can read your email back to you, or read web articles as you're getting dressed in the morning.

When you open Narrator, you wind up at a Welcome screen called Narrator Hub (Figure 8-39).

Tip: Instead of having to burrow through the Start menu to find Narrator, you can press ⊞+Ctrl+Enter at any time to start and stop it.

Figure 8-39:
The Narrator home screen offers a QuickStart tutorial, a full "Narrator guide" (manual), a list of "What's new," and the Settings dialog box. When it's open, the voice of Microsoft David (no relation) starts reading everything on the screen.

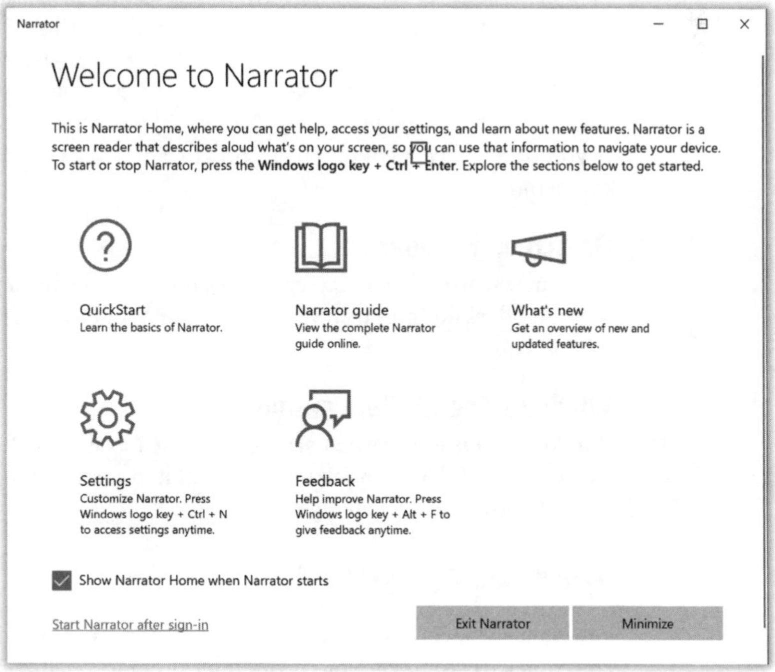

Narrator — □ ✕

Welcome to Narrator

This is Narrator Home, where you can get help, access your settings, and learn about new features. Narrator is a screen reader that describes aloud what's on your screen, so you can use that information to navigate your device. To start or stop Narrator, press the **Windows logo key + Ctrl + Enter**. Explore the sections below to get started.

(?)
QuickStart
Learn the basics of Narrator.

Narrator guide
View the complete Narrator guide online.

What's new
Get an overview of new and updated features.

Settings
Customize Narrator. Press Windows logo key + Ctrl + N to access settings anytime.

Feedback
Help improve Narrator. Press Windows logo key + Alt + F to give feedback anytime.

☑ Show Narrator Home when Narrator starts

Start Narrator after sign-in   Exit Narrator   Minimize

Touchscreen basics

Narrator is especially important on touchscreen computers; if you're blind, how else are you supposed to navigate the screen?

Drag your finger around the touchscreen; Narrator speaks everything you touch, so you can get a feel for the layout of things. You can also tap to hear a single item identified; you don't have to worry about opening something accidentally.

Of course, if touching something makes it say its name, then how are you supposed to open it? Simple: Add another tap. That is, you *double-tap* when a single tap usually works (or press-and-hold) and *triple-tap* when you'd ordinarily double-tap.

As you'll discover, mastering Narrator takes a lot of time and patience; it's something like a complete operating system in itself. You'd be wise to take the QuickStart tutorial.

To see the master cheat sheet of touch gestures in Narrator (and to hear it read to you), tap *three times with four fingers* against the screen. You'll learn essential tips like these:

To do this...	...Use this touch command
Stop Narrator from reading	Tap once with two fingers
Read current window	Swipe up with three fingers
Click	Double-tap
Double-click	Triple-tap
Start dragging	Tap with three fingers
Show/hide Narrator window	Tap with four fingers
Move to previous/next item	Flick left/right with one finger
Scroll	Swipe any direction with two fingers
Tab forward and backward	Swipe left/right with three fingers

If you don't have a touchscreen, press Caps Lock+1 to view the master list of commands.

On-Screen Keyboard

In the new world of touchscreen tablets, not everyone has a physical keyboard. Windows 10 offers this onscreen version (in your Windows Ease of Access folder), which is described on page 451.

Windows Speech Recognition

Windows offers a somewhat accurate speech-recognition feature, in your Windows Ease of Access folder. You can read all about it in a free appendix on this book's "Missing CD." Visit *missingmanuals.com*.

Windows PowerShell

PowerShell is a command console and scripting language. If you're a programmer, PowerShell lets you write your own simple programs, called *cmdlets* ("commandlets") that can perform all kinds of automated drudgery for you: copy or move folders, manipulate files, open or quit programs, and so on.

You harness all this power by typing up *scripts* in PowerShell's command line interface (which means no mouse, no menus, no windows—all text, like in the DOS days). In short, PowerShell is not for the layperson. If you're an *ambitious* layperson, however, a Google search for *PowerShell tutorial* unveils all kinds of websites that teach you, step by step, how to harness this very advanced tool.

Windows Security

Here's Windows 10's built-in antivirus software. Details are in Chapter 11.

Windows System

This folder in your Start menu is the home for seven techie tools that you may actually use from time to time.

Command Prompt

Command Prompt (in your Windows System folder) opens a *command line interface:* a black, empty screen with the time-honored *C:>* prompt, where you can type out instructions to the computer. This is a world without icons, menus, or dialog boxes; the mouse is almost useless.

Of course, the whole breakthrough of Windows was that it *eliminated* the DOS command line interface that was still the ruling party on the computers of the day. Most non-geeks sighed with relief, delighted that they'd never have to memorize commands again. Yet here's Microsoft's supposedly ultramodern operating system, complete with a command line! What's going on?

Actually, the command line never went away. At universities and corporations, professional computer nerds kept right on pounding away at the little *C:>* prompts, appreciating the efficiency and power such direct computer control afforded them.

You never *have* to use the command line. In fact, Microsoft has swept it far under the rug, expecting that most people will use the icons and menus of the regular desktop.

GEM IN THE ROUGH

Task Scheduler

Weirdly enough, not every app in Windows has an icon. Not every app is listed in the Start menu. A passel of obscure utility apps are available only by searching for them.

One of those is Task Scheduler, which you can use to run certain tasks automatically, according to a schedule. For example, you can schedule the Recycle Bin to empty itself, or email to check itself, or your drive to defragment itself.

For details, see the free PDF appendix to this chapter called "Task Scheduler." It's on this book's "Missing CD" at *missingmanuals.com.*

Tip: Quickest way to open the Command Prompt: type *command* into the search box, and then press Enter.

If you have time and curiosity, however, the Command Prompt lets you access corners of Windows that you can't get to from the regular desktop. (Commands for exploring network diagnostics are especially plentiful—*ping, netstat,* and so on.) It lets you perform certain tasks with much greater speed and efficiency than you'd get by clicking buttons and dragging icons. And it gives you a fascinating glimpse into the minds and moods of people who live and breathe computers.

Here are a few examples:

Command	Purpose	Example
control	Opens a Control Panel applet	*control date/time*
ping	Checks to see if a server is responding	*ping nytimes.com*
ipconfig	Reveals your PC's IP address	*ipconfig*
mkdir	Make directory (that is, create a folder)	*mkdir \Reports*
copy	Copy files from one folder to another	*copy c:\Reports*.* \Backup*

You can also type the true, secret name of any program to open it, quickly and efficiently, without having to mouse around through the Start menu. For example, you can type *winword* to open Word, or *charmap* to open Character Map.

To see the hundreds of commands at your disposal, consult the internet, which is filled with excellent lists and explanations. To find them, Google *Windows command line reference.* You'll find numerous ready-to-study websites that tell you what to type at the Command Prompt. (Here's an example from Microsoft: *http://bit.ly/bx0xo4.*)

Control Panel
See page 264 for details on this ancient settings app (in your Windows System folder).

File Explorer
Here, in your Windows System folder, is the actual icon for the main file- and window-management interface described in Chapter 2.

Run
When you want to open something with just a few keystrokes, the little Run command line window is there for you. See the free PDF appendix "Run Command" on this book's "Missing CD" page at *missingmanuals.com.*

Task Manager
This icon represents the all-purpose running-app manager described on page 213.

This PC
Don't be fooled by this item in the Windows System folder; it's not an app at all. It simply opens your This PC window, exactly as though you'd selected its name in any File Explorer window.

Windows Administrative Tools

This link simply opens the Windows Administrative Tools folder (page 355). It's full of apps—the exact same ones listed separately in the Start menu.

Xbox

Steady, there. Windows 10 does not come with a free Xbox.

But if you already *own* Microsoft's popular game console, you're in for a treat. This app is one of Microsoft's proudest Windows 10 features. It can perform a whole circus full of stunts that supplement an *actual* Xbox in your TV room.

For example, the Xbox app shows you all your stats, recently played games, and friends; you can message them, invite them, chat with them (by typing or by talking), or play games with them.

You can also use your tablet or laptop as a remote control for the Xbox (using it to change TV channels, for example, or pause playback).

Some companies are releasing games that you can play *between* a PC and a real Xbox, too.

The real eye-popper, though, is real-time *game streaming*. That's when you're sitting at your laptop or tablet in one room, playing games that are physically running on the Xbox One in another. You're seeing, hearing, and controlling the Xbox on your PC, using the PC as a second screen.

That's a huge benefit when you're playing a game on the Xbox in the TV room and some heartless family member comes in and demands to watch TV. Instead of being booted off your game, you can just take it anywhere else on the Wi-Fi network.

UP TO SPEED

Game Mode

Windows has a mode dedicated to giving you smoother, faster game performance for free.

It works by dedicating a big chunk of your PC's resources, like graphics-processor (GPU) cycles and main-processor (CPU) threads, to the game you're playing—at a cost to anything running in the background, including both programs you can see (like Spotify playing music or videos in a browser) and those you can't (like virus scans).

To turn on Game Mode, open the game, and then summon the Game Bar by pressing ⊞+G. Choose ⚙ to open the Settings, and turn on "Use Game Mode for this game."

Close the box; that's all there is to it. (You have to repeat this process for each game.)

Now for some expectation-setting. On a high-horsepower PC (like one you've built especially for gaming), you won't see any difference. Even on a modest PC like a budget laptop, you won't see a difference unless there's something running in the background. But on an average or cheap computer with some other programs open, Game Mode can make the difference between a stuttering game being unplayable and it being just bearable.

(Conversely, of course, Game Mode makes any programs that *are* running in the background slow to a crawl.)

The Guided Tour

If you've ever played an Xbox *game*, much of the Xbox *app* should look familiar (Figure 8-40):

- **Top left.** Here's a list of the Xbox games you've been playing recently. You'll need this list if you ever decide to try that game-streaming business, as you'll see in a moment.

Tip: If you click a game's cover art here, you open the "game hub"—the game company's own news feed.

Figure 8-40:
The Xbox app is a wireless global companion for your Xbox console at home—and for your universe of friends and rivals on the Xbox service. The Xbox app is a remote control for your Xbox, which also makes it possible to play games on your laptop that physically run on the Xbox elsewhere in the house.

- **Lower left.** Featured games from the Microsoft Store—that is, games the company dearly hopes you'll buy.

- **Center column.** This is your activity feed, exactly as it appears on the Xbox. It shows what your friends have been doing in their games and lets you comment on or "like" their achievements.

- **Right column.** Here's your list of friends and clubs—all of them, whether they're online at the moment or not. You can see what they're doing right now on their Xboxes ("Watching TV," "Blu-ray Player," "Halo," or whatever), send them messages, start a party chat, invite them to game sessions, watch their recorded game clips, and so on. (Click a friend's name to summon the Invite and Message buttons in a toolbar at top.)

Game Streaming

OK, here it is: the much-celebrated Xbox game streaming. Your Xbox One console is actually running the game, but you're playing it on a Windows 10 computer elsewhere on the same Wi-Fi network. Here's how to get it going.

First, the setup: The Xbox One and your Windows 10 machine have to be on the same network—very fast Wi-Fi or a wired network are recommended—and you have to sign in with the same Xbox account (gamertag) on both.

1. **Set up the Xbox One for streaming.**

   On the Xbox itself, go to ■→⚙→Preferences. Turn on "Allow game streaming to other devices." On the same screen, under "Enable the SmartGlass connection," select either "From any SmartGlass device" or "Only from profiles signed in on this Xbox."

2. **On your Windows 10 machine, open the Xbox app. Tap ≡ (top left) to open the menu column. Hit Connection.**

   The "Add a device" screen opens, and the app scans the network for Xbox One consoles.

3. **Select your Xbox's name.**

   If the fates are smiling, you're now connected. New options appear for streaming, power, and media remotes. You now have remote control of your Xbox One!

4. **Select Connect. Within the Xbox app, find a game you want to play. On its details screen, hit "Play from console" at upper right.**

   In just a moment, the game appears on your Windows 10 machine's screen. You can plug in a USB game controller, if you like, or just use the keyboard—but either way, you can marvel at the miracle of gaming that transcends the barriers of space and time.

   Well, sort of.

Tip: If your network isn't fast enough for smooth, crisp video, you may have to settle for smooth, less crisp video. In the Xbox app, open ■→⚙→XBox One, and try lowering the quality level until the gameplay stops stuttering.

Screenshots and Game DVR

If you do something extra-cool in a game, it's not enough just to brag about it; you've got to capture a picture of it (a screenshot) or record it as a video, using the Game Bar; see page 299.

Your Phone

This bare-bones app is dedicated to establishing a connection with your iPhone or Android phone; see page 251.

CHAPTER 9

The Edge Browser

Internet Explorer was the most famous web browser on earth, thanks in part to several years of Justice Department scrutiny. But it may have been too successful for its own good. Because it was built into Windows, because everyone used it, Internet Explorer became a prime target for hackers. Over the years, it had become old and slow, and riddled with holes and patches. In Windows 10, Microsoft decided to start over. It wrote a brand-new browser—called Edge.

Internet Explorer is still on your computer (in the Windows Accessories folder). If you care about it, read the free downloadable PDF appendix to this chapter, "Internet Explorer," on this book's "Missing CD" page at *missingmanuals.com*.

But as far as Microsoft's future is concerned, Edge is it. It's far faster and more modern than IE ever was—and much simpler. You cannot believe how much cruft Microsoft hacked out of it. A ton of stuff nobody used (Trusted Zones, anyone?) and a lot of shortcuts and refinements you may miss. (Microsoft says, "Give us time." With each version of Windows 10, Microsoft brings more features to Edge.)

Edge is designed to eat up very little screen space with controls, so the web pages you're reading get as much room as possible. Yet the big-ticket features you'd expect are in place, like bookmarks, a Downloads list, a History list, Reading view (text and graphics only—no ads or blinkies), private browsing, Find on Page, password storing, and Print.

Edge is a fresh start, a clean canvas, modernized and ready for the next 10 years. And the best news is that Edge now accepts extensions (feature plug-ins), just like the ones that make Chrome so attractive to so many people (*cough* ad blockers *cough*).

To open Edge, click its icon on the taskbar. It comes preinstalled there—a blue lowercase *e*, so as not to throw off people looking for the old Internet Explorer logo. It's also preinstalled on the right side of the Start menu.

Tip: There's one other sneaky way to open desktop Edge, one that may actually be quicker sometimes. Just type a web address—a *URL* (Uniform Resource Locator)—into any File Explorer window's address bar, and then hit Enter. Edge opens automatically and pulls up that page. (A web page URL usually begins with the prefix *http://*, but you can leave that part off when typing into the address bar.)

The Edge window is filled with tools designed to facilitate a smooth trip around the World Wide Web (Figure 9-1).

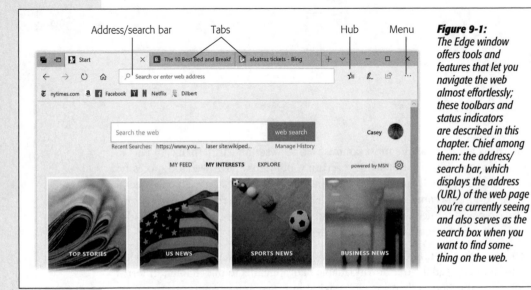

Address/search bar   Tabs   Hub   Menu

Figure 9-1:
The Edge window offers tools and features that let you navigate the web almost effortlessly; these toolbars and status indicators are described in this chapter. Chief among them: the address/search bar, which displays the address (URL) of the web page you're currently seeing and also serves as the search box when you want to find something on the web.

The Start Page

The first web page you encounter when Edge connects to the internet may be a "What's New in Windows 10" page, or the Microsoft Edge Tips page, or Microsoft's standard news starter page. Of course, there's an address bar so you can type a URL. But you may find web browsing more fun if you specify your *own* favorite web page as your startup page.

The easiest way to go about it is to follow the instructions shown in Figure 9-2. Your options include these:

- **Start page.** If you choose "Start page," Edge always opens with a news-headline page. You're supposed to tailor it to your own interests; hit Personalize, and choose news categories that interest you: Horoscopes, Parenting, Pets, Investing, NCAA Basketball, and so on.

Go to My Feed to reap what you've sown. Here are tiles representing individual stories from the web, on the topics you've set up on the Personalize tab.

Note: This customized Start page appears when you first open Edge (assuming you've chosen "Start page" in Settings). But when you open a new *tab*, you get a row of icons that represent Top Sites above the usual Start-page news items. Top Sites are Microsoft's calculations of the sites you visit most often. You can turn them off in ⋯→⚙→"Open new tabs with."

You can also get rid of one of the suggestions (point to it and click the ✕), prevent it from being replaced by Microsoft's subsequent suggestions (point to it and hit ⇥), or install a new site of your choosing (eliminate at least one of the tiles, hit the + tile, specify the new site, and then hit ⇥ to pin it).

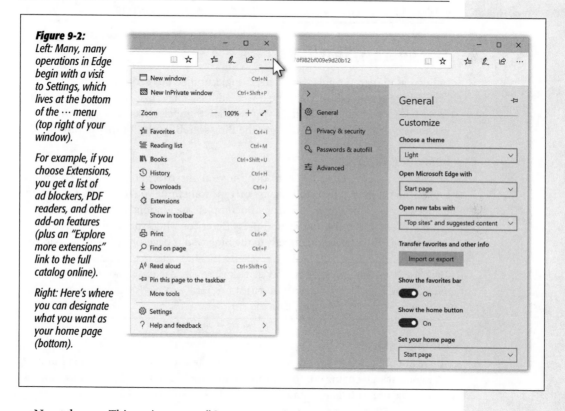

Figure 9-2:
Left: Many, many operations in Edge begin with a visit to Settings, which lives at the bottom of the ⋯ menu (top right of your window).

For example, if you choose Extensions, you get a list of ad blockers, PDF readers, and other add-on features (plus an "Explore more extensions" link to the full catalog online).

Right: Here's where you can designate what you want as your home page (bottom).

- **New tab page.** This option means "Open a new window with whatever I like to see when I create a new *tab*" (page 371)—which you determine using a drop-down menu here. It's called "Open new tabs with," and it offers its own three options: "Top sites" (icons for your most recently visited sites), "Top sites and suggested content" (a combination of those icons and your customized news start page), or "A blank page."

A blank page—an empty home page—makes Edge load very quickly when you launch it. Once this window opens, *then* you can tell the browser where you want to go today.

- **Previous pages.** Whatever pages you had open the last time you closed Edge.

- **A specific page or pages.** Lots of people like to be greeted every morning by a site like NYTimes.com or Weather.com. Or even several favorite sites, all loaded and ready for reading; that's a great way to avoid wasting time by calling up one site after another, because they'll all be loading in the background as you read the first one.

Tip: Edge offers light and dark modes, just as Windows itself does (page 154). To switch, open the ··· menu and then hit Settings; there's your "Choose a theme" drop-down menu. Try them all!

The Address/Search Bar

In Edge, as in many popular browsers, a single, unified box serves as both the address bar and the search bar. If you type a web address there, like *amazon.com,* pressing Enter takes you to that website; if you type anything else, like *cashmere sweaters* or just *amazon,* pressing Enter gives you the Bing search results for that phrase.

Searching the Web

Press Ctrl+L (or F4, or Alt+D) to deposit your insertion point inside the unified toolbar, just as in Internet Explorer. As you type something you're looking for—*phony baloney,* say—a drop-down menu of autocomplete suggestions appears beneath your typing. When you finish typing and press Enter (or when you choose one of those suggestions), Edge takes you directly to the Bing results page, or the page you selected.

Tip: You can turn off these suggestions. (They are, after all, provided courtesy of a two-way trip to Microsoft's servers, meaning that Microsoft knows what you're typing.) Hit ···→⚙→"Privacy and security"→"Show search and site suggestions as I type." Turn it off.

Adding Google

You're not obligated to use Microsoft's Bing search service. (There is, after all, another very good search engine out there. You might have heard of it.) Fortunately, you can make Edge use Google—or another search site—instead of Bing.

To begin, you must manually visit *google.com* (or another search site) at least once. Now open ··· →⚙→Advanced. (Why is this an advanced setting? Seems pretty basic to most people.) Scroll down and choose "Change search provider," hit "Add new," and select Google Search. Finally, choose "Set as default."

From now on, much to Microsoft's dismay, you'll be using Google instead of Bing for searching. As an added convenience, the names of any search services you add in this way appear in the "Search in the address bar with" pop-up menu. In other words, you can switch back and forth as you like.

Tip: Sure, Bing and Google are great for finding web pages on the internet. But Edge can also find words *on* a certain page. Press Ctrl+F. (Or hit ··· and then "Find on page.") In the "Find on page" toolbar that appears, type the text you're trying to find, and then use the < and > buttons to jump from occurrence to occurrence. (The Options drop-down menu lets you specify whether you require full-word matches and whether capitalization counts.)

Entering an Address

Because typing out internet addresses is so central to the internet experience—and such a typo-prone hassle—the address bar is rich with features that minimize keystrokes. For example:

- **You don't have to click in the address bar before typing;** just press Alt+D.

- **You don't have to type out the whole internet address.** You can omit the *http://www* and *.com* portions; if you press Ctrl+Enter after typing the name, Edge fills in those standard address bits for you.

  To visit *amazon.com*, for example, you can press Alt+D to highlight the address bar, type *amazon*, and then press Ctrl+Enter.

- **Even without the Ctrl+Enter trick,** you can still omit the *http://* from any web address. (Most of the time, you can omit the *www.,* too.) To jump to today's Dilbert cartoon, type *dilbert.com* and then press Enter.

- **When you begin to type into the address/search bar,** AutoComplete kicks in. Edge displays a drop-down list below the address bar, listing web addresses that seem to match what you're typing, as well as sites you've visited recently whose addresses match. To save typing, just select the correct complete address with your mouse, or use the ↓ key to reach the desired listing and then press Enter. The complete address you selected then pops into the address bar.

Topside doodads

Around the address/search bar, you'll find several important buttons. Some of them lack text labels, but all offer tooltip labels:

- **Back button (←), Forward button (→).** Click the ← button to revisit the page you were just on. (Keyboard shortcut: Alt+←)

  Once you've clicked Back, you can then click Forward (or press Alt+→) to return to the page you were on *before* you clicked the Back button.

- **Refresh button.** Click ↻ if a page doesn't look or work quite right, or if you want to see the updated version of a web page that changes constantly (such as a stock ticker). This button forces Edge to re-download the web page and reinterpret its text and graphics.

- **Stop (✕).** Click to interrupt the downloading of a web page you've just requested— by mistake, for example. (The ✕ replaces the ↻ icon when a page is downloading.)

- **Home** (⌂). Click to bring up your starter page, as described on page 366.

- **Reading view** (▯). This button opens the glorious Reading view (page 384).

- **Add to Favorites** (☆) bookmarks a page for reading later. You can list the page either as a Favorite (page 375) or a reading list item (page 383).

- **The Hub** (☲). Here's where everything you collect online winds up: favorites, reading list, browsing history, and recent downloads.

- **Markup** (🖉). Draw or type onto any web page; save it as a graphic (page 377).

- **Share** (🖅). Opens the Share panel so you can send a link to this page to other people or apps.

- **More actions** (⋯). This is Edge's More menu. There's a lot of stuff crammed into it, but you'll eventually find what you're looking for.

What's really cool in the May 2019 Update is that you can now install a few additional important tools on the toolbar. They're hiding in the ⋯→⚙→"Show in toolbar" submenu, and they include Reading list (page 383), Books (page 381), History (page 376), and Downloads (page 386). That's right: No longer must you burrow into a menu to find your History list!

You can use the same submenu to remove tools you use rarely or never (Markup 🖉, for example). Choose their names so the checkmark disappears—and so does the icon on your toolbar.

Scrolling Edge

Use the scroll bar, or the scroll wheel on your mouse, to move up and down the page—or to save mousing, press the space bar each time you want to see more. Press Shift+space bar to scroll *up*. (The space bar has its traditional, space-making function only when the insertion point is blinking in a text box or the address/search bar.)

UP TO SPEED

How Scroll Bars Work

These days, swiping with your finger or tapping the space bar are the most efficient ways to move down a page. But if you're a mouse addict, you can still operate the vertical scroll bar at the right edge of the window.

(It's ordinarily hidden until you move the mouse or touch the trackpad; to turn off the auto-hiding, visit ⊞→⚙→Ease of Access→Display→"Automatically hide scroll bars in Windows.")

In case this whole scroll bar thing is new to you, the scroll bar is a map of your entire document

or page. In the middle, there's a sliding, darker rectangle; its height represents how much of the page you're already seeing. For example, if the differently colored handle is one-third the height or width of the whole screen, then you're already seeing one-third of the page.

You can drag the handle to move around the page. You can also click or tap in the scroll bar track on either side of the handle to make the window scroll by one screenful.

You can also press the ↑ and ↓ keys to scroll. Page Up and Page Down scroll in full-screen increments, while Home and End whisk you to the top or bottom of the page.

Tabbed Browsing

Beloved by hard-core surfers the world over, *tabbed browsing* is a way to keep a bunch of web pages open simultaneously—in a single, neat window, without cluttering up your taskbar with a million buttons (Figure 9-3).

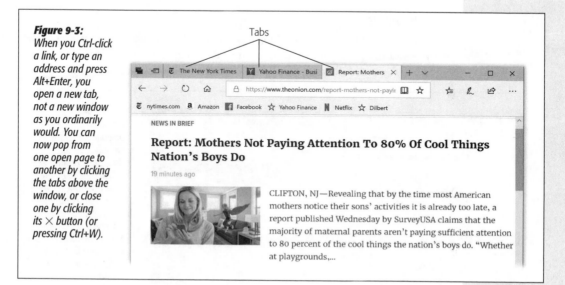

Figure 9-3:
When you Ctrl-click a link, or type an address and press Alt+Enter, you open a new tab, not a new window as you ordinarily would. You can now pop from one open page to another by clicking the tabs above the window, or close one by clicking its ✕ button (or pressing Ctrl+W).

Tabs

Tabs: The Missing Manual

Tabbed browsing unlocks a whole raft of Edge shortcuts and tricks, which are just the sort of thing power surfers gulp down like Gatorade:

- **To open a new, empty tab** in front of all others, press Ctrl+T (for *tab*), or click the + to the right of any existing tabs (you can see it in Figure 9-3). From the empty tab that appears, navigate to any site you want.

- **To open a link into a new tab,** Ctrl-click it. Or click it with your mouse wheel.

Note: Ctrl-clicking a link opens that page in a tab *behind* the one you're reading. That's a fantastic trick when you're reading a web page and see a reference you want to set aside for reading next, but you don't want to interrupt whatever you're reading now. But if you want the new tab to appear in *front*, then add the Shift key.

- **To close a tab,** click the ✕ on it, press Ctrl+W, or click the tab with your mouse wheel or middle mouse button, if you have one. (If you press Alt+F4, you close all tabs. If you press Ctrl+Alt+F4, you close all tabs *except* the one that's in front.)

- **Switch from one tab to the next** by pressing Ctrl+Tab. Add the Shift key to move backward through them.

- **Jump to a specific tab** by pressing its number along with the Ctrl key. For example, Ctrl+3 brings the third tab forward.

- **Open a duplicate of this tab** by pressing Ctrl+Shift+K. (Handy if your quest for information might branch out in a different direction.)

- **Close all?** When you close Edge, a dialog box appears asking if you really want to close *all* the tabs, or just the frontmost one. If you grow weary of answering that question, then turn on "Always close all tabs" before making your selection.

Tab Previews

Point to a tab's name without clicking to see a miniature of the page it represents. Better yet—hit the ∨ button (right end of the tabs) to open the special tab-preview bar shown in Figure 9-4, thereby viewing thumbnails of all your open tabs simultaneously.

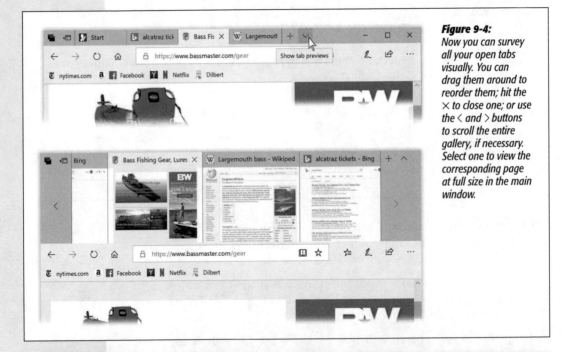

Figure 9-4:
Now you can survey all your open tabs visually. You can drag them around to reorder them; hit the ✕ to close one; or use the ‹ and › buttons to scroll the entire gallery, if necessary. Select one to view the corresponding page at full size in the main window.

The Tab Mute Button

It's one of the most annoying situations in all of computing: Sound is blaring from some tab somewhere, and you don't know which one. And you just want it to stop.

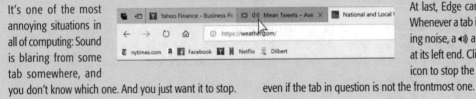

At last, Edge can help: Whenever a tab is making noise, a ◄)) appears at its left end. Click that icon to stop the racket, even if the tab in question is not the frontmost one.

Set-Aside Tabs

You can set aside a certain group of open tabs, all in a bunch, so you can pull them all up later with one quick click or tap. Imagine, for example, that you're planning a trip, so you've opened a bunch of tabs with flight, hotel, and sightseeing information. Or maybe you've opened a bunch of tabs related to some project you're researching.

With one click, you can file that complete set of tabs away. You'll be able to reopen them again with another single click, hours or years later (although there's no guarantee that the airfare you were looking at won't have changed; Edge stores only the pages' addresses, not their contents).

How to set tabs aside

Got some related tabs open? Great. Hit the ⬅ at top left. That's it: They're now memorized. You're welcome to set aside more than one group of tabs; just repeat this procedure as many times as you like.

Bringing tabs back

Choose the 🗔 icon at the far top left of the Edge window to open the "Tabs you've set aside" panel. Here they are, arranged chronologically, complete with miniatures to refresh your memory (Figure 9-5).

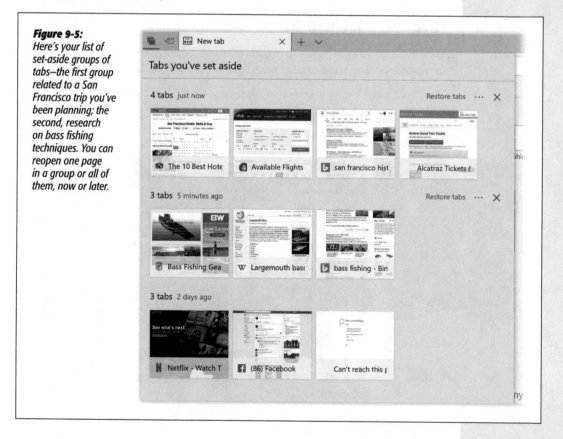

Figure 9-5:
Here's your list of set-aside groups of tabs—the first group related to a San Francisco trip you've been planning; the second, research on bass fishing techniques. You can reopen one page in a group or all of them, now or later.

At this point, here's some of the fun you can have:

- **Open one of the pages** by selecting it.

Note: These tabs reopen to the right of any tabs you already have open, which can be baffling if you're not ready for it. Some people close all their existing tabs first to avoid that tab sprawl.

- **Open all of the pages in a set-aside set** by choosing Restore tabs.
- **Remove a page from a set** by pointing to it and choosing ✕ (or right-clicking and choosing Remove).
- **Delete a group from the list** by choosing ✕.
- **Add a set-aside set to your Favorites** by choosing ··· and then "Add tabs to favorites." There's no real difference in storing a tab group in one or the other of these places, except that in Favorites, you can rename it, and it will appear in the Favorites lists of your other Windows machines (thanks to the magic of syncing).
- **Share a set-aside group with a fellow Windows 10 fan** (by email, message, or another method) by choosing ··· and then "Share tabs." The usual Windows sharing options appear (page 378).

Favorites (Bookmarks)

When you find a web page you might like to visit again, press Ctrl+D or hit the ☆ in the address bar. The Favorites pane appears; hit Add.

The page's name now appears in the ⭐≡ menu (on the Favorites pane). The next time you want to visit that page, click the ⭐≡—or press Ctrl+I—and choose the website's name in the list.

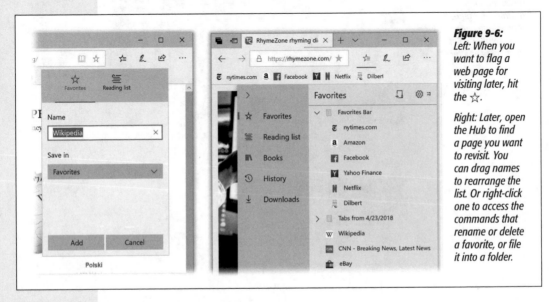

Figure 9-6:
Left: When you want to flag a web page for visiting later, hit the ☆.

Right: Later, open the Hub to find a page you want to revisit. You can drag names to rearrange the list. Or right-click one to access the commands that rename or delete a favorite, or file it into a folder.

Tip: Unfortunately, the Favorites menu covers up part of the web page you're reading. It hides itself soon enough, but you might also want to freeze it open so it doesn't cover the page. To do that, click the ⊣⋈ above the Favorites tab.

You can rearrange the bookmarks in your Favorites menu easily enough. Hit the ⭐≣ to open Favorites (Figure 9-6, right), and then drag things up and down in the list. You can also create folders to organize your favorites (hit ⊡).

Tip: Edge is perfectly happy to import the bookmarks you've carefully assembled in rival browsers. To do that, open ⋯→⚙→"Import or export" to begin. (You can even import them from several browsers simultaneously.)

The Favorites Bar

The Favorites panel is one way to maintain a list of websites you visit frequently. But choosing a Favorite requires two clicks. Favorites *toolbar* lets you summon a few, very select, *very* favorite web pages with only *one* click. (See Figure 9-7 for some handy tips.)

Figure 9-7:
If you right-click an icon on the Favorites bar, you'll discover that you can rename it or hide its name ("Show icon only").

You can also drag these icons around to rearrange them.

And you can add a site to the Favorites bar by dragging its icon from the address bar.

You make the toolbar appear by pressing Ctrl+Shift+B (for "bar"). Or the long way: Hit ⋯ →⚙→ "Show the favorites bar."

You can add a new bookmark to the Favorites bar in any of these ways:

• **If a page you'd like to enfavorite is open,** drag its icon (the tiny ⓘ or other symbol just before its name in the address bar) directly downward onto the Favorites bar to install it there.

- Click ☆—but in the resulting box (Figure 9-6, left), choose "Favorites bar" from the "Save in" drop-down menu.

- **Open the Hub (☆≡).** Drag an existing favorite into the Favorites Bar folder, as shown at right in Figure 9-6.)

Tip: In Edge, five important lists are hiding in the Hub—the panel marked by ☆≡. But there are direct keyboard shortcuts for all five, too. You've got Ctrl+I (Favorites), Ctrl+M (reading list), Ctrl+Y (Books), Ctrl+H (History list), and Ctrl+J (Downloads list).

History List

The *history* is a list of the websites you've visited. To see it, click ☆≡, and then ↺. Or install the History icon (↺) directly onto the address bar, as described on page 370. Or skip all that and just press Ctrl+H.

Figure 9-8 presents the world's shortest History class.

Tip: When the FBI comes around, don't forget you can erase the entire history with a click or tap on "Clear history," shown at top right in Figure 9-8.

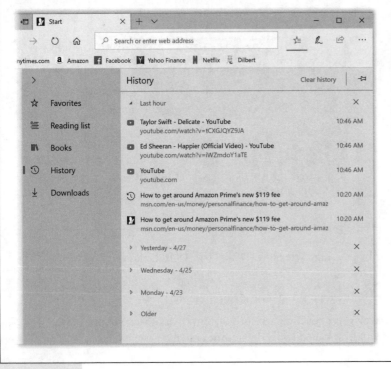

Figure 9-8:
You can expand or collapse the "folders" here (indicating days, weeks, and older time periods) with a click.

Handily enough, you can also delete any of these time-period browsing records with a click—on the ✕ button next to it.

Mark Up Your Web Pages

Microsoft (or at least its marketing team) is especially proud of this unusual feature: You can use drawing tools on any web page. Mark it up. Underline, circle, type comments (Figure 9-9).

Sadly, your graffiti doesn't show up on the real web; the rest of the internet doesn't get to see your handiwork (although that'd be fun!). But once you've marked up a page, you can preserve it as a graphic—send it to someone, capture it in OneNote, or whatever.

Note: These markup tools are also handy (actually, even handier) for annotating PDF documents.

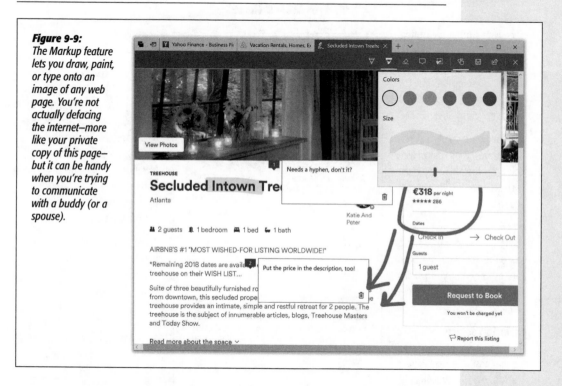

Figure 9-9:
The Markup feature lets you draw, paint, or type onto an image of any web page. You're not actually defacing the internet—more like your private copy of this page—but it can be handy when you're trying to communicate with a buddy (or a spouse).

All you have to do is click Add Notes (✐) in the top-right corner of Edge. The Markup toolbar appears, starring these tools:

- **Ballpoint Pen** (▽), **Highlighter** (▽), **Eraser** (◇). These standard markup tools are described starting on page 340.

- **Typed notes** (▢). Click or tap to open a little text box, where you can type your notes, observations, or corrections. You can create as many of these boxes as you like. They expand vertically to hold a lot of text, but you can't make them wider. You can move them, though, by dragging their numbered tags.

A 🗑 button appears in the corner of each for easy disposal later.

- **Clip** (✂️). This tool lets you copy a certain rectangle of the web page, ready for pasting into, for example, an email message or OneNote. When you open the tool, Edge tells you "Drag to copy region" in lettering big enough to see from Pluto. Drag diagonally and then release; the image is now on your Clipboard.

- **Touch writing** (✍️). As you'd guess, this mode lets you write on the screen using your finger—touchscreen and finger required). When this is turned off, dragging with your finger *scrolls* the page instead.) Select a pen tool before you begin.

UP TO SPEED

The Share Panel

The Share button (⤴) offers a quick, one-click way to send something (text, link, photo, video…) to somebody else (by email, Twitter, Facebook, text message, Nearby Sharing…).

This button pops up in all kinds of programs: File Explorer windows (on the Share tab); the Edge browser; the Photos app; and so on.

When you use this button, you're offered various ways to share the selected item. The choices vary, but you usually find them arranged in three sections:

Favorite contacts. Here are the people you've indicated are the most important in your life (page 326). Presumably, they're also the people you share the most stuff with. (Hit "More people" to see your complete, searchable Contacts list.)

Nearby Sharing. As you can read on page 564, the Nearby Sharing feature lets you shoot files and other material to nearby Windows 10 machines—wirelessly, without having to

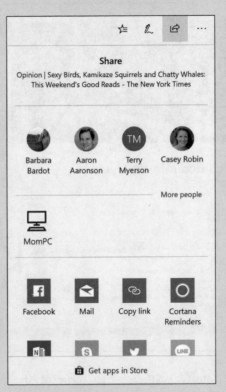

fuss with passwords, file sharing, mounting disks, and so on.

Apps and functions. At the bottom of the scrolling Share panel, you'll find icons for all apps, services, and commands that can receive whatever you're sending: Facebook, Twitter, Instagram, Skype, Mail, Messenger, Cortana Reminders, and so on—plus a handy "Copy" (or "Copy link") button to start you off.

There may be additional steps involved. For example, if you choose Mail, then Windows copies the selected material into a new, outgoing email message, or attaches the selected file to an outgoing message. Just add a few explanatory notes, address the message, and send.

Or, if you choose Facebook, the photo or text you're sharing appears in a new post, but you still have to edit it, choose the audience, and hit Post.

In any case, the Share menu is now standardized and recognizable across various parts of the Windows archipelago. That's less for you to learn, and more for you to share.

Save a Web Note

If you want to preserve the marked-up page for future generations, you can save it or send it.

If you hit the 🖫 icon, you're offered a choice of three places to save this Web Note (a graphic snapshot of your marked-up page):

- **OneNote.** Your image becomes a note "page" in OneNote (page 317).

- **Favorites.** The image becomes a bookmark you can call up later from within Edge. You'll be able to continue editing at that point. (You can choose which Favorites folder you want, and you can type a name for this marked-up image.)

- **Reading list.** The image is stored as an "article" that you can read—and edit—later (page 383).

Tip: Remember, you're just editing a graphic image at this point. When you reopen your Web Note from the Favorites or reading list panels, however, a "Go to original page" link appears at the top; it takes you to the live, original web page. (And there's a "Hide notes" button that temporarily hides all your markings.)

Send to Your Fans

The Share button (↪) opens the standard Share panel (see the box on the facing page), with whatever options appear there: your favorite contacts, Nearby Sharing, and various websites and apps (OneNote, Twitter, and Mail, and so on). That's handy if you want to email the marked-up web page image to prove a point.

Close

If you choose ✕, you return to regular web surfing and stop drawing. If you haven't exported or shared your masterpiece, and you decline to save your changes in the confirmation box, then your work is lost forever.

Cortana Meets Edge

Cortana, as you may recall from Chapter 5, is your voice-controlled personal assistant. Microsoft says she's at work in Edge, too, although you'll soon discover that there's very little resemblance to the cheerful assistant who lives on the taskbar.

Microsoft is referring to these fledgling features in Edge:

- **Instant answers in the address bar.** We're talking about weather, stocks, and definitions. Type *weather 10024* or *goog* or *define perspicacious* into the address bar, and a panel pops up with the temperature, stock price, or definition *even before you press Enter* (Figure 9-10). You never leave the page you were reading.

- **Instant info in an article.** You're reading along, and you encounter a reference to, let's say, vegan cooking. What is that, exactly? Highlight the text. Right-click it or hold your finger down on it. From the shortcut menu, choose "Ask Cortana about [your word]," and boom: A panel opens on the right side of the window with a lot more information about whatever it is you highlighted. A company, a person, a place, a word you need defined (Figure 9-10, middle).

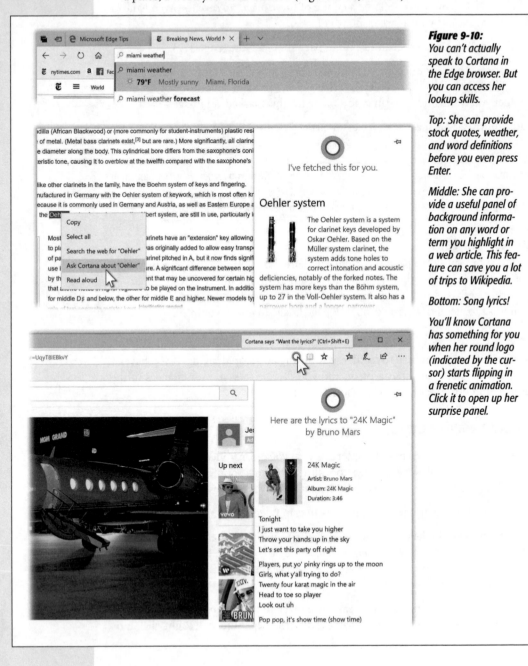

Figure 9-10:
You can't actually speak to Cortana in the Edge browser. But you can access her lookup skills.

Top: She can provide stock quotes, weather, and word definitions before you even press Enter.

Middle: She can provide a useful panel of background information on any word or term you highlight in a web article. This feature can save you a lot of trips to Wikipedia.

Bottom: Song lyrics!

You'll know Cortana has something for you when her round logo (indicated by the cursor) starts flipping in a frenetic animation. Click it to open up her surprise panel.

- **Shopping alternatives.** When you're poised to buy something on Amazon.com or another shopping site, you may spot the phrase "Want some other options?" in your Address Book. Choose that phrase to open a panel that shows the same item on other big shopping sites (Walmart, eBay, and so on); now and then, you'll discover that you can save money using a different site.

- **Song lyrics.** This one's good. Whenever you're watching a music video (for example, on YouTube), the Cortana logo in the address bar may do a little animated flip. That's your cue to click it to open a right-side panel that contains the full lyrics for the song.

- **Restaurant details.** Someday, Microsoft says, you'll be able to type the name of a restaurant into the address bar and marvel as a button appears that says, "I've got directions, hours, and more." Choose that link, and an info panel for the restaurant will appear—with directions, hours, and more!

Alas, Microsoft has to hand-rig each restaurant to this feature, so it's available for a relatively small number of them.

Edge as PDF (and Ebook) Reader

You may think of Edge as a web browser, but Microsoft has bigger plans for it. Now, more than ever, it's the primary Windows viewer for PDF documents and ebooks. You can annotate them, mark them up, adjust the font, layout, and background, and even have them read aloud to you. (What better audio background as you get dressed for work than your PC reading *The 7 Habits of Highly Effective People* to you for inspiration?)

Just double-click a PDF or EPUB (ebook) document. Windows proposes opening it in Edge; if you agree, it opens, clear and uncluttered. The experience varies slightly:

- **PDF documents.** Click or tap to reveal the toolbar. Its buttons let you scale the page up or down, rotate it, switch to a two-page layout, hear it read aloud, print it, save it, or expand it to full screen.

  To move through the pages, use the mouse, trackpad, or your finger on the touch-screen as usual—or tap the Page Up and Page Down keys (to move a page at a time) or the arrow keys (a line at a time).

Tip: If you've used the switch to turn *off* Continuous Scrolling, then tapping the down or right arrow key scrolls a full page at a time.

- **Ebooks.** At one point, Microsoft attempted an online ebook store; it flopped, and Microsoft closed it in May 2019. But you can still read non–copy-protected ebooks in the EPUB format from *any* source in Edge. The Hub (⭐≡) offers a Books tab, which lists any such books you've installed.

The toolbar at top has buttons for Table of Contents, Notes, Search, visual adjustments (such as font, size, background color, line spacing), Read Aloud, Grammar tools (see the Tip that follows), bookmark, and Full Screen. Figure 9-11 shows the idea.

Tip: If you opt to download the Grammar Tools app, this toolbar button offers a drop-down panel of assistive-reading options. *Syllables* adds hyphens between all syllables on every page of the ebook; some read-ers pro-bab-ly find that eas-i-er to read.

The *Nouns*, *Verbs*, and *Adjectives* switches highlight every occurrence of those parts of speech on the page—again, in an effort to help struggling readers.

To turn the pages of an ebook, tap the space bar, press your arrow keys, or swipe with your finger. Drag the slider at the bottom to leap through many pages.

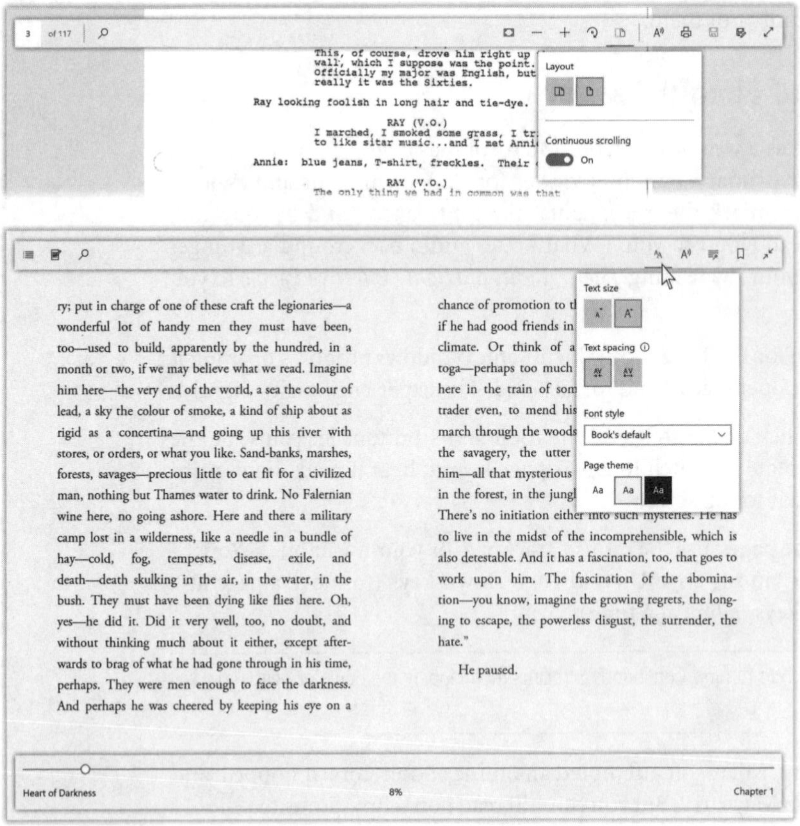

Figure 9-11:
Top: When you're reading a PDF document, the toolbar offers buttons for enlarging, rotating, or printing the file—or adjusting its layout.

Bottom: When you're reading an ebook, the menu shown here provides all the controls you need for adjusting the typeface, word spacing, font size, and background color.

New in the May 2019 Update: If you double-click a word (or tap with your finger), you get an instant dictionary definition; see page 386.

Tips for Better Surfing

Edge is filled with shortcuts and tricks for better speed and more pleasant surfing. For example:

Bigger Text, Smaller Text

When your eyes are tired, you might like to make a web page bigger. Fortunately, there are plenty of ways to zoom in or out of the whole affair:

- **If you have a touchscreen,** pinch or spread two fingers against the glass.

- **If you have a scroll-wheel mouse,** press the Ctrl key as you turn the mouse's wheel. (This works in Microsoft Office programs, too.)

- **Press Ctrl+plus or Ctrl+minus** on your keyboard.

- Hit ⋯ to see Zoom buttons staring you in the face.

Note: In Edge, there's no way to enlarge only the *text* on a page. You must enlarge or shrink the *entire* page.

Online Photos

Right-clicking an image on a web page produces a shortcut menu that offers commands like "Save picture as," "Copy," and "Share picture." (That last one opens the Share panel, where you get options like Facebook or Mail.)

So when you see a picture you'd like to keep, right-click it and choose "Save picture as." After you name the picture and then click Save, the result is a new graphics file on your hard drive containing the picture you saved.

The Reading List

The reading list, one of the options in the Hub (⊁≣), saves the names of web pages that you want to read later.

Unlike the similar feature in rival browsers, this one doesn't actually *store* the web pages on your computer so you can read when you're offline. You still need an internet connection to reopen one.

In other words, Edge's reading list feature does pretty much the same thing as Favorites or Bookmarks. (In fact, Windows 10 even synchronizes your reading list among your Windows 10 machines, just as it does Favorites. It's as though the web always keeps your place as you move from gadget to gadget.)

To add a page to the reading list, hit ☆, just as though you're about to add a Favorite. But in the panel that appears, select "Reading list." Edit the name, if you like, and then choose Add.

Later, to view your saved pages, open the Hub (⊁≣); then choose the "Reading list" (≣) tab. Select the story you want to reopen.

Memorized Passwords, Forms, and Credit Cards

Each time you type a password into a web page, Edge can offer to memorize it for you. Or your address, phone number, or credit card information—so you don't have to keep typing those into shopping sites, gaming sites, and so on. (Of course, use it with caution if you share an account on your PC with other people.)

It's easy to see all the passwords, forms data, and credit card info Edge has saved for you—and to delete the ones you want it to forget (see Figure 9-12).

This feature is a lot like the popular password/credit card keeper programs like 1Password and Dashlane—but it's free, and your passwords sync to your other PCs.

To see the on/off switches for this feature, hit ···→⚙→ "Passwords & autofill." And here they are: "Save passwords," "Save form data," and "Save cards." Each offers a Manage button, too, which opens a panel full of options for saving, editing, or deleting the memorized information (Figure 9-12).

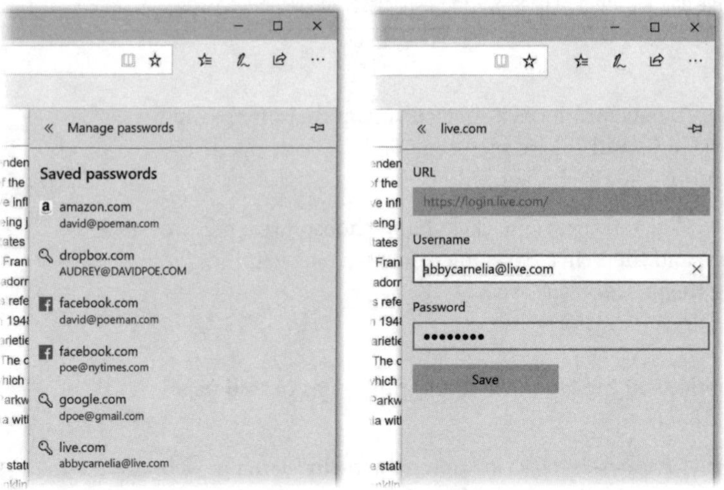

Figure 9-12:
Left: Here are all the websites for which Edge has memorized your passwords so you don't have to type them in every time you visit. Yes! You can make Edge forget one by hitting the ×, or you can double-click a row to edit its name/password combination (right).

Sharing Pages

Edge lets you tell a friend about the page you're looking at. You might find that useful when you come across a particularly interesting news story, op-ed piece, or burrito recipe. Hit the Share icon (🔗) to open the Share panel (page 378).

Reading View

How can people read web articles when there's Times Square blinking going on all around them? Fortunately, you'll never have to put up with that again.

The Reading view button (📖) at the top of the Edge window is amazing. With one click (or one press of Ctrl+R), it eliminates *everything* from your page except the text and photos. No ads, blinking, links, banners, promos, or anything else.

The text is also changed to a clean, clear font and size, and the background is made plain and pure. Basically, it makes any web page look like a printed book page or a Kindle page, and it's glorious (Figure 9-13). (Its looks and its controls have a lot in common with Edge's ebook-reading features, described on page 381.)

Figure 9-13:
Seriously, which way would you rather read an article? Like this (top)? Or in the calm peace of this (bottom)? Not only does Reader get rid of all the ads and clutter and blinking, but it even knits multipage articles together into one seamless, scrolling page, as though it's an ebook. Use the space bar or two fingers to scroll, as usual.

To exit Reading view, hit 📖 again. Best. Feature. Ever.

Here's some of the fun you can have in Reading view:

- **Display options.** Click or tap the screen to reveal a toolbar with options for changing the background color and type size, reading the page aloud, using Microsoft's grammar tools, printing the page, or expanding the window to full screen. Figure 9-11 shows the idea.

- **Definitions.** New in the May 2019 Update: In Reading view, double-click a word (or tap with your finger) to open a little box containing its definition—and even a 🔊 button so you can hear how it's pronounced.

- **Line focus.** Also new: Edge can highlight one line at a time in color (or two, or five), dimming the rest of the screen, to help you focus on what you're reading. This feature can be a big help to beginning readers or people with dyslexia, for example.

  To try it, click or tap the screen to open the controls toolbar; hit "Learning tools"→ "Reading preferences," and turn on "Line focus." Choose an icon for one, three, or five lines highlighted at a time. You'll see the effect right away. Use the arrow keys, or the arrow buttons on the screen, to move the highlighting and scroll the page as you read.

The Download Manager

When you click a link to download something from a web page, Edge records it in the Downloads list (Figure 9-14).

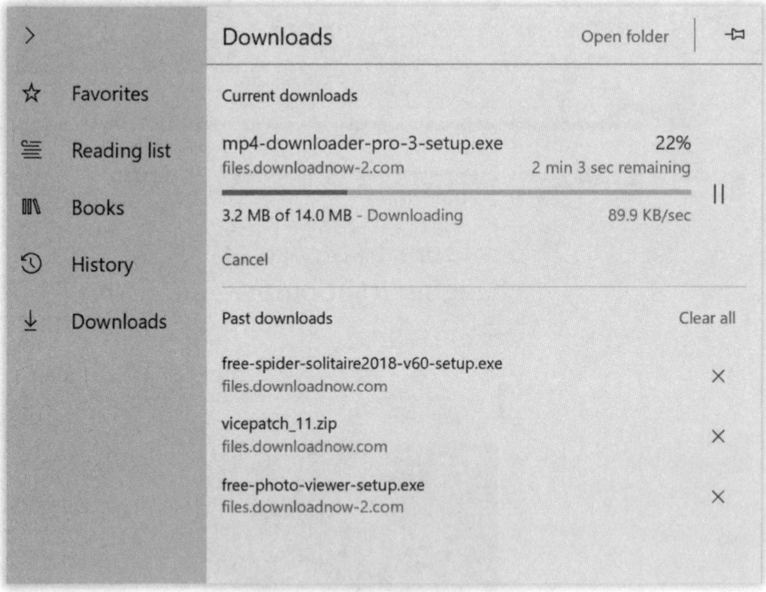

> **Figure 9-14:**
> *The Downloads window shows you whatever you're downloading now (complete with Pause, Resume, and Cancel buttons), along with a list of things you've downloaded recently. To have a look at your Downloads folder at the desktop, hit "Open folder."*

To view the list, open the Hub (✪≣), and then Downloads (↓). Click the ✕ to clear a downloaded item's name from the list, or "Clear all" to erase the entire list. You're not actually removing any files from your computer—you're just erasing the visual record of what you've downloaded.

Tip: Don't forget you can add the ↓ button to your toolbar, so you don't have to burrow into the Hub to find it every time. See page 370.

Stop Autoplay

There's nothing quite as obnoxious as a web page that begins to play a video, blaring sound, the instant the page opens. Or, worse, an ad. How about letting *us* decide if we want to play a video?

The Windows 10 May 2019 Update brings that control back to you—control you can exert either universally or on a site-by-site basis.

- **To stop all autoplay videos.** ⋯→⚙→Advanced. Use the "Media autoplay" pop-up menu.

- **To stop autoplay videos on just this site.** Hit the tiny icon just to the left of the site's address in the address bar (it might look like a little globe or a padlock)—the "Show site information" button. Choose "Media autoplay settings."

In either case, you're offered three options:

- **Allow.** What you're used to: You open a web page, and some video starts blaring at you, unbidden.

- **Limit.** Videos can play automatically, but only if they have no soundtrack or if the sound starts out muted. (If it's muted, you're supposed to click the little speaker icon to make it start playing.)

- **Block.** No videos will ever start playing automatically.

Printing Pages

The decade of chopped-off printouts is over. In Edge, when you press Ctrl+P or choose ⋯ and then Print, *all* the page's text is laid out to fit within the page.

The Print panel offers a handsome preview of the end result, plus controls like these:

- **Orientation** means Portrait, Landscape (upright or sideways).

- **Scale** affects the size of the image on the printed pages. "Shrink to fit" adjusts the printout so it won't be chopped off, but you can manually magnify or reduce the printed image by choosing the other percentage options in this menu.

- **Margins.** Do you want Narrow, Normal, Moderate, or Wide margins in your printout?

- **Headers and footers** hides or shows the header (the text at the top of the printout, which usually identifies the name of the website you're printing and the number of pages) and the footer (the URL of the web page and the date).

- **Clutter-free printing.** This option is a pure delight. As you'll immediately see in the preview, it eliminates ads, navigation bars, banners, and other distracting junk from the printout of certain articles, leaving them clean and easy to read. (Tragically, this option appears only when printing from a few websites.)

Tip: Lots of websites have their own "print this page" buttons. When they're available, use them instead of Edge's own Print command. The website's Print feature not only makes sure the printout won't be chopped off, but it also eliminates ads, includes the entire article (even if it's split across multiple web pages), and so on.

The Keyboard Shortcut Master List

Before you sail off into the Edge sunset, it's worth noting that surfing the web is one of the things most people do *most* with their PCs. As long as you're going to spend so much time in this single program, it's worth mastering its keyboard shortcuts. Once you've learned a few, you save yourself time and fumbling.

Page 597 in Appendix B offers a master list of every Edge keyboard shortcut known to Microsoft. Clip and save.

CHAPTER 10

Mail

M ail, Windows 10's built-in email program, is easy to use, beautiful, and offers a fast, fluid way to work, especially if you have a touchscreen. Mail even syncs with your other Windows 10 machines. Set up your accounts once, and find them magically waiting for you on any other phones, tablets, or PCs you may pick up. Finally, it's handy that Mail's messages notify you by appearing in the Windows 10 Action Center (page 96).

Note: The Mail app is simple to use, but that's another way of saying it's fairly rudimentary.

There are plenty of alternative mail programs, though—including Microsoft's own Windows Live Mail, which came with Windows 8 but not with Windows 10. It's a desktop program (rather than a Microsoft Store app), so it's far more complete. It's a free download, it works great in Windows 10, and you can find it on this book's "Missing CD" page at *missingmanuals.com*. In fact, there's a free PDF appendix to this book that describes it, on the same "Missing CD": "Windows Live Mail."

Setting Up

The first time you fire up Mail—or any email program, actually—your first job is to enter the details of your email account. When you open Mail for the first time, you're offered one button: "Add account."

On the next screen, you'll see that Mail comes ready to accommodate all kinds of popular email services (Figure 10-1): Gmail, Yahoo, Apple's iCloud, Outlook.com (any of Microsoft's free web-based email services, including Hotmail, Live.com, or MSN), and Exchange (the system most offices use). If you have any other service, hit "Other account" and fill in the details.

In general, all you have to fill in is your email address, password, and name, as it will appear in the "From" line when other people get messages from you. (See the box below for details on some of the weirder account types.)

When you click Done on the "All done" screen, you return to the Accounts setup screen so you can start over again with another account. Once you've completed this joyous task, you end up at your inbox, where you can start doing email.

Note: You can always add additional accounts later. Hit Accounts in the left-side panel; from the menu that appears, choose "Add account." That "Manage accounts" panel is also how you delete an account; select it, and then choose "Remove this account from your device."

If your settings were all correct, you get teleported directly into that account's inbox, ready to start processing email.

If you've set up more than one account, you switch among them in the left-side panel. (Depending on the window's width, you may just see the *icons* of the menu-column entries; click the $\mathcal{R}$ icon to see your list of accounts.)

And now, two cool inbox tips:

- **Unified inboxes.** Plenty of email programs let you combine the inboxes of all your accounts into a single, unified inbox, saving you the trouble of checking the inbox

---

UP TO SPEED

POP, IMAP, and Web-Based Mail

There are three kinds of email accounts—and Windows 10 Mail works with all of them.

Web-based mail. Some email accounts are designed to be accessed on a website, like the free accounts offered by Gmail, Yahoo, Hotmail, or Outlook.com.

IMAP accounts (Internet Message Access Protocol) are the latest type, and they're surging in popularity. IMAP servers keep all your mail online, rather than storing it solely on your computer; as a result, you can access the same mail from any computer (or phone), and you'll always see the same lists of mail. IMAP servers remember which messages you've read and sent, and they even keep track of how you've filed messages into mail folders. (Those free Yahoo and iCloud email accounts are IMAP accounts, and so are corporate Exchange accounts. Gmail and Outlook.com accounts are usually IMAP, too—yes, an account can be both.)

POP accounts are the oldest type on the internet. (POP stands for Post Office Protocol, but this won't be on the test.)

The big difference: A POP server transfers incoming mail to your computer; once it's there, it's no longer on the internet. (If you try to check your email on your phone, you won't see whatever messages were downloaded by your computer back at home.) Internet providers like Time Warner and Comcast usually provide email addresses as POP accounts.

Windows 10 Mail, unlike Windows 8 Mail, works with POP accounts. If they're from a big name like, well, Time Warner or Comcast, use the "Other account" option on the setup screen and supply your email address and password.

If Windows doesn't immediately recognize the provider name, then you need a way to enter the account details beyond the name and password (like the server addresses, authentication method, and so on).

For that purpose, there's an "Advanced setup" option at the bottom of the "Add account" screen. (You may have to scroll down to see it.) Hit that, choose "Internet email," and off you go.

---

for each account separately. But Windows 10 Mail goes a step further: It lets you create multiple combo inboxes, each containing the inboxes of just some of your accounts. You could combine your two personal accounts into one inbox and your three work accounts into another, for example.

To get started, choose ⚙→"Manage accounts"→"Link inboxes." In the resulting dialog box, you can specify exactly which inboxes to combine (and what you want to call the resulting inbox).

- **Pin your inbox.** You can also pin one account's inbox—or any other mail folder—to your Start menu (right side), for instant access and step-saving. For example, if you have a folder called Stuff to Do, or a folder called Reply to These, you might want them pinned on your Start menu.

To do that, right-click (or hold your finger down on) the folder you want to pin; choose Pin to Start. You'll find the pinned folder at the bottom of your Start menu. One click on that tile, and boom: You're in Mail, in that folder, reading the latest communiqués.

Figure 10-1:
Windows 10 Mail is surprisingly chummy with email services from its rivals, including Google, Yahoo, and even Apple.

Once you've chosen the service that provides your email account, enter your email address and password. (You can also create a new account right here, by clicking "Create account.")

The Amazing Expand-O-Window

Mail is one of Microsoft's *universal* apps, meaning that it runs identically on phones, tablets, and computers. Which really means that its layout *changes* to fit the screen size of the machine you're using. Which makes it hard for a computer-book author to anticipate what you might see on your screen.

In Mail's wildest dreams, it has a very wide screen, showing three columns:

- **First column:** The list of your email accounts, and the email folders for whichever one you're using now.

- **Second column:** The list of messages.

- **Third column:** The actual message body of whatever you've selected in the list.

As you can see in Figure 10-2, though, these columns do various degrees of collapsing or shrinking as the window gets narrower.

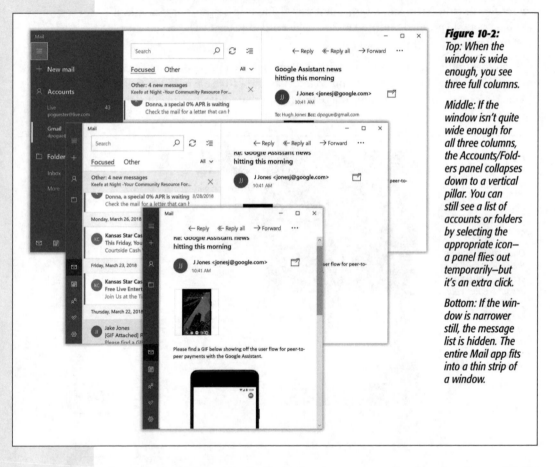

Figure 10-2:
Top: When the window is wide enough, you see three full columns.

Middle: If the window isn't quite wide enough for all three columns, the Accounts/Folders panel collapses down to a vertical pillar. You can still see a list of accounts or folders by selecting the appropriate icon—a panel flies out temporarily—but it's an extra click.

Bottom: If the window is narrower still, the message list is hidden. The entire Mail app fits into a thin strip of a window.

But wait, there's More! In the first column, you generally see only a few mail folders listed. But if you select More, a new column pops out, offering a list of standard subfolders, like Sent Items, as well as any subfolders you've created, like Cat Videos. If you'd like to keep any of the folders pinned to the Folders list, just right-click them and choose Add to Favorites.

Checking Email

If your email account offers "As they arrive" mail checking, then new messages show up on your computer as they arrive, around the clock.

If you have any other kind of account, or if you didn't turn that option on, then Mail checks for new messages automatically on a schedule—every 15, 30, or 60 minutes (see page 402). It also checks for new messages each time you open the Mail program.

Tip: You can also force Mail to check for new messages and send waiting ones on command—by hitting the Sync icon (🔄) above the message list. Or, if you have a keyboard, press Ctrl+M.

When new mail arrives, you'll know it. Mail can notify you, complete with a little chime, even when you're working in another app. And, of course, the Mail tile on the Start menu updates itself to show you the latest messages (a rotating display of their senders/subjects/first lines).

A new message is marked with a bold vertical line at its left edge. If you see a tiny > button next to the subject line, it's an indication that Mail is condensing several back-and-forths into a single line, for convenience; see Figure 10-3.

Note: If you're confused by the consecutive listing of emails that may, in fact, have been sent weeks apart, you can turn this feature off. Choose ⚙️→"Message list," and select "Individual messages" instead of "Grouped by conversation."

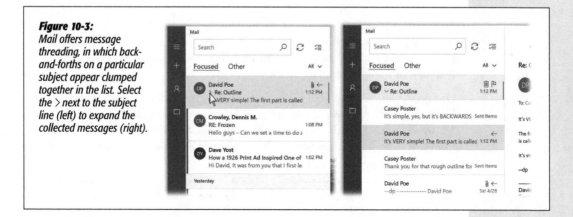

Figure 10-3:
Mail offers message threading, in which back-and-forths on a particular subject appear clumped together in the list. Select the > next to the subject line (left) to expand the collected messages (right).

You can flick your finger—or turn the mouse wheel, or two-finger drag on your trackpad—to scroll the message list, if it's long. Select a message to read it in all its formatted glory.

Focused Mail

When it comes to email overload, Microsoft says it feels your pain. That's why Mail tries to use artificial intelligence to sort your incoming messages into Focused

---

(meaning "important") and Other categories. You can see these two headings atop your message list, and you can click either one to see the messages Windows has put there (Figure 10-4). (This feature works on Microsoft accounts—addresses ending in *live.com, outlook.com, hotmail.com*, and so on—but may not work on other companies' email services.)

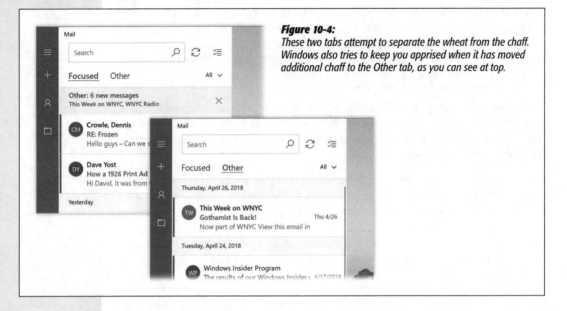

Figure 10-4:
These two tabs attempt to separate the wheat from the chaff. Windows also tries to keep you apprised when it has moved additional chaff to the Other tab, as you can see at top.

And what's an "important" message? Mail considers factors like what's in the message, who sent it to you, and how often you correspond with that person. In general, actual personal email lands in the Focused list, and junk mail, newsletters, special offers, and that kind of thing wind up in Other.

Of course, you can train Mail to do a better job. Right-click a message in the Focused list that you feel has been incorrectly filed; from the shortcut menu, choose either "Move to Other" (just this message) or "Always move to Other" (all future messages from this person). You can also perform this operation in the Other list, choosing "Move to Focused" or "Always move to Focused."

Tip: If this whole auto-filing system doesn't do much for you, you can also turn it off. Choose ⚙→"Focused inbox." Choose the account in question, and then turn off "Sort messages into Focused and Other."

What to Do with a Message

Once you've read a message, you can respond to it, delete it, file it, and so on. Here's the drill:

- **Read it.** The type size in email messages can be pretty small. Fortunately, you have some great enlargement tricks at your disposal. For example, on a touchscreen, you can spread two fingers to enlarge the entire email message. Or press Ctrl+plus or Ctrl+minus, just as in a web browser.

- **Next message.** Once you've had a good look at a message and have processed it to your satisfaction, you can move on to the next (or previous) message in the list. *Touchscreen or mouse:* Tap or click the message you want in the message list. *Keyboard:* Press the ↑ or ↓ keys.

- **Open an attachment.** You'll know when somebody has attached a file to a message you've received. A paper clip (📎) appears on the message in the message list, and an icon for the attachment appears at the top of the body. Tapping the attachment icon opens it right up.

- **Reply to it.** To answer a message, select Reply at the top of the message. If the message was originally addressed to multiple recipients, then "Reply all" sends your reply to everyone simultaneously.

Tip: If you have a keyboard, you can press Ctrl+R for Reply, or Shift+Ctrl+R for Reply All.

A new message window opens, already addressed. As a courtesy to your correspondents, Mail places the original message at the bottom of the window. At this point, you can add or delete recipients, edit the subject line or the original message, and so on. When you're finished, hit Send or press Ctrl+Enter.

- **Forward it.** Instead of replying to the person who sent you a message, you may sometimes want to pass the note on to a third person. To do so, hit Forward at the top of the message (or press Ctrl+F.) A new message opens, looking a lot like the one that appears when you reply; you're expected to start by filling in the To box. You may wish to precede the original message with a comment of your own, like "Frank: I thought you'd be interested in this joke about your mom."

- **Delete it.** Hit Delete at the top of the message. (There's no confirmation screen; on the other hand, you can recover the message from the "Deleted items" folder if you change your mind.)

Tip: If you have a touchscreen, you can swipe leftward across the message to delete it. (Some email services call this "Archive" instead.)

- **File it.** Most mail accounts let you create filing folders to help manage your messages. Once you've opened a message that's worth keeping, you can move it into one of those folders.

To do that, hit the ⋯ button, or right-click the message; from the shortcut menu, choose Move. Mail displays the folder list. Choose the one you want.

Alternatively, you can drag-and-drop messages into a new folder. (If the folder isn't immediately visible, drag the message onto the word "More" at the bottom of the folder list. When the full folder list appears, continue your drag until you reach the target folder.)

- **Flag it.** Sometimes you'll receive email that prompts you to some sort of action, but you may not have the time (or the fortitude) to face the task at the moment. ("Hi there…it's me, your accountant. Would you mind rounding up your expenses for 2005 through 2015 and sending me a list by email?")

That's why Mail lets you *flag* a message, summoning a little flag icon next to the message's name and giving a color tint to its row in the message list. These indicators can mean anything you like—they simply call attention to certain messages.

To flag a message in this way on a touchscreen, see Figure 10-5. If you have a mouse or trackpad, click the message in the list; the ⚑ icon appears at the right end. Click that icon to flag the message. (To clear the flag, repeat the procedure.)

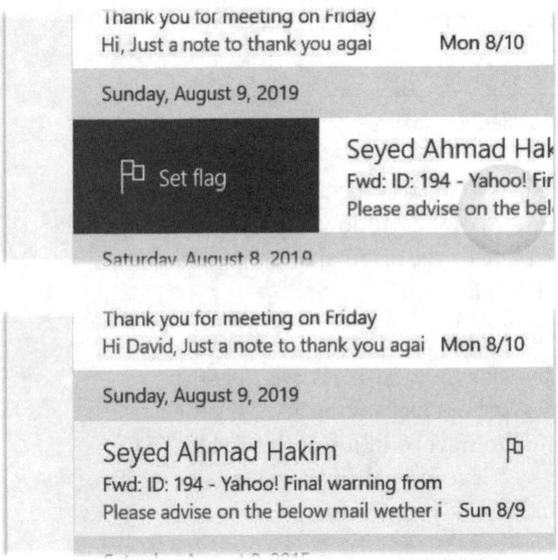

Thank you for meeting on Friday
Hi, Just a note to thank you agai   Mon 8/10

Sunday, August 9, 2019

⚑ Set flag   Seyed Ahmad Hak
                    Fwd: ID: 194 - Yahoo! Fir
                    Please advise on the bel

Saturday, August 8, 2019

Thank you for meeting on Friday
Hi David, Just a note to thank you agai   Mon 8/10

Sunday, August 9, 2019

Seyed Ahmad Hakim   ⚑
Fwd: ID: 194 - Yahoo! Final warning from
Please advise on the below mail wether i   Sun 8/9

Figure 10-5:
Swipe rightward across a message's name in the list (top). If your finger completes its journey, you've just flagged that message. It shows up with color and a flag (bottom).

- **Mark it as unread.** In the inbox, a bold, blue bar marks any message you haven't yet read. Once you've opened the message, the bar goes away. By choosing Mark as Unread, you make the boldface *reappear*. It's another great way to flag a message for later, to call it to your own attention. The boldface can mean not so much "unread" as "un–dealt with."

(This button changes to say "Mark as read" if you want to go the *other* way—to flag an unread message, or a bunch of them, as read; read on.)

To see the "Mark as unread" command, hit the More button at top right (···).

Tip: Got a keyboard? Press Ctrl+U for "Mark as unread," Ctrl+Q for "Mark as read."

Filing or Deleting Batches of Messages

You can select a message by clicking or tapping it, of course. But what if you want to file or delete a bunch of messages at once?

To select more than one at a time, so that all remain highlighted, hit the ⅍≡ above the message list. Suddenly, checkboxes appear.

Select each message you want to include; you don't have to tap the checkboxes themselves.

Tip: Once you've made the checkboxes appear, you can work down the list using the arrow keys; press Ctrl+Enter to add the checkmark to each message.

You can select as many messages as you like, scrolling as necessary. At that point, you can operate on them all at once—mark them as junk, flag them, delete them, or mark them as read or unread—using the buttons atop the list.

Message Folders

When you first tiptoe into Mail, you may notice, aghast, that your mail folders—Sent, Deleted, Drafts, Important, Work Stuff, and so on—aren't listed anywhere. Actually, they are there, but the list doesn't appear until you select More in the left-side panel. At that point, the folder list sprouts open (you can see it in Figure 10-6). Click a folder to see what's in it.

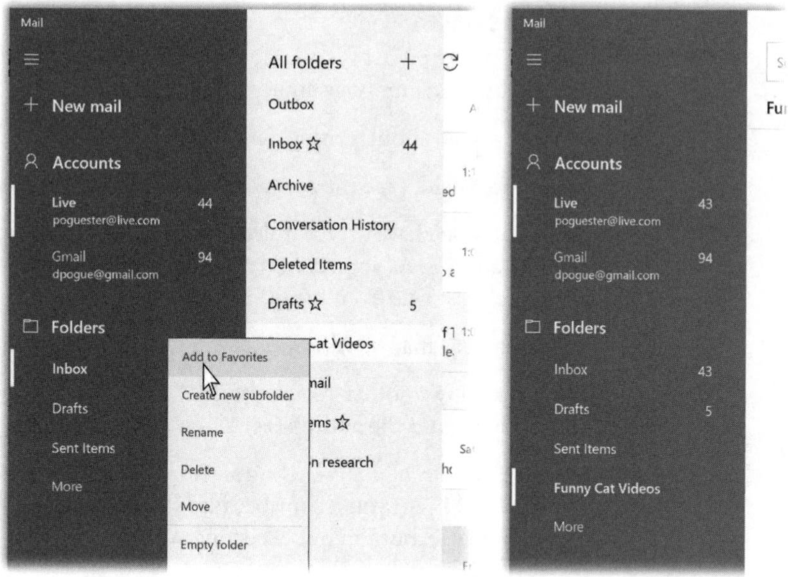

Figure 10-6:
Hit More to view the complete list of folders in your email account (left). Then right-click (or hold your finger down on) a folder's name in the "All folders" list; from the shortcut menu, choose Add to Favorites.

Right: Now it appears on the main Accounts panel, along with Inbox and Sent Items.

It's not especially convenient to have to open and close this pull-out drawer of folders, though. Fortunately, you can install the folders you use most often right onto the left-side pane; Figure 10-6 shows how.

Note: Right-clicking one of these folders in the left-side list gives you access to some important commands: You can rename a folder, delete it, empty it (delete all the email messages it contains), or remove it from the favorites that Mail keeps displayed here for your convenience. Another intriguing option is Pin to Start, which turns this folder into a tile on the right side of the ⊞ menu.

Moving Messages

To move messages among folders, you can drag them, select them, and then use the Move button on the toolbar, or right-click them and choose Move.

Searching

Praise be—there's a search box in Mail, right above the message list. After you type into it and press Enter (or tap ⌕), Mail hides all but the matching messages in the current mail folder; select any one of the results to open it.

Tip: Using the drop-down menu below the search box, you can specify that you want to search either the current folder only—or all folders.

Select any message in the list to read it. When you're finished, tap the × above the message list. Your full list is restored, and the search adventure is complete.

Writing Messages

To compose a new piece of outgoing mail, hit "+ New mail" in the top-left corner. A blank, new outgoing message appears (see Figure 10-7).

Here's how you go about writing a message:

1. **In the "To:" field, type the recipient's email address—or grab it from People.**

    Often, you won't have to type much more than the first couple of letters of the name or email address. As you type, Mail displays all matching names and addresses so you can choose one from the list instead of typing.

    You can add as many addressees as you like; just repeat the procedure.

2. **To send a copy to other recipients, hit "Cc & Bcc" to reveal the "Cc:" or "Bcc:" boxes. Then enter the address(es).**

    Cc stands for *carbon copy*. Getting an email message where your name is in the Cc line implies: "I sent you a copy because I thought you'd want to know about this correspondence, but I'm not expecting you to reply."

    Bcc stands for *blind* carbon copy. It's a copy that goes to a third party secretly—the primary addressee never knows who else received it. For example, if you send your co-worker a message that says, "Chris, it bothers me that you've been cheating the customers," you could Bcc your supervisor to clue her in without getting into trouble with Chris.

Each of these lines behaves exactly like the "To:" line. You fill each one up with email addresses in the same way.

3. **Type the topic of the message in the Subject box.**

It's courteous to put some thought into the subject line. (Use "Change in plans for next week," for instance, instead of "Yo.") Leaving it blank only annoys your recipient. On the other hand, don't put the *entire* message into the subject line, either.

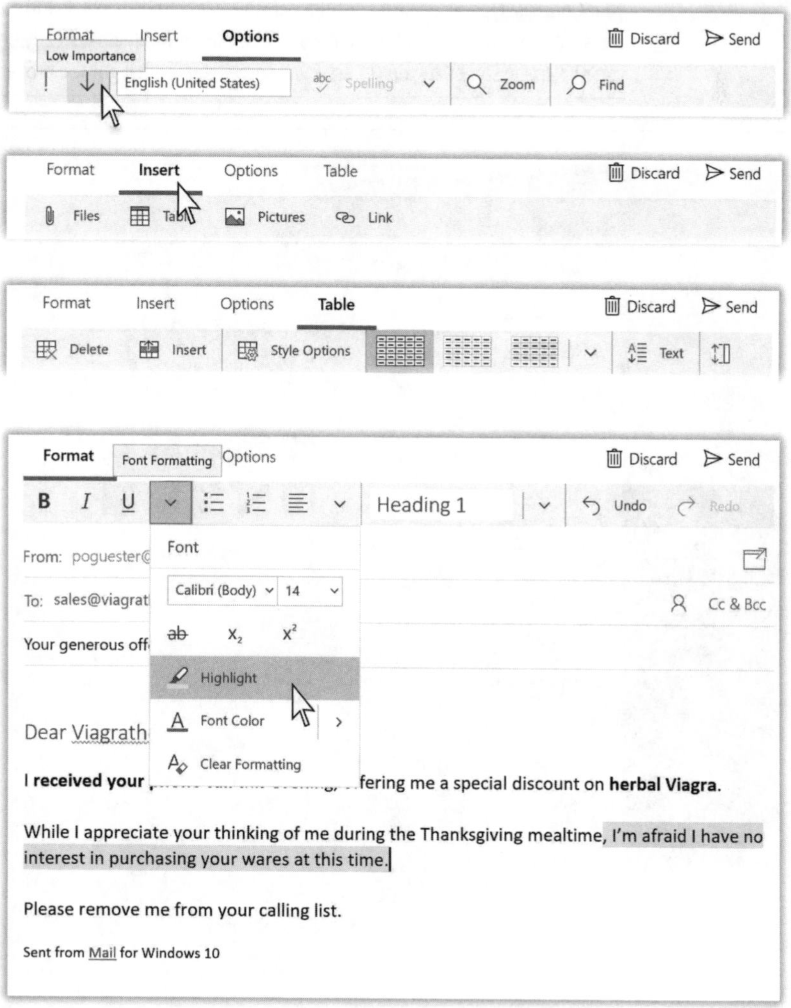

Figure 10-7:
Mail is unusually generous with email-writing tools. The various tabs at the top let you specify an importance level (top), insert all kinds of supplementary materials, like tables (second from top)—complete with full cell and formatting controls (third from top)—and format your text to within an inch of its life (bottom).

4. Type your message in the message area.

All the usual keyboard tricks apply (Chapter 3). Don't forget you can use Copy and Paste, within Mail or from other programs. Both text and graphics can appear in your message.

A wealth of formatting awaits on the Format bar (Figure 10-8). There are your font and style controls, plus options to create bulleted or numbered lists, indent paragraphs, add space before or after paragraphs, or even choose various canned styles (headings, emphasis, book titles, and so on).

Tip: If, as you prepare your message, you type an @ symbol, Mail promptly pops up a mini-window into your Contacts; type a couple letters of a person's name to highlight it, and press Enter to insert it into your message. Mail adds that address to the addressee list, if you hadn't already done so; it assumes that, hey, if you're blaming something on (or assigning something to) that guy, he probably deserves to know about it.

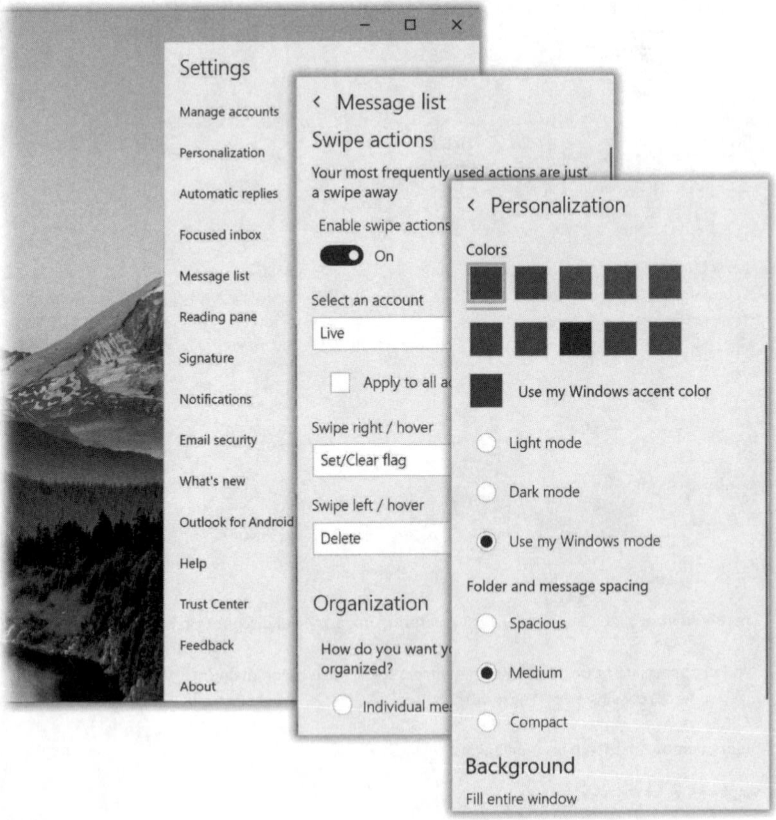

Figure 10-8:
Not everything on the Settings panel is, in fact, a panel of settings. (Trust Center, Feedback, and About just wound up here because they had nowhere else to go.)

But the "Personalization" and "Message list" panes, in particular, are worth your attention.

It's now very easy to insert emoji or a symbol, too—just choose Insert→Emoji to open the emoji palette. See Figure 10-9.

Tip: Actually, you can open the Emoji palette in any app, at any time, by pressing ■+period—but they're useful mostly in texts and emails.

Figure 10-9:
Once the Emoji palette is open, type the term you want to find: "pizza," "idea," "car," whatever.

Or use the category buttons on the bottom row—"Smiley faces and animals," "People," "Celebrations and objects," "Food and plants," "Transportation and places," and "Symbols"–to browse the complete collection.

If you choose the "People," you get a tiny skin-color swatch at top right that lets you specify a shade for your emoji people.

The ☺ reveals emoji you've used recently, for easy re-access.

Don't miss the three top icons, either. The center one offers kaomoji (pictures made of ASCII characters, like the "shrug" in the last line of this email); the rightmost one is full of typographical symbols like ©, ™, and §.

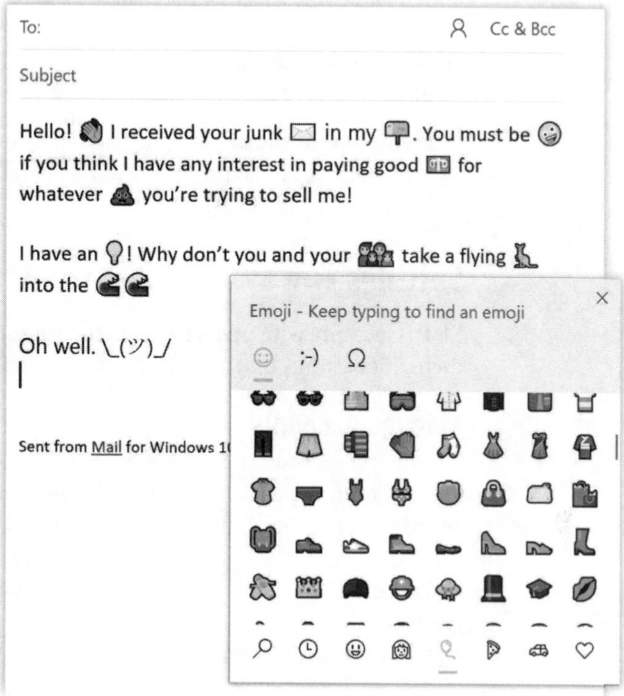

5. **Attach a file, if you like.**

On the Insert tab, the Files button opens the standard Open File dialog box. Tap the file you want to send, and then choose Open. You return to your message in progress, with the files neatly inserted as icons.

Here on the Insert tab, you can also insert a Table; a toolbar appears, with controls to format and adjust its rows and columns.

There's a Pictures button, too; choose a photo from your computer to insert into the message, whereupon a formatting toolbar appears with buttons for Rotate, Crop, Size, and so on. (Drag the round white dots to resize the photo, or the top center icon to rotate it.)

Finally, there's a Link button, which lets you insert a link to a web address.

Tip: A visit to the Options tab is an optional step. Here you can establish a Priority setting for the messages you're about to send; in Mail, you have only two choices—High (!) and Low (↓) importance. The good part about this system is that it lets your recipient see that an email you've sent is, for example, urgent. The bad part is that not every email program displays the priority of email (and even if your recipient's email program *does* display your message's priority, there's no guarantee it'll make him respond any faster).

The Options tab also includes an option to check your spelling and to hide any proofing marks that may have wound up in your message (for example if it was copied in from Word).

6. **To send the message, hit Send, or press Ctrl+Enter. Or hit Discard to back out of it.**

If you choose Discard, the message lands in your Drafts folder. Later, you can open the Drafts folder, tap the aborted message, finish it up, and send it. (Or delete it from there; Mail doesn't care.)

Settings Fun

Mail is teeming with preferences worth examining—and a few worth changing. To see them, hit Settings (⚙). On the Settings panel (Figure 10-8), pay a visit to these tabs:

Manage Accounts

On this panel, you see a simple list of the email accounts you've set up: Gmail, Outlook, iCloud, or whatever. Choose the one you want to open its settings box. You can choose "Add account" here, too, as described on page 389.

Note: Of course, Mail displays only email. If you turn on Contacts and Calendar for one of your accounts, then your lists of names and appointments show up elsewhere in Windows—namely, in the People and Calendar apps. Handily enough, Mail includes a Calendar button at lower left, for easy app hopping.

The settings available for each account type are different. But "Change mailbox sync settings" is always available.

Here's where you find settings like these:

- **Change mailbox sync settings.** How often do you want Mail to check for new messages? Usually, "As items arrive" is what you want. Some account types offer only "Every 15 minutes," "Every 30 minutes," and so on. (If you choose Manually, then Mail never checks unless you hit the Sync button.)

  "Download email from" specifies how far back you want your mail collection collected. (If you have a limited-storage device like a phone or a tablet, you might not want your whole lifetime of mail stored on it. "The last 3 months" might be a good choice.)

  Some services, like Google and corporate Exchange servers, offer more than email; they also maintain online calendars and address books. Under "Sync options," turn on the data types you want to display: Email, Contacts, and/or Calendar.

- **Delete account from this device.** Just what it says. "Delete account from the Microsoft Cloud" deletes this account, and its mail, from the internet—including all of your machines.

Manage Subscriptions

This link opens a web page where you can view and adjust the settings and payments for various Microsoft services: OneDrive storage, Microsoft Office subscriptions, Skype phone service, and so on. (Why is it in the Mail app?)

Personalization

On this pane, Microsoft has built in a raft of cosmetic controls to suit your personality and mood. Here you can choose a color scheme for the app, opt for the usual dark mode (white on black) or Light mode (black on white) designs, adjust the line spacing of your message list, and choose a photo as the Mail background. You'll see that photo in the message-body area when your window is wide enough to permit the three-column view, and no message is selected.

Using the Background Browse button, you can choose a photo of your own to install here. Maybe a photo of a couch and a remote control, to suggest a reward for getting through your email.

Ordinarily, this wallpaper fills only the space where you usually see the message body—when no message is open. But if you turn on "Fill entire window" then, by golly, the photo fills the entire program's window, including (in blurry form) the background of the left-side panel where your accounts appear.

Automatic Replies

Not all email services offer this option; but if you have a Microsoft service, like Outlook or Exchange, you might get a kick out of it. You're supposed to use this option

---

FREQUENTLY ASKED QUESTION

Canning Spam

Help! I'm awash in junk email! How do I get out of this mess?

Spam is a much-hated form of advertising that involves sending unsolicited emails to thousands of people. While there's no instant cure for spam, you can take certain steps to protect yourself from it.

1. **Above all, *never post your main email address online, ever.*** Use a different, dedicated email account for online shopping, website and software registration, and comment posting. Spammers have automated software robots that scour every web

page, recording any email addresses they find. These are the primary sources of spam, so at least you're now restricting the junk mail to one secondary mail account.

2. **Even then, when filling out forms or registering products online,** look for checkboxes requesting permission for the company to send you email or to share your email address with its "partners." And just say no.

3. **Buy an antispam program like SpamAssassin.**

---

for out-of-office automatic responses like, "I'm away on vacation until Monday, August 26." Turn this on when you leave, and specify the canned message.

Of course then you run the risk of sending these auto-replies to *every* incoming message, including newsletters you've signed up for (and spam you haven't). That's why "Send replies only to my contacts" is usually worth turning on, too, and why Mail lets you set up one auto-reply for people within your company and another for outsiders.

Focused Inbox

Here's the on/off switch for the "Focused inbox" feature described on page 393.

Message List

Here you can customize your swipe actions, a Mail feature that's based on typical smartphone mail apps. They let you operate on a message in the list by dragging your finger right or left across it.

When you first use Mail on a touchscreen, swiping to the *right* across a message in the list marks it as flagged (page 396), and to the *left* archives it (moves it out of the inbox and into the Archived folder).

But on this panel, you can redefine what the right swipe and left swipe do (or turn off the "Swipe actions" feature entirely). Your choices for swiping each direction include "Set/Clear flag," "Mark as read/unread," "Archive," "Delete," and "Move."

You might set things up so a left swipe deletes a message and a right swipe moves it to a new folder, for example.

The "Message list" pane also lets you turn off the first-line-of-the-body previews that show up in the message list; turn off the tiny photos of your correspondents; and turn off the appearance of attached photos right in the message body.

Why would you want to? Only Microsoft's focus groups know for sure.

Reading Pane

Here's what you've got on the Reading pane options:

- **Auto-open next item.** What this phrase leaves out is "when I delete a message." In other words, when you delete a message, what do you want to take its place in the Message pane—the next message on the list or your background photo?

- **Mark item as read.** When do you want Mail to indicate that you've actually read a message?

  Your options include "When selection changes" (that is, when you choose another message); "Don't automatically mark item as read" (that is, you have to mark it as read manually); and "When viewed in the reading pane." That last one makes Mail flag a message as read only after you've had it open long enough to actually read it (and you can change the number of seconds that implies).

- **Caret browsing** means that, when you're reading an email message, your up/down arrow (and Page Up/Page Down keys) move an insertion-point cursor through the text instead of simply scrolling the text.

  (Oh, and you can hold down the Shift key to select the text as you go. That's especially useful when you're selecting text on a web page or heavily laid-out email message, because it captures only the text in the current column. If you simply drag your mouse through a web page, you might also accidentally highlight stuff that's off to the side, like ads or list boxes or other stories. And when you copy and paste that selection, you wind up with a nightmare of intermixed text from different columns. Selecting text with, for example, Shift+arrow keys, prevents that phenomenon.)

  That's commonplace in word processing, of course, but Microsoft offers it to you here to use on a web page or when editing email.

- **External content.** Spammers, the vile undercrust of low-life society, have a famous trick. When they send you email that includes a picture, they don't actually paste the picture into the message. Instead, they include a "bug"—a piece of code that instructs your email program to *fetch* the missing graphic from the internet. Why? Because that gives the spammer the ability to track who has actually opened the junk mail, making their email addresses much more valuable for reselling to other spammers.

  That's a long explanation for a simple feature: If you turn this option off, then Mail does not fetch "bug" image files at all. You're not flagged as a sucker by the spammers. You'll see empty squares in the email where the images ought to be. The actual pictures don't appear until you manually select the "Download all images in this message" link.

Note: Graphics sent by normal people and legitimate companies are generally pasted right into the email, so they'll still show up just fine.

Default Font

New in the May 2019 Update: You can now choose a default font and style—the format all your outgoing messages will use. Here you can specify which account you want this font to affect (or use "Apply to all accounts"), and then go nuts with the formatting controls here. Hit Save.

Signature

A *signature* is a bit of text that gets stamped at the bottom of your outgoing email messages. It can be your name, a postal address, or a pithy quote. Here's where you enter the signature you want to use for outgoing messages from each of your accounts. (Also turn on "Use an email signature," of course.)

Notifications

Do you want Windows to let you know when new mail arrives from this account? If so, turn on "Show notifications in the action center," and then specify how you want to be notified. You can choose to "Play a sound," "Show a notification banner," or both. Remember, you can set things up differently for each email account.

Everything Else

The other items in the Mail Settings pane are mostly edge cases or marketing exercises. Namely:

- **Email security.** Well, hey! Here's where you can change the S/MIME Digital Signature and Encryption settings for certain kinds of email accounts. (Hint: probably not yours.)

- **What's new.** Opens a web page that describes what's new in this version of Mail.

- **Outlook for Android and iOS.** Opens a web page with links to the phone versions of Microsoft's Outlook email app.

- **Help.** Offers an Open Help button that, in turn, opens a very sparse Help web page for Mail.

- **Trust Center.** "Enable locally relevant content: Let Office connect to online services from Microsoft to provide functionality that's relevant to your usage and preferences." Ohhh, so *that's* what this does!

  That bit of prose is doublespeak for a much simpler meaning: "Let us send you ads based on what's in your email."

- **Feedback.** Opens the Feedback Hub app, where you can send Mail's programmers suggestions and complaints.

- **About.** Shows which version of Mail you have.

CHAPTER 11

Security & Privacy

I f it weren't for that darned internet, personal computing would be a lot of fun. After all, it's the internet that lets all those socially stunted hackers enter our machines, unleashing their viruses, setting up remote hacking tools, feeding us spyware, trying to trick us out of our credit card numbers, and otherwise making our lives an endless troubleshooting session. It sure would be nice if they'd cultivate some other hobbies.

In the meantime, these lowlifes are doing astronomical damage to businesses and individuals around the world—along the lines of $100 billion a year (the cost to fight viruses, spyware, and spam).

Microsoft has been making Windows steadily more secure for years. Evil strangers will still do all they can to make your life miserable, but they'll have a much, much harder time succeeding.

Note: Most of Windows' self-protection features have to do with *internet* threats—because, in fact, virtually all the infectious unpleasantness that can befall a PC these days comes from the internet. A PC that never goes online probably won't get infected. So this chapter covers many features of Windows 10's browser, Edge (covered in more detail in Chapter 9).

Lots of Windows' security improvements are invisible to you. They're deep in the plumbing, with no buttons or controls to show you. If you're scoring at home, they include features with names like application isolation, service hardening, Protected Mode, Network Access Protection, PatchGuard, Data Execution Prevention, Code Integrity, and everybody's favorite, Address Space Layout Randomization. They're all technical barricades that stand between the bad guys and your PC.

The rest of this chapter describes features that *aren't* invisible and automatic—the ones you can control.

Note: And does it work? Do all these tools and patches actually reduce the number of virus and spyware outbreaks?

Apparently, yes. The years of annual front-page headlines about national virus outbreaks—called things like Melissa (1999), Blaster (2003), and Sasser (2004)—seem to be over. There will always be clever new attacks—but they'll be much less frequent and much harder to write.

Note, however, that built-in security tools can't do the whole job of keeping your PC safe; you play a role, too. So heed these tips before you or your family go online:

- **Don't trust a pretty face.** It doesn't take much expertise to build a snazzy-looking website. Just because a website *looks* trustworthy doesn't mean you can trust it. If you're visiting a little-known website, be careful what you do there.

- **Don't download from sites you don't know.** The web is full of free software offers. But that free software may, in fact, be spyware or other malware. (Malware is a general term for viruses, spyware, and other Bad Software.) So be very careful when downloading anything online. Especially free movies and songs.

- **Don't click pop-up ads.** Pop-up ads are more than mere annoyances; some of them, when clicked, download spyware to your PC.

With all that said, you're ready to find out how to keep yourself safe when you go online.

Windows Security (the App)

After several decades, Microsoft finally built free antivirus software right into Windows.

But these days, virus protection is only the beginning. You now have a standalone app called Windows Security (formerly Windows Defender, formerly Defender Security Center). It's a master dashboard for Windows' complete arsenal of protection against PC disaster—not just virus infections (see Figure 11-1, top).

To see these realms of protection, open the Windows Security app.

On this one unified dashboard—the Home page—you'll find icons for "Virus & threat protection," "Account protection," "Firewall & network protection," "App & browser control," "Device security," "Device performance & health," and "Family options." The following pages cover these areas one by one.

Virus & Threat Protection

You can get all kinds of viruses, spyware, ransomware, and so on from the internet. This part of Windows Security, called Windows Defender Antivirus, is designed to protect you from all of it (Figure 11-1, bottom).

You usually get this nasty stuff in one of three ways. First, a website may try to trick you into downloading it. You see what looks like an innocent button in what's actually a phony Windows dialog box. Second, you may be sent an attachment by email that you foolishly double-click.

Third, you may get spyware or viruses by downloading a program you *do* want, without realizing it's a secret program in disguise. (That phenomenon is one advantage of the Microsoft Store; all *these* apps have been checked and found to be clean.)

Once installed, the malware may make changes to important system files, install ads on your desktop, or (in the case of ransomware) actually encrypt all your files, holding them hostage until you pay the anonymous creator hundreds of dollars.

Spyware can also do things like hijack your home page or search page so that every time you open your browser, you wind up at a web page that incapacitates your PC with a blizzard of pop-ups. *Keylogger* spyware can record your keystrokes, passwords and all, and send them to a snooper.

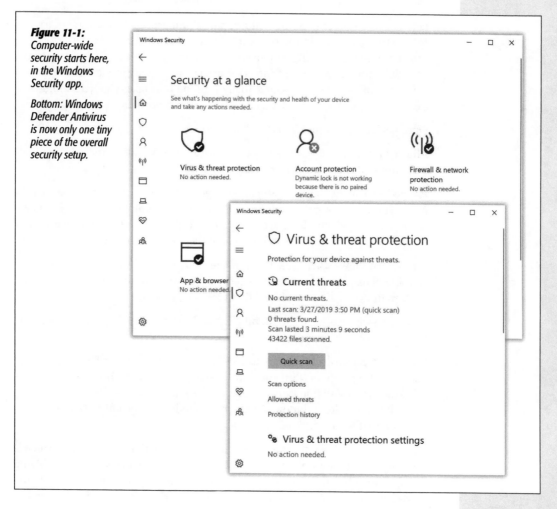

Figure 11-1:
Computer-wide security starts here, in the Windows Security app.

Bottom: Windows Defender Antivirus is now only one tiny piece of the overall security setup.

Freaked out yet? All right, then: Here's what you'll find on this screen:

- **Current threats.** A summary of any vulnerabilities Defender has found right now, along with the details of the most recent malware scan.

- **Quick scan.** Ordinarily, the program scans your PC continuously. But if you're feeling a little antsy, you can also trigger a scan manually, using this button. It tells Windows Security to inspect the folders that malware usually targets.

Tip: If, after running this scan, Windows feels that you really should run one of the more thorough scans, it'll tell you so after it's finished.

- **Scan options.** There are other kinds of scans, including Full scan (checks every single file in every single folder, and takes a long time) and Custom scan (you choose the folders).

  Let's hope you never need the Offline scan. It's for especially tough malware, like *rootkits* (infections so close to the heart of Windows that normal antivirus software can't even find it); usually, Windows lets you know if an Offline scan is necessary. Your PC shuts down and then enters a special virus-defense mode that can inspect your copy of Windows without actually running it. It takes about 15 minutes to clean your copy of Windows; then your PC restarts normally.

  Once you've made your choice, hit "Scan now."

- **Allowed threats.** This page simply lists software that Windows thought was malware, but that you allowed to run anyway.

- **Protection history.** Defender watches over your PC constantly, as a barrier against new virus and spyware infections. Each day, the program auto-downloads new *definitions files*—behind-the-scenes updates to its virus database, which keep it up to date with the latest viruses Microsoft has spotted in the wild.

  This screen shows when Defender most recently scanned your PC, how many of your files it inspected, how many infections it discovered, and what actions it took to clean things up. If you're lucky, that screen says "No recent actions."

  If any malware *has* been found, hit "Threat history" to go beyond the headline (see page 412).

- **Virus & threat protection settings.** Here's the on/off switch for Defender's automatic scanning cycles ("Real-time protection"). You'd basically be nuts to turn it off, which is why Windows frantically warns you, if you try, that you're leaving yourself vulnerable. (Windows also turns Defender *back on* after a "short time," a duration that Microsoft keeps secret.)

  This page also includes the on/off switch for Cloud-delivered protection, which is a big, big deal. It allows Windows to protect you even from malware that's evolving and spreading by the hour—even malware that's never been seen before. There's also a switch for Automatic sample submission, which lets you decide whether to send sample files from your PC to Microsoft for malware analysis. See the box below for details.

Nowadays, some malware gets sneaky: It works by turning off your security software! Tamper protection, new in the May 2019 Update, stops it in its tracks. It prevents background changes to your Windows Security settings, which can be changed only by opening the Windows Security app. Leave this on!

Controlled folder access is Microsoft's way of protecting you against ransomware (malicious software that holds system components hostage until you pay up). It's rather clever: It maintains a list of folders that you'd be really, really unhappy to lose to some overseas dirtbag and his greedy scheme. If any app tries to modify anything in these folders, Defender shuts it down (and notifies you in the Action Center).

The folder list starts out with your Documents, Pictures, Videos, Music, Favorites, and Desktop folders, but you can add other folders here. (Note that if you then move one of these folders, it's no longer protected.)

Note: Windows tries to figure out which programs have a legitimate need to access the folders on the list, but it doesn't always guess right. If it seems to be blocking an app that does deserve access, hit "Allow an app through Controlled folder access" and then choose its name.

While you're here, you can choose some **Exclusions** (folders, files, file types, or programs) that you *don't* want Defender to monitor for infection.

Finally, **Notifications** is where you can adjust how often Defender bugs you with messages in the Action Center about its activities. Some people, for example, turn off "Recent activity and scan results"—they don't want to be alerted every time Defender runs a scan and *doesn't* find anything amiss.

UP TO SPEED

Cloud-Delivered Protection: Death to First-Time Malware

In the old days, everybody got the same viruses. Remember ILOVEYOU and Blaster?

Nowadays, it's different. Want to hear a shocking statistic? According to Microsoft, *96 percent* of malware that Windows Defender blocks is found only once, on a single PC! That's how shape-shifty and fragmented viruses have become.

Clearly, trying to come up with a single virus-definitions file that protects everybody is an increasingly outdated approach. How on earth is Windows supposed to protect you against a virus that nobody has ever seen before?

With *cloud-delivered protection*. It's an artificially intelligent virus expert online.

Whenever Windows encounters suspicious-seeming code on your machine, it places a 10-second hold on running it. In the meantime, it uploads that file to Microsoft's cloud protection servers, which perform some AI analysis; if they determine that the file looks, smells, and feels like malware, Windows sends a "do not open" command back to your PC, and you're instantly protected.

Microsoft now knows about this new malware, and it instantly protects millions of *other* people, too.

Microsoft encourages you to leave "Automatic sample submission" turned on; that's the permission slip that lets your PC submit the bad file to Microsoft for analysis.

- **Virus & threat protection updates** reveals what definitions database you've got. And there's a big, fat "Check for updates" button to download the latest one right now.

- **Ransomware protection** is another way to access the "Controlled folder access" settings described already.

Now, Defender is certainly not the only antivirus program on the planet. It's not even the best one. Several rival antivirus programs are free for personal use. These do have their downsides—some nag you to buy the Pro versions, for example, and there's nobody to call for tech support.

Note: If you do install another antivirus program (Norton, Symantec, Avast, or whatever), Defender turns off automatically. You can still use it to run a malware scan, though.

In any case, the bottom line is this: If your PC doesn't have antivirus software working for you right now, then getting some should be at the top of your to-do list.

What happens when Defender finds malware

When Defender finds malware, it takes control. It puts the offending software into a quarantined area where it can't do any more harm, and it lets you know (with a notification) what it's found.

In "Protection history," you can look over the fruits of its labors like this:

- **Current threats.** A list of malware that Windows hasn't killed yet, along with a recommendation for your next step.

- **Quarantined threats.** Here's a list of the nasties that Windows has found and isolated. You see each program Defender has taken action on, the alert level, and the date. You can use "Remove all" if you don't recognize any of it, or you can just wait; Windows periodically empties out the quarantine area on its own.

  You can also select an item to view its details, and to view the buttons for Remove or Restore. (Restore means "It's fine. Put it back and let me run it"; of course, it's usually a terrible idea to run software that Windows has told you is malware.)

- **Allowed threats.** If Defender announces that it's found a potential piece of malware, but you allow it to run anyway, it's considered an allowed item. From now on, Defender ignores it, meaning that you trust that program completely. Allowed programs' names appear here.

  If you highlight a program's name and then click Remove From List, it's *gone* from the Allowed list, and therefore Defender monitors it once again.

Account Protection

This screen offers links to your Microsoft account (page 534), Windows Hello setup (page 549), and Dynamic Lock (page 554), all of which appear elsewhere in settings. Why are these controls repeated here? Because, in Microsoft's view, they have to do with protection, so they kind of fit.

Firewall & Network Protection

If you have a broadband, always-on connection, you're connected to the internet 24 hours a day. It's theoretically possible for some cretin to use automated hacking software to flood you with files or to take control of your machine. Fortunately, the Windows Defender *Firewall* feature puts up a barrier to such mischief.

The firewall acts as a gatekeeper between you and the internet. It examines all internet traffic and lets through only communications it knows are safe; all others are turned away at the door.

Every kind of electronic message sent to or from your PC—instant messaging, music sharing, file sharing, and so on—conducts its business on a specific communications channel, or *port*. Ports are numbered tunnels for certain kinds of internet traffic.

The firewall blocks or permits signals based on a predefined set of rules. They dictate, for example, which programs are permitted to use your network connection or which ports can be used for communications.

You don't need to do anything to turn on the Windows Defender Firewall. When you turn on Windows, it's already at work. But you *can* turn the firewall off.

Tip: It's perfectly OK to use both Windows Defender Firewall *and* another company's firewall software. If you're a supergeek, you can assign each to handle different technical firewall functions.

Here are the settings available to you.

Domain network, Private network, Public network

You can turn the firewall on or off independently for these three kinds of networks. A domain network is the one at a corporation, maybe where you work; a private network is your home network (Figure 11-2, top); and a public network means the kind at a coffee shop or airport.

For each kind, you can turn the firewall on or off. There's very little reason to turn it off, though, even if you decide to install another company's firewall; its installer turns off the Windows Defender Firewall if necessary.

Note: If you really are on a domain (Chapter 19), then you may not be allowed to make any changes to the firewall settings, because that's something the network nerds like to be in charge of.

You also might be tempted to turn off the firewall because you have a *router* that distributes your internet signal through the house—and most routers have *hardware* firewalls built right in, protecting your entire network.

Still, there's no harm in having *both* a hardware and a software firewall in place. In fact, having the Windows Defender Firewall turned on protects you from viruses you catch from other people on your own network (even though you're both "behind" the router's firewall). And if you have a laptop, this way you won't have to remember to turn the firewall on when you leave your home network.

For each kind of network, you can also turn on "Block all incoming connections, including those in the list of allowed apps." When you turn on this especially conservative option, your computer is pretty much completely shut off from the internet except for web browsing, email, and instant messaging.

Allow an app through firewall

The firewall isn't always your friend. It can occasionally block a perfectly harmless program from communicating with the outside world—a chat program or a game that you can play across the internet, for example.

Fortunately, whenever that happens, Windows lets you know with a message that says "Windows Defender Firewall has blocked some features of this program." Most of the time, you know exactly what program it's talking about, because it's a program you

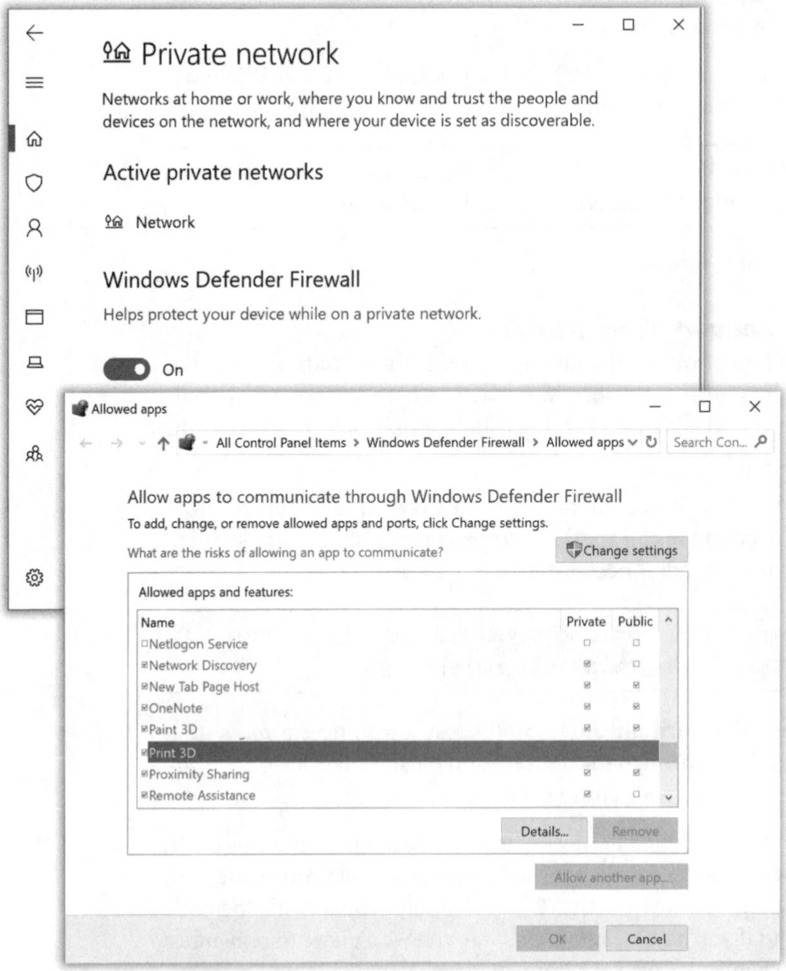

Figure 11-2:
Top: The Windows Defender Firewall window is basically a dashboard that tells you if your firewall is turned on, the name of your network, and what the settings are for each kind of network location.

Bottom: Here you can specify when each program is allowed to connect to the internet—independently for each kind of network you might be on (using the Private or Public checkboxes at far right). Turning off the checkbox at far left blocks the program completely. Click "Allow another app" to add a new program to this list so it won't bug you the first time you run it.

just opened *yourself*—a program you installed that might legitimately need internet access. In other words, it's not some rogue spyware on your machine trying to talk to the mother ship. Click "Allow access" and get on with your life.

Alternatively, you can set up permissions for your apps in advance, using this option. Click "Change settings," and proceed as shown in Figure 11-2.

Network and Internet troubleshooter
A link to a different Settings page, one filled with options designed to help you troubleshoot your network. Relevance to firewall settings: marginal.

Firewall notification settings
Lets you shush Windows if it seems to be notifying you too often that the firewall has blocked an app.

Advanced settings
The Defender Firewall screen gives you a good deal of control over how this firewall works. But it doesn't offer nearly the amount of tweakiness that high-end geeks demand, like control over individual ports, IP addresses, programs, and so on. It also offers no way to create a log (a text-file record) of all attempts to contact your PC from the network or the internet, which can be handy when you suspect that some nasty hacker has been visiting you in the middle of the night.

There is, however, an even more powerful firewall control panel. In an effort to avoid terrifying novices, Microsoft has hidden it, but it's easy enough to open. It's called Windows Defender Firewall with Advanced Security. You get there by choosing "Advanced settings" in the Defender Firewall window.

In the resulting box, you can open a port for some app that needs access. Suppose, for example, some game needs a particular port to be opened in the firewall. Click Inbound Rules to see all the individual "rules" you've established. In the right-side pane, click New Rule. A wizard opens; it walks you through specifying the program and the port you want to open for it.

Then again, if you're really that much of an Advanced Security sort of person, you can find Microsoft's old-but-good guide for this console at *http://bit.ly/hxR0i*.

Restore firewalls to default
Sure enough: This command restores all your firewall adjustments to their factory settings. (You're asked to confirm.)

App & Browser Control
This page is the home of SmartScreen, an anti-phishing technology (see the box on the next page). If you try to open a downloaded file (or app), or visit a website, that Microsoft knows is suspicious, it blocks your path with a warning banner (Figure 11-3).

SmartScreen works by comparing the file or site against a massive list of websites and file downloads that have been reported to Microsoft as unsafe.

This page offers four sets of controls:

- **Check apps and files.** When Windows discovers you're trying to open a program or a file download that's been reported as malware, how would you like it to respond? Block the app, just warn you, or go ahead and open it (Off)?

- **SmartScreen for Microsoft Edge.** When you're using Edge, and you try to open a known phishing site, what would you like it to do? Block you, just warn you, or go ahead and open it (Off)?

- **SmartScreen for Microsoft Store apps.** You remember Microsoft Store apps, right (page 233)? Sometimes, they reach to the web to retrieve data (think of, for

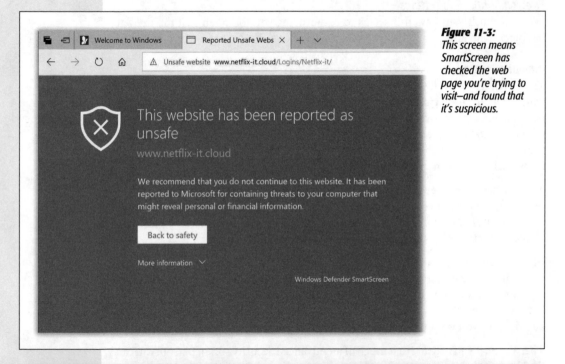

Figure 11-3:
This screen means SmartScreen has checked the web page you're trying to visit—and found that it's suspicious.

UP TO SPEED

Phishing 101

What's phishing? That's when you're sent what appears to be legitimate email from a bank, eBay, PayPal, or some other financial website. The message tells you the site needs to confirm your account information, or warns that your account has been hacked and needs you to help keep it safe.

If you, responsible citizen that you are, click the provided link to clear up the supposed problem, you wind up on what looks like the bank/eBay/PayPal site. But it's a fake, carefully designed to look like the real thing; it's run by a scammer. If you type in your password and sign-in information, as requested, then the next thing you know, you're getting credit card bills for $10,000 charges at high-rolling Las Vegas hotels—the scammer has collected your sign-in information. The fake sites look so much like the real ones that it can be extremely difficult to tell them apart.

example, a weather app). If you choose Warn here, then Windows will alert you if it thinks an app is trying to pull *suspicious* data from the web.

- **Exploit protection.** Microsoft once developed a sophisticated tool for corporate tech geeks called the Enhanced Mitigation Experience Toolkit (EMET). It was intended to block many common avenues of hacker attack.

EMET (or a variation thereof) is now built into Windows. It's *still* intended for corporate network administrators, though, as you can probably tell by the controls' names here ("Validate exception chains [SEHOP]" and "High-entropy ASLR," anyone?). For best results, leave these options at their factory settings.

If you know exactly what you're doing, and you suspect that one of these blockades is causing glitches in one of your programs, you can select "Exploit protection settings" and make adjustments on an app-by-app basis.

Device Security

The controls here vary by machine, but here's what you may see:

- **Core isolation.** Here's yet another defense against the dark arts whose name means nothing to most people. These are *virtualization-based security* (VBS) tools; they're Microsoft's response to the methods used by the WannaCry and Petya ransomware attacks, which managed to evade Windows' existing protections. Turning on core isolation prevents nastyware from inserting its own sinister code into important pieces of Windows.

- **Security processor.** Some PCs come with a special chip called a TPM (trusted platform module), whose purpose is to store the encryption "keys" for your particular machine. That way, even if you use BitLocker (page 529) and some thug steals your hard drive, he won't be able to do anything with it.

- **Secure boot.** This feature prevents a nasty type of malware called a rootkit from sneaking onto your device. Don't turn it off unless it's causing problems for one of your drivers.

Device Performance & Health

Hey, it's a dashboard within a dashboard! This screen summarizes the health of your storage, drivers, battery, and apps.

Family Options

"Family options" is Microsoftese for what you probably know as parental controls. They're described on page 424.

Five Degrees of Web Protection

Since most of the dangerous things that happen to a computer or its owner—viruses, ransomware, stolen data—stem from ill-advised adventures on the web, it makes sense that Microsoft has poured a lot of effort into making its Edge browser safe. Here are some of the ways Edge protects your computer, your privacy, and you.

Privacy and Cookies

Cookies are something like web-page preference files. Certain websites—particularly commercial ones like Amazon.com—deposit them on your hard drive like little bookmarks so they'll remember you the next time you visit. On Amazon, in fact, a greeting says, "Hello, Casey" (or whatever your name is), thanks to the cookie it uses to recognize you.

Most cookies are perfectly innocuous—and, in fact, are extremely helpful. They can let your PC sign into a site automatically or let you customize what the site looks like and how you use it.

But fear is on the march, and the media fan the flames with tales of sinister cookies that track your movement on the web. Some websites rely on cookies to record which pages you visit on a site, how long you spend on a site, what kind of information you like to find out, and so on.

If you're worried about invasions of privacy—and you're willing to trade away some of the conveniences of cookies—then Edge is ready to protect you.

Cookie options

In the Edge browser, choose ⋯→Settings→"Privacy and Security." Scroll down to the Cookies pop-up menu. It offers three choices:

- **Block all cookies.** No cookies, no exceptions. Websites can't read existing cookies, either.

- **Block only third-party cookies.** A first-party cookie is created by the site you're currently visiting. (These kinds of cookies generally aren't privacy invaders; they're

---

FREQUENTLY ASKED QUESTION

Sherlock Edge

How does the Edge browser know what's a phishing site and what's not?

Edge uses three bits of information to figure out whether a site is legitimate or a phishing site.

Its first line of defense is a Microsoft-compiled, frequently updated database of known phishing sites that—believe it or not—sits right on your own hard drive. Whenever you head to a website, Edge consults that database. If the website appears in the list, you'll get a warning. (The database is compiled from several companies that specialize in phish

tracking, including Cyota, IID, and MarkMonitor, as well as from direct feedback.)

Second, Edge uses *heuristics,* a sort of low-level artificial intelligence. It compares characteristics of the site you're visiting against common phishing-site characteristics. The heuristics tool helps Edge recognize phishing sites that haven't yet made it into the database of known sites.

Finally, Edge quietly sends addresses of some of the sites you visit to Microsoft, which checks them against a frequently updated list of reported phishing sites (not the database on your PC).

---

the Amazon type described already, designed to sign you in.)

Third-party cookies, though, are deposited on your hard drive by a site other than the one you're currently visiting—often by an advertiser. Needless to say, this kind of cookie is more objectionable. It can track your browsing habits and create profiles about your interests and behaviors.

- **Don't block cookies.** All cookies are OK. Websites can read existing cookies.

Note: Some sites don't function well (or at all) if you reject all cookies. So if you choose "Block all cookies," and you run into trouble browsing your favorite sites, then return here and change the setting to "Block only third-party cookies."

History: Erasing Your Tracks

The most visible tracks you leave when you surf the web are on the History list. It's a menu, right there for anyone to see, that lists every website you've visited recently. In the Edge browser, you can view the History list by choosing ☆≡ and then the ⟳ tab. (Or just press Ctrl+H.)

Some people find that record-keeping unnerving. So:

- **To delete just one particularly incriminating History listing,** click the ✕ to its right.

- **To delete your entire history from one day (or week),** click the ✕ to *its* right.

  Actually, you can delete any of the history "folders" here—like Yesterday, Last Week, or Older—the same way.

- **To erase the entire History menu,** hit "Clear history" at the top.

This is good information to know; after all, you might be nominated to the Supreme Court someday.

The Pop-Up Blocker

The world's smarmiest advertisers inundate us with *pop-up* and *pop-under* ads: nasty little windows that appear in front of the browser window or, worse, behind it, waiting to jump out the moment you close your browser window. They're often deceptive, masquerading as error messages or dialog boxes…and they'll do absolutely anything to get you to click inside them.

Pop-ups are more than just annoying; they're also potentially dangerous. They're a favorite trick that hackers use to deposit spyware on your PC. Clicking a pop-up can begin the silent downloading process. That's true even if the pop-up seems to serve a legitimate purpose—asking you to participate in a survey, for example.

Edge, fortunately, has a pop-up *blocker*. It comes automatically turned on; you don't have to do anything. You'll be browsing along, and then one day you'll see the "Pop-up blocked" message at the bottom of your window (Figure 11-4).

Note that Edge blocks only pop-ups that are spawned *automatically*, not those that appear when you click something (like a seating diagram on a concert-tickets site). And it doesn't block pop-ups from your local network.

Figure 11-4:
Edge has spared
you from the
spawn: a pop-up
window you
haven't asked for.

Overriding the pop-up blocker

Sometimes, though, you *want* to see the pop-up. Some sites, for example, use pop-up windows as a way to deliver legitimate information. In those situations, click one of the two buttons:

- **Allow once** lets this website's pop-ups through just for this browsing session. Next time, pop-ups will be blocked again.

- **Always allow** does what it says; pop-ups from this site will always appear.

Turning off the pop-up blocker

Many internauts are partial to other companies' pop-up blockers, like Adblock Plus or Pop Up Blocker. In that case, you'll want to turn off Edge's version.

To do that in the Edge browser, choose ⋯→⚙→ "Privacy and security." Turn off "Block pop-ups."

InPrivate Browsing

If not everything you do on the web is something you want your spouse/parents/boss/teachers to know about, then Microsoft has heard you.

FREQUENTLY ASKED QUESTION

The Wisdom of Edge

How does the pop-up blocker know a good pop-up from a bad one, anyway?

Edge generally tries to distinguish between pop-ups that are necessary for a site to run and those that are dangerous or just annoying.

Although it doesn't always succeed, there is some logic behind its thinking. At the factory setting, some pop-ups get through. For example, it allows pop-ups that contain "active content"—for example, important features that are integral to the proper functioning of a website: seating charts, flight-details screens, and so on.

Finally, if you already have a spyware infection, pop-ups may appear constantly; the pop-up blocker isn't designed to block spyware pop-ups.

You might be shocked to see the kinds of information your browser stores about you. History entries aren't the only tracks you leave as you browse. Behind the scenes, it stashes your cookies, of course, plus passwords and information you type into web forms (your name and address, for example). Your hard drive also keeps *cache* files—graphics and text files that make up the web pages themselves, stored to speed up their reappearance if you visit those sites again.

Every modern browser offers a feature like Microsoft's InPrivate browsing, which lets you surf wherever you like within a single browser window. Then, when you close that window, *all* your tracks are wiped out. No History items, no cookies, no saved password list, no AutoFill entries, and so on. In other words, what happens in InPrivate browsing stays in InPrivate browsing.

To start InPrivate browsing, hit ··· →"New InPrivate window." A new window opens (Figure 11-5). Nothing you do in this window—or in the tabs within it—will be remembered in any way.

Tip: Alternatively, you can right-click Edge's icon on the taskbar; from the shortcut menu, choose "New InPrivate window."

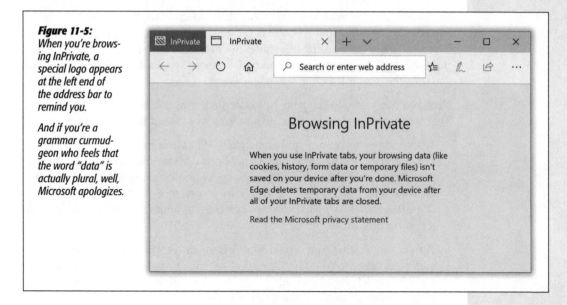

Figure 11-5:
When you're browsing InPrivate, a special logo appears at the left end of the address bar to remind you.

And if you're a grammar curmudgeon who feels that the word "data" is actually plural, well, Microsoft apologizes.

Browsing InPrivate

When you use InPrivate tabs, your browsing data (like cookies, history, form data or temporary files) isn't saved on your device after you're done. Microsoft Edge deletes temporary data from your device after all of your InPrivate tabs are closed.

Read the Microsoft privacy statement

To stop InPrivate browsing, close the window. Open a new Edge window to continue browsing "publicly."

Do Not Track

You know how there's a "Do not call" list? If you register your phone number with this list, telemarketers are legally forbidden to call you.

Now there's a "Do not track" list, too. If you turn this feature on in your browser—like Edge—then web advertisers are supposed to not track your web activities, which they like to do in order to market to you better.

There's a difference, though. Advertisers' respect for your Do Not Track setting is *optional*. There's no law that says they have to obey it. As a result, it's essentially a useless feature.

If you care, you can find the Do Not Track setting like this: Click ⋯→⚙→ "Privacy and security." Turn on "Send Do Not Track requests," if it's not on already.

Hotspot Security

One of the greatest computing conveniences is the almighty public wireless hotspot, where you and your Wi-Fi–enabled laptop can connect to the internet at high speed, often for free, in public places around the world.

But unless you're careful, you'll get more than a skinny latte from your local café if you connect to its hotspot—you may get eavesdropped on as well. It's possible for hackers sitting nearby, using free shareware programs, to "sniff" the transmissions from your laptop. They can intercept email messages you send, names and passwords, and even the images from the web pages you're visiting.

Now, you don't have to sell your laptop and move to the Amish country over this. There are a few simple steps that will go a long way toward keeping you safe:

- **Tell Windows you're on a public network.** When you first connect to a wireless network, Windows asks whether it's a public or a private one. Choosing Public gives you extra protection. Technically speaking, Windows turns off *network discovery*, the feature that makes your PC announce its presence to others on the network. (Unfortunately, lurking hackers using special scanning software can still find you if they're determined.)

- **Turn off file sharing.** You certainly don't want any of your overcaffeinated neighbors to get access to your files. Open the Start menu. Start typing *sharing* until you see "Manage advanced sharing settings" in the results list; click it. In the resulting window, turn off all the Sharing options.

- **Watch for the padlock.** You generally don't have to worry about online stores and banks. Whenever you see the little padlock icon in your web browser (or whenever the URL in the address bar begins with "https" instead of "http"), you're visiting a secure website. Your transmissions are encrypted in both directions and can't be snooped.

- **Look over your shoulder.** Hacking isn't always high-tech stuff; it can be as simple as "shoulder surfing," in which someone looks over your shoulder to see the password you're typing. Make sure no one can look at what you're typing.

- **Don't leave your laptop alone.** Coffee has a way of moving through your system fast, but if you have to leave for the restroom, don't leave your laptop unattended. Pack it up into its case and take it with you, or bring along a lock you can use to lock it to a table.

- **Use a virtual private network (VPN).** If somebody intercepts your "Hi Mom" email, it may not be the end of the world. If you're doing serious corporate work, though, and you want maximum safety, you can pay for wireless virtual private network (VPN) software that encrypts all the data you're sending and receiving. Nobody will be able to grab it out of the air using snooping software at a hotspot.

  For example, HotSpotVPN (*hotspotvpn.com*) costs about a hundred bucks a year. You get a password, user name, and the internet address of a VPN server.

  See page 461 for more on setting up a VPN connection.

Protect Your Home Wireless Network

Public wireless hotspots aren't the only ones that present a theoretical security risk; your wireless network at home harbors hacker potential, too. It's theoretically possible for so-called war drivers (people who drive around with laptops, looking for unprotected home Wi-Fi networks) to piggyback onto home networks to download child pornography or to send out spam.

This one's easy to nip in the bud:

- **Use a password on your Wi-Fi.** When you first set up your Wi-Fi router (your base station or access point), you're offered the chance to create a password for your network. Take that chance. (Wireless routers have offered three different types of password-protected encryption over the years, called WEP, WPA, and WPA2. If it's available, choose the most modern, most secure one, which is WPA2.)

  You then have to enter the password when you first connect to that hotspot from each wireless PC on your network.

Note: You won't have to type this password every time you want to get onto your own network! Windows offers to memorize it for you.

- **Ban unwanted PCs.** Many routers include a feature that lets you limit network access to specific computers. Any PC that's not on the list won't be allowed in. The feature is called MAC address filtering, although it has nothing to do with Mac computers. (It stands for media access control, which is a serial number that uniquely identifies a piece of networking hardware.)

Not all routers can do this, and how you do it varies from router to router, so check the documentation. In a typical Linksys router, for example, you sign into the router's administrator screen using your web browser and then select Wireless→Wireless Network Access. On the screen full of empty boxes, type the MAC address of the PC that you want to be allowed to get onto the network.

Note: To find out the MAC address of a PC, press ■+R to open the Run dialog box. Type *cmd* and press Enter. Type *ipconfig/all*, and press Enter. In the resulting info screen, look for the Physical Address entry. That's the MAC address.

Type all the MAC addresses into the boxes on the Linksys router, click Save Settings, and you're all done.

- **Place your router properly.** Placing your Wi-Fi router centrally in the house minimizes the "leaking" of the signal into the surrounding neighborhood.

Family Features (Parental Controls)

Many parents reasonably worry about the volatile mixture of kids+computers. They worry about kids spending too much time in front of the PC, rotting their brains instead of going outside to play stickball in the street like we did when we were their age, getting fresh air and sunshine. They worry that kids are playing disgusting, violent video games. They worry that kids are using programs they really shouldn't be using, corrupting themselves with apps like PowerPoint and Quicken. (That's a joke.)

Above all, parents worry that their kids might encounter upsetting material on the internet: violence, pornography, hate speech, illegal drug sites, and so on.

Fortunately, Windows comes with parental controls that give you a fighting chance at keeping this stuff off your PC: "Microsoft family features." They're easy to use and impressively complete.

Specifically, there are four features to protect your youngsters:

- **Blocking inappropriate websites** from their impressionable eyes.
- **Setting daily time limits** on their computer, Xbox, and phone use.
- **Monitoring which programs they're using,** and limiting games and apps they buy from the Microsoft Store.
- **Sending you activity reports so you know what they're up to.** Each week, you'll get emailed a report for each of your kids that summarizes which websites they've visited, what words they've searched for online, how much time they spent on the computer each day, which programs and games they've used this week, and what apps they've downloaded from the Microsoft Store.

Setting Up Family Features

Before you can set up parental controls, some housekeeping is required. You, the parent, are presumably in charge of the computer and should therefore have an administrator account (page 536). And it must be password-protected; if it's not, then the kid whose innocence you're trying to preserve can just sign in as you and turn parental controls off.

Your child, on the other hand, must have what Microsoft calls a child account (Figure 11-6). And it has to be a Microsoft account, meaning that it's stored online, not on your computer.

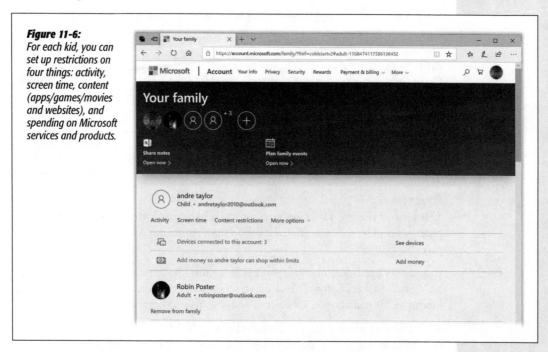

Figure 11-6:
For each kid, you can set up restrictions on four things: activity, screen time, content (apps/games/movies and websites), and spending on Microsoft services and products.

The process of creating that account gets pretty intrusive; you'll have to supply your phone number, provide a credit card number, agree to a 50-cent charge, decline Microsoft's offer to sell your kid's information to advertisers, and approve of an agreement that talks about what kinds of personal information about your kid will be exposed online (especially in Xbox land).

In any case, the step-by-steps for creating a child account begin on page 538.

Once you've created a child account, you can turn on the parental controls in the Windows Security app, among other places. In Windows Security, choose "Family options," and then choose "View family settings."

You land on a special page on the Microsoft website where you can set up the guardrails for your youngster.

Note: If this is your first time setting up family protection, hit "Create a family group." You're asked to enroll your family members, one by one. Each one requires a Microsoft account and a cellphone number or email address, which Microsoft will use to invite them to join the family. The following pages assume you've already added your family-mates to the group.

The main screen is a list of your family members (Figure 11-6).

Tip: In the "More options" drop-down menu, you'll find a "Remove from family" command, which you might use in the event of a *really* ugly rebellious-teen episode.

Select a kid's name to open his main screen. Here are your options, arranged as headings across the screen:

Activity

On this screen, you see your youngster's recent activity: a complete list of web searches, websites visited, apps and games used, and total amount of screen time. You can also turn off activity tracking (or just the weekly email reports).

Tip: This screen even tallies your kid's phone time, provided that it's an Android phone and that you've installed the Microsoft Launcher app on it.

Screen time

This feature (Figure 11-7) lets you control when your little tyke can use the computer—a much more automated method than constant "Why don't you go out and play?" nagging.

You can set up time limits independently for the Xbox and the PC, or you can turn on "Use one schedule for all devices" to set the same amount of screen time for both machines. (If you choose "One hour," that means one hour on *each* machine.)

You have two ways to limit this account holder's brain-rotting time: by total number of hours each day, or by specific times of the day (no computer on school nights, for example):

- **Hours of availability.** Click the graph to indicate the hours during which computer use is OK. You might create an early-morning and an after-school block, for example (Figure 11-7, bottom).

- **Time limits.** Use the "Time limit" pop-up menu to specify a total screen-time maximum for each day of the week *within* the "available" hours. No more than three hours on school days, for example (cumulatively). Of course, these limits apply only to this one computer.

Your rugrats won't be able to sign in outside of the permitted hours. And if they're signed in when the time block ends, they get a "time remaining" warning or two, and then they're dumped off, with a message that they're out of time. (Their programs and windows remain open in the background, in suspended animation until the next approved time slot.)

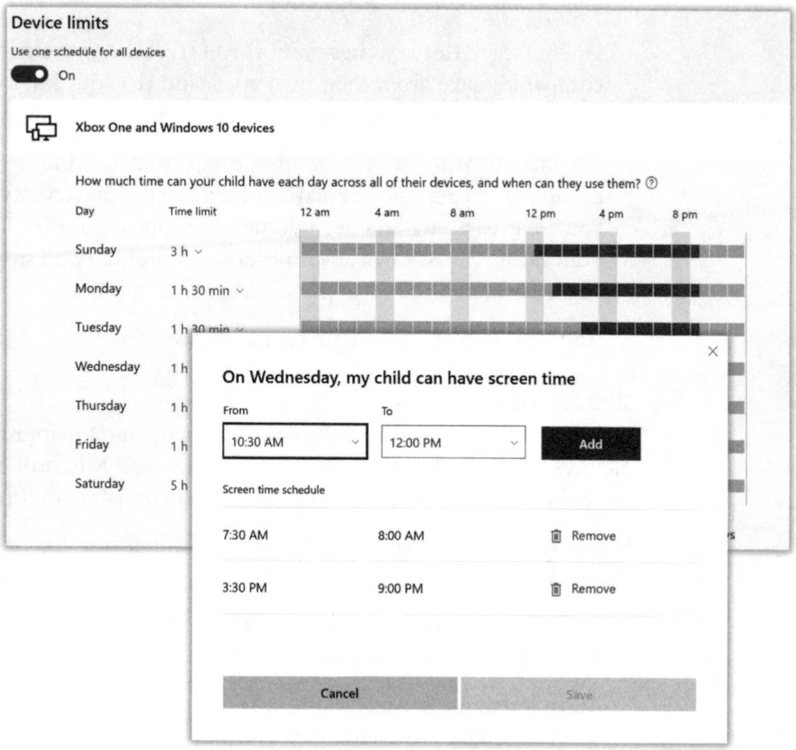

Figure 11-7:
For each kid, you can set up two kinds of time restrictions. First, you can set up various windows during the day when the PC or Xbox is available for use. Second, you can establish how much total screen time the kid can use during those hours.

Content restrictions

This option offers some very simple protections from having your youngsters go nuts on the Microsoft Store, or experiencing violent or sexy games or movies:

- **Ask a parent.** If you turn on "Needs adult approval to buy things" for a child account, your tiny tot won't be able to download anything from the Microsoft Store without your OK. (The approval-seeking process is electronic and instantaneous and can be long-distance.) You may also want to turn on "Email me when my child gets stuff," for extra Big Brotherishness.

- **Block inappropriate apps, games & media** lets you prevent your kid from playing anything Microsoft deems to be a mature game or movie, without your approval.

  Use the pop-up menu ("Allow apps and games rated for") to limit apps by age—for example, if you choose "10-year-olds," then your little darling can download and play anything intended for 10 and under. (To see what game-industry ratings these ages correspond to, choose "View allowed ratings.")

If your child tries to open a program that's off-limits, you'll be notified and given a chance to OK it or block it. (Your choices will be reflected in the "Always allowed" and "Always blocked" lists here.)

Of course, all this assumes that (a) you trust the age ratings the game and movie companies have given their own apps, and (b) your kid won't try to play any of the thousands of games that do *not* come from the Microsoft Store.

Fortunately, you have two more tools at your disposal: You can block an app or a game *after* your kid has played it. On the Recent Activity screen for your child, you see everything he's been doing on Windows 10 PCs. The beauty is that you, even sitting across town at your office, can monitor and stop stuff that upsets you. Click Block to block an app or a website, on the spot.

And then hope that the damage hasn't been done.

Web browsing

Web filtering prevents your youngsters from opening inappropriate websites—dirty pictures, hate speech, and so on. You can either trust Microsoft's ever-evolving "blacklist" of known naughty sites, or you can add individual web addresses to the blocked list.

Here's where you can control what happens when your kid tries to surf the web on a Windows 10 machine:

- **Block inappropriate websites.** This is the master on/off switch for filtering. (And who decides what's inappropriate? Microsoft.)

- **Add a website you want to allow.** Your little ragamuffin is allowed to use any sites whose addresses you add here.

- **Add a website you want to block.** And she's *not* allowed to visit any sites whose addresses you add *here*.

By the way: This feature works only in Microsoft's browsers, Edge and Internet Explorer. So what stops your kid from just using Chrome or Firefox to download porn? This feature also blocks access to those other browsers! (You can, of course, scroll up to the "Apps, games and media" area and unblock them. They show up once your kid has, in fact, attempted to open them.)

Spending

Here you can add money to your kids' Microsoft account (good for buying games and apps online), and review what they've bought.

Find my child

You've heard of "Find my Phone"? Well, now you can see the current location of your lost offspring on a map. Unfortunately, it works only in the unlikely event that he (a) owns a Windows phone, or (b) owns an Android phone with the Microsoft Launcher app installed.

Privacy from Windows

As you're probably aware, privacy is a big thing these days. Facebook, Google, and other companies have sheepishly admitted that they've been harvesting insane amounts of data about their customers—and, in some cases, selling it in unsavory ways.

Therefore, Microsoft has gone to great lengths to reveal the kinds of information it collects from you, to allow you to shut off this collection, and even to let you delete the data it's collected so far.

To see all this, choose ■→⚙→Privacy. Here's what you'll find.

General

These on/off switches govern the kinds of information about you that's sent to Microsoft (Figure 11-8).

- **Let apps use advertising ID.** Ordinarily, you're identified (not by name, but by a serial number) to advertisers who pay Microsoft for this kind of data. As a result, if you download a lot of trout-fishing apps, you might begin to see more ads for fishing gear within apps. (This option has nothing to do with websites; it affects ads displayed *within apps*. There aren't many of those. Yet.)

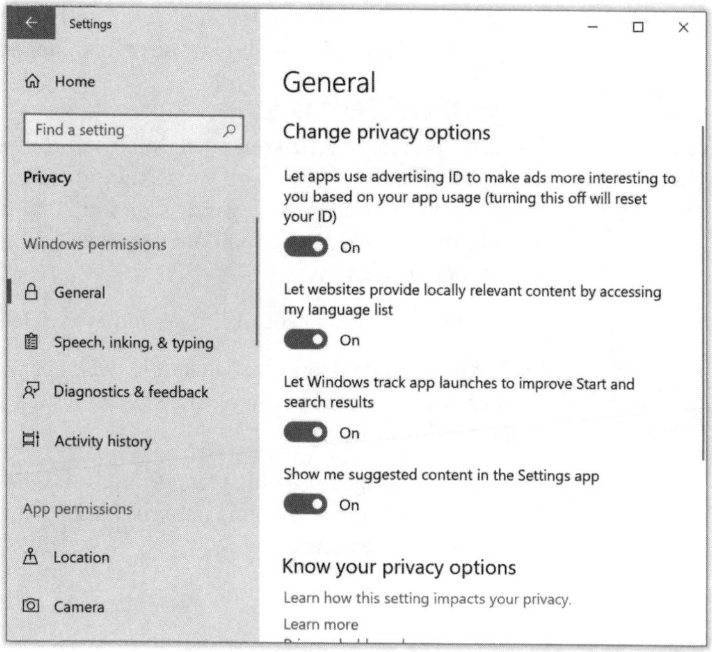

Figure 11-8:
Nowadays, you get two sets of controls: one that offers protections against Windows' own data harvesting, and another for blockades against your apps' data grabs.

If you turn this option off, your app data won't be shared with advertisers—and you'll see general ads within your apps, rather than ads tailored to the sorts of interests you seem to have.

- **Let websites provide locally relevant content by accessing my language list.** Websites may tailor the kinds of information they show you, based on the languages you've enabled on your machine. For example, if you've turned on French, then some sites might display their articles in French, for your convenience, or they might show you news stories about French-speaking countries.

- **Let Windows track app launches to improve Start and search results.** When you open the ⊞ menu and start typing the name of an app to search for it, the apps that Windows thinks you most likely want appear at the top of the results list. This option provides the data to help it make that determination; this data also shapes the "Most used" apps list (page 27).

- **Show me suggested content in the Settings app.** Microsoft says your various Settings panes may occasionally display little bits of text that help you "discover new features within Settings, or suggest new content and apps you may find interesting." Few people have actually witnessed this feature in action, but in any case, here's the Off switch.

Speech, Inking, & Typing

To improve the accuracy of speech recognition and handwriting recognition, Microsoft analyzes your voice and handwriting, which of course means collecting data from you. You can turn all this off here, but you will no longer be able to speak to Cortana, and the accuracy of Windows' autocomplete typing suggestions and handwriting recognition will decline, because those will no longer be personalized to your style.

Diagnostics & Feedback

Like any operating-system purveyor, Microsoft routinely collects behind-the-scenes records of what's happening on your PC (and millions of others). All of this data is collected and poured into a gigantic data soup that Microsoft's engineers can study to find patterns—and thereby eliminate crashes, make things faster, and improve the next Windows versions.

This dashboard lets you control, view, and even delete this stuff:

- **Diagnostic data.** Here you can specify whether you want only Basic data sent to Microsoft (what PC you have and whether it's OK) or Full data (what you've been *doing* on your PC).

- **Improve inking and typing recognition.** Is it OK to send anonymized records of your handwriting and typing patterns back to the mother ship, so Microsoft can improve future accuracy?

- **Tailored experiences.** Suppose you've said it's OK for Microsoft to collect some of this data. Is it OK for the company to *use* that data to shape the tips and ads it shows you?

- **Diagnostic data viewer.** For the first time, you can see the data Microsoft is collecting from your PC, using this option. Hit "Diagnostic Data Viewer" to download the free app required to show it to you.

  Hint: Unless you're a programmer, it won't mean much to you. Unless this is your kind of nonfiction reading:

```
"name": "Microsoft.Windows.Graphics.D3D11.CreateDevice"
"time": "2019-05-04T10:03:41.6305563Z"
"iKey": "o:0a89d516ae714e01ae89c96d185e9ae3"
"flags": 257
```

- **Delete diagnostic data.** As an even more generous act of self-sacrifice, Microsoft is now willing to let you delete whatever data it's collected from your PC, with a quick click or tap on this button.

- **Feedback frequency.** Very occasionally—verging on never, in fact—Windows might display a dialog box asking you to rate some app or feature. Here you can shut off those queries, or adjust (up or down) how often Windows is allowed to ask.

Activity History

You know how Windows can resume the activity (like web browsing) you were recently pursuing on a different Windows device? To pull that off, it has to monitor what you were *doing* on your other devices; these are the on/off switches.

Similarly, the Timeline (page 210) is designed to show tiles for the apps and documents you've worked on using *all* your machines, all your accounts. Here you can turn certain Microsoft accounts off, hiding them from the Timeline.

Finally, there's a link here that takes you to the Microsoft web page, where you can investigate or erase all the activity Microsoft has collected about you.

Privacy from Your Apps

The miracle of the modern app is that it can help you in astounding ways. By analyzing your data, your movements, and your computer, it can make you more efficient and save you a lot of steps.

For example, a movie app can tell you which movies are playing nearby—because it has learned *where you are* by consulting your tablet's GPS. Or an email program can autocomplete somebody's email address, saving you time—because it has consulted your People app.

But plenty of people are creeped out by the notion of software following their movements around town, tracking the websites they visit, or even listening to their world through the built-in microphone.

Fortunately, the ⊞→⚙→Privacy screen offers individual on/off switches that shut down your apps' access to every conceivable shred of useful data about you and your PC. Here's what the tabs do on that screen.

Location

This item (Figure 11-9) is generally intended for tablets and laptops—computers that get moved around. It refers to apps that function best if they know where you are: a movie-listing app, for example, that can show you what's playing at local theaters.

Of course, letting such apps know where you are also means that your location might get transmitted to the software companies that wrote those apps. Here's where you can take control of the whole process:

- **Allow access to location on this device.** Hit Change, and then the on/off switch, to shut off location tracking for your computer: all apps, all accounts (administrator account required).

- **Allow apps to access your location.** This switch is the master on/off switch for giving your *apps* access to your location. Turn it off, and all the apps listed lower

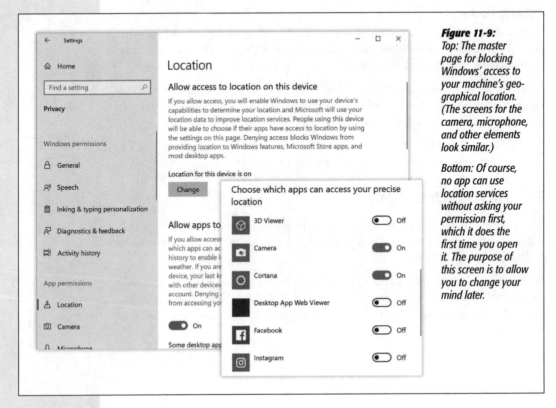

Figure 11-9:
Top: The master page for blocking Windows' access to your machine's geographical location. (The screens for the camera, microphone, and other elements look similar.)

Bottom: Of course, no app can use location services without asking your permission first, which it does the first time you open it. The purpose of this screen is to allow you to change your mind later.

down on this screen turn off simultaneously. Turn it on, and you can adjust them individually. (This control, unlike the first one, is available independently to every account holder on this PC. You, the paranoid, might want location services shut off; your spouse, who likes Uber to know where to send the driver, might prefer it on.)

Tip: There's a tile for the identical function on your Quick Actions center (page 97).

- **Default location.** What location should Windows and your programs use if they can't figure out where you really are?

- **Location history.** Windows stores your location for 24 hours on the PC; during that time, apps that need to know where you are (a weather app, Lyft) can access it. But if you've been somewhere shady, and you're running for Congress, you can hit Clear to delete that data for now.

- **Choose which apps.** Finally, the main event: On/off switches for each app's access to your location (Figure 11-9, bottom).

- **Geofencing.** Some apps turn features on and off only when you're within a speci-fied geographic area (a geofence). Apps that remind you when you get to a loca-tion ("Pick up milk when you're near the grocery"), provide discounts at specific stores or attractions, or "check in" at certain locales all rely on the geofence feature.

  This item tells you whether or not any of your apps are using a geofence—not that there's anything you can do about it.

Camera, Microphone, Contacts, Calendar...

Many items on this Settings screen list the various parts of your machine—both hardware features and apps like the Calendar and People apps—that various apps might want to access.

Each of these panels offers controls that mimic the Location options already described:

- **Allow access on this device.** This is the master Off switch for all apps, all accounts—your entire PC. Administrative privileges required.

- **Allow apps.** Then comes the master switch for just your account. "No app is going to use *my* camera!" you might declare, when you've had a particularly rough night.

- **Choose which apps.** Then comes the list of apps that seek to use this component of your computer, complete with on/off switches.

The panels that follow this model include Camera, Microphone, Voice activation (apps listening for spoken commands), Notifications, Account info, Contacts, Calendar, Phone calls, Email, Tasks (to-do list), Messaging, Documents, Pictures, Videos, and File system (the ability to access any files at all).

A few other items on this list are missing the "on/off for the entire computer" con-trol—you get only an on/off switch for your account, plus control over individual apps. These items include Radios (Bluetooth, Wi-Fi, and cellular, if you have it), Other devices (mainly, advertising "beacons" in stores), Background apps (which apps are allowed to run in the background), and App diagnostics.

Note: For many of these screens, the "Choose which apps can access" list is probably empty on your machine. That's because you don't have any apps that seek to access the corresponding component of your computer.

Part Four:
Hardware and Peripherals

4

Tablets, Laptops & Hybrids

I f its recent experiments with Windows show anything at all, it's that Microsoft is betting on the future of mobile. Fewer and fewer computers will be tethered to desks. More and more will be carried around—and most of them will have touchscreens. Microsoft believes that so strongly that it's designing all its new apps to have big, fat, widely spaced buttons for finger touches.

But touchscreen friendliness isn't the only nod Windows 10 makes to easing the lives of road warriors. This chapter covers a motley collection of additional tools for anyone who travels.

Battery Saver

It's common for smartphones to have a battery-saver mode. That's where the phone, upon dropping to a low level of battery remaining, switches off a lot of nonessential background activities and features to save power. The screen dims, there are fewer animations, email and Facebook don't get checked in the background—all in the name of extending your phone's battery long enough to get you through the day.

And now the same feature comes to Windows laptops and tablets.

You can turn it on manually by opening the Action Center (■+A, or tap ▢ on the taskbar, or swipe in from the right on a touchscreen) and hitting "Battery saver."

Or you can wait until your battery hits 20 percent remaining, which is when Battery Saver kicks in automatically.

In Battery Saver mode, your screen dims (screen brightness is one of the biggest power drains). Apps running in the background go to sleep. You don't get notifications from apps. Things generally calm down and slow down, and your battery lasts a lot longer.

You can adjust or override most of those features, by the way. In ■→۞→System→ Battery, you can fiddle with these switches (Figure 12-1):

- **Turn battery saver on automatically…** If you turn off this switch, you can still use Battery Saver—but you'll have to turn it on yourself.

- **[percentage slider].** Battery Saver likes to kick in when your battery charge hits 20 percent. But using this slider, you can change that threshold. You can set it to anything from 5 percent to 100 percent. (100 percent would mean "on all the time.")

- **Battery saver status until next charge.** This option is available only when you're actually running on battery, and it means "Turn off Battery Saver when I plug in."

- **Lower screen brightness while in battery saver.** What if you can't stand your screen dimming? You can turn off that aspect of Battery Saver here (but of course you won't get as much battery savings).

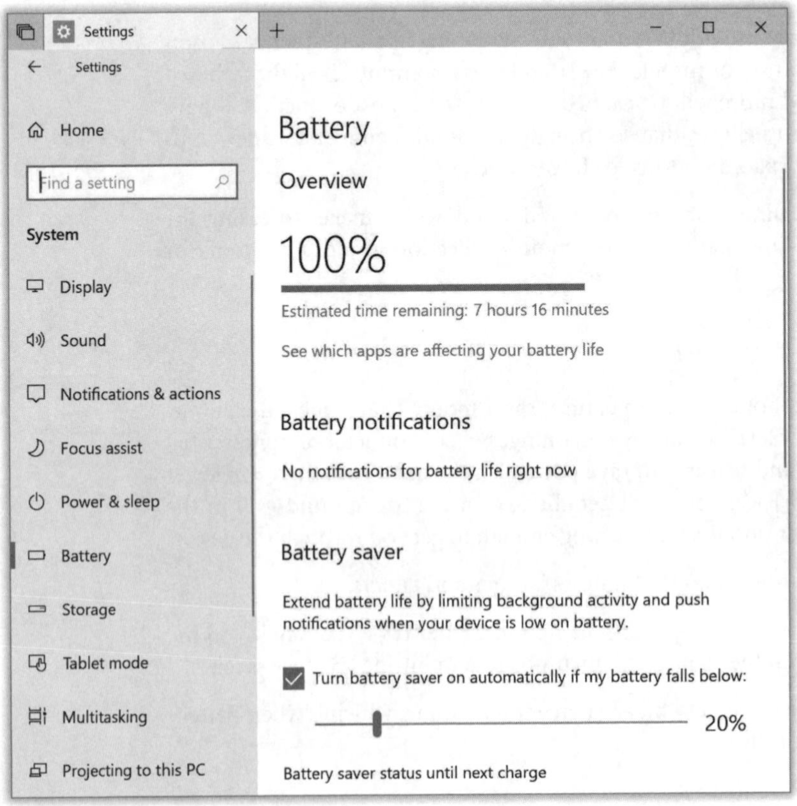

Figure 12-1:
Here it is, expressed as a percentage, in huge numbers: your current battery charge.

If Windows has anything to tell you about your battery (for example, that it needs replacing), you'll see it here, under "Battery notifications."

"Battery saving tips" takes you to Microsoft's web page for battery-saving suggestions.

Battery Detective Work

Windows 10 also offers a screen that sleuths out which apps have been eating up the most power in the hours, day, or week. It's all waiting on ■▪→⚙→System→Battery; choose "See which apps are affecting your battery life."

This screen (Figure 12-2) shows exactly which apps are gulping down the most power. You can specify the time period you're seeing: "6 hours," "24 hours," or "1 week." And you can limit the list to "Apps with usage" (programs you've actually used since the last charge), "All apps," or "Always allowed apps."

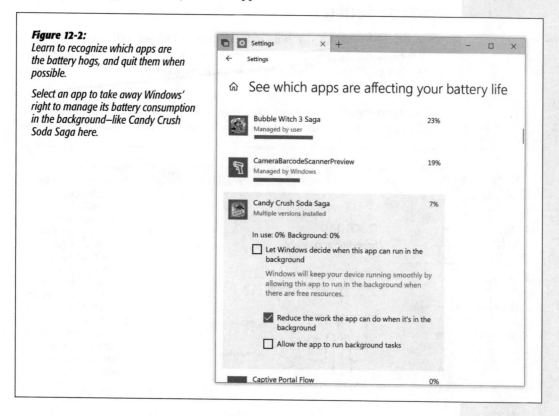

Figure 12-2:
Learn to recognize which apps are the battery hogs, and quit them when possible.

Select an app to take away Windows' right to manage its battery consumption in the background—like Candy Crush Soda Saga here.

So what are "Allowed apps"?

Windows prefers to manage your apps' battery usage all by itself. For example, when an app is in the background, Windows might throttle it (slow it down) whenever a foreground app needs to do some processing.

But you can override Windows' control of your apps, thus turning them into "allowed apps." They're programs that are allowed to keep running at full power in the background, even in Battery Saver mode.

To do that, on this screen, select an app's name to expand its details panel (Figure 12-2). Turn off "Let Windows decide." You're giving this app full reign to run at full speed and power, battery be damned.

Some apps (from the Microsoft Store) offer other checkboxes, like "Reduce the work the app can do when it's in the background" and "Allow the app to run background tasks." They give you even more control—and take even more control away from Windows' own app-management smarts.

Trackpad Settings

If your laptop has a trackpad (hint: it does), then visit ■■→⚙→Devices→Touchpad (Figure 12-3). It's the control center for trackpad settings. They vary by trackpad, but here's what you'll find on one of Microsoft's Surface tablets (which has a "precision touchpad"):

- **Touchpad on/off.** Yes, you can actually turn off your trackpad. You might do that when you've got a mouse connected, so you don't hit the trackpad by mistake and

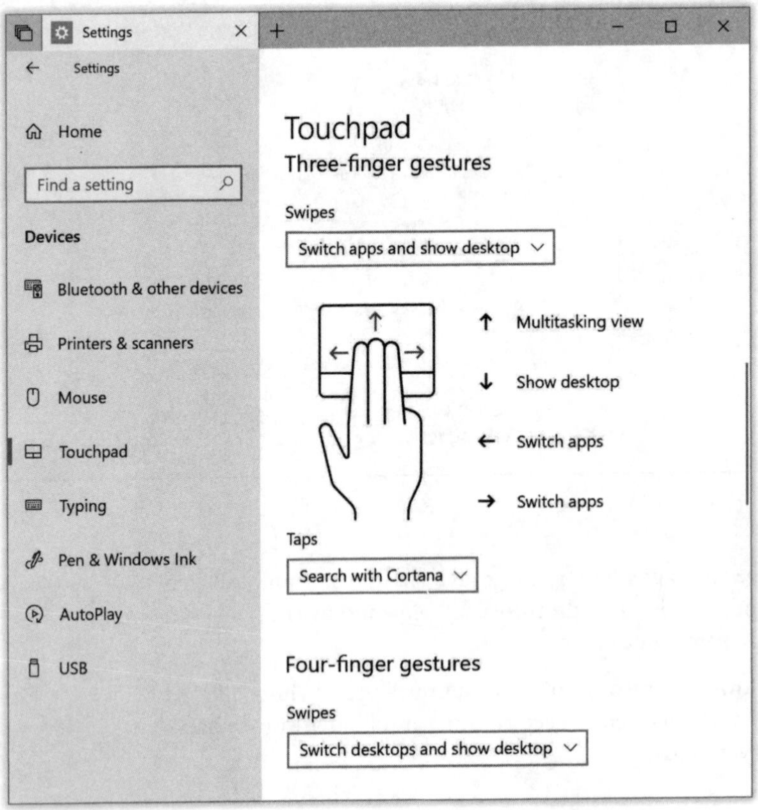

Figure 12-3:
The Swipes drop-down menu offers canned sets of gestures for swiping multiple fingers up, down, left, or right. For example, if you choose "Switch apps and show desktop," then (as the diagram indicates) swiping left or right with three fingers switches apps; three fingers upward opens the Timeline, and three fingers down reveals the desktop.

trigger errant clicks. Then again, just turning off "Leave touchpad on when a mouse is connected" is a more efficient way of addressing that problem.

- **Change the cursor speed.** At the lowest setting, sliding your finger across the entire trackpad barely budges the pointer; at the highest, the cursor screams across the entire screen with barely a hint of finger movement (which might be handy if you have a huge monitor).

- **Touchpad sensitivity.** You get four options for clicking, right-clicking, and selecting, from "Most sensitive" to "Low sensitivity." If you find yourself accidentally triggering clicks while you're typing, then choose a lower setting.

- **Taps.** Modern trackpads are *multitouch*, meaning they can detect more than one simultaneous finger touch. They therefore permit all kinds of cool shortcuts, which you can turn on and off here. You might have "Tap with two fingers to right-click" turned on, for example. This is also where you can designate the lower-right corner of your trackpad as the "right-click" button. (Or, if you find yourself *accidentally* triggering right-clicks, you can turn these checkboxes off.)

- **Scroll and zoom.** The most involved settings here relate to two-finger scrolling, which—along with mouse scroll wheels—has made scroll bars largely obsolete. Out of the box, "reverse scrolling" is enabled: You drag two fingers *up* the trackpad, and the page scrolls *up*. That seems logical if you're used to scrolling on a tablet or a smartphone, but it feels backward for longtime scroll-bar lovers. Fortunately, you can reverse the scrolling direction by choosing "Down motion scrolls down" here.

- **Pinch to zoom.** This feature works just as it does on a phone, at least in some apps (Photos, Edge, Microsoft Office apps, and a few others): Draw two fingers together on the trackpad to zoom out of a photo or document, or spread two fingers apart to zoom in (magnify).

- **Three-finger gestures, Four-finger gestures.** If your laptop offers these choices, and you're willing to put in the time to learn them, they can make you much faster on your laptop, because your trackpad hand never needs to leave its home base (to use the keyboard, for example). See Figure 12-3.

  You can even specify what happens when you *tap* with three fingers (or four fingers). For example, you might use the drop-down menu to choose Search with Cortana or Action Center, making one of those functions just a three-finger tap away.

- **Reset your touchpad.** If you've made a mess of these controls, this button restores the factory settings.

Getting Online

There are all kinds of ways to get onto the internet these days:

- **Wi-Fi.** Wireless hotspots, known as Wi-Fi, are glorious conveniences, especially if you have a laptop, tablet, or hybrid. Without stirring from your hotel bed, you're online at high speed. Sometimes for free.

- **Ethernet.** The beauty of Ethernet connections—that is, *wires*—is that they're superfast and supersecure. No bad guys sitting across the coffee shop, armed with shareware "sniffing" software, can intercept your email and chat messages, as they theoretically can when you're on wireless.

  Connecting to an Ethernet network is usually as simple as connecting the cable to the computer. That's it. You're online, quickly and securely, and you never have to worry about connecting or disconnecting.

  Most broadband wired connections require no setup whatsoever. Take a new PC out of the box, plug the Ethernet cable into your cable modem, and you can begin surfing the web instantly. That's because most cable modems, DSL boxes, and wireless base stations use DHCP. It stands for "dynamic host configuration protocol," but what it means is "We'll fill in your Network Control Panel automatically." (Including techie specs like IP and DNS Server addresses.)

  If for some reason you're not able to surf the web or check email the first time you try, it's remotely possible that your broadband modem or your office network doesn't offer DHCP. In that case, you may have to fiddle with the network settings manually. For details, see the free PDF appendix called "Deep-Seated Networking Options." It's on this book's "Missing CD" at *missingmanuals.com*.

- **Cellular modems.** A few well-heeled individuals enjoy the go-anywhere bliss of USB cellular modems, which get them online just about anywhere they can make a phone call. These modems are offered by Verizon, Sprint, AT&T, and so on, and usually cost $60 a month.

  To make the connection, turn on the cellular gadget (phone, MiFi, whatever). After about 20 seconds, the name of your private Wi-Fi hotspot shows up in the list, as shown in Figure 12-4.

POWER USERS' CLINIC

Secret Hotspots

It's entirely possible to be standing right in the middle of a juicy, strong Wi-Fi hotspot—and not even know it. It turns out that the hotspot's owner can choose whether or not it should broadcast its name. Sometimes, he might want to keep the hotspot secret—to restrict its use to employees at a coffee shop, for example, so the customer riffraff can't slow it down. In these cases, you'd have to know (a) that the hotspot exists, and (b) what its name is.

Sometimes you see "Unidentified network" right there in the list of available hotspots. If so, great—select it, enter the name and password, and off you go.

If not, open the Network and Sharing Center (Control Panel→Network and Internet→Network and Sharing Center). Select "Set up a new connection or network." On the next screen, choose "Manually connect to a wireless network," and then hit Next.

Now enter the network's exact name and password. You'll probably want to turn on "Start this connection automatically," too, if you think you might encounter the hotspot again.

When you click Next, you'll get a notification that you've successfully connected (if, in fact, you have).

- **Mobile Hotspot.** Tethering, what Microsoft calls Mobile Hotspot, is letting your cellphone act as a glorified internet antenna for your PC, whether connected by a cable or a Bluetooth wireless link. See page 446.

- **Dial-up modems.** It's true: Some people still connect to the internet using a modem that dials out over ordinary phone lines. They get cheap service but slow connections, and their numbers are shrinking. High-speed internet is where it's at, baby!

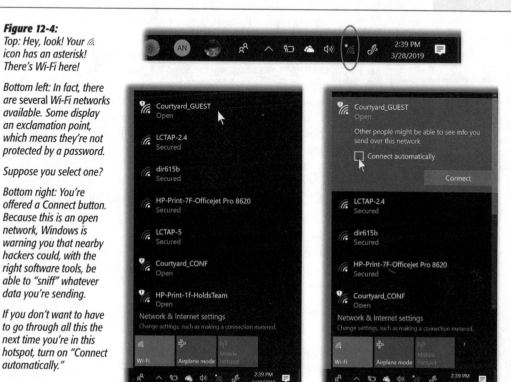

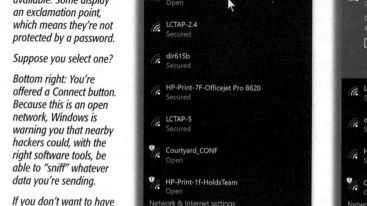

Figure 12-4:

Top: Hey, look! Your 🛜 icon has an asterisk! There's Wi-Fi here!

Bottom left: In fact, there are several Wi-Fi networks available. Some display an exclamation point, which means they're not protected by a password.

Suppose you select one?

Bottom right: You're offered a Connect button. Because this is an open network, Windows is warning you that nearby hackers could, with the right software tools, be able to "sniff" whatever data you're sending.

If you don't want to have to go through all this the next time you're in this hotspot, turn on "Connect automatically."

Connecting to a Wi-Fi Hotspot

Almost every computer today has a built-in Wi-Fi antenna, officially known as 802.11 (Wi-Fi) wireless networking technology. Wi-Fi can communicate with a wireless base station up to 300 feet away, much like a cordless phone. Doing so lets you surf the web from your laptop in a hotel room, for example, or share files with someone across the building from you.

Sometimes you just want to join a friend's Wi-Fi network. Sometimes you've got time to kill in an airport or on a plane that has Wi-Fi, and it's worth a $7 splurge for half an hour. And sometimes, at some street corners in big cities, Wi-Fi signals bleeding out of apartment buildings might give you a choice of several free hotspots to join.

If you're in a new place, and Windows discovers, on its own, that you're in a Wi-Fi hotspot, then the *(i. icon sprouts an asterisk. And where is the *(i. icon? It's in two places:

- **On the taskbar** (Figure 12-4, top).

- **On the Quick Actions panel** (hit the ▭ icon on the taskbar).

Figure 12-4 shows you how to proceed. Along the way, you'll be offered the "Connect automatically" checkbox; if you turn it on, you'll spare yourself all this clicking the next time your PC is in range. It'll just hop on that network by itself.

Tip: If you point to the *(i. taskbar icon without clicking, you see the network's name. And if you right-click the icon, you get links to a troubleshooting app and the Network & Internet Settings pane.)

Most hotspots these days are protected by a password. It serves two purposes: First, it keeps everyday schlumps from hopping onto that network; second, it encrypts the connection so hackers armed with sniffing software can't intercept the data you're sending and receiving.

When You Can't Get On

There are a bunch of reasons why your *(i. icon might indicate that you're in a hotspot, but you can't actually get online:

- **It's locked.** If the hotspot's icon doesn't have an exclamation point (*(i.), then the hotspot is password-protected. That's partly to prevent hackers from "sniffing" the transmissions and intercepting messages, and partly to keep random passersby like you off the network. Anyway, you need the password.

- **The signal isn't strong enough.** Sometimes the Wi-Fi signal is strong enough to make the hotspot's name show up, but not strong enough for an actual connection.

- **You're not on the list.** Sometimes, for security, hotspots are rigged to permit only specific computers to join, and yours isn't one of them.

- **You haven't signed in yet.** Commercial hotspots (the ones you have to pay for) don't connect you to the internet until you've supplied your payment details on a special web page that appears automatically when you open your browser.

- **The router's on, but the internet's not connected.** Sometimes wireless routers are broadcasting, but their internet connection is down. It'd be like a cordless phone that has a good connection back to the base station in the kitchen—but the phone cord isn't plugged into the base station.

Memorized Hotspots

If you turned on "Connect automatically," then whenever your laptop enters this hotspot, it will connect to the network automatically. You don't have to do any tapping at all. Behind the scenes, Windows is capable of piling up quite a list of these hotspots, representing a bread-crumb trail of the hotspots you've used at every hotel, airport, coffee shop, and buddy's house.

You're welcome to peek at this list at any time—and to clean it out, purging the hotspots you'll never need again. To see it, proceed as shown in Figure 12-5.

Figure 12-5:
To see your PC's memorized Wi-Fi hotspots, open ■→⚙→Network & Internet→Wi-Fi; choose "Manage known networks."

To remove a memorized hotspot, choose its name and then Forget.

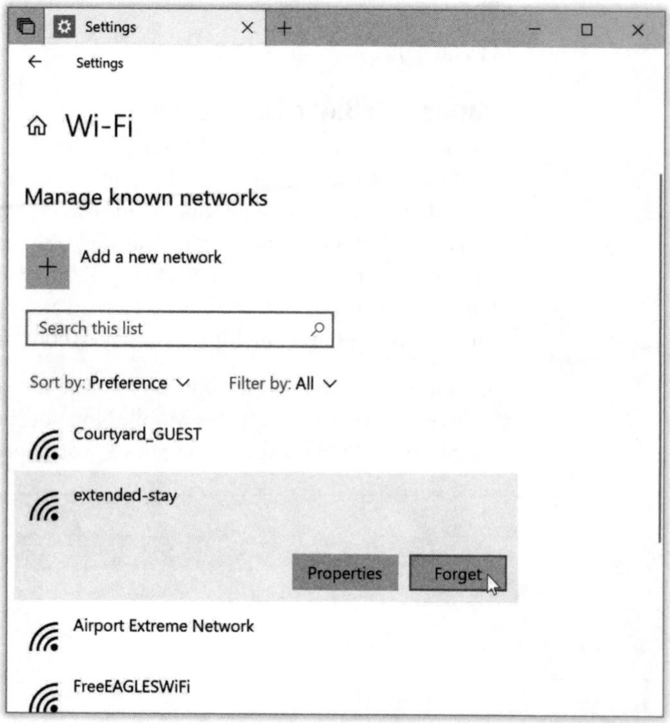

Commercial Hotspots

Choosing the name of the hotspot you want to join is generally all you have to do—if it's a home Wi-Fi network.

Unfortunately, joining a commercial hotspot—one that requires a credit card number (in a hotel room or an airport, for example)—requires more than just connecting to it. You also have to sign into it before you can send so much as a single email message.

To do that, open your browser. You see the "Enter payment information" screen either immediately or as soon as you try to open a web page of your choice. (Even at free hotspots, you might have to click OK on a welcome page to initiate the connection.)

Supply your credit card information or (if you have a membership to this Wi-Fi chain, like Boingo or T-Mobile) your name and password. Click Submit or Proceed, try not to contemplate how this $8 per hour is pure profit for somebody, and enjoy your surfing.

The Mobile Hotspot

Here's a wild concept that may take your brain a moment to comprehend. The Mobile Hotspot feature (sometimes called Internet Sharing, or tethering) lets one computer broadcast its internet connection to any other nearby machines over Wi-Fi. The first computer can be online over an Ethernet wire, using a cellular connection, or even connected to Wi-Fi itself.

Let's take these scenarios one at a time.

Sharing a Cellular Connection

Suppose your Windows 10 tablet or laptop has a cellular modem inside. It can provide its cellular internet signal to nearby computers—laptops, for example. The nice part is that they can therefore get online almost anywhere there's cell coverage. The less-nice part is that the connection isn't always blazing fast, and you have to pay your cell company for the privilege. (It's usually $20 or $30 on top of your regular monthly phone plan; for that, you're allowed to send and receive, say, 2 gigabytes of data each month. If you go over the limit, you pay overage fees. Good luck with that.)

Here's a typical example: Suppose you have a cellular Surface Pro tablet. You open ■→⚙→Network & Internet→Mobile Hotspot (Figure 12-6). You turn it on. Where it says "Share my Internet connection from," you choose the Surface's cellular connection.

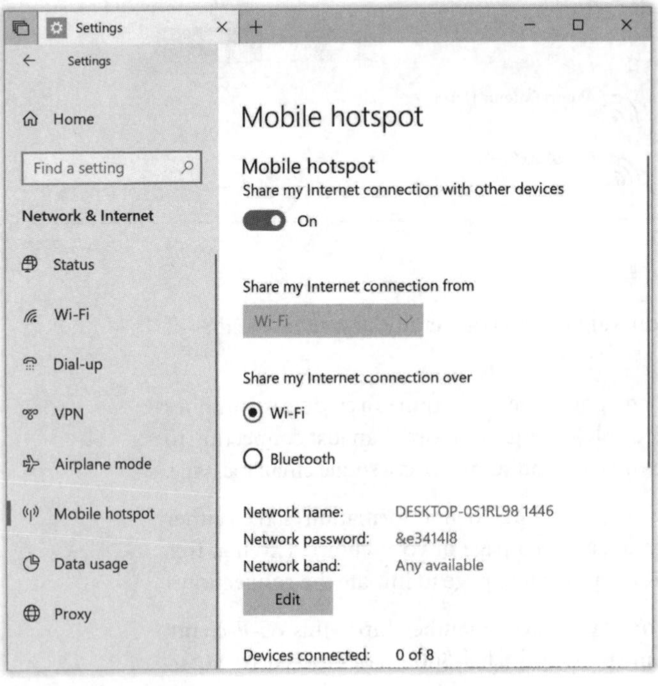

Figure 12-6:
"Mobile Hotspot" means creating a Wi-Fi network from your internet-connected computer for nearby Wi-Fi gadgets to enjoy. It doesn't matter how the primary computer is getting its internet connection, which can be super-handy.

You make note of your homemade hotspot's name and the password Windows makes up for it. (Or hit Edit and make up your own name and password.)

Tip: In the future, on the machine doing the broadcasting, you can start or stop the internet sharing by clicking the Mobile Hotspot tile on the Action Center (page 97).

On your laptop, choose your Surface's name as you would any other Wi-Fi hotspot. Presto: Your laptop is online.

Now, tethering eats up your tablet's battery like crazy. So you probably shouldn't count on watching Netflix on your laptop via your tablet. But for email, emergency web checks, and other mobile crises, tethering is a convenient feature. And when you're on the road for a couple of weeks, it's a heck of a lot cheaper than paying your hotel $13 a night for Wi-Fi.

Sharing an Ethernet Connection

You can use Mobile Hotspot for a totally different scenario, too: when one computer has a wired Ethernet connection, and you'd like it to broadcast that signal to nearby machines over Wi-Fi. (This, of course, assumes the main computer also has Wi-Fi circuitry.) Your savings: one Wi-Fi router or repeater.

The steps are the same as described already—except, of course, that for "Share my Internet connection from," you choose Ethernet.

Sharing a Wi-Fi Connection

Why would anyone want to use the Mobile Hotspot feature to share their Wi-Fi internet connection with other computers—over Wi-Fi?

Here's a good reason: so only one person has to pay for the hotel's or airport's Wi-Fi. Other family members can slurp down a copy of that connection without having to pay again and again.

This time, of course, you'd choose Wi-Fi from the "Share my Internet connection from" drop-down menu.

Tip: If you have a Windows phone that you've paired with a PC—like a laptop—then you get a special treat. As long as both have Bluetooth turned on, and you've paired your phone with the laptop (page 251), then the laptop can turn on the previously established Mobile Hotspot feature on the phone *automatically*, by remote control, so you don't have to get up and slog across the room.

To make this happen, ensure that "Turn on remotely" is turned on. From now on, when you're on the laptop, you'll see the phone's mobile hotspot listed as an available Wi-Fi network. Just choose its name as usual, confident that it will turn itself on—and then off again, saving battery power, when you're finished.

Find My Device

There are very few feelings quite as sickening as realizing that you've left your laptop or tablet somewhere. Fortunately, Windows 10 has a feature that can help—if your lost machine still has power and is still online. If you suspect your machine has been stolen, you can even lock it remotely, signing off any accounts and ensuring that Location Services is turned on so you can track its movements.

None of this magic does you any good, however, unless Find My Device is turned on. That switch is in ■→⚙→Update & Security→"Find my device."

Later, when the devastating discovery strikes you, visit *account.microsoft.com/devices*.

Once you sign in, you arrive on the Devices page of your Microsoft account web page, which lists each of your machines (Figure 12-7, top). Open the missing machine to view its details screen (middle), hit "Find my device," and proceed as shown in Figure 12-7, bottom.

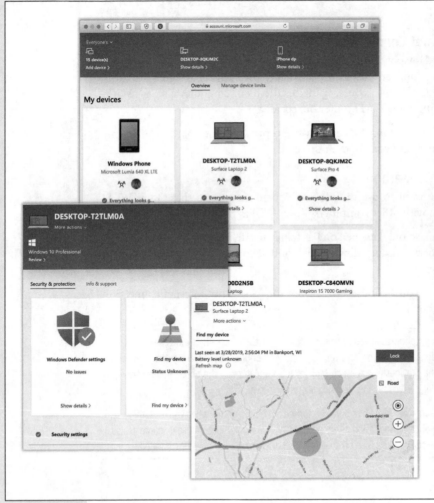

Figure 12-7:

Top: This website shows all your Windows gadgets, and even any iPhone and Android phones you've set up in the Your Phone app.

Middle: The details screen shows its current protection and location status.

Bottom: Even if your gadget is dead or off, this map shows its most recent location. Alas, you can't make it beep, display a message, erase itself, or change its password remotely. You can use the Lock button to remotely sign out of all accounts, display the Lock screen, and ensure that Location Services is turned on so you can track its movements. Good luck chasing it down.

For Hybrid PCs Only: Tablet Mode (Continuum)

No matter how hard Microsoft's engineers pound their heads against their conference-room tables, they can't make one thing change: Touchscreen devices are not the same as regular PCs. Your finger and a mouse are not the same thing. They have radically different degrees of precision.

But grafting together two completely different operating systems, as Microsoft did in Windows 8, was not the solution.

In Windows 10, Microsoft came up with a less drastic approach, designed for hybrid machines: tablets with detachable keyboards, like Microsoft's own Surface. The solution involves two parts:

- **Tablet mode.** In Tablet mode, you're pretty much back to Windows 8. The Start menu becomes the Start *screen*, filling the monitor. Every app runs in full-screen mode—no overlapping windows. The onscreen keyboard pops up automatically when you're in a place where you can type.

- **Continuum.** This simply means "Enters Tablet mode every time you detach the keyboard." Whenever you take your tablet out of its dock, or pull off its keyboard, or fold its keyboard behind the screen, the touch-friendly Tablet mode kicks in automatically.

Note: You can try out Tablet mode even if you don't have a touchscreen, although there's not much point to it. Tablet mode is designed to make Windows 10 more finger-friendly.

Here's what the two modes do.

Manual Tablet Mode

To turn on Tablet mode, hit the ▯ on your taskbar (or press ⊞+A) to open the Action Center, and then hit "Tablet mode."

Here's what you'll see:

- **Start menu.** The most dramatic change in Tablet mode is that the Start menu goes full-screen, as shown in Figure 12-8. But you still have access to your "All apps" menu (hit the ⊯ near the top-left corner), and you still have access to the left side of the Start menu (hit the ☰ at the top-left corner).

- **Taskbar.** You'll notice that the taskbar is a bit simpler, too. On the left, only four icons remain: the ⊞ button, a ← button (returns you to the Start menu from whatever app you're using), Cortana, and Task View/Timeline.

  The usual taskbar icons for open programs, and the programs you use often, are hidden.

Tip: You can bring them back, however. In ⊞→⚙→System→"Tablet mode," turn off "Hide app icons on the taskbar in tablet mode."

- **Apps full screen.** In Tablet mode, every app fills the entire screen. You can still split the screen as described on page 47, though.

- **A Close button.** Since every app fills the screen, you won't have much use for the Minimize and Maximize buttons. All that remains in the upper-right corner of an app window is the × button—and even that's hidden.

If you have a mouse or a trackpad, point to the top edge without clicking; you'll see a title bar slide into view, complete with the × you need to close the app.

On a touchscreen, drag your finger all the way down the screen, from above to below, in one smooth motion. You'll see the app follow, shrink, and disappear.

Figure 12-8:
The idea behind Tablet mode is to make Windows much easier to navigate with a finger. Tiny menus and tiny taskbar icons are mostly hidden.

If you buy a Windows tablet, in fact, it starts up in Tablet mode like this out of the box.

Auto-Tablet Mode

Now that you know about Tablet mode, Windows 10 has another offer: Would you like Tablet mode to start up *automatically* when you take away the keyboard?

(That question makes the most sense if you have a hybrid tablet—one whose keyboard comes off or flips around to the back. For best results, do not try ripping the keyboard off a *regular* laptop.)

Yes, this is the feature that Microsoft marketing executives call "Continuum," although that term does not actually appear in Windows.

In ▦→⚙→System→"Tablet mode," you have two sets of controls. The first set controls what happens when you sign into your account. (In other words, different people may see something different when they sign in.)

This drop-down menu offers you a choice of "Use tablet mode," "Use desktop mode," or "Use the appropriate mode for my hardware" (that is, use desktop mode if the keyboard is attached).

The second drop-down menu wants to know what happens when you attach or detach your hybrid's keyboard:

- **Nothing.** Choose "Don't ask me and don't switch."

- **Automatically switch to or from Tablet mode.** "Don't ask me and always switch."

- **Ask before switching.** This is the factory setting: When you detach or attach the keyboard, Windows asks if you want to pop into or out of Tablet mode.

And while you're here: Two switches let you opt to hide all the little app icons on your taskbar, or the entire taskbar itself, when you're in the Mode.

The Onscreen Keyboard

If your computer has a physical keyboard, or if your tablet has a removable one, great! But touchscreens generally don't have moving keys. That's why, whenever you tap in a spot where typing is required, you can summon the onscreen keyboard (Figure 12-9). Just hit the keyboard button on the system tray (lower right of your screen).

Note: If you don't see the keyboard icon, then right-click (or hold your finger down on) the taskbar; from the shortcut menu, choose "Show touch keyboard button."

In general, this keyboard works pretty much like any keyboard you've ever used, with a few exceptions:

- **The keys don't move.** Of course not—it's a piece of glass! The keys do everything they can, though, to tell you when they've been struck. They change color and make little sounds.

- **It has a symbol/number layout.** Two, actually. Tap the "&123" key to change all the letter keys into symbol keys: !, @, %, $, &, and so on. Tap the Ω to view a second set of them—less common symbols like ©, <, >, and other currency symbols and brackets. And a numeric keypad appears at the right end of the keyboard.

  To return to the regular alphabet keyboard, tap the "abc" key.

- **It's a shape-shifter.** See the little 🖼 icon at top left? It sprouts a choice of five icons: tablet keyboard, mini keyboard, split two-thumb keyboard, normal keyboard, and handwriting panel (see Figure 12-9).

- **It's also a Swype keyboard.** On phones, people love the Swype and SwiftKey keyboards; in these systems, you don't have to *tap* each key to spell out a word. Instead, you rapidly and sloppily drag your finger *across* the glass, hitting the letters you want and lifting your finger at the end of every word. The software figures out which word you were going for.

Sounds bizarre, but it's fast and very satisfying. And pretty—your finger leaves a sort of fire trail as it slides across the glass.

Believe it or not, all the keyboards on your touchscreen Windows 10 machine offer this swipe-to-type keyboard. Try it!

- **You can remove the margins.** Ordinarily, the keyboard stretches all the way across your screen. But the middle row of the pop-out panel circled in Figure 12-9 offers a slightly narrower one that eliminates the side margins. Once those margins are gone, you can drag the keyboard to wherever you want it on the screen.

Tip: The bottom row of that pop-out panel offers one-tap access to the Region & Language and Typing pages of Settings, described on pages 255 and 249.

- **It has emoji.** Tap the smiley-face key (☺) to change all the letters into a huge array of tiny smileys and other icons, also called emoticons or emoji (Figure 12-9,

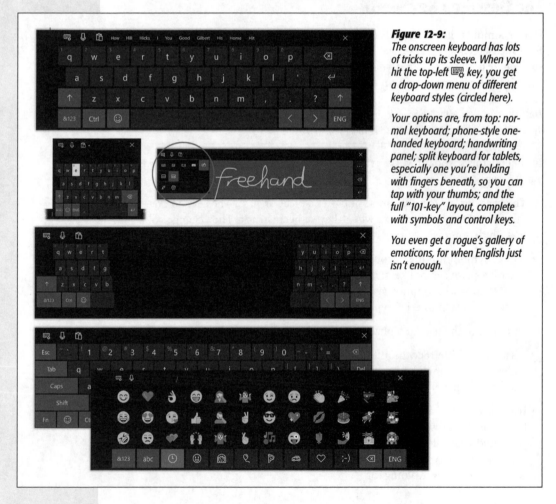

Figure 12-9:
The onscreen keyboard has lots of tricks up its sleeve. When you hit the top-left ⌨ key, you get a drop-down menu of different keyboard styles (circled here).

Your options are, from top: normal keyboard; phone-style one-handed keyboard; handwriting panel; split keyboard for tablets, especially one you're holding with fingers beneath, so you can tap with your thumbs; and the full "101-key" layout, complete with symbols and control keys.

You even get a rogue's gallery of emoticons, for when English just isn't enough.

bottom). These are available wherever you type, but they're most appropriate when you're typing in a chat room or *maybe* an email message. (And, even then, plenty of people would argue that they're *never* appropriate.)

The bottom row displays buttons for seven pages full of emoji, plus a ;-) button for kaomoji (emoji made of regular typed characters). The ⏲ displays symbols you've used recently for easier retrieval.

- **Its modifier keys are sticky.** If you want to press Shift+D, for example, or Ctrl+N, you don't have to *hold down* the Shift or Ctrl key. Just tap the modifier key (Shift, Ctrl, Alt) and *then* the letter that goes with it.

- **Caps Lock is there.** Just as on a phone, you can lock down the Shift key to type in ALL CAPITALS by *double*-tapping it. It lights up to show that it's locked down. (Tap it again to unlock it.)

- **Its letter keys are hiding punctuation and accents.** To produce an accented character (like é, ë, è, ê, and so on), keep your finger pressed on that key for about a second.

The comma sprouts a semicolon (;) option, but the period and the question mark— oh, baby. Their secret palettes contain a wealth of other punctuation marks (dash, colon, parentheses, exclamation point, number sign/hashtag, at symbol, slash, hyphen, and so on) that save you from having to call up the special-symbols layout.

Tip: Most keys on the symbol keyboard sprout variations, too; for example, the $ key offers an array of alternate currency symbols.

- **The double-space-bar trick is available.** If you press the space bar twice, you get a period, a space, and an automatically capitalized next letter—exactly what you want at the end of a sentence. (It's the same trick that saves you fussing on the iPhone, Windows Phone, Android phones, BlackBerry, and so on.)

Note: The on/off switch for this feature is in ⊞→⚙→Devices→Typing.

- **There are cursor keys.** See the ⟨ and ⟩ keys to the right of the space bar? Those don't mean "greater than" and "less than." They're arrow keys. They move your cursor left and right through the text.

- **There are typing suggestions.** When you've typed the beginning of a word that Windows can guess—*lun,* for example—a row of AutoComplete suggestions appears above the keyboard, proposing suggestions: *lung, lunch,* and *luncheon,* for example.

If one of those choices is indeed the word you wanted, tap it; Windows inserts it into whatever you were typing. Once you get used to this feature, you can save a lot of time and typos.

You can turn off the suggestions, if you like, in ⊞→⚙→Devices→Typing.

- **There's a full 101-key PC keyboard layout, too.** The standard Windows 10 keyboard layout was designed to make the letter keys big and easy to type. Microsoft chose

---

to hide a lot of the other stuff you'd find on a real keyboard, including numbers, Tab, Esc, and so on.

But if you'd prefer an onscreen version of the real thing, Windows can accommodate you. The standard drop-down menu of keyboard layouts offers the full 101-key PC keyboard (Figure 12-9, bottom).

When you're finished typing, tap the ✕ at the top right of the keyboard; it goes away, returning the full screen area to your command.

Keyboard Settings

In ⊞→☼→Devices→Typing, you'll find a raft of options that govern the onscreen keyboard: "Show text suggestions as I type," "Add a period after I double-tap the Spacebar," "Capitalize the first letter of each sentence," and so on. They're described in detail on page 249.

In the meantime, note how easy it is to jump to these settings: Tap ⌨ at top left of the onscreen keyboard, and then ☼.

Handwriting Recognition

The accuracy of Windows' handwriting recognition has come a very long way—which is great news if you have a tablet. Hey, if tablets can decipher doctors' handwriting, surely you can get your tablet to recognize yours.

In Windows 10, Microsoft has killed off the yellow two-line Input Panel of previous Windows versions. Instead, handwriting transcription is built right into the palette of available keyboards (Figure 12-9, second from top, right). It lets you handwrite text anywhere you can type: Microsoft Word, your email program, a web browser, and so on.

To make Windows recognize your handwriting, open any program where you would otherwise type.

Now open the handwriting panel. It's a window that automatically converts anything you write into typed text. To view this panel, start by summoning the regular onscreen keyboard (tap ⌨ on the taskbar).

Once the onscreen keyboard appears, tap ⌨ (top left); then tap the Handwriting icon (✐, circled in Figure 12-9). Now the handwriting panel is ready to use. Just write on the line.

The "digital ink" doesn't just sit there where you wrote it. A split second after you finish each word, Windows transcribes that word into typed text in your document, converted from your handwriting.

For your inking pleasure, a button at the right end of the panel serves as the Enter key. Hit the ··· icon at top right to open a miniature palette: left and right cursors, space bar, Backspace, a button to get you the emoji keyboard, and the "&123" button for punctuational and numerical fun. If you tap to pull up one of those other keyboards, just hit the ✐ button to toggle back.

Tip: In the May 2019 Update, a similar handwriting input panel pops up automatically whenever you tap in a text-entry area with a digital stylus.

Fixing Mistakes

Windows' handwriting recognition is amazingly accurate. It is not, however, perfect. Fortunately, it's got some tools to help.

First, don't miss the row of alternative transcribed words above your handwriting. Tap a word to insert it. Second, if *you* make a mistake as you write, strike out the word (drag your finger or pen across it, right to left). Windows vaporizes just that word.

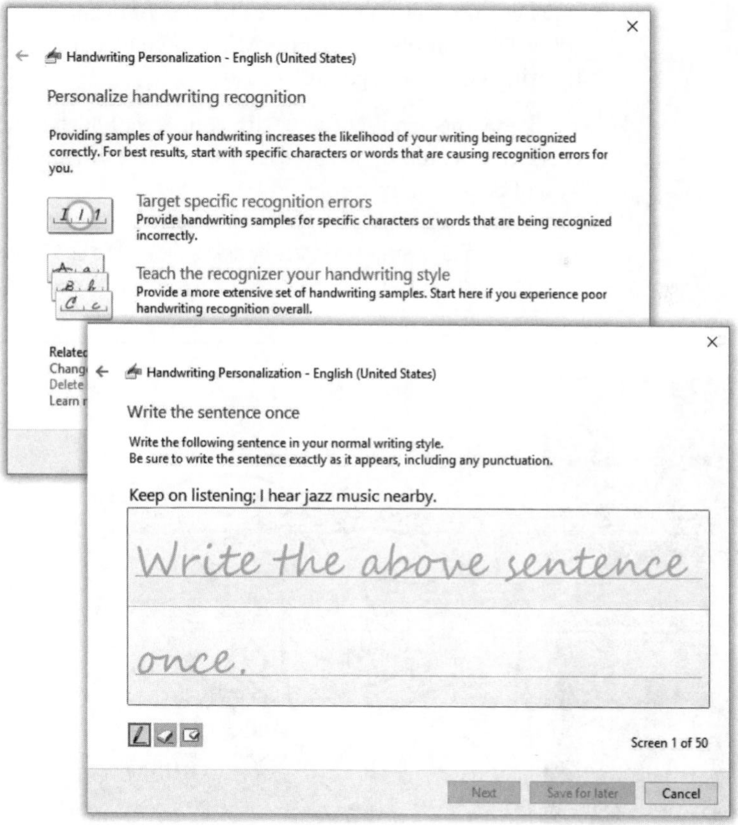

Figure 12-10:
Top: The handwriting training wizard offers you the chance to fix certain recognition errors (good if you've been at it awhile), or to teach it your general style (best if you're just starting out).

You're offered the chance to write either sentences or numbers, symbols, and letters; for best accuracy, you should work through both. More than once, in fact. They're not brief exercises—the Sentences option involves about 50 screens (bottom)—but it's all for a good cause.

← 📖 Handwriting Personalization - English (United States)   ✕

Personalize handwriting recognition

Providing samples of your handwriting increases the likelihood of your writing being recognized correctly. For best results, start with specific characters or words that are causing recognition errors for you.

Target specific recognition errors
Provide handwriting samples for specific characters or words that are being recognized incorrectly.

Teach the recognizer your handwriting style
Provide a more extensive set of handwriting samples. Start here if you experience poor handwriting recognition overall.

← 📖 Handwriting Personalization - English (United States)   ✕

Write the sentence once

Write the following sentence in your normal writing style.
Be sure to write the sentence exactly as it appears, including any punctuation.

Keep on listening; I hear jazz music nearby.

Write the above sentence once.

Screen 1 of 50

Next   Save for later   Cancel

Training Windows to Know Your Handwriting

Windows does amazingly well at understanding your handwriting right out of the box. But if you plan to use it a lot, you should *train* it. You provide samples of your handwriting, and Windows studies your style.

Open ⊞→⚙→Devices→Pen & Windows Ink, and choose "Improve recognition." Proceed as shown in Figure 12-10.

After working through the exercises, you can start using handwriting recognition—with better accuracy.

Windows Ink Workspace

Microsoft still believes touchscreens are the future. The company can't believe some people still buy laptops whose screens aren't touch-sensitive.

So Microsoft continues to sweeten the pot for people who *do* buy into the touchscreen thing. For example, if you buy a Microsoft tablet or touchscreen laptop, it thanks you by bringing you a wagon full of gifts.

You know the pen that came with your recent Surface tablet? You can program the clicker on the top to do some cool stuff—like opening the Ink Workspace, a collection of pen-friendly apps.

Tip: You can also open the Workspace by clicking the ✐ icon on the taskbar. If you don't see it, right-click a blank spot on the taskbar; from the shortcut menu, choose "Show Windows Ink Workspace button."

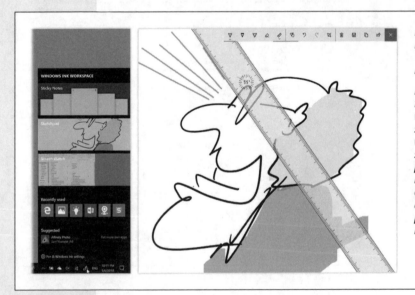

Figure 12-11:
Left: The entryway to the Windows Ink Workspace is this taskbar panel.

Right: Sketchpad's coolest feature is a virtual ruler, which you can use as a straightedge. Rotate it with two fingers on the screen, and then make perfectly straight lines by keeping your stylus, cursor, or finger pressed against it. There's even a protractor, hiding in the Ruler toolbar icon.

They include:

- **Sticky Notes.** Same app described on page 342; this is just a reminder that it's Ink-enabled, meaning you can jot down words or drawings with your stylus.

- **Sketchpad.** This is a super-simple app for free-form drawing (Figure 12-11). Make sketches, capture brainstorms, use it as the traditional back of a napkin. Its toolbar offers a marker, a pencil, and a highlighter, each with a drop-down menu of color choices. There's an eraser, too.

- **Screen sketch.** The instant you choose this tool, it captures a screenshot—and opens it with the usual drawing tools (same ones as in Sketchpad), so you can draw on it or annotate it. The Share button completes the transaction.

The best part of all of this: You can set up the pen-clicker thing to bring up the Ink Workspace even before you've signed in—at the Lock screen. Finally, a tablet is as useful as a legal pad. You're getting the phone number of somebody attractive? Click your pen and start writing, without first signing in like some kind of nerd.

(All of this, Microsoft says, may also work with other companies' Bluetooth pens.)

Controlling Your PC, Long Distance

Windows provides several avenues for accessing one PC from another across the network—or across the internet. If you're a road warrior armed with a laptop, you may be delighted by these features. If you're a corporate employee who used to think you could escape the office by going home, you may not.

The three most common scenarios for using these remote access features are (1) helping someone by viewing their screen remotely, (2) connecting to your office network from your PC at home, and (3) controlling your home PC remotely using a laptop.

These pages cover two of those systems of connecting:

- **Quick Assist.** This feature is for troubleshooting or teaching. It lets you see and take control of someone else's PC from across the internet (or lets someone else see and take control of yours). Don't get any hackery ideas: The other person must be seated at his computer, must give you permission, and can watch everything you do.

  Fortunately, Quick Assist is incredibly easy to set up and get going.

- **Virtual private networking (VPN).** In this system, you use the internet as a secure link between the host and the remote machine. The remote computer behaves exactly as though it has joined the network of the host system—usually your company's network.

The third feature, called Remote Desktop, lets you take control of an *unattended* PC—presumably your own, back at home. It requires a Pro version of Windows, plus a good deal of setup and some scavenging through the technical underbrush. But when you're in Tulsa and a spreadsheet you need is on your PC in Tallahassee, you may be grateful to have it in place.

In this age when your documents, photos, calendar, address book, email, and other stuff is all online anyway, Remote Desktop is somewhat less useful than it once was. If you're interested in diving in, though, see the free PDF appendix "Remote Desktop." It's available on this book's "Missing CD" at *missingmanuals.com*.

Quick Assist

You may think you know what stress is: deadlines, breakups, downsizing. But *nothing* approaches the frustration of an expert trying to help a PC beginner over the phone—for both parties.

The expert is flying blind, using Windows terminology the beginner doesn't know. Meanwhile, the beginner doesn't even know what to describe. Every little step takes 20 times longer than it would if the expert were simply seated in front of the machine. Both parties are likely to age 10 years in an hour.

Fortunately, that era is at an end. Windows' Quick Assist feature lets somebody having computer trouble extend an invitation to an expert, via the internet. The expert can actually see the screen of the flaky computer, control the mouse and keyboard, and make technical tweaks—running utility software, installing new programs, adjusting hardware drivers, even editing the Registry—by long-distance remote control. Quick Assist really *is* the next best thing to being there.

The fine print

A few notes about Quick Assist:

- **It requires that both PCs are running** Windows 10 Anniversary Update (the 2016 update) or later.

- **The expert must have a Microsoft email account,** like a Hotmail account.

- **Quick Assist doesn't transmit sound.**

- **Quick Assist requires fairly fast internet connections** on both ends.

Tip: If one of these requirements is a deal killer, you can always use the older Remote Assistance feature, which is similar but more complex to set up. Instructions are on this book's "Missing CD" at *missingmanuals.com*, in a free PDF appendix called "Remote Assistance."

Quick Assist security

Now, most people react to the notion of remote assistance with stark terror. What's to stop some troubled teenager from tapping into your PC in the middle of the night, rummaging through your files, and reading your innermost thoughts?

Plenty. You, the expert, have no access to the other person's computer until she enters a six-digit code that you provide. The code has a time limit: If she doesn't respond within 10 minutes, then the electronic door to her PC remains shut.

Finally, she must be present *at her machine* to make this work. The instant she sees something fishy going on, a quick tap on her Esc key disconnects her.

Making the connection

OK. You, the knowledgeable person (perhaps the owner of a book about Windows 10), have received a panicked call from a clueless relative. Let's call him Uncle Frank.

1. **You:** Open Quick Assist. The quickest way is to type *quick assist* in the ⊞ search box.

   Hit "Assist another person" (Figure 12-12, top left). Now you're shown a six-digit security code (top right). You have 10 minutes to communicate it to Uncle Frank; this screen offers to copy it to your Clipboard (so you can text it, for example) or to email it.

2. **Uncle Frank:** Opens his own copy of Quick Assist. Types in that six-digit code and hits "Share screen" (Figure 12-12, top left again).

Figure 12-12:
Quick Assist really is quick. You, the helper, encounter only three dialog boxes.

First (top left), hit "Assist another person." Second (top right), read or send the security code to the person you're trying to help out. Third (lower left), specify whether you just want to see the other guy's screen or actually control it.

The floundering helpee sees only two dialog boxes. First, he sees the same box you did at the beginning (top left)—but his job is to enter the code you've sent him and then hit "Share screen."

He then sees the box at lower right, where the Allow button explicitly grants permission for you to invade.

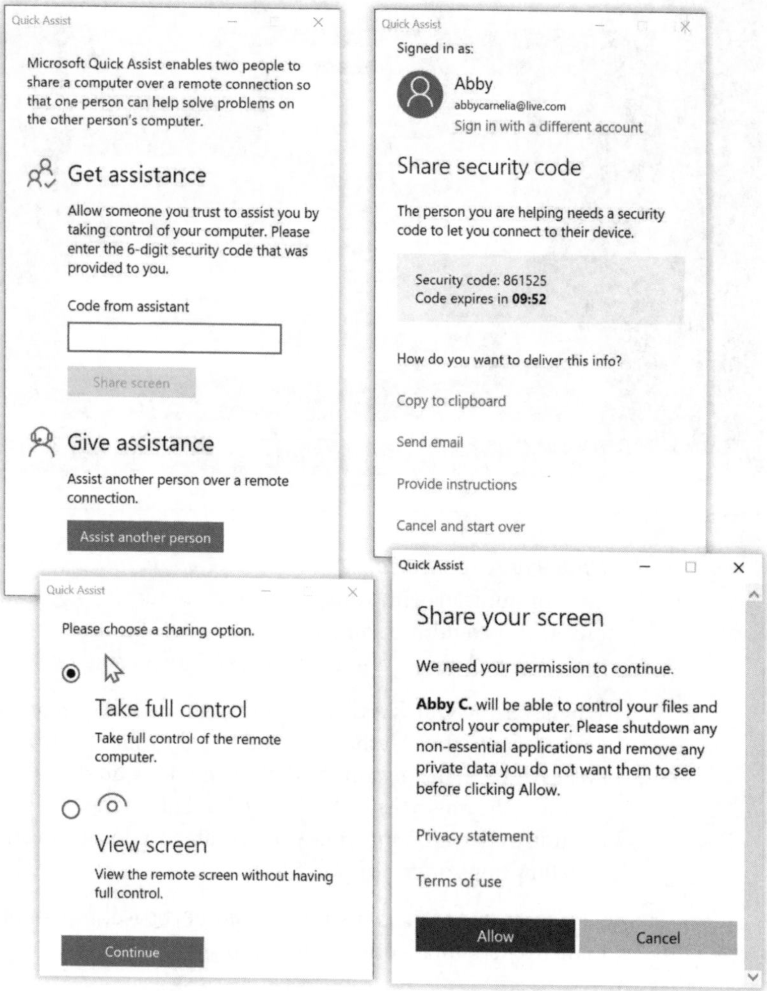

3. **You:** Specify how much control you want. Your choices are "Take full control" of Uncle Frank's screen, or just "View screen" (Figure 12-12, lower left).

4. **Uncle Frank:** On the "Share your screen" screen, hits Allow (Figure 12-12, lower right).

And that is all. A window opens on your screen, bordered in yellow, showing exactly what's on Uncle Frank's screen (Figure 12-13). You can now see what he's doing—and what he's doing wrong.

Figure 12-13:
This is what your entire screen looks like; Uncle Frank's screen appears entirely within the big window.

Once you're connected

To communicate with your troubled comrade, it's a great idea to talk on the phone. (Yeah, you could use something like Skype, but that might slow down your Quick Assist video. You can also type back and forth; read on.)

Whenever the Quick Assist program's window is selected, you can use your mouse, keyboard, and troubleshooting skills to do whatever work you need to do. You can do anything to the distant PC that the novice would be able to do—and you can't do anything the novice isn't allowed to do. (For example, if Uncle Frank doesn't have an administrative account, you won't be able to do administratory things for him like installing apps or creating accounts.)

Of course, he can use his mouse and keyboard, too—but if you're both trying to maneuver simultaneously, things can get annoying.

While the helping is going on, you can use these toolbar buttons:

Tip: If you're not sure which icon is which, choose ⋯ (top right) to make text labels appear.

- **Select Monitor.** Useful only if Uncle Frank has multiple screens.

- **Annotate.** Turns your cursor into a marker, so you can write on Uncle Frank's screen. He'll see any circles, arrows, and other shapes you write, as you write them. You can use the top-left icon to choose a different pen color; there's an Erase tool up there, too. Hit Exit (top right) to stop annotating (and remove any annotations you've just drawn).

- **Actual size/Fit screen.** This button is designed to handle situations where Uncle Frank's screen is larger than yours. If you click "Fit screen," his screen shrinks down small enough to fit inside your Quick Assist window, and this button becomes "Actual size." If you click "Actual size," his screen appears at full size on yours, but you'll have to use scroll bars to move around.

- **Restart.** Restarts his PC. Once it comes to life, he's offered a one-click invitation to let you reconnect and continue the help session.

- **Task Manager.** Opens Task Manager (page 213) on Uncle Frank's PC.

- **Reconnect.** In case the connection goes down in mid-help.

- **Pause.** Your screen goes black. (Frankly, *Uncle Frank's* Pause button—on the little Quick Assist panel at the top center—probably makes more sense; it lets him do something personal without your seeing. He can also hit the ✕ to end the session.)

- ⋯ **(Details).** Does nothing but add text labels to the buttons on the toolbar.

When your job is done, choose the black square End button—or wait for your grateful patient to click his own End button.

Virtual Private Networking

All over the world, frequent travelers connect to distant homes or offices using *virtual private networking*. VPN is a fancy way of saying, "Your remote computer can become part of your host network over the internet."

What corporations like most about VPN is that it's extremely secure. The information traveling between the two connected computers is encoded (encrypted) using a technology called *tunneling*. Your connection is like a reinforced steel pipe wending its way through the internet to connect the two computers.

To create a VPN connection, the host computer has two important requirements. If you're VPNing into a corporation or a school, it's probably all set already. Otherwise:

- **It must be on the internet at the moment you try to connect.**

- **It needs a fixed IP address.** See the Note on the next page.

On the other hand, the remote computer—your laptop—doesn't have any such requirements. It just needs an internet connection.

> **Note:** Several of the remote-connection methods described in this chapter require that your home-base PC have a *fixed, public* IP address. (An IP address is a unique number that identifies a particular computer on the internet. It's made up of four numbers separated by periods.)
>
> If you're not immediately nodding in understanding, murmuring, "Ahhhhh, right," then download the bonus appendix available on this book's "Missing CD" page at *missingmanuals.com*. The free PDF supplement you'll find there is called "Getting a Fixed, Public IP Address."

Setting up your laptop

In general, the big network bosses who expect you to connect from the road have already set up the VPN software on *their* end. They may even have set up your laptop for you, so that dialing in from the road requires only one quick click.

But if not—if you want to set up your remote PC yourself—open ▦→⚙→Network & Internet→VPN→"Add a VPN connection" (Figure 12-14, top). Fill in the blanks.

You'll need the server name or registered IP address of the VPN host—that is, the computer you'll be tunneling into.

If you fill in your user name and password now, and turn on "Remember my sign-in info," you won't have to retype it every time you connect. If you're connecting to a

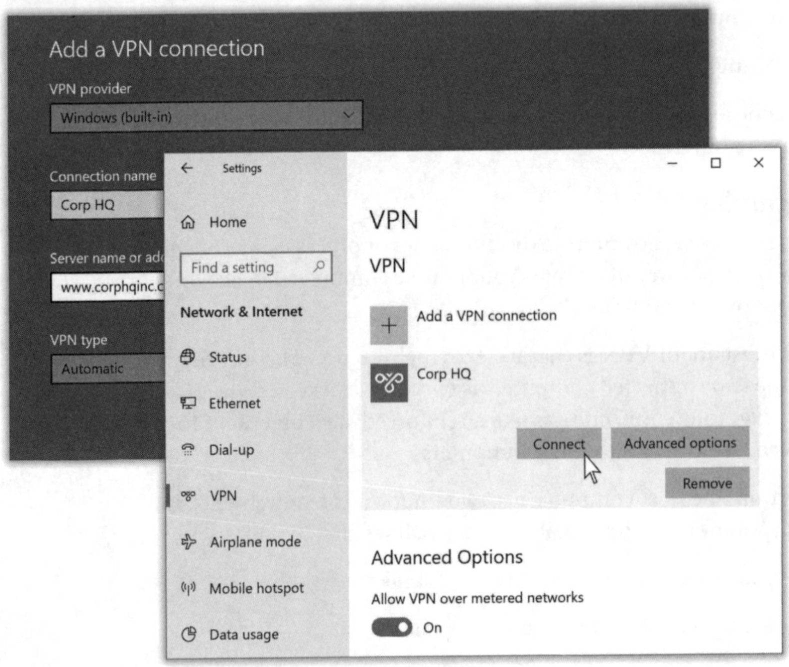

Figure 12-14:
Top: Here's where you set up your VPN connection, using the technical specs provided by the corporate IT person who takes care of you.

Bottom: Once you've set up the VPN, it shows up here, in Settings, ready for clicking and connecting.

server at work or school, your system administrator can tell you what to type here. If you're connecting to a computer you set up yourself, specify its public IP address. (See the previous Note.)

This is *not* the private IP address on your home network, and definitely not its computer name (despite the fact that the New Incoming Connection wizard told you that you would need to use that name); neither of these work when you're signed into another network.

It doesn't matter what you type as the Connection name; that's just for your reference.

Finally, click Save.

Connecting to the VPN

All you've done so far is create a *VPN connection*—a stored, clickable icon for connecting to the mother ship. When the time comes to make the actual connection, here's what you do:

1. Open ▦→⚙→Network & Internet→VPN.

   Or open the Action Center (▦+A) and hit VPN. Either way, the VPN pane of Settings opens up (Figure 12-14, bottom).

2. **Select the icon of the VPN connection you made earlier, and then click Connect.**

   If you entered your name and password (and turned on "Remember my sign-in info") when you created the VPN connection, you hop directly onto the distant network. If not, you're asked to enter your name and password—take this final step:

3. **Type your user name, password, and, if required by the network administrator, the domain name. Then click OK.**

When you make the VPN connection, you've once again joined your home or office network. You should feel free to transfer files, make printouts, and even run programs on the distant PC. (If you open the Network icon in your system tray, you'll see that you're connected, and you'll see a Disconnect option.)

Changing your VPN settings

If the VPN connection doesn't work the first time—it hardly ever does—you can make some adjustments. Just reopen the panel of PC Settings where you created the VPN connection in the first place, tap its name, and then tap "Advanced options." Keep your company's highly trained network nerd nearby to help you.

Three Obscure Mobility Features

Windows 10 still harbors three ancient features for laptop luggers:

- **Windows Mobility Center** is a handy, centralized hub for managing laptop settings: brightness, volume, battery, Wi-Fi, external projector connection, and so on. Today, most of its functions have moved to the Quick Actions panel (page 97).

- **Offline Files.** The ancient *offline files* feature lets your laptop carry away files that generally live on your office network. Then, when you return and connect your laptop to the office network, Windows automatically copies your edited documents back to their original locations on the network. Truth is, using a VPN or your OneDrive is a newer, much better way to work on documents from afar.

- **Windows To Go,** in the Enterprise edition of Windows 10, lets your IT overlords create a complete Windows world *on a flash drive* that can be used to start up any laptop—even your own. It contains a copy of Windows, whatever programs the bosses want you to have, documents, the works.

Each of these three features is described in appropriately named PDF appendixes to this chapter on this book's "Missing CD" page at *missingmanuals.com*.

CHAPTER 13

Printing, Fonts & PDFs

Technologists got pretty excited about "the paperless office" in the 1980s, but the PC explosion had exactly the opposite effect. Thanks to the proliferation of inexpensive, high-quality printers, the world generates far more paper than ever. Fortunately, there's not much to printing from Windows 10.

And since they seem like vaguely printing-related subjects, this chapter also covers Windows' font technologies and one of the best features in Windows 10: the ability to turn any document into a PDF document with one click. OK, two.

Installing a Printer

A printer is a peripheral device—something outside the PC—and as such, it won't work without a piece of *driver software* explaining the new hardware to Windows. In general, getting this driver installed is a simple process. It's described in more detail in Chapter 14.

The good news, though, is that Windows comes with the drivers for thousands of printers, of all different brands, ready to be installed. Read on.

USB Printers

If the technology gods are smiling, here's the entire set of instructions for installing a typical inkjet USB printer:

1. **Connect the printer to the computer; turn it on.**

   A notification appears (Figure 13-1, top), and that's it. You're ready to print. No driver operations, no setup. Next time you print something, you'll see the printer's name in the Print dialog box.

The backup plan

In certain situations, the printer doesn't "just work" when you plug it in. Maybe it's wireless. Maybe it's older.

In that case, here's Plan B: Open ⊞→⚙→Devices→"Printers & scanners" (Figure 13-1, bottom). Choose "Add a printer or scanner." Now Windows shows you the printer's name; select it, hit "Add device," and off you go.

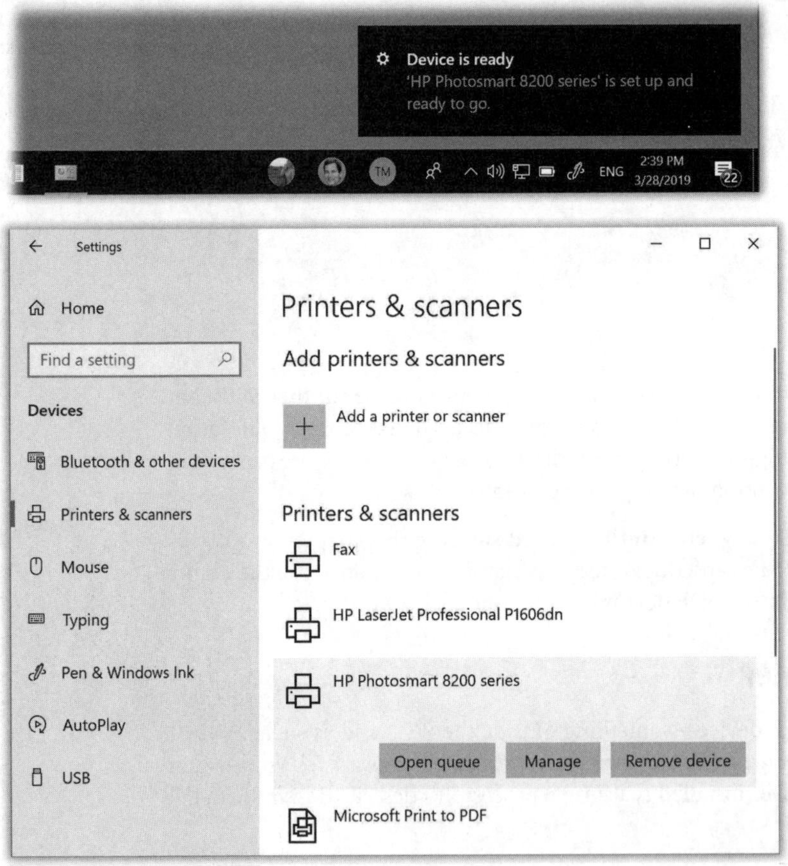

Figure 13-1:
Top: When you plug in a typical inkjet printer, Windows discovers it instantly. Mission accomplished.

Bottom: Now and then, you may have to visit the "Printers & scanners" page of Settings. It lists the printers your PC already knows about.

The backup backup plan

If you have a *really* old printer, its drivers might not be compatible with Windows 10. Check the manufacturer's website, such as *epson.com* or *hp.com,* or a central driver repository like *windrivers.com* to see if there's anything newer.

In dire situations, you might have to call upon the mighty powers of the "Find a printer by other options" wizard. Open ⊞→⚙→Devices→"Printers & scanners," hit "Add a printer or scanner," and then choose "The printer that I want isn't listed," and walk through the friendly onscreen guidance.

Network Printers

If you work in an office where people on the network share a single printer (usually a laser printer), the printer usually isn't connected directly to your computer. Instead, it's elsewhere on the network; your PC's Ethernet cable or wireless antenna connects you to it indirectly.

In general, there's very little involved in ensuring that your PC "sees" this printer. Its icon simply shows up in your Print dialog box.

Printing

Once you've connected a printer or three, printing is little more than a one-click operation.

After you've created a document you want to see on paper, start the printout. The object is simply to find the Print command; it shouldn't be hard. For example, in Mail and the Edge browser, it's in the More (···) menu. In Microsoft Office programs Word and Excel, it's in the File menu. The steps differ depending on which kind of app you're using:

Printing from Microsoft Store Apps

If you're printing from a Microsoft Store app (page 233), like most of the built-in Windows 10 programs, you wind up at the Print dialog box (Figure 13-2).

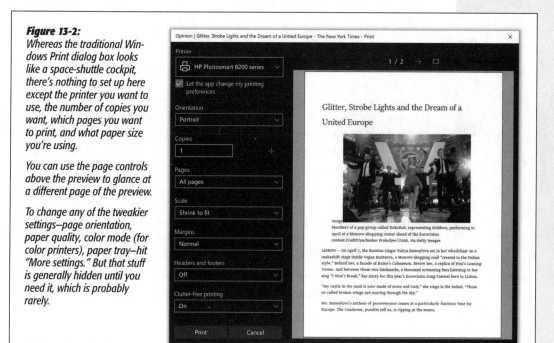

Figure 13-2:
Whereas the traditional Windows Print dialog box looks like a space-shuttle cockpit, there's nothing to set up here except the printer you want to use, the number of copies you want, which pages you want to print, and what paper size you're using.

You can use the page controls above the preview to glance at a different page of the preview.

To change any of the tweakier settings—page orientation, paper quality, color mode (for color printers), paper tray—hit "More settings." But that stuff is generally hidden until you need it, which is probably rarely.

Printing from Desktop Programs

In a desktop program—a *non*–Microsoft Store app—choose File→Print, click the Print button on the toolbar, or press Ctrl+P. The old Print dialog box appears, as shown in Figure 13-3.

This dialog box, too, changes depending on the program you're using—the Print dialog box in Microsoft Word looks a lot more intimidating than the WordPad version—and the printer model. But you'll usually find these basics here: a choice of printers, number of copies, and so on. Don't miss:

- **Preferences/Properties.** Clicking this button opens a version of the printer's Properties dialog box, where you can change the paper size you're using, whether you want to print sideways on the page (landscape orientation), what kind of paper—or photo paper—you're using, and so on. Here you're making changes only for a particular printout; you're not changing any settings for the printer itself. (The specific features of this dialog box depend on the program you're using.)

- **Page Range.** If you want to print only some of the pages, click the Pages option and type in the page numbers you want (with a hyphen, like *3-6* to print pages 3 through 6).

Tip: You can also type in individual page numbers with commas—like *2, 4, 9*—to print only those three pages—or even add hyphens to the mix, like this: *1-3, 5-6, 13-18.*

Click Current Page to print only the page where you've placed the blinking insertion point. Click Selection to print only the text you selected (highlighted) before opening the Print dialog box. (If this option button is dimmed, it's because you didn't highlight any text—or because you're using a program that doesn't offer this feature.)

- **Print.** The Print drop-down list that might appear in the lower-left section of the dialog box offers three options: "All pages in range," "Odd pages," and "Even pages."

  Use the Odd and Even pages options when you have to print on both sides of the paper but your printer has no special feature for this purpose. You'll have to print all the odd pages, turn the stack of printouts over, and then run the pages through the printer again to print the even pages on the other side.

- **Application-specific options.** The particular program you're using may add a few extra options of its own to an Options tab in this dialog box.

When you've finished making changes to the print job, click OK or Print, or press Enter. You don't have to wait for the document to emerge from the printer before returning to work on your PC. (Just don't put your machine to sleep until it's finished printing.)

Tip: During printing, the tiny icon of a printer appears in your system tray. Pointing to it without clicking produces a pop-up tooltip that reveals the background printing activity.

Printing from the Desktop

You don't necessarily have to print a document while it's open in front of you. You can, if you wish, print it directly from the desktop or from a File Explorer window in a couple of ways:

- **Right-click the document icon,** and then choose Print from the shortcut menu. Windows opens the program that created it—Word or Excel, for example. The document is then sent automatically to the default printer.

- **If you've opened the printer's own print queue** (Figure 13-4), then you can drag any document icon directly out of a File Explorer window into the list of waiting printouts. Its name joins the others on the list.

These methods bypass the Print dialog box and therefore give you no way to specify which pages you want to print, or how many copies. You just get one copy of the entire document.

Controlling Printouts

Between the moment you click OK in the Print dialog box and the arrival of the first page in the printer's tray, there's a delay. Usually, it's brief, but when you're printing a complex document with lots of graphics, it can be considerable.

Fortunately, the waiting doesn't necessarily make you less productive, since you can return to work on your PC, or even quit the application and go watch TV. An invisible program called the *print spooler* supervises this background printing process. The spooler collects the document that's being sent to the printer, along with all the codes the printer expects to receive, and then sends this information, little by little, to the printer.

To see the list of documents waiting to be printed—the ones that have been stored by the spooler—open the printer's window (Figure 13-4).

Tip: While the printer is printing, a printer icon appears in the system tray. As a shortcut to opening the printer's window, just double-click that icon.

This window lists the documents currently printing and waiting—the *print queue*. They print in top-to-bottom order.

You can manipulate documents in the queue in any of these ways during printing:

- **Put one on hold.** To pause a document, right-click its name, and then choose Pause from the shortcut menu (Figure 13-4). When you're ready to let the paused document continue to print, right-click its listing and choose Resume.

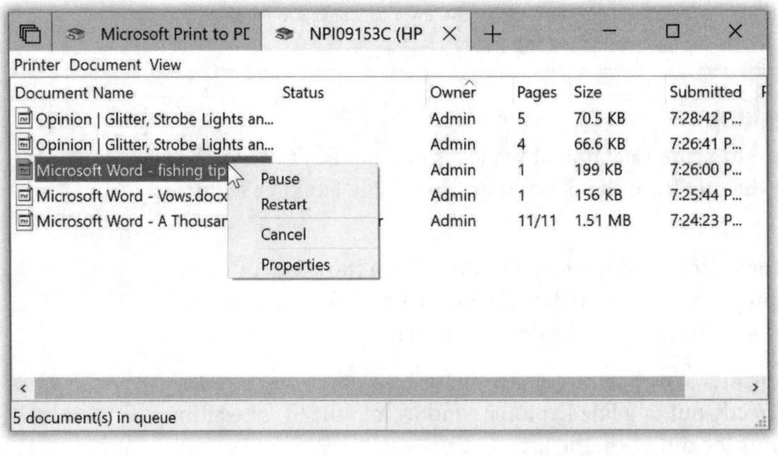

Figure 13-4:
By right-clicking documents in this list, you can pause or cancel any document in the queue—or all of them at once.

- **Put them all on hold.** To pause the printer, choose Printer→Pause Printing from the window's menu bar. You might do this when, for example, you need to change the paper in the printer's tray. (Choose Printer→Pause Printing again when you want the printing to pick up from where it left off.)

- **Add another one.** As noted earlier, you can drag any document icon directly *from its disk or folder window* into the printer queue. Its name joins the list of printouts-in-waiting.

- **Cancel one.** To cancel a printout, click its name and then press the Delete key. If you click Yes in the confirmation box, the document disappears from the queue; it won't print. (Or right-click it and choose Cancel from the shortcut menu.)

- **Cancel all of them.** To cancel the printing of all the documents in the queue, choose Printer→Cancel All Documents.

Note: A page or so may still print after you've paused or canceled a printout. Your printer has its own memory (the *buffer*), which stores the printout as it's sent from your PC. If you pause or cancel printing, you're only stopping the spooler from sending *more* data to the printer.

- **Rearrange them.** To rearrange the printing order, start by right-clicking the name of one of the printouts-in-waiting; from the shortcut menu, choose Properties. On the General tab, drag the Priority slider left or right. Documents with higher priorities print first.

Printer Troubleshooting

If you're having a problem printing, the first diagnosis you must make is whether the problem is related to *software* or *hardware.* A software problem may mean the driver files have become damaged. A hardware problem means there's something wrong with the printer, the port, the cable, the toner, the ink, or whatever.

If you're guessing it's a software problem—fairly likely—reinstall the printer driver. Open ■→⚙→Devices→"Printers & scanners," select the printer's icon, and then choose "Remove device" from the shortcut menu. Then reinstall the printer as described at the beginning of this chapter.

If the problem seems to be hardware-related, try these steps in sequence:

- **Check the lights or the LED panel readout** on the printer. If you see anything other than the normal "Ready" indicator, then check the printer's manual to diagnose the problem.

- **Turn the printer off and on** to clear any memory problems.

- **Check the printer's manual** to learn how to print a test page.

- **Check the cable** to make sure both ends are firmly and securely plugged into the correct ports.

- **Test the cable.** Use another cable, or take your cable to another computer/printer combination.

If none of these steps leads to an accurate diagnosis, don't forget that Windows has its own troubleshooting tools. In ■→⚙→Devices→"Printers & scanners," choose "Get help with your printer" (on the right side of the screen) to get started.

Fancy Printer Tricks

Windows, in its effort to be all operating systems to all people, is full of additional printer-related tricks. You can schedule printouts (to take advantage of low-traffic office hours); create a separator page that prints to identify each document and its owner (handy when you share a busy printer); and fiddle with your printer's color settings. If you're interested, you can read about all this in the free PDF appendix to this chapter, "Fancy Printer Settings," available on this book's "Missing CD" page at *missingmanuals.com.*

Fonts

Some extremely sophisticated programming has gone into the typefaces that are listed in the Fonts dialog boxes of your word processor and other programs. They use *OpenType* and *TrueType* technology, meaning that no matter what point size you select for these fonts, they look smooth and professional—both on the screen and when you print. (And if that seems obvious, you obviously didn't live through the jagged-fonts era of the late '80s.)

Managing Your Fonts

Windows comes with several dozen great-looking fonts: Arial, Book Antiqua, Garamond, Times New Roman, and so on. But the world is filled with additional fonts. You may find them on websites or in the catalogs of commercial typeface companies. Sometimes you'll find new fonts on your system after installing a new program, courtesy of its installer.

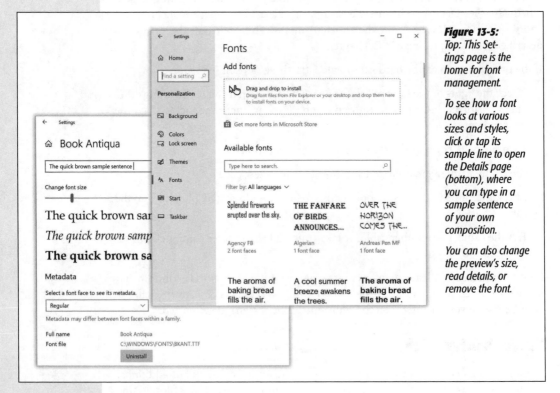

Figure 13-5:
Top: This Settings page is the home for font management.

To see how a font looks at various sizes and styles, click or tap its sample line to open the Details page (bottom), where you can type in a sample sentence of your own composition.

You can also change the preview's size, read details, or remove the font.

The hub of all fonts on your machine is in ■→⚙→Personalization→Fonts (Figure 13-5). You can perform four janitorial tasks here:

- **Add new fonts.** Choose "Get more fonts in Microsoft Store." Off you go to a searchable catalog of free or cheap font files. The beauty of this font source is that soon after you hit Get, you're offered an Install button that, yes, installs the font on your system, making it ready to use in your programs.

- **Install a font.** The Microsoft Store, of course, is not the keeper of all fonts. You can find thousands of free or cheap fonts on other sites, which you download as files. Once you have one, you can install it either by double-clicking (and then clicking Install) or by dragging it into the "Drag and drop to install" box (Figure 13-5). Now the font is available to use in your programs.

- **Preview fonts.** When you choose a font's tile, the details page opens (Figure 13-5).

- **Remove fonts.** Select a font's name to open its details page. Choose Uninstall, and then confirm.

You see the changes immediately reflected in your programs' Font dialog boxes; you don't even have to quit and reopen them.

The Fonts Folder

The Fonts display in Settings is actually just a front end for the fonts *folder*, which is in your *Local Disk (C:)* ❯ *Windows* ❯ *Fonts* folder. It may not be as pretty, but it offers a more direct way to do the following:

- **Add a font you've downloaded.** Drag its file icon into this window (or right-click the font and then click Install).

- **Remove a font.** Select its icon in this folder and then hit Delete on the toolbar. You can also choose to show or hide specific fonts in your programs.

PDF Files

Many a software manual, brochure, Read Me file, and downloadable "white paper" come as PDF (portable document format) files. In the beginning, you needed the free program called Adobe Reader if you hoped to open or print these files. In Windows 10, they open up in the Edge browser, for your perusing pleasure.

In fact, in Windows 10, you can turn *any document* (in any program with a Print command) into a PDF file—a trick that once required a $250 program called Adobe Acrobat Distiller.

Why would you want to create a PDF? Consider these advantages:

- **Other people see your layout.** When you distribute a PDF file, other people see precisely the same fonts, colors, page design, and other elements you put in your original document. And here's the kicker: They get to see all this even if they don't *have* the fonts or the software you used to create the document.

- **It's universal.** PDF files are very common in the Windows, Mac, Unix/Linux, and even smartphone worlds. When you create a PDF file, you can distribute it (by email, for example) without worrying about what kinds of computers your correspondents are using.

- **It has very high resolution.** PDF files print at the maximum quality of any printer. A PDF file prints great both on cheapo inkjets and on high-quality image-setting gear at professional print shops. (Right now you're looking at a PDF file that was printed at a publishing plant.)

- **You can search it.** A PDF file may look like a captured graphic, but behind the scenes, its text is still text; the Search feature can find a word in a PDF haystack in a matter of seconds. That's an especially handy feature when you work with electronic software manuals in PDF format.

Opening PDF Files

There's nothing to opening a PDF file: Just double-click it. Edge takes over from there and opens the PDF file on your screen. You can scroll through it, change the background or type, have it read out loud, or zoom in and out (using the Zoom commands in the ··· menu). See page 381 for more on Edge's PDF mode.

Creating PDF Files

Opening, schmopening—what's really exciting in Windows 10 is the ability to create your *own* PDF files.

Just use the standard Print command as you always do—but in the spot where you'd specify which printer you want to use, choose Microsoft Print to PDF; see Figure 13-6.

Note: All right, technically Windows alone creates *screen-optimized* PDF files: compact, easy-to-email files that look good onscreen but don't have high enough resolution for professional printing. For high-end purposes and more optimization for specific uses (web, fancy press machines, and so on), you still need a program like Adobe Acrobat, Illustrator, or InDesign.

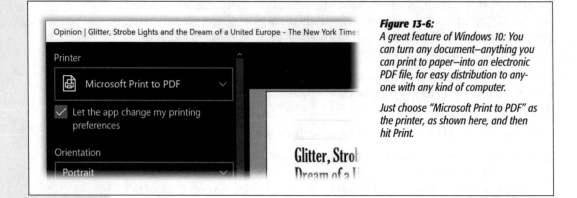

Figure 13-6:
A great feature of Windows 10: You can turn any document—anything you can print to paper—into an electronic PDF file, for easy distribution to anyone with any kind of computer.

Just choose "Microsoft Print to PDF" as the printer, as shown here, and then hit Print.

Faxing

In the increasingly rare event that your PC has a built-in fax modem—and is connected to a phone line—it can serve as a true-blue fax machine. This feature works like a charm, saves money on paper and fax cartridges, and may even spare you the expense of buying a physical fax machine.

You even get a dedicated program, Windows Fax and Scan, for the purpose of managing faxes. For step-by-step instructions, find the free downloadable PDF appendix, "Faxing from Windows 10," on this book's "Missing CD" page at *missingmanuals.com*.

Scanning

Faxing isn't the only technology that turns paper into digital bits. Scanning is the other—and that, too, is a talent of Windows Fax and Scan.

First, install your scanner (and its driver) as described in Chapter 14.

Load it up with the page you want to scan. Open the Windows Fax and Scan program. (You can find it with a quick search.)

Click New Scan. The New Scan dialog box appears. Click Preview to trigger a quick, temporary scan so you can see how the document will look after the scan (Figure 13-7). If it all looks good, click Scan.

Figure 13-7:
In this box, you have the chance to specify what sort of thing you want to scan–picture? document?–and specify its resolution and color settings.

Choose 300 to 600 dots per inch resolution (dpi) for professional scans; for everyday scanning, 150 to 200 dpi is plenty. The more dots, the bigger the resulting file.

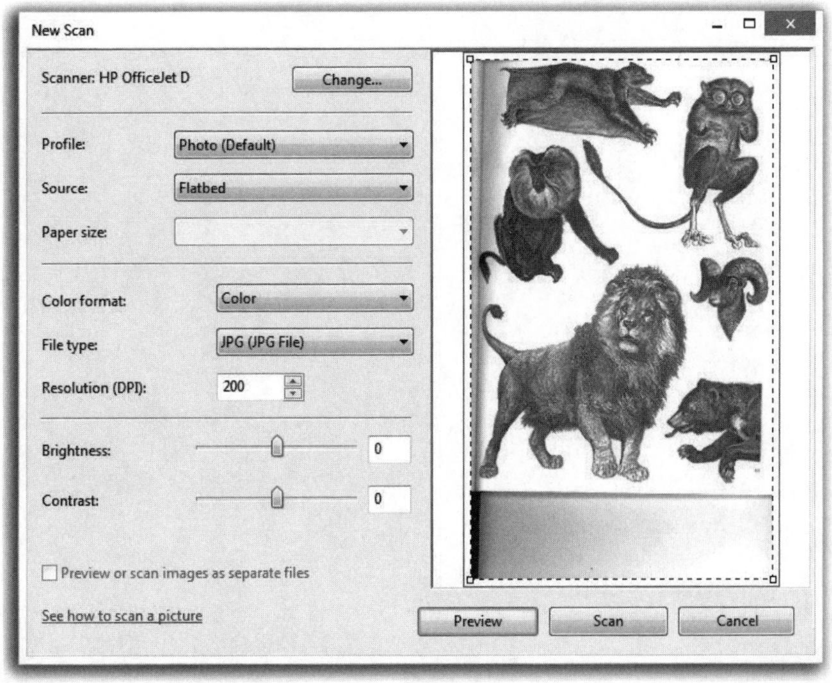

Once the document has magically turned into a graphic in your Scan list, you can do all kinds of neat things with it: Forward it as a fax or an email attachment (click Forward as Fax or Forward as E-mail on the toolbar); export it as a JPEG, GIF, BMP, TIFF, or PNG document (click "Save as" on the toolbar); print it; or delete it.

Hardware & Drivers

If your Windows machine is a tablet, good for you. You probably won't have to spend much time mucking around with peripherals and their drivers. But if you have a regular PC, adding new gear is part of the fun. Hard drives, flash drives, cameras, phones, printers, scanners, network cards, video cards, keyboards, monitors, game controllers, and other accessories all make life worth living.

Before you can use a piece of equipment new to the PC, you must hook it up and install its *driver,* the software that lets it talk to the rest of the PC.

The driver issue was once a chronic, nagging worry for the average Windows fan. Drivers conflicted; drivers went missing; drivers went bad; drivers went out of date.

Fortunately, Microsoft has made strides in addressing the driver problem. Windows 10 comes with thousands upon thousands of drivers for common products already built in, and Microsoft deposits dozens more on your hard drive, behind the scenes, with every Windows update. Chances are good you'll live a long and happy life without ever having to lose a Saturday manually configuring new gizmos, as your ancestors did.

Most of the time, you plug in some new USB gadget, and bam—it's ready to use. You don't have to install anything, walk through any wizards, or sacrifice any animals.

This chapter counsels you on what to do when the built-in, autorecognized drivers don't do the trick.

Note: Chapter 13 contains additional hardware-installation details specific to printers.

External Gadgets

Over the years, various engineering organizations have devised an almost silly number of connectors for printers, scanners, and other *peripherals*. The back, side, or front of your PC may include any of these connector varieties.

USB Ports

Man, you gotta love USBs (Universal Serial Bus). The more of these jacks (also called connectors or ports) you have, the better.

The USB port itself is a compact, thin, rectangular connector that's easy to plug and unplug. It often provides power to the gadget, saving you one more cord and one more bit of clutter. And it's hot-pluggable, so you don't have to turn off the gadget (or the PC) before connecting or disconnecting it.

Tip: Be careful, though, not to yank a USB flash drive or hard drive out of the PC when it might be in the middle of copying files.

USB accommodates a huge variety of gadgets: USB hard drives, scanners, mice, phones, keyboards, printers, palmtop cradles, digital cameras, camcorders, and so on.

Most modern PCs come with at least two USB ports, often on both the front and back panels.

Note: Today's USB gadgets and PCs offer *USB 3.0* jacks—a faster, enhanced form of USB. You can still plug the older, slower USB 1.1 and 2 gadgets into USB 3.0 jacks, and vice versa—but you'll get the older, slower speed.

USB-C

After 20 years of USB, the world's electronics companies got together and (over the course of three years) designed its successor: USB-C. It's fantastic.

UP TO SPEED

Of Hubs and Power

If your PC doesn't have enough built-in USB jacks to handle all your USB devices, then you can also attach a USB *hub* (with, for example, four or eight additional ports), in order to attach multiple USB devices simultaneously.

Whether the USB jacks are built in or on a hub, though, you have to be aware of whether they're *powered* or *unpowered* jacks.

Unpowered ones just transmit communication signals with the USB gadget. These kinds of USB gadgets work fine with unpowered jacks: mice, keyboards, flash drives, and anything with its own power cord (like printers).

Powered USB jacks also supply current to whatever is plugged in. You need that for scanners, webcams, hard drives, and other gadgets that don't have their own power cords but transmit lots of data.

The bottom line? If a gadget isn't working, it may be because it requires a powered jack and you've given it an unpowered one.

This connector can carry power, video, audio, and data—simultaneously. It can, in other words, replace a laptop's power cord, USB jacks, video output jack, and headphone jack.

A USB-C cable is identical top and bottom, so you can't insert it the wrong way. It's identical end for end, too, so it doesn't matter which end you grab first. It feels more secure than USB when you insert it; you get a physical click instead of just relying on friction to hold it in.

USB-C can charge your gadget faster and transfer data faster than what's come before, too. It's tiny—about the same size as a micro-USB—so the same cable can charge your phone and tablet and laptop. And the brand doesn't matter. My Samsung USB-C cable can charge your Surface tablet and his Apple MacBook.

Second, you can already buy phones, tablets, and laptops that come with USB-C jacks—from Google, Microsoft, Nokia, Apple, and others.

Eventually, the USB-C payoff will be gigantic, convenient, and universal. In the meantime, we're in for a couple of years of transition and fumbling with adapters that accommodate all our old USB gear: flash drives, hard drives, scanners, printers, cameras, and so on.

Other Jacks

At one time, the backs of PCs were pockmarked with all manner of crazy jacks: serial ports, PS/2 ports, SCSI ports, parallel ports, keyboard ports. Today, all these connectors are rapidly disappearing, thanks to the all-powerful superiority of USB and USB-C.

Here's what else you may find on the modern PC, though:

- **Video (VGA), DVI, or DisplayPort.** These are all ways to connect a second monitor or a projector. The older but widely compatible VGA is a narrow female connector with 15 holes along three rows. The DVI (digital visual interface) jack has 24 pins and is designed for modern LCD screens. And DisplayPort, which is intended to replace VGA and DVI (but retain compatibility via adapters), looks like a USB jack with one diagonally clipped corner.

- **HDMI.** Handy! This kind of jack sends high-def video *and* audio to an HDTV set or an external monitor.

- **SD card reader.** Pop the SD memory card out of your camera and straight into this slot to import the photos. Sweet.

Connecting New Gadgets

In books, magazines, and online chatter about Windows, you'll frequently find people talk about *installing* a new component. In many cases, they aren't talking about physically hooking it up to the PC—they're talking about installing its driver software.

But remember the insanely complete collection of drivers—especially for USB gadgets—that comes with Windows. When you plug the thing into the PC for the first time, Windows autodetects its presence, digs into its trunk for the driver, and installs it automatically. A flurry of notifications appear.

If Windows can't find the driver, then a dialog box appears, suggesting that you insert whatever software-installation disc came with the gadget.

And now, the fine print:

- **Usually plugging the device in is all it takes.** Sometimes, though, you're supposed to install the driver before connecting the gizmo (check the manual).

- **Usually the device should be turned off before you plug it in.** Again, though, check the manual, because some devices are supposed to be switched on during the installation.

In either case, your gear is now completely installed—both its hardware and its software—and ready to use.

Troubleshooting Newly Installed Gear

If, when you connect a new component, Windows doesn't display a "successfully installed" message, that means it probably can't "see" your new device.

Before panicking, try restarting the PC. If you still have no luck, try the Add Hardware Wizard described in the Note below. (And if even *that* doesn't work, contact the manufacturer.)

Note: The ancient Add Hardware Wizard has been put on an ice floe and sent out to sea. It's for very old, pre–Plug-and-Play gadgets (what Microsoft calls "legacy hardware") that Windows doesn't autorecognize when you plug them in. For details, see the free PDF appendix to this chapter called "Add Hardware Wizard." It's on this book's "Missing CD" at *missingmanuals.com*.

Bluetooth Gadgets

Bluetooth is a short-range, low-power, wireless *cable-elimination* technology. It's designed to connect gadgets in pairings that make sense, like cellphone+earpiece, PC+wireless mouse, phone+portable speaker, or PC+cellphone.

Now, you wouldn't want the guy in the next cubicle to be able to operate *your* PC using *his* Bluetooth keyboard. So the first step in any Bluetooth relationship is *pairing*, or formally introducing the two gadgets that will be communicating. Figure 14-1 shows how that goes.

To pair two gadgets, open ■→⊛→Devices. Make sure Bluetooth is On. (The only reason to turn it off is to save a tiny bit of battery power.) Select "Add Bluetooth or other device," and then Bluetooth.

The PC automatically starts searching for nearby Bluetooth gadgets within range (see Figure 14-1)—nearby mice, keyboards, cellphones, and so on. Usually, it finds the one you're trying to pair. Just click the one you want, and then click Pair.

When it's all over, the new gadget is listed in the panel, in the list of Bluetooth stuff you've previously introduced to this computer. (You can click it and then click "Remove device" to get rid of the pairing, when that day comes.)

Note: Windows 10 now has a special speed-pairing feature for Bluetooth mice. All you have to do is turn the mouse's pairing mode on (there's usually a special button for this)—and boom. A notification appears on your computer's screen, offering a Connect button. You don't have to visit Settings at all. At the outset, this feature works only with new Microsoft mice; Logitech brand auto-pairing is in the works.

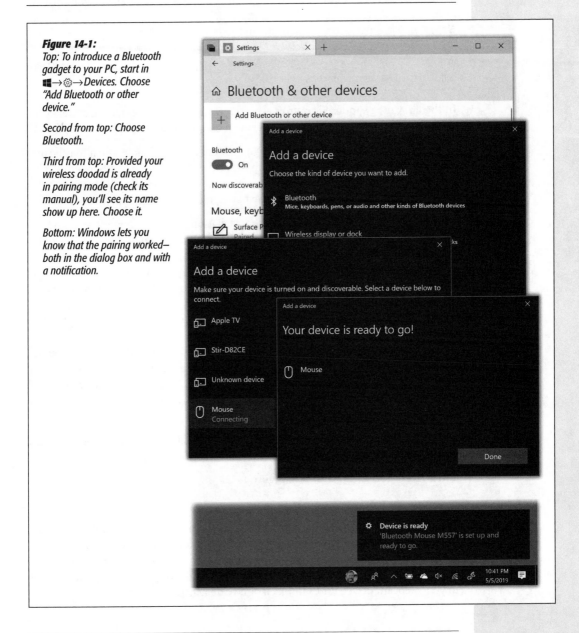

Figure 14-1:
Top: To introduce a Bluetooth gadget to your PC, start in ■→⚙→Devices. Choose "Add Bluetooth or other device."

Second from top: Choose Bluetooth.

Third from top: Provided your wireless doodad is already in pairing mode (check its manual), you'll see its name show up here. Choose it.

Bottom: Windows lets you know that the pairing worked—both in the dialog box and with a notification.

Driver Signing

Every now and then, when you try to install the software for one new gadget or another, you see a warning box that says "Windows can't verify the publisher of this driver software."

It's not really as scary as it sounds. It's just telling you that Microsoft has not tested this driver for Windows 10 compatibility and programming solidity. (Technically speaking, Microsoft has not put its digital signature on that driver; it's an *unsigned driver*.)

Note: In very rare circumstances, you may also see messages that say "This driver software has been altered" or "Windows cannot install this driver software." In those cases, go directly to the hardware maker's website to download the official driver software; Windows is trying to warn you that hackers may have gotten their hands on the driver version you're trying to install.

In theory, you're supposed to drop everything and contact the manufacturer or its website to find out if a Windows 10–certified driver is now available.

In practice, just because a driver isn't signed doesn't mean it's no good; it may be that the manufacturer simply didn't pony up the testing fee required by Microsoft's Windows Hardware Quality Labs. After all, sometimes checking with the manufacturer isn't even possible—for example, it may have gone to that great dot-com in the sky.

So most people just plow ahead. If the installation winds up making your system slower or less stable, you can always uninstall the driver, or rewind your entire operating system to its condition from before you installed the questionable driver. (Use System Restore, described on page 509, for that purpose. Windows automatically takes a snapshot of your working system just before you install any unsigned driver.)

The Device Manager

The Device Manager (Figure 14-2) is an extremely powerful tool that lets you troubleshoot and update drivers for gear you've already installed. It's a master list of every component that makes up your PC: drives, keyboard, trackpad, screen, battery, and so on. It's also a status screen that lets you know which drivers are working properly and which ones need some attention.

The quickest way to open the Device Manager is to right-click the ⊞ button, which makes the secret Utilities menu appear; choose Device Manager.

You arrive at the screen shown in Figure 14-2.

The Curse of the Yellow ! Badge

A yellow circled exclamation point next to the name indicates a problem with the device's driver. It could mean that either you or Windows installed the *wrong* driver, or that the device is fighting for resources with another component. It could also mean that a driver can't find the equipment it's supposed to control. That's what happens to your webcam driver, for example, if you've detached the webcam.

The yellow badge may also be the result of a serious incompatibility between the component and your computer, or the component and Windows. In that case, a call to the manufacturer's help line is almost certainly in your future.

Tip: To find out which company created a certain driver, double-click the component's name in the Device Manager. In the resulting Properties dialog box, click the General tab, where you see the name of the company, and the Driver tab, where you see the date the driver was created, the version of the driver, and so on.

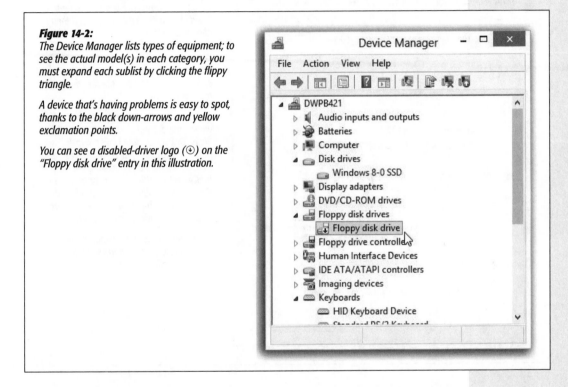

Figure 14-2:
The Device Manager lists types of equipment; to see the actual model(s) in each category, you must expand each sublist by clicking the flippy triangle.

A device that's having problems is easy to spot, thanks to the black down-arrows and yellow exclamation points.

You can see a disabled-driver logo (⊘) on the "Floppy disk drive" entry in this illustration.

Duplicate devices

If the Device Manager displays icons for duplicate devices (for example, two modems), then remove *both* of them. (To remove a device, click Uninstall in the dialog box shown in Figure 14-3.) If you remove only one, Windows will just find it the next time the PC starts up, and you'll have duplicate devices again.

When the PC starts up again, Windows finds the hardware device and installs it (only once this time). Open the Device Manager and make sure there's only one of everything. If not, call the manufacturer's help line.

Resolving resource conflicts

If the yellow-! problem isn't caused by a duplicate component, then double-click the component's name to find an explanation of the problem.

Updating Drivers

If you get your hands on a new, more powerful (or more reliable) driver for a device, you can use the Device Manager to install it. Open the dialog box shown in Figure 14-3, and then hit the Update Driver button. The Update Device Driver wizard walks you through the process.

Intel(R) PRO/1000 MT Network Connection Properties ☒

| Events | Resources | Power Management |
| General | Advanced | Driver | Details |

Intel(R) PRO/1000 MT Network Connection

Driver Provider: Microsoft
Driver Date: 3/23/2018
Driver Version: 8.4.13.0
Digital Signer: Microsoft Windows

Driver Details	To view details about the driver files.
Update Driver...	To update the driver software for this device.
Roll Back Driver	If the device fails after updating the driver, roll back to the previously installed driver.
Disable	Disables the selected device.
Uninstall	To uninstall the driver (Advanced).

OK   Cancel

Figure 14-3:
To get here, double-click a component listed in your Device Manager and then choose the Driver tab. Here you find four buttons and a lot of information. The Driver Provider information, for example, lets you know who's responsible for your current driver—Microsoft or the maker of the component.

Hit the Driver Details button to find out where on your hard drive the actual driver file is. Or click Update Driver to install a newer version, the Roll Back Driver button to reinstate the earlier version, the Disable button to hide this component from Windows until you change your mind, or the Uninstall button to remove the driver from your system entirely—a drastic move.

(If the buttons here are dimmed, click the General tab, click "Change settings," and then authenticate.)

Roll Back Driver

Suppose that you, the proficient PC fan, have indeed downloaded a new driver for some component—your scanner, say—and successfully installed it. Life is sweet—until you discover that your scanner no longer scans in color.

In this situation, open the dialog box shown in Figure 14-3 and click Roll Back Driver. Windows, forgiving as always, instantly undoes the installation of the newer driver and reinstates the previous driver.

Part Five: PC Health

5

Maintenance, Speed & Troubleshooting

Your computer requires periodic checkups and preventive maintenance—pretty much like you, its human sidekick. Fortunately, Microsoft has put quite a bit of effort into equipping Windows with special tools, all dedicated to making your system stable and fast. Here's a guide to keeping your PC and its hard drive humming.

The Action Center

If you're looking for the best place to go for at-a-glance information about the current state of your PC's maintenance and internet security, open the Action Center. To do so, press ■+A, or click the tiny ▢ on your system tray.

Here, all in one place, are all the security and maintenance messages Windows wants you to see. Be grateful; they *used* to pop up as individual nag balloons on the system tray all day. Now they accumulate here.

You can read the full scoop on the Action Center on page 96. For now, it's enough to remember that this is the place to check to see how your Windows updates, security scans, and PC backups are doing.

Windows Update

Microsoft intends to update your copy of Windows 10 continuously and automatically, over the internet, as it develops new features and plugs new security holes, through a feature called Windows Update.

You may have noticed the word "automatically" casually slipped into that paragraph. This is the controversial part: For the first time in Windows history, *you can't decline*

Microsoft's Windows updates. If your PC is connected to the internet, you'll get each update, whether you like it or not.

There's a persuasive argument for automatic updates. Microsoft and other security researchers constantly find security holes—and as soon as they're found, Microsoft rushes a patch out the door. But creating a patch is one thing; actually getting that patch installed on millions of copies of Windows has been another thing entirely.

That's where Windows Update comes in. When Microsoft releases a security fix, it will be delivered straight to your PC and get automatically installed.

Note: In fact, it's Microsoft's *patches* that usually alert hackers to the presence of security holes in the first place! They used to be able to exploit the fact that not everyone had the patch in place instantly.

What to Do if a Minor Update Glitches Your Computer

For most people, most of the time, getting automatic Windows updates is the safest, best way to go. It's fairly unlikely that an update will mess things up for you—and potentially dangerous to turn off Microsoft's ability to protect you from new viruses.

But what if it happens? What if that blue moon comes to pass, and an update makes your computer start crashing or acting weird? In that case, you can uninstall the update—and then prevent it from auto-reinstalling until you learn that a fixed driver or updated update is available.

To do that, open ■→⚙→Update & Security→Windows Update; choose "View update history," and then "Uninstall updates." Proceed as shown in Figure 15-1.

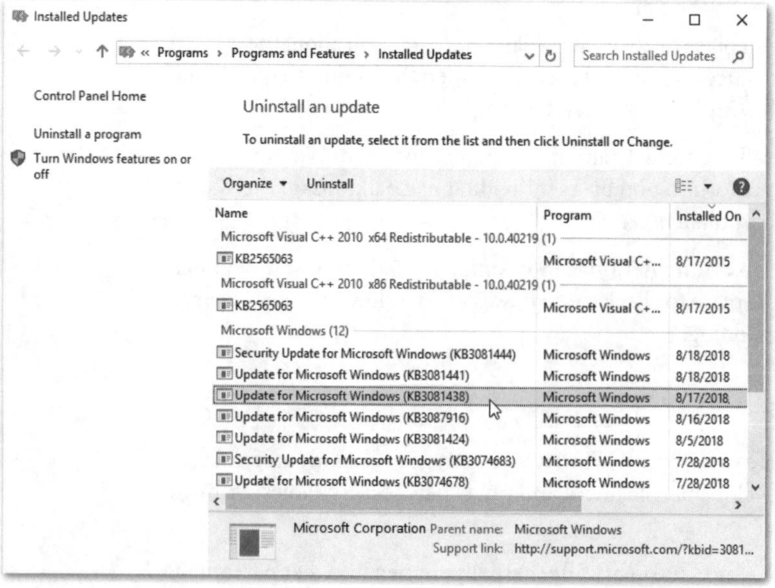

Figure 15-1:
Since updates, for most people, are automatic, you might not even realize you've been upgraded until you consult this list. Most of them are probably security updates (antivirus, antispyware patches).

To remove one you don't want, just select it and then hit Uninstall.

Note: If the update in question messed up one of your drivers, you can surgically remove just that driver. Open the Device Manager (page 482), right-click the device with the bad driver, choose Uninstall Device from the shortcut menu, and confirm by clicking "Delete the driver software for this device if available."

Prevent an Update from Reinstalling Itself

So you've successfully undone a problematic update. Great! But if you just sit back on the couch now, Windows Update will just install it right back again.

To prevent that from happening, Microsoft offers a weird little program called the "Show or hide updates troubleshooter." You can grab it by Googling that name, or you can find it on this book's "Missing CD" page at *missingmanuals.com*.

Download it, and then proceed like this (these are the steps to take *after* uninstalling the balky update as described already):

1. **On the opening screen (Figure 15-2, top), hit Next.**

   You arrive at the second box shown in Figure 15-2.

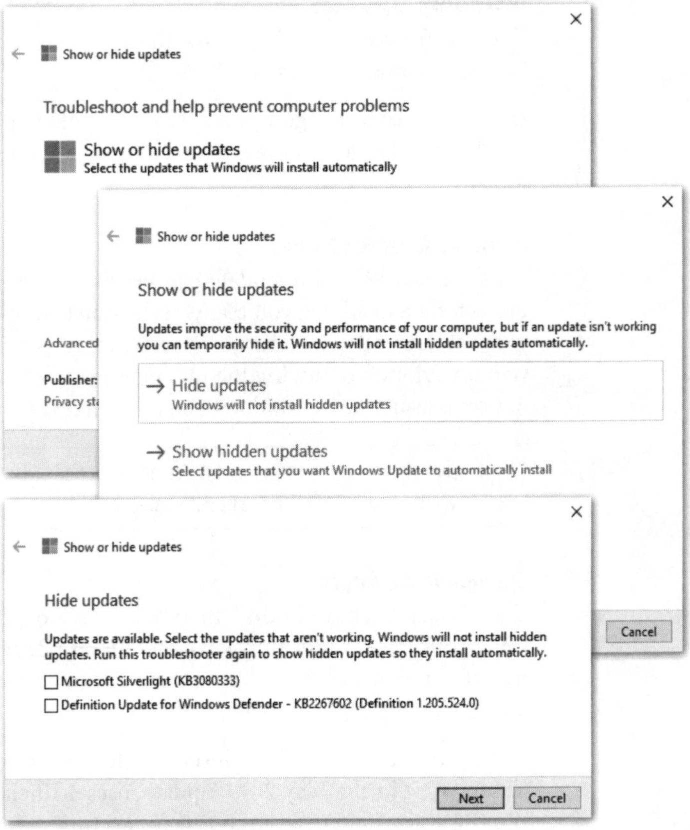

Figure 15-2:
When this app says "hide," what it means is block. It means: "This is a problematic update that you've already uninstalled (as described on page 489 of Windows 10 May 2019 Update: The Missing Manual), *and I shall now prevent it from installing ever again."*

2. **Hit "Hide updates."**

   Windows shows you all the updates you've uninstalled (or that have been down-loaded but not yet installed), as shown in Figure 15-2, bottom.

3. **Turn on the update(s) you want to block, and then hit Next.**

   After a moment of contemplation, the app says, "Troubleshooting has completed."

Note: You should ignore the message in the box that shows the glitchy update with a happy little green "Fixed!" checkmark. Nothing has been fixed.

The update has been blocked. Microsoft won't try to install it again until you want it.

Later, when you determine that the update is now safe to install—maybe you've read online that it's been fixed—run this little app again. This time, in step 2, hit "Show updates." Turn on the update(s) you want to permit, and then hit Next.

At its next opportunity, Microsoft will send that update to you again—and install it automatically.

Installing Updates

The control center for Windows Update awaits at ⊞→⚙→Update & Security→ Windows Update (Figure 15-3).

Here you'll see what's going on with your updates, plus a few other options—conces-sions to people who've always resented the aggressiveness of Microsoft's auto-updating feature.

Pause updates for 7 days

Sometimes a Windows update can be disruptive. If you're in the middle of some project, on a deadline, you really, really don't want to have to troubleshoot or learn your way around new features. If you turn this switch on, then Windows will patiently wait a week before forcing the update on you. (New in the May 2019 Update: This option is available in Windows 10 Home, not just Pro.)

Tip: If 7 days is too long or too short, hit "Advanced options." Under "Pause updates," you can choose any time between 0 and 35 days for the update-pausing.

Change active hours

Click "Change active hours," then "Change," to tell Windows when you're usually using your PC— for example, 9 a.m. to 6 p.m. During these hours, Windows won't restart automatically to accommodate a new update. (Yes, it used to do that. Yes, it used to make people crazy.)

Or turn on "Automatically adjust active hours for this device based on activity." That feature, new in the May 2019 Update, uses artificial-intelligence smarts—based on your PC usage patterns—to choose restart times when they're least likely to bug you.)

View update history

Here's where you can see all the updates you've received—and uninstall them if you're not pleased.

Figure 15-3:
Most of the time, you'll see "You're up to date." But sometimes you'll see that an update is downloading, bringing you some little gift (like an updated antivirus database) or a big gift (like juicy new features).

Advanced options

Here are a few not-really-that-advanced options:

- **Receive updates for other Microsoft products when you update Windows.** Ordinarily, Windows Update is about making changes to *Windows*. But what if there are updates to Office, Skype, Minecraft, or other Microsoft programs? Here's where you authorize automatic updates to those programs, too.

- **Download updates over metered data connections.** In other words: Do you still want your computer to download updates over cellular connections (this means you, tablet owners)? Updates are big, and data usually costs money.

- **Restart this device as soon as possible.** New in the May 2019 Update: Instead of waiting for a good time, when you won't be bothered, any update that requires restarting will restart the PC instantly. Turn this on if being out of date gives you anxiety.

- **Show a notification when your PC requires a restart to finish updating.** When you've got an update that requires a restart, but your PC hasn't yet restarted, you'll see a Windows Update icon with an orange dot in the system tray as a reminder.

- **Pause updates.** As described previously.

- **Choose when updates are installed.** This option, available only in the Pro, Enterprise, Education, and S versions of Windows, lets you fine-tune and extend the delays. You can hold off on installing "feature updates" (like, say, the October 2019 Update) for up to a year, or "quality updates" (bug fixes and security patches) for up to a month. (Clearly, there's some overlap with the "Pause updates" feature. Also clearly, Microsoft has had a lot of complaints over the years about updates and restarts being shoved down our throats.)

- **Delivery Optimization.** Every time Microsoft sends out an update, it has to send out *hundreds of millions of copies*. That an unbelievable amounts of identical data flooding out over the internet airwaves. If you've got several PCs, each of them has to download that same data, redundantly, from Microsoft.

  In Windows 10, your PC can join thousands of others in a peer-to-peer network, passing bits of update code to *one another*. In other words, all those machines become part of Microsoft's distribution system, passing along bits of Windows updates to other people. Now one of your computers can download an update and then pass pieces of it along to the others without having to download them again.

  Overall, the idea can save huge amounts of bandwidth and storage on the internet. It can also get these updates to you faster, with a much lower consumption of internet data if you're on an office network.

  All of this is really kind of a cool idea. But if your internet service has a monthly limit, you might worry that your computer sending out those bits of updates to other people online might eat up data unnecessarily.

  Fortunately, this feature doesn't kick in at all if you're using a cellular connection. If you're on a Wi-Fi network with monthly data limits, though, you should inform Windows so it doesn't eat up your allotment by sending bits of update to strangers online. You can turn the whole thing off, using the master switch on this Settings page. Or leave it on and choose "PCs on my local network." That way, you get the benefit of bandwidth and data savings (by sharing update bits among your own computers), without worrying about becoming part of the larger internet data-sharing network and running up your data bill.

Uninstalling a Major Windows Version

The discussion so far has concerned the relatively minor updates and patches that come along weekly or monthly. But there are also the whoppers, the twice-a-year Windows 10 updates that are so important, they get their own names, like "Fall Creators Update" or "May 2019 Update."

What happens if you install one of *those*, and it turns out to be a disaster? If you realize your mistake within about 10 days, no big deal. Open ⊞→⚙→Update & Security→Recovery, and choose "Go back to the previous version of Windows 10."

(After 10 days, Windows deletes the files from your previous version; you can't roll back without doing a complete reinstallation.)

Note: Rolling back like this is especially handy if you've signed up for the Windows Insider Program (page 263), and you've just received a new build that's too buggy to work with.

Troubleshooting Tools

These days, a first-time Windows owner probably doesn't even know what you mean by the phrase "blue screen of death." PCs don't crash nearly as often as they used to.

But there are still about a million things that can go wrong and about a million troubleshooting tools to help you—or somebody you've begged to help you—solve them. Here's the, ahem, crash course.

Figure 15-4:
Here's your master list of troubleshooters (top). Along the way, you might be invited to take a step, or check a setting, that Windows thinks could help; you can accept it or reject it. Every now and then, you get lucky, and Windows fixes the problem (bottom).

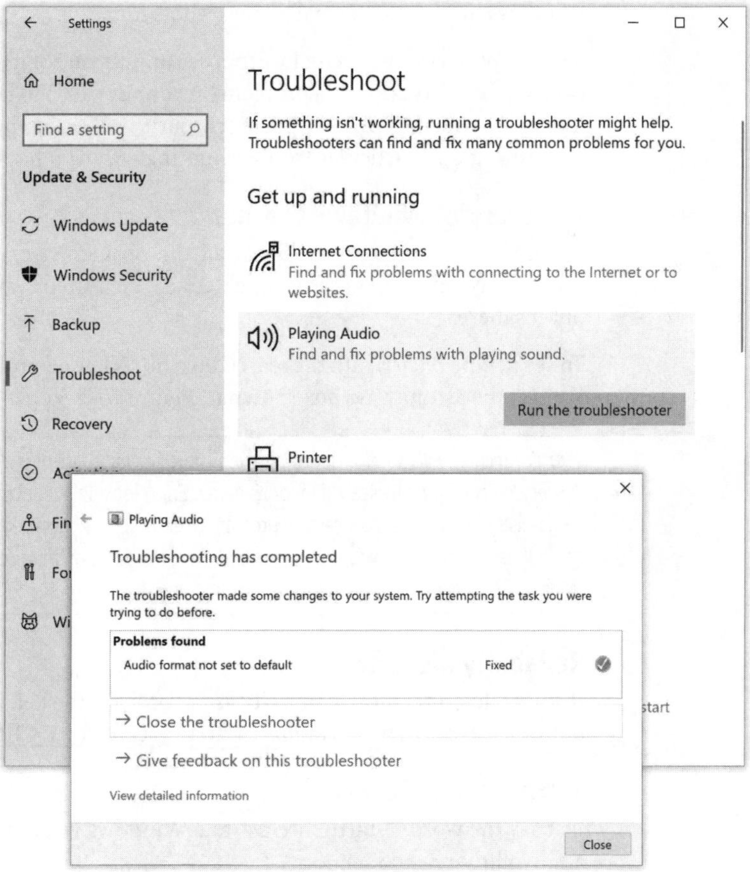

Windows Troubleshooters

A troubleshooter is an automated, step-by-step "wizard" that's supposed to analyze some problem you're having and fix it automatically. Basically, it's Windows trying to fix itself, and you can guess how often *that* works.

Still, every now and then, a troubleshooter will fix some glitch, and you'll be glad you spent the time.

In the olden days, you'd have to open ⊞→⚙→Update & Security→Troubleshoot. As you can see in Figure 15-4, Microsoft has built 17 troubleshooting wizards for you, arrayed in categories such as Internet Connections, Playing Audio, and Video Playback. You could select one and then hit "Run the troubleshooter" to get started.

But in the May 2019 Update, troubleshooters have taken two steps forward. First, Windows fixes some problems automatically and invisibly. "For example, we may automatically restore default settings for critical services, adjust feature settings to match your hardware configuration, or make other specific changes required for Windows to operate normally," says Microsoft.

Second, Windows may actually propose running one of its troubleshooters; a notification appears ("We can fix a problem on your device") to let you know. If you click the message, or open ⊞→⚙→Update & Security→Troubleshoot, you'll see that Windows is featuring one particular troubleshooting wizard it hopes will help.

The Diary of Windows Crashes

Windows maintains a tidy list of all the problems you've been having with your machine. Needless to say, this little item isn't featured very prominently in Windows, but it's there.

To see it, type *reports* into the search box; hit "View all problem reports" in the results. You get the astonishing box shown in Figure 15-5 (top).

Tip: For techies, Windows includes an even more technical list of the goings-on on your PC: the Event Viewer. You can find it by searching for its name. Enjoy looking over eye-glazing lists of every log Windows keeps—lists of happenings concerning programs, setup, security, services, and more. You can sort, filter, and group these events. But if you can understand the significance of these obscure messages, you shouldn't be reading a Windows book—you should be writing one.

Reliability Monitor

If you prefer to get the bad news in visual form, try the Reliability Monitor (Figure 15-5, bottom). To see it, type *reliability* into the search box. Click "View reliability history."

Startup Items Revealed

Just say the words "startup items" to a Windows veteran, and you're sure to witness an involuntary shudder.

Startup items are programs that load automatically when you turn the computer on, without your invitation. Some are icons in the system tray. Some are designed to assist antivirus or iPod syncing apps. Some run in the background, invisibly.

But all of them use memory, and sometimes they can slow down your machine. And in older Windows versions, they were annoying and complex to manage.

Now, sometimes, there are on/off switches for the startup items in the programs themselves, in menus called Settings, Preferences, Options, or Tools. That's a clean, direct way to shut something up, but it won't help you with invisible startup items—those you didn't even know were running.

In Windows 10, the Task Manager has a tab called Startup Items. It's a startup/shutdowner's dream come true.

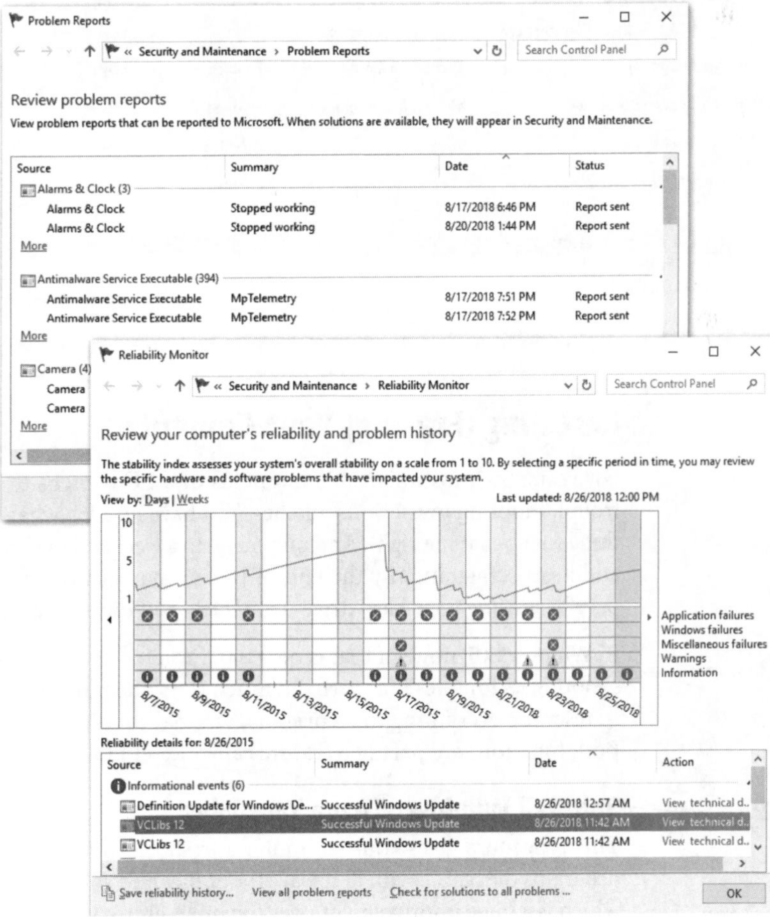

Figure 15-5:
Top: Diary of a typical Windows machine. It's a list of all the things that have gone wrong recently. Double-click one to open a screen of techie details that could be useful to a tech-support rep.

Bottom: Here's a mighty graph of your crashes stretching back one year, which explains why your PC has seemed so cranky lately. Each icon shows something that went wrong—a crash, a freeze, an error message. Click a column to see everything that happened that day.

If you see a lot of crashes following, for example, an installation or system change, you might have spotted yourself a cause-and-effect situation. You now have a clue to your PC's recent instability.

To open the Task Manager, right-click the Start menu and, from the shortcut menu, choose Task Manager. Now click its Startup tab, and proceed as shown in Figure 15-6.

Tip: If your computer is having startup *problems*—it can't even start up—then it's time to open the Windows toolbox of tools known as the Recovery Environment. See page 499.

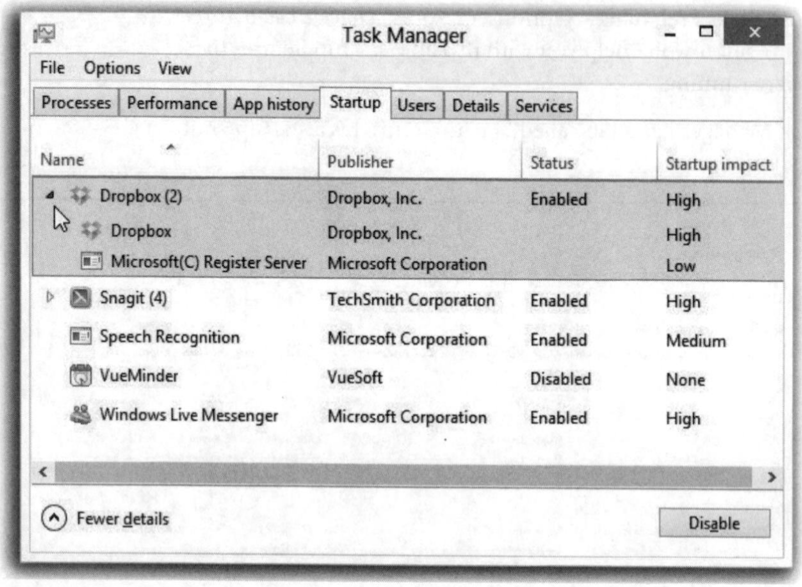

Figure 15-6:
To see what secret software is loading at startup time, open the Task Manager's Startup tab.

The "Startup impact" column shows you how much time and memory each item is sucking away from your computer's startup sequence.

The handy Disable button lets you turn off any selected item with one click.

Resetting (Erasing) Your Computer

For years, the most miserable moments of a PC owner's existence have been spent troubleshooting mysterious glitches. You have no idea what went wrong, but something isn't behaving right. And off you go to a weekend of Googling, troubleshooting, and head-scratching. By the end of it, you may just be inclined to do a "nuke and pave"—erasing your hard drive completely and reinstalling everything from scratch.

In Windows 10, none of that is necessary. You have two incredibly powerful troubleshooting techniques that perform much the same purpose as a nuke and pave—that is, resetting everything to its original, virginal condition—but require far less effort. Both functions are part of a feature called Reset PC.

Reinstall Windows, Leave Your Files

This procedure gives your computer a fresh, clean copy of Windows 10 and all the programs that came with it. It leaves your files and your Microsoft Store apps in place, which is a huge improvement over the nuke-and-pave tradition. It's a powerful trick to remember when your computer just isn't behaving right.

But it erases all your *drivers, Windows settings, and programs you've installed* (the ones that didn't come with Windows itself). Any programs and drivers you've installed since getting Windows 10, you'll have to reinstall after the procedure.

(For your reconstructing convenience, Windows displays a thoughtful list of all the programs that are about to be deleted. You'll find this same list on a text file on your desktop after the reset is over.)

1. **Open ⊞→⚙→Update & Security→Recovery. Under "Reset this PC," choose "Get started" (Figure 15-7, top).**

   Now you see the intriguing options shown in Figure 15-7.

2. **Choose "Keep my files" (Figure 15-7, middle).**

   At this point, you may be warned that other people are logged in, or that you'll lose your ability to rewind to an earlier Windows version (page 509).

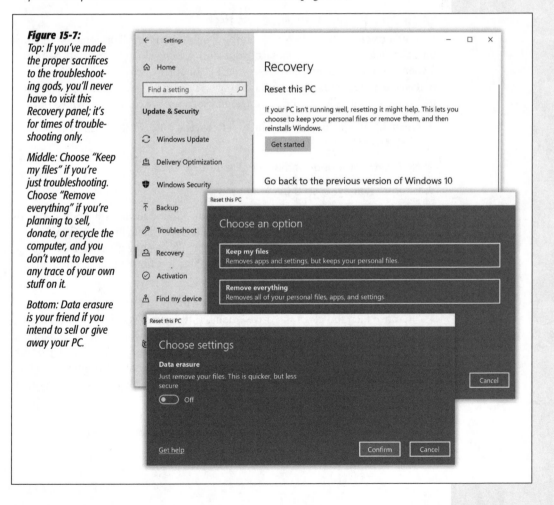

Figure 15-7:
Top: If you've made the proper sacrifices to the troubleshooting gods, you'll never have to visit this Recovery panel; it's for times of trouble-shooting only.

Middle: Choose "Keep my files" if you're just troubleshooting. Choose "Remove everything" if you're planning to sell, donate, or recycle the computer, and you don't want to leave any trace of your own stuff on it.

Bottom: Data erasure is your friend if you intend to sell or give away your PC.

In most cases, the "Additional settings" box appears now. It lets you know that it intends to restore all the apps and settings that came with the PC once this is over. In other words, it won't leave your PC completely empty.

(If you'd rather retain your files but *eliminate* all the PC's factory-installed apps, hit "Change settings," hit the On switch so it turns off, and then hit Confirm.)

Windows says it's "Ready to reset this PC," and offers to show you a list of the apps you'll have to reinstall when this process is over.

3. **Click Reset.**

After a moment, your freshly cleaned computer comes to. Your files and original programs are intact, but your settings, plus any programs and drivers you've installed, are gone.

And so, in most cases, are the glitches.

Erase Your PC Down to Windows Itself

In more dramatic situations—for example, you're about to sell or donate your computer and want to make sure none of your stuff is going along for the ride to the new owner—you can also *completely reset* your PC. In other words, you're sending it back to its factory-fresh condition, with nothing on it except Windows and the programs that came with it. All your files, settings, and software are completely wiped out.

1. **Open ■→⚙→Update & Security→Recovery. Under "Reset this PC," choose "Get started."**

Now you see the options shown in Figure 15-7, middle.

2. **Choose "Remove everything."**

A new dialog box appears (Figure 15-7, bottom). Windows lets you know it intends to "Just remove my files. This is quicker, but less secure." In other words, Windows will erase everything you've ever done to this PC, leaving it with a fresh copy of Windows and the apps that come with it. This is a fine option if you intend to reinstall stuff and keep using the PC.

If you select "Change settings," you'll be able to hit an Off switch. Now you're in "Remove files and clean the drive" mode. In this case, Windows will erase your files *and* scrub those storage spaces with digital static, which will make it almost impossible for even a sleuth or recovery company to resurrect your deleted files. (This takes longer, but it's the option to use if you're planning to donate or sell the computer.) Hit Confirm to return to the "Additional settings" box.

3. **Hit Next.**

You get one more warning, one final reminder that you're about to erase every program you've installed on your PC.

4. **Hit Reset.**

The resetting process takes a long time. When it's all over, your computer is empty except for Windows and the apps it came with. It's shiny clean and ready to donate or reuse yourself.

Note: On some computers, there's a third option called "Restore factory settings." It's the same thing as "Remove everything," except that it also restores whatever version of Windows came on the PC from the store.

Windows Recovery Environment

You might play by all the rules. You might make regular backups, keep your antivirus software up to date, and floss twice a day. And then, one day, you get your reward: The PC won't even start up. You can't use any of Windows' software troubleshooting tools, because you can't even get to Windows.

In that most dire situation, Microsoft is pleased to offer what's known to techies as WinRE (Windows Recovery Environment), shown in Figure 15-8. It's a special recovery mode, loaded with emergency tools: System Reset, System Refresh, System Restore, System Image Recovery, Safe Mode, and on and on.

Windows Recovery Environment is a pure, protected mode that's separate from the normal workings of Windows—a place to troubleshoot without worrying about changes that have been made by any software, good or bad.

If the problems you're having are caused by drivers that load just as the computer is starting up, for example, then turning them all off can be helpful. At the very least, WinRE allows you to get into your machine to begin your troubleshooting pursuit. It's a menu most people never even know exists until they're initiated into its secret world by a technically savvy wizard.

It used to be easy to open this screen; you just pressed the F8 key at the right moment during startup. But that trick doesn't work in Windows 10. Some machines start up so fast that you'd have only milliseconds to hit the F8 key at just the right time.

Instead, WinRE appears *automatically* if the computer hasn't successfully started up after two attempts. If it doesn't, or if you're impatient, you can get to it manually.

The steps differ depending on how much trouble you're having getting the computer going. Choose *one* of these four techniques:

- **Hold down the Shift key as you click Restart.** (To find the Restart button, open the ■ menu, select ⏻, and then select Restart.)

- **In ■→⚙→Update & Security→Recovery,** under "Advanced startup," click "Restart now."

- **Start up from a Windows disc or a flash drive.** At the Windows Setup screen, hit Next; then choose "Repair your computer." (This technique works even if the computer is too sick to start up normally.)

• **If you're a command-line kind of person,** here's how you open the Recovery Environment from the command console: Type *shutdown.exe /r /o* and press Enter.

In each case, you arrive at the "Choose an option" screen. Follow the sequence shown in Figure 15-8 to get to the Startup Settings menu.

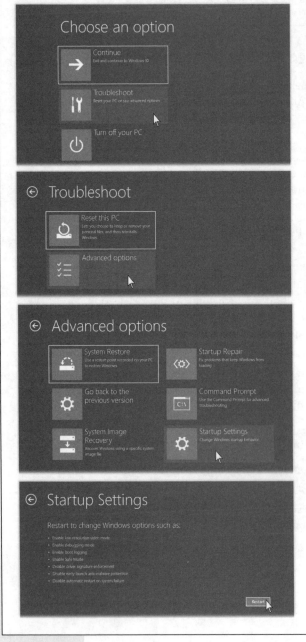

Figure 15-8:
Welcome to the Windows Recovery Environment. Somewhere in this series of screens, you'll encounter every conceivable troubleshooting tool.

The first one is the "Choose an option" screen. If you select the Troubleshoot option here, you get the Troubleshoot screen (second from top). Here, for your troubleshooting pleasure, is another version of the Reset command (page 496).

If you click "Advanced options," you arrive at the "Advanced options" screen (third from top). This is a good place to recover data from a System Restore backup (page 509) or from a system image (page 506), or to rewind to the last version of Windows you'd installed, or to run Startup Repair, an automated mode that checks for, and replaces, missing or damaged system files.

But if you choose Startup Settings (which, on smaller screens, may require hitting "See more recovery options"), you arrive at this explanatory screen (bottom). Hit Restart, and once the PC comes to, you finally arrive at the actual, true-blue Startup Settings menu.

Use the arrow keys to walk through the Startup Settings options, or type the corresponding number key or function key to choose one. Here's what the Startup Settings menu commands do:

1. **Enable low-resolution video mode.**

   In this mode, your PC uses a standard VGA video driver that works with all graphics cards, instead of the hideously ugly generic one usually seen in Safe Mode. Use this option when you're troubleshooting video-display problems—problems that you're confident have less to do with drivers than with your settings in the Display control panel (which you're now ready to fiddle with).

   Of course, VGA means 640 × 480 pixels, which looks huge and crude on today's big monitors. Do not adjust your set.

2. **Enable debugging mode.**

   Here's an extremely obscure option, intended for very technical people who've connected one PC to another via a serial cable. They can then use the second computer to analyze the first, using specialized debugger software.

3. **Enable boot logging.**

   Same as Normal, except that Windows records every technical event that takes place during the startup in a log file named *ntbtlog.txt* (in your Windows folder).

   Most of the time, you'll use the boot logging option only at the request of a technician you've phoned for help. After confirming the operating system startup, the technician may ask you to open ntbtlog.txt in Notepad and search for particular words or phrases—usually the word "fail."

4. **Enable Safe Mode.**

   Safe Mode starts up Windows in a special, stripped-down, generic, startling-looking startup mode—with the software for dozens of hardware and software features *turned off.* Only the very basic components work: your mouse, keyboard, screen, and disk drives. Everything else is shut down and cut off. In short, Safe Mode is the tack to take if your PC *won't* start up normally, thanks to some recalcitrant driver.

   Once you select the Safe Mode option on the Startup menu, you see a list, filling your screen, of every driver Windows is loading. Eventually, you're asked to sign in.

   Your screen now looks like it was designed by drunken cavemen, with jagged, awful graphics and text. That's because in Safe Mode, Windows doesn't load the driver for your video card (on the assumption that it may be causing the very problem you're trying to troubleshoot). Instead, Windows loads a crude, generic driver that works with *any* video card.

   The purpose of Safe Mode is to help you troubleshoot. If you discover that the problem you've been having is now gone, you've at least established that the culprit was one of the now-disabled startup items or drivers. If this procedure doesn't solve the problem, then contact a support technician.

5. Enable Safe Mode with Networking.

This option is exactly the same as Safe Mode, except that it also lets you load the driver software needed to tap into a network or onto the internet—an arrangement that offers a few additional troubleshooting possibilities, like being able to access drivers on another PC or from the internet.

6. Enable Safe Mode with Command Prompt.

This variation of Safe Mode is for power users who are comfortable typing out text commands at the command prompt.

7. Disable driver signature enforcement.

As a way to protect your PC, Windows uses a technique called driver signature enforcement, which is designed to load only drivers verified to be valid. Of course, there are plenty of times when drivers aren't verified but are in fact usable. If you suspect that to be the case, choose this option; Windows will load all your drivers.

8. Disable early-launch anti-malware protection.

Bad guys often release a *rootkit* (a virus-like bit of software), which installs a driver that loads into memory when your computer starts up. Since it's there before your antivirus software has loaded, it's difficult to detect and remove. As revenge, Microsoft created Early-Launch Anti-Malware Protection (ELAMP), a window of opportunity for certain antivirus programs to load before all other drivers. That way, the antivirus software can scan any other drivers that load and, if they're malware, block them.

Ah—but what if one of these antivirus programs identifies a driver as evil but it's not? Then you won't be able to start up at all. In that situation, you'd want to turn ELAMP off using this option. Once you've started up, update your virus software or remove the questionable driver. The next time you start up, ELAMP will be turned on again.

9. Disable automatic restart on system failure.

Under normal conditions, Windows automatically reboots after a system crash. Choose this option if you don't want it to reboot.

If you press F10 instead of choosing one of those nine options, you're offered the chance to return to the Windows Recovery Environment. If you press Enter, you start the operating system in its usual fashion, exactly as though you'd never summoned the Startup Settings menu to begin with. It lets you tell the PC, "Sorry to have interrupted you…go ahead."

Thanks to these powerful startup tools, there are fewer reasons than ever to pay $35 for the privilege of talking to some technician following a script.

Two Obscure Speed Boosts

Every PC seems to get slower the longer you own it. Fortunately, in Windows 10, here and there, nestled among the 50 million lines of code, you'll find a couple of free tricks that may give your PC a speed boost:

- **SuperFetch** attempts to keep your most frequently used programs in RAM (memory), ready to go, all the time, based on your work patterns.

- **ReadyBoost** lets you use a USB flash drive as an additional cache (a chunk of superfast memory) for frequently used data.

For details on both features, see the free PDF appendix to this chapter called "Two Speed Boosts." It's on this book's "Missing CD" at *missingmanuals.com*.

Backups & File History

T here are two kinds of people in the world: those who have a regular backup system—and those who *will*.

You'll get that grisly joke immediately if you've deleted the wrong folder by accident, made changes you regret, or (worst of all) had your hard drive die. All those photos, all that music you've bought online, all your email—gone. It's *painful*.

Yet the odds are overwhelming that, at this moment, you do not have a complete, current, automated backup of your computer. Despite about a thousand warnings, articles, and cautionary tales a year, guess how many people do? About *4 percent*. Everybody else is flying without a net.

If you don't have much to back up—you don't have much in the way of photos, music, or movies—you can get by with copying stuff onto a flash drive or using a free online backup system like Dropbox or your OneDrive. But those methods leave most of your stuff unprotected: all your programs and settings.

What you really want, of course, is a backup that's rock-solid, complete, and *automatic*. You don't want to have to remember to do a backup, to insert a drive, and so on. You just want to know you're safe.

If you use Windows in a corporation, you probably don't even have to think about backing up your stuff. A network administrator generally does the backing up for you.

But if you use Windows at home, or in a smaller company that doesn't have network nerds running around to ensure your files' safety, you'll be happy to know about the various tools that come with Windows 10, all dedicated to the proposition of making safety copies.

What's confusing is that there are three different backup mechanisms in Windows these days, some of which Microsoft is trying to de-emphasize by hiding them. Here's a quick overview:

- **System images.** A complete clone of your entire hard drive, including all your files, all your apps, and Windows itself. Strangely buried in Windows 10, but useful—the only option that will get you back up and running if your entire drive dies (or gets stolen).

- **System Restore.** A "snapshot" of your copy of Windows, as it was when it was last working well. You can rewind to a snapshot when, for example, a new app or upgrade seems to foul things up.

- **File History.** For rewinding *individual documents* to earlier drafts—or recovering them if they've gotten deleted or damaged.

Note: Of course, these are only the backup features of Windows 10 itself. You can also buy non-Microsoft backup programs, many of which have more features.

This chapter covers these three systems in order.

System Images

When your hard disk crashes, you lose more than just your personal files. You also lose your operating system—*and* all the programs you've installed, *and* all their updates and patches, *and* all your settings and tweaks. It can take you a very long time to restore your PC to that state.

A *system image* solves the problem easily. This feature (called Complete PC Backup in the Windows Vista days), creates a perfect snapshot of your entire hard drive at this moment: documents, email, pictures, and so on, *plus* Windows, *and* all your programs and settings. Someone could steal your entire hard drive, or your drive could die, and you'd be able to install a new, empty one and be back in business inside of an hour.

It's a good idea to make a fresh system image every few months, because you'll probably have installed new programs and changed your settings in the interim.

Note: For the techies scoring at home, a system image is a .vhd file, the same kind that's created by Microsoft's Virtual PC software—and, therefore, you can mount it using Virtual PC, if you like.

Make the Image

To make a system image, open the old Control Panel (type *control pan* into the ⊞ search box). Open "Backup and Restore (Windows 7)." Never mind that "Windows 7" part—it still works in Windows 10.

Choose "Create a system image" (Figure 16-1, top); proceed as shown in Figure 16-1.

No matter where you store the image, you'll need a *lot* of empty disk space. Not as much as your entire PC drive, because you won't be backing up empty space or temporary files. But a lot.

Note: You can keep multiple system images around—representing your PC's world at different times—if you back up to discs or hard drives. If you save to a network location, though, you can keep only the most recent system image.

Figure 16-1:
Top: On this Control Panel screen, start the process with "Create a system image."

Bottom: Your options: a hard drive (must be NTFS formatted), a stack of CDs or DVDs, or (if you have the Pro or Enterprise editions of Windows) another computer on the network.

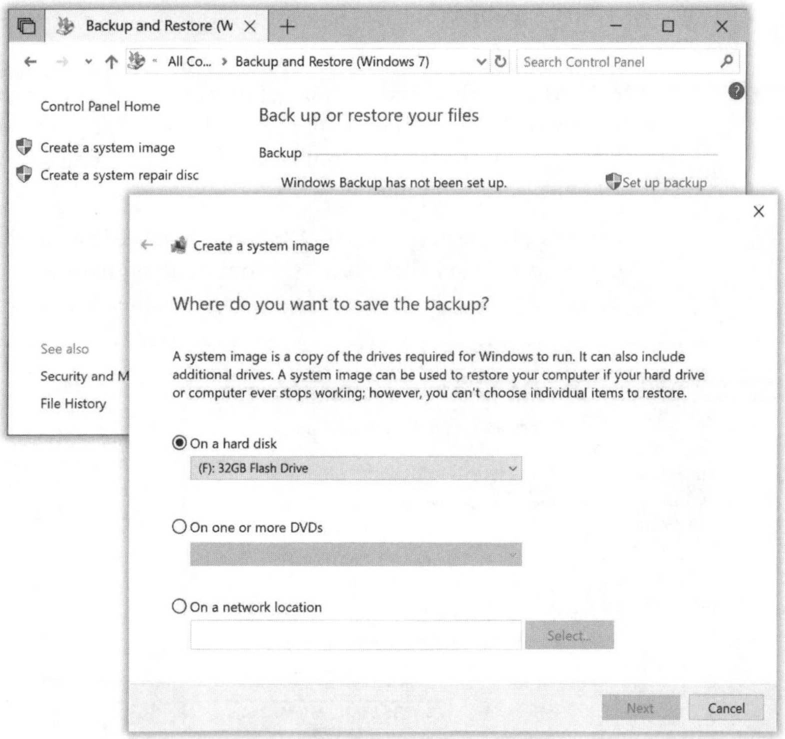

When you hit Next, you're offered a list of all your computer's drives and informed how much storage space the backup will need. You may, if you wish, include other drives as part of the system image, so they'll be restored, too, if the worst should come to pass. (Your Windows drive is automatically selected; you're not allowed to include the drive you're saving the image *onto*.)

Choose "Start backup"; the backup begins. You'll be prompted if you need to insert new discs.

Restore the Image

Suppose disaster strikes: Your hard drive is trashed. Fortunately, restoring your entire system using a system image is easy. You just have to open the Windows Recovery Environment (page 499):

- **If your PC is running,** hold down the Shift key as you hit Restart. (To find the Restart button, select ⊞→⏻.)

- **If the PC won't even start up,** start up from a Windows DVD, flash drive, or system repair disk. At the Windows Setup screen, hit Next; then choose "Repair your computer."

Once you see the "Choose an option" screen, click Troubleshoot, then "Advanced options," and then System Image Recovery. (You can see this sequence of screens illustrated in Figure 15-8 on page 500.) In the System Recovery Options dialog box that appears, choose an administrator's account. Enter the appropriate password, and then click Continue.

On the next screen (Figure 16-2), choose "Use the latest available system image (recommended)," and click Next. (Of course, if you have some weird agenda, you can also choose an older system image using the other option here.)

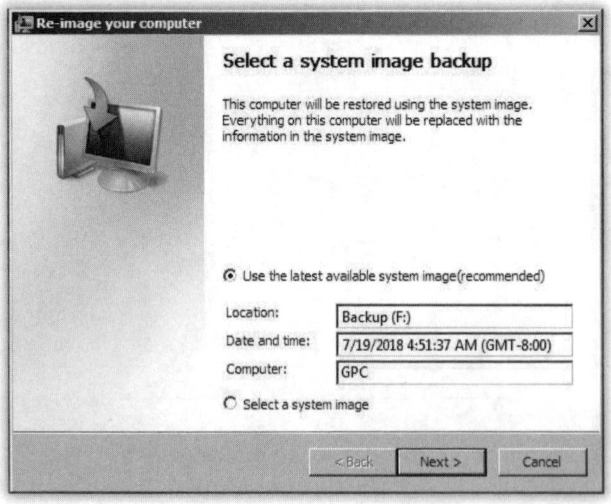

Figure 16-2:
Here's the payoff for your diligent system imaging. Windows is about to turn your current, messed-up computer back into the model of PC health it was the day you made the image.

When prompted, find the drive or disc that contains your system image. When you click Next, you see the "Choose additional restore options" dialog box, which offers some complicated options. The key element worth inspecting is the "Format and repartition disks" option:

- **If this option is turned on,** then every disk and partition will be formatted and partitioned to match the system image. (If this box is turned on and dimmed, then you have no choice.)

- **If you can't turn on this checkbox**—it's dimmed and unchecked—then you're probably restoring a system image from one partition to another on the same disk. Clearly, Windows can't erase the disk it's operating from.

The "Only restore system drives" option does what it says: leaves your other drives alone.

When you click Finish and then Yes in the confirmation box, the long, slow restoration process begins. And the rest, as they say, is history recreated.

Just remember that this process *reformats your hard drive,* and in the process *wipes out all your data and files.* They'll be replaced with the most recent snapshot (system image) you've made. Of course, you may well have a *regular* backup that's more recent; you can restore that as the final step.

Note: If you were thinking of using a system image to turn a new PC into a replica of your old, crashed one, be warned: You can't restore a system image to a new PC's hard drive if it's smaller than the old one. (Yes, even if the data on the backup drive would easily fit on the target drive.)

System Restore

As you get more proficient on a PC, pressing Ctrl+Z—the keyboard shortcut for Undo—eventually becomes an unconscious reflex. In fact, you can sometimes spot Windows veterans twitching their Ctrl+Z fingers even when they're not near the computer—after knocking over a cup of coffee, locking the keys inside the car, or blurting out something inappropriate in a meeting.

Windows offers the mother of all Undo commands: System Restore. This feature alone can be worth hours of your time and hundreds of dollars in consultant fees.

The pattern of things going wrong in Windows usually works like this: The PC works fine for a while, and then suddenly—maybe for no apparent reason, but most often following an installation or configuration change—it goes on the fritz. At that point, wouldn't it be pleasant to be able to tell the computer, "Go back to the way you were yesterday, please"?

System Restore does exactly that. It "rewinds" your copy of Windows back to the condition it was in before you, or something you tried to install, messed it up. Best of all, System Restore *doesn't change your files.* Your email, pictures, music, documents, and other files are left up to date.

Tip: If your PC manages to catch a virus, System Restore can even rewind it to a time before the infection—*if* the virus hasn't gotten into your documents in such a way that you reinfect yourself after the system restore. An up-to-date antivirus program (page 408) is a much more effective security blanket.

In fact, if you don't like your PC after restoring it, you can always restore it to the way it was *before* you restored it. Back to the future!

Turning on System Restore

In the latest versions of Windows 10, the System Restore feature comes turned off. It's not protecting you until you turn it on.

To do that, open the System Protection dialog box shown in Figure 16-3. Choose Configure, and then "Turn on system protection." Use the slider to designate a maximum amount of disk space you're willing to dedicate to this feature (see the box on the facing page.) Click OK.

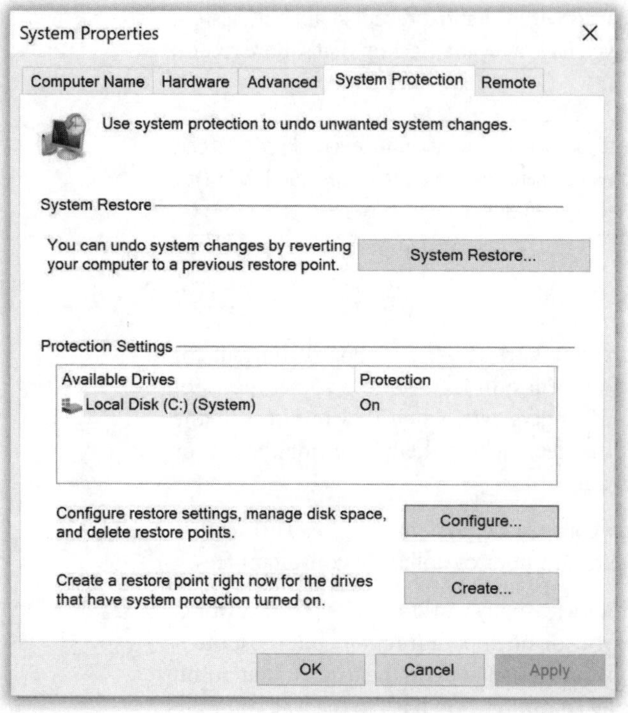

Figure 16-3:
Here's your command center for all System Restore functions.

To get here: Start typing restore *into the* ■ *search box until you see "Create a restore point." Choose it.*

Hit Configure to turn this protection feature on. Use Configure to delete all restore points and limit disk space.

Select System Restore to perform the actual rewinding of your system.

System Restore will now take periodic memorized snapshots, called *restore points*, of your copy of Windows. In particular, Windows will create landing points for your little PC time machine at the following times:

- **Every time you install a new program,** a new device driver, or a Windows Update.

- **Whenever you feel like it**—for instance, just before you install a new component.

When the worst comes to pass, and your PC starts acting up, you can use System Restore to rewind your machine to its configuration the last time you remember it working well.

Manual Restore Points

To create one of these checkpoints *manually*, open the System Protection dialog box (Figure 16-3). At the bottom of that box, hit Create to make and name a new manual restore point. (Windows adds a date and time stamp automatically.)

Performing a System Restore

If something goes wrong with your PC, here's how to roll it back to the happy, bygone days of late last week:

1. **Open the System Protection dialog box (Figure 16-3).**

   The steps are described on the previous pages.

2. **Click System Restore.**

   The "Restore system files and settings" welcome screen appears (Figure 16-4, top).

   Windows is suggesting that you rewind only as far as the most recent change you made to your machine—a software installation, for example. In Figure 16-4 at top, you can see that the most recent restore point was made when you installed a new device driver. If your computer suddenly started acting up, well, you've got your culprit.

POWER USERS' CLINIC

System Restore vs. Your Hard Drive

Ever wonder where Windows stashes all those backup copies of your operating system? They're in a folder called System Volume Information, which is in your Local Disk (C:) window. Inside *that* are individual files for each restore point. (System Volume Information is generally an invisible folder, but you can make it visible by following the instructions on page 572. You still won't be allowed to move, rename, or delete it, however—thank goodness. In fact, you won't even be able to look inside it.)

As you can imagine, storing all these copies of your Windows configuration consumes quite a bit of disk space. That's why System Restore lets you limit how much of your drive

is allowed to fill up with restore points. Click Configure in the System Protection dialog box (Figure 16-3); you get a slider that lets you cap the percentage of the drive that can be swallowed up with restore-point data. When your drive gets full, System Restore starts deleting the oldest restore points as necessary.

In times of strife, there's also a nuclear option here: the Delete button. Note, however, that this deletes not just all your restore points, but also the backups of all your *documents* (those created by the File Histories feature described starting on page 513).

You've been warned. Be careful out there.

If that seems like the right restore point, click Next, and then Finish; that's all there is to it. If it seems like you might want to rewind your computer to an even earlier point, though, read on:

3. **Choose "Choose a different restore point."**

The list of all memorized restore points appears (Figure 16-4, bottom).

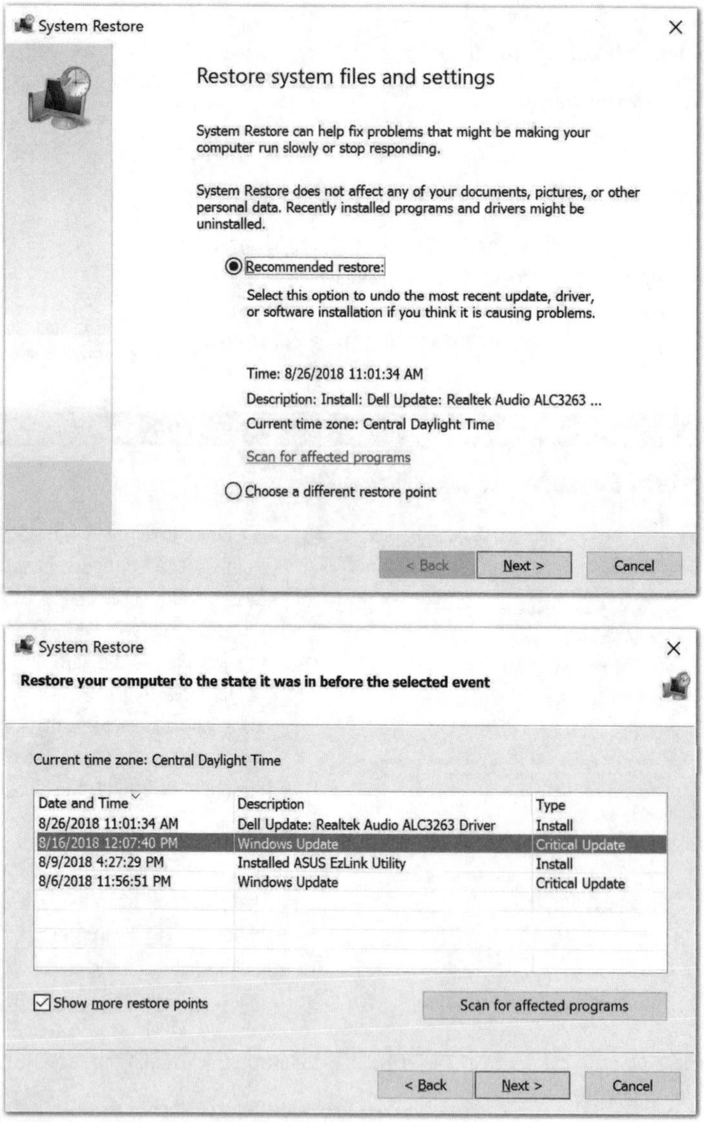

Figure 16-4:

Top: Windows suggests rewinding your computer to the most recent change you made to it. Most often, that's what you want.

Bottom: You can, however, also hit "Choose a different restore point" to view a list of older restore points Windows or you have made, anticipating just this moment. You're shown the date and time of each restore point, as well as why the restore point was created—for example, because you installed a new piece of software, or because you applied a Windows Update. That's a clue as to which restore point you should use.

Bottom: You can now see which software elements this system rewind will affect.

4. **Choose a restore point, and then select "Scan for affected programs."**

Now Windows thoughtfully displays a list of which apps and drivers will be affected if you go through with the restore. Remember: Any apps and drivers you've *installed* since that point will be deleted; any apps and drivers you've *deleted* since then will be put back! You're literally rewinding your computer.

5. **If all looks good, choose Close, and then Next.**

You have one more chance to back out: Windows displays the date and time of the restore point, shows you which drives will be affected, gives you another chance to create a password-reset disk, and asks if you *really* want to go back in time.

6. **Click Finish. In the confirmation box, click Yes.**

Windows goes to town, reinstating your operating system to reflect its condition on the date you specified. Leave your PC alone while this occurs.

When the process is complete, the computer restarts automatically. When you sign in again, you're back to the past—and with any luck, your PC runs smoothly. (None of your emails or files are disturbed.)

If it didn't work—if you only made things worse—then repeat step 1. At the top of the System Restore welcome screen, you'll see an option called Undo System Restore. It lets you *undo* your undoing.

Or, of course, you can click "Choose a different restore point" if you think that maybe you didn't rewind your PC back far *enough* and want to try again with a different restore point.

Turning System Restore Off

You really shouldn't turn off System Restore. It's incredibly useful to hit rewind and get a smoothly running PC, even if you never do find out what the trouble was.

But if you're an advanced power user with no hard drive space to spare—is there such a person?—then open the System Protection tab of the System Properties box (shown in Figure 16-3). Click Configure, click "Disable system protection," and then click OK. (See the box on page 511 for details.)

In the "Are you sure?" box, click Yes. That's it. You're flying without a net now, baby.

File History

System Restore is an amazing, powerful, career-saving feature—but it's awfully self-interested. It cares only about protecting *Windows*.

How can you rewind your *documents* to their earlier, healthier, or pre-edited conditions?

File History is a time machine for documents in the same way System Restore is a time machine for your system software. It's an incredible safety net against damage, accidental modification, or late-night bouts of ill-advised editing. It automatically backs up files in your libraries, on the desktop, in your address book, and on your OneDrive. If anything bad happens to the originals, you're covered. You can also rewind documents to specific dates—if, for example, you decide your novel was better before you tinkered with it last week. It's a lot like the Time Machine feature on the Mac.

Note: There was a similar but less sophisticated feature in Windows 7 called either Previous Versions or Shadow Copy, long gone now.

The beauty of File History is that it's automatic and invisible. And to save time and disk space, File History bothers copying only the files that have changed since the last restore point was created.

Set Up File History

The File History feature has its own dashboard in ■→⚙→Update & Security→ Backup (Figure 16-5, top).

File History works best if you direct it to create its backups on some other drive—not the one the files are on now. The whole point, after all, is to provide protection against something going wrong—and disk failure is a big something. So you're supposed to use an external drive—even a flash drive with decent capacity will do—or another computer on the network.

If there's already a second drive connected to your computer, Windows cheerfully begins using it to store the backups. If you've got more than one, hit "Add a drive" and choose it.

And that, dear reader, is it. If the "Automatically back up my files" button is on, then your computer is backing up your files automatically, once every hour. Isn't peace of mind wonderful?

File History Options

On the ⚙→Update & Security→Backup screen, the "More options" link takes you to a wonderland of additional settings (Figure 16-5, bottom):

- **Back up now.** If you can't wait for the hourly backup, this button lets you trigger a backup now.

- **Back up my files [when].** Ordinarily, File History quietly checks your computer once an hour. If any file has changed, it gets backed up at the end of the hour. These follow-up backups are quick; Windows backs up only what's changed.

  So, should disaster strike, the only changes you can lose are those you've made within the past 59 minutes.

  With this drop-down menu, though, you can specify different backup intervals— anything from "Every 10 minutes" to "Every 12 hours" or just "Daily."

- **Keep my backups [how long].** This menu lets you specify how *long* you want Windows to hang on to the old versions of your documents. Maybe after a year, for example, it's OK for those old backups to start self-deleting, to save space on the backup drive. Or "Until space is needed," meaning that older backups self-delete to make room for new ones when the backup disk is full.

- **Back up these folders.** Unless you start meddling, Windows automatically backs up your entire personal folder—that is, everything in your own account folder: documents, photos, music, videos, settings, and so on (page 25). But by using the "Add a folder" button, you can tell File History to back up folders that *aren't* in your personal folder.

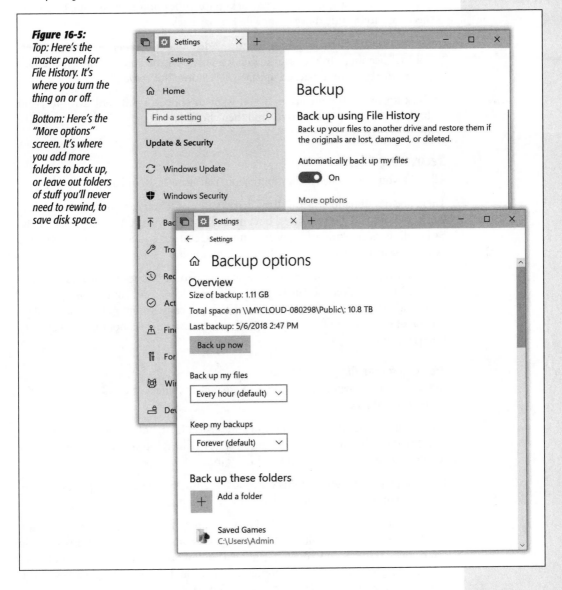

Figure 16-5:
Top: Here's the master panel for File History. It's where you turn the thing on or off.

Bottom: Here's the "More options" screen. It's where you add more folders to back up, or leave out folders of stuff you'll never need to rewind, to save disk space.

- **Exclude these folders.** The whole point of File History is to have a backup of all your files. It's conceivable, though, that you might want to exclude some files or folders from the File History treatment. First, you might not want certain, ahem, private materials to be part of your data trail.

  Second, you might want to save space on the backup drive, either because it's not as big as your main drive or because you'd rather dedicate its space to more backups of the essential stuff. For example, you might decide not to back up your collection of downloaded TV shows, since video files are enormous. Or maybe you use an online photo-sharing website as a backup for your photos, so you don't think it's necessary to include those in the File History backup.

  To omit certain files and folders, choose "Add a folder" (under the "Exclude these folders" heading). In the resulting dialog box, navigate your computer, choose a folder you don't need backed up, and hit "Choose this folder."

- **Back up to a different drive.** If you want to choose a different drive for your backups, hit "Stop using drive," and then choose a new one. (The backups on the original drive are still safe.)

Recovering Files

All right, you've got File History on the job. You sleep easy at night.

Then, one day, it happens: Your hard drive crashes. Or you can't find a file or folder you know you had. Or you save a document and then wish you could go back to an earlier draft. Some kind of disaster—sunspots, clueless spouse, overtired self—has befallen your files. This is File History's big moment.

Do a ⊞ search for *file history*; in the results list, choose "Restore your files with File History." The old Control Panel opens up (Figure 16-6, top). Your job is to find the file in question, either because it's been deleted or because you want to rescue an older version of it. There are four ways to go about it: browsing, Ribboning, searching, or Properties-ing.

Browsing for the file

In the window shown in Figure 16-6, double-click folders as usual, looking for the file in its usual place.

If it's been deleted, of course, you won't find it—at least, not in *today's* listing. But if you click the ◄ button, the entire window slides to the right; you're viewing endlessly scrolling *versions* of the current window, going back in time.

If you scroll back far enough this way, you'll eventually see the missing file reappear. You've rewound time to a point before it went missing.

Scrolling back in time is also useful when you want to find an earlier *version*, or draft, of a document. And how will you know which version you're looking at? Because you can *double-click* an icon to open it, right within this window (Figure 16-6, bottom). You can keep clicking the ◄ button even when the document is open, so you can watch its contents change in real (backward) time.

Once you've found the file in question, click the big green Restore button. Magically enough, the lost or outdated file or folder is brought back from the dead.

File History prides itself not just on recovering files and folders, but also on putting them back where they came from.

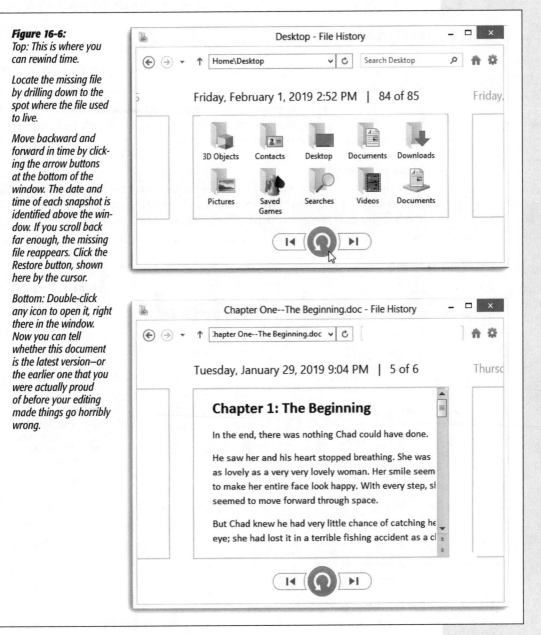

Figure 16-6:
Top: This is where you can rewind time.

Locate the missing file by drilling down to the spot where the file used to live.

Move backward and forward in time by clicking the arrow buttons at the bottom of the window. The date and time of each snapshot is identified above the window. If you scroll back far enough, the missing file reappears. Click the Restore button, shown here by the cursor.

Bottom: Double-click any icon to open it, right there in the window. Now you can tell whether this document is the latest version—or the earlier one that you were actually proud of before your editing made things go horribly wrong.

Tip: You can also tell File History to put the file or folder into a *new* location. To do that, right-click its icon; from the shortcut menu, choose "Restore to," and then choose the new folder location.

If you recover a different version of something that's still there, Windows asks if you want to replace it with the recovered version—or if you'd rather keep both versions.

Ribbon rewinding

You don't actually have to bother with the Control Panel when you want to restore a file. There's a History button on the Ribbon's Home tab in every File Explorer window.

In other words, you can start the recovery process by opening the folder that contains (or used to contain) the file you want. Or find the icon of the file you want to rewind. In either case, click that History button. You wind up in exactly the same spot illustrated in Figure 16-6; the recovery process is the same.

Searching for the file

Once you've opened the window shown in Figure 16-6, here's another way to find the missing or changed file: Type into the search box at the top of the window. That's handy if you can't remember what folder it was in. See Figure 16-7.

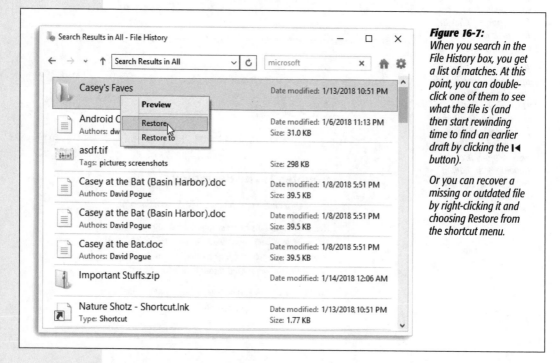

Figure 16-7:
When you search in the File History box, you get a list of matches. At this point, you can double-click one of them to see what the file is (and then start rewinding time to find an earlier draft by clicking the ◀ button).

Or you can recover a missing or outdated file by right-clicking it and choosing Restore from the shortcut menu.

The Properties dialog box

The fourth way to rewind a file or folder is to right-click its icon (or hold your finger down on it); from the shortcut menu, choose "Restore previous versions." The

Properties dialog box opens for that item, where you can click the tab called Previous Versions.

Note: Question: If you have to click the Previous Versions tab anyway, why choose "Restore previous versions" from the shortcut menu instead of Properties? Answer: Who knows? Both commands do exactly the same thing.

Anyway, the result is a list of previous versions of your document. Each one is date-stamped. To inspect a version to see if it's the one you want, select it and then hit Open. (You can also use the button's drop-down menu to choose "Open in File History," which takes you to the box shown at the bottom of Figure 16-6.)

When you've found the one you want, click Restore; Windows cheerfully recovers the older version of that file or folder and puts it back where it used to be (or where the current version sits). Or you can save it into a different folder by using the Restore button's drop-down menu ("Restore to").

The USB Recovery Drive

Here's the sneaky surprise: Your computer may have come with an invisible "hard drive" (a partition of your main drive). It's about 5 gigabytes in size.

When the day comes when your computer won't start up, you'll be glad you had this "separate" disk. On it, Microsoft has provided some emergency tools for fixing drive or software glitches, restoring files, and even reinstalling Windows.

Better yet, you can create a USB flash drive that does the same thing. That's handy if (a) your computer does not have a recovery partition, or (b) you wouldn't mind deleting the recovery partition from your drive, so you can use the space for your own files.

Note: Techies, the *recimg* command is no longer in Windows 10.

1. **Do a search for *recovery drive*; in the results list, choose "Create a recovery drive."**

   Authenticate if necessary.

   Before you click the first Next button in the Recovery Drive wizard, note the checkbox called "Back up system files to the recovery drive." If that's turned on, then your flash drive will be able to reinstall a copy of Windows on your machine—a great safety net. (If you turn this box off, then your flash drive will contain troubleshooting tools only; you'll have to figure out some other way to reinstall Windows, if it comes to that.)

   Be sure that "Copy the recovery partition from the PC to the recovery drive" is selected.

2. **Hit Next. Insert a USB flash drive into your computer.**

   The message on the screen tells you how much space the flash drive needs—and that the flash drive is about to be *erased*.

3. **Select the USB drive's name; hit Next; hit Create.**

Windows copies the recovery image and recovery tools to your flash drive. It takes awhile. At the end, you can choose Finish (to keep your PC's recovery partition) or "Delete the recovery partition from your PC" to free up the disk space.

Using Your Recovery Drive

Should trouble ever strike, you can start up the computer from that flash drive, even if (especially if) it can't start up normally on its own.

Note: Truth is, if your PC is having a problem, your first thought should be to use one of the reset options at this point (page 496); the recovery process will be faster and more convenient. Proceed with your recovery drive only if the Reset thing doesn't help get your PC going again.

Turn on the computer with the flash drive inserted. The "Choose an option" screen (page 497) appears. (Welcome to the Recovery Environment; hope you enjoy your stay.)

Select Troubleshoot and then "Recover from a drive."

Now the Windows virtual paramedics spin into action. They'll *delete all your files, programs, settings, and drivers*, leaving behind only a fresh, clean installation of Windows 10, as though it's day one.

CHAPTER 17

The Disk Chapter

To make life easier for you, the terminology of objects on your computer screen precisely mirrors the terminology of the real world. You use the computer to create *files*, just as in the real world. You put those files into *folders*, just as in the real world. And you put those folders into *filing cabinets*—

Well, OK. The metaphor goes only so far.

There is a term for the larger storage entity that holds all those files and folders, though: disks.

Nobody uses floppy disks anymore, and even CDs and DVDs are rapidly disappearing. But spinning hard drives are still cheap, big, reliable, and common, and SSDs (solid-state drives) are popular in laptops, despite their relatively high cost and small capacity.

In any case, this chapter is all about storage and disks: cleanups, defragmentation, compression, encryption, analysis, and management.

Note: Some of the features mentioned in this chapter—dynamic disks, disk compression, and EFS (encrypting file system)—all require the *NTFS file system* on your computer's disk drives. That's probably what you're using on your main hard drive, because Windows 10 requires it.

But many other kinds of disks—memory cards, flash drives, and so on—use the older FAT32 file system instead. You won't be able to use NTFS tricks on them.

Storage Sense: More Gigs, Yours Free

Your PC sits at the unhappy pinch point between two opposing trends: the growing size of today's files (videos, photos, music) and the shrunken size of our available storage (the non–hard disks on today's laptops).

But Windows 10 can help—by reclaiming swaths of wasted space on your drive.

The feature is called Storage Sense. Once you turn it on, it automatically deletes these kinds of files to make more room:

- **Temporary files.** Various programs create invisible files in tucked-away places as "scratch pads" for the work they do. Unfortunately, they then sometimes forget to delete those files. Storage Sense to the rescue!

- **Recycle Bin files.** Storage Sense autodeletes files you threw into the Bin more than 30 days ago (or 1 day, 14 days, or 60 days ago).

- **Forgotten downloads.** If you downloaded stuff more than 30 days ago (or 1 day, 14 days, or 60 days ago) and then left it, unchanged, in the Downloads folder, Storage Sense figures it's ripe for deleting.

- **Old versions of Windows 10.** If you upgraded to the Windows 10 May 2019 Update from an earlier Windows version, and everything seems to be going well, there may not be much point in keeping all those old gigabytes of Windows around. They do, after all, eat up 13 gigs per version.

If you like the idea of Storage Sense, open ⊞→⚙→System→Storage and turn it on.

While you're here, hit "Configure Storage Sense or run it now." On the resulting screen (Figure 17-1, lower left), you can specify:

- **When Storage Sense should do its cleanups.** You might choose daily, weekly, monthly, or only when your drive is running out of space.

- **How old temporary files have to be.** The Temporary Files pop-up menus offer to auto-delete files that have been rotting untouched in your Recycle Bin and Downloads folders for a long time.

- **Whether to nuke local OneDrive copies.** As you know from page 141, Windows generally copies your online OneDrive files onto your PC so they're available even when you're not online. But that, of course, eats up a lot of disk space.

  The OneDrive pop-up menu tells Windows to auto-delete *local* OneDrive files (the copies on your PC) that you haven't touched in awhile. This feature never affects the online OneDrive copies (nor files on any other synced machines).

- **Free up space now.** Storage Space usually kicks in automatically, in the background, when you're not doing much on your PC. But if you need space right now, you can hit "Clean now" to run it on the spot. (It's still governed by the what-and-when settings on this screen.)

What's Eating Up Your Disk

As you can see in Figure 17-1, there's a handy "how full is my disk" graph at the top of the ■■→⚙→System→Storage screen.

Below that, you get a breakdown of the *kinds* of files filling your hard drives: pictures, videos, music, documents, and so on. Then you can select one of *those* graphs to drill down even further. Eventually, you burrow all the way to a details screen that lets you inspect the underlying storage-occupiers.

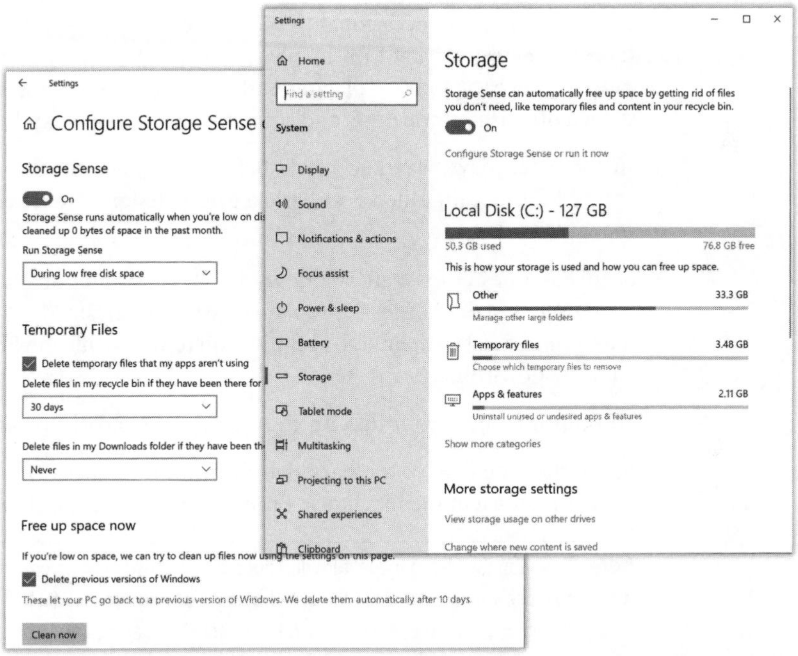

Figure 17-1:
Top right: Here's a list of your drives and how full they are. Click one to open its details screen, a breakdown of which kinds of files are eating up space. At this point, you can click a category to open a File Explorer or Settings window, where you can inspect and delete the stuff that's overrunning your storage.

Bottom left: This page lets you control which items Storage Sense deletes—and when.

Actually, you can do more than inspect them; you can remove them. For example:

- **Apps & features.** Select this bar to open the screen described on page 253, where it's easy to start deleting programs you don't need anymore.

- **Pictures, Music, Videos, Documents, Desktop, OneDrive.** Hit one of these graphs, and then the resulting View button, to open a File Explorer window containing that file type for inspection and cleaning. (These tallies show what's in your Pictures, Music, Videos, Documents, and OneDrive *folders*. If you have pictures, music, videos, and documents in other folders, they're not counted here.)

- **Mail.** "Manage mail" opens your Mail app, so you can delete some mail to save space.

- **Maps** refers to offline maps (regions you've saved to your computer so you can view them without an internet connection later; see page 313). Hit "Manage maps" to open a Settings page that lists your offline maps for easy purging.

- **Temporary files** may offer the most fruitful spring cleaning of all. Here are links to all kinds of cache files, temporary files, and other junk Windows doesn't really need. Turn on the checkboxes that seem promising, and then hit "Remove files," to reclaim what's sometimes a ton of space.

Hard Drive Checkups

It's true: Things can occasionally go wrong on the surface of your hard drive. Maybe there's a messed-up spot on its physical surface. Maybe, thanks to a system crash, power outage, or toddler playing with your surge suppressor, your computer gets turned off without warning, and some files are left open and stranded.

In the olden days, way back even before Windows XP, fixing your disk required running a program called ScanDisk, a utility designed to detect and, when possible, repair drive damage.

ScanDisk doesn't exist in Windows 10. But its functions, and many more, have been overhauled. Many disk problems are automatically detected and automatically fixed—and most of them don't require you to wait while the PC repairs itself. There's a lot less downtime.

You can also check your disk on command—the old disk-checking procedure.

Right-click the icon of the hard drive you want to check (in the This PC window). From the shortcut menu, choose Properties; click the Tools tab, and click Check.

Note: Geeks fondly refer to the feature described here as *chkdsk* (apparently named by someone with no vowels on his keyboard). You get to the geek-friendly, text-only version of it by typing *chkdsk* in a Command Prompt window. But the method described here is much better looking.

Volumes Defined

You won't get far in this chapter, or in most PC chat rooms, without understanding a key piece of Windows terminology: *volume.*

For most people, most of the time, volume means "disk." But technically, there's more to it than that—a distinction that becomes crucial if you explore the techniques described in this chapter.

If you open your This PC window, you see that each disk has its own icon and drive letter (C:, for example). But each icon isn't necessarily a separate disk. It's possible that you, or somebody in charge of your PC, has split a single disk into multiple *partitions* (page 583), each with a separate icon and drive letter. Clearly, the world needs a term for "an icon/drive letter in the This PC window, whether it's a whole disk or not." That term is *volume.*

Disk Management

"Disk management" isn't just a cool, professional-sounding skill—it's the name of a built-in Windows maintenance program that lets you perform all kinds of operations on your hard disk. To open it, right-click the Start menu; from the shortcut menu, choose Disk Management. (Only administrator account–holders are welcome.)

You arrive at the window shown in Figure 17-2. At first glance, it appears to be nothing more than a table of every disk (and *partition* of every disk) currently connected to your PC. In truth, the Disk Management window is a software toolkit that lets you *operate* on these drives.

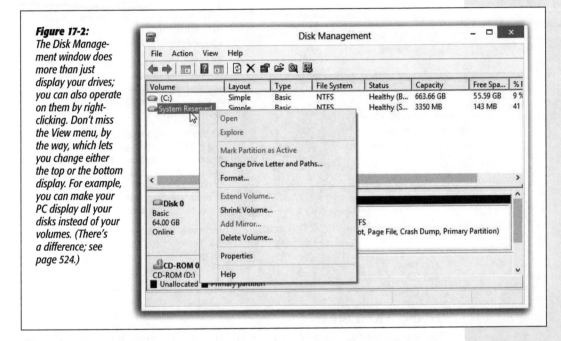

Figure 17-2:
The Disk Management window does more than just display your drives; you can also operate on them by right-clicking. Don't miss the View menu, by the way, which lets you change either the top or the bottom display. For example, you can make your PC display all your disks instead of your volumes. (There's a difference; see page 524.)

Change a Drive Letter

As you've probably noticed, Windows assigns a drive letter to each disk drive associated with your PC. In the age of floppy disks, the floppy drives were always A: and B:. The primary internal hard drive is generally C:; your CD/DVD drive may be D: or E:; and so on. Among other places, you see these letters in parentheses following the names of your drives in the This PC window.

Windows generally assigns these letters in the order you install new drives to your system. You're not allowed to change the drive letter of any startup hard drive (the C: drive and, if you're set up for dual booting, any other boot drives).

You can, however, override the *other* drives' unimaginative Windows letter assignments easily enough, as shown in Figure 17-3. Your computer won't run any faster, but you may feel a tiny surge of pride at how much better organized you feel.

Note: If Windows is currently using files on the disk whose drive letter you're trying to change, Disk Management might create the new drive letter assignment but leave the old one intact until the next time you restart the computer. This is an effort to not pull the rug out from under any open files.

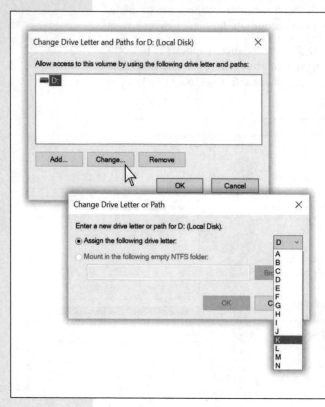

Figure 17-3:
Right-click a drive icon. From the shortcut menu, choose Change Drive Letter and Paths.

Top: In this dialog box, click Change.

Bottom: Next, choose a letter that hasn't already been assigned. Click OK, and then approve your action in the confirmation box. Note that if you change a drive's letter, shortcut icons pointing to files on it no longer work.

And although you can change the drive letter of a USB drive (like an external hard drive or a flash drive), it won't stick. Next time you attach it, Windows will just give it the first available letter.

It's also possible, by the way, to turn a drive into a "folder," with its own letter (technically known as mounted drives, junction points, or drive paths). You could do that, for example, to expand the capacity of your main hard drive—by installing a second hard drive that masquerades as a folder on the first one.

For details, see the free PDF appendix to this chapter called "Turn a Drive into a Folder." It's on this book's "Missing CD" at missingmanuals.com.

Partition a New Drive

The vast majority of Windows PCs have only one hard drive, represented in the This PC window as a single icon.

Plenty of power users, however, delight in *partitioning* the hard drive—dividing its surface so it appears on the screen as two different icons with two different names. At that point, you can live like a king, enjoying the following advantages (just like people who have two separate hard drives):

- **You can keep Windows 10 on one of them** and Windows 8.1 (for example) on the other, so you can switch between the two at startup. This feature, called *dual booting,* is described on page 583.

- **You can keep your operating system(s) separate from folders and files.** In this way, you can perform a clean install of Windows (page 581) onto one partition without having to worry about losing any of your important files or installation programs. Or you can keep your files safely on one partition while you install and reinstall different operating systems, or different versions of them, on the other.

Now, in earlier Windows days, partitioning a hard drive using the tools built into Windows required first erasing the hard drive completely. Fortunately, Windows' Disk Management console can save you from that hassle, although making a backup before you begin is still a smart idea. (The short version: Right-click the disk's icon in Disk Management; from the shortcut menu, choose Shrink Volume. In the Shrink dialog box, specify how much space you want to free up, and then click Shrink. Then turn the free space into a new volume, as described next.)

Note: Partitioning is an advanced kind of surgery that involves erasing disks and moving lots of files around. *Do not proceed* unless you have a backup and you're a technically confident soul.

Creating a partition

In the Disk Management window, free space (suitable for turning into a partition of its own) shows up with a black bar and the label "Unallocated."

To create a new partition, right-click one of these unallocated segments. From the shortcut menu, choose New Simple Volume (if this option isn't available, right-click the disk and choose Initialize Disk). A wizard appears; its screens ask you to make some decisions:

- **How big you want the volume to be.** If you're dividing up a 500 GB drive, for example, you might decide to make the first volume 300 GB and the second 200 GB. Begin by creating the 300 GB volume (right-clicking the big Unallocated bar). When that's done, you see a smaller Unallocated chunk still left in the Disk Management window. Right-click it and choose New Simple Volume *again,* this time accepting the size the wizard proposes (which is *all* the remaining free space).

- **What drive letter you want to assign to it.** Most of the alphabet is at your disposal.

- **What disk-formatting scheme you want to apply to it.** Windows 10 requires NTFS for the system drive. It's far safer and more flexible than the old FAT32 system.

  Consider FAT32 only if, for example, you plan to dual-boot Windows 10 with Linux, Mac OS X, or an old version of Windows. (FAT32 might be the only file system all those operating systems can recognize simultaneously.)

When the wizard is through with you, it's safe to close the window. A quick look at your This PC window confirms that you now have new "disks" (actually partitions of the same disk), which you can use for different purposes.

Encrypting Files and Folders

If your Documents folder contains nothing but laundry lists and letters to your mom, then data security is probably not a major concern for you. But if there's some stuff on your hard drive that you'd rather keep private, Windows can help you out. The

Encrypting File System (EFS) is an NTFS feature, available in the Pro and Enterprise versions of Windows, that stores your data in a coded format that only you can read.

The beauty of EFS is that it's effortless and invisible to you, the authorized owner. Windows automatically encrypts your files before storing them on the drive, and decrypts them again when you want to read or modify them. Anyone else who signs into your computer, however, will find these files locked and off-limits.

If you've read ahead to Chapter 18, of course, you might be frowning in confusion. Isn't keeping private files private the whole point of Windows' *accounts* feature? Don't Windows' *NTFS permissions* keep busybodies out already?

Yes, but encryption provides additional security. If, for example, you're a top-level agent assigned to protect your government's most closely guarded egg salad recipe, you can use NTFS permissions to deny all other people access to the file containing the information. Nobody but you can open the file.

However, a determined intruder could conceivably boot the computer using *another* operating system—one that doesn't recognize the NTFS permissions—and access the hard drive using a special program that reads the raw data stored there. But if you had encrypted the file using EFS, that raw data would appear as gibberish, foiling your crafty nemesis.

Using EFS

You use EFS to encrypt your folders and files in much the same way that you use NTFS compression. See Figure 17-4.

Depending on how much data you've selected, it may take some time for the encryption process to complete. Once the folders and files are encrypted, they appear in File

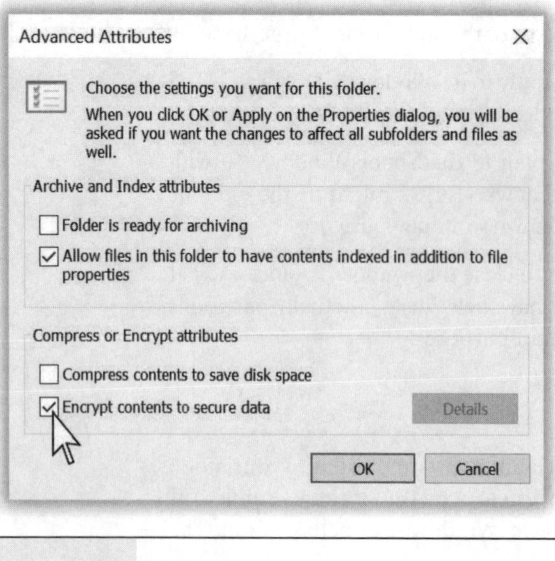

Figure 17-4:
To encrypt a file or folder using EFS, turn on the "Encrypt contents to secure data" checkbox (at the bottom of its Properties dialog box). If you've selected a folder, a Confirm Attribute Changes dialog box appears, asking if you want to encrypt just that folder or everything inside it, too.

Explorer in a different color from your compressed files (unless you've turned off the "Show encrypted or compressed NTFS files in color" option).

Note: You can't encrypt system files or any files in the system *root folder* (usually the Windows folder). You can't encrypt files and folders on FAT32 drives, either.

Finally, note that you can't both encrypt *and* compress the same file or folder. You can, however, encrypt files that have been compressed using another technology, such as .zip files or compressed image files.

After your files have been encrypted, you may be surprised to see that, other than their color, nothing seems to have changed. You can open them the same way you always did, change them, and save them as usual. Windows is just doing its job: protecting these files with the minimum inconvenience to you.

Still, if someone with a different account tries to open one of these files, a message cheerfully informs them that they don't have the proper permissions to access the file.

EFS Rules

Any files or folders you move *into* an EFS-encrypted folder get encrypted, too. But dragging a file *out* of one doesn't unprotect it; it remains encrypted as long as it's on an NTFS drive. A protected file loses its encryption only in these circumstances:

- **You manually decrypt the file** (by turning off the checkbox in the Properties box).

- **You move it to a FAT32 or exFAT drive.**

- **You transmit it via a network or email.** When you attach the file to an email or send it across the network, Windows decrypts the file before sending it on its way.

By the way, even if passing evildoers can't *open* your private file, they can still *delete* it—unless you've protected it using Windows' permissions feature (to learn more, see "NTFS Permissions" on this book's "Missing CD" at *missingmanuals.com*). Truly protecting important material involves using these security features in combination.

Six Disk Utilities You'll Rarely Need

If you're of a technical persuasion, you may feel gratified to know that Microsoft has equipped Windows with an arsenal of advanced drive management tools. Each is described on a free PDF appendix to this chapter. Here's what lies in store:

- **BitLocker Drive Encryption.** EFS is a great way to keep prying eyes out of individual files. But when million-dollar corporate secrets are at stake, a knowledgeable thief could swipe your laptop, nab your flash drive, or even steal the hard drive out of your desktop PC.

  When you turn on BitLocker Drive Encryption, your PC automatically encrypts (scrambles) everything on an *entire drive*, including all of Windows itself. If the bad guy tries any industrial-strength tricks to get into the drive—reprogramming the startup routines, for example, or starting up from a different hard drive—BitLocker presents a steel-reinforced password screen. No password, no decryption.

In Windows 10, you also get BitLocker to Go—a disk-encryption feature for removable drives like USB flash drives. Even if you lose your flash drive, it's worthless without the password.

- **Storage Spaces.** A RAID array is a bunch of drives installed inside a single metal box; clever software makes them look like one big drive to a computer. The files on a RAID system can be recovered even if one of the hard drives dies, thanks to a fancy encoding scheme.

  The Windows feature called Storage Spaces offers the same benefits as RAID systems without anywhere near the same complexity or inflexibility.

- **Dynamic Disks.** Before Storage Spaces came along, there were other ways to tell Windows to treat multiple drives as one. Even today, you can still create *dynamic disks, basic disks,* and *spanned volumes*—all methods of slicing and dicing your actual disks in clever ways.

- **Disk Cleanup.** This ancient predecessor to Storage Sense is still around, too.

- **Disk Defragmenter.** If your hard drive is very full for a long time, it may run out of space to "lay down" big new files. It winds up splitting them across multiple spaces on the disk's surface. Over time, this *file fragmentation* slows down your PC.

  Today, Windows defragments your drive in the background, but the old Disk Defragmenter app is still around for the benefit of historians and control freaks.

- **Disk Quotas.** When several people share a PC, one glutton may become overzealous about downloading stuff. Using the Windows "quota management" feature, you can limit the amount of disk space each account holder is allowed to use.

Each of these features and apps is described in a free PDF appendix, named appropriately, on this book's "Missing CD" at *missingmanuals.com*.

6

Part Six:
The Windows Network

Accounts (and Signing In)

F or years, teachers, parents, tech directors, and computer lab instructors struggled to answer two difficult questions: How do you rig one PC so several different people can use it throughout the day without interfering with one another's files and settings? And how do you protect a PC from getting fouled up by mischievous (or bumbling) students and employees?

Today's answer: Use a multiple-user operating system like Windows. Anyone who uses the computer must *sign in*—supply a name and password—when the computer turns on.

Since the day you installed Windows 10 or fired up a new Windows 10 machine, you've probably made a number of changes to your setup—fiddled with your Start menu, changed the desktop wallpaper, added some favorites to your web browser, downloaded files onto your desktop, and so on—without realizing that you were actually making these changes only to *your account.*

Ditto with your web history and cookies, Control Panel settings, email stash, and so on. It's all part of your account.

If you create an account for a second person, then when she turns on the computer and signs in, she'll find the desktop looking the way it was factory-installed by Microsoft: basic Start menu, standard desktop picture, default web browser home page, and so on. She can make the same kinds of changes to the device that you've made, but nothing she does will affect your environment the next time *you* sign on.

In other words, the multiple-accounts feature has two benefits: first, the convenience of hiding everyone else's junk and, second, security that protects both the PC's system software and everyone's work.

Behind the scenes, Windows stores *all* these files and settings in a single folder—your personal folder, the one that bears your name. (Technically, your personal folder is in the *This PC > Local Disk (C:) > Users* folder.)

Note: Even if you don't share your PC with anyone and don't create any other accounts, you might still appreciate this feature because it effectively password-protects the entire computer. Your PC is safe from unauthorized casual fiddling when you're away from your desk (or if your laptop is stolen)—especially if you tell Windows to require your sign-in password anytime the screen saver has kicked in (page 164).

If you're content simply to *use* Windows, that's really all you need to know about accounts. If, on the other hand, you've shouldered some of the responsibility for *administering* Windows machines—if it's your job to add and remove accounts, for example—read on.

Local Accounts vs. Microsoft Accounts

For most of Windows' history, any account you created on your PC was a *local* account, meaning *stored on the computer itself*. All your stuff—your files, email, settings, passwords—sat on the PC itself.

Seems obvious, right? Where else would you store all those details?

Today, there's an answer to that: online.

In Windows 10, you have the option to have Microsoft store your account details online ("in the cloud," as the marketing people might say). You don't sign in with a name like "Fizzywinks"; instead, you sign in with an *email address* that you've registered with Microsoft. If your name and password match, you've just succeeded in signing in with your *Microsoft account* instead of with a local one.

And why is that a good thing? Because it means you can sign into *any Windows 8 or 10 computer anywhere*—your other laptop, a friend's PC, another company's—and find yourself instantly at home. You won't have your files, music collection, and movies, of course (unless you've stored them on your OneDrive). But you will find every possible account-related element ready and waiting, even on a computer you've never used before. Here's what you'll find:

- **Your email, Twitter, Facebook, LinkedIn, Hotmail, and other accounts.** You're supposed to link *these* to your Microsoft account. After that, no matter what computer you use, your People app, Skype program, and other address books will always be up to date and fully loaded.

- **Your online photos.** Once again, your Microsoft account can store your links to services like Flickr and Facebook, so their contents are automatically available when you sign into any Windows 8 or 10 machine.

- **Your OneDrive.** Any files you've stashed on OneDrive (page 140) are available to you.

- **Your settings.** Here are your wallpaper, color scheme, Cortana settings, and many other settings. Many programs store their settings as part of your Microsoft account, too.

- **Your Xbox world.** As described on page 361, Windows 10 can show you all the details of your online Xbox universe; let you play an Xbox game on your computer; and let you play certain games against someone with an Xbox (while you're on a Windows 10 machine). All that requires a Microsoft account.

- **Your web world.** Your browser bookmarks (Favorites), browsing history, and even stored website passwords will be there waiting for you in Edge.

Note: Your passwords don't get synced until you make each computer a "trusted PC." When you first sign into a new Windows 8 or 10 computer, a message asks if you want to "Trust this PC." If you do, you're asked to confirm that this is your message account by replying to an email or text message.

- **Your Microsoft Store apps.** You can install a Microsoft Store app on up to 81 Windows machines. They don't show up automatically when you sign into a brand-new computer, but you can open the Microsoft Store app and click "Your apps" to re-download them.

A Microsoft account is also, of course, your Microsoft wallet; you can use your Microsoft ID to buy apps, music, videos, and games from Microsoft. It's also what you use to sign in if you have an Xbox (possible) or a Windows Phone (unlikely).

In fact, you can't download new Microsoft Store apps from the app store *at all* without a Microsoft account.

A Microsoft account still lets you into your PC when you don't have an internet connection. You can turn off as many of the syncing features as you like, for privacy's sake. The company swears it won't send anything to the email address you use. And it's free. In general, it's the best way to sign into Windows.

And what about the alternative—a local account? If you have only one computer (and therefore don't need the syncing business) and don't plan to buy anything online, it's fine, too. In fact, Windows 10 is much kinder to local accounts than Windows 8 was; for example, you can now use the built-in apps like Mail, Calendar, and People without having a Microsoft account.

You can always convert any account from Microsoft to local or vice versa.

Accounts Central

To set up and survey your computer's accounts, open ■→⚙→Accounts. You see the panel shown in Figure 18-1.

Here are all the accounts you've created so far. Here, too, is where you can create new accounts, edit the ones you've already made, or delete them, as described in the following pages.

First, though, it's important to understand the differences between the two account types you may see in Settings: *Administrator* and *Standard*. Read on.

The Types of Accounts

On your own personal PC, the word "Administrator" probably appears under your name in the panel shown in Figure 18-1. As it turns out, that's one of two kinds of accounts you can create.

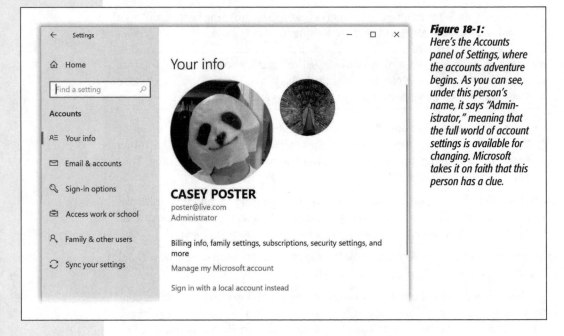

Figure 18-1:
Here's the Accounts panel of Settings, where the accounts adventure begins. As you can see, under this person's name, it says "Administrator," meaning that the full world of account settings is available for changing. Microsoft takes it on faith that this person has a clue.

Administrator accounts

Because you're the person who installed Windows, the PC assumes that you're one of its *administrators*—the technical wizards who will be in charge of it. You're the teacher, the parent, the resident computer genius. You're the one who will maintain this PC and who will be permitted to make system-wide changes to it.

You'll find settings all over Windows (and all over this book) that *only* people with administrator accounts can change. For example, only an administrator is allowed to do the following:

- **Create or delete** accounts and passwords.
- **Make changes** to certain Control Panel programs.
- **See and manipulate** *any* file on the machine.
- **Install new desktop programs** (and certain hardware components).

Note: You don't need to be an administrator to install a Microsoft Store app, though.

Standard accounts

There's another kind of account, too, for people who *don't* have to make those kinds of changes: the standard account.

Now, for years, people doled out administrator accounts pretty freely. You know: The parents got administrator accounts, the kids got standard ones. The trouble is, an administrator account is a kind of security hole. Anytime you're signed in with this kind of account, any nasty software you may have caught from the internet is *also,* in effect, signed in—and can make changes to important underlying settings on your PC, just the way a human administrator can.

Put another way: A virus you've downloaded while running a standard account will have a much harder time infecting the rest of the machine than one you downloaded while using an administrator account.

Today, therefore, Microsoft recommends that *everyone* use standard accounts—even you, the wise master and owner of the computer!

So how are you supposed to make important Settings changes, install new programs, and so on?

That's gotten a lot easier. Using a standard account no longer means you can't make important changes. In fact, you can do just about everything on the PC that an administrator account holder can—if you know the *password* of a true administrator account.

Note: Every Windows 10 PC must keep at least one administrator account on hand, even if that account is rarely used.

Whenever you try to make a big change, you're asked to *authenticate yourself.* As described on page 558, that means supplying an administrator account's password, even though you, the currently-signed-in person, are a lowly standard account holder.

If you have a standard account because you're a student, a child, or an employee, you're supposed to call an administrator over to your PC to approve the change you're making. (If you're the PC's owner, but you're using a standard account for security purposes, you know the administrator password, so it's no big deal.)

Now, making broad changes to a PC when you're an administrator *still* presents you with those "prove yourself worthy" authentication dialog boxes. The only difference is that you, the administrator, can click Continue (or tap Enter) to bypass them, rather than having to type in a password.

You'll have to weigh this security/convenience tradeoff. But you've been warned: The least vulnerable PC is one on which everyone uses a standard account.

Adding an Account

To create a new account, open ■→⚙→Accounts. The top tab, "Your info," represents your account information—the account Windows created when you installed it (Figure 18-1).

Select "Family & other users." If you see some accounts listed here, then maybe you created them when starting up Windows 10 for the first time, or maybe you created them in an earlier version of Windows (and Windows imported them).

The steps for adding another account depend on whether it's for a family member or not. What's the difference? Well, if it's a family member, then when you sign into any other Windows 10 computer, the rest of your family's accounts will appear on that machine, too, ready to use.

Also, if it's a family member who's a *kid*, you'll get periodic email reports on what he's been doing with his computer time, as described on page 424.

Finally, a family member *must* sign in with a Microsoft account, as described on page 534. If you want to create a local account, you have to use the "Other users" option described in a moment.

Adding a Family Member

Let's start with the steps for adding a family member. Assuming that you are, in fact, signed in with an administrator account, start at ▉→⚙→Accounts→"Family & other users." Figure 18-2, top, shows you what this screen looks like.

> **Note:** Your Settings screens may refer to either "people" or "users," but the steps are the same either way.

Select "Add a family member." Now you see the screen shown at bottom in Figure 18-2.

Choose either "Add a child" or "Add an adult," and then enter the email address for that person's Microsoft account. It doesn't have to be a Microsoft email address (like one that ends in *@hotmail.com, @live.com,* or *@outlook.com*).

And what if this relative of yours has no email address? Choose "The person I want to add doesn't have an email address." You'll be given the chance to create a free Outlook.com email address, which will become this person's Microsoft account.

You'll also be offered "Use a phone number instead." That's right: Family members can now use their phone numbers as their Microsoft IDs. Either way, enter the address or number and then hit Confirm, and then Close.

You wind up on the "Your family" screen again (Figure 18-2, top), where your new family member's Microsoft account appears. You've created the account! Behind the scenes, Microsoft has sent an invitation to the email address or phone number you've specified. Until the person accepts the invite, the word "pending" appears next to the account name on this screen.

After they accept the invitation, though, new family members can sign into this computer (or any other Windows 8 or 10 machine).

> **Note:** You may notice that next to your family members' names on the "Your family" screen, it says "Can sign in." That's your cue that if they're very, very naughty, you can block them. Hit Block, and then Block in the confirmation box, to prevent them from logging in. Once they've apologized, you can always unblock them.

Adding Someone Else

You can add a new account for someone who's *not* a family member, too.

This time, you'll have the chance to create a *local account* (page 534), which lets the person sign in with his name instead of an email address. (Of course, a local account doesn't offer the syncing and other features of a Microsoft account; it exists only on *this* computer.)

Tip: It's perfectly OK to create an "Other users" account even for someone who *is* a family member. You'd do that if you wanted your relative to have a local account, for example, or if you wanted to create an account for an adult relative who does *not* need control over the kids' accounts.

Figure 18-2:
Top: This is the master list of people for whom you've set up accounts on this machine. There are two lists: One for family members (whose accounts will show up automatically when you sign in on another Windows 10 machine), and one for "Other users."

Bottom: Windows wants to know if this is a child (whose online activities you can monitor and control) or an adult (who will be able to monitor the kids and change their settings).

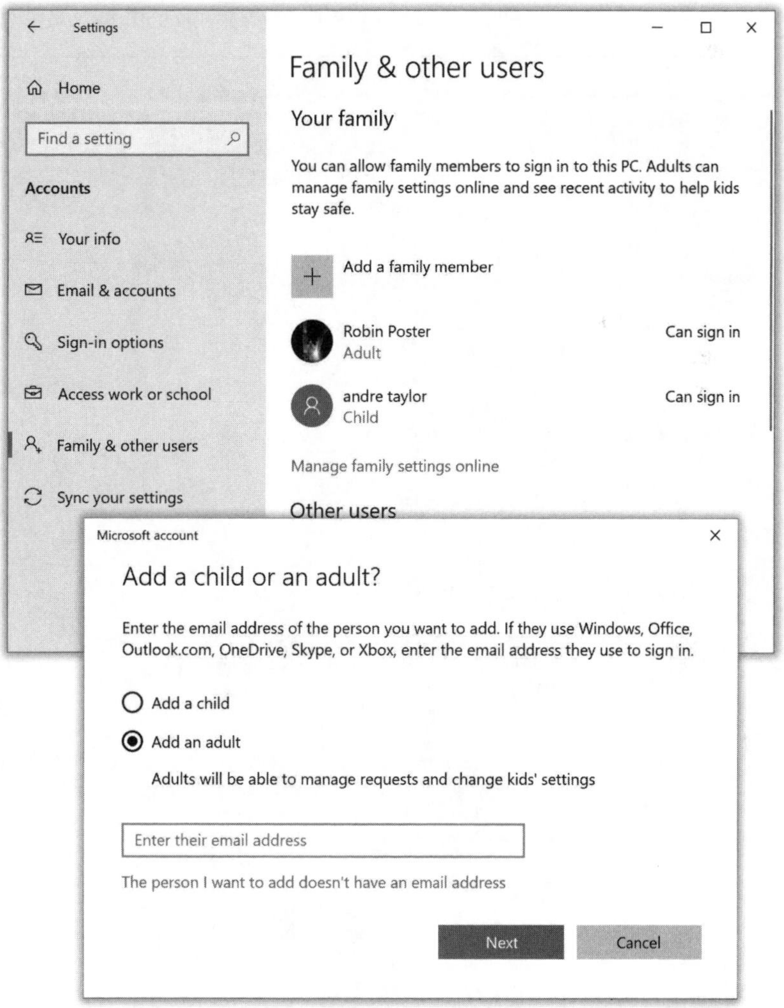

The fun begins, as always, on the ▦→⚙→ Accounts→ "Family & other users" screen. Under "Other users," select "Add someone else to this PC" (Figure 18-3).

Windows now wants to know: "How will this person sign in?"

- **If he has a Microsoft account:** Enter the email address or cellphone number on record for his Microsoft account in the box. Click Next and then Finish. The deed is done: He can now sign into this computer, or any Windows 8 or 10 computer, with that email address or phone number and his Microsoft account password.

- **If this person has an email address but it's not a Microsoft account:** Hit "I don't have this person's sign-in information."

  On the next screen, you can enter the person's regular email address; you can sign up for a Microsoft (@outlook.com) address by hitting "Get a new email address"; or use the person's phone number ("Use a phone number instead").

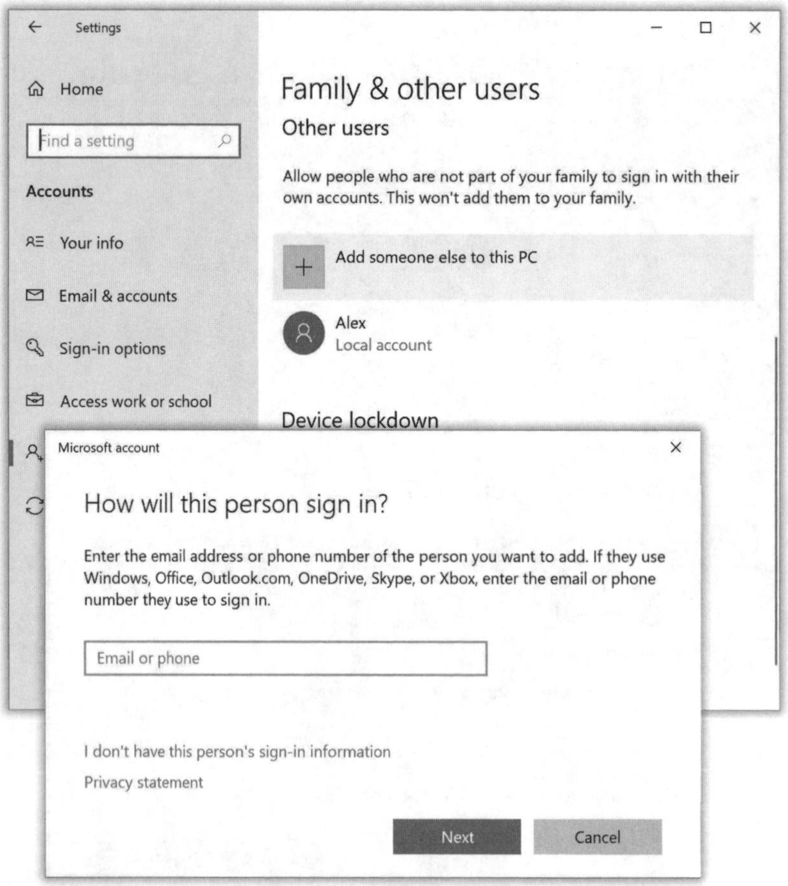

Figure 18-3:
Top: You're about to create an account for a non–family member (or a family member who doesn't want a Microsoft account).

Bottom: This is where things get tricky. You're about to tell Windows that this person has a Microsoft account, doesn't have one but wants one, or doesn't have one but doesn't want one.

Within a few minutes, your new account holder receives an invitation, at that address or phone number, from Microsoft. When he clicks "Accept invitation," he's taken online to a web page where he can complete the process of turning that email address into a proper Microsoft account (complete with a complex password). At that point he'll be able to sign into any Windows 8 or 10 machine with his email address and that password.

- **To create a local account:** Click "The person I want to add doesn't have an email address." On the next screen, click "Add a user without a Microsoft account." You wind up on the "Create an account for this PC" screen, where you can make up a name and password.

Tip: Having a local account means you can make up a very simple password, or no password at all—an attractive time-saver if this is your home computer and you don't have (or aren't worried about your) housemates. To set that up, just leave both password blanks empty. Later, whenever you're asked for your password, leave the Password box blank. You'll be able to sign on and authenticate yourself that much faster each day.

If you provide a password, you must also set up three security questions (and answers): for example, "your first pet's name," "your childhood nickname," and "your oldest cousin." Later, when you sign in and can't remember your password, you'll be able to choose "Reset password" on the login screen. You'll be offered the chance to answer your three security questions in order to make up a new password.

After a moment, you return to the Accounts screen, where the new account holder's name joins whatever names were already there. You can continue adding new accounts forever or until your hard drive is full, whichever comes first.

POWER USERS' CLINIC

The Other Administrator Account

This will sound confusing. But there's another kind of administrator account: *the* administrator account.

This is an emergency backup account with full administrator powers and *no password.* Even if you delete all your other accounts, this one still remains, if only to give you some way to get into your machine. It's called Administrator, and it's ordinarily hidden.

Most people see it only in times of troubleshooting, when they start up their PCs in Safe Mode (page 501). It's the ideal account to use in those situations. Not only does it come with no password assigned, but it's also unlimited. It gives you free power over every file, which is just what you may need to troubleshoot your computer.

Back in Windows XP, the problem was, of course, that anyone who knew about it could get into Windows with full administrator privileges—and no need to know a password. Your kid, for example, could blow right past your carefully established parental controls—and let's not even consider what a virus could do.

So in the more security-minded Windows 10, the secret administrator account is still there, but it's disabled. It comes to life *only* if you're starting your PC in Safe Mode.

(That's on a standard home or small-office PC. On a corporate domain network, only a networking geek who's got a domain admin account can start up in Safe Mode. You know who you are.)

Tip: If you never had the opportunity to set up a user account when installing Windows—if you bought a PC with Windows already on it, for example—you may see an account named Owner already in place. Nobody can use Windows unless there's at least *one* administrator account on it, so Microsoft is doing you a favor here.

Just double-click it and click "Change the account name" to change the name "Owner" to one that suits you better. Make that account your own using the steps in the following paragraphs.

Editing an Account

Although the process of creating a new account is swift and simple, it doesn't offer you much in the way of flexibility. You don't even have a chance to specify the new person's account picture (rubber ducky, flower, or whatever).

That's why the next step is usually *editing* the account you just set up. You make these sorts of changes in two places: in Settings, and (for Microsoft accounts) online.

Changing the Account Type

If you're signed in with an administrator account, you have the power to change other people's account types (your choices: administrator or standard). To do that, open ⊞→⚙→Accounts→"Family & other users."

Select the account name, choose "Change account type," and use the drop-down menu to choose Administrator or Standard User. Hit OK.

Changing Picture, Password, or Microsoft Account

On the "Your info" tab of ⊞→⚙→Accounts (Figure 18-1), you can make changes *only to your own account*. So if you've just created a new account for somebody, she'll have to sign in, open this panel, and make the following changes herself:

- **Change your picture.** The usual sign-in screen displays each account-holder's name, accompanied by a little picture. When you first create the account, however, it assigns you a generic silhouette.

  To choose something more personal, hit "Browse for one" (to choose an existing picture from your hard drive) or Camera (meaning "Take a picture of my head right now, using the computer's camera").

Note: You may see other photos here. They represent account pictures you've used in the past, for easy re-selection.

- **Switch to a Microsoft or local account.** If you have a local account, you can switch to a Microsoft account, or vice versa; either way, the button to click is right there at the top of your Accounts panel.

  To change a local account to a Microsoft account: Click "Sign in with a Microsoft account instead." You're led through creating a Microsoft account to call your own. *To change a Microsoft account to a local account:* Click "Sign in with a local account instead." After you enter your password, you'll be asked to make up a name and password for a local account.

- **Change your sign-in options.** Windows lets you sign in with many different kinds of "passwords": a regular typed password, a four-digit number, a picture password (you draw lines on a photo you've selected), face or fingerprint recognition (on specially equipped machines), and so on. On the "Sign-in options" panel, you can create or change whatever you've set up. Details start on page 545.

- **Change the wallpaper, color scheme, notifications, and other settings.** All the settings you make in PC Settings apply *only to your account.*

And if you've created a Microsoft account, guess what? Most of these settings are stored online—and if you sign into another Windows 8 or 10 computer somewhere, you'll find all your settings instantly recreated on that machine.

Settings You Change Online

Remember—a Microsoft account is stored on the internet. It should come as no surprise, then, that Microsoft offers a website where you can make a lot of additional changes to your account.

On the ⊞→⚙→Accounts→"Your info" screen (Figure 18-1), click "Manage my Microsoft account." Off you go into your web browser, where you arrive at the peculiar page shown in Figure 18-4.

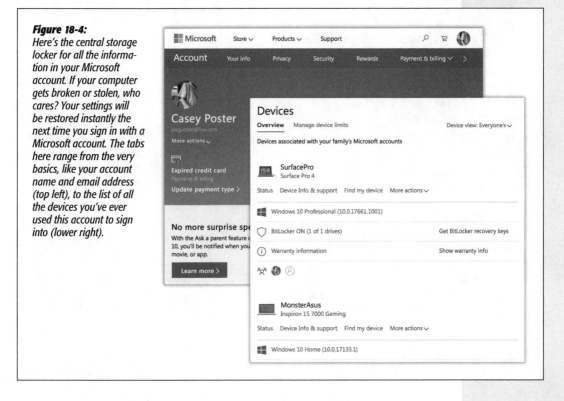

Figure 18-4:
Here's the central storage locker for all the information in your Microsoft account. If your computer gets broken or stolen, who cares? Your settings will be restored instantly the next time you sign in with a Microsoft account. The tabs here range from the very basics, like your account name and email address (top left), to the list of all the devices you've ever used this account to sign into (lower right).

On this page, you can change settings like these:

- **Your info.** Edit your name (again). Change your account photo. Change the email or phone number associated with your Microsoft account.

Tip: Using the "More actions"→"Edit profile"→"Contact info" screen, you can not only change the address or phone number associated with your Microsoft account, but you can also set up additional ones. If you have three email addresses, for example, you can register all three, so you don't have to remember which one you've hooked up to your Microsoft account. Or when you sign into a Windows 10 machine, you can use whichever involves the least typing.

- **Payment & billing.** Here's the master list of stuff you've bought online from Microsoft: music, movies, apps, and so on. You can see your purchase history, change your credit card info, redeem gift cards, and so on.

- **Devices** is the list of computers you've signed into using your Microsoft account (Figure 18-4, bottom). There are links to get help with one, find it (page 447), buy accessories for it, or remove it from the list.

POWER USERS' CLINIC

Sync Settings

It's one of the best parts of the Microsoft account system: Whenever you sign into a Windows 8 or 10 computer, all your settings are in place. Your desktop picture, your color scheme, your web bookmarks—the works. If you have a desktop PC at home and a laptop on the road, well, you're all set; everything is consistent as you move from computer to computer.

There are two reasons you may not love this idea, however.

First, maybe there's some reason that you don't want a certain setting synced. Maybe you use your laptop exclusively when you're in France and don't want your English-language preference synced. Maybe you want independent bookmarks on each machine.

Second, maybe the privacy implications freak you out. Maybe you don't want your laptop browsing history showing up on the family PC in the living room. Or maybe you just don't want Microsoft knowing about your activity at all.

Sync your settings

Sync Windows settings to other devices using poguester@live.com.

How does syncing work?
Sync settings
● On

Individual sync settings

Theme
● On

Web browser settings
● On

Passwords
● On

Language preferences
● On

In any case, there are on/off switches for most of the sync settings. To find them, open ■→⚙→Accounts→"Sync your settings."

At the top: a master switch for the whole concept of syncing your settings. That's the one to flip if the whole idea just feels creepy. Below that: individual switches for various categories of settings.

In most cases, the descriptions tell you what gets synced for each switch. But some additional settings you might not guess: "Theme" governs your choice of theme, yes, but also your screen-saver settings and taskbar configuration. And "Language preferences" also stores your preferences for the Windows spell-checker.

- **Subscriptions.** Here's the dashboard for all the monthly payments you're making to Microsoft: for Office 365, Xbox Live, extra OneDrive storage, and so on. Here, too, is where you cancel one of these accounts, change credit cards, and see when the next renewal and payment dates are.

- **Family.** Here's the master list of family-member accounts you've set up, as described earlier in this chapter—along with links to each person's screen-time limits, website and game restrictions, and so on (page 424). You can also add and remove accounts here.

- **Rewards.** How much does Microsoft want you to use its Bing search page instead of Google, and its Edge browser instead of Chrome? Enough to bribe you. For every search you do in a day using Bing, you earn five Rewards points. You also get five points an hour for using the Edge browser. You can also get points by buying stuff from the Microsoft Store. Earn enough points, and you can cash in for an Amazon or Starbucks gift card, Xbox and Windows gift cards, Microsoft Store gift cards, and more. Anyway, here's the dashboard for your progress.

- **Privacy.** Here's your chance to see much of the data Microsoft has collected about you—search history, browsing history, locations, voice-command history, movie and TV watching, and so on—and, if you like, to delete it. Of course, almost everybody realizes that these big tech companies track our actions. But to see all of your data here, date-stamped, shivering and naked—well, it gives one pause.

- **Security.** Change your password, change your other credentials, see where you've signed in recently.

  Here, too, is your opportunity to delete your Microsoft account—for example, when you buy that Mac you've always wanted. (Joke! That's a joke.)

  To do that, choose "More security options"; sign in; scroll down; and choose "Close my account." You'll be guided through the process of closing down your association with Microsoft. (What do you want to do about your subscriptions? Your leftover account balance? Your kid accounts?)

Seven Ways to Sign In

As you know from Chapter 1, which you've carefully memorized, you can sign into your account using any of several methods (Figure 18-5). Typing out a password is one of them, yes, but everybody hates passwords. So in Windows 10 you have all these ways to prove you're you:

- **Draw three lines, dots, or circles** on a photo you've selected.

- **Type in a four-digit number.**

- **Type a traditional password.**

- **Use your fingerprint,** if your computer has a built-in fingerprint scanner.

- **Just look at the computer's camera.** If it recognizes your face, it signs you in.

• **Look into your computer's eye scanner** until it recognizes the iris of your eye.

Note: Those last three ways require specialized equipment; most computers don't offer them. They're part of a Windows 10 feature called Windows Hello. These days, in fact, Windows Hello does more than sign you into your PC. It can also sign you into a few apps (including Dropbox, Enpass, and OneDrive)—and, in theory, even certain websites, although they're hard to find.

• **Skip the security altogether.** Jump directly to the desktop when you turn on the machine.

So how do you specify which method you want? It all happens on the "Sign-in options" screen shown in Figure 18-5. Just follow the admirably simple steps in the sections that follow.

Note: Every account still requires a regular text password; you'll need it when, for example, installing new software or making system-wide Control Panel changes. The drawing-lines thing, the four-digit thing, the no-password-at-all thing, and Windows Hello are all *additional* ways to sign in.

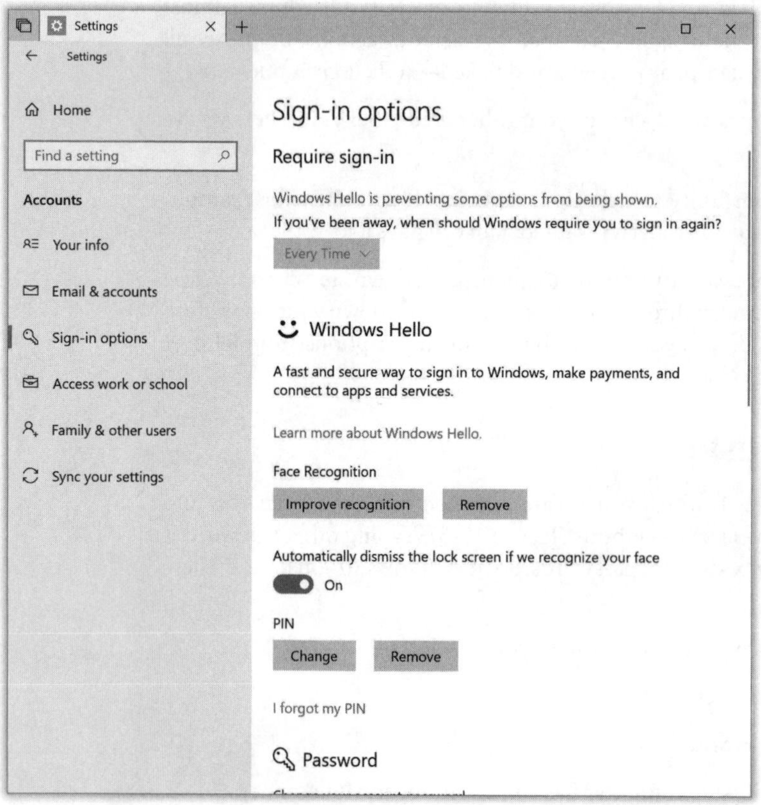

Figure 18-5:
Windows 10 gives you a wide variety of ways to sign in—ways that don't involve having to type in a password. Here in ⊞ → ⚙ → Accounts → "Sign-in options," you can scroll down, and down, and down, to see all of them. Most people won't see the Windows Hello section here—it appears only if your computer has special sign-in hardware—but the ones who do see it will have a blast signing in.

If you do have a Windows Hello–compatible machine, there's a quicker way to get to this screen: On the Lock screen itself, select "Sign-in options."

Creating a Picture Password

This little stunt is perfect for touchscreens, especially tablets that lack physical keyboards, because it's so much easier than typing a password.

The password screen will show a photograph you've chosen. You draw three lines or taps on top of it, something like what's in Figure 18-6. The idea is that only you know how and where to draw these lines and taps. That's your security.

Note: Truth is, picture passwords aren't as secure as typed passwords. One reason is that bad guys might be able to learn your photo fingerstrokes by watching you from across the room.

But an even greater security hole is the finger grease you leave behind on your touchscreen. If you drag the same lines over and over, an evildoer can learn your fingerstrokes just by studying the finger-grease marks when the screen is turned off. You've been warned.

Here's how to set up a picture password:

1. **Open ⊞ → ⚙ → Accounts. Choose "Sign-in options."**

   The "Sign-in options" screen appears (Figure 18-5).

2. **Under "Picture password," hit Add. Enter your current typed password to prove you're not a criminal, and hit OK.**

   Now a screen appears where Windows explains the rules. Time to choose your photo!

Figure 18-6:
The rules are simple: Choose a photo from your Pictures folder. Draw three lines on it—circles, curves, or lines. Don't forget them! (Although, if you do, the world won't end; you can always use your regular typed password instead.)

Later, you'll recreate those gestures to unlock the tablet, which is easier than having to type some password. (The lines don't appear when you actually sign in. Wouldn't want some bad dude sitting next to you to catch on!)

3. **Hit "Choose picture."**

You're now shown the contents of your Pictures folder. Choose the one you want to draw on, and then hit Open (lower-right corner).

You now arrive at a "How's this look?" screen, showing how the picture will appear on the sign-in screen. If the photo isn't perfectly suited to your screen dimensions, you can drag it around to fit the screen better.

4. **Pick "Use this picture."**

Now, on the "Set up your gestures" screen, you're supposed to draw on the photo—three taps, lines, or circles in any combination (Figure 18-6). On a baby photo, for example, you might circle the baby's mouth, tap her nose, and then draw an invisible antenna right out of her head. Just don't forget what you did.

You're asked to repeat the three gestures in the same order to make sure you and Windows have both got it.

If all went well, Windows says, "Congratulations!" If not—if your two tries weren't similar enough—it prompts you to perform this step again.

5. **Hit Finish.**

Now test your picture password. In the ⊞ menu, click your account photo (far-left column); from the shortcut menu, choose "Sign out." You arrive back at the Lock screen.

Dismiss it with a swipe up or a keypress (and, if you see the names of more than one account, tap yours). You arrive at the Picture Password screen, with your photo magnificently displayed. Draw your three lines or taps, as you've set them up. If you do a good enough job, Windows signs you into your account.

If you give up, you can always tap "Sign-in options" and just type the darned password.

The Four-Digit Passcode (PIN)

You might not think that a four-digit passcode, or PIN (personal identification number), is as secure as a full-blown, "f8sh^eir23h*$$%23"-style password. But in one way, it's actually more secure—because it's local. It's stored only on this computer. It's useless to your enemies or faraway hackers, even if they guess it, because it works only when you're physically sitting in front of your machine.

Note: Here again, you still have to create a regular text password for your account—as a backup method, if nothing else.

---

1. **Open ⊞→⚙→Accounts. Choose "Sign-in options."**

You see the screen shown in Figure 18-5.

2. **Under PIN, select Add. Enter your current typed password to prove that you're
you, and hit OK.**

   Now make up a four-digit PIN (personal identification number): the last four digits
   of your mom's phone number, the month and year of your birthday—whatever.

3. **Enter your chosen PIN into both boxes, and then hit Finish.**

Next time you sign in, you'll be able to use your PIN instead of a password (Figure 18-7). You don't even have to press Enter; after you type the fourth digit, bam—you're signed in.

Note: You'll also be offered a link that says "Sign-in options" (Figure 18-7). When you choose that, you're offered icons that represent all the sign-in options you've created so far: picture password, PIN, Windows Hello biometric, and regular typed password. So if you can't get in one way, you can try a different method.

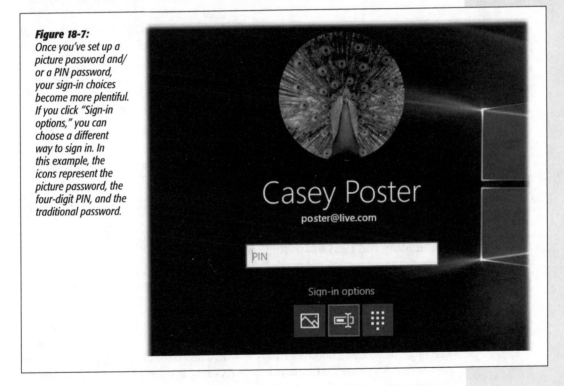

Figure 18-7:
*Once you've set up a
picture password and/
or a PIN password,
your sign-in choices
become more plentiful.
If you click "Sign-in
options," you can
choose a different
way to sign in. In
this example, the
icons represent the
picture password, the
four-digit PIN, and the
traditional password.*

Face Recognition

Here's an absolutely brilliant feature: instant face recognition. When you sit down in front of your computer, it recognizes your face and unlocks the computer instantly. You can't fool it with a photograph, a 3D model of your head, or even an identical twin!

This stunt requires an Intel RealSense depth-sensing camera, a fairly sophisticated device that actually uses *three* cameras—infrared, color, and 3D—in combination.

Some tablets and laptops have it, for example (including Microsoft's own Surface machines), and you can buy this camera as a USB peripheral.

If you're one of the lucky ones, you'll know it, because in ⊞→ ⚙ → Accounts→ "Sign-in options," you'll see a heading for Windows Hello Face. Hit Add to get started, and then "Get started" to *really* get started.

Enter your PIN. (Yes, Windows Hello requires you to set up both a password and a PIN, so you'll be able to get into your machine if something goes wrong with either your RealSense camera or your face.)

Now you're asked to look into the camera. After just a couple of seconds, an "All set!" message appears; Windows has learned what you look like.

Tip: If you wear glasses, hit "Improve recognition" and look into the camera again, this time without them (or with them, if you didn't wear them the first time). Now Windows Hello will recognize you either way.

At this point, note the "Automatically unlock the screen if Windows recognizes your face" option. It saves you one additional click—the one required to dismiss the Lock screen—before the recognizing happens.

Fingerprint, Iris

If your PC has a fingerprint reader or eye scanner, you'll see other Windows Hello options in Settings: Fingerprint and Iris.

The procedures are exactly like the one described above, except this time when you hit "Set up," you're asked to touch your finger to the reader a few times, or hold your eye up to the eye scanner.

When it's over, you'll be able to sign in just by touching your fingertip to the reader, or peeking into the eye reader—fast and secure.

Eliminating the Password Requirement

The usual computer book takes this opportunity to stress the importance of a long, complex password. This is excellent advice if you create sensitive documents and work in a big corporation.

But if you share the computer only with a spouse, or with nobody, you may have nothing to hide. You may see the multiple-users feature more as a convenience (keeping your settings and files separate) than a protector of secrecy and security. In these situations, there's no particular urgency to the mission of thwarting the world's hackers with a password.

That is, you may prefer to blow *past* the password screen, so you can get right down to work. You may wish you could *turn off* the requirement to sign in with a password.

No password required when waking

With one click or tap, you can eliminate the requirement for entering a password when you *wake* the computer. (You still need it when you turn it on or restart it.)

Open ▦→⚙→Accounts→"Sign-in options." There, under "Require sign-in," you can change the usual setting ("When PC wakes up from sleep") to the much more convenient one: "Never."

Now you won't be asked for your password when you just wake the machine after it's gone to sleep.

No password required, ever

With a little more work, you can eliminate the requirement to enter your password even when you're restarting the machine:

1. **Open the Run dialog box (press ▦+R.) In the Run box, type** *netplwiz.* **Hit OK.**

   You now find yourself in the little-seen User Accounts dialog box (Figure 18-8, top). Most of the functions are the same as what you'd find in the Settings panel for accounts—it's just that you don't have to slog through several screens to get things done. Here you can add, remove, or edit accounts, all in a single screen.

Figure 18-8:
Top: Here's the User Accounts box. It's where you find the master switch for the requirement to enter a password when you sign in.

Bottom: In this box, enter your user name and your text password. You're telling Windows to sign you in automatically from now on.

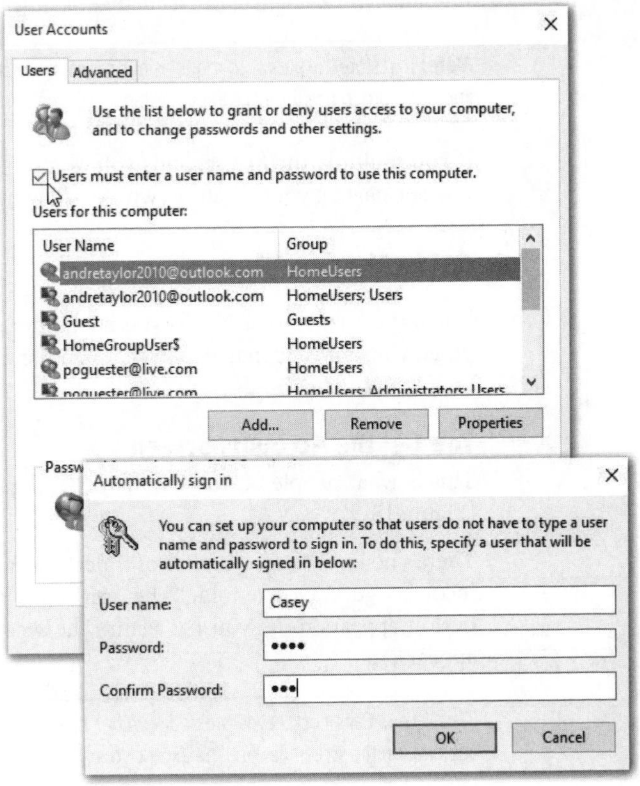

But this older Control Panel program also offers a few features that you don't get at all in the new one. For example:

2. **Turn off "Users must enter a user name and password to use this computer." Hit OK.**

You've told Windows you want to sign in automatically. Now you have to tell it *who* gets to sign in automatically (Figure 18-8, bottom).

This lucky individual won't have to specify any name and password at sign-in time and can instead turn on the PC and cruise directly to the desktop. (This feature works only at startup. If you choose "Sign out" from the Start menu, the standard sign-in dialog box appears so other people have the opportunity to sign in.)

3. **Enter your account name and password (and the password again); hit OK.**

This is your real text password, not some measly four-digit PIN.

The next time you restart your computer, you'll gasp in amazement as it takes you all the way to the desktop without bothering to ask for your password. It's a great setup, provided you recognize the security hole it leaves open.

Note: To restore the password requirement, repeat these steps—but turn *on* "Users must enter a user name and password to use this computer" in step 2.

If you multiply the five seconds you've just saved by the thousands of times you'll wake or start up your machine, why, you'll wind up with literally *minutes* of free time!

After You've Signed In

When it comes to the screens you encounter when you sign into a Windows computer, your mileage may vary. What you see depends on how your PC has been set up. For example:

You Get the Accounts Screen

This is what people on standalone or workgroup computers see most of the time (Figure 18-9).

There's no limit to the number of times you can try to type in a password. With each incorrect guess, you're told, "The user name or password is incorrect," and an OK button appears to let you try again. The second time you try, your password hint appears, too.

Tip: If your Caps Lock key is pressed, another balloon lets you know. Otherwise, because you can't see anything on the screen as you type except dots, you might be trying to type a lowercase password with all capital letters.

You Zoom Straight to the Desktop

If you're the *only* account holder, and you've set up no password for yourself, you can cruise all the way to the desktop without any stops. The setup steps appear on page 551.

This password-free scenario, of course, is not very secure; any evildoer who walks by your machine when you're in the bathroom has complete access to all your files (and protected websites). But if you work in a home office, for example, where the threat of privacy invasion isn't very great, it's by far the most convenient arrangement.

Figure 18-9:
To sign in, click your account name or icon. If no password is required for your account, then you proceed to your desktop with no further interruption.

If there is a password associated with your account, you see a place for it. Type your password and then press Enter.

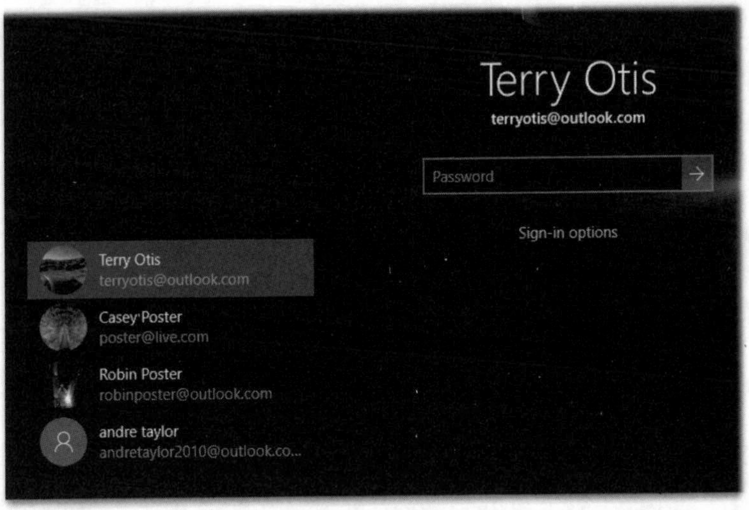

You Get the "Press Ctrl+Alt+Delete to Begin" Message

You or your friendly network geek has added your PC to a domain while installing Windows and activated the "Require Users to Press Ctrl+Alt+Delete" option. This is the most secure configuration, and also the least convenient.

The Forgotten Password Disk

You already know that Windows contains a handy *hint* mechanism for helping you recall your password if you've forgotten it.

But what if, having walked into a low-hanging branch, you've forgotten both your password *and* the correct interpretation of your hint? In that disastrous situation, you don't have to fling your worthless PC into the river quite yet. You have a few more options:

- **If you've forgotten your Microsoft account password,** you can go online to reset it at *account.live.com/password/reset.*

- **On a corporate network,** the system administrator can reset your password.

- **Someone with an administrator account** can sign in and change your password for you. Even *you* can do that, if you know the password for another admin account.

- **If you've forgotten your *local* account password,** you can use a Password Reset Disk.

This disk is a clever solution-in-advance. It's a USB flash drive that you can use like a physical key to unlock your account in the event of a forgotten password. The catch: You have to make this disk *now*, while you still remember your password.

To create it, insert a USB flash drive. Then search for *password reset;* in the results, select "Create a password reset disk." (If it doesn't open, open the Control Panel manually by right-clicking the Start menu and choosing its name; then search for *password reset,* and select "Create a password reset disk.")

The Forgotten Password wizard appears. Click through it, supplying your current password when asked. When you click Finish, remove the disk or flash drive. Label it, and don't lose it!

Don't leave it in plain sight, though; anyone with that drive can now get into your stuff.

Note: Behind the scenes, Windows saves a file onto the flash drive called *userkey.psw.* You can guess what that is.

When the day comes when you can't remember your password, leave the Password box empty and hit Enter. You wind up back at the sign-in screen; this time, in addition to your password hint, you see a link called "Reset password." Insert your Password Reset flash drive and then click that link.

A Password Reset wizard now helps you create a new password (and a new hint to remind you of it). You're in.

GEM IN THE ROUGH

Dynamic Lock: The Invisible Phone Leash

Windows 10 can use some high-tech tricks to unlock your PC when you sit down at it—face recognition, fingerprint, or whatever. But it can also use a high-tech trick to lock your PC when you step away from it.

This feature, called Dynamic Lock, involves pairing your smartphone or smartwatch with your PC using Bluetooth. Because Bluetooth has a limited range—about 30 feet—your PC knows when the phone or watch has broken its wireless connection. Which means you're no longer at your desk. Which means your PC should be locked.

> **Dynamic lock**
>
> Windows can lock when devices paired to your PC go out of range.
>
> ☑ Allow Windows to automatically lock your device when you're away

To bring this about, pair your phone or watch with your PC, as described on page 251. Then, in ⊞→⚙→Accounts→ "Sign-in options," scroll down to "Dynamic lock" and turn on "Allow Windows to automatically lock your device when you're away."

And that's it. Next time you walk away from your PC with the phone in your pocket, after about a minute, the PC will notice your absence—and thoughtfully lock itself for your protection.

Even though you now have a new password, your existing Password Reset Disk is still good. Keep it in a drawer somewhere for use the next time you experience a temporarily blank brain.

Deleting or Suspending Accounts

It happens—somebody graduates, somebody gets fired, somebody dumps you. Sooner or later, you may need to delete an account from your PC.

If you're signed in with an administrator account, you have the power to kill off other people's accounts. To do that, open ⊞→⚙→Accounts→"Family & other users."

Select the account name, choose "Change account type," and hit either Remove (to remove a local account) or Block (to prevent a Microsoft account holder from signing in; you can re-Allow them later, if necessary). Use the drop-down menu to choose Administrator or Standard User. Confirm by choosing "Delete account and data" or "Block."

A few more points about deleting accounts:

- **You can't delete the account you're signed into.**

- **You can't delete the final administrator account.** One must remain.

- **You can create a new account with the same name and password** as one you deleted earlier, but in Windows' head, it's still not the same account.

- **Don't manipulate accounts manually** (by fooling around in the Users folder). Create, delete, and rename them using only Settings or the Control Panel. Otherwise, you'll wind up with duplicate or triplicate folders in the Users folder, with the PC name tacked onto the end of the original account name (Bob, Bob.DELL, and so on)—a sure recipe for confusion.

Tip: If you're an administrator, don't miss the Users tab of the Task Manager dialog box. (Press Ctrl+Shift+Esc to get to the Task Manager.) It offers a handy, centralized list of all the people signed into your machine and contains buttons that let you sign them off or disconnect them. This can be handy whenever you need some information, a troubleshooting session, or a power trip.

The Guest Account

Believe it or not, administrator and standard aren't the only kinds of accounts you can set up on your PC.

A third kind, called the guest account, is ideal for situations when somebody is just visiting you for the week. Rather than create an entire account for this person, complete with password, hint, little picture, and so on, you can just switch on the guest account.

Guest accounts are pretty standard in computers these days, but you wouldn't think so if you just poked around Windows 10; Microsoft has buried the feature under mounds of dust and rubble, and you can get to it only if you have Windows 10 *Pro*.

To turn on the guest account, in the search box, type *lusrmgr.msc*. In the results, choose "lusrmgr.msc."

The crazy window shown in Figure 18-10 appears; proceed as shown in the figure. (You can read more about this window in a free PDF appendix to this book. See "Local Users Console" on the "Missing CD" at *missingmanuals.com*.)

Now, when the visitor tries to sign in, she can choose Guest as the account. She can use the computer but can't see anyone else's files or make any changes to your settings.

When the visitor is finally out of your hair, healthy paranoia suggests that you turn off the guest account once again. (To do so, follow precisely the same steps, except turn "Account is disabled" on again.)

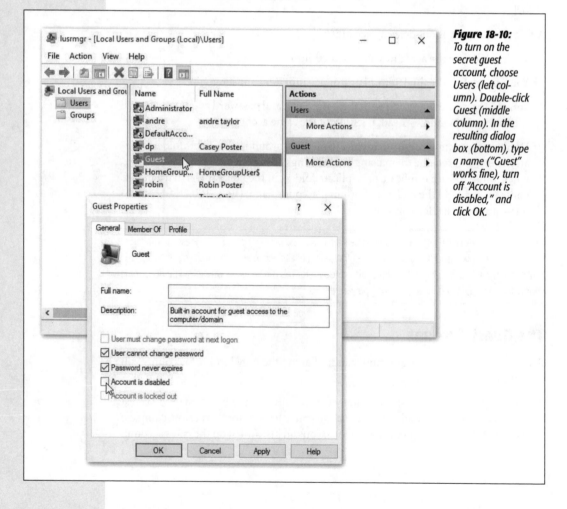

Figure 18-10:
To turn on the secret guest account, choose Users (left column). Double-click Guest (middle column). In the resulting dialog box (bottom), type a name ("Guest" works fine), turn off "Account is disabled," and click OK.

Fast User Switching

Suppose you're signed in and you've got things just the way you like them. You have 11 programs open in carefully arranged windows, your web browser is downloading some gigantic file, and you're composing an important speech in Microsoft Word. Now Robin, a co-worker/family member/fellow student, wants to duck in to do a quick email check.

In the old days, you might have rewarded Robin with eye-rolling and heavy sighs, or worse. To accommodate the request, you would have had to shut down your whole ecosystem—interrupting the download, closing your windows, saving your work, and exiting your programs. You would have had to sign out completely.

Thanks to Fast User Switching, however, none of that is necessary. See Figure 18-11.

The words "Signed in" beneath your name indicate that you haven't actually signed off. Instead, Windows has *memorized* the state of affairs in your account—complete with all open windows, documents, and programs—and shoved it into the background.

Figure 18-11:
To sign in while someone else is signed in, just press the magic keystroke ■ (to open the Start menu), and then click the current person's account photo. Boom: There's the list of people with accounts on this machine, including you.

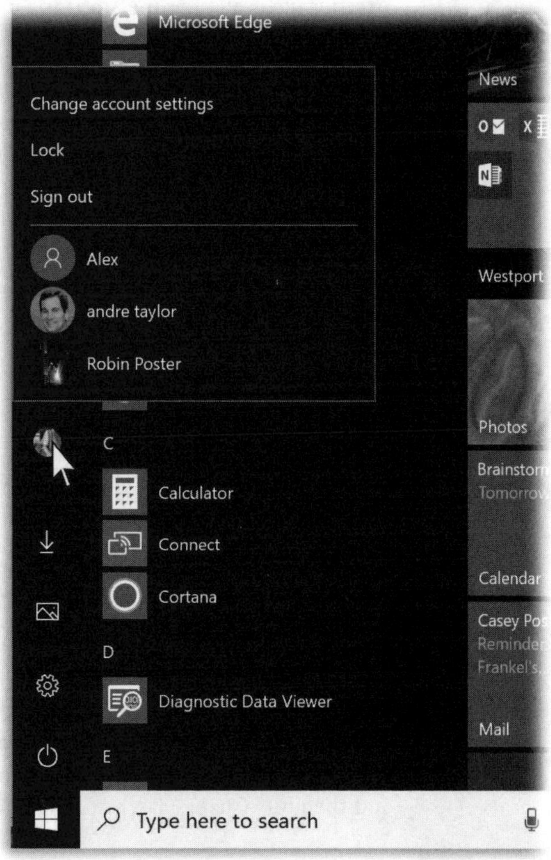

Robin can now click the Robin button to sign in normally and do a little work or look something up. When Robin signs out, the Accounts screen comes back once again, at which point *you* can sign back in. Without having to wait more than a couple of seconds, you find yourself exactly where you began, with all your programs and documents still open and running—an enormous time-saver.

Authenticate Yourself: User Account Control

Work in Windows long enough, and you'll encounter the dialog box shown in Figure 18-12 at top. It appears anytime you install a new program or try to change an important setting on your PC. (Throughout Windows, a colorful 🛡 icon next to a button or link indicates a change that will produce this message box.)

Clearly, Microsoft chose the name User Account Control (UAC) to put a positive spin on a fairly intrusive security feature; calling it the IYW (Interrupt Your Work) box probably wouldn't have sounded like so much fun.

Why do these boxes pop up? In the olden days, nasties like spyware and viruses could install themselves invisibly, behind your back. That's because Windows ran in *Administrative mode* all the time, meaning it left the door open for anyone and anything to make important changes to your PC. Unfortunately, that included viruses.

Windows 10, on the other hand, runs in *standard* mode all the time. Whenever somebody or some program wants to make a big change to your system—something that ought to have the permission of an *administrator* (page 536)—the UAC box alerts you. If you click Continue, Windows elevates (opens) the program's permissions settings just long enough to make the change.

Most of the time, *you* are the one making the changes, which can make the UAC box a bit annoying. But if that UAC dialog box ever appears by *itself,* you'll know something evil is afoot, and you'll have the chance to shut it down.

How you get past the UAC box—how you *authenticate yourself*—depends on the kind of account you have:

- **If you're an administrator,** the UAC box generally doesn't appear at all. Even when you click a link marked with a 🛡 icon, you either blow right past it or get the simple "Yes/No" box shown at top left in Figure 18-12.

- **If you're a standard account holder,** the UAC dialog box requires the password (or sign-in PIN number) of an administrator (Figure 18-12, top right). You're supposed to call an administrator over to your desk to indicate his permission to proceed by entering his own name and password.

The UAC interruptions don't come along *nearly* as often as they used to, in earlier versions of Windows 10. But if even the few remaining interruptions are too much for you, you can turn them off altogether. Open the ⊞ menu. Type *uac;* select Settings, and then hit "Change User Account Control settings."

You get the dialog box shown at bottom in Figure 18-12. If you drag the slider all the way to the bottom, you won't be interrupted by UAC boxes at all.

This truly isn't a good idea, though. You're sending your PC right back to the days of Windows XP, when any sneaky old malware could install itself or change your system settings without your knowledge. Do this only on a PC that's not connected to a network or the internet, for example, or maybe when you, the all-knowing system administrator, are trying to troubleshoot and the UAC interruptions are slowing you down.

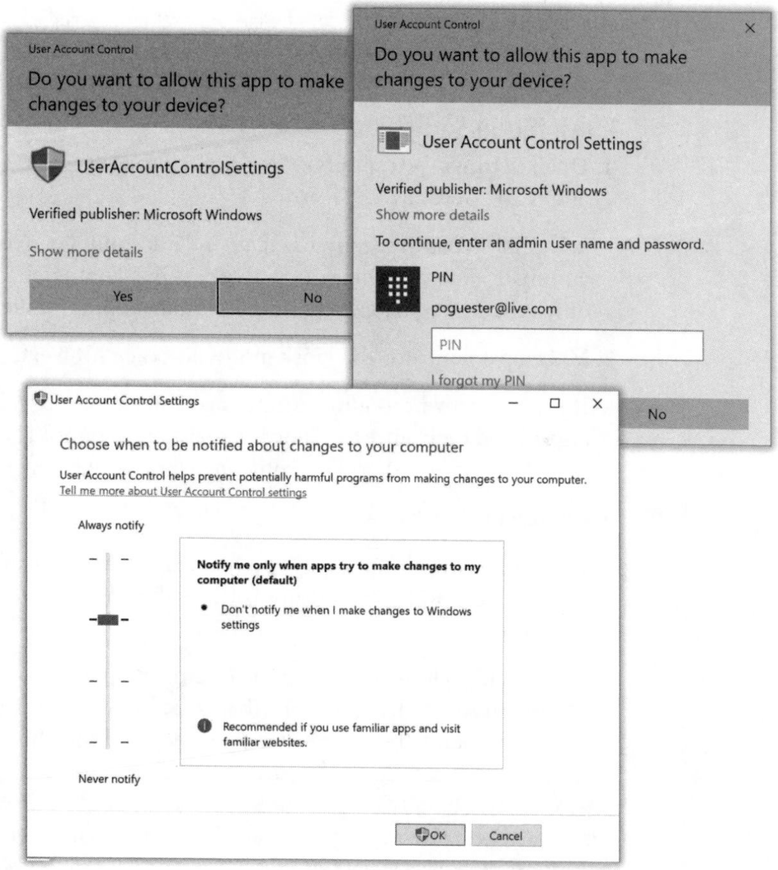

Figure 18-12:
Top: When you try to make a major change to Windows, like deleting an account or installing a program, Windows wants to make absolutely sure that it's you and not some virus doing the changing. So it stops the show to ask for confirmation that it's you out there.

If you're an administrator, just hit Yes (left). If not, you'll have to get an Administrative account holder to authenticate (right).

Bottom: This dialog box offers a nuisance slider; you control where Windows stands on the security/interruption continuum by dragging it up (more alarmist) or down (no interruptions at all).

Kiosk Mode (Assigned Access)

In kiosk mode, which Microsoft also calls "Assigned access," you can turn your entire PC into a super-limited appliance that's locked in one particular app. Whoever's using the machine can't leave the app, can't get to the desktop, can't make any changes to your system, and doesn't see any notifications.

You might use kiosk mode in these situations:

- **You want to turn the PC into an appliance that does only one thing** at your business: a restaurant booking app, for example, or a card-catalog search program in a library.

- **You want to set up a demo or self-running slideshow** at, say, a trade show.

- **You want to help someone with motor-control difficulties** (or a tween with self-control difficulties).

Tip: It's possible to create a kiosk mode that runs more than one app, but this feature is clearly aimed at professional system administrators who use technical provisioning apps. If that sounds like you, visit *docs.microsoft.com/en-us/windows/configuration/lock-down-windows-10-to-specific-apps.*

Kiosk Mode Setup

1. **Open Settings→Accounts→"Family & other users." Choose "Assigned access," and then "Get started."**

   Your first step is to specify, or create, a PC account (see Chapter 18) that will open automatically when you turn on the machine. That's right: Kiosk mode is so locked down that it doesn't even permit the usual account holders to use the computer.

2. **Make up a name for the kiosk mode, and then hit Next.**

   If there are any non-administrator accounts (page 537) on your machine, you're also offered the chance to "Choose an existing account." That's handy if you're trying to set up a limited world for someone who's very young or very old, for example.

3. **Choose the kiosk app.**

   This will be the one and only app that runs. Alas, you can't choose any old app to run in kiosk mode (at least not without the administrator tools described in the Tip above).

   Your choice is limited to the basic Microsoft apps—those that have been written to run "above the Lock screen" (that is, before you've dismissed the Lock screen). Choose its name from the list you see here, and then hit Next.

Note: If you select Microsoft Edge, the browser—a common choice—you'll encounter two additional dialog boxes. The first asks which of two modes you want for the browser (full-screen or only partially locked down), and what URL (web address) you want to open automatically when your kiosk starts up. See Figure 18-13 for details.

---

4. **Hit Close.**

Running Kiosk Mode

Now that you've set things up, log into the account you've designated as the kiosk account in step 2. (No password or login is required on the Login screen; just hit the "Sign in" button that appears.)

When you sign in, you'll discover a weird world. The chosen app fills the screen; there's no Start menu, no taskbar, no apparent way out.

But of course there is a way out: If you have a keyboard, press Ctrl+Alt+Delete. If you have a tablet, press the ■ button five times. You return to the Login screen, so you can sign in with a different account—yours, for example—and use the computer as usual.

If you now return to Settings→Accounts→"Family & other users" and hit "Assigned access," you'll find that you can take control in any of these ways:

- **Change the kiosk app.** Choose the app's name, and then hit "Change kiosk app."

- **Get rid of the special kiosk account.** Choose the existing account name, and then hit "Remove kiosk." (If you chose an existing account, it's not deleted—it just turns back into a normal Windows account.)

Figure 18-13:
If you choose Microsoft Edge, the browser, as your kiosk app, you specify how you want it to work. "As a digital sign or interactive display" means that your app will show only a single web page of your choosing, full screen; the idea is that people will interact very little (for example, it's a building directory or restaurant payment app) or not at all (besides reading a menu or seeing an ad). The other choice, "As a public browser," gives people a full-blown web browser, although they can't customize it, and when they hit the "End session" button, all of their tracks (cookies, stored passwords, and so on) are wiped away.

If you're creating a "public browser," you also get to choose a timeout period, after which the whole thing resets on your original startup URL. That's handy if, say, you're a library, and the starting URL is the main "Search the card catalog" page. Five minutes (or whatever) after the last patron does a search for a book, the browser auto-switches back to the starting page, ready for the next bookworm.

Advanced Features Worth Mentioning (Maybe)

Microsoft designed Windows in an era when only techies used PCs. Lately, though, it has been taking strides to make Windows appear simpler and cleaner.

But the old techie features are still there, hiding.

Here are three advanced topics you can read more about in free online appendixes to this book:

- **Local Users & Groups.** The Local Users & Groups console offers the same options as the ⊞→ ⚙ → Accounts page described in this chapter—but for the technically proficient, it provides a few extra options. One is the ability to create account *groups*—named collections of account holders, all of whom have the same access to certain shared files and folders.

- **Profiles.** Every document, icon, and preference setting related to your account resides in a single folder: the one bearing your name in the *Local Disk (C:) > Users* folder. To network geeks, that folder is known as your *user profile.* Each account holder has a user profile. But your PC also has a couple of profiles that aren't linked to human beings' accounts.

- **NTFS Permissions.** *NTFS permissions,* a core part of Windows' security system, let you specify exactly which co-workers are allowed to open or edit which files and folders on your machine. This introduces a lot of complexity; entire books have been written on the topic.

To find the free PDF appendixes that describe these features, visit this book's "Missing CD" at *missingmanuals.com.*

CHAPTER 19

Sharing Files on the Network

Almost every Windows machine on earth is connected to the Mother of All Networks, the one we call the internet. But most PCs also get connected, sooner or later, to a smaller network—some kind of home or office network.

If you work at a biggish company, then you probably work on a *domain network*—the centrally managed type found in corporations. In that case, you won't have to fool around with building or designing a network; your job, and your PC, presumably came with a fully functioning one (and a fully functioning geek responsible for running it).

Within your home or small office, though, you can create a simpler network that you set up yourself. Your PCs are connected either by Ethernet wires or over a wireless Wi-Fi network.

Being on a network means you can share all kinds of stuff among the various PCs that are connected:

- **Files, folders, and disks.** No matter what PC you're using on the network, you can open the files and folders on any *other* networked PC, as long as the other PCs' owners have made those files available for public inspection. That's where *file sharing* comes in, and that's what this chapter is all about.

  The uses for file sharing are almost endless. It means you can finish writing a letter in the bedroom, even if you started it downstairs at the kitchen table—without having to carry a flash drive around. It means you can watch a slideshow drawn from photos on your spouse's PC somewhere else in the house. It means your underlings can turn in articles for your company newsletter by depositing them directly into a folder on your laptop.

Tip: File sharing also lets you access your files and folders from the road, using a laptop. See Chapter 12 for more on this road-warrior trick.

- **Music and video playback.** Windows Media Player can *stream* music and videos from one PC to another on the same network—that is, play in real time across the network, without your having to copy any files. In a family situation, it's super-convenient to have Dad's Mondo Upstairs PC serve as the master holding tank for the family's entire music collection—and be able to play it using any PC in the house.

- **Printers.** All PCs on the network can share a printer. For instructions, see the free PDF appendix called "Fancy Printer Properties." It's on this book's "Missing CD" at *missingmanuals.com*.

Note: Your network might include a Windows 10 PC, a couple of Windows 7, 8, XP, or Vista machines, older PCs, and even Macs. That's perfectly OK; all these computers can participate as equals in this party. This chapter points out whatever differences you may find in the procedures.

File Sharing 1: Nearby Sharing

Setting up file sharing traditionally requires a lot of steps. (Even the HomeGroups concept, the Windows 7 attempt to simplify the process, was so baffling that Microsoft eliminated it in April 2018.)

Today, Windows 10 offers a feature called Nearby Sharing, which is a loving homage to (or maybe a shameless rip-off of) a Mac feature called AirDrop.

Nearby Sharing is a breakthrough in speed, simplicity, and efficiency. There's no setup, no passwords, nothing to email. It lets you transmit files or links to someone else's PC up to 30 feet away, instantly and wirelessly. You don't even need an internet connection; it works on a flight, a beach, or a sailboat in the middle of the Atlantic.

It requires PCs with the April 2018 Update of Windows or later.

Nearby Sharing Setup

To get things ready, open ⊞→⚙→System→ "Shared experiences." Here you have three choices to make:

- **Nearby sharing on/off.** Shocker: The feature doesn't work unless it's turned on.

Tip: There's also an on/off tile for Nearby Sharing on the Action Center (page 96), for your convenience.

- **I can share or receive content from.** Your choices are "Everyone nearby" (including total strangers, by the way) or "My devices only" (you'll use it only for moving files and photos among your own machines—computers that are signed into the same Microsoft account).

Note to the paranoid: If you choose "Everyone nearby," it's true that total strangers could mischievously attempt to send you files. But it's also true that when a "Do you want to accept?" notification appears on your screen, you can always just hit Decline.

- **Save files I receive to.** Where do you want incoming files to go? Windows, of course, proposes your Downloads folder.

Sending a File with Nearby Sharing

You begin the sending process from Windows 10's modern Share button, which is usually marked by a ↪. You'll find it in two general places: at the desktop and in your apps. Here's how you send stuff using Nearby Sharing:

- **Start in a File Explorer window.** Right-click a file's icon. From the shortcut menu, choose Share. The Share panel appears, as shown in Figure 19-1. (See page 378 for more on the Share panel.)

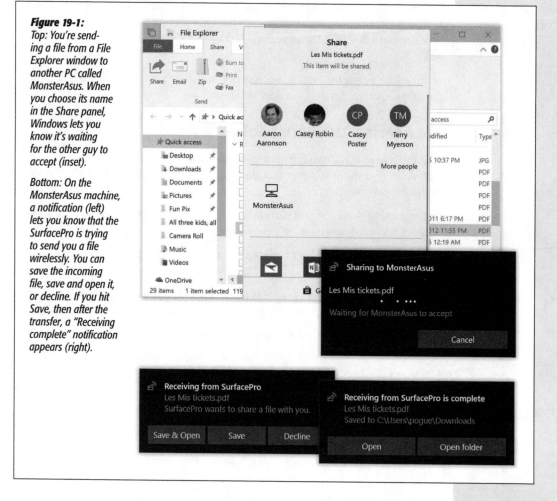

Figure 19-1:
Top: You're sending a file from a File Explorer window to another PC called MonsterAsus. When you choose its name in the Share panel, Windows lets you know it's waiting for the other guy to accept (inset).

Bottom: On the MonsterAsus machine, a notification (left) lets you know that the SurfacePro is trying to send you a file wirelessly. You can save the incoming file, save and open it, or decline. If you hit Save, then after the transfer, a "Receiving complete" notification appears (right).

After a moment, the icons of any other Windows 10 machines show up, as shown in Figure 19-1. (Well, at least any others that are turned on, have Nearby Sharing turned on, and are within range.)

Note: If *you* don't have Nearby Sharing turned on, then the middle of the Share panel says "Tap to turn on nearby sharing." Click or tap that message to get started.

Select the icon of the PC you want to receive the file you're trying to send.

- **Start in an app.** Nearby Sharing is also available in any app that bears a Share button (⤴), and therefore has the Share panel. That includes Photos (send pictures or videos), Edge (send links), News (send articles), Paint 3D (send your artwork), People (send someone's "card"), and Maps (send whatever place or directions you're looking at).

Either way, a notification lets you know the other PC has yet to accept (Figure 19-1, top).

In a moment, a message appears on the other PC's screen, asking if the owner *wants* to accept your file (Figure 19-1, lower left). That person can choose either Save (to save the file to that PC's Downloads folder), Save & Open (which also opens the file), or Decline.

If the receiver opts for one of the Save buttons, after a moment, the transaction is complete. Quick, effortless, wireless, delightful.

File Sharing 2: "Share a Folder"

Nearby Sharing is, of course, fantastically convenient in many, many situations. "Hey, Casey, can you shoot me over that document?" "Oooooh, can I have that photo?" "Where are we meeting, again?"

Unfortunately, Nearby Sharing isn't otherwise a replacement for Windows' traditional network file-sharing system, for several reasons:

- **Any computers that aren't running Windows 10's April 2018 Update** or later are shut out.

- **Nearby Sharing requires people at both computers;** you can't grab a file from, for example, your own upstairs PC while you're on your laptop in the kitchen.

- **Nearby Sharing is only for *transferring* files;** you can't actually *open* a file while it's sitting on another PC.

In what Microsoft cleverly calls the "share any folder" method of file sharing, you can make any folder available to other people on the network. You can even set up elaborate *sharing permissions* that grant individuals different amounts of access to your files.

Better yet, files you share this way are available to other people on the network *and* other people with accounts on the *same computer.*

Here's how to share a file or folder on your PC:

1. **In a File Explorer window, open the window that contains the files or folders you want to share. On the Ribbon's Share tab, choose the names of the people you want to share with.**

   The names of this PC's other account holders all appear here, in this cramped scrolling list (Figure 19-2, top). You can click to share with one person.

   Or, to share with more than one person, click "Specific people" to open the "Choose people to share with" dialog box (Figure 19-2, bottom). You wanted individual control over each account-holder's access? You got it.

Note: The steps for sharing a *disk* are different. See page 569.

Figure 19-2:
Top: The Ribbon offers insta-sharing with any individual. Or, if you want more than one person to get in on the fun, choose "Specific people" to open...

Bottom: ...this box.

Use the drop-down menu at the top to choose an account holder's name. Or type it out, if you prefer.

After each name, click Add. Then use the Permission Level drop-down menu to specify permissions: either Read ("look but don't touch") or Read/Write ("you can edit and even delete stuff"). Click Share when you're finished.

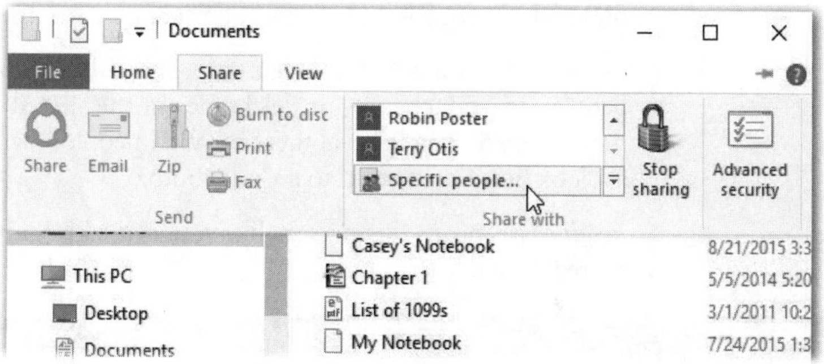

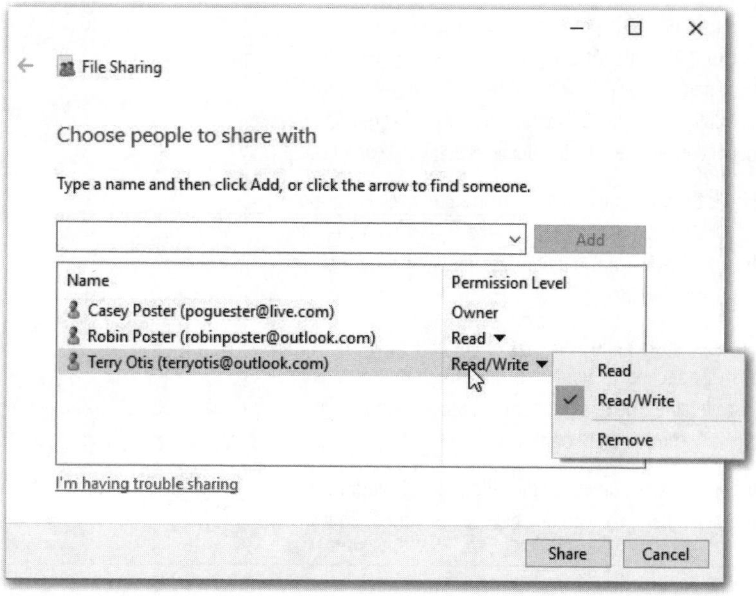

2. **Choose a person's name from the upper drop-down menu, and then click Add.**

   This is the list of account holders (Chapter 18)—or account-holder *groups,* if someone has created them.

   If the person who'll be connecting across the network doesn't yet have an account on your machine, choose "Create a new user" from this drop-down menu. ("Create a new user" isn't some kind of sci-fi breakthrough. You're creating an account for an *existing* person.)

   The name appears in the list. Now your job is to work through this list of people, specifying *how much* control each person has over the file or folder you're sharing.

3. **Click a name in the list. Click the ▼ in the Permission Level column and choose Read or Read/Write.**

   Read means "look but don't touch." This person can see what's in the folder (or file) and can copy it, but she can't delete or change the original.

   Contributors (available for folders only—not files) have much broader access. These people can add, change, or delete files in the shared folder—but only files *that they put there.* Stuff placed there by other people (owners or co-owners) appears as "look but don't touch" to a Contributor.

   Read/Write means this person, like you, can add, change, or delete any file in the shared folder.

UP TO SPEED

Public Networks, Private Networks, and How to Switch

Throughout this chapter, throughout this book, and throughout your life with Windows, you'll encounter references to your network being "discoverable" or "not discoverable," or Public or Private. Microsoft introduced this terminology out of concern for you, the public—but it's still complicated.

Here's the problem: When you're in a *public* Wi-Fi hotspot—at a coffee shop, for example—bad guys with the right hacker software can, in theory, get into your computer. You wouldn't want that.

So when you've told Windows you're on a public network, things attached to your machine, like printers, are not discoverable. The bad guys can't see them on the network. *Nobody* can see them on the network.

When you're at home or at the office, though, your network is private. Bad guys couldn't get in if they tried. So it's OK to share printers and files with other computers within your home or office.

That's the explanation, but here's the punch line: You can share files and printers only if Windows thinks you're on a private network—your own network.

So here's how you change Windows' mind about what kind of network yours is:

Open ⊞→⚙→Network & Internet. On the left, choose how you're connected (Wi-Fi or Ethernet). Choose the name of your current connection.

On the next screen, the buttons you want are Public (you're on a public network, and you'd rather lock things down) or Private (the network is private, and it's OK to share files and printers).

Note: Your name shows up here as Owner. You have the most power of all—after all, it's your stuff.

4. **Click Share.**

The "Your folder [or file] is shared" dialog box appears. This is more than a simple message, however; it contains the *network address* of the files or folders you shared. Without this address, your colleagues won't know you've shared stuff and will therefore have a tough time finding it.

Note: If you've shared some files, you may see an interim message that appears before the "Your files are shared" box, warning you that Windows is about to adjust the access permissions to the folder that encloses them. That's normal.

5. **Click "e-mail" or "copy" (Figure 19-3).**

The "e-mail" link opens a new, outgoing message in your email program, letting the gang know you've shared something and offering them a link to it. The "copy" link copies the address to the Clipboard so you can paste it into another program—which is your best bet if Mail isn't your email program of choice.

Tip: To stop sharing a folder or file, click it. Then, from the Share tab of the Ribbon of whatever window contains it, choose "Stop sharing."

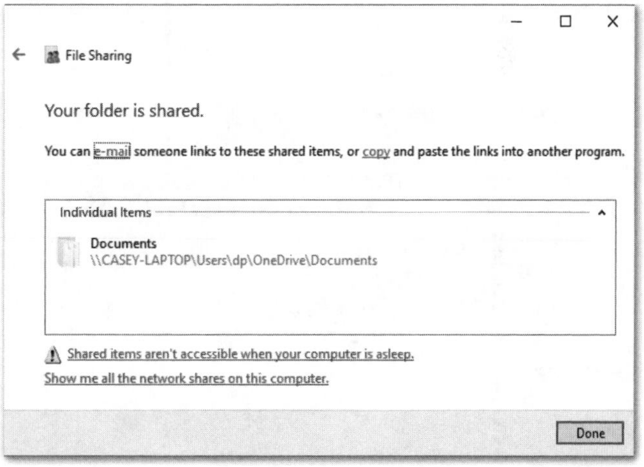

Figure 19-3:
Windows wants to make absolutely sure you—and those you share your files with—know what you've done. So click "e-mail" to start an outgoing message in your email program with the link to your shared goods, or click "copy" to park that link on your Clipboard for future sharing. Wouldn't want the wrong people sniffing around the wrong personal files, now.

Advanced Folder Sharing—and Disk Sharing

The "share any folder" wizard described in the previous pages might seem fairly complex, but look on the bright side: It replaces an older method that was even more complicated.

And guess what? That method is still available. Here's a quick review of this alternate route (which is, by the way, the *only* way to share entire *disks*):

1. **Right-click the folder or disk you want to share. If it's a folder, choose Properties from the shortcut menu, and then click the Sharing tab. If it's a disk, choose "Share with"→"Advanced sharing."**

   At this point, you *could* click the Share button (if you're operating on a folder, anyway). You'd arrive at the dialog box shown in Figure 19-2 (bottom) where you could specify the account holders and permission levels, just as described earlier. But don't.

2. **Click Advanced Sharing. Authenticate, if necessary.**

   The Advanced Sharing dialog box appears.

3. **Turn on "Share this folder." (See Figure 19-4, top.) Next, set up the power-user sharing options.**

   For example, you can limit the number of people who are browsing this folder at once. You can click Permissions to fine-tune who can do what (Figure 19-4,

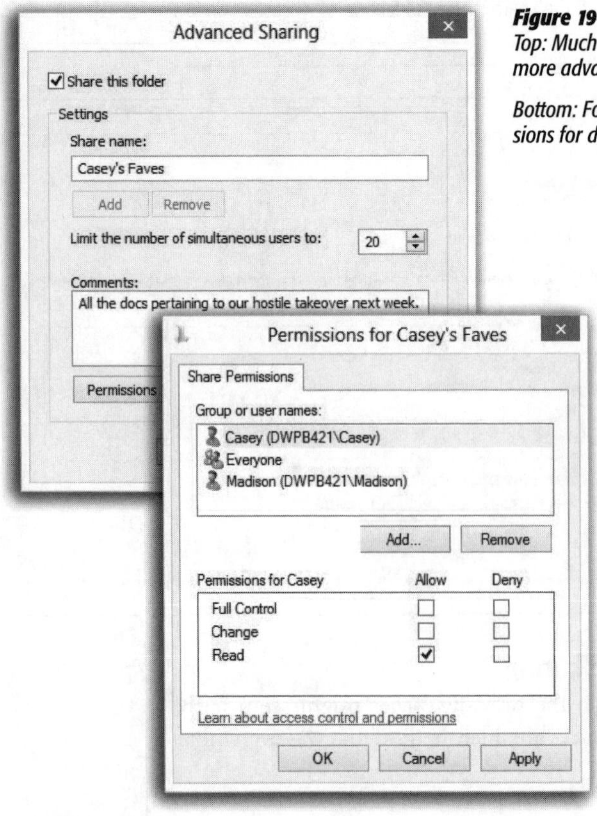

Figure 19-4:
Top: Much finer-tuned sharing features are available in this more advanced box.

Bottom: For example, you can specify personalized permissions for different individuals.

bottom). And you can edit the "Share name"—in fact, you can create *more than one* name for the same shared folder—to make it more recognizable on the network.

Notes on File Sharing

And now, the fine print on sharing files:

- **Sharing a folder also shares all the folders inside it,** including new ones you may create later.

  On the other hand, it's OK to *change* the sharing settings of a subfolder. For example, if you've shared a folder called America, you can make the Minnesota folder inside it off-limits by making it private. To do this, right-click the inner folder, choose Properties, click Sharing, click Advanced Sharing, and use the dialog box shown in Figure 19-4.

- **Be careful with nested folders.** Suppose, for example, you share your Documents folder, and you permit other people to change the files inside it. Now suppose you share a folder *inside* Documents—called Spreadsheets, for example—but you turn *off* the ability for other people to change its files.

  You wind up with a strange situation. Both folders—Documents and Spreadsheets—show up in other people's Network windows. If they double-click the Spreadsheets folder directly, they won't be able to change anything inside it. But if they double-click the Documents folder and then open the Spreadsheets folder inside *it*, they *can* modify the files.

Hiding Folders

If a certain folder on your hard drive is really private, you can hide the folder so other people on the network can't even *see* it. The secret is to type a $ symbol at the end of the *share name*.

For example, if you name a certain folder My Novel, anyone else on the network can see it (even if they can't read the contents). But if you name the folder *My Novel$*, it won't show up in anybody's Network window. They won't even know it exists.

GEM IN THE ROUGH

Sharing Disks

You can share files and folders, of course, but also *disks*.

Sharing an entire disk means every folder on it, and therefore every file, is available to everyone on the network. If security isn't a big deal at your place (because it's just you and a couple of family members, for example), this feature can be a time-saving convenience that spares you the trouble of sharing every new folder you create.

On the other hand, people with privacy concerns generally prefer to share individual *folders*. By sharing only a folder or two, you can keep *most* of the stuff on your hard drive private, out of view of curious network comrades. Actually, sharing only a folder or two does *them* a favor, too, by making it easier for them to find the files you've made available. This way, they don't have to root through your entire drive looking for the folder they actually need.

Note: Technically, there's yet another kind of sharing: *Public-folder* sharing. Every PC has a Public folder. It's free for anyone on the network to use, like a grocery store bulletin board. Super-convenient, super-easy.

Yet you should probably skip this method, for two reasons. First, you have to move files *into* the Public folder before anyone else can see them; you can't leave them where they're sitting, as you can with the other sharing methods.

Second, in Windows 7 and 8, the Public folders containing your shared files sit inside *libraries*—but in Windows 10, Microsoft has hidden away the whole libraries feature. (The main Public folder still exists—but it's in your *(C:)* > *Users* folder.) The bottom line is that even if you share files by putting them into one of the Public folders, nobody on your network will be able to find them!

Accessing Shared Folders

Now suppose you're not you. You're your co-worker, spouse, or employee. You're using your laptop downstairs, and you want access to the stuff that's in a shared folder on the Beefy Main Dell computer upstairs. Here's what to do:

1. **Open any File Explorer window.**

   The navigation pane at left shows a Network heading. Click its > button, if necessary, to see icons for all the computers on the network (Figure 19-5, top). The same navigation pane is available in the Save and Open dialog boxes of your programs, too, making the entire network available to you for opening and saving files.

   If you *don't* see a certain computer's icon here, it might be turned off, or off the network. It also might have *network discovery* turned off; that's the feature that lets a PC announce its presence to the network (see the box on page 568).

   And if you don't see any computers at *all* in the Network window, network discovery might be turned off on *your* computer.

2. **Double-click the computer whose files you want to open.**

   If you're on a corporate domain, you may first have to double-click your way through some other icons, representing the networks in other buildings or floors, before you get to the actual PC icons.

POWER USERS' CLINIC

Unhiding Hidden Folders

As sneaky and delightful as the hidden-folder trick is, it has a distinct drawback—*you* can't see your hidden folder from across the network, either. Suppose you went to the upstairs PC on the network and want to open something in your hidden My Novel folder (which is downstairs in the kitchen).

Fortunately, you can—if you know the secret.

On the upstairs computer, press ▉+R. In the Run dialog box, type the path of the hidden folder, using the format *Computer Name**Folder Name*. For example, enter *kitchen**my novel$* to get to the hidden folder called "My Novel$" on the PC called "Kitchen." (Capitalization doesn't matter.) Click OK to open a window showing the contents of your hidden folder.

If you don't have an account on the PC you're invading—an account with the same name and password as you have on your own PC—then the Connect To box now appears (Figure 19-5, bottom).

Here you have to fill in the name and password of an account on the *other* computer. This, of course, is a real drag, especially if you access other people's files frequently. Fortunately, if you turn on "Remember my credentials," you'll never see this box again. The next time you want to visit the other PC, you'll be able to double-click its icon for instant access.

Tip: In the unlikely event that you want Windows to *stop* memorizing your password, search for *credential* and select Credential Manager in the results. You see a list of every name/password Windows has memorized for you. You can use the options here to add a new memorized name/password, or expand one of the existing items in the list to remove it ("Remove from vault") or edit it.

Figure 19-5:
Top: The computers on your network are arrayed before you! Double-click the one you want to visit.

Bottom: Supply your account name and password as it exists on the distant PC, the one you're trying to access.

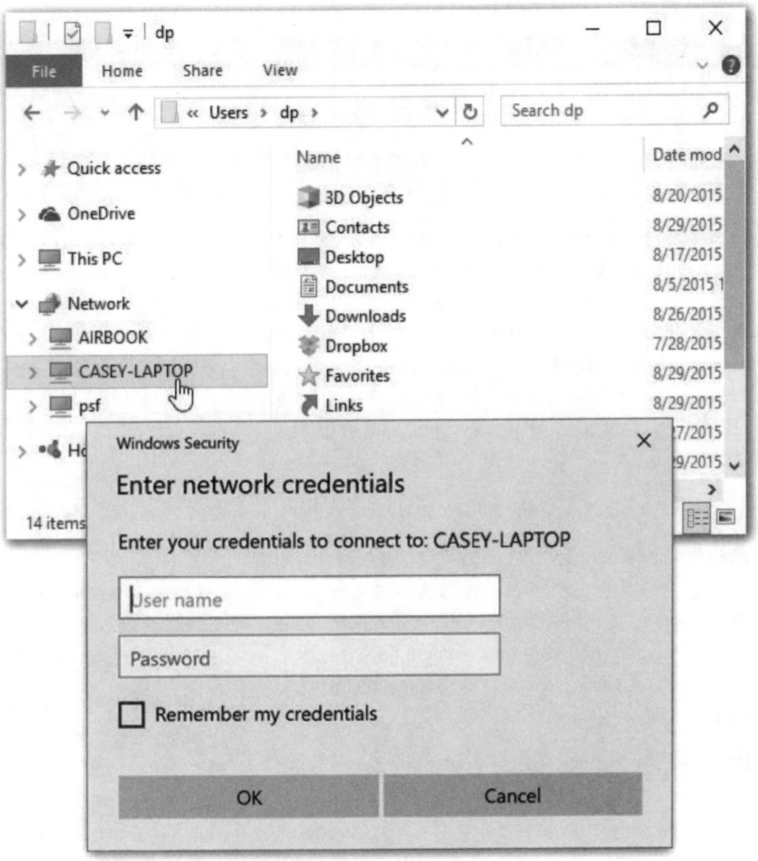

3. **Click OK.**

If all went well, the other computer's window opens, presenting you with the icons of its shared folders and disks.

Tip: Working with the same shared folders often? Save yourself a lot of time and burrowing—make a desktop shortcut of it right now!

Once you've opened the window that contains the shared folder, grab your mouse. Right-click the shared item and drag it to the desktop. When you release the mouse, choose "Create shortcuts here" from the shortcut menu. From now on, you can double-click that shortcut to open the shared item directly.

Once you've brought a networked folder onto your screen, you can double-click icons to open them, drag them to the Recycle Bin, make copies of them, and otherwise manipulate them exactly as though they were icons on your own hard drive. (Of course, if you weren't given permission to change the contents of the shared folder, you'll have less freedom.)

FREQUENTLY ASKED QUESTION

FTP Sites and Other Online Disks

How do I bring an FTP server, or one of those web-based backup drives, onto my PC?

The trick to bringing these servers online is to open the Computer window. On the Ribbon's Computer tab, click "Add a network location." When the wizard appears, click Next. Then, on the second screen, click "Choose a custom network location." Click Next. Finally you arrive at the critical screen, where you can type in the address of the website, FTP site, or other network location you want your new shortcut to open.

Into the first text box, type any of these network addresses:

The UNC code. A UNC code pinpoints a particular shared folder on the network. For example, if you want to open the shared folder named FamilyBiz on the computer named Dad, enter *dad**familybiz*. Capitalization doesn't matter. Or, to open a specific file, you could enter something like *dad**finances**budget.xls*.

http://website/folder. To see what's in a folder called Customers on a company website called BigBiz.com, enter *http://bigbiz.com/customers*. (You can't just type in any old

web address. It has to be a website that's been specifically designed to serve as a "folder" containing files.)

ftp://ftp.website/folder. This is the address format for FTP sites. For example, if you want to use a file in a folder named Bids on a company site named WeBuyStuff.com, enter *ftp://ftp.webuystuff.com/bids*.

What happens when you click Next depends on the kind of address you specified. If it was an FTP site, you're offered the chance to specify your user name. (Access to every FTP site requires a user name and password. You won't be asked for the password until you actually try to open the newly created folder shortcut.)

Click Finish. Your network shortcut now appears in the Network Location area in the Computer window. The wizard also offers to connect to and open the corresponding folder.

You can work with these remote folders exactly as though they were sitting on your own hard drive. The only difference is that because you're actually communicating with a hard drive via the internet, the slower speed may make it feel as if your PC has been drugged.

Tip: There's one significant difference between working with "local" icons and working with those that sit elsewhere on the network. When you delete a file from another computer on the network (if you're allowed to do so), either by pressing the Delete key or by dragging it to the Recycle Bin, it disappears instantly and permanently, without ever appearing in the Recycle Bin.

You can even use Windows' Search feature to find files elsewhere on the network. This kind of searching can be very slow, however.

Sharing Between Macs and PCs

These days, Microsoft and Apple don't consider each other enemies. Microsoft makes all kinds of apps that run on Macs and iPhones; Apple makes most of its online services available to Windows machines. Everybody wins.

If you have both Mac and Windows machines on the same small network, they can "see" each other just fine.

Share PC Folders, Open on the Mac

Here's how to prepare your PC for network invasion by Macs:

1. **Make your PC "discoverable" on the network.** Type *sharing* into the ⊞ search box; choose "Manage advanced sharing settings." The resulting screen offers three expandable sections: "Private," "Guest or Public," and "All Networks."

2. **Make sure "Turn on network discovery"** and "Turn on file and printer sharing" are turned on under *Private*.

Tip: Under "All Networks," you can turn on "Turn on sharing so anyone with network access can read and write files in the Public folders." That way your Mac friends can also get at the files in the Public folders of all account holders on this PC.

3. **The payoff—now you can access your PC folders.** On your Mac, open any desktop (Finder) window. In the sidebar at left, click Network (Figure 19-6, top). It's under the Shared or Locations heading, depending on your macOS version.

Tip: If you don't see your Windows computer on your Mac, it may be because the machines don't all have the same *workgroup* name. (A workgroup is a cluster of networked machines.)

To see what your Windows 10 machine's Workgroup name is, type *workgroup* into the ⊞ search box; click "Show which workgroups this computer is on."

On the Mac, open →System Preferences→Network. Click Advanced→WINS, and make sure the same workgroup name appears in the Workgroup box.

After a moment—it could be a very long moment, like 10 minutes—the icons of the PCs on your network show up. Proceed as shown in Figure 19-6.

Once you've opened your PC→Users→Personal folder, you'll have access to all the stuff in your Windows account, ready to open and edit as usual.

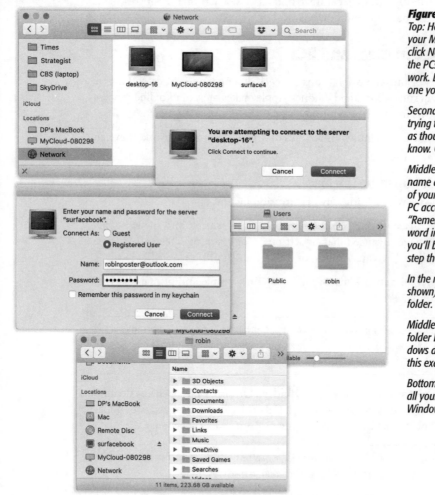

Figure 19-6:
Top: Here you are on your Mac. When you click Network, you see the PCs on your network. Double-click the one you want to open.

Second from top: You're trying to access the PC, as though you didn't know. Click Connect.

Middle left: Enter the name and password of your Windows PC account. Turn on "Remember this password in my keychain" so you'll be able to skip this step the next time.

In the next window (not shown), open the Users folder.

Middle right: Open the folder bearing your Windows account's name (in this example, "robin").

Bottom: Boom! Here's all your stuff from the Windows PC.

Share Mac Folders, Open on the PC

When it comes to networking, Macs are people, too.

Windows is perfectly capable of letting you rifle through a Mac's contents from across the network. Here's how to set that up:

1. **Make your Mac "discoverable" on the network.** On the Mac, choose →System Preferences. Click Sharing, and proceed as shown in Figure 19-7.

Tip: Before you close the Sharing window shown at top in Figure 19-7, you might notice that a line in the middle of the dialog box says "Windows users can access your computer at smb://192.168.1.203." Those numbers are the Mac's IP address. You'd need it only if you decided to access the Mac by typing its address into the Run dialog box—a last-resort method of connecting.

2. **The payoff—now you can access your Mac folders.** On your PC, open any desktop (File Explorer) window. In the sidebar at left, click Network. The Mac shows up like any other icon. When you click the Mac's name, the "Enter network credentials" box appears, as shown at bottom in Figure 19-5.

Tip: If the Mac's icon doesn't show up, you may have to get forceful. In the ■ search box, type *run* and press Enter. In the Run dialog box, type the Mac's IP address as noted in the previous Tip. Precede it with two backward slashes, like this: *102.168.1.203*. When you press Enter, the "Enter network credentials" box appears; continue with these steps as though nothing had gone wrong.

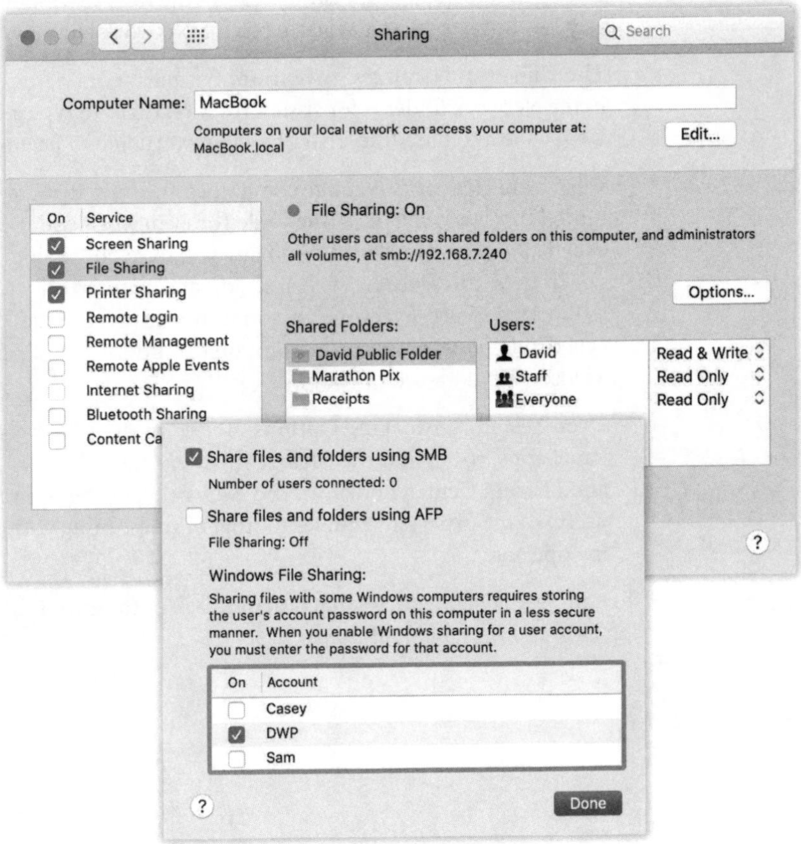

Figure 19-7:
Top: On your Mac, in the Sharing pane of System Preferences, make sure File Sharing is turned on. Click Options.

Bottom: Turn on "Share files and folders using SMB." Then specify which Mac accounts you want to be able to access from the PC; enter their passwords as necessary. Click Done.

Enter your Mac account name and password, and turn on "Remember my credentials" (so you won't be bothered for a name or password the next time you perform this amazing act). Click OK.

Now your Mac home folder opens on the screen before you. You can edit those files exactly as though they were in a folder on your PC. Détente has never been so easy.

For Further Study

Windows networking is a nearly limitless subject—and a rewarding career specialty all its own. There are a few more topics that are beyond the scope of this book, but you can find out more about them in free downloadable appendixes to this chapter:

- **Mapping Shares to Drive Letters.** Using this trick, you can assign a *letter* to a particular shared disk or folder on the network. Just as your hard drive is called C: and your floppy drive is A:, you can give your Family Stuff folder the letter F: and the backup drive in the kitchen the letter K:. And why bother? Because these disks and folders now appear directly in the My PC window. Getting to them this way can be faster than navigating to the Network window.

- **The Universal Naming Convention.** For hard-core nerds, double-clicking icons in the Network folder is for sissies. It's way cooler to type a folder's or document's *UNC* code into the address bar of a window: *\\laptop\documents\salaries 2019.docx*.

- **Corporate Networks.** In huge companies, the ones that are Microsoft's bread and butter, the sprawling, building-wide (or even worldwide) company networks are called *domain* networks. In a domain, you have only a single name and password, which gets you into every shared PC and printer on the network that you're authorized to use. Everyone's account information resides on a central computer called a *domain controller*—a computer so important, it's usually locked away in a closet or a data-center room.

- **Deep-Seated Networking Options.** Buried in the Windows Settings and Control Panel apps, you'll find the Change Adapter Options screen, the ancient Network and Sharing Center, and advanced Network Sharing options. All of these can be useful to the expert in troubleshooting or fine-tuning your networking and sharing options.

To find the PDF appendixes that describe each of these topics, visit this book's "Missing CD" at *missingmanuals.com*.

Part Seven: Appendixes

7

Installing & Upgrading to Windows 10

W hen Windows 10 debuted in 2015, learning how to upgrade a Windows 7 or Windows 8 PC was critically important. These days, though, the chances that your pre-2015 PC is still running Windows 7 or 8—or still running at all—are fairly small. If that's your intention, see the free PDF appendix called "Upgrading from Windows 7 or 8.1." It's on this book's "Missing CD" at *missingmanuals.com*.

This appendix, then, covers all *other* aspects of Windows 10 May 2019 Update installation, like how to install a fresh copy, how to make a bootable flash drive, and how to navigate the Setup Assistant that everyone encounters after a clean install—or when turning on a new PC for the first time.

The Upgrade to the May 2019 Update

If you're running some flavor of Windows 10, then getting the May 2019 Update described in this book is no big deal: It happens automatically. You'll see a notification that it's available to install, and it will require a restart. But the point is that you have nothing to go out and download. The Windows Update feature described on page 487 takes care of it.

The Clean Install

Upgrading—moving from an older version of Windows to a newer one—retains all your existing settings and data files. Sounds great, right? Who wouldn't want to avoid having to redo all those settings?

Well, there are two situations when you might want to perform a clean install:

- **When you're working with an *empty* PC or hard drive**—one that doesn't already have Windows on it. Maybe it's a PC you built yourself.

- **When you want to "nuke and pave."** Sometimes, as a troubleshooting step, or because you feel like your PC has grown too slow to bear, you may want to reformat your disk, wiping out everything on it. You wind up with a fresh system, 100 percent free of any little glitches and inconsistencies that have built up over the years. (Of course, you'll also have to take the time to reinstall all your programs, reconfigure your personalized settings, recreate your network connections, and so on.)

A clean install requires that you first make a Windows 10 installation flash drive or DVD, as described on page 588.

The process is identical to the one described there—right up until you reach the "Which type of installation do you want?" screen (Figure A-1, top).

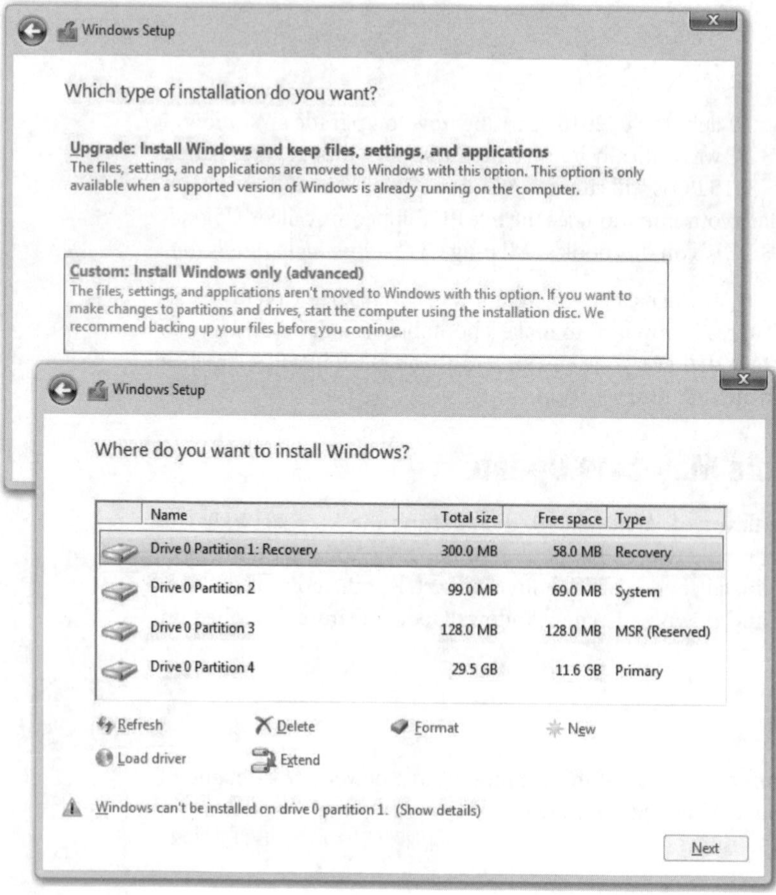

Figure A-1:
Top: Use the buttons on this screen to indicate whether you want a clean installation or an upgrade installation.

Bottom: You have to install Windows onto its own partition.

Here, instead, you should choose "Custom: Install Windows only (advanced)." That's the clean-install option.

From there, you proceed to the "Where do you want to install Windows?" screen.

It shows you a list of the *partitions* on your hard drive (Figure A-1, bottom). Unless you've set up your hard drive for dual booting as described in the box below, you probably have only one.

Select the name of the partition (or choose some unallocated space) on which you want to install Windows, and then hit Next. If you see a "Drive options (advanced)" link at the bottom of this window, you can use it to delete, create, or format partitions. To create a dual-boot situation, you have to *erase a partition completely* to make it ready for Windows 10.

After the formatting process is complete, click Next.

The Setup program begins copying files to the partition you selected and, eventually, restarts the computer a time or two.

POWER USERS' CLINIC

Dual Booting

In the advanced setup known as dual booting, you install Windows 10 onto the *same* PC that contains an older version of Windows, maintaining both of them side by side. Then, each time you turn on the machine, it asks you which operating system you want to run for this computing session.

Dual booting comes in handy when you have some program or hardware gadget that works with one operating system but not the other. For example, if you have a scanner with software that runs on Windows 7 but not Windows 10, you can start up in 7 only when you want to use the scanner.

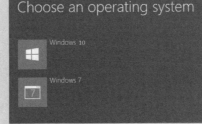

If you intend to dual boot, keep this in mind: You can't install both operating systems onto the same hard drive partition. If you did, your programs would become horribly confused.

Instead, keep your two Windows versions separate using one of these avenues:

Buy a second hard drive. Use it for one of the two operating systems.

Back up your hard drive, erase it completely, and then *partition* it, which means dividing it so each chunk shows up with its own icon, name, and drive letter. Then install each operating system on a separate disk partition, using the "clean install" instructions in this appendix.

If you're less technically inclined, you might prefer to buy a program like Acronis Disk Director. Not only does it let you create a new partition on your hard drive without erasing it first, but it's also flexible and easy.

There's just one wrinkle with dual booting: If you install Windows 10 onto a separate partition (or a different drive), as you must, you won't find any of your existing programs listed in the Start menu, and your desktop won't be configured the way it is in your original operating system. You'll generally wind up having to reinstall every program into your new Windows world, and to reestablish all your settings, exactly as though the Windows 10 "side" were a brand-new PC.

Suddenly, the screen looks colorful and the typography modern. You've entered the Setup Assistant, described next.

The Windows 10 Setup Assistant

If you've just bought a brand-new PC, you don't have to install Windows 10; it's already installed and activated. But you don't go straight to the desktop when you turn it on. Instead, you have to punch through a slew of setup screens (Figure A-2)—made

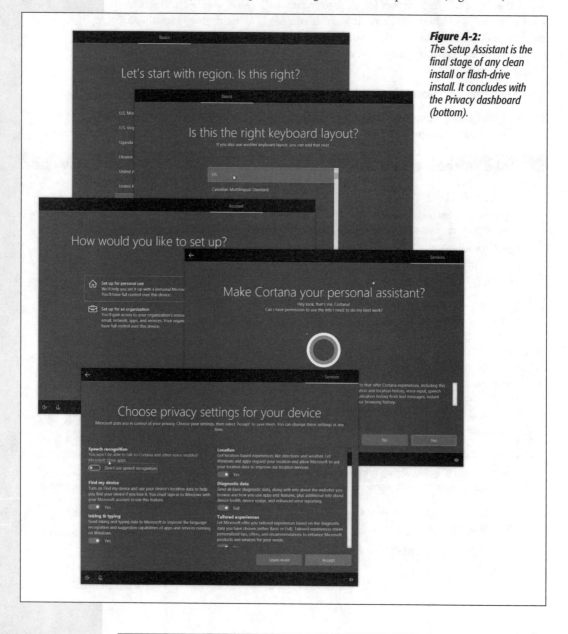

Figure A-2:
The Setup Assistant is the final stage of any clean install or flash-drive install. It concludes with the Privacy dashboard (bottom).

more pleasant by Cortana, whose voice walks you through them (and even lets you confirm each screen by saying "Yes").

Tip: Or you can shut her up by hitting the microphone icon (🎤) at lower left.

You also enjoy a variation of this Setup Assistant after you perform a clean install (page 581).

Here are some of the screens you may see (Figure A-2). Keep in mind that you may see more or fewer screens (for example, your computer maker—Dell or whatever—can insert its own screens along the way):

- **Continue in selected language?** Choose the language you want, then hit Yes.

- **Hi there! I'm Cortana, and I'm here to help.** Yes, she could be very helpful if you're visually impaired, because she starts talking aloud here. Just be patient while she finishes her canned speech; among other things, it lets you know that you can shut her voice up by hitting the microphone icon (🎤) at lower left.

Tip: Even if you've silenced Cortana, you can still speak the names of the buttons in the Setup Assistant to proceed from screen to screen ("Yes" or "Next," for example).

- **Let's start with region. Is this right?** Make sure Windows has identified your country correctly; hit Yes.

- **Is this the right keyboard layout?** Choose the country whose keyboard you're used to; then hit Yes.

- **Want to add a second keyboard layout?** Up to you; hit Skip if not.

- **Let's connect you to a network.** Here are all the available Wi-Fi networks, plus an Ethernet option. Choose the one you want to join, hit Connect, specify whether you want this computer to be discoverable on the network (page 568), and enter that password if necessary.

- **Windows 10 License Agreement.** Enjoy the law firm's output; hit Accept.

- **How would you like to set up?** Choose "Set up for personal use" unless you're at work, under the watchful eye of a professional IT person who will control many of your computer's settings. (In that case, choose "Set up for an organization.") Then hit Next.

- **Sign in with Microsoft.** Enter the email address you've registered as your Microsoft account (page 534); if you don't have one, hit "Create account" to take care of that essential task. Then hit Next.

- **Enter your password.** After you type it, hit Next.

- **Use your face to sign in faster and more securely.** This screen appears only if your PC has a Windows Hello-compatible camera; see page 549 for details.

- **Set up a PIN.** Set up a personal identification number (see page 548 for background); a four-digit number *and* your password is much more secure than just a password. Hit "Set a PIN," enter your chosen code twice, and then hit OK.

- **Link your phone and your PC.** See page 251 for details. Hit "Do it later" to pass for now, or enter your number, hit Next, and finish that setup process.

- **Protect your files with OneDrive.** Windows is asking if you want to set up OneDrive as your automatic backup system. A nice idea, if you've got the space. Hit "Only save files to this PC" if you decline; otherwise, hit Next.

- **Make Cortana your personal assistant?** Cortana is Microsoft's Siri: a voice-activated assistant, as described in Chapter 5. No reason to turn her off unless you don't like the idea of your queries being sent to Microsoft's servers. (Also turn on "Let Cortana respond to 'Hey Cortana'" if you'd like to be able to ask things of Cortana without having to click a button first; she'll be listening for her name at all times.)

  Choose No or Yes.

- **Choose privacy settings for your device.** This screen (Figure A-2, bottom) is a big deal; it lays out every single kind of information Windows would like to collect from your PC to send back to Microsoft.

  Of course, the *reason* it's harvesting data is to make possible the features listed here: Speech recognition, Find my device, Inking & typing, and so on.

UP TO SPEED

The 7 GB of Reserved Space

If you read the articles about the May 2019 Update before it actually came out, your eyebrows might have popped right off your forehead. Microsoft, they said, intends to set aside 7 gigabytes of disk space for its own purposes.

That's right: Windows intends to steal 7 gigs you paid for, making it off-limits to you. What the heck, Microsoft!?

OK. First of all, you don't get this Reserved Storage feature unless either (a) you buy a new PC with the May 2019 Update already on it, or (b) you perform a clean install (page 581). Otherwise, this whole business doesn't affect you.

Reserved Storage is intended to solve an occasional source of headaches: trying to install a new app or Windows update when your drive is nearly full. Every installation requires some disk space—the installer you download, and other temporary files, have to go somewhere. And if the disk is full, ugly, crashy things can happen. Reserved Storage gives those installers a little working room, no matter how full your drive seems.

(And what if some installer needs more than 7 GB? In that case, Windows fills up the reserved space and then uses regular, visible disk space for the overflow. And it walks you through the process of freeing up disk space or using a USB flash drive as overflow storage.)

By the way: Windows doesn't always set aside exactly 7 GB. It may reserve more or less space, depending on your PC. For example, if you switch among multiple languages, Windows will reserve more space. If you uninstall features you're not using (in ⚙️→Apps→"Apps & features"→"Manage optional features"), it may reserve less.

In any case, you can't turn off Reserved Storage if you have it, and you can't turn it on if you don't. All you can do is trust that Windows is always trying to do the right thing.

You can turn off these switches individually; a message lets you know, as you do so, exactly which features you *won't* have as a result.

Note: Depending on the laws where you live, this central privacy dashboard screen may be broken up onto several successive screens, but the idea is the same.

Choose Accept. You can always review or change your privacy settings in ▦→⚙→ Privacy.

After a moment, the triumphant word "Hi" appears on your screen. That's your signal that the installation has gone well.

After another minute or two, you arrive at the desktop; Microsoft Edge opens to a welcome screen containing details about the May 2019 Update.

Jobs Number 1, 2, 3...

Once you've installed Windows 10, you can start using the computer however you like. But if you're smart, you'll make these tasks your first order of business:

- **Transfer files from your old computer, if necessary.** The old Windows Easy Transfer program no longer comes with Windows, so you'll have to use file sharing (page 564), an external hard drive, or something like your OneDrive to bring all your stuff over.

Tip: If it's worth money to do the job right, programs like Laplink PCmover or Todo PCTrans can bring over not just your files and programs, but also your settings and every last shred of your old PC's account.

- **Customize the Start menu (page 22).**
- **Add users.** That means adding *accounts* to a PC that will be used by more than one person, as described in Chapter 18.
- **Turn on Windows Defender.** If you have a new PC, and it came with a trial version of antivirus software like Norton or McAfee, you'd be wise to mutter, "But Windows comes with its own antivirus software!"

Well done! Now uninstall the trialware and turn on Windows Security (page 408).

The adventure begins!

The Installation Flash Drive

If you want a "disk" you can use to install Windows 10, you have to create it yourself. You might want such a drive so you can reinstall Windows 10 on some future date, in a pinch, or so you can install it efficiently onto multiple machines.

That's why Microsoft offers the Media Creation Tool. It downloads Windows 10 and copies the installer to a flash drive (or DVD) that you supply. Then you'll always be ready to reinstall Windows if the need arises.

Create the Flash Drive

The routine goes like this:

1. **On your PC, go to the Windows 10 download page (Figure A-3).**

   For the U.S. edition of Microsoft Windows, that address is *microsoft.com/en-us/software-download/windows10*.

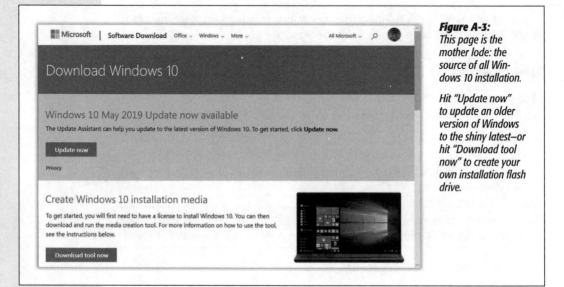

Figure A-3:
This page is the mother lode: the source of all Windows 10 installation.

Hit "Update now" to update an older version of Windows to the shiny latest—or hit "Download tool now" to create your own installation flash drive.

2. **Click "Download tool now."**

   Your browser offers you a choice of Run or Save. Choose Run.

   Authenticate yourself as described on page 558.

3. **On the legalese screen, hit Accept.**

   After some more time elapses, you're asked: "What do you want to do?" Your choices are "Upgrade this PC now" or "Create installation media (USB flash drive, DVD, or ISO file) for another PC" (Figure A-4).

   Do you want to upgrade your computer right now? Or make an installation flash drive (or disc) that you can use to upgrade other machines?

   If you choose "Upgrade this PC now" (and then hit Next), the installer springs into action, as described in the next section.

   But suppose your intention here has been to create an installation flash drive or DVD.

Now you arrive at a language/edition/architecture screen.

4. **Use the drop-down menus to specify your language, Windows 10 edition, and architecture.**

Or just leave "Use the recommended options for this PC" turned on.

The *architecture* means 32-bit or 64-bit, corresponding to the kind of computer you have. (If you're not sure, open ■→⚙→System→About. Under "Device specifications," you'll see what kind of machine you've got.)

5. **Hit Next.**

Now you're asked what kind of installation drive you want to create: A flash drive or an ISO file (for burning a DVD).

6. **Choose "USB flash drive" or "ISO file" (Figure A-4, bottom).**

Insert a blank flash drive of at least 8 gigabytes. Windows goes to town, building you an installer on that drive. (If the drive wasn't blank before, Windows erases it first.)

If you don't have a flash drive, you can opt for the ISO option. It creates a disk image of the type described on page 149. You can install directly from this file, or you can burn it onto a blank DVD, if that's how you prefer to go.

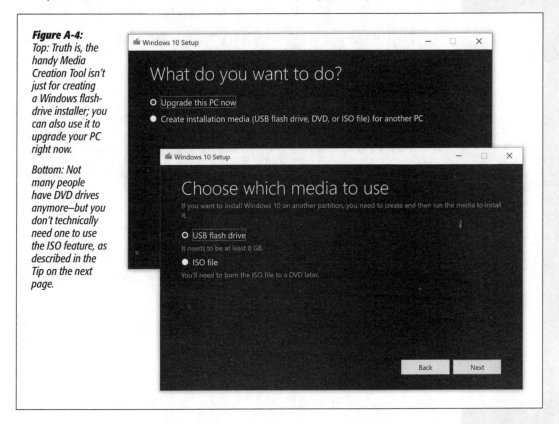

Figure A-4:
Top: Truth is, the handy Media Creation Tool isn't just for creating a Windows flash-drive installer; you can also use it to upgrade your PC right now.

Bottom: Not many people have DVD drives anymore—but you don't technically need one to use the ISO feature, as described in the Tip on the next page.

Tip: Once you create the ISO file, you can convert it into a DVD (if your machine has a DVD burner) using a DVD-burning program. But you can also install Windows 10 directly from the ISO file!

To do that, *mount* the ISO file by right-clicking its icon; from the shortcut menu, choose Properties. On the General tab, click Change; choose Windows Explorer as the program to use to open ISO files. Hit Apply.

Right-click the ISO file and select Mount. Double-click the ISO file to see what's inside it—including the app called setup.exe. Open it to begin the Windows 10 installation.

Install from the Flash Drive or DVD

Whether you start the upgrade cycle straight from the Update Assistant or from a flash drive or DVD, the actual process is pretty much the same.

You have only a short checklist left to follow:

- **Update your virus program and scan for viruses—and then turn it off.** If you're updating an existing copy of Windows, *turn off* your virus checker. Also turn off auto-loading programs like non-Microsoft firewall software and web ad blockers.

- **Gather updated, Windows 10–compatible drivers** for all your computer's components. Graphics and audio cards are particularly likely to need updates, so be sure to check the manufacturers' websites—and driver-information sites like *windrivers.com* and *driverguide.com*—and download any new drivers you find there.

- **Plug in.** If it's a laptop or tablet you're upgrading, keep it plugged in to power during the upgrade. If its battery dies midway through, you're in trouble.

- **Back up your world.** Use File History (page 513). Upgrades that go wrong are very rare. But you don't want to be that one in a million who loses files.

If you've gone to all this trouble and preparation, the Windows installation process can be surprisingly smooth. The Windows 10 installer is much less painful than the ones for previous versions of Windows—and takes much less time, too, maybe 30 minutes.

OK, ready? With your PC turned on, insert the flash drive or DVD containing the Windows 10 installer, and then shut down the PC.

Now start the computer; just after it chimes, hold down any key.

Note: That's *usually* the trick for starting up from a DVD or a flash drive. If it doesn't work, and the computer starts up into your existing Windows version, then you probably have to fool around with the machine's BIOS or UEFI settings. To find out how you do that, you'll have to visit your computer maker's website and hunt for details, since it's different for every computer model. Sorry.

Eventually, the Install Windows page appears. Now you're in for a lengthy screen-by-screen interview process that goes like this:

- **Language to install.** Specify your language, regional preferences, and keyboard language; hit Next.

- **Install now.** Yep; hit "Install now."

- **Enter the product key to activate Windows.** Your product key (serial number) is the proof you've actually bought Windows 10; the product key number came in the confirmation email that Microsoft sent you.

    You may, of course, choose "I don't have a product key" instead, but you'll get persistent nags to buy one until you finally do.

- **Applicable notice and license terms.** Yay, lawyers! Choose "I accept the license terms." Hit Next.

- **Which type of installation do you want?** Choose "Upgrade: Install Windows and keep files, settings, and applications" (Figure A-1, top).

Now the installation begins; this is the time-consuming part. The PC will restart a couple of times along the way; that's normal.

Eventually, things on the screen start looking a lot more modern; you've arrived in the Setup Assistant. Continue as described on page 584.

Master List of Keyboard Shortcuts & Gestures

H ere it is, by popular, frustrated demand: The master list of every secret (or not-so-secret) keystroke in Windows 10. Clip and post to your office wall (unless, of course, you got this book from the library).

General Windows shortcuts

Open or close the Start menu	⊞
Open or close the Action Center	⊞+A, four-finger tap
(At the desktop:) Highlight notification area	⊞+B
Speak to Cortana	⊞+C (see page 180)
Display the desktop	⊞+D, three-finger swipe down
Open File Explorer to the "Quick access" list	⊞+E
Open Feedback Hub, attach screenshot (bug reports)	⊞+F
Search for computers (if you're on a network)	Ctrl+⊞+F
Open Settings	⊞+I
Open the Quick Connect panel (wireless A/V)	⊞+K
Lock your computer or switch accounts	⊞+L
Lock the screen in its current orientation	⊞+O
External-screen mode (Duplicate, Extend, and so on)	⊞+P
Search	⊞+Q, ⊞+S, three-finger tap
Open the Run dialog box	⊞+R
Clipboard history	⊞+V
Open secret Utilities menu	⊞+X
Switch input between desktop and Mixed Reality	⊞+Y

Show available commands in a full-screen app	⊞+Z
Open the System Properties dialog box	⊞+Pause (or +Break)
Switch to the app that just displayed a notification	Ctrl+⊞+B
Select all items in a document or window	Ctrl+A
Display properties for the selected item	Alt+Enter
Open a menu (some apps)	Alt+underlined letter
"Click" a menu command (or other underlined command)	Alt+underlined letter
Open Task Manager	Ctrl+Shift+Esc
Open Snip & Sketch app (for screenshots)	⊞+Shift+S
Take a screenshot (saved to Screenshots folder)	PrtScn
Take a screenshot (copied to Clipboard)	Alt+PrtScn

File Explorer

Open a new window	Ctrl+N, ⊞+E
Close the current window	Ctrl+W
Minimize all windows	⊞+M
Create a new folder	Shift+Ctrl+N
Display the bottom/top of the active window	End/Home
Display all subfolders under the selected folder	Num Lock+* on numeric keypad
Show/hide Preview pane	Alt+P
Display the contents of the selected folder	Num Lock+Enter on numeric keypad
Collapse the selected folder	Num Lock+minus (-) on numeric keypad
Collapse the current selection (if expanded), or select parent folder	←
Open the Properties dialog box for selected item	Alt+Enter
Back to the previous folder	Alt+←, Backspace
Next folder	Alt+→
Display the current selection (if it's collapsed), or select the first subfolder	→
Open the parent folder	Alt+↑
Display all folders above the selected folder	Ctrl+Shift+E
Enlarge/shrink file and folder icons	Ctrl+mouse scroll wheel, or pinch/spread two fingers on the laptop trackpad
Select the address bar	Alt+D, Ctrl+L
Select the search box	Ctrl+E, Ctrl+F
Delete the selected item and move it to the Recycle Bin	Delete (or Ctrl+D)

Delete the selected item without moving it to
the Recycle Bin first   Shift+Delete

Rename the selected item   F2

Scroll to top, bottom of window   Home, End

Taskbar

Cycle through programs on the taskbar   ⊞+T

Open the calendar/time panel   Alt+⊞+D

Open another window in a program   Shift-click a taskbar button

Open a program as an administrator   Ctrl+Shift-click a taskbar button

Show the window menu for the program   Shift+right-click a taskbar button

Show the window menu for the group   Shift+right-click a grouped
                                                         taskbar button

Cycle through the windows of the group   Ctrl-click a grouped
                                                         taskbar button

Open the first, second (and so on) program
pinned to the taskbar   ⊞+1, ⊞+2…

Open another window in the first, second (and
so on) pinned taskbar program   Shift+⊞+1, Shift+⊞+2…

Open another window in the first, second (and
so on) pinned taskbar program as administrator   Ctrl+Shift+⊞+1…

Switch to the last window in first, second (and
so on) program pinned to the taskbar   Ctrl+⊞+1, Ctrl+⊞+2…

Open a jump list for the first, second (and
so on) program pinned to the taskbar   Alt+⊞+1, Alt+⊞+2…

Touchscreen (Tablet mode) gestures

Right-click   Hold finger down one second

Task View   Swipe in from left edge

Action Center   Swipe in from right edge

Scroll   Slide across screen

Zoom in/zoom out (Maps, Photos, and so on)   Spread or pinch two fingers

Select next AutoComplete suggestion   Swipe across onscreen space bar

Close app   Drag from the top of the screen
                                                        to the bottom

Open app into a split screen   Drag its title bar against the right
                                                        or left edge of the screen

Switch apps   Swipe in from left edge

Virtual desktops

Task View (Timeline)   ⊞+Tab, swipe up with three
                                                        fingers on trackpad

New virtual desktop   Ctrl+⊞+D

Switch between virtual desktops	Ctrl+⊞+←, Ctrl+⊞+→, four-finger swipe
Close the current desktop	Ctrl+⊞+F4

Managing windows

Close the window	Alt+F4
Close the document (in apps that let you have multiple documents open)	Ctrl+F4
Open the shortcut menu for the active window	Alt+space bar
Switch among open programs	Alt+Tab, three-finger horizontal swipe
Use the arrow keys to switch among open programs	Ctrl+Alt+Tab
Task View/Timeline	⊞+Tab
Cycle screen elements in a window or the desktop	F6
Display the shortcut menu for the selected item	Shift+F10
Refresh the active window	F5 (or Ctrl+R)
Maximize the window	⊞+↑
Maximize the window, maintain width	⊞+Shift+↑
Restore window, maintain width	⊞+Shift+↓
Minimize all windows	⊞+M
Restore minimized windows to the desktop	⊞+Shift+M
Snap window to the side of the screen	⊞+←, ⊞+→ (or drag window against the edge of the screen)
Move window to the previous/next monitor	⊞+Shift+←, ⊞+Shift+→
Restore/minimize the window	⊞+↓
Minimize all but the active window	⊞+Home
Peek at desktop	⊞+comma (,)
Highlight a Windows tip	⊞+J (press again to highlight whatever the tip is talking about)

Languages and keyboard layouts

Next language and keyboard layout	⊞+space bar
Previous language and keyboard layout	⊞+Ctrl+space bar
Switch the input language when multiple input languages are enabled	left Alt+Shift
Switch the keyboard layout when multiple keyboard layouts are enabled	Ctrl+Shift
Turn Chinese input method editor on/off	Ctrl+space bar
Change the reading direction of text in right-to-left reading languages	Ctrl+right Shift or Ctrl+left Shift

Inside apps

Start dictation	⊞+H
Open emoji panel	⊞+;
Zoom in or out (Magnifier)	⊞+plus, ⊞+minus
Zoom in or out (web, mail, and so on)	Ctrl+turn mouse's scroll wheel
Go back a screen (most Microsoft Store apps)	Alt+←
Make the menu bar appear (some apps)	Alt or F10
Open the next menu to the right, or open a submenu	→
Open the next menu to the left, or close a submenu	←
Cancel the current task	Esc
Copy the selected item	Ctrl+C (or Ctrl+Insert)
Cut the selected item	Ctrl+X
Paste the selected item	Ctrl+V (or Shift+Insert)
Undo an action	Ctrl+Z
Redo an action	Ctrl+Y
Move the cursor to the beginning of the next word	Ctrl+→
Move the cursor to the beginning of the previous word	Ctrl+←
Move the cursor to the beginning of the next paragraph	Ctrl+↓
Move the cursor to the beginning of the previous paragraph	Ctrl+↑
Select a block of text	Shift+Ctrl with an arrow key
Select more than one item in a window, or select text within a document	Shift+any arrow key
Select multiple individual items in a window or on the desktop	Ctrl+any arrow key+space bar

Edge browser

Highlight address bar	Alt+D, F4
Add *http://www.* and *.com* to the text in address bar	Ctrl+Enter
New window	Ctrl+N
New InPrivate window	Shift+Ctrl+P
Refresh page	F5, Ctrl+R
Stop loading page	Esc
Scroll down a screenful	space bar (or Page Down)
Scroll up a screenful	Shift+space bar (or Page Up)

Zoom in/out	Ctrl+plus, Ctrl+minus
Return to 100 percent zoom	Ctrl+0 (that's a zero)
Close all tabs	Alt+F4
View Reading List	Ctrl+M
View History list	Ctrl+H
View Favorites	Ctrl+ I
View Downloads	Ctrl+J
Hide or show Favorites bar	Ctrl+Shift+B
Open home page	Alt+Home
Reading view on/off	Shift+Ctrl+R
Previous page (Back)	Backspace, Alt+←
Forward a page	Alt+→
Add to Favorites	Ctrl+D
Find text on this page	Ctrl+F
Find copied text on this page	Shift+Ctrl+L
Print	Ctrl+P
Open a new tab	Ctrl+T
Next tab	Ctrl+Tab
Previous tab	Shift+Ctrl+Tab
Open link in a new window	Shift-click
Open link in new background tab	Ctrl-click (or scroll wheel–click, or middle button–click)
Open link in new foreground tab	Shift+Ctrl-click (left or middle button)
Open URL in the address bar in a new tab	Alt+Enter
Duplicate this tab	Ctrl+K
Switch to tab 1, 2, 3...	Ctrl+1, Ctrl+2, Ctrl+3...
Switch to last tab	Ctrl+9
Cycle through tabs	Ctrl+Tab
Cycle backward through tabs	Shift+Ctrl+Tab
Close tab	Ctrl+F4, Ctrl+W
Reopen last closed tab	Shift+Ctrl+T
Turn on caret browsing	F7

Photos app

Select thumbnail (and enter Selection mode)	space bar
Select another thumbnail (in Selection mode)	Enter
Show/hide toolbar (on an open photo)	space bar
Scroll thumbnails	arrow keys
Previous/next open photo	←, →

Zoom in/out	⊞+plus, ⊞+minus
Back to actual size	⊞+0
Previous screen	Esc
Save	Ctrl+S
Print	Ctrl+P
Rotate	Ctrl+R
Enhance the open photo	Ctrl+E
Resize the cropping area	Shift+arrow keys
Move the cropping area	Ctrl+arrow keys
Begin slideshow from open photo	F5
View photo details	Alt+Enter
Save this photo as your Lock screen image	Ctrl+L

Dialog boxes

Open the selected drop-down menu	F4
Move forward through tabs	Ctrl+Tab
Move back through tabs	Ctrl+Shift+Tab
Move forward through options	Tab
Move back through options	Shift+Tab
Perform the command (or select the option) that goes with that letter	Alt+underlined letter
Checkbox on/off	Space
Select highlighted command	Enter
In Save/Open dialog boxes, go up one folder level	Backspace

Game Bar

Open Game Bar (to record screen, for example)	⊞+G
Save the last 30 seconds as a video	Alt+⊞+G
Start/stop video recording	Alt+⊞+R
Take a screenshot of current window	Alt+⊞+PrtScn
Show/hide recording timer	Alt+⊞+T

Ease of Access

Open the Ease of Access page in Settings	⊞+U
Turn Filter Keys on and off	right Shift for eight seconds
Turn High Contrast on or off	left Alt+left Shift+PrtScn (or PrtScn)
Turn Mouse Keys on or off	left Alt+left Shift+Num Lock
Turn Sticky Keys on or off	Shift five times
Turn Toggle Keys on or off	Num Lock for five seconds
Open Narrator	Ctrl+⊞+Enter

Magnifier

Open Magnifier	⊞+plus (+) key
Exit Magnifier	⊞+Esc
Zoom in or out	⊞+plus or +minus
Preview the desktop in full-screen mode	Ctrl+Alt+space bar
Switch to full-screen mode	Ctrl+Alt+F
Switch to lens mode	Ctrl+Alt+L
Switch to docked mode	Ctrl+Alt+D
Invert colors	Ctrl+Alt+I
Pan in the direction of the arrow keys	Ctrl+Alt+arrow keys
Resize the lens	Ctrl+Alt+R

Index

THE MISSING CD

There's no
CD with this book—
you just saved $5.00!

Instead, every single bonus appendix and piece
of downloadable software mentioned in this book
is available at *missingmanuals.com* (click the
Missing CD icon). There you'll find
a tidy list of links, organized
by chapter.